Language and Society

World Anthropology

General Editor

SOL TAX

Patrons

CLAUDE LÉVI-STRAUSS
MARGARET MEAD†
LAILA SHUKRY EL HAMAMSY
M. N. SRINIVAS

MOUTON PUBLISHERS · THE HAGUE · PARIS · NEW YORK

Language and Society

Anthropological Issues

Editors

WILLIAM C. McCORMACK
STEPHEN A. WURM

MOUTON PUBLISHERS · THE HAGUE · PARIS · NEW YORK

General Editor's Preface

The mystery of a language itself is as tantalizing as any in nature, perhaps more so because of the way languages, and the phenomenon of language itself, impinge on everything else that is human. Four companion volumes sample these connections and the methods by which they can be understood. The present book looks particularly at how language operates in societies as people move and cultures change. It has the advantage of dealing with these subtle phenomena worldwide, owing to its origin in a uniquely representative international Congress.

Like most contemporary sciences, anthropology is a product of the European tradition. Some argue that it is a product of colonialism, with one small and self-interested part of the species dominating the study of the whole. If we are to understand the species, our science needs substantial input from scholars who represent a variety of the world's cultures. It was a deliberate purpose of the IXth International Congress of Anthropological and Ethnological Sciences to provide impetus in this direction. The *World Anthropology* volumes, therefore, offer a first glimpse of a human science in which members from all societies have played an active role. Each of the books is designed to be self-contained; each is an attempt to update its particular sector of scientific knowledge and is written by specialists from all parts of the world. Each volume should be read and reviewed individually as a separate volume on its own given subject. The set as a whole will indicate what changes are in store for anthropology as scholars from the developing countries join in studying the species of which we are all a part.

The IXth Congress was planned from the beginning not only to include as many of the scholars from every part of the world as possible, but also with a view toward the eventual publication of the papers in high-quality volumes. At previous Congresses scholars were invited to bring papers which were then read out loud. They were necessarily limited in length; many were only summarized; there was little time for discussion; and the sparse discussion could only be in one language. The IXth Congress was an experiment aimed at changing this. Papers were written with the intention of exchanging them before the Congress, particularly in extensive pre-Congress Sessions; they were not intended to be read aloud at the Congress, that time being devoted to discussions — discussions which were simultaneously and professionally translated into five languages. The method for eliciting the papers was structured to make as representative a sample as was allowable when scholarly creativity — hence self-selection — was critically important. Scholars were asked both to propose papers of their own to suggest topics for sessions of the Congress which they might edit into volumes. All were then informed of the suggestions and encouraged to re-think their own papers and the topics. The process, therefore, was a continuous one of feedback and exchange and it has continued to be so even after the Congress. The some two thousand papers comprising *World Anthropology* certainly then offer a substantial sample of world anthropology. It has been said that anthropology is at a turning point; if this is so, these volumes will be the historical direction-markers.

As might have been foreseen in the first post-colonial generation, the large majority of the Congress papers (82 percent) are the work of scholars identified with the industrialized world which fathered our traditional discipline and the institution of the Congress itself: Eastern Europe (15 percent); Western Europe (16 percent); North America (47 percent); Japan, South Africa, Australia, and New Zealand (4 percent). Only 18 percent of the papers are from developing areas: Africa (4 percent); Asia-Oceania (9 percent); Latin America (5 percent). Aside from the substantial representation from the U.S.S.R. and the nations of Eastern Europe, a significant difference between this corpus of written material and that of other Congresses is the addition of the large proportion of contributions from Africa, Asia, and Latin America. "Only 18 percent" is two to four times as great a proportion as that of other Congresses; moreover, 18 percent of 2,000 papers is 360 papers, 10 times the number of "Third World" papers presented at previous Congresses. In fact, these 360 papers are more than the total of *all* papers published after the last International Congress of Anthropological and Ethnological Sciences which was held in the United States (Philadelphia, 1956).

The significance of the increase is not simply quantitative. The input of scholars from areas which have until recently been no more than subject matter for anthropology represents both feedback and also long-awaited theoretical contributions from the perspectives of very different cultural, social, and historical traditions. Many who attended the IXth Congress were convinced that anthropology would not be the same in the future.

The fact that the Xth Congress (India, 1978) was our first in the "Third World" may be symbolic of the change. Meanwhile, sober consideration of the present set of books will show how much, and just where and how, our discipline is being revolutionized.

In addition to its three companion volumes — *Language and man, Language and thought*, and *Approaches to language* — others in this *World Anthropology* series which the reader will find interesting treat human interaction and social, biological, cultural and historical variations and developments.

Chicago, Illinois   SOL TAX
15 February 1979

Preface

A General Session on "Language in Anthropology" of the IXth International Congress of Anthropological and Ethnological Sciences (Chicago, Fall 1973) was organized by McCormack at the invitation of Professor Sol Tax, President of the Congress. It evolved over more than a year on the basis of relevant papers volunteered to the Congress, and an equal number of papers solicited by McCormack, notably at international linguistics congresses in Europe in 1972, under gratefully acknowledged travel support from The Canada Council of Ottawa and The Wenner-Gren Foundation for Anthropological Research, Inc., of New York City. What started out as a single session ultimately divided into subsessions, of which four major topical ones have yielded the *World Anthropology* volumes entitled *Language and man, Language and thought, Approaches to language*, and *Language and society*.

Wurm joined this undertaking at the invitation of Professor Tax upon the recommendation of McCormack, and he assumed full responsibility for the conduct and written summary of the session discussions at Chicago. Those were based on precirculated papers. Wurm chaired essentially all subsessions of this General Session, i.e., an opening informal subsession, the four formal topical subsessions plus a fifth one on language in anthropology at large, and four ad hoc gatherings of self-selected membership. In this, and at his invitation, he was accompanied by Dr. Nguyen Dang Liem of The University of Hawaii, acting as his assistant and discussion coordinator throughout. Wurm's subsequent provision of written summaries of discussions was aided by the prepared texts of formal discussants and tapes of most proceedings.

For three years from mid-1972 until finalization of resultant books, Anna Pikelis McCormack acted as administrative and editorial associate to McCormack for this General Session. All operations behind the scenes have carried the stamp of her extraordinary competence. For further and efficient assistance, she joins McCormack in thanking Mrs. Charlotte Stewart, secretary for the Department of Linguistics of The University of Calgary.

The subsession on language and society was entitled "Language in Many Ways" at Chicago, and had for its discussion theme "language behavior of individuals and groups: problems in description, verifiability, interpretation and theoretical import." Only an hour of time was available for it, thus discussion was restricted to the two formal discussants and the authors of papers in the subsession. However, all Congress members were explicitly free to contribute additional comments, verbally or in writing, on other occasions.

Editorial discretion for the present volume on *Language and society* rested solely with McCormack. The papers by Baha Abu-Laban and Evangelos A. Afendras were secured after the Congress and were therefore not susceptible to discussion at the Congress.

The University of Calgary   WILLIAM C. McCORMACK
Calgary, Alberta, Canada
7 April 1975

Table of Contents

SECTION SIX: DISCUSSION

SECTION ONE

Introductory

Introduction

WILLIAM C. McCORMACK

LANGUAGE IN MANY WAYS

The IXth ICAES subsession at which most papers in this volume were discussed (see "Preface") was planned to explore the role which socially-learned cultural values might have in instigating the patterned phenomena which sociolinguistics investigates. Thus the subsession was entitled "Language in many ways" by way of stimulating discussion of how sociolinguistic study of language use and the means for interpreting language variation might proceed if hybridized with anthropology's view that language, culture, and society are systematically interrelated concepts because each represents an aspect of learned behavior. Formal discussant Michael A. K. Halliday clarified this theme, and his insightful comments on subsession papers sketch, among other things, a framework for viewing language habits and variation as the outcome of social experiences lived according to particular cultural-semantic styles. Generally in agreement with some points of view in psychological anthropology (e.g. Wallace 1970:34–36), Halliday expects variation to be the norm within communities which enjoy a cultural identity. Formal discussant John B. Pride, however, strongly resisted all *a priori* compartmentalization of phenomena, including the much debated dichotomy between micro- and macro-sociolinguistics (see Fishman 1971:43–56), and the present volume enjoys greater richness of thought because of it. Pride, who sees his thinking about speech–act analysis as convergent with sociological ethnomethodology (see Mehan and Wood 1975), has here stated a very contemporary view that neither language nor social structure enjoys autonomy but are enacted jointly out of rule-governed, socially situated, pragmatic transactions about the rights (status) and obligations (role) of interlocutors. Due to these significantly differing viewpoints of Halliday and Pride, the "Summary of Discussion" by co-editor Wurm, below, amounts to a key theoretical section of this book. Wurm's summary of Halliday's remarks on a large sample of the subsession papers shows how Halliday's ontogenetic and semiotic view of language as a projection or special realization of a meaningful social–cultural system (see Halliday 1975) encompasses the variety of interests represented by authors in the subsession. Pride, on the other hand, who actively participated in the informal as well as the formal subsessions on language, is revealed to have drawn the dimensions of his own critical and interactionist sociolinguistics much more independently, and his comments reference the other papers in this book to lesser degree than his own.

A noteworthy feature of this "Summary of Discussion" is that debate on the relative merits of psychological versus sociological explanation for language phenomena is virtually absent, and discussants appear to accept as axiomatic that language will be interpreted as part of the system of social meanings with which it is found to be associated. Possibly because the collectivity of members in the subsession had talked themselves out over the issue on a previous occasion (see McCormack and Wurm 1978), "psychologism" (Wisdom 1970:277), of which the linguist Noam Chomsky's subjectivist philosophy is the prime contemporary example in the history of scientific thought (e.g. Chomsky 1975:6–7, 21–27, 120ff.), here went neglected. That is not for want of a paper generally sympathetic to the cognitive deterministic viewpoint of Chomsky which might have stimulated further debate, e.g. the paper by Levine and Crockett. Nor is it for want of Ornstein's drawing attention to the underrepresentation of analysis based on universals of bilingualism, a topic which by the scientific fashions of 1973 was viewed chiefly as contributory to psychology. Nevertheless it happened, so that we can accord Eric Hamp, serving as formal discussant for the preceding relevant subsession, the final thought-provoking word on the subject. The question he posed is whether psychologically-oriented generative semantics, correlational sociolinguistics, and ethnography of communication are not "simply three names for one ideal, each named by a worker starting from his own vantage point of interest — a question, then, of emphasis, of elaboration and formalization, and of perspective?" (in McCormack and Wurm 1978; see also Lindenfeld's rejoinder in "Summary of Discussion" below; Hymes 1976:237, *passim*).

Turning at last to the papers of which the present volume is composed, those start with a Section 2 on the social meaning of language, and in Sections 2 through 5 provide us with results of original research into sociolinguistic processes affecting language use and variability, the world over. Quantitatively speaking, the major strength of this volume lies in that category of sociolinguistics which Bright (1966) labeled "application," and of which he further stated subcategories of research interest to be language as an index of social structure, languages in culture–area matrices undergoing change, and language planning. Regarding language planning in particular, Section 5 features the topics of language in education and national planning, so that whatever else it may be — and the terminology of specialists in this subject remains notably fluid (Rubin 1973; Wurm 1977) — language planning can be seen as a response to the dynamics of modernization. At the same time, papers of Section 3 on sociolinguistic-survey techniques are relevant to language-planning procedures, and papers of Section 4 which treat of language and social–cultural change as interactive and alternating possibilities for social groups' adapting to local circumstances are relevant to cost/benefit evaluation of language policies. A case might be made that studies of codeswitching and pronominal address forms in Section 2, as examples of natural socially- and culturally-situated speaker choices, also have some bearing on the ultimate understanding of community decision about the use and allocation of functions to the available language varieties through language planning (see Hymes 1976:226).

THE SOCIAL MEANING OF LANGUAGE: CODESWITCHING

It is a basic premise in sociolinguistics that any full account of meaning in language must include attention to how that language indexes the cultural context of speech acts and the social statuses and roles of both speakers and addressees (see Silverstein 1972, 1975, 1976). Phenomenological study of such indexing is usually complicated by a human propensity to codeswitch during speech — whether from speech style to speech style, dialect to dialect, language to language, and/or combinations thereof — and Section 2 of this book elucidates a variety of theoretical positions from which to analyze and understand codeswitching as a peculiarity of the social meaning of language.

In the opening paper, and as grounded in an analysis of social pragmatics, Pride argues that sociolinguistics is still far from providing a functional account of rules for appropriate codeswitching speech behavior of any kind (now see also Gumperz 1977), and proposes a unique cognitive framework by which perhaps to do so. Scotton, on the other hand, finds that the somewhat mechanistic social-exchange model, today most familiar from the work of the social behaviorist George Homans (Ritzer 1975:152ff.), still serves adequately for her theoretical explanation of bilingual codeswitching as a "safe choice" for the speaker in East Africa. Lindenfeld would generalize to sociolinguistic research of all kinds the experimental methods from social psychology used by Ervin-Tripp (1964) to study Japanese-English bilingual codeswitching. But Pascasio and Hidalgo find that bilingual codeswitching in the Philippines is predicted by the long-familiar concept of institutional "domain," i.e., by typified classes of recurrent situations for speech (see, e.g. Weinreich 1953:87–88; Fishman 1974a:1657–1661; Fishman et al. 1971:568–569).

An approach to codeswitching in which speaker choice is interpreted in relation to a culture's needs for a variety of expressive styles, and inclusive of a "normal" codeswitching style (Hymes 1976:223), is the ethnographic description of speaking as the speaking occurs in given cultural contexts. This approach is employed in the papers by Dakubu, Sampson, and Vanek. Vanek's study of polite pronominal usage in Czech, which contains social–cultural data for at least two generations of speakers, was singled out by discussant Halliday as good evidence for the sociolinguist's axiom that meaning in language is socially learned, and against the myth of autonomous syntax that has motivated formal, particularly Chomskyan generative, grammar (see Labov 1970).

SOCIOLINGUISTIC SURVEY: METHODS, TECHNIQUES, RESULTS

Section 3 opens a diversified critique of sociolinguistic methods and techniques with two papers that plainly reveal the scientifically murky nature of understandings about black–white speech relationships in the U.S.A. To a nonspecialist, who is not enlisted by one or other of at least three schools of thought in these matters (see Wolfram 1974; Dillard 1975), the arguments, pro and con, about alleged correlations between speakers' skin-pigmentation on the one hand, and black–white dialect markers, admittedly colored by sex, age, social class, ideology, and place of residence, on the other, do not exactly have the weight of test results from crucial experiments. In the first of the two papers here, McDavid eschews such dialectics by disclaiming that his inventory of prestige features from American dialect-atlas materials refers to "white English," and saying that "there is much to be explored before the scholars can justifiably dichotomize [American speech] on the basis of race or ethnic antecedents." As for scholarly debate on the methodology of urban sociolinguistics, McDavid states as his own the traditional dialect geographers' position (e.g. Kurath 1968) of skepticism about urban sociolinguistic methods of the 1960's which made so little use of the data or experience gained (e.g. about regional differences in educated speech) during compilation of the *Linguistic Atlas of the United States and Canada*. In the second of the two papers, Smith criticizes the urban sociolinguists' oversimplified picture of the linguistic sociology of black Americans, especially that synchronic structured-variability model for abstracted grammar in social dialects, which has generalized standard-

English features at the formal end of a speech continuum and black dialectal features at the other end. While this familiar model may have pedagogical value for teachers of some American children who are victimized in some localities because of their speech (see Bolinger 1975:369; Burling 1973; Traugott 1976), its referencing of "black English" to low status may just ignore the existence and cultural valuation of certain high black varieties, or registers, in black communities. Also, there seems to be no way at present to define a clearly bidialectal speaker of "black English" except by noting the fact that he is of the middle class. Without longitudinal studies, one does not know if black bidialectalism arises from linguistic insecurity, from upper-middleclass role-playing, to assert ethnic identity, or what (see Hoover 1978:83).

Pandit finds similar shortcomings in the American approach to interpreting sociolinguistic survey data from India, and his account of socially significant speech variation in that country weights (as does Smith) the personal style of the speaker and his use of language as a symbol of political–religious identity (see McCormack 1975). However, relatively stable class or caste variables are not altogether ruled out, inasmuch as Pandit notes that "literate/illiterate, rural/urban are also relevant factors in understanding the speech variation" (see Bean 1974a). On another issue, Bean has pointed out that pronominal address systems everywhere presuppose that "subordination is expressed only through the feature 'socially close,' leaving no way to signify the addressee's social distance" (Bean 1978:114). But Pandit, accounting for the high-caste Indian's relative propensity for formal, ritualistic, and "Sanskritic" speech — to which can be added that socially anonymous non-Brahmins may pass for Brahmins by doing likewise (McCormack 1960, 1968) — claims for the Indian caste-system context (see Marriott and Inden 1974) that "if a Brahmin can maintain his social distance by the choice of a [formal] variant in his speech . . . he is in no danger of losing his caste while talking to a non-Brahmin" (see Bean 1974b:106). In South India, forms of address would seem to violate also another general conversational rule, namely, that politeness is defined by "the speaker's acting as though his status were lower than that of the addressee" (Lakoff 1972:911). Finally, and as Khubchandani elucidates in his paper here, India represents a sociocultural context where census returns "reveal an individual's allegiance and esteem for a particular language (in response to the census category for identification of his mother tongue), sometimes even in contradiction of his actual speech habits." A striking example is the country's "Urdu population," which appeared to have undergone a population explosion with the decennial national census of 1961, due to a new Muslim fashion of reporting Urdu for a mother tongue as a marker of Muslim religious identity. Of course, secondary analysis of these data should not exclude the possibility that the inflated population figures were meant to call attention to Muslim availability as a voting bloc in anticipation of elections in some linguistic regions of the nation (see McCormack 1967). Such a hypothesis accords with Jolly's discussion, in this book, of the appearance of multilingualism as a socially marketable resource among a group of tribal students of northeastern India.

The selection of social criteria to explain linguistic variation in the survey techniques of correlational sociolinguistics is always subject to risk of reflecting observer bias and resulting in ambiguous results. Three innovative approaches to sociolinguistic survey techniques proposed by authors of papers in Section 3 reduce the influence of the observer on the selection of predictor variables. Ure describes her language-diary technique, primarily with respect to its pedagogical application with Ghanaian children, but its value as a technique for gathering self-report data so as to overcome sampling bias is noted by Afendras in this volume. Equally original is Yamamoto's technique of charting features of discourse in relation to his classification of "culture spaces" that interrelate with sociolinguistically relevant features of interlocutor status in a Japanese hamlet. This method has been elsewhere reported as adaptable to description of Hopi ritual performances (Voegelin and Voegelin 1972). Finally, Ornstein describes the work of his research project on "relational bilingualism" among Mexican-American college students, in which theory focuses on the problem of how language repertoire and social roles interrelate among bilingual/bicultural individuals versus monolingual/ monocultural individuals. The paper reports on socioeducational and language-skills testing by the project's research team, and so may be compared with similar progress reports from other longitudinal studies of bilingual (albeit primary school) education in North America (see Cohen 1975; Lambert and Tucker 1972; Lambert, Tucker, and d'Anglejan 1973).

John Ross's report on the Orléans project describes clearly how sociolinguistic survey procedures were operationally altered during the course of a research project that never had innovation in survey techniques for a goal. Starting with all the advantages of working in the modern Western society of France — e.g. the ease of employing stratified random-sampling procedures — the researchers nevertheless informally made more and more use of ethnography of communication (see Hymes 1967, 1974a, 1974b) as the study progressed, because the interpretation of variation in syntactic features of French came to "depend more on direct sociological observation set in a linguistic perspective."

An experienced craftsman's approach to sociolinguistic survey is exemplified here by Southworth's complex sociolexicological analysis of the Tamil word for "curry." For reasons predictable from the ethnosociology of caste (Marriott and Inden 1974) and spelled out by Southworth, Indian expressions relating to food and drink illustrate dialect-splitting along the social boundaries between castes. Words for "curry" in the Dravidian sister-language of Kannada show that linguistic innovation among Brahmin castes can accord with the principle of the " 'flight' of the elite" (Bright 1960), and Southworth's data support this hypothesis in that cross-dialectal interference of meaning (cf. Smith 1969) accounts for some Brahmin speakers' avoidance of the unmarked (or normal) lexical form entirely.

Two remaining papers in Section 3 deal with gender differences in English-language styles, and both advance our knowledge of survey-based research reported in part earlier. Thus Warshay now adds age and marital-status variables to reanalyze the findings in her earlier study of "Instrumental and affective language styles in sex status" (1969), and finds that the magnitude of correlations between verbal-stylistic markers, e.g. the correlation between fluency measures and femaleness, is reduced among married, as contrasted with unmarried, persons. One notes that her selection of "status" (see Lakoff 1973, 1975) rather than "role" (Crosby and Nyquist 1977; Key 1972) for a predictor variable represents an observer's approximation of what, in Piagetian perspective, is the mature view expectable from her college-educated subjects (Kohlberg and Ullian 1974).

In their paper, Levine and Crockett provide a statistical and psychological interpretation of gender-differentiated features of pronunciation in a representative cross-sectional sampling of speech in a North Carolina community of the U.S.A. Their first report on this small town (Levine and Crockett 1966) showed that urban sociolinguistic techniques could be generalized beyond the megalopolis (Weinreich, Labov, and Herzog 1968:181), and their subsequent observation (Crockett and Levine 1967) of "women's relatively great responsiveness or susceptibility to external norm pressure" and "men's relatively great conformity [to peers]" was later replicated elsewhere (Labov 1973; Trudgill 1972). Here, Levine and Crockett ask "Why?" the gender difference, in relation to participation in local community speech mores, and as measured by their new "mode score." Their data — which now may be expected to interest sociobiologists, too, because of focusing on the more differentiated choices of women (see Daly and Wilson 1978:76–79, 259–260) — provide two hypotheses, one based on sampling probabilities (women's lowered chances to contribute to community norms), and the other rooted in female psychology (women's "ambivalent" cognitive set). Also, their data on expressive phonological patterning lead them to posit for an idealized speaker the psychological faculty of sociolinguistic competence, which must include knowledge of "an enormous stock of statistical information" (see Shuy 1969).

SOCIOLINGUISTIC APPROACHES TO SOCIAL AND
CULTURAL CHANGE

Authors in Section 4 bring a variety of perspectives — i.e. social–cultural, evaluative, demographic, linguistic, and social psychological — to bear on the analysis of language use and language attitudes in acculturation situations. Viewed narrowly in terms of language planning, their papers can be said to describe the political cultures of socially subordinate groups that resist any displacement of mother tongue notwithstanding the imperatives to linguistically homogenize which flow from situations of government assimilationist policies, breakdowns of spatial and social isolation, and demographic factors such as migrations, changes of political boundaries, and war (Lieberson 1975). Hopefully, anthropological readers will view these papers also more broadly in the light of Weinreich's (1953) assertion of close parallelism between studies of the consequences of languages in contact and studies of acculturation processes generally (for the relevance of traditional philology, see also Bright 1973). The concept of "identity" (Robbins 1973), duly illuminated in the present papers, seems particularly promising for cross-disciplinary research on social and cultural change (McCormack 1975). From the standpoint of contribution to anthropology, for example, linguistic and other nonanthropological studies of bilingualism contain some of the best self-report data — i.e. data on "identity" — that is available in print (see Fishman et al. 1971).

The papers by Apte, Guboglo, and Heye, on immigrant groups in widely separated culture areas of the world, confirm Weinreich's (1953) insight that local and historical circumstances are crucial to predicting the attitudes of bilingual speakers toward language in culture-contact situations (see Hymes 1976:226; and on like considerations affecting attitudes toward social authority, see LeVine 1960). Apte's paper breaks new ground for the sociolinguistics of India by showing that a South Indian speech community which maintains its linguistic identity in a host region is neither ideologically separatist nor unified by any formal association that would cross the Brahmin/non-Brahmin caste division within the speech group. The speech community as a whole appears to enjoy psychological "immunity" (see Boulding 1963:134) to language shift under conditions of migration, and Heye's study of German speakers in Brazil shows the same to be true of them.

Relative to social–historical and comparative analyses of the appearance of monolinguistic nationalism, objective explanations of the appearance of multilingualist ideology within a given political system are rare (see Fishman 1972). Here, Muthiani applies social psychological thoughtways about group dynamics to interpret the acceptance and maintenance of multilingualist ideology in Kenya. He observes that although his interlocutors are descended from many different tribal peoples of Kenya, language choices related to three linguistic-ethnic stereotypes all exemplify consensual norms for behavior by bilingual speakers. Since his data picture bilingual speakers' adjusting their language choices to their perceptions of hearers and to their own self-perceptions, one gathers that the social rewards for conformity to Kenya's miltilingualist ideology include an opportunity for (some) lower-ranking persons to use choice of a lingua franca as a symbolic means to avoid social stigmatization (see Samarin 1966:198).

Cultural oppression in acculturative situations can be expressed through official rules that restrict the range of functions permitted to the language varieties associated with relatively weak social groups. Albó and Pulte both describe such cases for us and discuss what might be expected if this situation changed to permit the weak groups full employment of their cultural–linguistic resources.

One thing linguistic anthropologists and sociolinguists themselves can usefully do by way of cooperating in situations of cultural–linguistic change is to collect field data on cultural specialists' performances of traditional verbal art. Armstrong points out that such performances express cultural values but in the acculturative setting tend to have little or no popular institutional support for preservation and publication. He thus recommends tape-recording African oral literature now, as one means to insure a permanent opportunity for interpretation of it. Texts with known cultural functions are, of course, useful too for improvement of language instruction and advancement of linguistic theory (see BREDA 1976).

As for some accomplished applied sociolinguistics, Darnell reports here on the cooperation between herself and Cree women in producing culturally appropriate Cree language-learning materials for Cree children in the province of Alberta, Canada. While the women strongly valued the oratorical style of old Cree, they chose to use contemporary conversational Cree for the children's storybooks, on grounds that it was easier to learn. Much work was devoted to devising a writing system for the language, and it would be interesting to know whether previous experiences of discrimination in English-language schools occurred and affected the group's choice of a script that does not resemble the English alphabet.

In open recognition of past discrimination, and in response to ethnic-group and other minority-group demands for improvement of their cultural–linguistic status within school systems, affluent industrialized countries like the U.S.A. and Canada have for some years been providing official encouragement to cultural self-study and teacher-training programs aimed at disadvantaged communities. Treuba describes one such program for Mexican–Americans. In spite of the program's meeting with a mixed reception by the people it serves, its philosophy of bilingualism/biculturalism appears to be gaining ground.

However, it seems too that demographic factors are at once basic to language maintenance by minority groups and also rarely subject to local control in urban industrialized countries because the economies of such countries are normally integrated on a national scale. As Lewis demonstrates from his comparison of Wales with the U.S.S.R., migration dictated by economic considerations has more effect on the maintenance or loss of cultural–linguistic identity than "education, social ideology and philosophy together with the actual operation of a political policy."

MODERNIZATION AND THE SCIENCE OF LANGUAGE PLANNING

With Section 5, we come to consider directly a few of the ways in which sociolinguistics may contribute to planning for social and cultural change. In general, the contribution is most likely to be through helping to evolve an interdisciplinary science of language planning. The evolution of that science, as of any science, entails theoretical synthesis (see Fishman 1976; Haugen 1971, 1973; Hymes 1973, 1976; Lambert 1967a), but for language planning as an activity that is "by definition" relevant chiefly to situations of development and/or modernization, it is helpful to refer to C. S. Peirce's 1903 semiotic conception of normative science (see Potter 1967:25ff.) for an understanding of how that synthesis may ultimately be achieved. Peirce argued that normative science was a branch of philosophical inquiry, and so was basically a nonspecialist (we might say "interdisciplinary") encounter with the theoretical problem of prediction in human affairs. Ethics, for which his preferred term was "practics," would be the normative science *par excellence*, and should formulate theoretical rules for conduct that ought to be followed. However it was assumed that practics could, but normally would not, permeate the activities of those kinds of people adept at the practical skills in conducting those affairs to which its theoretical rules applied. In this last respect, at least, language planning is now recognizably a theoretical normative science which is able to predict that in the actualization of language-policy matters:

the final approaches to such problems tend to be very vague solutions — compromises between the two possible extremes of total planning and total laissez-faire; or the planning action may be vigorous but the implementation of the plans inadequate, or the results nullified either through other, contradictory official actions or the lack of some necessary official action (Wurm 1977:346).

At the present time, some formal conceptualizations for a theoretical science of language planning are already in place. Thus it is almost ten years since Haugen (1969) subdivided language-planning procedures according as they relate to policy decisions (or selection of reference norms), to codification (in grammars and dictionaries), to elaboration (of the code's functions), and to implementation. To these features, Rubin (1971) added evaluation, such as is necessary for administration of any social-action program (see Suchman 1967; Wurm 1971). Fishman (1974b) added still more components of theory, according to the insights of Ferguson (1968), plus of Neustupný (1970) and others of the Prague school of linguistics.

More recently, though, language-planning theorists have taken great interest in details of the development of applied linguistics in the People's Republic of China, where language research is altogether applications-oriented (Ferguson 1975a), and of which it is said that, "There is no near parallel to this massive planned language change taking place anywhere else in the world" (Ferguson 1975b; see also Lehmann 1975; Light 1978). Further, Kumanëv here describes Soviet governmental success in achieving mass literacy within the U.S.S.R. in less than a generation, and it is common knowledge that the trend in social sciences in the West since the 1960's has been toward applications as well. Cutting through all political boundaries, Maraini here questions the notion that any script such as the Roman alphabet can best serve all communicative needs of any population, and shows how the advantages of ideographic scripts for rapid scanning of texts may well offset the learning difficulties they pose.

It remains to be seen how these two great streams of attention to language planning will advance the evolution of language planning as a normative science. For the time being, we here illustrate the range of language-planning activities in a partial way, with a diversity of papers on language in education on the one hand, and on language in national planning on the other. Since the general political–cultural motivations (see Hymes 1976:225–226) for popular as well as sociolinguistic interest in reshaping these two institutional domains derive fairly obviously from the dynamics of modernization, extended comment on the matter seems unnecessary here.

One paper which represents both topics is Fishman's project report on national language planning *vis-à-vis* samples of literate and school-related populations of students, teachers, and parents in the nations of Israel, Indonesia, and India. Sophisticated quantitative analysis of massive data indicated that

for adults their primary group memberships (ethnic, religious, linguistic) and their basic social experiences (education, occupation) most strongly determine their attitudinal/cognitive and overt usage responses to language planning. On the other hand, students are (still) responding largely on attitudinal/informational bases. . . .

Fishman sees a functional role for school and college populations in effectuating the social goals established by central planning agencies, "since informational/attitudinal manipulation is generally easier than fostering demographic change in occupation, social class, education, etc." Independently supporting Fishman's observation that youth-age groups, specifically students, are openminded toward proposals tor language reform, the Silvermans' paper on a proposed introduction of the artificial Esperanto language into U.S. language-learning programs claims that "many university students in the United States would be supportive of the goals of the international language [Esperanto] movement if they were made aware of its existence."

Further to the subject of language in education, sociolinguists have always been sensitive to the problems faced by schoolchildren who speak language varieties containing socially stigmatized nonstandard phonological or grammatical features and therefore suffer from being negatively stereotyped by their teachers. Under such circumstances, remedial teacher-training about the sociolinguistic facts of life is indicated, for such features of speech may be taken to signal probable cultural qualities such as social-class or ethnic background but not also "wholly fanciful, nonexistent attributes" of individual linguistic competence or personality (Allport 1958; Burling 1971, 1973 especially ch. 2; Fowler 1971:263–266, 272–273; Giles and Powesland 1975:107–110; Spolsky 1974:2033). That the hearer in such cases is victim of a learned cognitive set to stereotype is demonstrated here by Giles and colleagues, who experimentally instructed a panel in Wales to indicate preferences for standard as against nonstandard pronunciations of French, and found that they had none.

For a totally different perspective on the issue of social tolerance of linguistic diversity, Décsy's reconstruction of past language policy in the Danube Basin shows that Old Hungary fell within a larger culture area characterized by early Greek and Byzantine attitudes of toleration for linguistic pluralism (Lewis 1976), and of itself once showed a special adjustment of its multilingualism to farflung civilizational contacts. However, a post-World War II emphasis on practical instruction within modern Hungary is reflected in a realignment of language policy to fit the claims of internal linguistic–ethnic constituencies, in such a way that none of the presently subsidized five major languages is able to fulfill the internationally functional roles vacated by German, Latin, and Greek.

In the case of a province of western Canada, as Abu-Laban discovered from content-analysis of representations to a 1972 Alberta Cultural Heritage Conference, East European immigrants and their descendants are clearheaded and articulate on the value of bilingual schooling for inculcating respect for the total spectrum of cultural–linguistic groups in Canada. Lieberson (1970) had already made the point that schooling should be bilingual if minorities were to consolidate cultural–linguistic identity. Whatever argument persuaded the Albertan authorities, it is now the fact that Ukrainian/English bilingual schooling exists in Alberta.

Moving now to language planning at national levels, an analogy for what is likely to happen to a modernizing culture when group action toward modernization goals proceeds by favoring a single language for communication exists in the history of legal reform where "the very [functional] forces that support this movement [toward a unified, uniform, hierarchic, and rational legal system] and are released by it deflect it from its apparent destination" (Galanter 1966:164). Such is the anomaly that emerges from Ferguson's and Dil's survey of universals in language planning and national development, which reveals that amidst modernization the forces for language plurality considerably offset those for language uniformity. Moreover, one of their hypotheses, that, *"The development process tends toward [language] differentiation along functional lines* . . . within single languages or . . . by the use of one or more different functional allocations [of extant languages in the community]," is borne out independently by Verdoodt's sociolinguistic profile of the new African nation of Burundi. Burundi is unimodal in that a single language is the mother tongue of over 95 percent of the population, yet at the time of Verdoodt's study, it was the French language which had been allocated the modernizing functions.

The normal complexities of interactive process between national development and language planning are immensely multiplied in India, a giant of pluralism in almost every sense, and by now many years along the road to modernization. As Krishnamurti here shows, India is a prime case of competing models for language cultivation within its component states, even though most states have now had boundaries reorganized to contain their respective majority linguistic–cultural groups. Lexical expansion of the major vernaculars to enable communication about modern technological civilization has generally followed the principle of diglossic complementarity of high and low prestige forms, with the high forms taken largely from Sanskrit roots, but for Tamil, in particular, Krishnamurti finds that diglossia (see Ferguson 1959) has delayed the spread of mass literacy, and even that, "The diglossic situation has inhibited the growth of an educated spoken variety" (see Pride 1971). Pandit has made the point strongly in this volume that communication in India is not hampered by grassroots multilingualism (see Khubchandani 1975), and Lakshmanna and Yadava tell us about sociological networks operating for the communication of modern-type messages in rural southern and northern India, respectively, in spite of the language diversity (see Lerner 1958, 1963).

As for special utilization of the concept of "network" in sociolinguistics, Afendras suggests that tracing networks of popular response to centralized language-planning policies is a method for evaluating local implementation of the policies (Rubin 1971, 1973) such as to possibly result in important revisions to the policies at the center. According to Cheng, just such revisions at the center, to accord more with local needs, have been necessary in Taiwan. It is rare that sociolinguists have been able to forestall the need for major revisions in language planning, by having the opportunity to carry out detailed and influential sociolinguistic studies in advance (e.g. Ohannessian, Ferguson, and Polomé 1975), but here Brann describes how government foresight in Nigeria enabled a sociolinguistic contribution to a sophisticated plan for development of a multilingual public-school curriculum.

CONCLUSIONS

The charter for this book has been the objectivist position that if language, culture, and society are conceptually interrelateable, then this must be shown to be so not only in the minds of investigators but also as predictive of sociolinguistic patterns. From the latter it would follow that the understanding of speech acts, of values and habits of cultural perception, and of normative functions for group action and sociability requires that these phenomena be treated together and not be severally reserved to the domains of specialized disciplines.

The limitations of a narrowly specialist linguistics have been shown here by, for example, Halliday's interpretation of Vanek's study, which in turn is in the genre of a classic study of pronominal address (Brown and Gilman 1960) that repeatedly demonstrates precisely this point. Conversely, sociology and anthropology ignore sociolinguistic data at their peril (see Lambert 1967b), when Sampson can find here that her study of Chaucerian pronominal usage reveals "information about the [contemporary] class structure of the society that was not available before." Third, and *pace* nonlinguistic cultural anthropology, Dakubu's study of Ga stylistic codeswitching here presents one local expression of the universal verbal differentiation, or marking, of social distance between interlocutors, which Ervin-Tripp has speculated functions in facilitating a person's learning to manipulate "major social dimensions and categories of groups" (Ervin-Tripp 1976:152) and which may also bear a functional relationship to the kinds of moral and intellectual development that occur through Piagetian "decentration" processes (see Laurendeau and Pinard 1962:7–9).

If disciplinary exclusivity has from the present perspective "by definition" had serious shortcomings for many kinds of intellectual understandings before, those shortcomings would only proliferate vis-à-vis evolution of a science of language planning. Sociolinguistics has hitherto been resistant to *a priori* definition of its scope and content (see Piaget 1973), and perhaps, as scholarship is everywhere increasingly enlisted in the formidable task of serving the people, it is just as well that its open-endedness be cherished. As Karam has summed up (1974:108):

Regardless of the type of language planning, in nearly all cases the language problem to be solved is not a problem in isolation within the region or nation but is directly associated with the political, economic, scientific, social, cultural, and/or religious situation.

REFERENCES

ALLPORT, G. W.
  1958   *The nature of prejudice*. Garden City, New York: Doubleday Anchor.
BEAN, S. S.
  1974a   Linguistic variation and the caste system in South Asia. *Indian Linguistics* 35:277–293.
  1974b   "An exploration into the semantics of social space in Kannada," in *Structuralism in South Indian studies*. Edited by H. Buck and G. Yocum, 96–114. Chambersburg, Pa.: Wilson Books.
  1978   *Symbolic and pragmatic semantics, a Kannada system of address*. Chicago: University of Chicago Press.
BOLINGER, D.
  1975   *Aspects of language*. 2nd ed.; New York: Harcourt, Brace, Jovanovich.
BOULDING, K.
  1963   *Conflict and defense: a general theory*. New York: Harper Torchbooks.
BREDA
  1976   Summary of working paper: Symposium on the problems of education in the mother-tongue in a sub-region of Africa. *ALSED Newsletter*, No. 5 (June): 6–8. Paris: UNESCO (Anthropology Language Sciences and Educational Development).
BRIGHT, W.
  1960   Social dialect and language history. *Current Anthropology* 1:424–425.
  1966   "Introduction: the dimensions of sociolinguistics," in *Sociolinguistics*. Edited by W. Bright, 11–15. The Hague: Mouton.
  1973   "North American Indian language contact," in *Current trends in linguistics*, volume ten. Edited by T. A. Sebeok, 713–726. The Hague: Mouton.
BROWN, R. W., A. GILMAN
  1960   "The pronouns of power and solidarity," in *Style in language*. Edited by T. A. Sebeok, 253–276. Cambridge, Mass.: MIT Press.
BURLING, ROBBINS
  1971   Talking to teachers about social dialects. *Language Learning* 21 (2):221–234.
  1973   *English in black and white*. New York: Holt, Rinehart, and Winston.
CHOMSKY, NOAM
  1975   *Reflections on language*. New York: Random House, Pantheon Books.
COHEN, A. D.
  1975   *A sociolinguistic approach to bilingual education*. Rowley, Mass.: Newbury House.

CROCKETT, H. J., JR., L. LEVINE
1967   Friends' influences on speech. *Sociological Inquiry* 37:109–128.
CROSBY, F., L. NYQUIST
1977   The female register: an empirical study of Lakoff's hypotheses. *Language in Society* 6:313–322.
DALY, M., M. WILSON
1978   *Sex, evolution, and behavior.* North Scituate, Mass.: Duxbury Press.
DILLARD, J. L.
1975   Review of: *The study of social dialects in American English*, by W. Wolfram and R. Fasold. *Language in Society* 4:367–375.
ERVIN-TRIPP, S. M.
1964   "An analysis of the interaction of language, topic, and listener," in *The ethnography of communication.* Edited by J. J. Gumperz and D. Hymes, 86–102. *American Anthropologist* (Special Publication) 66(6) Part 2.
1976   "Speech acts and social learning," in *Meaning in anthropology.* Edited by K. H. Basso and H. A. Selby, 123–153. Albuquerque: University of New Mexico Press.
FERGUSON, C. A.
1959   Diglossia. *Word* 15:325–340.
1968   "Language development," in *Language problems of developing nations.* Edited by J. A. Fishman, C. A. Ferguson, and J. Das Gupta, 27–35. New York: John Wiley.
1975a Linguistics serves the people: lessons of a trip to China. *Items* 29 (March): 5–8. New York: Social Science Research Council.
1975b Applied linguistics in China. *Linguistic Reporter* 17 (4):3, 10. Arlington, Va.: Center for Applied Linguistics.
FISHMAN, J. A.
1971   *Sociolinguistics: a brief introduction.* Rowley, Mass.: Newbury House.
1972   *Language and nationalism.* Rowley, Mass.: Newbury House.
1974a "The sociology of language: an interdisciplinary social approach to language in society," in *Current trends in linguistics* 12, part 3. Edited by T. A. Sebeok, 1629–1784. The Hague: Mouton.
1974b "Language planning and language planning research: the state of the art," in *Advances in language planning.* Edited by J. A. Fishman, 15–33. The Hague: Mouton.
1976   *Bilingual education.* Rowley, Mass.: Newbury House.
FISHMAN, J. A., R. L. COOPER, R. MA
1971   *Bilingualism in the barrio.* (Indiana University Language Science Monographs, Vol. 7). Bloomington: Indiana University; The Hague: Mouton.
FOWLER, W.
1971   "Cognitive baselines in early childhood: developmental learning and differentiation of competence rule systems," in *Cognitive studies, volume two.* Edited by J. Hellmuth, 231–279. New York: Brunner/Mazel; London: Butterworth.
GALANTER, M.
1966   "The modernization of law," in *Modernization: the dynamics of growth.* Edited by Myron Weiner, 153–165. New York and London: Basic Books.
GILES, H., P. F. POWESLAND
1975   *Speech style and social evaluation.* (European Monographs in Social Psychology 7.) London, New York and San Francisco: Academic Press.

GUMPERZ, J. J.
1977   "Sociocultural knowledge in conversational inference," in *Georgetown University Round Table on Languages and Linguistics 1977.* Edited by M. Saville-Troike, 191–211. Washington, D.C.: Georgetown University Press.

HALLIDAY, M. A. K.
1975   "Language as social semiotic: towards a general sociolinguistic theory," in *The first LACUS forum, 1974.* Edited by Adam and V. B. Makkai, 17–46. Columbia, S.C.: Hornbeam Press.

HAUGEN, E.
1966   "Linguistics and language planning," in *Sociolinguistics.* Edited by W. Bright, 50–71. The Hague: Mouton.
1969   "Language planning, theory and practice," in *Actes du Xe Congres International des Linguistes, Bucarest.* Edited by A. Graur, 701–711. (Reprinted in: *The ecology of language: essays by Einar Haugen.* Edited by A. S. Dil, 287–298. Stanford: Stanford University Press, 1972.)
1971   The ecology of language. *Linguistic Reporter,* Suppl. 25 (Winter): 19–26. (Reprinted in: *The ecology of language: essays by Einar Haugen.* Edited by A. S. Dil, 325–339. Stanford: Stanford University Press, 1972.)
1973   The curse of Babel. *Daedalus: Journal of the American Academy of Arts and Sciences* (Summer): 47–57. (Reprinted in: *Language as a human problem.* Edited by E. Haugen and M. Bloomfield, 33–43. New York: W. W. Norton, 1974.)

HOOVER, M.
1978   Community attitudes toward black English. *Language in Society* 7:65–87.

HYMES, D. H.
1967   "Models of the interaction of language and social setting," in *Problems of bilingualism.* Edited by J. Macnamara, 8–28. (*Journal of Social Issues* 23.)
1973   On the origins and foundations of inequality among speakers. *Daedalus: Journal of the American Academy of Arts and Sciences* (Summer): 59–86. (Reprinted in: *Language as a human problem.* Edited by E. Haugen and M. Bloomfield, 45–71. New York: W. W. Norton, 1974.)
1974a "Ways of speaking," in *Explorations in the ethnography of speaking.* Edited by R. Bauman and J. Sherzer, 433–451. Cambridge: Cambridge University Press.
1974b *Foundations of sociolinguistics: an ethnographic approach.* Philadelphia: University of Pennsylvania Press.
1976   Towards linguistic competence. *Sociologische gids* 76:217–239.

KARAM, F. X.
1974   "Toward a definition of language planning," in *Advances in language planning.* Edited by J. A. Fishman, 103–124. The Hague and Paris: Mouton.

KEY, M. R.
1972   Linguistic behavior of male and female. *Linguistics* 88:15–31.

KHUBCHANDANI, L. M.
1975   Language planning in modern India. *Language Planning Newsletter* 1 (1):1, 3–4. Honolulu: East-West Centre.

KOHLBERG, L., D. Z. ULLIAN
1974   "Stages in the development of psychosexual concepts and attitudes," in

Sex differences in behavior. Edited by R. C. Friedman, R. N. Richart, and R. L. Van de Wiele, 209–222. New York and Toronto: J. Wiley.

KURATH, H.
1968   *The investigation of urban speech and some other problems confronting the student of American English.* (Publication of the American Dialect Society, 49.) University, Ala.: University of Alabama Press.

LABOV, W.
1970   The study of language in its social context. *Studium Generale* 23:30–87. (Revised as chap. 8 in his *Sociolinguistic patterns.* Philadelphia: University of Pennsylvania Press, 1972.)
1973   "The social setting of linguistic change," in *Current trends in linguistics,* volume eleven. Edited by T. A. Sebeok, 195–251. The Hague: Mouton. (Revised as chap. 9 in his *Sociolinguistic patterns.* Philadelphia: University of Pennsylvania Press, 1972.)

LAKOFF, R.
1972   Language in context. *Language* 48 (4):907–927.
1973   Language and woman's place. *Language in Society* 2 (1):45–80.
1975   *Language and woman's place.* New York: Harper and Row.

LAMBERT, W. E.
1967a   "A social psychology of bilingualism," in *Problems of bilingualism.* Edited by J. Macnamara, 91–109. (*Journal of Social Issues* 23.)
1967b   The use of "tu" and "vous" as forms of address in French Canada: a pilot study. *Journal of Verbal Learning and Verbal Behavior* 6 (4):614–617.

LAMBERT, W. E., G. R. TUCKER
1972   *Bilingual education of children: the St. Lambert experiment.* Rowley, Mass.: Newbury House.

LAMBERT, W. E., G. R. TUCKER, A. D'ANGLEJAN
1973   Cognitive and attitudinal consequences of bilingual schooling: the St. Lambert project through grade five. *Journal of Educational Psychology* 65:141–159.

LAURENDEAU, M., A. PINARD
1962   *Causal thinking in the child.* New York: International Universities Press.

LEHMANN, W. P., *editor*
1975   *Language and linguistics in the People's Republic of China.* Austin: University of Texas Press.

LERNER, D.
1958   *The passing of traditional society: modernizing the Middle East.* Glencoe, Ill.: Free Press.
1963   "Toward a communication theory of modernization," in *Communication and political development.* Edited by L. W. Pye, 327–350. Princeton: Princeton University Press.

LEVINE, L., H. J. CROCKETT, JR.
1966   Speech variation in a Piedmont community: postvocalic *r. Sociological Inquiry* 36:186–203.

LEVINE, R. A.
1960   The internalization of political values in stateless societies. *Human Organization* 19:51–58.

LEWIS, E. G.
1976   "Bilingualism and bilingual education: the ancient world to the Renaissance," in *Bilingual education: an international sociological perspective.*

By Joshua A. Fishman, with an appendix by E. Glyn Lewis, 150–200. Rowley, Mass.: Newbury House.

LIEBERSON, S.
1970 *Language and ethnic relations in Canada.* New York: J. Wiley.
1975 The course of mother-tongue diversity in nations. *American Journal of Sociology* 81:34–61.

LIGHT, T.
1978 U.S. applied linguistics delegation to the People's Republic of China: a report. *Linguistic Reporter* 20 (7): 4–5, 8. Arlington, Va.: Center for Applied Linguistics.

McCORMACK, W. C.
1960 "Social dialects in Dharwar Kannada," in *Linguistic diversity in South Asia: studies in regional, social, and functional variation.* Edited by C. A. Ferguson and J. J. Gumperz, 79–91. (*International Journal of American Linguistics* 26 (3): No. 3; also, Bloomington, Ind.: Research Center in Anthropology, Folklore and Linguistics [Publ. No. 13].)
1967 "Language identity," in *Chapters in Indian civilization: vol. II, British and modern period.* Edited by J. W. Elder, 435–465. Madison, Wis.: Department of Indian Studies, University of Wisconsin. (second ed.; Dubuque, Iowa: Kendall/Hunt Publishing Co., 1970.)
1968 "Occupation and residence in relation to Dharwar dialects," in *Structure and change in Indian society.* Edited by M. B. Singer and B. S. Cohn, 475–485. (Viking Fund Publications in Anthropology, No. 47.) Chicago: Aldine.
1975 "Language identity of a Friesian town: symbol, stereotype, or social communication?," in *Proceedings of the XIth International Congress of Linguists, Bologna, 1972, Vol. II.* Edited by L. Heilmann, 165–170. Bologna: Società editrice il Mulino.

McCORMACK, W. C., S. A. WURM, *editors*
1978 *Approaches to language: anthropological issues.* The Hague and Paris: Mouton.

MARRIOTT, M., R. INDEN
1974 Caste systems. *Encyclopaedia Britannica* 3:982–991.

MEHAN, H., H. WOOD
1975 *The reality of ethnomethodology.* New York: J. Wiley.

NEUSTUPNÝ, J. V.
1970 Basic types of language problems. *Linguistic Communications* 1:77–98. (Reprinted in: *Advances in language planning.* Edited by J. A. Fishman, 37–48. The Hague: Mouton, 1974.)

OHANNESSIAN, S., C. A. FERGUSON, E. C. POLOMÉ, *editors*
1975 *Language surveys in developing nations: papers and reports on sociolinguistic surveys.* Arlington, Va.: Center for Applied Linguistics.

PIAGET, J.
1973 *Main trends in interdisciplinary research.* New York: Harper and Row. (Originally chap. 7 in *Main trends of research in the social and human sciences, Part 1.* The Hague and Paris: Mouton/UNESCO, 1970.)

POTTER, V. G.
1967 *Charles S. Peirce on norms and ideals.* Amherst, Mass.: University of Massachusetts Press.

PRIDE, J. B.
1971 *The social meaning of language.* London: Oxford University Press.

RITZER, G.
1975 *Sociology: a multiple paradigm science.* Boston: Allyn and Bacon.

ROBBINS, R. H.
1973   "Identity, culture, and behavior," in *Handbook of social and cultural anthropology*. Edited by J. J. Honigmann, 1199–1222. Chicago: Rand McNally.

RUBIN, J.
1971   "Evaluation and language planning," in *Can language be planned?* Edited by J. Rubin and B. Jernudd, 217–252. Honolulu: University Press of Hawaii.
1973   "Introduction," in *Language planning: current issues and research*. Edited by J. Rubin and R. Shuy, v–x. Washington, D.C.: Georgetown University Press.

SAMARIN, W. J.
1966   "Self-annuling prestige factors among speakers of a Creole language," in *Sociolinguistics*. Edited by W. Bright, 188–217. The Hague: Mouton.

SHUY, R. W.
1969   "Sociolinguistic research at the Center for Applied Linguistics: the correlation of language and sex," in *International days of sociolinguistics*, 849–857. Rome: 2nd International Congress of Social Science of the Luigi Sturzo Institute.

SILVERSTEIN, M.
1972   "Linguistic theory: syntax, semantics, pragmatics," in *Annual review of anthropology, volume one*. Edited by B. J. Siegel, A. R. Beals, and S. A. Tyler, 349–382. Palo Alto, Calif.: Annual Reviews.
1975   "Linguistics and anthropology," in *Linguistics and neighboring disciplines*. Edited by R. Bartsch and T. Venneman, 157–170. Amsterdam: North-Holland Publishing Co.
1976   "Shifters, linguistic categories, and cultural description," in *Meaning in anthropology*. Edited by K. H. Basso and H. A. Selby, 11–55. Albuquerque: University of New Mexico Press.

SMITH, R. B.
1969   Interrelatedness of certain deviant grammatical structures in Negro nonstandard dialects. *Journal of English Linguistics* 3:82–88.

SPOLSKY, B.
1974   "Linguistics and the language barrier to education," in *Current trends in linguistics* 12, Part 3. Edited by T. A. Sebeok, 2027–2038. The Hague: Mouton.

SUCHMAN, E. A.
1967   *Evaluative research: principles and practice in public service and social action programs*. New York: Russell Sage Foundation.

TRAUGOTT, E. C.
1976   "Pidgins, creoles, and the origins of vernacular black English," in *Black English: a seminar*. Edited by D. S. Harrison and T. Trabasso, 57–93. Hillsdale, New Jersey: L. Erlbaum Associates.

TRUDGILL, P.
1972   Sex, covert prestige and linguistic change in the urban British English of Norwich. *Language in Society* 1:179–195.

VOEGELIN, C. F., F. M. VOEGELIN
1972   "Dependence of selectional restrictions on cultural spaces," in *Studies for Einar Haugen*. Edited by E. S. Firchow, K. Grimstad, N. Hasselmo, and W. A. O'Neil, 535–553. The Hague: Mouton.

WALLACE, A. F. C.
1970   *Culture and personality*. Second ed.; New York: Random House.

WARSHAY, D. W.
1969 "Instrumental and affective language styles in sex status." Unpublished doctoral dissertation, Ohio State University.

WEINREICH, U.
1953 *Languages in contact: findings and problems.* Fourth printing; The Hague: Mouton, 1966.

WEINREICH, U., W. LABOV, M. I. HERZOG
1968 "Empirical foundations for a theory of language change," in *Directions for historical linguistics*. Edited by W. P. Lehmann and Y. Malkiel, 95–195. Austin: University of Texas Press.

WISDOM, J. O.
1970 "Situational individualism and the emergent group-properties," in *Explanation in the behavioural sciences*. Edited by Robert Borger and Frank Cioffi, 271–296. Cambridge: Cambridge University Press.

WOLFRAM, W.
1974 The relationship of white southern speech to vernacular black English. *Language* 50:498–527.

WURM, S. A.
1971 "Language policy, language engineering and literacy in New Guinea and Australia," in *Current trends in linguistics* 8, Part 2. Edited by T. A. Sebeok, 1025–1038. The Hague: Mouton. (Revised in: *Advances in language planning*. Edited by J. A. Fishman, 205–220. The Hague: Mouton, 1974.)
1977 "Pidgins, creoles, lingue franche, and national development," in *Pidgin and creole linguistics*. Edited by A. Valdman, 333–357. Bloomington, Ind.: Indiana University Press.

SECTION TWO

Social Meaning of Language

A Transactional View of Speech Functions and Codeswitching

J. B. PRIDE

TALK ABOUT TALK

A basic assumption of many sociolinguistic investigators today is that, ideally, "perception of the categories that are being measured" should be that of both the investigator and his informant (Gumperz and Hymes 1972:15). What the informant says largely constrains, if it does not altogether control, what the investigator can validly say and how he says it. As Frake (1972:110) has put it: "Information about what is 'same' and what is 'different' can only come from the interpretations of events made by the people being studied . . . we must attend to the way of Yakan talk about talking." In a similar vein, Abrahams (1972) observes: "As in other parts of Afro-America, on St. Vincent there is a good deal of talk about talk"; and he goes on to show that this kind of behavior amounts to important data in its own right, lending itself to structural analysis and having in particular a good deal to do with values in relation to choice of language. Thus, "talking sweet" and "talking bad" can be seen, he shows, as linguistic reflections of "the worlds of 'acting behaved' and 'acting rude'," behaviors which are "counterpoised for purposes of entertainment" on social occasions and which may be of some significance for the way things are going — sociolinguistically — in this part of the world. In general, sociolinguistic research convinces in such cases as when, e.g. "by living in Yakan households during the entire field period, the investigator was continually exposed to conversations related to litigation" (Frake 1972:107); or when, say, "rapping" is both discussed and enacted by informants "in a public park" (Mitchell-Kernan 1972:171).

Generally speaking, however, talk about talk should not be taken at

---

This paper supercedes an earlier version entitled "Facts of speech in sociolinguistics."

face value: Ervin-Tripp (1972) points to various grounds for distrusting informants' reports about their own behavior (e.g. "Some speakers cannot remember the language in which they just spoke") and claims that behavioral rules and reports about them are "likely to be systematically different" — systematically indeed in the implications, for example, of Labov's "principle which holds quite generally in New York City: that those who used the highest percentage of a stigmatized form in casual speech were the most sensitive in stigmatizing it in the speech of others" (Labov 1972a: 532). Blom and Gumperz (1972) likewise reveal how their Norwegian informants show "clear signs of disapproval" on noticing — or having pointed out to them — "violations of co-occurrence rules" in their own use of what (to them) should have been either distinctly Bokmål or Ranamål. Then a particularly valuable section of Albert's rewarding essay on "Culture patterning of speech behaviour in Burundi" (1972) is that which relates such patterning to the business of fieldwork ("locating verbal and other cues by which individuals signal either ignorance of the subject on which they are pretending to give information or intentional distortion" (1972:98). And to return to Frake and the Yakan people he was studying, a necessary condition for an activity such as "litigation" will, he shows, be their ability to recognize it as such, reference to it having at the same time to be assessed as "lying," "joking," etc. in relation to the "conditions under which it is congruous" to state that this is what one is doing.

Much depends on the extent to which members of a speech community share views concerning the place of language (its varieties, uses, users, etc.) in their lives. Shared norms, values, interpretations of all sorts, are in fact as basic as anything else in the definition of most speech communities. They have indeed pride of place in the view that "the speech community is defined not by the presence or absence of a particular dialect or language but by the presence of a common set of normative values in regard to linguistic features" (Gumperz and Hymes 1972:513; see also Labov [1964] where the point is made explicit with regard to the New York speech community). So too will the kinds and degrees of identification between the investigator and the speech community he is studying matter a great deal. This holds good whether or not any particular investigation draws upon "participant analysis," as do those of Labov and his colleagues (1968), Mitchell-Kernan (1971), and others, into "Black English" in the United States. And it holds good even in respect of sheer observation: in Labov's view (1972b), observation of what people do is "the most difficult of all the methods" he discusses, these being the use of texts, elicitations, intuitions, and observations (see, for example, his revealing discussion, [1969] of the problems encountered in the elicitation and observation of "nonstandard" English). Identification between speech community and investigator is certainly an essential prerequisite for the exploration of many interesting linkages among such factors as: what people do (i.e. linguistically), think they do, say they do, think/say others do/think/say, hear themselves/others doing, consider best to do/say, think/say others consider best to do/say, and so forth. The list can soon become quite large, embracing such considerations as what people (including scholars of various persuasions) consider best for others to do, and (not least) how ordinary people account for all these various behaviors and assumptions. Hoenigswald (1966) applied the expression "folk linguistics" to the study of widespread views about language; one might say then that current sociolinguistics is increasingly (but of course by no means exclusively) concerning itself with the many ramifications of folk linguistics.

One very clear example of the importance of data which shows how speech communities (and speech communities within speech communities) see their linguistic situation is that of "Black English" in the United States. Thus, in certain communities in California there are polarized norms which on the one side value speech which is not ethnically marked and on the other discount ethnic marking as, in itself, neither good nor bad; so that "country-flat" speech, say, may or may not be accounted "bad" speech, and vice versa, according to what one might wish to call the subspeech community (Mitchell-Kernan 1971: esp. 43–50). Another good example is that of "diglossia," wherever this may be found. Ferguson's well-known definition (1959) goes as follows:

Diglossia is a relatively stable language situation in which, in addition to the primary dialects of the language (which may include a standard or regional standards), there is a very divergent, highly codified (often grammatically more complex) superposed variety, the vehicle of a large and respected body of written literature, either of an earlier period or in another speech community, which is learned largely by formal education and is used for most written and formal spoken purposes but is not used by any sector of the community for ordinary conversation.

Ferguson's examples do not include that of diglossia in India, but what McCormack (1970) says is further proof of the extent of this phenomenon:

Take any major Indian language for your example, and you will find that ordinary speech is made up of codes for signaling directives to act and manipulate things, but there exists also a prestigious, pedantic, STYLE of the language which is employed to dress up the virtues of a text and/or to display the virtuosity of the writer or performer of the text. By extension, this latter style gets used by anyone who knows it, in all kinds of social situations, to accent the relatively high status of the speaker and to underscore the relatively great importance of the matter being talked about. Both the speaker and hearers mutually value this sign of importance in the particular social situation, and it is comparatively irrelevant whether what the speaker says is intelligible to his hearers or not (1970: 232; original emphasis).

With reference to Arabic, however, Nader (1962) interestingly shifted the focus of attention from the single prestigious "high" variety to the many different ways in which one particular Arabic speech community, the Lebanese, have rated their various colloquial ("low") dialects according to appropriateness for use in different situations or for different purposes ("such as when a person wishes to be stiff or relaxed, honest, amusing, or ambivalent"). In other words, the various low dialects (or languages) in situations of diglossia will be likely to have their own particular values, albeit different in kind from those of the single high style.[1] Fishman (1972) on the other hand sees diglossia in a rather different light: "The high culture values with which certain varieties are associated and the intimacy and folksiness with which others are congruent are both derivable from domain-appropriate norms governing characteristic verbal interaction" (1972:451). The crucial factor may ultimately be whether or not the informant himself (adequately representative, one hopes, of the speech community or communities to which he belongs) sees the diglossia situation as essentially a matter of domains or as one of values, his perspective amounting that is to say to very real data in itself, a kind of definition of what is to be sociolinguistically described and explained.[2]

[1] Compare the recent attention given to alternative values inherent in nonstandard varieties of English used in the United States. Labov, who has been at the forefront of such work, suggests the functioning of "other values, at a deeper level of consciousness, which reinforce the vernacular speech forms of New York City" (quoted from "On the mechanism of linguistic change," now in Gumperz and Hymes [1972:533]). Then there are the pages (491–501) on "Pressures from below" and "Differences in linguistic attitudes of various subgroups" in *The social stratification of English in New York City*. The principle is further elaborated in Labov, Cohen, Robins and Lewis (1968:vol. 2, pp. 217ff.). Thus, on pages 217 and 218 the authors state: "It has now been established in a sufficient number of cases that certain speech forms are highly valued in terms of the middleclass scale of job suitability. In SSENYC, Negro subjects showed as much or more sensitivity to these social markers as white subjects (Labov 1966:442–446, 652–655). We observe these values being imposed throughout adolescence; the average adult reaches full agreement with the system of social norms in his early twenties (Labov 1965). But when we examine the overall sociolinguistic structure, it appears that people systematically deviate from these norms, and this systematic deviation forms the complex system which we wish to explain. Part of the reason that workingclass speakers do not conform more closely to the middleclass norms which they endorse is that they acquire these norms after their productive capacity has been formed. It is also possible that many never get enough practice in SE forms to achieve productive control. But we must also consider the possibility that the middleclass norms such as job suitability are not the only ones which are operating to maintain this structure — that there are other norms which reinforce and give value to working class speech. Such opposing norms would be covert in the test situation, and may indeed be difficult to observe in any case, since they are further removed from conscious attention than most social norms". Specific detail in support of this view is given in various places in these volumes, e.g. in vol. 2, p. 248, figs. 4–20a, 4–20b, and 4–20c, which, along with the accompanying discussion (pp. 247–266), show that even (or especially?) for the conventionally prestigious (r) variable subjective reactions differ very considerably, for the subjects studied, according to whether suitability for a job, toughness, or friendship is the governing consideration.
[2] One's data will always be incomplete without at the same time some understanding of

Everything said so far applies from the most "macro" to the most "micro" levels of analysis (see Pride and Holmes 1972: Introduction): the same general considerations will usually apply whatever the level. Let us show this further by taking a particularly "micro" analysis — Ervin-Tripp's schematic model of her own rules of address language, which (as she says) are cast rather in the form of a computer flow chart comprising a series of binary selectors (1972:218ff.). Although her own main informant, and representative of the "academic circle" she knows (1972:222), what she has done is to "expand" the analysis of Brown and Ford (1961) to account for details of her own forms of address. Presumably this works, but a good deal of further informant testing must have been necessary to check that the system — AS a system, as well as in its details — works also for the wider speech community indicated. Brown and Ford's original informants had after all been a remarkably heterogeneous collection. Otherwise, three particular aspects of her analysis prompt a number of more general reflections.

FIRST, there is the question of the number and types of linguistic outcomes. The seven considered incorporate title, Mr./Mrs./Miss, kin title, first/last name, and zero. But one is bound to ask whether these are necessarily more important, more self-evidently central, to the business of addressing people, than for example opening expressions like "excuse me," "heh!," "look," etc. The latter must add up to a very large list indeed, may be spoken moreover in different meaningful ways, and as often as not are used WITHOUT formal address terms such as the seven chosen by Ervin-Tripp. (One cannot, incidentally, help noting that choice of zero must surely suit more than "children whose names are unknown." Missing dimensions involved here will have much to do with the unfolding of discourse: how often — and with what purpose in mind — one names one's addressee, and so forth.) This point is not being made so much as a criticism of what Ervin-Tripp HAS done as a reflection on what somebody COULD do — with of course a good deal of participant analysis.

SECOND, the selector labelled "dispensation," which "creates a locus

---

what seems to the informant to LINGUISTICALLY mark his norms of usage — not merely in piecemeal detail, but also in more structural terms. He may for example recognize and attribute certain linguistic features as "a superordinate category of mistakes" (Mitchell-Kernan's phrase), or as relatively more (or less) "correct," or even as some ideal target to be aimed at but never reached. An interesting light in which to consider these matters is again that of diglossia in Arabic. Kaye (1972), largely following T. F. Mitchell, seriously questions whether the superposed ("high") variety is not rather a collection of what he wishes to call "ill-defined" (Mitchell suggests "less easily described") varieties of an essentially ideal ("mostly prescriptive") nature, imperfect imitations of a "language" (?) native to none. As always, but here very particularly, the feelings and reactions and linguistic behaviors generally of informants matter a great deal: "one can elicit from the same informant in successive sentences forms like /θaláaθa/, /taláata/, and /saláasa/ 'three'," or, "when told that there are colloquial dialects which have /ra?aa/ but no /šaaf/, they almost die in utter amazement," and so on.

for the expression of individual and situational nuances" (1972:221), not further elaborated, could cover a multitude of factors which would enable those concerned (analysts and informants alike) not so much to predict what is going to happen as to interpret what has happened.[3] One is inclined to feel that "nuances" is not quite the right word here. There may well be additional situational factors to take account of but there seems nothing to say about them that would merit them either this label or their allotted place in the model alongside "individual" nuances. Is it to this place, for example, that one is to shepherd all such potentially important situational factors as "length of acquaintanceship" (distinguishable from "friend"), identity of third parties, topic (which can have a powerful effect on most other aspects of language use), social class (distinguished from "rank"), ethnic group (which can vary within a given academic community), and so forth.

THIRD, there is the awkward fact that so many of the answers that matter in real life are of the form "yes in some respects but no in others" or else couched in terms of graded points on a scale or simply indeterminate. Therefore the extent to which informants themselves will WANT or be ABLE to see the picture in terms of dichotomies will always matter a great deal. The factor of "length of acquaintanceship," for example, (which does not figure in Ervin-Tripp's scheme) may seem by its very nature to defy binary interpretation, while two categories which she does use ("friend or colleague" and "adult") might well prove equally difficult, when the question is put, to see in yes/no terms.[4] What may seem on the face of it to amount to an informant's inarticulate hesitations could,

---

[3] Sankoff (1972) spells out a useful threefold distinction between (a) predictive approaches in analysis which can define certain limits on appropriateness in choice of language; (b) interpretive approaches (such as that of Gumperz and Hernandez 1971) which recognize the frequent "futility" of deterministic models in the face of "individual speech strategies"; and (c) statistical-correlative approaches (such as that of Labov 1966) which seek to show the meaningfulness of sheer relative proportions among alternative linguistic choices (be these languages, dialects, Labov's "phonological variables," or whatever) — where, that is to say, alternation itself is appropriate. Note that (a), (b), and (c) are by no means necessarily exclusive of each other. Referring to Blom and Gumperz (1972) and Fishman (1972) respectively, the editors (Gumperz and Hymes) state: "In both this and the preceding chapter there is the concern of relating individual choices to relatively stable patterns, but whereas Blom and Gumperz align themselves with the view that the latter are generated from the former, Fishman treats the individual choices as being derived from stable patterns" (Gumperz and Hymes 1972:436). Whatever the precise meanings of the expressions "generated" and "derived" might be, most of us would perhaps prefer to back both these horses.
[4] Note too that one's reservations about a generally binary interpretation of linguistic phenomena must apply as forcefully to linguistic outcomes as to situationally-disposing factors: all such oppositions as "restricted" and "elaborated" codes, "situational" and "metaphorical" codeswitching (see below), "standard" and "nonstandard" speech, "formal" and "informal" speech, and so on, both in general and in particular instances, are always best regarded as suspect to begin with. Hymes suggests that the prevalence of such dichotomies in sociolinguistics "shows how preliminary is the stage at which we work" (1972:50).

when properly understood, alter one's view of things. There might, for example, be cumulative evidence (revealed in just this sort of way) that at such and such a point choice of language — or of interpretation — tends to be difficult; and incidentally "point" could mean variously point in the model, in the discourse, in some personal or interpersonal history, even in history (see e.g. Brown and Gilman's observations [1960] in this respect concerning the *tu–vous* distinction in European languages). There may be difficulty in identifying the various factors which have governed, or are governing, or could govern choice of language; there may be corresponding difficulty in identifying what has been, is being, or could be chosen; or there may be difficulty arising from the ways in which various factors governing choice of language seem to pull in different directions, or in some way to fit uneasily together, or at the very least to need careful handling by the producer — not to mention careful interpretation by the receiver. Friedrich (1972) speaks of inferences the reader might gather from the Russian novel of the "felicitous union of personal respect and an affection whose strength was not mitigated by overt restraint," signalled often by "explicit Вы combined with paralinguistic Мы" (1972:298).[5] Stylistic balances of this sort are not necessarily easily achieved.

Finally, one should consider the role of informant opinion in the proper understanding of processes of borrowing and codeswitching between languages (or dialects). Processes of borrowing can be enriched by possibilities for the assimilation or, alternatively, non-assimilation of whatever is borrowed into the patterns (phonological, grammatical, etc. — these may indeed not tally in these respects) of the borrowing language. Whiteley's illuminating study (1967) of borrowings from English into Swahili in Tanzania provides a detailed commentary on the various borrowing mechanisms concerned. It would e.g. probably be no exaggeration to suggest that Swahili offers itself to the user in three potential guises, according to patterns of borrowing — none or very little, assimilated, and unassimilated, taking their place alongside strategies of codeswitching between Swahili, English, and local vernaculars, as in many parts of East Africa. In such ways, as Whiteley (1973) put it, "people tend to manipulate their language skills to their own advantage" (1973:ch. 13). In the same volume (1973:ch. 4), Parkin shows how codeswitching in what he calls "transactional conversations" might emphasize similarities or differences in cultural (or alternatively political) stereotypes of ethnic groups, or (alternatively again) socioeconomic

[5]   One is reminded of one of Geertz's observations (1960) on "linguistic etiquette" in Javanese, about how the use of "high and low honorifics" might e.g. "resolve the conflict between familiarity and respect" (1960:257); hence also of Tanner's study (1967) of bilingualism among an Indonesian élite, for whom — as for many others — the strength of "everyday Indonesian" lies to some extent in its role as "neutral" language with which the speaker can sidestep the need to express (as he would otherwise have to do, in Javanese) one or another set of power or solidarity relationships inhering in the situation.

interests; or might emphasize solidarity or assertiveness; and so on. He calls these "critical speech events." Knowledge about these, as about so much else, can only arise out of, in effect, listening to talk about talk.

SPEECH FUNCTIONS

Language behaviors of all kinds (whether these take the form of terms and expressions for addressing others, or codeswitching, or anything else) can serve purposes of what Goffman has called "impression management," perhaps reflecting "dilemmas of choice," generally contributing to "transactional bargains" in which, for each participant, "the value gained . . . is greater or equal to the value lost" (Barth 1966). This is certainly a fruitful context in which to look into the notion of "speech functions."

I have argued elsewhere (1971b:100, 110) that this particular concept (expressed that is to say in "speech acts") might be related usefully to the componential analysis of "statuses" on "status dimensions" ("cordiality," "reverence," "sexual distance," and so forth), statuses being points at which particular combinations of particular "rights and duties" apply. Let us paraphrase very briefly the main argument of Goodenough (1965) on this subject. Goodenough approaches the characterization of social identities (husband, wife, physician, etc.) and — more basically — identity relationships (husband–wife, physician–patient, etc. — he believes these are probably limited in number for each identity) in terms of the constellations of rights and duties which normally apply to them in the society in question. The latter are in turn taken as reflecting particular statuses on particular status dimensions ("deference," "cordiality," "reverence," "affection," "sexual distance," "emotional independence," etc.). So that any one identity relationship will have its rights and duties, as it were, assigned to it in ways which can be explained by reference to different statuses on different status dimensions. Social identities are themselves selected according to occasion and setting and may enter into several identity relationships simultaneously (i.e. identities will include such as "old," "young," "man," "woman," etc. as well as "husband," "physician," etc., hence allowing a person to assume more than just one identity relationship at any one time). The "role" of an identity will be made up of the aggregate of all its rights and duties. Goodenough also discusses the problem of finiteness and suggests that Miller's postulation (1956) that "the greatest number of discriminations that can be made consistently on one dimension seems to be about seven (plus or minus two)" may well apply. He goes on to suggest that stylistic alternatives for the same duties are to be expected ("like allomorphs of a morpheme in language") and that breaches of duty or the enactment of more duties than are required could incur displeasure or convey flattery, etc. Thus, finally, he says:

Methods that allow us objectively to measure such things as anger, insult, flattery, and the gravity of offenses, and that help us to appreciate the poetic justice of events in alien cultural contexts, such methods, I submit, are not exercises in sterile formalism (1965:20).

Bearing in mind the essential qualification (which will be returned to below) that no kind of componential analysis (such as this) is immune from situational modification, the invitation which Goodenough's model holds out to the sociolinguist should be clear. Choice of language, that is to say, may in itself amount to the expression of rights and duties just as well as any other form of behavior might, reflecting, that is to say, the operation of statuses on status dimensions (as appropriate to identities in identity relationships . . .). "Speech functions" then can be understood very profitably in corresponding terms as basically statuses on status dimensions (or clusters of statuses on several status dimensions) and expressed in "speech acts." In other words, Goodenough's model can provide a conceptual framework for a fuller understanding of the linguistic expression of various kinds and degrees of, say, "deference," "cordiality," etc. One should note that Goodenough himself admits more than merely pluses and minuses into the resultant tables which he constructs, making use rather of entries such as "allowed," "disapproved," "forbidden," etc. (see his Table 3 [1965:14]). This extra sensitivity to what is meant by the bare terms "rights" and "duties" would certainly be important in any linguistic perspective.

Speech functions then would variously embody clusters of statuses, their manner of clustering being perhaps rule-governed in some way. Suppose now we take "advice" as one kind of everyday speech function. Advice presumably amounts to something like the linguistic expression of a right on the part of the speaker to convey to the listener information which could potentially be beneficial to the listener providing he acts on it. More than this, however, the MANNER of giving advice may vary according to how the speaker sees (and wishes to express) various other statuses, on various dimensions, characterizing his identity relationships with the listener: e.g. relative amount of relevant knowledge might be a factor or deference due to education/sex/age and so forth (i.e. different kinds of deference dimensions), or solidarity arising from shared ethnicity (or from any other shared group identity) or from long acquaintanceship (etc.), power of various sorts (not necessarily amounting to the same thing as deference), and so forth.

The essence of the whole matter, however, has not yet been reached: namely that speech functions and speech acts relate to each other as composite LINGUISTIC SIGNS, equally constituted of "what" and "how," "function" (or "content") and "form," "structure" and "substance." "Meaning" derives not so much from relationships between the two as from their fusion. At the same time, practical analysis, and discussion, will always demand a degree of separation (on an "as if" basis) — the particular relationships we are interested in being those between status rules on the one side and structural–linguisitic form on the other. Very little has been said so far about the latter, partly because the major linguistic dimensions even of any single speech act in ordinary everyday English have yet to be explored in any depth. The range of variation may be vast: a field such as say "commands and requests" might be made up of alternative ways of speaking, at various levels of analysis, meaningfully different to all concerned, which probably run into millions (Pride 1973a). Theoretically, it seems essential that the LINGUISTICS of, say, "the language of commands and requests," of "advice," etc., that is to say, the study of systematic means for the expression of particular speech functions, must ultimately match whatever system of interconnecting statuses and status dimensions can be found to apply. Indeed, the two systems must theoretically be identical in any final analysis — the one functional, the other formal, coming together in the one linguistic sign.[6] Everyday labels for speech functions ("advice," "suggestion," "warning," "hinting," "informing," and so on) are at once a guide to the territory and a veritable sociolinguistic puzzle as well. Labels of this sort refer not so much to distinctions in status on single status dimensions as to distinctions between clusters of statuses on several dimensions at once; everyday usage is hardly likely to indicate straightforwardly what are the relevant single constituent status dimensions and statuses.

Further than all this, speech functions may tend also to be characterized by sociocultural values; as values can override institutionalized social structure in ordinary life, so may speech functions reflect this fact. E.g. "advice" may on occasion, indeed rather frequently, serve the primary purpose of reinforcing the solidarity that comes from shared values — rather than of conveying something, and expecting some response, as of right. It may express concern, sympathy, exasperation,

---

[6]   De Saussure (1966) still deserves extensive quotation on this concept. Here is one extract, from Baskin's translation of the *Cours*: "A succession of sounds is linguistic only if it supports an idea. Considered independently, it is material for a physiological study, and nothing more than that. The same is true of the signified as soon as it is separated from its signifier. Considered independently, concepts like 'house,' 'white,' 'see,' etc., belong to psychology. They become linguistic entities only when associated with sound-images; in language, a concept is a quality of its phonic substance just as a particular slice of sound is a quality of the concept" (p. 103). One might add to this that many "slices of sound" may jointly amount to a quality of a single overriding concept, as well as individually contributing to each constituent concept, yielding a many–many entity which is no less a linguistic sign. In addition, while a composite semantic field of, say, "commands and requests" will find expression in many different forms (see Pride 1973a, for English), each single form of expression may also function in various other semantic fields and contexts.

self-importance, masculinity, or whatever. Values are as much a part of the social fabric as are more overtly apparent rights and duties, but rather define the USES MADE of them — ways of juxtaposing different kinds of status relationships, assigning priorities, ignoring statuses altogether, or indeed asserting new kinds of status. E.g. "sympathetic advice" could, on occasion, highlight the solidarity of shared sex and/or age and/or experience (there must be status scales of shared experiences) over and above whatever deference would normally be owed to the other's greater socioeconomic attainments or over and above whatever duties are owed (or not owed) to total strangers and so forth. Judicious (or injudicious) choice of language can serve to reflect or emphasize or disguise incompatibilities among statuses. Or one can give up on language — "dilemmas of choice" being such as to force one to silence (see e.g. Basso 1972; Philips 1970), or indeed to the use of another language altogether (see Tanner 1967).

At the beginning of this section reference was made to Barth's social anthropological theory of "transactional bargains" in which participants are seen as endeavoring to match statuses with each other so as to maximize the value that might accrue. Study of the linguistics of everyday speech functions in these (or any other) terms has virtually not yet begun. One reason for this may lie in the still widely prevailing tendency to bypass or to minimize the importance of the factor of "context of situation." Everything we have referred to so far is subject to variation according to situation. What may count as advice in one situation may not be permissible at all in another or might count as something else in a third. More generally, the warning which Whiteley (1966) gave against any too mechanical application of Goodenough's earlier methods (1956) of componential analysis — "Both Goodenough's significata and his connotata belong to a conceptual model which is constantly under review from the social context" (1966:149) — still applies to the later work and derivations from it. Only if one accepts this will one be in a position to look for "rules" which may conceivably be general across all situations: rules such as e.g. "the more deference, the less familiarity," or "the greater the familiarity the greater the range of linguistic expression," and so forth. If, of course, any such tendencies can be shown to be general across language and speech community boundaries, as well as across situational boundaries within the one language and speech community, then they must be taken as possible universals, universal speech functions and speech acts. For example, the dimensions of power and solidarity have frequently attracted hypotheses in sociolinguistics of this sort.

One fundamental situational variable is the native informant's view of things. But what general form might the responses of informants take to questions about speech functions and speech acts? How much could one get out of comments of for example the sort: "Yes, that way of putting things would certainly count as an apology, in the circumstances — seems to show about the right amount of deference, I would say, not too much friendliness . . . (etc.)"; or: "I'm not sure what this kind of language amounts to at all, it might be some kind of apology but I get the feeling he'd be laughing at me . . ."; and so on? Alternatively, comments of one sort or another could perhaps be elicited with reference to real language which has already occurred naturally. Here more would be wanted than single-word labelling, though even this is not necessarily easy or unilluminating — as an earlier reference to Frake's investigations (1972) into what counts as "litigation" among the Yakan has made clear. Alternatively again, on being presented not with a piece of text but instead with a speech-functional gloss to a text (i.e. minus text) an informant might volunteer: "I suppose I'd say something like 'Why don't you try doing it this way . . .'." Quite clearly, much would depend on the questions (who asks them how, etc.); on whether the texts are real or imaginary, identified or anonymous; and on many other such factors. One imagines that responses (interpretations and/or linguistic expressions) could be revealing of what informants BELIEVE would be appropriate (or possible, or correct, etc.), in relation to what does happen in practice. In other words, we would be entering into what was earlier referred to as the potential "ramifications of folk linguistics." Informant responses of this general sort could certainly reflect the "modes of practical reasoning used by researcher and subject alike" postulated by the sociological ethnomethodologist — these amounting, it has been suggested, to an important part of the "first order of business in social research" (Gumperz and Hymes 1972:304, on Garfinkel). Indeed, the various theoretical links between what we have been discussing, on the one hand, and sociological ethnomethodology, on the other, may in certain respects be quite close. Garfinkel (1972) for instance, states of one example he gives: "To recognize WHAT is said means to recognize HOW A PERSON IS SPEAKING, e.g. to recognize that the wife, in saying 'Your shoes need heels badly,' was speaking narratively or metaphorically, or euphemistically, or double-talking" (1972:320) — or, we are implying, advisingly, commandingly, appealingly, and so forth (Pride 1973b).

One should certainly not seek one-to-one relationships (statistical or otherwise) between "situational" (speech function) and "linguistic" (speech act) variants. Much that may seem at first sight to be predictable may turn out to be interpretive on closer inspection (see Note 3). To take one example to close this section: the "ten discriminations" which for Friedrich constitute a system that "predicts with accuracy the usage in new texts," (1972:299), i.e. terms of personal address in nineteenth-century Russian novels, include several which might be difficult to isolate and vouch for on independent grounds, that is to say, predict from; e.g. there are "informality of topic," "emotional affinity or antipathy," "common purpose," "dislike or deprecation bred of familiarity," and so on. Interestingly, Friedrich adds a footnote in which he contrasts the notion of "society," as referring to "the regularities that may be observed, measured, or otherwise determined . . .," with that of "culture," as made up of "the structured set of . . . norms, values, attitudes, feelings, and ideas . . ." (1972:273). This is immediately followed in the main text, however, by the statement: "In what follows I shall attempt to demonstrate how speech usage is determined by cultural principles." Part of the difficulty here is that the culture that is said to determine speech usage cannot so easily be itself determined by the investigator. Or to put this another way, the usage which Friedrich goes on to tell us so much about is itself a prime example of a sociolinguistic sign. In the terms of the present discussion, the language of personal address, like everything else that is meaningful in language, is a composite of both form and function. Functionally, what is involved are different degrees of status (in English: "Sir/Charlie/Boy/You idiot . . ."), of different kinds ("Hullo old chap/ Hullo luv/Hi Charlie . . ."), given varying emphases ("Yes,/SIR/Come on, LITTLE man . . ."), co-occurring with others in variously appropriate sequences ("Look mate why don't you just clear out of here/Look mate please don't let me keep you here one moment longer I know how busy you are" . . .), co-occurring with others simultaneously ("explicit Вы combined with paralinguistic Мы": above), observably happening or descriptively potential (see Appendix) and always appropriate to various other situational factors — including not least the transactional intentions of participants.

TRANSACTIONAL CODESWITCHING

The difficulty of correctly estimating what ARE the cultural principles which "determine" (more exactly: are embodied in) speech usage is well illustrated by the study of codeswitching in the northern Norwegian community of Hemnesberget carried out by Blom and Gumperz (1972). The authors make here a basic distinction between a "situational" type of codeswitching which is governed by situational norms and what they call "metaphorical" codeswitching in which "contextually marked modes of speaking are used in other than their normal context" (Gumperz and Hymes 1972:18), hence serving to "enrich" a situation rather than to redefine it. One must question, however, the authors' interpretation of this important distinction. Metaphorical switching is surely not normally characterized (i.e. in contradistinction to situational switching: 1972:424) by no "significant change in definition of participants' mutual rights and obligations" (1972:425). Nor does such an interpretation square with the statement made a few lines later, that one has here "the enactment of two or more different relationships among the same set of individuals" (1972:425). This is very likely to be the case, but, if so, the enactment of or even allusion to such relationships can have everything to do with the definition, or re-definition, of situations in terms of "rights and obligations." The real distinction seems to be rather that in the one case wider sociocultural norms are, so to speak, relatively dominant, while in the other it is the individual who is tending to assert his own view of the rights and obligations (also values) that seem to him to apply, or that he wishes to assert. The contrast "situational redefinition": "metaphorical enrichment" is perhaps as fundamentally mistaken (at any rate as incomplete) as would be the view that social situations in general cannot CHANGE quite radically upon being given some added — even fleeting — element of "enrichment." Use of one language, or dialect, or style, or even single variant, in the mainstream of another, or otherwise outside of its "normal context," can undoubtedly alter the status situation as well as merely added to it, though of course it need not do this. "Metaphorical" codeswitching which e.g. "reflects a de facto recognition of their own nonlocal identification" (1972:431), as when a speaker might wish to "validate his status as an intellectual" (1972:430), might (for the students concerned) amount to a significant assertion of the relevance to their present situation of rights and duties (as well as values) attached to or associated with some other situation — amounting therefore to a "re-definition" of the present situation. Furthermore, if this type of codeswitching is indeed characterized by the breakdown of structural linguistic boundaries between the codes concerned (1972:429ff.), this need not necessarily imply that "situational" boundaries have become blurred to a corresponding extent. Blom and Gumperz maintain that the students "fail to maintain the situational barrier between the dialects and the standard" (1972:434) but one is surely prompted to ask: might they not rather be proving capable, linguistically, as entrepreneurs, of juxtaposing two sets of values, and/or rights and duties, without at all failing to discriminate ("maintain the situational barrier") between them?[7] Codeswitching of this sort may certainly not be normative for the community concerned, yet it may be perfectly systematic (even if not consciously so) from the point of view of interpersonal relationships which involve rights and duties of one sort or another. The concrete question then is: what ARE the statuses and status dimensions which combine to give the right to indulge in this type of codeswitching?

The example just discussed suggests that there may be no less than sixteen types of codeswitching which, in different ways, incorporate just these alternatives. This is to say, there may be codeswitching behaviors which: (a) either (1) do or (2) do not maintain relatively clearcut struc-

---

[7]   On the social-anthropological role of the entrepreneur see Barth (1966).

tural–linguistic distinctions between the codes concerned (be these languages, dialects, levels, varieties, styles, or whatever); (b) display a relative dominance of (1) wider sociocultural norms (call this therefore
"normative codeswitching") or of (2) more individual or minority
("non-normative") tendencies; (c) appear to be either (1) clearly systematic or (2) apparently nonsystematic from the point of view of
(d) — (1) domains (see Fishman) or of (2) interpersonal relationships.
Any one instance of codeswitching may of course belong to more than
one of these sixteen (or any other) categories.

A simple branching diagram (Figure 1) will illustrate what has just
been said:

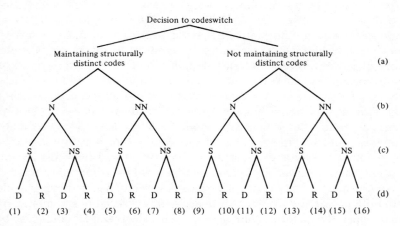

Figure 1. Types of codeswitching
Key: N = normative, and NN = non-normative; S = systematically related, and NS = not
systematically related to D = domains, or to R = interpersonal relationships

The applicability of any such layout will be subject to one's reservations
concerning analysis as prediction or as interpretation (the latter applying
particularly to cases of apparently nonsystematic codeswitching), also
concerning the use of binary alternatives. One has, for instance, to take
account of theoretical problems involved in deciding what are and what
are not "coexistent systems," as opposed to linguistic continua; of ways of
speaking which seem to answer to several (as opposed to just two)
degrees of normativeness, or of "solidarity" (see below), and so forth. In
other words, the kind of taxonomy indicated above comes dangerously
close to being yet another plus–minus view of something which could be
far more complex.

The factors listed are also, of course, incomplete. One could make a
host of further distinctions concerning, for example, how many and what

types of code are available ("standard"/"vernacular," "major"/"minor," "language"/"dialect," and so forth); psychological types of bilingualism (e.g. "compound"/"coordinate"); measures of proficiency; rapidity of codeswitching; frequencies (as opposed to norms) of use; channels of communication; relationships between what people do do/think they do, etc.; not to mention all kinds of speech functions which may be being served. With a few more such variables, and employing even a merely binary approach, our modest sixteen is soon raised to three or more figures. Branching from (a), e.g. one might distinguish the codes that are being switched as EITHER languages OR as dialects; thence switching EITHER between "standard" and "vernacular" OR between "vernacular" and "vernacular" (triglossia situations — common enough in the world at large — give at least four alternatives: H with M, M with L, H with L, and L with another L; see e.g. Abdulaziz [1972]), that is to say EITHER as normative OR as non-normative behavior. Branching from (d), interpersonal relationships can be estimated in terms of the relevance OR irrelevance of power AND/OR solidarity, domains in terms of the relevance OR irrelevance of spoken AND/OR written media;[8] and so on. With just these arbitrary (yet important) additions, and taking triglossic codeswitching into account, the figure has incidentally already reached 512. Not all these possibilities could be easily exemplified, needless to say, yet many probably could, and there seems no necessary reason why any should be impossible. Consider e.g. the single case of rather indistinct codeswitching between two vernacular languages which, for the community at large, is non-normative, yet, taking interpersonal relationships having to do with both power and solidarity into account, appreciably systematic; on top of which the factor of domain (variously categorizable) could also be playing a major part.

Let us go back, however, and look briefly at a few examples of the sixteen original categories, with particular reference to their transactional potentialities:

(1) The structurally-distinct, normative, systematically domain-oriented codeswitching of, say, Fishman's hypothetical "government functionary in Brussels" who "generally speaks standard French in his office, standard Dutch at his club, and a distinctly local variant of Flemish at home" (1972:438); transactionally speaking, we could say here that if Fishman's government functionary slips into Dutch in his office, then the reason may lie in altered status relationships or in the fact that values have overridden the status quo in some way or another. The same kind of thing could be said about any other example of this kind of codeswitching: e.g. about the language behavior of school children who succeed in shifting between a "standard" classroom language and a "vernacular" play-

---

[8]   Strictly speaking, channel of communication is not in itself a subcategory of domain.

ground language, or indeed about Blom and Gumperz's "situational switching" in Norway.

(2) — as (1), but rather relationship-oriented, as in rural parts of Kenya between Swahili and English, according to factors like the need for "privacy" or for "added authority" (Whiteley 1973:ch. 13). Let us quote Whiteley directly on transactional codeswitching in this context:

People tend to manipulate their language skills to their own advantage. Thus a man wishing to see a Government officer to renew a licence, for example, may state his request in Swahili to the girl typist as a suitably neutral language if he does not know her. To start out in English would be unfortunate if she did not know it, and on her goodwill depends his gaining access to authority reasonably quickly. She may reply in Swahili, if she knows it as well as he does and wishes to be co-operative; or in English if she is busy and not anxious to be disturbed; or in the local language if she recognises him and wishes to reduce the level of formality. If he, in return, knows little English, he may be put off at her use of it and decide to come back later; or, if he knows it well, he may demonstrate his importance by insisting on an early interview and gain his objective at the loss of goodwill from the typist. The interview with the officer may well follow a similar pattern, being shaped by the total repertoire available to each on the one hand, and on the other by their respective positions in relation to the issue involved.

In a similar sort of way, the transactional meaningfulness of Geertz's account of switching from one level of Javanese to another according to the need to establish particular balances between power and solidarity relationships (1960) is very clear; so too with Rubin's binary interpretation (1968:526) of bilingual (Spanish and Guarani) codeswitching in Paraguay, seen in terms of formal/informal, non-intimate/intimate, and serious/non-serious: "It seems as though when we speak Guarani, we are saying something more intimate and something which is sweeter to us" (1968:524). Compare the rather similar motives which occasionally influence choice of Spanish or of English within the New York Puerto Rican community where, incidentally, what Rubin's informants say about Guarani is closely reflected in what Hoffman's (Hoffman 1968) informants say about Spanish (when asking for a favor: "I'll just speak in Spanish a little more. You know, a little more affectionately. You know the Spanish." On this, see also Pride [1971b:104]). Finally, the transactional implications of what Salisbury (1962) has to say about choice of language by host and by guest in the New Guinea Highlands are very evident and raise interesting questions concerning crosscultural differences in these respects. The main variables concerned in the case he cites are: choice of host language or guest language, the indication of bilingual competence or incompetence (i.e. one's own or the other party's), and choice of host's language as "at home" language or of guest's language as "foreign" language. This is one of many communities where what Wolff (1959) calls a "pecking order of intelligibility" works in favour of being able, rather than unable, to understand the other man's language.

(3) applies wherever codeswitching takes place irrespective of changes in domain; this is more usually the case within the restrictions imposed within one or a few overriding domains, e.g. "nonrural" and "nonformal" in Paraguay — given which, what matters are not further distinctions of domain but rather distinctions of intimacy, seriousness, predicated language proficiency, sex, etc. (Rubin 1968). These are precisely the kinds of consideration which as often as not have to be weighed in the balance. "The head doctor of the Luque hospital said that in selecting a language in which to address his patients, he considered which language they might be more comfortable in and tried to encourage them to use it, too" — regardless of other considerations that seemed to point in the direction of the other language? (3), in other words, is as (2), but makes specific reference to points in the system where not only have relationships become relevant but further distinctions of domain have become irrelevant. Conversely, (4) is as (1), with reference to the irrelevance of relationships: e.g. if Flemish is spoken at home and French in the office, quite regardless of any changes in interpersonal relationships. In bilingual homes and offices, this state of affairs would, one feels, be rare.

(5) and (6) introduce all the problems involved in defining "normative" in the first place. What may be normative for a wider community may not be so for some minority group within it, and vice versa. What is expected in Hemnesberget may be out of place in Oslo. An immigrant or otherwise minority community may codeswitch between its native language (e.g. at home) and the dominant community language (at work) in a way that is quite "foreign." For such a minority group, the problem of deciding just how to communicate with children in the family who come home knowing more of the larger community's language than any other member (and needing it moreover to progress in school — and beyond) can become acute. Denison (1971) points to the changing role of Italian in just such a situation in one part of northern Italy; Gorman (1971) analyses intergenerational codeswitching in Kenya, with particular reference to the increasing use of English in schools; and indeed such examples can easily be multiplied. Gorman shows how patterns of codeswitching with the family in Kenya tend to be more complicated as one moves down the generational ladder. Statuses and status dimensions governing choice of language — like "politeness" to older generations, age relationships among siblings, sex, and whatever status feelings are associated with particular topics — have to be recognized, weighed in the balance, and resolved in what are essentially transactional bargains. In these cases, note that transactional codeswitching may have the ultimate purpose of simply identifying what the new norms are, or are going to be.

(7) and (8) may be exemplified perhaps by switching between Spanish

and English in parts of Texas, described as "what seems almost random language mixture," which "tends to be disparaged and referred to by pejorative terms such as Tex Mex," and which is "rarely reported in the literature and frequently dismissed as abnormal" (Gumperz 1972). Gumperz and Hernandez (1971) state that this sort of usage is "very persistent," even among the educated; and that even though it is held in disrepute, it occurs "whenever minority language groups come in close contact with majority language groups under conditions of rapid social change" (1971:112). They suggest further however that it tends to carry *tu–vous* connotations of distance and warmth (1971:113) — hence bringing it, to this extent, into our type (6).

(9) and (10) appear to be jointly illustrated in Mitchell-Kernan's transciption of a dialogue showing "signifying" in Black English (Mitchell-Kernan 1972:170ff.). Very considerable overlapping of dialects may take place in such uses of language but systematically related, it would appear, to both domains and relationships. Signifying is language having "multi-level meanings," and may show e.g. "relatively formal or literary expressions . . . spoken with typically black phonology and black grammar" (1972:172). Such language is quite normative for the particular population in question.

(11) and (12) could be reflected e.g. in Bailey's comment on codeswitching habits in Jamaica:

A given speaker is likely to shift back and forth from Creole to English within a single utterance, without ever being conscious of this shift. Most observers of language in Jamaica have encountered extreme difficulty in distinguishing between the various layers of the language spectrum, and indeed the lines of demarcation are very hard to draw (Bailey 1965:1, see also Bailey 1971; de Camp 1971).

Whether such behavior is in fact normative, or in what respects it is, is difficult to say. Labov's explanation (1971:450) suggests that it is not: "Whenever a subordinate dialect is in contact with a superordinate one, linguistic forms produced by a speaker of the subordinate dialect in a formal context will shift in an unsystematic manner towards the superordinate" — in which case it belongs under (15) and (16).

(13) is well shown in the use of Hindi and Punjabi (recognized as distinct languages in the Indian Constitution) in certain domains, such that "codeswitching styles" emerge in which "the particular linguistic object of imitation must be established through empirical research" (Gumperz 1962). Standard normative grammars, Gumperz observes, do not refer to these ways of speaking. The transactional nature of this kind of linguistic mutual accommodation is, in principle, apparent from its characteristic use in the market place.

(14) can be illustrated by the "metaphorical switching" of Blom and

Gumperz. Note, in addition to what has been said already, that Fishman (1972) has claimed that codeswitching of this sort is ultimately related to norms which have to do with domains (i.e. domain-normative usage is merely being referred to out of context). His point underlines the fact that domains and relationships are not necessarily mutually exclusive (or distinguishable) factors in any case. Similarly, Sankoff's example (1972:45) of the choice of Neo-Melanesian and Buang in parts of New Guinea on the same occasion to refer to the "local community" and to the "modern, outside world respectively" may be difficult to assign exclusively to domain OR to interpersonal usage. What is clear is that transactional considerations are as central here as, e.g. in type (2).

Finally, (15) and (16) might be further illustrated by the use of non-normative forms of Black English spoken by children ("I gots to go," "he can gets hurt," etc.) in ways that do not easily lend themselves to any systematic explanation.

Most of the foregoing examples of codeswitching can be interpreted in terms of the putting into effect, or manipulation, of status relationships. That is to say, they are "transactional" in nature. The literature of codeswitching is indeed full of examples which, explicitly or (more often) implicitly, show the operation of transactional processes. In this sense, therefore, acts of codeswitching are speech acts, their functions tantamount to what we have described as speech functions.

APPENDIX: AN ANALOGY

One way of clarifying just what are the main features of any concept is to place it side by side with some other basic concept from another part of the same (or "same") discipline. If a rough analogy can be established, so much the better. Let us take distinctive feature phonology as, so to speak, our adjacent conceptual world.

Distinctive feature theory seeks to characterize the more traditional phoneme as a rather arbitrary or "informal" clustering of fewer and more fundamental binary oppositions of a physiological and/or acoustic nature, these being conceivably finite even for all languages taken as a whole. E.g. Chomsky and Halle (1968) accept thirteen distinctive features (we shall call these "D.F.'s") for forty-six or so phonemes of American English. D.F.'s, of course, have nothing to do with "meaning" in any normally accepted sense of the term, whereas phonemes certainly do. So that one can say that, in respect of the presence or absence of a component of meaning, there is nothing at all analogous in D.F. phonology to the speech function. Nor for that matter is the phoneme analogous to the speech function. What would be analogous to the phoneme would be something that contrasts with others of its kind both functionally and physically, a composite of speech FUNCTION and speech ACT — a complete functioning entity or linguistic SIGN. Such a unit has not been unambiguously named in the sociolinguistic literature.

This may be the point to observe that overlaps among D.F.'s (allowing for such statistical considerations as those gone into e.g. by Wheeler [1972]) have been said to give "natural classes" of phonemes. Note that Wheeler (1972:99) is concerned to introduce or reintroduce D.F.'s in order to establish intuitively salient natural classes which would be otherwise indefinable. If there is an analogy here, it would be of the kind that argues for natural classes of linguistic signs compounded of both speech acts and speech functions, indicated, that is to say, by evidence of overlaps among the linguistic features making up speech acts. This is the sort of assumption that is made in Pride (1973a), in which a composite field of "commands and requests" is identified (or, in a sense, generated) on what may well seem to be overly structural–linguistic grounds. The question is, therefore, just what is analogous to what? Strictly speaking, the most exact analogy would be this: that where the D.F. table in phonology places phonemes (horizontally) against D.F.'s (vertically), yielding pluses and minuses in the body of the table, our analogous picture would have to incorporate linguistic signs (composed of speech functions/acts) horizontally, against a vertical column of structural–linguistic features; and of course, in place of pluses and minuses, there would be indications of types and degrees of appropriateness. Let us proceed therefore on this basis.

Phonemes, in the traditional view, contrast functionally; as everyone knows, this is a significant part of their definition. The "minimal pair" in their case (yielding word, or morpheme, contrasts such as for instance "pen":"pin") should therefore find its analogy in ours, the larger functional frame in this case being the "speech event." In other words, speech events can be regarded as contrasting (functionally) by virtue of their speech function/act constitution. Now, since it is claimed that the permissibility of some given phoneme or set of phonemes in a particular place in a sequence of phonemes (of word length or shorter) can be referred to the D.F. makeup of the sequence as a whole, so, analogously, we should ask whether sequences (or co-occurrences) of speech functions/acts might be referred to constraints upon sequences or co-occurrences of linguistic features. That is to say, one is asking how far and in what respects considerations of sheer grammaticality inhibit the expression of otherwise possible clusterings of speech functions: what are some of the things that CAN be said in the language, but only via roundabout routes?

Constraints upon sequences of speech functions/acts have been studied for English by Schegloff (1968), among others. Simultaneous occurrences of distinguishable speech functions/acts, as in the case, e.g., of "advice which has a touch of threat about it," "signifying" along with "rapping" (see Mitchell-Kernan 1972) and so on, are likely to be no less rule-governed, in terms of allowable or even of more or less obligatory linguistic features, than are more sequentially ordered co-occurrences. The more obligatory, or appropriate, or predictable, such linguistic co-occurrences, the more apparent becomes a further analogy, namely with those contextually-conditioned variants of phonemes called allophones — the phonetic values of which may, as it were, stray into the territory of neighboring phonemes. In other words, in our present terms, one would be dealing with the conditioning circumstances implied in the sort of statement that might read: "not surprisingly in the circumstances, his advice amounted to a kind of threat . . ." Further than this, the generative linguist's well-known distinction between the "three adequacies" seems also to apply. Firstly, the goal of "observational adequacy" aims to present, in phonology, the data of observed "performance," e.g. in such a statement as: "the word 'brick' occurs in English." Similarly, there is a category of "advice" in English, instances of which can be observed; sequences of, say, warning and advice can be observed within the same utterance; so too can more or less simultaneous occurrences of warning and advice ("All I can say is you'd better get out of here or else . . ."). Secondly,

"descriptive adequacy" concerns the potential of the language user's "competence," i.e. what could be produced even though it might not happen to have been
observed as yet; thus: "a word 'blick' — e.g. if borrowed from another language — would count phonologically as English, whereas 'bnick' would not."
Analogies here would have to recognize speech functions/acts (or sequences or
co-occurrences of these) which, although apparently novel in themselves, are
nevertheless not felt to violate structural–linguistic rules which would disallow
them. Thirdly, "explanatory adequacy" seeks to explain the notion of competence. The gist of the present paper is that part of the explanation must lie NOT in
structural–linguistic constraints but rather in constraints upon co-occurrences of
statuses — constraints which are shared by (hence serve to define) the speech
community.

Generative phonology seeks therefore to present rules of observational,
descriptive, and explanatory adequacy in terms of D.F. symbols (+ or −) which
apply at particular places in the structures of words, taking account both of the
morphological structures of those words and of their syntactic roles in sentences.
Thus, in terms of descriptive adequacy, it might be shown that a word form
"blick" would break some rule which is not stateable in less than 17 D.F.
symbols, "bnik" would break a rule with 7 symbols, and "brzk" a rule with only 4
symbols. If the series 17-7-4 seems (as it has been suggested) to reflect one's
feelings of increasing "deviance," a logical question would seem to be whether
different sequences (or relatively simultaneous co-occurrences) of speech func-
tions/acts could or should be analogously measured for deviance, with reference
to structural–linguistic rules of one sort or another (logically, generative-semantic
rules?). There are good reasons, however, why any such measurement of
sociolinguistic deviance in these terms would be fundamentally mistaken. To
begin with, one would have to work entirely with binary oppositions rather than
with graded status points since only then would one be enabled to establish a clear
line between redundant and distinctive features (Harms 1968:15). Such a line is
necessary, since the numbers of symbols (17-7-4, mentioned above) reflect
degrees of deviance only if, for the word in question, one can specify in the first
place what are its irreducibly nonredundant ("classificatory"; Harms 1968:14)
features rather than merely its total D.F. configuration. But even if one accepts
the theoretical rightness of binary oppositions, there is still the telling point that
judgments of redundancy among linguistic features must ultimately be those of
informants; i.e. only by making use of informants (including of course himself)
will the investigator ascertain what are the linguistic features that define non-
redundantly the precise nature of observed and/or potential speech func-
tions/acts.[9] This seems to be a virtually impossible task, however neat-looking
the model that someone some day may come up with.

Anyway, using this analogy, one would be asking for precise measurements, by
informants, of "deviance" — deviance, that is to say, from the dictates of binary-
choice rules. But deviance, as a single cover term, is a misleading enough way of
putting what is ultimately involved, even in phonology. In language, whatever the
level of analysis, one has at the very least to be aware always of the possibility that
one has to do with more than uniform sets of rules drawn upon properly (or else
deviantly), whatever the occasion. Phonologically, for instance, words in very

[9]   The services of informants are necessary on both sides of our analogy: e.g. only they can
show (however difficult it might be to get them to do this) what are OPERATIONALLY the
nonredundant D.F.'s of acceptable word forms in the language, features which are in
effect — consciously or unconsciously — listened for in another's speech or monitored in
one's own.

informal speech may, as a normal feature, admit of D.F. structures which one would not expect to find in more formal speech; and of course many other situational factors can alter the picture too. Phonological deviance, that is to say, must relate to many situational factors. Phonological rules tend, of course, to be more, or less, relative to situations of use. To take a very simple example, the D.F. structures both of "won't" and of "will not" realize rules which are more general (in the sense that there is nothing situationally-specific about the phoneme sequences /o:n/, /o:nt/, etc.) and rules which are less general ("won't," as a word, will tend not to appear at all in very formal or stilted language). The "glottal stop" in English is generally restricted to informal situations of use, or to particular users. And so forth. One must expect to find that structural–linguistic rules which bear upon the expression of speech functions are similarly more, or less, specific to situations: what may count as a piece of advice in one situation may count as something else in another — or may not be permissible at all.

But what is the point of this farfetched analogy anyway? It is to emphasize the gulf that separates some of the unquestioned assumptions of most linguists today from what seems, to this writer at least, to be some of the realities of LANGUAGE. In 1929 Sapir wrote: "It is peculiarly important that linguists, who are often accused, and accused justly, of failure to look beyond the pretty patterns of their subject matter, should become aware of what their science may mean for the interpretation of human conduct in general. Whether they like it or not, they must become increasingly concerned with the many anthropological, sociological, and psychological problems which invade the field of linguistics." Nearly half a century has passed since then, new generations of linguists have come and gone, but not many have been weaned away from the secure concerns of their parent discipline: its "informal" passing references to whatever is situationally meaningful, its characteristic reliance on clearcut binary alternatives, its neglect of the natural language behavior and responses of informants, and all the rest of it. One suspects that Sapir was right; that it is, after all, a question of status.

REFERENCES

ABDULAZIZ, M. H.
  1972 Triglossia and Swahili-English bilingualism in Tanzania. *Language in Society* 1 (2).
ABRAHAMS, R.
  1972 The training of the man of words in talking sweet. *Language in Society* 1:15–31.
ALBERT, E. M.
  1972 "Culture patterning of speech behaviour in Burundi," in *Directions in sociolinguistics*. Edited by J. J. Gumperz and D. H. Hymes, 72–105. New York: Holt, Rinehart and Winston.
BAILEY, B. L.
  1965 *Jamaican creole syntax*. London: Cambridge University Press.
  1971 "Jamaican creole: can dialect boundaries be defined?", in *Pidginisation and creolisation of languages*. Edited by D. H. Hymes, 341–348. London: Cambridge University Press.
BARTH, R.
  1966 *Models of social organisation*. Occasional paper no. 23. London: Royal Anthropological Institute.

BASSO, K. H.
1972   "To give up on words: silence in Western Apache culture," in *Language and social context*. Edited by P. P. Giglioli, 67–87. Harmondsworth: Penguin.

BLOM, J.-P., J. J. GUMPERZ
1972   "Social meaning in linguistic structures: codeswitching in Norway," in *Directions in sociolinguistics*. Edited by J. J. Gumperz and D. H. Hymes, 407–434. New York: Holt, Rinehard and Winston.

BROWN, R. W., M. FORD
1961   Address in American English. *Journal of Abnormal and Social Psychology* 62:372–385.

BROWN, R. W., A. GILMAN
1960   "The pronouns of power and solidarity," in *Style in language*. Edited by T. Sebeok, 253–276. Cambridge, Massachusetts: M.I.T. Press.

CHOMSKY, N., M. HALLE
1968   *The sound pattern of English*. New York: Harper and Row.

DE CAMP, D.
1971   "Toward a generative analysis of a post-creole speech continuum," in *Pidginisation and creolisation of languages*. Edited by D. H. Hymes, 349–370. London: Cambridge University Press.
1972   Hypercorrection and rule generalisation. *Language in Society* 1:87–90.

DE SAUSSURE, F.
1966   *Course in general linguistics*. Edited by C. Bally and A. Sechehaye. Translated by W. Baskin. London: P. Owen.

DENISON, N.
1968   Sauris — a trilingual community in diatypic perspective. *Man* (new series) 3:578–594.
1971   "Some observations on language variety and plurilingualism," in *Social anthropology and language*. Edited by E. Ardener, 157–185. ASA Monograph 10. London: Tavistock.

ERVIN-TRIPP, S.
1972   "On sociolinguistic rules: alternation and co-occurrence," in *Directions in sociolinguistics*. Edited by J. J. Gumperz and D. H. Hymes, 213–250. New York: Holt, Rinehart and Winston.

FERGUSON, C. A.
1959   Diglossia. *Word* 15:325–340.

FISHMAN, J. A.
1972   "Domains and the relationship between micro- and macrosociolinguistics," in *Directions in sociolinguistics*. Edited by J. J. Gumperz and D. H. Hymes, 435–453. New York: Holt, Rinehart and Winston.

FRAKE, C. O.
1972   "Struck by speech: the Yakan concept of litigation," in *Directions in sociolinguistics*. Edited by J. J. Gumperz and D. H. Hymes, 106–129. New York: Holt, Rinehart and Winston.

FRIEDRICH, P.
1972   "Social context and semantic feature: the Russian pronominal usage," in *Directions in sociolinguistics*. Edited by J. J. Gumperz and D. H. Hymes, 270–300. New York: Holt, Rinehart and Winston.

GARFINKEL, H.
1972   "Remarks on ethnomethodology," in *Directions in sociolinguistics*. Edited by J. J. Gumperz and D. H. Hymes, 301–324. New York: Holt, Rinehart and Winston.

GARVIN, P. L.
1959 The standard language problem: concepts and methods. *Anthropological Linguistics* 1 (3):28–32.
GEERTZ, C.
1960 "Linguistic etiquette". Chapter 3 of *The religion of Java*. Glencoe, Illinois: The Free Press.
GOODENOUGH, W. H.
1956 Componential analysis and the study of meaning. *Language* 32: 195–216.
1965 "Rethinking 'status' and role'," in *The relevance of models for social anthropology*. Edited by H. Banton, 1–24. ASA Monograph 1. London: Tavistock.
GORMAN, T. P.
1971 "Socio-linguistic implications of a choice of media of instruction," in *Language use and social change*. Edited by W. H. Whiteley, 198–200. London: Oxford University Press.
GUMPERZ, J. J.
1962 "Hindi-Punjabi code-switching in Delhi," in *Proceedings of the Ninth International Congress of Linguists*. Edited by H. G. Lunt, 1115–1125. The Hague: Mouton.
1972 "Verbal strategies in multilingual communication," in *Language and culture diversity in American education*. Edited by R. Abraham and R. Troike. New York: Prentice-Hall.
GUMPERZ, J. J., E. HERNANDEZ
1971 "Cognitive aspects of bilingual communication," in *Language use and social change*. Edited by W. H. Whiteley, 111–125. London: Oxford University Press.
GUMPERZ, J. J., D. H. HYMES, *editors*
1972 *Directions in sociolinguistics*. New York: Holt, Rinehart and Winston.
HARMS, R. T.
1968 *Introduction to phonological theory*. Englewood Cliffs, N.J.: Prentice-Hall.
HAUGEN, E.
1966 Language, dialect, nation. *American Anthropologist* 68:922–935.
HOENIGSWALD, H. M.
1966 "A proposal for the study of folk-linguistics," in *Sociolinguistics*. Edited by W. Bright. The Hague: Mouton.
HOFFMAN, G.
1968 "Puerto-Ricans in New York: a language-related ethnographic summary," in *Bilingualism in the barrio*. Edited by J. A. Fishman. U.S. Department of Health, Education and Welfare.
HYMES, D. H., *editor*
1971 *Pidginisation and creolisation of languages*. Cambridge: University Press.
HYMES, D. H.
1972 "Models of the interaction of language and social life," in *Directions in sociolinguistics*. Edited by J. J. Gumperz and D. H. Hymes, 35–71. New York: Holt, Rinehart and Winston.
KAYE, A. S.
1972 Remarks on diglossia in Arabic. *Linguistics* 81:32–48.
LABOV, W.
1964 "Phonological correlates of social stratification," in *The ethnography of communication. American Anthropologist* 66:164–176.

1966   *The social stratification of English in New York City*. Washington, D.C.: Center for Applied Linguistics.

1969   "The logic of non-standard English," in *Linguistics and the teaching of standard English to speakers of other languages or dialects* (Georgetown University Monograph Series on Languages and Linguistics 22). Edited by J. Alatis, 1–44.

1971   "The notion of 'system' in creole languages," in *Pidginisation and creolisation of languages*. Edited by D. H. Hymes, 447–472. London: Cambridge University Press.

1972a "On the mechanism of linguistic change," in *Directions in sociolinguistics*. Edited by J. J. Gumperz and D. H. Hymes, 512–538. New York: Holt, Rinehart and Winston.

1972b Some principles of linguistic methodology. *Language in Society* 1:97–121.

LABOV, W., P. COHEN, C. ROBINS, J. LEWIS
1968   *A study of the non-standard English of negro and Puerto Rican speakers in New York City* (ERIC). New York: Columbia University Press.

McCORMACK, W.
1970   "Language identity: an introduction to India's language problems," in *Chapters in Indian civilisation*, volume two. Edited by J. W. Elder, 209–241. Dubuque, Iowa: Kendall-Hunt.

MILLER, G. A.
1956   The magical number seven, plus or minus two: some limits on our capacity for processing information. *Psychological Review* 63:81–97.

MITCHELL-KERNAN, C.
1971   *Language behaviour in a black urban community*. Monograph number 10, Language Behavior Research Laboratory, Berkeley: University of California.

1972   "Signifying and marking: two Afro-American speech acts," in *Directions in sociolinguistics*. Edited by J. J. Gumperz and D. H. Hymes, 161–179. New York: Holt, Rinehart and Winston.

NADER, L.
1962   A note on attitudes and the use of language. *Anthropological Linguistics* 4:24–29.

PHILIPS, S. U.
1970   "Acquisition of rules for appropriate speech usage," in *Monograph Series on Languages and Linguistics* 23. Georgetown University.

PRIDE, J. B., J. HOLMES, *editors*
1971a *The social meaning of language*. London: Oxford University Press.

1971b "Customs and cases of verbal behaviour," in *Social anthropology and language*. Edited by E. Ardener, 95–117. ASA Monograph 10. London: Tavistock.

1973a An approach to the (socio-) linguistics of commands and requests in English. *Archivum Linguisticum* 4 (new series).

1973b Directions in sociolinguistics: review article. *Language in Society* 2 (2).

PRIDE, J. B., J. HOLMES, *editors*
1972   *Sociolinguistics*. Harmondsworth: Penguin.

RUBIN, J.
1968   "Bilingual usage in Paraguay," in *Readings in the sociology of language*. Edited by J. A. Fishman, 512–550. The Hague: Mouton.

SALISBURY, R. F.
1962   Notes on bilingualism and linguistic change in New Guinea. *Anthropological Linguistics* 4, 7:1–13.

SANKOFF, G.
  1972 "Language use in multilingual societies: some alternative approaches," in *Sociolinguistics*. Edited by J. B. Pride and J. Holmes, 33–51. Harmondsworth: Penguin.
SAPIR, E.
  1929 "The status of linguistics as a science," in *Selected writings of Edward Sapir*. Edited by D. G. Mandelbaum. Berkeley and Los Angeles: University of California Press.
SCHEGLOFF, E. A.
  1968 Sequencing in conversational openings. *American Anthropologist* 70:1075–1095.
TANNER, N.
  1967 Speech and society among the Indonesian élite: a case study of a multilingual society. *Anthropological Linguistics* 9:15–40.
WHEELER, M. W.
  1972 Distinctive features and natural classes in phonological theory. *Journal of Linguistics* 8:87–102.
WHITELEY, W. H.
  1966 Social anthropology, meaning and linguistics. *Man* 1, 2:139–157.
  1967 "Loanwords in linguistic description: a case study from Tanzania, East Africa," in *Approaches in linguistic methodology*. Edited by I. Rauch and C. T. Scott, 125–143. Madison, Wisconsin: University of Wisconsin Press.
  1973 *Language in Kenya*. Nairobi: Oxford University Press.
WOLFF, H.
  1959 Intelligibility and inter-ethnic attitudes. *Anthropological Linguistics* 1, 3:34–41.

Extralinguistic Variables and Linguistic Description

ANTHONY L. VANEK

Linguists in the mid-twentieth century have gradually come to reformulate their basic task from one of describing (by any means that permit prediction) the corpus of correct utterances in a language to a view in which the linguist's statements claim to reflect the reality of formulating grammatical utterances for the (native) speaker of a language. This has been a laudable trend, and it has greatly increased the psychological validity of what linguists say about the realities they study. Yet few have taken the step from recognizing language behavior as rule-governed to realizing that linguistic rules cannot be written in isolation from man as a speaking being. It will be the contention of this paper that linguistic rules, to reflect social reality for speakers of a language appropriately, will have to use *non*-linguistic information. The corollary of such a position is that what linguists have generally referred to as "extra linguistic" features of language are also rule-governed.

The example to be used here is that of the so-called politeness pronouns in Czech. Such an analysis as I present has normally been treated, if at all, as an "extralinguistic" variation which is not part of the formal description of Czech (and other languages having comparable phenomena). I will demonstrate, in contrast, that the use of personal pronouns in Czech in a way which on the surface violates the grammatical features of the pronouns is actually rule-governed and socially explicable by rules like those which linguists have always written for pronoun use (except that some of the information is social).

The Czech pronoun *ty* 'thou' refers to single address; the pronouns *vy* 'you', *on* 'he', and *oni* 'they' may also, however, be used in reference to a single person in address. Similarly the pronoun *já* 'I' may, under specifiable circumstances, be replaced by *my* 'we', or *on* 'he'. The final two forms are not politeness pronouns in the traditional use of this term, but are included in this analysis because they form the reciprocal of the politeness relationships of direct address to a single person. If the use of the first set of forms is socially conditioned, then one might expect similar social features to determine the appropriate use of the second set.

There has been some previous discussion, in both anthropology and linguistics, of the way in which languages express respect or relative status of speaker and addressee. This is perhaps most notable in the attention paid to "honorific" forms of address. Obviously such expressions of respect will be culturally-specific in the status relationships they reflect; however, it is equally clear that every language will have some form of recognition for status differences, even if only the basic ones of age, sex, and generation.

Choice of pronoun in the examples to be considered below will depend on feature specification changes in the pronominal NP under conditions which are clearly determined extralinguistically. The normal form of address for himself by the (male) speaker of Czech is *já*. However, this is not the only option. In each of the following examples of direct speech the speaker is the King of Bohemia, George of Podiebrady:

1. *Já Jiří z Poděbrad prohlašuji že . . .*
   I, George of Podiebrady, proclaim . . .
2. *My Jiří z Poděbrad, král český, prohlašujeme že . . .*
   We, George of Podiebrady, King of Bohemia, proclaim . . .
3. *Já váš král k vám dnes mluvím, lide český . . .*
   I, your King, am speaking to you today, Czech people . . .
4. *On váš král k vám dnes mluví, český . . .*
   He, your king, is speaking to you today, Czech people . . .

The use of the plural pronoun *my* in place of the singular form *já* is generally described as the "royal we" or *pluralis maiestaticus* if the speaker is an individual of high political and social prestige. When used by less prestigious persons, it may be referred to as the "editorial we." This shift in grammatical number from (1) to (2) depends on the high social status of the speaker. In examples (3) and (4), the situation is reversed and the speaker is striving to put himself on the same level as his audience. The king thus encourages unity among his people by recognizing himself as one of them.

The speaker in these two instances changes the grammatical feature specification of person or number in the NP in which he refers to himself. He does not, however, change the feature specification of the social context since he is still the speaker and not the addressee. His semantic singularity also persists, since the NP continues to have an individual referential index rather than a set index. That is, the NP requires a singular rather than a plural predicate.

Tentatively, then, we have isolated two social features which are necessary to determine the appropriate pronoun for reference to oneself in direct address. The first might be characterized as ± respect and the second as ± equalization of status.

Now let us turn to the pronouns of politeness which refer to the addressee rather than to the speaker:

5. *Ja ti Jane sděluji, že jsi byl pozván na tuto recepci.*
   I am informing thee John that thou hast been invited to this reception.
6. *Ja vám Jane sděluji, že jste byl pozván na tuto recepci.*
   I am informing you John that you have been invited to this reception.
7. *Ja mu Jane sděluji, že (je) byl pozván no tuto recepci.*
   I am informing him John that (he) has been invited to this reception.
8. *Ja jim Jane sděluji, že (jsou) byl pozván na tuto recepci.*
   I am informing them John that (they) have been invited to this reception.

In the above four sentences, the NP *Jane* 'John' refers to a single addressee. This NP, however, concurs not only with the expected pronoun *ti* 'thee', but in addition with the second *plural* pronoun *vy*, 'you', the *third* singular pronoun *mu* 'him', and the *third plural* pronoun *jim* 'them'. Both number and person can, therefore, be altered to reflect relative social status of the speaker and addressee. The differences in the conditions for use of these various forms in Czech are named, the traditional terms being *tykání* 'thouing', *vykání* 'youing', *onkání* 'heing' and *onikání* 'theying'.

The use of these four forms of address is linked to changing social conditions in Czechoslovakia. The generation that grew up between the turn of the century and World War II uses all of the forms. The generation that grew up during the War and since tends to use only *tykání* and *vykání*. This clearly reflects social change from a more to a less status-oriented society. All four terms continue to exist in the language and may, indeed, be understood, but the usage of them has changed.

The pronoun of address *onkání* was used to persons thought to be of consequence because of their social status. For example, it was employed by servants to the children of their employers, by children of the upper classes among themselves (especially in formal contexts). In contrast, employers addressed their servants as *ty*, the same pronoun used among themselves by members of the lower classes. We may formalize this notion in a feature of ± consequential to account for the feature shift from second to third person in NP's of direct address to a single person.

Turning now to *tykání* and *vykání*, we find another criterion of use of polite pronouns. *Vykání* was, and still is, used to address persons who command respect, either by virtue of specific position, age or status, or in the social experience of a specific speaker. *Vykání* could, for example, be used to a policeman, a mayor, a judge, a manager, a teacher, any appreciably older person, or a blind date. *Tykání* is used in the absence of such respect, for example, among friends, within the family, to small children. This notion may be formalized by a feature of ± accordance of respect which accounts for the feature change from singular to plural for NPs of speech to a single addressee.

The features of "consequence" and "respect" are distinguishable. The older generation uses both to decide between *vykání* and *onikání*. The former is used for those who command respect because of office, position or age, but such individuals may not be considered by the speaker to be persons of social consequence, e.g. a policeman. The most formal address, *onikání*, is used only where the two features are both present. For example, an old servant will address his employer as *oni* 'they', while addressing the children of that employer as *on* 'he'; the children are respected because they share the social status of their parents but, being children, are of little social consequence. Members of the upper classes formerly addressed one another as *oni* unless they were close friends and close in age, in which case *onikání* might be replaced by *onkání* or *tykání*.

Let us now return to the pronoun forms used by a speaker in referring to himself. We postulated that use of the third person pronoun *on* indicates the speaker's intention to put himself on the level of the addressee(s). We will assume that everyone considers himself to be a person of consequence in his own eyes; if this is so, the normal feature of the speaker NP in this regard is + consequential. The form *on* is then − consequential and may be loosely equated with an expression of modesty.

It is now possible to collapse the rules for pronoun choice of speaker and addressee into two rules. The NP affected by these rules is the pronominal NP, since the lexical NP will not reflect the shifts in feature value (although titles used in direct address may reflect the same features).

9.

NUMBER SHIFT:

X   NP: [+Pro]   Y
                  (+respect)
                  $\left\{\begin{matrix}[+1\ ]\\ [+11]\end{matrix}\right\}$

1   2   3
1   2:[(p1]   3

10.

PERSON SHIFT:

X   NP: [+Pro   ]   Y
                  [a 1   ]
                  [− a 11   ]
                  (− a csqnl)

1   2   3 $\Rightarrow$
1   2: [− 1]   3
1   [− 11]

These rules are ordered with respect to each other, the number shift rule always preceding the person shift rule.

The features of consequence and respect are not contained in the lexical item. Because pronouns of politeness are used only in addressing a person or in reference to the speaker, it is a necessary condition that they can be associated only with + human nouns. Let us consider the following hypothetical example in which individual XY knows 200 other individuals well enough to refer to them other than as *člověk* 'person', *muž* 'man', *žena* 'woman', *dítě* 'child', *hoch* 'boy', *dívka* 'girl'. The referential indices of these 200 persons are specified in his mind in terms of name, sex, physical characteristics, behavioral characteristics, or other identifying information; each individual can be referred to as *Jan, my mother, my father, our policeman, my neighbor*, etc. Individual XY must also associate with each of these people the additional information that 100 of them command his respect and 60 are, to him personally, persons of consequence. He will then associate the feature + respect with 100 of these referential indices and the feature + consequential with 60 of them. Person XY would then use *vykání* in addressing 45 of the 200 persons, *onikání* in addressing 55, *onkání* in addressing 5 and *tykání* in addressing 100.

The association of features such as respect and consequence with the referential index is necessarily based on extralinguistic criteria. Indeed, the association is not necessarily a static one in the case of the relationship of any two given individuals. For example, if a Czech boy meets a girl, he will accord her respect and refer to her as *vy*; when he has known her for some time and they are friends, he will consider her his equal and will address her as *ty*. This means he will change the feature that accompanies her referential index from + respect to − respect.

However, this change in social relationship is governed by the feature of respect (and consequence) which we have postulated and the two extralinguistically determined features do affect linguistic processes. If we are to explain the form of the Czech politeness pronouns and resulting subject–verb agreement we will have to incorporate features such as the two proposed here into our linguistic description. It is not enough for the linguist to argue that sentences are semantically synonymous when such pronoun shifts are made. The features of respect and consequence affect meaning in the sense that the relationship between speaker and addressee (which may be open to manipulation by either party, as in the case of the King of Bohemia in our initial examples) is part of the meaning of the utterance. Only by including rules based on social interaction in our linguistic rules can we accurately describe the politeness pronouns. Certainly this principle can be applied to other languages with politeness formulas of various sorts; equally certainly, there are other kinds of grammatical rules which will have to incorporate so-called "extralinguistic" criteria to adequately explain the way speakers use their language.

Sociolinguistic Aspects of Pronoun Usage in Middle English

GLORIA PAULIK SAMPSON

Pronouns of address are of interest in sociolinguistics because they can reflect socially-determined linguistic variability. The present study is concerned with expressing regularities underlying such variability in the form of generative rules which characterize normal pronoun use.

Pronouns are found in all languages. And in all languages they are defined by linguists as referring to the same categories of expression; e.g., personal pronouns, demonstrative pronouns, relative pronouns and so forth. But, as Emile Benveniste (1971:217) has pointed out, pronouns are not a unitary class, but are of two different types. Some pronouns belong to the syntax of a language and others belong to what he terms "instances of discourse." Benveniste defines "instances of discourse" as the "discrete and always unique acts by which the language is actualized in speech by a speaker" (1971:217). Such instances of discourse are perhaps more profitably viewed as "contexts of situation" as the latter construct was developed by Malinowski (1956:307), Firth (1957:18), and most recently by Halliday (1973:49). "Context of situation" includes not only the clearly linguistic aspects of instances of discourse but also the participants involved in the instance, the particular channel of communication used, and the role relations among the participants. In describing role relations and the like, it should be evident that extensive knowledge of the social system and the culture of the participants is necessary.

Benveniste's classes of pronouns might be termed "syntactic" and "deictic." An example of a syntactic pronoun would be the relative pronoun as treated by George Lakoff (1971:331). Pronouns characteristic of instances of discourse are I and YOU. More precisely, "I is the individual who utters the present instance of discourse containing the linguistic instance I" (Benveniste 1971:218). By introducing the situation of address, a reciprocal definition of you is obtained. "YOU is the individual spoken to in the present instance of discourse containing the linguistic instance YOU" (Benveniste 1971:218). This constant and necessary link to the instance of discourse constitutes the feature that unites to the pronouns I and YOU a series of deictic forms which belong to various classes (pronouns, adverbs, adverbial phrases). Some examples of these forms are "this," "these," "today," "a week from tomorrow." Benveniste notes with regard to these forms that the deixis is contemporary with the instance of discourse that carries the indicator of person. That is, the critical feature of these deictic forms is that they are linked to a specific instance of discourse. These forms are empty or nonreferential and become full only when a speaker introduces them into an instance of discourse. "Their role is to provide the instrument of a conversion that one could call the conversion of language into discourse" (Benveniste 1971:220). Their use marks the process of the appropriation of language by the speaker on his own behalf.

It should be noted, by the way, that if Benveniste's analysis is correct, then certain other syntactic phenomena become part of this process of LANGUAGE AS AN ACTIVITY MANIFESTED IN INSTANCES OF DISCOURSE. Tense and aspect, for example, are also dependent upon the actualization of an instance of discourse. Also certain uses of the definite and indefinite articles in English may be subsumed here. Hence, an examination of deixis, in particular pronouns of address, may help shed some light on presently intractable portions of grammar and lexis.

The present study views the pronouns of address in specific instances of discourse, or, more precisely, in the context of situation. This study builds upon a knowledge of the social structure and the belief system of the society in which the pronouns are used. The model therefore links social structures and linguistic forms.

The data are drawn from Geoffrey Chaucer's *The Canterbury tales* which was written between 1387 and 1400. The data consist of 3,502 instances of use of Middle English THOU and YE forms ("thou," "thee," "thy," "thine," and "ye," "yow," "your" are the syntactic variants).

Table 1 is a schematization of part of the model proposed to account for second-person pronoun usage. A given pronoun use may appear on any one of three LEVELS OF DISCOURSE: the link, the tale, or the literary level. The first two correspond to the traditional separation of link versus tale. In the links the pilgrims address one another. In the tales of pilgrims tell stories about various characters. The literary level of discourse covers situations in which a pilgrim assumes an explicit role as narrator and directly addresses his audience.

In applying the model, the first decision made about an instance of pronoun use between members of an addresser–addressee dyad is what level of discourse it is being used on. The next decision is what DOMAIN the addresser and addressee are functioning in. Varying status criteria operate in the domains. Members of the addresser–addressee dyads are positioned in the social domain according to dimensions such as birth, occupation and wealth. Kinship positions are based on a person's place within his family. Ideational positions assume that one member of the dyad is nonhuman. Nonhumans are gods, animals, and personifications of emotions, such as Lust or Woe.

Table 1. A model of the use of second person pronouns

Lexical entry	Levels of discourse	Domain	Position scales
		Social	– – – – – – – – – – – –
	Link	Kinship	– – – – – – – – – – – –
Second		Ideational	– – – – – – – – – – – –
Person			
Singular		Social	– – – – – – – – – – – –
Pronoun	Tale	Kinship	– – – – – – – – – – – –
		Ideational	– – – – – – – – – – – –
	Literary	Narrative	
		Citatory	

The sociological assumption underlying the notion of domain is that a person's status can be stated only with respect to some reference group. The model reflects reference groups when persons are ranked on a scale within the relevant domain. E.g., when a king is talking to one of his subjects, both are positioned on a status scale in the Social Domain. When a king is talking to his daughter, both are positioned in the Kinship Domain. When a king prays to a god, both are ranked in the Ideational Domain. Thus the concept of status is characterized in the model by the ranking of positions in accordance with the standards of a specific scale in a given domain.

Each domain contains at least one POSITION SCALE. The position scales are vertical arrangements of the statuses available to persons in the society of Chaucer's time. They exemplify the kinds of social stratification that existed. Of course there are many varieties of social status, such as economic, political, etc. This model is based on the assumption that prestige status is the major determinant of pronoun use in *The Canterbury tales*.

Further, while there are many positions vertically on a scale, it is assumed that certain adjacent positions can be grouped together (i.e. made equivalent to one another). These groupings, which are emic as opposed to etic, formalize the sociological construct of social class.

The notion of prestige status can be broken down into two components: (1) style of life, which refers to occupation, income, and attitudes, and (2) social participation. Evidence for these two components was gathered from an examination of the sumptuary laws of medieval England (laws governing how people may dress) and from codes of etiquette of the time, such as John Russell's *The boke of nurture* and Wynkyn de Worde's *The boke of keruynge*.

It is suggested that there were five social classes in Chaucer's England. These are, from highest to lowest:
5. Royal Class,
4. Knight Class,
3. Squire Class,
2. Mediocre Class,
1. Laboring Poor Class.
Each of the twenty-three pilgrims and eighty-four persons in the tales the pilgrims tell are placed on the status scales. Both lay people and clergy are ranked in these classes. The class structure is the basis for attitudes and pronoun use shown by both pilgrims in the links and characters in the tales.

Every instance of second-person pronoun use (3,502 instances) was coded on a computer card. The social statuses of the members of each addresser–addressee dyad were also coded and a program was written to sort the cards in accordance with a series of rules postulated to account for pronoun use. A statistical test was applied to see how well the rules matched the data. Most of the rules for which there were sufficient data were confirmed.

In addition to the specific formal features of the model discussed above, there are several other important non-obvious aspects of it. First, the model is comprehensive. Pronoun usage of all classes represented in *The Canterbury tales* is examined. In contrast, Brown and Gilman (1968:261) deliberately exclude from their classic study informants from working class families. Further, no systematic view was taken of society. Earlier pronoun studies, such as that of Kocher (1967), use terms such as teacher, policeman, villager to describe the social statuses of the users of the pronouns. Yet these are all atomistic terms and no picture of the overall social structure emerges. Built into the present model is the assumption that the society is structured. While such an assumption may seem obvious to sociologists, a precise statement as to the membership of the various social classes and the primary determinants of social class do not seem to have been built into earlier pronoun usage studies.

Second, the model addresses itself to the question of what pronouns are actually used, in contradistinction to what pronouns people think they might use in a hypothetical situation. Examination of actual instances of use may reveal more underlying parameters governing use than would an inspection of hypothetical uses.

Third, the model assumes face-to-face contact of dyad members (addresser–addressee).

Fourth, as the subsequent discussion of the rules will show, features such as social class, sex, and age are not considered extralinguistic. These features are the environments in lexical rules.

Fifth, the distinction between "inappropriate" with respect to infelicitous use and "ungrammatical" as the latter term is presently used by linguists is a difference of degree and not of kind. That is, advocates of a competence/performance distinction might suggest that "inappropriateness" as a judgment belongs to the performance arena and "ungrammaticality" belongs to the competence arena. When linguists consider the question of the ungrammaticality of a given instance, however, they must and do ask the questions "Ungrammatical for whom?" and "Ungrammatical for what corpus of English?" Thus, even the notion of grammaticality as linguists presently use it is context-of-situation dependent.

Sixth, non-use of the pronoun suggested by the rules of the model causes certain inferences to be drawn. (The notion of "inference" is borrowed from Schegloff (1972:112).) The speaker may be regarded as insolent, ignorant, defiant, angry, and so forth. Because of such inferences, inappropriate uses of the pronouns can be accounted for.

The last non-obvious assumption embodied in the model is that communication, from the point of view of meaning, involves not just similarity of referent but similarity of universe of discourse or "context of culture" as that term is used by Malinowski (1956). Understanding between people is possible through language because of mutual recognition of the set of presuppositions (context of culture) underlying an utterance. The purpose of the model is to make explicit the shared presuppositions governing pronominal usage.

While the lexical rules which follow below are appropriate only for the society represented in *The Canterbury tales*, the underlying regularities expressed in them in fact are not unique to that society. Earlier published studies of pronoun usage indicate in general that the second-person plural form of the pronoun is used by inferiors to superiors. The relative ranks of the persons involved may be on any one of several scales, including those based on kinship, intimacy, or ascribed social status as determined by education, job, or the like. Equals may use either the plural or singular pronoun reciprocally. Superiors use the singular pronoun when addressing inferiors.

Not all the rules of the model are given below. The ones discussed are a representative sample to illustrate some of the principle features of the rule component of the model.

1. 2PN → *thou*/([aHuman], [−aHuman])

Rule (1) predicts that the second-person singular pronoun ("thou" or its allomorphs) will be used reciprocally between human beings and anything characterized as nonhuman in Middle English. Its format simply follows the standard alpha notation of Chomsky (1965). The notation to the left of the comma indicates an addresser, that to the right of the comma indicates an addressee. In cases where the addresser is nonhuman and the addressee is human, this rule predicted 91 percent of the uses. In cases where the addresser was human and the addressee was nonhuman, the rule predicted 87 percent of the occurrences. This is out of a total of 343 dyadic transactions.

$$2.\ 2PN \rightarrow \begin{cases} ye/ & \left(\begin{bmatrix} +\text{Family} \\ -\text{Male} \\ +\text{Generation elder} \end{bmatrix}, \begin{bmatrix} +\text{Family} \\ +\text{Male} \\ +\text{Generation elder} \end{bmatrix} \right) \\ \\ thou/ & \left(\begin{bmatrix} +\text{Family} \\ -\text{Male} \\ +\text{Generation elder} \end{bmatrix}, \begin{bmatrix} +\text{Family} \\ +\text{Generation younger} \end{bmatrix} \right) \end{cases}$$

The topmost portion of Rule 2, an example of a rule operation on members of a dyad in which both addresser and addressee are members of the Kinship Domain, predicts that wives will address their husbands with YE forms (or their allomorphs). (Again, the addresser is characterized by the features listed to the left of the comma.) Out of 708 instances of use the rule was confirmed for 97 percent of these.

$$3.\ 2PN \rightarrow \begin{cases} ye/ & (a,\ b)\ \text{where}\ b \geqslant a \geqslant 3\ \text{or}\ b > a\ \text{and}\ a < 3 \\ thou/ & (a,\ b)\ \text{elsewhere} \end{cases}$$

Rule 3 is actually a schema of twenty-five separate rules governing pronomial use among members of the five prestige classes in the Social Domain. In this schema, *a* refers to the addresser, and *b* to the addressee. It should be recalled that the social classes are ranked in order. The number 5 indicates the highest class (Royal Class), whereas the number 1 refers to the lowest class (Laboring Poor). The middle class in the strict sense of the term is number 3 (Squire Class). The rule states that when the addresser is of middle class or higher he will use YE forms to his equals or to those higher than he is. If the addresser is of a class LOWER than the middle class, he will use YE forms to anyone higher than he is in rank. THOU forms are used to his equals and his inferiors. In all but two groups of dyads in the Social Domain where there were sufficient data, this schema was confirmed.

4. 2PN ⟶ *thou*/(—,—)   where Discourse is LITERARY
                                                      and Domain is CITATORY

Rule 4 states that a second-person pronoun is realized as a THOU form in a quotation. Statuses of addresser and addressee are irrelevant. The rule is confirmed in 125 of the 133 occurrences *The Canterbury tales* (94 percent of instances).

As mentioned above, this listing of the rules is not exhaustive, but merely an illustrative sample drawn from the entire set of rules.

Because the rules permitted pronoun usage to be examined with precision, the nature of the exceptions to these rules could be inspected too. The question arises as to the inferences which are drawn when deviations from predicted use occur. These deviations are termed "pronominal switching."

First, it is clear from the text that changes of emotional state on the part of the addresser are concurrent with pronominal switching. Thus, switching indicates anger, love and so forth. Also included in this category are special motives such as mockery and intent to deceive.

Second, changes of role within a single status are concomitant with pronominal switching. For example, in "The Clerk's Tale" a member of the highest class (Royal Class) uses YE forms to a member of the lowest class (Laboring Poor). The model predicts that THOU forms should occur. When these exceptions to the rule are examined, however, it can be seen that the member of the Royal Class is courting the member of the lowest class, and he finally asks her to marry him. This courtship occasion evokes a special role and this is concurrent with a special use of the pronouns. It should be noted, by the way, that if "friend" is considered a role change, then assumption of this role by members of a dyad causes switching to THOU forms only in the Squire Class. (Members of the two classes lower than Squire always use reciprocal THOU forms.) Friends in the Knight and Royal classes use reciprocal YE forms. This supports the analysis of medieval pronoun usage in Brown and Gilman's study (1960:255).

Third, certain verbs co-occur with instances of switching. E.g., requests using forms such as "help" and "pray" (the latter verb has the meaning "to beseech") when used by an addresser co-occur with switched forms only. Yet subcategorization of verbs into verbs of beseeching, verbs of command, verbs of request, verbs of loving, and so forth, is only of very limited value because it is more common for a sentence to display not a member of such a class of verbs, but rather a paraphrase of the intent described by the verb. Contrast the sentence (a) "Pity us," with the sentence (b) "Let some drops of pity fall upon us." Until a theory of paraphrase is available which provides a formal mechanism for the linguist to analyze sentence (b) as equivalent to (a), it is not possible to formalize the phenomenon of pronoun switching which is concurrent with the use of certain categories of verbs or their paraphrases.

Last, the model revealed instances of possible social conflict. The main thrust of the model was focused elsewhere, but this revelation might be viewed as an interesting byproduct which could provide further independent verification for at least some assumptions built into the model.

A priori it might be expected that social conflict if extant would be greatest between adjacent classes, and it would be particularly abrasive where there might be some social mobility such that a member of one class or the other could rise into or fall out of a given class. This suggests that the rules postulated to underlie pronoun use would be highly confirmed, e.g., in those exchanges between members of the Royal Class and other classes, inasmuch as Royal status is ascribed. Persons cannot of their own volition enter the class, except by marrying into it or being born to it. On the other hand, a member of the Squire Class could, due to ill fortune, fall to the status of Mediocre, and it is remotely possible that a Mediocre could rise to Squire. Therefore, it can be predicted that Squires might be very careful to use THOU forms to members of the Mediocre Class, whereas members of the Mediocre Class might be somewhat unwilling to admit to their lower status and would be less prone to use YE forms to members of the Squire Class. This hypothesis in fact is confirmed. Members of the Squire Class use THOU to members of the Mediocre Class in 93 percent of all instances. But the members of the Mediocre Class use YE forms to the members of the Squire Class in only 47 percent of the instances. It can be confirmed that this pattern of usage is due to true class conflict and not due to a mistake in the model of having one class too many. The reasoning is as follows. Members of the Squire Class use YE forms to one another. If the members of the Mediocre Class were then really members of the Squire Class (that is, if no Mediocre Class existed), they too would use YE forms to one another AND to those members of the Squire Class to whom they presently use YE forms only half the time that they should. Thus the patterning of pronoun usage among the social classes provides information about the class structure of the society that was not available before.

Results of the present study suggest that a concern with the activity of language reveals interesting facts not only about language but also about the society engaged in that activity.

REFERENCES

BENVENISTE, EMILE
1971 "The nature of pronouns," in *Problems in general linguistics.* Translated by Mary Elizabeth Meek, 217–222. Coral Gables, Fla.: University of Miami Press.
BROWN, ROGER, ALBERT GILMAN
1960 "The pronouns of power and solidarity," in *Readings in the sociology of language.* Edited by Joshua A. Fishman, 252–276. The Hague: Mouton.
CHAUCER, GEOFFREY
1957 "The Canterbury tales," in *The works of Geoffrey Chaucer* (second edition). Edited by F. N. Robinson, 1–265. Boston: Houghton Mifflin.
CHOMSKY, NOAM
1965 *Aspects of the theory of syntax.* Cambridge, Mass.: The M.I.T. Press.
DE WORDE, WYNKYN
1868 "The boke of keruyinge," in *Early English text society.* Edited by Frederick J. Furnivall, 261–288.
FIRTH, J. R.
1957 *Papers in linguistics, 1934–1951.* London: Oxford University Press.
HALLIDAY, M. A. K.
1973 *Explorations in the functions of language.* London: Edward Arnold.
KOCHER, MARGARET
1967 Second person pronouns in Serbo-Croatian. *Language* 43:725–741.
LAKOFF, GEORGE
1971 "Presupposition and relative wellformedness," in *Semantics.* Edited by Danny L. Steinberg and Leon A. Jakobovits, 329–340. Cambridge: University Press.
MALINOWSKI, B.
1956 "The problem of meaning in primitive languages," supplement to C. K. Ogden and I. A. Richards, *The meaning of meaning* (tenth edition), 296–336. New York: Harcourt, Brace and World.
RUSSELL, JOHN
1868 "The boke of nurture," in *Early English text society.* Edited by Frederick J. Furnivall, 115–228.
SCHEGLOFF, EMANUEL A.
1972 "Sequencing in conversational openings," in *Advances in the sociology of language*, volume two. Edited by Joshua A. Fishman, 91–125. The Hague: Mouton.

Codeswitching as a "Safe Choice" in Choosing a Lingua Franca

CAROL MYERS SCOTTON

THE PHENOMENON OF CODESWITCHING

When many members of a society can speak more than one language, switching between two or more languages in the same conversation is a common phenomenon. Some reasons for codeswitching have been fully discussed in sociolinguistic literature (Gumperz 1970; Stewart 1968; Fishman 1970; Parkin 1974, among others). But in this paper we wish to present another explanation for codeswitching which is, to some extent, an overview of all other explanations. We reason codeswitching often takes place because the switcher recognizes that the use of either of two languages has its value in terms of the rewards and costs which accrue to the user. The switcher chooses a "middle road" in terms of possible rewards and decides to use both languages in a single conversation.

Such an interpretation of codeswitching presupposes a general sociolinguistic theory which views language transactions in multilingual groups as EXCHANGES in which participants choose a language by weighing the relative costs and rewards incurred in that choice. The possibility and attractiveness of alternative outcomes and/or alternative relationships figure implicitly in any choice. Here we draw data to support these propositions largely from East Africa.

Four main reasons for codeswitching have been put forth in the past:

1. Lack of knowledge of one language or lack of facility in that language on a certain subject. This lack necessitates switching from one language to another for certain parts of the conversation. For example, a Kikuyu university student in Nairobi reported that although he usually speaks Kikuyu with his younger brother, in a session in which he was helping him with his geometry homework he had to switch constantly to English to discuss certain points: "*Atīrīrī* angle *niati* has *ina* degree

eighty; *nayo* this one *ina mirongo itatu. Kuguori*, if the total sum of a triangle *ni* one-eighty *ri* it means the remaining angle *ina ndigirii mirong mugwanja.*"

2. The second reason for codeswitching is its use in excluding certain persons present from a portion of the conversation if it is known that these persons do not know the language used for switching. For example, many educated young people in East African use English as "the language of love and sex." They can speak English to discuss their affairs of the heart and to exchange information on sex in front of parents and others who do not know English, and their secrets will remain unknown.

A specific example of switching for the purpose of exclusion occurred in a conversation among six Kikuyu men who were thinking of setting up a business together. The "chairman" began the session in Kikuyu. But then one man complained that the initial investment mentioned by the chairman was too great. Discussion in Kikuyu followed. Then the chairman intervened and said in English that a large initial investment was necessary to make the venture worthwhile. He added that anyone who could not come up with the specified sum of money was not qualified to join such a venture. He chose English for this statement for two reasons: first, to gain support from the English-speaking members who were also, not by chance, the wealthier ones and the ones whom he thought would agree with his line of reasoning; second, to let the English speakers know of his attitude toward those members who were arguing for a small initial investment without actually insulting them directly. As non-English speakers, they missed the bluntness of his point.

3. Codeswitching is also used as a stylistic device to indicate a change in the "tone" of the conversation at a certain point, or to signal the introduction of a subject more or less more formal than what had been under discussion. We see codeswitching put to this use in the following examples. Two educated Nigerian men were conversing in standard English at a party in Lagos. A rather overly dressed, attractive woman passed. The one conversant dropped his standard English to say in pidgin English, "Look wetin dat woman carry put for body" (indicating that her attire represented quite a production). In Nairobi, a Tanzanian was asking a Kenyan for a loan of money. The conversation began in Swahili with an explanation of the circumstances which caused the request. But when the actual subject of borrowing was raised, the Tanzanian switched to English, as if to indicate he was aware of the seriousness of the request. ". . . *Nina shida ya lazima sana ya pesa kwa sasa. Naomba sana unisaidie*" 'I have a great need of money right now. I ask you to help me.' And then in English: "Well, this is the first time since I knew you, I think, to borrow money. I know money can break our friendship."

4. A man may use codeswitching in an attempt to impress another with his virtuosity in several languages or at least in one prestige language.

David Parkin (1974) reports such a use of codeswitching in several conversations between market sellers and customers in Nairobi. For example, the seller may greet the prospective customer in the customer's own first language in a rather overt attempt to gain favor and therefore a sale.

While all of the above reasons for codeswitching are valid, they all can be subsumed under an explanation which views a desire to attain as high rewards as possible and as low costs as possible as the determining factor in any language choice. After all, although it is true a person may switch TO a language for any of the reasons already discussed, the underlying fact of the situation is that he has chosen to handle a conversational encounter is such a way as to REQUIRE two languages, not one, in the first place. Switching presupposes two languages (or more) and the CHOICE TO USE two languages presupposes a desire for a "safe return" — some rewards from the use of each language, we argue.

To support this hypothesis of codeswitching, we will present data from a study conducted in Kampala, Uganda in 1968–1970 on patterns of language use.[1] One of the most interesting findings of this study was the large amount of switching between English and Swahili which was observed and reported to take place between Africans, each of whom claimed some facility in English. Since English is decidedly the prestige language in Kampala, why should these persons — largely whitecollar workers with aspirations of upward mobility — use Swahili when it does not seem "necessary"?

Consider this situation which we encountered in our Kampala study. Two men meet, both claiming to speak some English. Although the more educated respondent can always establish or reinforce his status as being educated by using only English, in many situations the costs of such a move might cancel most of his rewards. This would be the result if the person spoken to has a weak command of English. An encounter in English would "cost" this man by exposing his poor English. (Our studies — discussed later — show that ability to speak English is used as a socioeconomic indicator in Kampala.) If high costs are inflicted upon the person spoken to, he will reject, or at least avoid, further such encounters with the persons who choose the costly language. Therefore the better English speaker could gain status by using English but lose the other man as a friend. Is such a gain worth it? If instead the good English speaker uses some Swahili, it is true he will not receive the undiluted reward of having his educated status acknowledged through his command of English, but he can be sure that his costs (in terms of creating uneasiness, resentment, etc.) will not be high. Therefore our better English speaker, faced with the need for a lingua franca and realizing the possible

[1]   For a more complete picture of the Kampala study than is presented here, see Scotton (1972).

costs and rewards involved in the available language, may choose to use both languages in the same conversation. This choice of Swahili/English represents a "safe return." Rewards involving socioeconomic status will not be as high as those possible with the choice of English alone, but neither will costs involving personal relationships be high. One respondent in our Kampala study explained the heavy use of the Swahili/English combination by persons who could speak English as follows: "Most people here live in mixed societies [i.e. persons of varying socioeconomic levels may live side by side, especially in municipal housing estates]. They prefer using some Swahili to avoid the suspicion that they use English because they are proud. If they use Swahili, they cannot be mistaken [as proud]."

Dire consequences can result in terms of costs incurred when a person who is ill-prepared to speak only the prestige language forsakes the middle road of combining that language with another language which he knows better. The following exchange took place between two Kikuyu men on a Nairobi bus:

1. *Niatia, Karanja?* 'How are you, Karanja?'
2. *Nikwega.* 'Fine.'
1. *No uraruta wira?* 'Are you still working in the same place?'
2. *Niwega.* 'Yes.'
1. By the way, what sort of work do you do there? [Note the switch to English only]
2. Dealing with debits.
1. What? [Obviously not understanding]
2. I usually deal with credits and debts of the company.
1. *Ati?* 'What?'
2. Debts.

Speaker one then kept silent for the rest of the journey. He appeared embarrassed because obviously he did not understand the meaning of the English word "debts" or "debits." Therefore he was unable to continue the conversation in the language he had initiated, English.

This view of codeswitching as a means of mitigating possible costs and maximizing rewards is complementary to a model which we wish to propose to explain the choice of a lingua franca in general. This model and the propositions involved are empirically based on data from a study of language choice in Kampala, Uganda. Hopefully, the model is precise enough to explain some of the questions arising from the Kampala data and to permit testing, but general enough to permit predictions applicable to other multilingual situations.

THE KAMPALA STUDY

Kampala, the capital of Uganda, is typical of many African cities. Its inhabitants once must have been a fairly homogenous, stable group, but, as of 1973, the city was the home of a constantly changing, very diverse population. It attracts the socially and economically aspiring African from all parts of Uganda. It used to be a center as well for persons from neighboring countries, but political developments have changed this situation somewhat. Kampala's population according to the 1969 census, was about 330,000.

Having little in common in terms of a first language, Ugandans and others need a lingua franca to communicate with each other when they move to Kampala.[2] English, as the official language of Uganda, is something of a lingua franca, but it is not really widely spoken. Twenty-eight percent of the men and 13 percent of the women questioned in the nationwide Uganda Language Survey of 1968 claimed they could hold a conversation in English.[3] Luganda has to some extent been a lingua franca in the past but our study shows it is now a poor third behind both English and Swahili. Swahili, the long-standing lingua franca of large parts of East Africa, has always had some importance as a lingua franca in Uganda, although of a lesser order than in Kenya and Tanzania. Today Swahili is the official language of Tanzania and it has gained currency in Kenya although English remains the official language there. Our study show Swahili is used widely today in Kampala.

METHODOLOGY OF THE STUDY

The immediate aim of the Kampala study was to report on patterns of language use and attitudes toward various languages and their socio-psychological correlates in several samples in Kampala. Situations calling for a lingua franca were of most interest.

[2] Kampala is located in the heartland of Buganda, the African kingdom which is now an administrative unit of independent Uganda. The people of Buganda, the Baganda, are the largest ethnic group in Uganda (about 16 percent of the population), and until recently they were the most powerful politically. Their language, Luganda, is, of course, widely used in Kampala among Baganda, but these days it does not figure prominently as a lingua franca.

About two-thirds of Ugandans are speakers of Bantu languages, as are the Baganda. The Bantu speakers live mostly in the southern half of the country where Kampala is located. There are three non-Bantu groups in Uganda: Western and Eastern Nilotic speakers and speakers of certain Central Sudanic languages. Western Nilotics make up about 14.5 percent of the total population, Eastern Nilotics make up just over 11 percent, and the Central Sudanic speakers make up almost 5 percent. All of these groups are represented in Kampala. (Figures are from the 1959 census, the last one which divided respondents by ethnic group.)

[3] See Ladefoged, Glick and Criper (1971) for more details on the Uganda Language Survey.

The findings of the study are based both on structured observations and on an interview[4] which was administered to a statistically representative sample of heads of households living in two Kampala areas. Because of limited financial resources and the unwieldiness of the problem of drawing a sample from the entire African population of Kampala, our only choice was to sample several areas. These areas were judged to be representative of the African working population of Kampala as a whole, on the basis of my observations and those of my assistants, the opinions of others familiar with the demographic makeup of the city, and preliminary surveys which we conducted in several areas. However, our sample remains statistically representative only of those areas from which it was drawn, not the whole city.

Our core sample ($n = 223$) represents a stratified random sample of a housing estate (Naguru Housing Estate) run by the city council and of a private housing area in another part of the city.[5] The sample includes about 25 percent of the heads of households in the areas. Ten percent of the sample are women.

In the analysis of the interview data we used several different computer programs, but most significantly a program in multiple linear regression analysis which provided two types of findings: (a) simple linear correlations holding between responses to various questions, and (b) significant determining variables in accounting for variance in response to questions. The percentage of variability in response to any question which can be accounted for to the significance level was also calculated, with the variables listed in order of their importance.

CHOOSING A LINGUA FRANCA

Three major concepts underlie the propositions which we put forth to

[4] Responses to the interview were checked by observation of actual language use in representative places of work, shops, markets, buses, bars, homes, etc. The observations were conducted over a period of two years and the survey was accomplished in the second year. The interviewee took between forty-five and ninety minutes to complete the questionnaire. The language used was either English or Swahili or a combination of the two, or sometimes a combination including Luganda as well. Two assistants did the interviewing and made observations; I accompanied them in some interviewing to be sure the procedure was standardized and also did some observing on my own. Both assistants are Baluyia men from Western Kenya and had been residents in Kampala for five years.

[5] For comparative purposes, we added three smaller samples, totalling eighty respondents, to our core sample. One group is predominately Baganda, one group is from a low income area, and the third group represents relatively high-income civil servants. Because of the way they were chosen, we cannot claim these smaller samples are statistically representative of any larger groups. Findings reported here refer to the core sample (which is statistically representative of its population) unless otherwise noted. Interestingly enough, results for the overall sample ($n = 303$ including the core sample) follow very closely those for the core sample alone.

explain the findings of the Kampala study and choice of a lingua franca in general:

1. The overall framework proposed by Thibaut and Kelley (1959) which sees social interaction as a process of exchange. The exchange is made in terms of a balancing of costs and rewards by the participants in the social process so that each participant achieves an outcome satisfying to himself — given his possibilities.

2. The concept that social norms provide the individual with a social reality or frame of reference (Sherif 1967; Festinger 1950). As Katz and Lazarsfeld (1955:55) point out, "The function of the group [is] as a provider of meanings for situations which do not explain themselves." That new and supra-individual qualities (which therefore do not necessarily reflect individual preference) arise in the group situation and become norms is the conclusion of Sherif (1967).

3. The concept of role-taking as opposed to simply role occupation. This concept is rooted at least in part in the work of George Mead (1934), but has been explained most clearly by Turner (1962:23). He writes:

The idea of role-taking shifts emphasis away from the simple process of enacting a prescribed role to devising a performance on the basis of an imputed other-role. The actor is not the occupant of a position for which there is a neat set of rules — a culture or set of norms — but a person who must act in the perspective supplied in part by his relationship to others whose actions reflect roles that we must identify.

In explaining choice of a lingua franca, we make use of all these concepts in concert. For example, in regard to role-taking, we reject any interaction theory (possibly also based on Mead's ideas) which insists the main focus is on relatively independent individuals taking ad hoc roles in social situations. Such a view denies a pattern to group relationships; it jumps directly from individuals to the level of "culture." For example, we do not see language choice as a "happening" which can unfold as a unique event. While we wish to make use of the idea that role-taking (here, language choice) is a dynamic process, we stress that any choice is inevitably restrained by group affiliations and norms. The "choice" arises at all in that some individuals are more successful than others in assessing the potentialities of a situation — in terms of costs and rewards — and thereby in making wise choices. Further, an interaction theory which explains linguistic behavior largely in terms of the individuality of encounters must be rejected on other grounds. Such a theory cannot meet our most important goal, that of prediction. How can we predict if everything is individualized?

Yet our Kampala findings show us that, while we cannot individualize language choice, neither can we say that it is entirely predetermined by demographic factors such as educational level, age, etc. It is true that in some Kampala situations demographic variables explain a great deal of variance in response. For example, in our overall sample 56.8 percent of variance in reported choice of a lingua franca with an Asian stranger at work can be explained by the combination of the demographic variables, claimed English ability, and educational level. But in other situations, such as the reported choice of lingua franca with neighbors, only 30.3 percent of the variance in response can be explained to a level of statistical significance by all or any of the demographic variables considered.

The striking amount of language switching between Swahili and English reported for the respondents who claim to speak English well is one of the most interesting findings of the Kampala study. If we considered the demographic profiles of these respondents, we would expect English alone to be a more typical choice. Yet, for example, with co-workers of a different ethnic group, the choice Swahili/English is reported by 40 percent (55 out of 139) of those claiming competence in English.

The problem with demographic variables as predictors of language choice is that they are one-way referents which treat speakers as single-faceted individuals. But speech involves interaction. Therefore, while we do not dismiss an individual's socioeconomic profile, we must also consider the effect of extra-individual cultural pressures which influence behavior in any interaction.

We must also be wary of relying heavily on the social situation or domain itself as the prime predictor of linguistic behavior. As many researchers have pointed out, language choice does vary according to domains such as family, neighborhood, occupation, etc. (Fishman et al. 1968; Fishman 1970; Gumperz 1966; Hymes 1962, among others). But we see domain or classes of situation as very weak predictors of linguistic behavior in a specific situation. This is because we have no explicit, demonstrable criteria by which to classify all situations. The terms "formal: informal," "public: private," "transaction: personal" have been used for situations. But on what basis is one to say, for example, that a conversation with a neighbor is necessarily less formal, less public, or more personal than a conversation with a shopkeeper?

Even while we recognize the inexactness of situational categories, we realize it would be difficult or impossible to discuss variation in language choice without reference to one situation or domain as DIFFERENT from another. Our quarrel is with the reliance of dichotomies of situations (informal versus formal, etc.) as the crucial factor in predicting language choice.

We argue that the theoretical concept proposed here — that linguistic behavior is an exchange based on viable social norms which determine the way in which costs and rewards accrue for all situations in the same way — gives us the encompassing explanation we are looking for. This concept can include, but need not make paramount, any of the factors we have been discussing: (1) It allows for the influence of demographic variables. These variables provide the individual with his socioeconomic profile (and his linguistic competency) from which he "starts." (2) The concept does not deny the centrality of individual encounters and/or classes of encounters (i.e. situations or domains), but it does not make the encounter itself the basis of linguistic behavior. Rather, language choice itself depends upon how these existing situations are viewed through the lens provided by societal and special group norms.

Depending upon the special group norms which an individual brings to the situation (determined by his socioeconomic profile), coupled with the general cultural norms applying to all individuals in a particular society, the individual will assess the situation and decide on the behavior which he believes will give him the best return in costs and rewards. Individuals will choose differently largely in terms of their differences in socioeconomic background. General societal norms will tend to iron out great differences which could result if socioeconomic backgrounds were the only determining factor.

This theory puts foremost in the mind of the speaker the social function of a linguistic choice. That is, the speaker figuratively asks himself, what will the choice of this particular language "mean" to me? Will it mean gains or losses in terms of various kinds of status?[6]

[6]   Thus we see that language choice depends upon how the existing situations and possible consequences are viewed through the lens provided by norms. Therefore we avoid reliance on social situations as direct predictors of behavior and also avoid the accompanying need to define such situations discretely. We still need to know that situation X is "different" in some ways from situation Y, but the important point is that we need not polarize X from Y, since our explanation does not rely on this.

This view that social norms are preeminent in determining linguistic behavior is not new, of course. Among writers who have discussed the part of norms in language choice is William Labov (1968:251), who writes: "The speech community is not defined by any marked agreement in the use of language elements, so much as by participation in a set of shared norms; these norms may be observed in overt types of evaluative behavior, and by the uniformity of abstract patterns of variation which are invariant in respect to particular levels of usage."

Let us look now in detail at the model illustrating this theoretical concept: The individual, defined by his own socioeconomic profile, sees the social situation through the lens of social norms. The most important feature of the model is that the individual sees the situation (and possible outcomes) only in these terms. The individual then makes his judgment concerning social reality on the basis of what he has seen (the situation) and how he has seen it (the norms). Social reality, of course, as distinct from physical reality, is somewhat different for each individual. It is comprised of an individual's view of what is going on about him and his assessment of his appropriate part in these goings on. He makes a judgment of the potential costs and rewards inherent in any linguistic behavior, given his view of social reality. In this light, he chooses to speak a certain language or combination. Next, interaction with other participants occurs. Now the individual assesses the balance of costs and rewards he is receiving in the interaction. At this point, he may consider the matter of what costs and rewards would be involved in alternative relationships outside his present one. He will decide whether the continuation of his present relationship is desirable. He may decide to continue the present interaction, but he may decide the costs and rewards he is receiving do not represent a "good return." Therefore he may make a re-assessment of the social situation and make an alternative language choice of view of the interaction — that is, in view of the choices of others.

Costs and rewards are defined here as abstract units comprised of behavioral features which determine a person's self-esteem and his special group and overall group esteem. By rewards, we mean certain positive satisfactions a person receives. By costs, we refer to factors creating anxiety in any form. Rewards have a positive effect on self-esteem, and costs a negative effect. Just what are costs and rewards becomes a relative matter dependent upon the values of the society in which the encounter takes place. See Figure 1 for the model illustrating this theoretical concept.

THE KAMPALA FINDINGS

We can use the model in Figure 1 to explain linguistic practices found in Kampala. First, let us look at linguistic competence there. Although English is the official language, it is only spoken to any real degree by Ugandans with at least six years of primary schooling. Of the variance in response for claims to speak English, 57.5 percent can be accounted for by a person's educational level alone. In our sample of members of the Kampala working force, 24 percent claimed to know no English at all and another 14 percent said they could speak only a little English.

A knowledge of Swahili, which has no official standing in Uganda, is much more widespread, our findings indicate. Only 3 percent of our sample claimed to know no Swahili. It is true that 42 percent did say they could speak only "a little" Swahili, but the point is that the sizeable majority of 97 percent claim at least the possibility of some kind of conversation in Swahili.

Luganda, the first language of the indigenous ethnic group of the Kampala area, is known by Kampala residents in general, but not as widely as Swahili. Twenty-three percent of the non-Baganda in the sample said they spoke no Luganda at all, and another 30.5 percent claimed to speak only a little Luganda. (With persons from his own ethnic group, the typical respondent speaks his own first language. Lingua francas are used mainly for outside contact, our findings show.)

There is no question but that the ability to speak English is used as a socioeconomic indicator in Kampala. Respondents claiming to speak English well reported in overwhelming numbers that they would use English only in a number of situations where status-raising was at stake. For example, asked what language they would use with an Asian stranger in their place of work, just over 68 percent of those respondents who claimed English competence said they would use English only. (English "competence" is defined as the ability to ask and answer questions in English.) Further, another part of our study showed that the ability to speak English well is directly correlated with a well-paying and/or high-

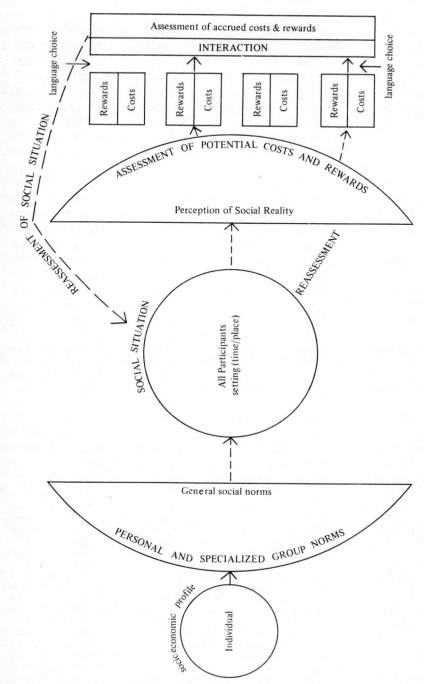

Figure 1. A model for predicting language choice

status job. Tape recordings of Africans speaking English with various degrees of proficiency were played in the interview. The respondents were asked to rate the speakers according to possible jobs they might hold. The better English speakers were judged to have the better jobs. A similar test with tape-recorded speakers of Swahili yielded, in general, responses of "no opinion" about possible jobs. This is an indication that Swahili performance is not correlated with socioeconomic status.

Still, even though a performance in English conveys an educated, high status image, in many situations the educated Africans in our sample use either Swahili only or the combination Swahili/English. Why is this? In terms of our model for explaining language choice, we would argue that in certain situations the use of English only is judged to give a "poor return." In line with our contention that social norms influence an individual's language choice, we would argue that the speaker need not attach the value of prestige to a language as a precondition to using it. For example, in Kampala the educated man may think that Swahili is mainly the language of the uneducated, but he himself will still use it because of the force of certain norms. In writing about norms, Thibaut and Kelley (1959:240), among others, make the point that social norms stand above individual preferences:

In general, it may be said that norms develop under circumstances in which individuals would not regularly behave in a certain manner of their own accord. The behavior or mode of behavior specified by a norm is not that which all individuals would consistently perform because of its intrinsic value to them.

Even an individual's seemingly personal behavior and attitudes may be byproducts of interpersonal relations. Thus, individuals may use Swahili not because of any positive image its use projects, but in accord with a norm stemming from Swahili's obvious usefulness in intergroup communication and because of its neutral connotations.[7]

---

[7]   If we assume the population recognizes the widespread knowledge of Swahili in Kampala, a person who initiates a conversation in Swahili presumes nothing about his companion except that he will be able to understand Swahili. Use of another language — English or any ethnically tied language — makes specific socioeconomic presumptions.

Also, the specific endorsement of the usefulness of Swahili by the sample as a whole, including the educated groups, indicates that the choice of Swahili will almost always be at least functional. Seventy-four percent of the core sample answered both English and Swahili to the question: "Considering your child's future life in East Africa, what language(s) would it be useful for him to study in school?" And 84 percent agreed with the statement: "All government employees in Kampala dealing with the public should be required to know Swahili." Forty-three percent favored Swahili as the national/official language in Uganda.

Another factor promoting the use of Swahili is the distinct feeling in Kampala that Swahili is a "safe" language. Almost all persons claiming ability in Swahili reported learning it on their own (only 12 percent of the sample said they had any schooling in Swahili). But only those who had school experience at a level insuring lengthy study of English reported knowing more than a little English. This willingness to "teach yourself Swahili" but not English can be explained, at least in part, by our finding that Swahili is hardly used as a

PATTERNS OF LANGUAGE CHOICE

The educated man in our Kampala sample makes three main choices for his lingua franca: Swahili alone with distinctly less educated persons, English alone with persons of established or potentially high status, and the combination Swahili/English with peers.

It seems significant that the most Swahili/English switching which was reported and observed occurred in situations for which an appropriate course of action is least clear. These "middle" situations include conversations with one's peers at work and chats with neighbors. For example, the neighbors, 51 percent of the core sample claim to speak Swahili only, but still 20 percent say they speak the combination Swahili/English in this situation. English only is not a viable choice, with only 4 percent reporting it. Among those in the sample claiming English competence, 37 percent said they speak Swahili only with neighbors, and 29.5 percent reported the Swahili/English combination. With co-workers of a different ethnic group, 39 percent of the entire core sample speak Swahili only, but 28 percent speak Swahili/English. At an evening social event, 38 percent said Africans such as themselves would speak Swahili/English, and 33 percent said they would speak Swahili only, while 18 percent believed English only a possible choice.

These same middle situations are also those for which language choice can be least defined in terms of the socioeconomic profile of the speaker or other demographic values. That is, regression analysis fails to point to demographic factors which can account for a high percentage of variance in response. In the more "set" situations certain demographic factors do emerge to account for a good deal of variance. For example, an impressive 56.4 percent of variance in response in the core sample for a conversation with an Asian stranger at work, and 46.8 percent of variance in a conversation with a well-dressed African stranger at work can be accounted for by the demographic variables entered in the program — notably, claimed English ability as the factor which emerges first and educational level as the second factor. But the variables we considered can account for only 35.3 percent of variance in response for a conversation with African co-workers of different ethnic groups. And only 25.3 percent of variance with African neighbors of different ethnic groups can be accounted for by these variables. (Again, however, claimed English ability and educational level emerge first.)

Our best example of a "middle" situation is a conversation between

---

socioeconomic indicator, while ability in English is. A person in any position need not fear a poor performance in Swahili will affect his status in the minds of his listeners. Further, the use of Swahili — with its lack of connections with education — carries with it no pretensions.

co-workers of different ethnic groups. In some aspects this is a situation which is formal and in which status-raising is possible, but in other aspects it is informal, since one is speaking with peers. For the core sample as a whole, Swahili alone is the most important choice, as we noted earlier. But if we just look at the group of English competents (139 out of the total core sample of 223), we see that they use Swahili and English about equally. However, the key point to note is that most of this usage comes through combining Swahili with English: 40 percent say they use Swahili/English, English only is used by only 21 percent, and Swahili only, 18 percent. Obviously, English competents — who presumably could try English only — prefer a safe, middle course which makes use of both languages when they are in an ill-defined situation such as a conversation with peers.[8]

As soon as the situation at work becomes more clearly one in which status-raising is possible, the amount of Swahili/English used goes down and the amount of English only goes up. This is as we would expect: the combination Swahili/English is a choice the educated man can "afford" to make only with his peers. In choosing Swahili/English, he manages to walk a fine line. He shows his education and he also maintains his image as a compatriot who is not above using the language "of the *wananchi* [people]." But as soon as he encounters strangers of potential high status, persons in higher positions, persons from another race, the educated respondent tends to jettison Swahili and will try to get his rewards strictly in terms of the educated status he can project by using English. True, the choice of English only could "cost" dearly if our educated respondent does not perform well, but it is a gamble he seems willing to take.

Thus the language patterns concerning the use of English only and Swahili/English which we found with African co-workers are almost reversed when Asian co-workers are present. While 40 percent of the English competents spoke Swahili/English with African co-workers, only 29 percent will speak it when Asians are present. While 21 percent spoke only English with African co-workers, 41 percent will speak only English with Asians.

With an Asian stranger who enters the place of work and even with a well-dressed African stranger, English only is the dominant choice. With bosses of any race, again, English only is the main choice of those who claim to speak it well.

[8]   We interviewed a special group ($n = 28$) of relatively highly educated civil servants. This sample is not statistically representative of any large group of civil servants, but it is still worth noting that even this highly educated group uses a good deal of the Swahili/English combination with co-workers. Thirty-six percent said they use Swahili/English with peers at work; 42 percent use English only and 7 percent use Swahili only. Even with neighbors, 32 percent use Swahili/English. But with a well-dressed African stranger at work — a situation where one's socioeconomic status is at stake — 82 percent would use English only, and only 14 percent would use Swahili/English, they reported.

Interestingly enough, it is really the amount of Swahili only and English only used — not the Swahili/English combination — which seems to be affected by differences in educational level. Let us look at the response of the English competents to the question "What language do you speak with co-workers of a different ethnic group?", according to educational level. We see that in the group of English competents who attained an educational level between Primary 6 and 8, 52 percent say they would use Swahili/English in this situation. Equally, 42 percent of those with a higher level (up to Senior 4) would use Swahili/English. But otherwise, the two groups react quite differently. While 32 percent of the Primary 6–8 group would use English only, 68 percent of the Senior 1–4 group would. Whereas 73 percent of the Primary 6–8 group would use Swahili only, 27 percent of the Senior 1–4 group would do so. Clearly, the combination Swahili/English is a middle road.

CONCLUSION

We have put forth the hypothesis that the major overall cause of language switching is the attempt to receive the best of two potential sets of costs and rewards patterns, especially in situations where there is uncertainty about the outcome. Therefore, in many Kampala situations, for example, we find heavier reported use of the combination Swahili/English than of either language alone. This codeswitching is notably a feature of conversations between middle-level educated peers who claim to speak English well and who also can speak Swahili. Switching combining other languages, such as English/Luganda and Swahili/Luganda, also occurs, especially in conversations where Baganda are most numerous.

To support our hypothesis we have produced statistical evidence showing the situations in Kampala in which the most codeswitching occurs and also data on the type of people who do the most switching.

The point is that the speaker attempts to obtain rewards and offset costs in two ways. Use of Swahili or a local vernacular defines his status in terms of one set of features: he is a "common" man without pretensions; use of English adds another set of features without cancelling the first: he is able to express himself in English and therefore establishes an identity as educated and probably economically successful.

Such codeswitching with the same purpose occurs in every multilingual society. The only real variable is the precise values attached to the languages involved in terms of costs and rewards. Consider this example from rural Western Kenya. A brother who runs a wholesale shop greets his sister, who has come to buy a few grams of salt. Both are Babukusu (a subgroup of the Baluyia). The brother greets the sister in their own first language, Lubukusu. But he soon switches to Swahili, the locally recognized language of trade. "This codeswitching reminds the sister that the shop is run as a business geared to profit-making," reported our respondent about this incident. "By continuing to speak some Lubukusu, he lets his sister know that he remembers their relationship, but by speaking some Swahili, he reminds her that he is a businessman and that she cannot ask for more free salt." Use of Swahili alone in this situation would have offended the sister. But use of Lubukusu alone would not have accomplished the brother's aim. Therefore he chooses the middle course of codeswitching for a safe return.

REFERENCES

FESTINGER, LEON
1966   "Informal social communication," in *Current perspectives in social psychology* (revised edition). Edited by Edwin P. Hollander and Raymond G. Hunt, 416–427. New York: Oxford University Press.
FESTINGER, LEON, STANLEY SCHACHTER, KURT BLACK
1950   *Social pressures in informal groups*. Stanford, Calif.: Stanford University Press.
FISHMAN, JOSHUA A.
1970   *Sociolinguistics, a brief introduction*. Rowley, Mass.: Newbury House.
FISHMAN, JOSHUA A., ROBERT L. COOPER, ROXANNA MA, *et al.*
1968   *Bilingualism in the barrio*. Final report on OECD-1-7-062817. Washington, D.C.: Office of Education.
GUMPERZ, JOHN J.
1966   "On the ethnology of linguistic change," in *Sociolinguistics*. Edited by William Bright. The Hague: Mouton.
1970   "Verbal strategies in multilingual communication," in *Report of the twenty-first annual round table meeting on linguistics and language studies*. Edited by James Alatis, 129–148. Monograph series on Languages and Linguistics 23. Washington, D.C.: Georgetown University Press.
HYMES, DELL
1962   "The ethnography of speaking," in *Anthropology and human behavior*. Edited by T. Gladwin and William C. Sturtevant, 13–53. Washington, D.C.: Anthropological Society of Washington. (Reprinted 1968 in *Readings in the sociology of language*. Edited by Joshua A. Fishman, 99–138. The Hague: Mouton.)
KATZ, ELIHU, PAUL F. LAZARSFELD
1955   *Personal influence*. Evanston, Ill.: The Free Press.
LABOV, WILLIAM
1968   The study of language in its social context. *Studium Generale* 23(1):30–87. (Revised and reprinted 1972 in *Sociolinguistic patterns*, Edited by William Labov, 183–259. Philadelphia: University of Pennsylvania Press.)
LADEFOGED, PETER, RUTH GLICK, CLIVE CRIPER
1971   *Language in Uganda*. Nairobi: Oxford University Press.
MEAD, GEORGE
1934   *Mind, self and society*. Chicago: University of Chicago Press.

PARKIN, DAVID J.
1974   "Language switching in Nairobi," *Language in Kenya*. Edited by W. H. Whitely, 189–216. Nairobi: Oxford University Press.

SCOTTON, CAROL MYERS
1972   *Choosing a lingua franca in an African capital*. Edmonton, Canada: Linguistic Research, Inc.

SHERIF, MAUZAFER
1967   *Social interaction*. Chicago: Aldine Press.

STEWART, WILLIAM A.
1968   "Distribution of French and Creole in Haiti," in *Georgetown University roundtable selected papers on linguistics 1961–1965*. Edited by Richard J. O'Brien. Washington: Georgetown University Press.

THIBAUT, JOHN, HAROLD KELLEY
1959   *The social psychology of groups*. New York: John Wiley and Sons.

TURNER, RALPH
1962   "Role taking: process versus conformity," in *Human behavior and social processes*. Edited by Arnold Rose. Boston: Houghton Mifflin.

Other People's Words: An Aspect of Style in Ga Songs

M. E. KROPP DAKUBU

1. INTRODUCTION

Among the Gas, a people of Ghana, the most widely practiced forms of verbal art are probably the libation and the song. Gas also have talking drums and talking horns, which must be considered verbal, although not oral, art forms. These however are reserved for specially skilled male performers in formal situations usually associated with state ceremonial. Libations and songs, on the other hand, are performed by all ranks of people, on all kinds of occasions, and by both sexes. Libations are more likely to be performed by men than by women, usually by the oldest person present, and lend a certain amount of formality to any occasion. Songs, on the other hand, are sung on all kinds of occasions, very often by old and young and both sexes together, although specific sets of songs may conventionally be sung mainly by one sex, or by the young, or on a particular kind of occasion.

It is a recognized feature of Ga songs that they frequently incorporate words and larger expressions from other languages (Nketia 1958:79–80). The most formal varieties of Ga verbal art, the talking drums and horns, are entirely in the Akan language, a phenomenon which is not peculiar to the Gas and is accounted for by historical relationships between the Gas and Akan-speaking states, especially Akwamu, and the role of Akwamu in the development of the Ga stool organizations (Wilks 1959). That is, these musical forms are derived from Akan forms and were introduced together with the political institutions with which they are associated. Libations are normally in Ga, but often incorporate Akan phrases and appellations. However, libations are made entirely in Akan for certain purposes. This author has recorded two such performed by the priestess, a Ga, of a "foreign" god, Tigare, at her house in the Ga town of Nungua.

This paper is concerned with the use of non-Ga linguistic material in songs sung by people whose normal language of daily use is Ga, and particularly songs in which more than one language appears. Many groups of Gas sing songs, or whole groups ("types") of songs, that are wholly in another language. Many of the popular churches in the Accra area sing hymns in Akan and in English, often somewhat garbled. Field reported songs in the "Obutu" language (Field 1937:5). These are songs belonging to the observance of certain ceremonial cycles, especially Kplejo, apparently obtained from a southern Guan ethnic stock which was absorbed into the Ga-speaking community at an early stage of its known history. At least the opening lines of the famous prayer *Awo! Awo!* (Hammond 1970:61) are probably in this language, although much of it is in Akan. There are also sets of songs which are entirely in Akan, sung for religious, state or recreational purposes. These have probably in the main been taken over wholesale from Akan traditions but there is also evidence that some have undergone change and expansion since their adoption. Thus Akaja, a song type which is entirely in Akan, although it is apparently unknown in Akan-speaking areas, contains at least one song apparently drawn from the Akan type called Adenkum (Dakubu 1972). All the Asaayere songs quoted in Hammond (1970) are in Akan.

This paper will deal with song types that, unlike those mentioned above, are not monolingual within their own domain. Actually, probably not even the above are completely exclusive linguistically. In Akaja, for instance, the vocalizations for the accompanying *odonno* drums are partly in Ga.

Within the multilingual song types, this paper is concerned especially with songs that are mainly in one language but contain elements from another. The phenomenon has two aspects. Ga contains a very large number of loanwords. With respect to borrowing, the relationship between the vocabulary of Ga and that of Akan is comparable to that between English and French. There are also a considerable number of recent loans from English. Many loans, especially from Akan, are thoroughly assimilated and not felt as foreign. Others, while they may be quite commonly used, are nevertheless recognized by the users as of foreign origin. It sometimes appears in songs that such words are being deliberately manipulated. The second aspect of the matter is the occurrence of nominal phrases of several words or even clauses from another language. In such a case there is rarely any doubt that the line or half-line is intended to be in a different language from the rest of the song.

In songs that are basically in Ga, Akan is by far the most frequent language to appear in these ways. Songs sung in Akan occasionally have a word or two in Ga. English words also occur, but not, in the material to hand, English phrases or clauses. Ewe only occurs in one song, but in a quite extensive passage. Only one instance of Hausa, a single word, has been noted.

2. PATTERNS OF MULTILINGUALISM

Before describing the use of foreign linguistic material in detail, it is relevant to indicate the extent of the multilingualism in the community that sings these songs.

The author of this paper has conducted a survey of the languages spoken by members of a Ga patrilineage centered on Accra. One-hundred and twelve members were surveyed, of all ages from fourteen years up. About two-thirds of the respondents are males; farmers, traders, tradesmen, students and clerical and technical workers are included. Many of the songs to be discussed were collected from members of this group. An additional twenty-three persons were surveyed, also from central Accra, whose formal education ranged from none to university and of whom ten are female. Of this total of 135 people, 111 (82 percent) knew Akan, more than half of them claiming good ability. More women claimed to know it than men, although more men claimed to know it well. Seventy-eight (58 percent) claimed knowledge of English, although many only claimed to know it slightly. In Ghana, school children are (at least in theory) taught English as a subject in the first three primary grades, and are taught in English thereafter. Therefore anyone who has spent any time at all in school is at least familiar with a few English words. Although it was not brought out in the survey, many people in Accra with no schooling at all are able to use a form of "broken English."

Thirty-three persons (24 percent) claimed knowledge of Ewe, and nineteen (14 percent) knew Hausa. Knowledge of French, Dangme and Yoruba was claimed by seven, six and three persons, respectively. Except for French, which is tied to secondary schooling, knowledge of these languages seems to depend on a person's social contacts. Except for Yoruba, a history of travel outside the Ga-speaking area does not seem to be a crucial factor, unless relative excellence is taken into account. That is, more than half of those who claim to know another language had learned it outside its home area. Of the 135 persons surveyed, only three claimed to be monoglots.

The author's impression is that this sample is probably fairly typical of Gas generally. It is striking that the order of frequency with which knowledge, however slight, of a language is claimed is the same as the order of frequency with which it occurs in Ga songs: Akan definitely first, then English, and then, at a considerable distance, Ewe and Hausa. French, Dangme and Yoruba do not occur in the song types to be dealt with here, although Field noted the occurrence of Dangme in religious songs of Tema and Teshie (1937: 16, 74). No one claimed to know "Obutu" or Awutu, but apparently songs in this language are not understood by the singers (1937:5). Such songs are not sung by the patrilineage which provided the bulk of the subjects for the survey.

3.   USE OF EXOTIC MATERIALS IN SONGS

This section will deal primarily with the language of songs belonging to five "types": Suolei 'mind your tail!', Tuumatu 'jump [and] I will jump' Kaadiohefɛosɛɛ 'don't mind about your beauty'; Sookpoti and Adaawe. These will hereafter be referred to respectively as S, T, K, Skp and A. Complete texts of the songs as recorded that are discussed in this paper are to be found in the Appendix. The author collected eleven Suolei, of which two contain Akan material. Most of these songs have to do with family strife and the part played in it by witches, but one of those containing Akan material admonishes girls to be hard-working. Of the three Sookpoti collected, two contain Akan material, and all are concerned with death. Two Adaawe songs were collected by the author; and sixty-one were published by Hammond. Of the latter thirteen contain Akan material, including three that are entirely in Akan. Four others prominently feature an English loanword with "overseas" associations, namely paoda 'toilet powder', sigareti 'cigarette', and meele 'steamship'. These songs are recreational songs sung mainly by young women.

Of eleven K songs collected by the author, four contain Akan material, and one has an English word. Of fourteen T songs, plus one collected by Professor J. H. Nketia in 1955, three are in Akan, one of them including one Ga and one English word, and one including a Hausa word. One other T song has Akan material. Six have English words, and another has English and a passage in Ewe. Both K and T songs are mainly about death and the fragility of life. They are sung principally by groups of women at wakes and festivals, although they were sung for the author by men.

It might be emphasized that some of the Adaawe and almost all the other songs are about death or family strife or both. There is no question of foreign words being used for comic effect.

3.1.   *Foreign Words in Textual Structure*

3.1.1.   AUGMENTS. It is a typical feature of the songs studied that many lines are augmented by a word that has little to do directly with the meaning of the line but serves as a kind of emotional decoration. An augment may occur at the beginning or end of a line, or occasionally in the middle. Very often the augment is in a different language from the rest of the song. In a Tuumatu song that is otherwise in Akan, the first line begins with an augment in Ga:

> *T-1*   ei <u>Kwɛmɔ</u>! [Ga] obi ba fɛfɛɛfɛ [Akan]
> Hwɛ deɛ ɔayɛ ná ɔda adeka mu [Akan].
>
> Hey <u>Look</u>! Somebody's beautiful child
> See what he has done and he is lying in a coffin.

In a song that is otherwise in Ga, a line occurs with an Akan augment:

> *T-2*   Mana eko ooo
> Kaakɛɛ eko oo
> ao <u>Mi adɔ</u> kaakɛɛ noko oo.
>
> I will get some
> Don't say some
> alas <u>My love</u> don't say anything.

One *K* song has a line with an English augment in the middle:

> *K-1*   Mi nyɛ baagbo ei
> Mi tsɛ baagbo ɛi
> Ni mi nyɛ baagbo ni makpɛ tso
> Ni mi nyɛ baagbo <u>fɛɛsi</u> ni naa gbe gbi
> Ni mi na mi nyɛɛɛ pii.
>
> My mother will die
> My father will die
> My mother will die and I will carve a tree [make a coffin]
> When my mother will die <u>first</u> that final day
> When I get I can't do much.

Adaawe songs occasionally have augmented lines. In the following, a song that is mainly in Ga has a line in Akan with an augment consisting of a loanword from Akan into Ga:

> *A-1*   Ayiwa ei ei ei
> Bɔni o fite mi ei, saamɔ mi ei [Ga]
> <u>Mɔbɔ</u>, munya bi a mu som [Akan].
>
> Ayiwa [a name]
> As you spoiled me, repair me
> <u>Pity</u> oh, if you get some, you keep it.

3.1.2. PARADIGMATIC TREATMENT OF FOREIGN WORDS. Sometimes sets of foreign words, or foreign and Ga words, appear in sets whose members substitute for each other in the structure of the song text. These are often systems of augments. In the Adaawe song just quoted, the Akan–Ga augment mɔbɔ is later replaced by an anglicism:

A-1   Ayiwa ei ei! ei ei!
Bɔni o fite mi ei, saamɔ mi ei,
<u>Mɔbɔ</u> oo, munya bi a nu som.

Ayiwa ei ei! ei ei!
O bɔ ajwamaŋ o ma sigarɛti ei,
<u>Polisi</u> oo, munya bi a mu som.

Ayiwa
You act as a prostitute you give out cigarettes,
<u>Police</u> oh, if you get some, keep it.

In the following *T* song, three "English" words form an augment system, which is run through and then repeated in reverse order. A second augment system of Ga words is introduced halfway through the song.

T-3   <u>Tsale</u> ei, looflɔ ewo mi kooŋ.
Basabasa hiɛ mi ei.
ao <u>diɛ</u> oo, looflɔ ewo mi kooŋ.
Basabasa hiɛ mi ei.
Jɔle ei, <u>ŋmɛnɛ</u>, looflɔ ewo mi kooŋ,
Bɔni a sumɔɔ a feɔ mi.
Jɔle ei, <u>kwɛmɔ</u>, looflɔ ewo mi kooŋ,
Bɔni a sumɔɔ no a feɔ mi.
ao <u>diɛ</u> oo, <u>ŋmɛnɛ</u>, looflɔ ewo mi kooŋ,
Bɔni a sumɔɔ nakai a hiɔ mi.
ei <u>tsale</u> ei, looflɔ ewo mi kooŋ.

<u>Chum</u>, a bird has put me in the bush,
Uselessness has hold of me.
<u>Dear</u>, a bird has put me in the bush,
Uselessness has hold of me.
<u>Sweetie</u>, <u>today</u>, a bird has put me in the bush.
As they like they do to me.
<u>Sweetie</u>, <u>look</u>, a bird has put me in the bush,
As they like, that they do to me.
<u>Dear</u>, <u>today</u>, a bird has put me in the bush,
As they like thus they treat me.
<u>Chum</u>, a bird has put me in the bush.

In the following *K* song, the two words underlined are not augments, but in the structure of the text they form a paradigm of meaning that has at least three features: names of small non-mammalian animals; defendant/aggressor; humanity/death. The paradigm can also be characterized as the lexical realization of a topicalized subject.

K-2   ei, Bo <u>waa</u>, te o baafee tɛŋŋ?
Nklaŋ lɛ, e shɛɛɛ gbeyei.

You <u>snail</u>, what will you do?
<u>Army ant</u>, he has no fear.

<u>Waa</u> 'snail', standing for humanity on the defensive, is a strictly Ga word. <u>Nklaŋ</u> 'army ant' is an Akan word, which is sometimes used in Ga, but has a purely Ga synonym gãgãa.

3.1.3. TRANSLATION AS A STYLISTIC DEVICE. Sometimes a line in a song appears first in one language and then in another. This occurs particularly in *Skp*, *S*, and to some extent in *A*. The central lines of one Sookpoti song are as follow:

Skp-1   Owu dade nda baako ei [Akan]
          Gbele klante efooo mokome too, o nu lo?

          Death's cutlass doesn't cut just one person.

The device occurs in two Suolei songs. In one of them, the fourth line occurs first half in Twi and half in Ga, and is later repeated completely in Akan:

S-1   Wɔ tsili okɔtɔ, [Akan] ha ni o nine ashε e nɔ [Ga]
        Wɔ tsili okɔtɔ, oma ɔsaŋ ka nɔ [Akan]

        You catch river-crab, let your hand reach it.

Immediately after the second occurrence, the second part is reiterated in Ga, but with a variation:

        Kε o nine shε e nɔ, feemɔ lε
        Bɔni o sumɔɔ.

        If your hand reaches it, treat it
        As you like.

In an Adaawe song of three lines, the first is in Ga, the second in Akan, and the third is essentially a translation of the Akan line into Ga, combining it with the first:

A-2   Kε o lé gbãla ei! [Ga]
        Aware fofro tisεε oja [Akan]
        Kε o le gbãla e tamɔ la [Ga].

        If you don't know marriage!
        New marriage is like fire.
        If you know marriage it is like fire.

3.2. *Semantic Aspects*

The larger part of the foreign words used in songs that are otherwise mainly in Ga seem to be divisible into two groups. Much of it, especially the Akan, refers to trouble and death. Most of the rest consists of insults or endearment. The two groups overlap somewhat, because abusive words often accuse the insulted person of killing.

3.2.1. TROUBLE AND DEATH. The Ga word for 'death', gbele, occurs rarely in the Ga songs studied, even though this is the major topic of most of them. The instance in *Skp-1* quoted above (section 3.1.3) is the only example I have found, and there it is introduced first in Akan, then translated into Ga. In a *K* song, the Akan word for 'death' is strikingly used in lines that are otherwise in Ga:

> *K-3*   Owuo kitee, ni wɔ sɛɛ ni maba.
>
> Death go ahead, and in future I will come.

In K-1, quoted in Section 3.1.2 above, the army ant, named here by an Akan word, stands for death, while the snail stands for humanity and is named in Ga. In another song, the world of the dead is named in Akan:

> *K-4*   Tsɛ mi o bi mi ei,
>   Kɛ mi aka ya sama ade.
>
> Call me and ask me,
> Don't send me to the world of ghosts.

In a Sookpoti song, most of the lines are in Ga, except the first line which is a lament, setting the mood of the song. It is sung first in Akan and then in Ga translation, as discussed in Section 3.1.3. The key word is amane 'trouble'.

> *Skp-2*   Maaka mi dɛɛbi, amanea mahu [Akan]
>   Mi kɛɛ mi daabi, amane ni mi na [Ga]
>
> I have said my no, trouble I have got.

In Adaawe songs, when trouble or especially death is named it is always named in Akan. For example:

> *A-3*   Mi ya he numo ei ei! [Ga]
>   Numo yɛ owuo [Akan].
>
> I went and got gossiped-about,
> Gossiped-about is death.

> *A-4*   Owu sɛɛ fie, Soobene. [Akan]
>
> Death spoiled the house, Soobene [a name].

There is a long Tuumatu song which tells the story of a lorry accident near the village (Kweiman) where the song was recorded. Most of the key words in the story are recent and recognized English loans: plosui 'police', diitsi 'ditch', sojafonyo, 'soldier', lɔle 'lorry'. The victims are taken to Korle Bu, meaning the hospital, not the lagoon, where a woman victim laments in Ewe. The underlined words are Ewe, the rest is Ga:

> *T-4* E ka shi aahunu ni e bɔi yaafo
> Ni e kɛɛ a mɛ ku lo,
> Va, slɔnyɛ ei.
>
> She lay down and began to weep
> And she said ah I have died,
> Come, husband.

3.2.2. INSULT AND ENDEARMENT. Akan words are often used where an insult is required. In a Suolei song which exhorts girls to work hard so that when they get married they will not starve, the lazy girl is insulted thus:

> *S-2* Mi shayoo bi lɛ, madɔ me yɛfum nti, ŋmaa he gbɔmɔ.
>
> My mother-in-law's daughter, "I like my stomach,"
> food person [person who likes food without work].

In essence, the Ga descriptive insult ŋmaa he gbɔmɔ is a repetition of or variation on the Akan phrase madɔ me yɛfum nti.
    More seriously, a killer witch is named in Akan in a Kaadiohefɛosɛɛ song:

> *K-5* Ofie tamfo, [Akan] ni o shaa no fiaa no [Ga].
>
> House enemy, that burns everything.

In a Tuumatu song that was not well understood by the singers but appears to be in Akan, the Hausa abusive word for "liar" occurs as an augment:

> *T-5* Ana ei aja ei yooyoo
> Nama see yo se obi wamma oo, kariya.
>
> Mother, father,
> [?] if somebody will come, liar.

Most of the English words that occur as augments are endearments, die 'dear', jɔle 'sweetie' [jolly], tsale 'chum' [Charlie]. These all occur in the song *T-3* quoted in Section 3.1.2 above. An Akan endearment mi adɔ 'my love' has also been noted, in *T-2* quoted in Section 3.1.1 above. Such words are not limited to foreign words, for Ga sũɔlɔ 'lover' also occurs as an augment:

T-4   Sowa ei, baakwɛ naakpɛ sane ei,
Suɔlɔ ei, baakwɛ naakpɛ sane ei.

Sowah, come see something marvellous.
Lover, come see something marvellous.

An English-derived word for "brother" is used as what might be called an endearing addressive in another *T* song:

T-6   ei Wɔ yaasɛɛtsi lo.
Beni wɔ tee, wɔ kɛ Ajeite ko ya kpɛ,
"Ataa Ajeite, niŋgbɛ o yaa yɛ biɛ?"
Ajeite ba jie naa,
"ao Bla Ago, ŋmɛnɛ, a wo mi shikpɔŋ mɔɔŋ ei."

We went to find it.
When we went, we met a certain Ajeite.
"Father Ajeite, where do you go here?"
Ajeite replied,
"Alas, Brother Ago, today they have put me in the prison of earth."

English bla and indigenous ataa here belong to an addressive paradigm in the initial position of two structurally parallel sentences. The use of the English verb sɛɛtsi [search], which is here used as the indigenous verb tao would be, can perhaps be explained as belonging to the trouble and death category of usage, since it is being used for the sad act of visiting a new grave. The Ga word ŋmɛnɛ is an example of an augment occurring mid-line. It does not mean that the person had been buried the same day.

Adaawe songs are often abusive, and the most insulting abuse is often in Akan, for example:

A-5   Koshitsɛ Lamte [Ga]
We nim atsia adene. [Akan]

Koshi's father Lamte,
Your face is hard [you are wicked].

4.   ATTITUDES TO OTHER LANGUAGES

The remarks made below are no more than ideas and tentative suggestions. One piece of research into attitudes to languages has been carried out in Ghana, by direct questionnaire methods (Ansre n.d.; Berry 1969). That work is not particularly relevant here because, although it was carried out near Accra, it sought to discover attitudes prevailing among a mixed group of immigrants into the area and only a small proportion of the respondents were Gas.

It might be useful to look at less self-conscious attestations of attitudes, such as remarks made in texts originally recorded for quite another purpose. Such evidence, however, is difficult to assemble and to interpret. I shall make an attempt to consider some of the attitudinal factors underlying the use of foreign linguistic resources as it has been described above, based on statements made in various kinds of recorded texts at various times. Since the quantity of relevant text is very slight, the discussion is only exploratory.

If one were to ask the singers why they use non-Ga words or lines in Ga songs, they would probably say that they are for beauty, or because they like it, or something of that sort; and there is a sense in which this is the best answer. Although Ga songs consist largely of repeated lines, more often than not a line is changed slightly each time it is repeated. The continual introduction of subtle variations seems to be an important part of the aesthetic, and translation into another language or introduction of a decorative word from another language is a popular way of doing this. As was seen in Section 2 above, familiarity with the languages used for this purpose is a widespread feature of the Ga language community, so there is nothing strained about the procedure. It need not reflect any great admiration for these languages per se, but it probably does reflect the desirability of knowing them.

The question remains of why the particular foreign words and expressions used are of the types they seem to be. The text of any of these songs is not absolutely fixed. There is considerable leeway for the individual performer, particularly in the style of repetition, and in the choice of what have been called augments (see Section 3.1.1). Thus the singer has most choice precisely where foreign words most often occur. It is therefore not the case that the use of exotic words reflects only the taste and linguistic ability of whoever first made the song.

Recorded references to Akans have two sides. On the one hand, many groups of Gas have historical and social links with their nearest Akan-speaking neighbors, the inhabitants of Akwapim. For example, an account of the founding of the village of Oyarifa saw it as the product of the friendship and cooperation of a Labadi man (Ga) and an Aburi man (Akwapim). Certain Ga lineages, including that of the singers of the Suolei songs discussed above, trace descent directly from Akan groups. On the other hand, the wars against the Ashanti (and also the Ewe) in the last century are very much alive in the memory of the same people and are commonly referred to in libations. However, there is no evidence in my material of any real hostility towards Akan or Akans, although I recorded one or two quite rude remarks about Ewes. This is not the likely explanation of the fact that mention of death and abusive terms are so often in Akan.

It seems to me that this is best accounted for on the general principle of distancing. This has two aspects; first, that bad things come from outside, and secondly, that to mention something explicitly bad in a language other than your own somehow weakens it, or keeps it at a distance. The songs discussed go in for a great deal of circumlocution. Thus although the theme of Tuumatu, Kaadiohefɛosɛɛ and Sookpoti is death, death itself is rarely named, and when it is, it is almost always named in Akan. The same is true of the closely related theme of witchcraft as a cause of death or misfortune. I suggest that this does not reflect any particular attitude toward Akans or the Akan language but a very general separation of Ga and non-Ga, which is related to oppositions of us and them, here and there, life and death, even good and bad; Akan is simply the most widely known non-Ga language handy for the purpose. Of course, there are many ambivalences and ambiguities and even downright contradictions in the relations among these oppositions, which I am not prepared to analyze at this time.

In Ghana, the popular opinion among non-Gas is that Ga is a language full of obscenity and abuse. Among university students the most widely used rude words are in Ga. But in all the songs considered there are very few explicitly abusive Ga words. Adaawe songs are sometimes abusive in Ga, but only through accusing a person of a particular kind of behavior. For example:

> A-6   Osu oblayei, tawa nyɛ fɔɔ lo?
>
> Osu young women, do you cut [use] tobacco?

and

> A-1   O bɔ ajwamaŋ o ma sigarɛti ei.
>
> You practice prostitution you give out cigarettes.

In the second example, all the lexical items are in fact loanwords, from Akan (ajwamaŋ, possibly bɔ in this usage, and probably ma) and English (sigarɛti). But when a person is insulted for what he inherently is, an Akan expression is generally used, as ofie tamfo 'house enemy' in K-5, and we nim atsia adene 'you are wicked' in A-5. The Ga word apasafo 'malicious gossiper' occurs in S-2. This is clearly a loan from Akan, but it is doubtful whether the singer is conscious of this. Although abusive, it is not as serious an accusation as the two which are certainly in Akan. The contrast between the popular idea of Ga as an abusive language and the handling of verbal abuse in Ga songs supports the proposition that undesirable things are kept at a distance by being put into someone else's language. In the popular stereotype of Ga they have apparently come to be associated with the language itself, but I find no evidence that the stereotype is objectively true of Ga as used by Gas, nor of a widespread equivalent stereotype among Gas with respect to Akan.

The frequent use of mild endearments from English (as well as from Ga and Akan) is possibly associated with a popular impression that in English both endearments and abuses (like "fool" and "idiot") are used very freely. In several Adaawe songs, Europe and European ways seem to be regarded as fascinating and desirable, probably because associated with wealth, but also somewhat disreputable, being associated with loose behavior as, for example, in the lines from *A-6* and *A-1* quoted above. This may be another factor behind the occurrence of such words as die and jɔle.

Ultimately, Akan and English words occur in Ga songs because these are the languages of powerful states whose cultures exerted what might have been an overwhelming influence on Ga culture and the Ga language for a long time, and still do. This fact seems to rest rather lightly on the singers of Ga songs. They seem far more interested in what they can do with this additional material than in what it may ever have done to them.

APPENDIX

Following are the texts of the songs referred to by number in the paper. They are the complete texts as recorded by the author, except the Adaawe texts, which are from Hammond (1970). All of these songs are of the type described by Nketia (1958:80) as popular, that is, not part of the ritual of either cult or court. The alphabet is the new one proposed by the Ga Orthography Committee of the Ghana Ministry of Education. The tones marked are speech tones. Word division is according to grammatical (systemic) principles and is not the orthographic division. Spelling of languages other than Ga reflects the pronunciation of the Ga singers.

Adaá!weè

These are songs sung by young women in villages on moonlit nights.

A-1 In Hammond's text, each of the three-line stanzas is sung by the leader and then repeated by the chorus.

(a) Ayiwá ei ei
Bɔ́ní ó 'fitè mi ei, saámɔ mì ei.
Mɔ́bɔ̀ oo, múnyà bí à mú som. [Akan]

(b) Ayiwá ei ei! ei ei!
A kɛɛ́ a ya kpèé mì ei, a kɛ mi tee,
A kɛ mi nyié kòkoó tsèi ashĭshi.

(c) Ayiwá ei! ei ei!
Bení miifo mi gbelè, míifo mi wàla.
Mɔ́bɔ̀, moko bí àwúsã.

(d) Ayiwá ei ei! ei ei!
Bɔní ò kɛ mi étèe, o kɛ mi ábà.
Mɔ́bɔ̀, moko bí àwúsã.

(e) Ayiwá ei ei! ei ei!
     O bɔ ajwamaŋ o ma sigarétì ei.
     Polísì oo, múnyà bí à mú som.

(a) Ayiwa [a name]
     As you have spoiled me, repair me.
     Pity oh, when you get some, keep it.
(b) Ayiwa,
     They said they would marry me, they went with me,
     They walked with me under the cocoa trees.
(c) Ayiwa,
     When I am weeping for my death, I am weeping for my life.
     Pity, somebody's child an orphan.
(d) Ayiwa,
     As you have taken me, you should bring me [you have pushed me
        around].
     Pity, somebody's child an orphan.
(e) Ayiwa,
     You practice prostitution and hand out cigarettes.
     Police oh, when you get some, keep it.

A-2   The first line is given by the leader, repeated by the chorus, again by the
      leader. Then the chorus sings the following:

      Kɛ̀ ò lé gbàla ei,
      Aware fofro tisɛɛ oja. [Akan]
      Kɛ̀ ò le gbãla e tamɔ la.

      If you don't know marriage,
      New marriage is like fire.
      If you know marriage it is like fire.

A-3   The two lines are sung by the leader, then repeated twice by the chorus.

      Mi ya hé nùmó ei ei!
      Numo yɛ owuo. [Akan]

      I went and got gossiped-about.
      Gossiped-about is death.

A-4   The last line is repeated four times, leader and chorus alternating.

      Leader: Wɔ yaa ei, Soobéne.
      Chorus: É!shɛ́kò mí nɔ̀ ei, Soobéne.
      Leader: Wɔ yaa ei, Soobene.
      Chorus: Aa aa ei, Soobene.
      Leader: Owu sɛɛ fie, Soobéne. [Akan]

            We go, Soobene.
            It hasn't reached me, Soobene.
            We go, Soobene.
            Death spoiled the house, Soobene.

A-5   The first line is given by the leader and the second by the chorus, before
      the leader sings the first four-line stanza through, after which the
      chorus repeats the second line. The same pattern is repeated with the
      second four-line stanza.

(a) Kóshitsὲ Lamté ei.
We nim atsia adene. [Akan]
A ya tsέ gbɔmɔ́ lὲ a kε ywiê.
Kɔkɔdéne fὲ bo anunyam.
(b) Ataá Làmté ei
We nim atsia adene.
Bení à ya tsέ gbɔmɔ́ lὲ kε ba
Kɔkɔdéne fὲ bo anunyam.

(a) Koshi's father Lamte,
Your face is hard [you are wicked].
They sent for the person to talk with him.
Frog has more respect than you.
(b) Father Lamte,
You are wicked.
When the person was sent for and brought
Frog has more respect than you.

A-6 The first line is sung by the leader, and the rest by the chorus.

Osú òbláyèi ei, tawá nyὲ foɔ lό?
Mi yε dεŋ, mi yε dεŋ? [Akan]
Kéjée tàwá wɔ̀ foɔ daa.
Ablotsiri a yεbεkɔ [Akan]
Hei, wɔ ŋfo lɔɔ.

Osu young women, don't you use tobacco?
What shall I do, what shall I do?
Isn't tobacco we use all the time.
Europe that we go to,
Hey, we use alum.

Kaádìóhèfέosὲε

These songs are generally sung by women's groups, at wakes and festivals.

K-1 The last two lines were repeated several times at the end.

Mí nyὲ baágbo ei.
ei Mí tsὲ baágbo ei.
Ní mi nyὲ baágbo nì mákpε tsò
Ní mi nyὲ baágbo fεèsi ní nàagbe gbĩ.
ei ei No hewɔ ni mí !na mi nyεεε pìi.
ei Ádèsã naabú ei ei,
No hewɔ no hewɔ
No hewɔ mí nyεεε makwê.
Naabú ei, nò hewɔ no hewɔ
No hewɔ mí nyεεε makwê,
Mɔ fέε mɔ̀ naabú !lε ei ei ei.

My mother will die.
My father will die.
When my mother will die and I will make a coffin.

When my mother will die first on that final day.
Therefore when I get I can't do much.
Person's mouth,
Because of that because of that
Because of that I can't look.
Mouth, because of that because of that
Because of that I can't look,
Everybody's mouth.

K-2   ei Bo waá!a té à baá!fee tɛŋŋ?
Nkĺàŋ lé !lɛ è shéee gbeyèi.
ei Bo waá!a, ŋkĺàŋ ba,
Té ò baá!fee tɛŋŋ?

You snail, what will you do?
As for the army ant, he isn't afraid.
You snail, army ant comes,
What will you do?

K-3   The last two lines were repeated six times. The phrase *ni maba* was
repeated the 2nd, 4th and 5th. The Akan word *owuo* was deleted the
5th.

ei Kítèe, ní wɔ sèɛ ní ma!ba.
Owúo kitèe, ní wɔ sèɛ ní ma!ba oo.
O tsū́ a ba tsɛ mì ei kítèe
Owuo ei, ei wɔ sɛɛ ei,
Ké ò bá !lɛ, bà átsɛ mì ei, kítèe,
Owuo ei, wɔ sɛɛ ni maba.
O tsū a ba tsɛ mi ei kitee,
Owuo ei, wɔ sɛɛ ni maba.

Go ahead, and in future I will come.
Death go ahead, and in future I will come.
You sent to call me go ahead
Death, in future,
If you come, come to call me, go ahead,
Death, in future I will come.
You sent to call me, go ahead,
Death, in future I will come.

K-4   Tsɛ́ mì ó bi mì ei,
Kɛ mi áka yà sáma ade.

ei Bí mì ei
Kɛ mi áka yà oo.

Kéji mi !tsɛ o ŋà
Bí mì ei, tsɛ́ mì ó bi mì ei,
Kɛ mi áka yà sáma ade.

Ké mì feé bò nó!ko
Bí mì ei, bí mí ei,
Kɛ mi áka yà sáma ade.

Kéji mi !tsɛ o ŋà ei
Tsé mì ó bi mì ei
Kɛ mi áka yà sáma ade.

Call me and ask me,
Don't send me to the ghost world.

Ask me,
Don't send me.

If I have called your wife
Ask me, call me and ask me,
Don't send me to the ghost world.

If I do something to you
Ask me, ask me,
Don't send me to the ghost world.

If I have called your wife
Call me to ask me
Don't send me to the ghost world.

K-5   Ofie tamfo [Akan]
     Ajee, ofie tamfo ei.
     Ní ò shãa nó fiaa no
     Mí ya he tòo, máwo lè.
     Hei ei, máwo lè.
     Ofie tamfo ei.
     Ma wo lɛ mawo lɛ
     Mawo lɛ ei,
     Ofie tamfo.

     House enemy,
     Alas, house enemy.
     You burn everything.
     I will go get a goat and put it on it.
     I will put it on it.
     House enemy.
     I will put it on it. [repeated]
     I will put it on it,
     House enemy.

Soókpoti

Skp-1   The first group of lines is sung twice, and twice again between the
     second and third groups.

(a)   Owú ei, ei ei, òwú ei, òwú ei
     Owú dàdé ǹda baakũ ei. [Akan]
     Owú ei.
     Gbélè klańtè é!fooo mòkomé too, o nù ló?
(b)   É!fooo mòkomé a!kɛ gbelè adédà.
     E!bāaa mòkomé.
     Gbélè klańtè é!fooo mòkomé too, o nù ló?
(c)   A kɛέ mi !nyɛɛɛ mayà ei.

A kɛé mi a!kɛ mi !nyɛɛɛ Ashanté mayà.
Ashanté Blɔfó bàá!fo mi !yi.

(a) Death, death, death,
Death's cutlass doesn't cut one person.
Death.
Death's cutlass doesn't cut just one person, have you heard?
(b) He doesn't cut one person with death's billhook.
It doesn't slash one person.
Death's cutlass doesn't cut just one person, have you heard?
(c) I was told I couldn't go.
I was told that I could go to Ashanti.
Ashanti European [? executioner] will cut my head.

Skp-2   Maákà mí dèɛbí àmanéà máhū. [Akan]
Mi kɛé mi dàabí àmane ni mi ná.
Sumɔɔ lɔbí.
Maákà mí dèɛbí àmanéà máhū.
Abonú!a sà̰ĭ sɔ́ŋŋ.
Be fɛ́ɛ bè ní mi nyè baágbo
Mákpè tsò adékà mi kɛ lɛ áwò mĭ.
Béni mi nyè gbó mì damɔ ta naa.
Mí sùmɔɔ lɔbí.
Maákà mí dèɛbí àmanéà máhū.

I have said my no, trouble I have got.
I have said my no, trouble I have got.
Dear lover.
I have said my no, trouble I have got.
Lemon [very bitter] matters.
Any time that my mother will die
I will make a coffin and put her in it.
When my mother died I stood before a war.
My dear lover.
I have said my no, trouble I have got.

Súolèí

S-1   Mí nyɛ ò le jí !ko mabò ei.
Bé!ɛ nàkāi hewɔŋ.
Gã mɛi fɛ́ɛ.
Wɔ tsili okɔ́!tɔ, há ni o nìne áshè e nɔ.
Bɔ́ni à sumɔɔ.

Moko ya heju hé ni à ba sɛɛ daní è wamɔɔ e he.
Kó mabò ei.
Bé!ɛ nàkāi nɔ́ŋŋ.
Ní à yɔ́ɔ̀ daa né!ɛ.
Wɔ tsili okɔ́!tɔ, o ma ɔsáŋ ka nɔ̀. [Akan]
Ké o nìne shɛ e nɔ feémɔ lè
Bɔní ò sumɔɔ.

Had I known I could have shouted.
Since it is so.

All Ga people.
You catch river-crab, let your hand reach it.
As you like.

One goes to the bathroom and comes back before he scratches himself.
I would have shouted.
Since it is so.
As one stays always.
You catch river-crab, let your hand reach it.
If your hand reaches it do with it
As you like.

S-2   Mí shàyoo bí !lɛ, madɔ ŋyɛfũ nti, ŋmàa he gbɔmɔ.
Dàni ò feé no!ko ni ò nyɛ yaá!kɛɛ̀
"Bo ó nàa wa fe ó nyɛ̀ naa."
O feé no!ko o tsɛ̀ yaá!kɛɛ̀ bo
"Ó nàa wa fe ó tsɛ̀ naa."
Mɛ́ɛ̀ yoo nɛ́?
Béni è tee gbãla e ŋɔ e nijĩ́ ényɔ̀ e kɛ wo e lagbaŋ ni e tá shĩ̀.
Apásafo yìŋtolɔ ya gba e nyɛ̃ kɛ e tsɛ á!kɛ hɔ̃mɔ miŋye lɛ.
E náaa ni!ŋ è ye.
Nyé kwɛà shayoo bí !lɛ, madɔ ŋyɛfũ nti, ŋmaa he gbɔmɔ.

My mother-in-law's child, "I like my stomach," food person.
Before you did something and your mother would say
"You are prouder than your mother."
You did something and your father told you
"You are prouder than your father."
What kind of woman is this?
When she was married she took her two hands and put them in her lap
    and sat down.
Malicious gossiper went and told her mother and her father that she
    was hungry.
She didn't get anything to eat.
Look at mother-in-law's child, "I like my stomach," food person.

Tuúma!tu

T-1   This song, in Akan, may be sung when a corpse is being placed in the
       coffin.

ei Kwémɔ, òbí bà féfɛɛfɛ
Shwé dìɛ waáyè ná ɔda adékà mú.

ei Jɔle ei, obí bà féfɛɛfɛ
Shwé dìɛ waáyè ɔda adékà mú oo.

Look, somebody's beautiful child
Look what he has done and he is lying in a coffin.

Darling, somebody's beautiful child
See what he has done and he is lying in a coffin.

T-1   ao Mána e!ko, mana e!ko
       oo Kaá!kɛɛ nokò.

ao Mána e!ko
Ajeíte kàá!kɛɛ e!ko ei.

ao Mána e!ko oo
Kaá!kɛɛ e!ko ei.
Mi adɔ́ kàá!kɛɛ nokò ei.

alas I will get some, I will get some
oh Don't say anything.

alas I will get some
Ajetey don't say something.

alas I will get some
Don't say something.
My love don't say anything.

T-3   Tsalé ei, lòóflɔ̀ éwò mì kooŋ.
Basabasa hié mì ei.
ao Dié oo ŋmé!nɛ lòóflɔ̀ éwò mi kooŋ.
Basabasa hié mì ei, hei
Jɔle ei ŋmé!nɛ lòóflɔ̀ éwò mi kooŋ.
Bɔní à sumɔɔ a féɔ̀ mi.
ei Jɔle ei kwémɔ lòóflɔ̀ éwò mi kooŋ
Bɔní à sumɔɔ no a féɔ̀ mi ei.
ao Dié oo ŋmé!nɛ lòóflɔ̀ éwò mi kooŋ.
Bɔní à sumɔɔ nakãi a híɔ̀ mi.
ei Tsalé ei lòóflɔ̀ éwò mi kooŋ.
Basabasa hĩé mì ei, ei.

Chum, a bird has put me in the bush.
Uselessness has hold of me.
alas Dear, a bird has put me in the bush.
Uselessness has hold of me.
Sweetie, today a bird has put me in the bush.
They do to me what they like.
Sweetie look a bird has put me in the bush
They do to me what they like.
alas Dear oh today a bird has put me in the bush.
As they like so they treat me.
Chum a bird has put me in the bush.
Uselessness has hold of me.

T-4   The first four lines were repeated.

ei Níí ei ŋmé!nɛ ó !tsū mì ó !tsū mì a ei
Míŋyà Sentse ní ma!ba ei
Bení mi bàa, bení mashè Ayí Mèń!sã
Náà plósùi lɔ́lè étèe diĩtsi ei.

Ajeíte Kwàshí bà ákwɛ nàakpɛ sane ei.
Sówà ei bà ákwɛ nàakpɛ sane ei.
Sũɔlɔ ei baákwɛ nàakpɛ sane ei.
Odaí Kwàámì ei ba ákwɛ nàakpɛ sane ei.

O míni sàne? Míni sàne?
Plósui lɔ́!le !lɛ etèe diĩtsi.

Kweímàŋ obláhi̇̀i bú kɛ̀ tee
Ní à ya ákwê
Ní à ya ákwê
Sójàfónyò mfó yè mĩ.
Obláyòó lɛ̀ lɛ́ !lɛ è hí!ŋmɛ lɛ̀ jwa.

Alóo àmɛ fɛ́ɛ kɛ̀ tee Gã.
A kɛ amɛ ya shwié Kɔ̀ɔle Bú.
E ká shĩ aahũ̀ù ni e bɔ̃ì yaafó,
Ni e kɛɛ́ â mɛ kú !lo.
Va, slɔ̃nyɛ ei.
Slɔ̃nyɛ ei, mɛ ku lo,
Slɔ̃nyɛ ei. jɔle ei, slɔ̃nyɛ ei,
Slɔ̃nyɛ ei, mɛ ku lo.
Slɔ̃nyɛ ei, jɔle ei, slɔ̃nyɛ. [Ewe]

ei Dié ei, míni tsūmɔ̀ nɛ́?
Míŋyà Sentse ní ma!ba ei.

Sir, today, you had sent me you had sent me
I was going to Senchi and I would come
When I come, when I will reach Ayi-Mensa [a village]
Behold a police wagon had gone in the ditch.

Adjeite Kwashi come to see something marvellous.
Sowa come to see something marvellous.
Lover come to see something marvellous.
Odai Kwami come to see something marvellous.

Oh what is the matter? what is the matter?
The police wagon had gone in the ditch.
Young men of Kweiman hurried and went
And went to see
And went to see
A soldier was crying inside.
The young woman, her eye was broken.

So they all went to Accra.
They were deposited at Korle Bu.
She lay down and began to weep,
And she said ah I have died.
Come, husband.
Husband, I have died,
Husband, darling, husband,
Husband, I have died.
Husband, darling, husband.

Dear, what sending is that?
I was going to Senchi and I would come.

T-5   This song, apparently in Akan, is not entirely understood.

Ana ei aja ei yoo yoo
Ana ei aja ei yoo yoo, yoo yoo
Námà see yo se obí wamba o wamba o o, kariya.

Ana ei aja ei ana ei
Ana ei aja ei ana ei
E mamá teoyo obiwɔmba oo, kaliya.

Mother, father,
Mother, father,
[?] somebody come, somebody come, liar.

Mother, father, mother
Mother, father, mother
[?] somebody come, liar.

T-6   ei Wɔ ya ásɛɛtsì ló.
Béni wɔ̀ tee wɔ kɛ Ajeíte kò ya kpe.
"Ataá Ajeíte niŋgbè o yaa yɛ bí!ɛ?"
Ajɔíte bà jié nàa.
"áò Blâ Ágo oo, ŋmé!nɛ, á wò mi shikpɔ́ŋ mɔɔ́ŋ éì"

We went to find it.
When we went we met a certain Ajeitey.
"Father Ajeitey where are you going here?"
Ajeitey replied.
"alas Brother Ago, today, I have been put in the prison of earth."

REFERENCES

ANSRE, G.
n.d.   "Madina, three polyglots, and some implications for Ghana." Unpublished manuscript.
BERRY, JACK
1969   The Madina project, Ghana (Language attitudes in Madina). *Research Review* 5, 61–79.
DAKUBU, M. E. KROPP
1972   Akaja, a Ga song type in Akan. *Research Review* 8.
FIELD, M. J.
1937   *Religion and medicine of the Ga people.* London: Oxford University Press.
HAMMOND, E. O.
1970   *Obɔade lalai.* Accra: Bureau of Ghana Languages.
NKETIA, J. H.
1958   Traditional music of the Ga people. *Universitas* 3:76–81.
WILKS, IVOR
1959   Akwamu and Otublohum: an eighteenth-century Akan marriage arrangement. *Africa* 29:390–402.

How Role-Relationships, Domains, and Speech Situations Affect Language Use Among Bilinguals

EMY M. PASCASIO and ARACELI HIDALGO

Within the last few years, a number of studies have been conducted on the relationship between language behavior and various psychological and social factors such as the setting, the roles of the participants, the topics of conversation, the functions of the interaction, and the views of inter-locutors concerning each of the foregoing. In bilingual settings these social and psychological factors are frequently expressed by codeswitch-ing (Ervin-Tripp 1964; Fishman 1968a; Fischer 1964; Hymes 1964; Labov 1968; Mackey 1966; Rubin 1968; Tanner 1967).

Hasselmo (1961) in his description of Swedish-American codeswitch-ing, attributed switching to the participants, the topic, and the location. Rubin (1968) found that factors such as intimacy and informality were useful in describing the use of Spanish and Guarani in Paraguay. Fischer (1964) has taken a specific setting, the family, to show the significance of patterns of address drawing upon several different domains (kinship, pronouns, personal names).

In the attempt to ascertain and describe accurately the language domi-nance configuration of the bilingual individual, Fishman (1964) has proposed a complex framework of description organized in terms of several sources of variance in language behavior. Sources of variance that Fishman has isolated are media variance (written, read, and spoken language), role variance (inner speech, comprehension, and production), situational variance (formal, semiformal, informal, and intimate) and domain variance.

The final preparation of this manuscript was done at the East-West Culture Learning Institute in Honolulu, Hawaii, where the principal investigator is currently doing sociolin-guistics research. We are grateful for the facilities that have been extended to us. This study is part of a bigger research project on Philippine bilingualism being conducted at the Ateneo Language Center, which is funded by the Faura Research Center Inc., Manila, Philippines.

Several studies on language usage and bilingual proficiency have been made using domains of social interaction as a context in which language behavior is analyzed and described (Edelman 1969; Cooper and Greenfield 1969b; Mangulabnan 1971). Several devices have also been designed to measure degree of bilingualism (Fishman 1968b; Mackey 1966; Macnamara 1967; Lambert 1967).

In a study made by Fishman and Greenfield (1970) the hypothesis that language used is associated with major clusters of complementary community values and varies with domains of social interaction in the community was tested. Specifically, it was hypothesized that Puerto Ricans in New York associate Spanish with values such as intimacy and solidarity and that Spanish is used in domains such as family and friendship while English is associated with status differentiation and is used in domains such as religion, education and employment.

Two experiments in which domain was conceived to be a complex of social situations which include three components: PERSON, PLACE, and TOPIC were designed to test this hypothesis. The results obtained showed that the use of Spanish and English for conversation differs according to domain. The use of Spanish was reported primarily for the domain of the family, secondarily for the domains of friendship and religion, and then least of all for the domains of education and employment. The reverse holds for English. In the first experiment, language preference varied according to person, place, and topic. In the second experiment, in which a different technique was used, difference in language preference was due mainly to difference in person and minimally to differences in topic and place.

The five domains used in the Fishman-Greenfield (1970) study, which were intuitively isolated, were family, friendship, religion, education, and employment. The problem is, in the description of the language behavior of the Filipino bilingual, what domains may be isolated as speech domains in that they have a significant effect on language behavior? This problem arises because in an exploratory investigation at the Ateneo Language Center (Bautista et al. 1971) on language fluency, results obtained suggested that the language in which 100 highschool students are fluent does not vary significantly for the domains of school and recreation/neighborhood.

The Filipino bilingual lives in a social world of different domains and the extent of his interaction or participation in these domains differ to some degree. It is not surprising, therefore, that his degree of bilingualism or the character of his language use differs over these ranges of social settings.

It is the objective of the present study to determine whether the intuitively isolated domains of home, school, and social gatherings have a significant effect on reported language used. In other words, is there a significant difference in language used for the domains of the home, school, and social gatherings? Other problems that this study attempts to examine are: (1) Does role-relationship have a significant effect on language used for each domain? (2) Do diverse speech situations have a differential effect on language used?

Interlocutors having role-relationships that are assumed to exist in the domain of the home are parents, older relatives, household helpers, and friends including brothers or sisters. Interlocutors having role-relationships that are assumed to exist in the domain of the school are professors, administrators, rank and file personnel, and schoolmates. Interlocutors with role-relationships that are assumed to exist in the domain of social gatherings such as parties, greetings, rallies, etc., are older people (authorities, host or hostess, etc.), particular girlfriend or boyfriend, friends (acquaintances), and strangers. These varying interlocutors may be generally classified as those belonging to the peer group of Ego, i.e. Ego and the peer group have an equal social level, those above the peer group; and those below.

Role-relationships are implicitly recognized and accepted sets of mutual rights and obligations between members of the same sociocultural system. One of the ways in which members reveal such common membership to each other, as well as their recognition of the rights and obligations that they owe to each other, is through appropriate variation of the way(s) they talk to each other (Fishman 1971).

Speech situations assumed to exist in the different domains are casually conversing, asking a favor, asking and giving information, giving a command, complimenting, persuading, and arguing.

Specifically, the problems this study aims to investigate are as follows:
1. Does domain have an effect on language used?
   a. Does domain have an effect on language used with interlocutors above the peer group level?
   b. Does domain have an effect on language used with interlocutors of the peer group level?
   c. Does domain have an effect on language used with interlocutors below the peer group level?
   d. Does domain have an effect on language used in a particular speech situation?
2. Does language used vary significantly from role-relationship to role-relationship within the same domain? In other words, do interlocutors have an effect on language used?
3. Do speech situations have an effect on language used?

METHODOLOGY

Technique

A device was constructed to gather self-reported data on the use of language. In order to study the effect of each of the three domains of social interaction on language usage, each of the seven speech situations was combined with the three domains of each of the categories of inter-locutors (above peer group level, at peer group level and below peer group level).

Thus the speech situations, casually conversing, asking a favor, asking and giving information, giving a command, complimenting, persuading, and arguing appeared in combination with the home domain, the school domain, and the domain of social gatherings respectively. Above peer group level interlocutors combined with each domain (parents and older relatives for the home, professors and administrators for the school, and older people and particular girlfriend or boyfriend for social gatherings) as did peer group level (friends, brothers, sisters for the home, school-mates for the school, and friends for social gatherings) and below peer group level (household helpers for the home, rank-and-file personnel such as secretaries, cafeteria personnel, etc., for the school, and strangers such as gate crashers at social gatherings).

In order to study the effect of role-relationships on language usage, each of the seven speech situations was combined with each interlocutor in each domain.

The instrument required the subjects to respond to the question of what language they used when interacting in a stated domain, a specified interlocutor, and a specified speech situation by checking along a five-point scale where 5 = always English, 4 = more English than Filipino, 3 = equal English and Filipino, 2 = more Filipino than English and 1 = always Filipino.

The data-gathering instrument was entirely in English and adminis-tered without time limit.

Subjects

The subjects included in this study were 150 freshmen college students, fifty of whom came from the Ateneo de Manila University, fifty from Saint Theresa's College, and fifty from Santo Tomas University. Fifty percent were female and 50 percent were male.

The samples were so selected because it is the purpose of this study to determine the language-dominance configuration of students entering college, particularly those entering private colleges of known high academic standards and coming from upper middleclass and middleclass Philippine homes. It is planned that the results of the study will be compared to the results of a similar study to be carried out later in which the subjects are freshmen college students of private colleges and where a good number of the students come from lowerclass homes.

Scoring

Responses were converted into their equivalent points and then added for each of the three domains. These total scores were used to determine the effect of domain as a whole on language used.

Responses for the seven speech situations were totalled for each inter-locutor in each of the three domains and were used to determine the effect of domain on language used with each interlocutor. These responses were also used to determine the relationships within a single domain on language used.

For the problem of whether domain has an effect on language used in a particular speech situation, responses for this speech situations "casually conversing" and "asking and giving information" were totalled for each domain. Only these two were selected of the seven speech situations as these two are more likely to exist in each domain and with each inter-locutor than are the rest of the speech situations.

The responses used to determine if speech situations have an effect on language used were those for the seven speech situations with friends, sisters, brothers for the home domain, and with other people (authorities, host or hostess, etc.) for the domain of social gatherings.

Results

Table 1 shows the mean scores and standard deviation on self-reported usage of English and Filipino in the domains of the home, the school, and social gatherings. In the first row are the mean scores and standard deviations for each domain as a whole. The means were derived from all of the four interlocutors in every domain. For instance, the mean score for the home domain was derived from the subjects' scores on language used in the seven speech situations with parents, older relatives, siblings and friends, and household helpers.

In the second row, the mean scores and standard deviations for each domain were derived from interlocutors that are above the peer group level. Only the scores from parents, professors, and older people in social gatherings were considered. Scores from other interlocutors who are also above the peer group level such as older relatives, school administrators, and special girlfriend or boyfriend were not considered because this would make the above the peer group level of two sources while the other levels would have one source each.

In the third row are mean scores and standard deviations for each domain when interlocutors are those of peer level such as siblings, schoolmates and friends, while in the fourth row are mean scores and standard deviations for each domain when interlocutors are those below the peer group level such as household helpers, rank-and-file personnel, and strangers.

Table 1.   Mean scores and standard deviations obtained for language used in the domains of home, school and social gatherings

		Home	School	Social gatherings
1. Domains as a whole (n=85)	M	64.7764	106.7764	98.3764
	s.d.	20.7411	16.4212	23.6672
2. Above peer group level (n=93)	M	17.7090	30.1827	27.2473
	s.d.	7.3302	5.2135	6.8023
3. Peer group level (n=93)	M	22.5379	21.8279	20.8064
	s.d.	5.8338	5.9759	6.4728
4. Below peer group level (n=91)	M	9.1978	23.3736	22.7252
	s.d.	4.7049	7.4371	8.6024
5. Casually conversing with all interlocutors (n=100)	M	7.7300	14.6800	12.4800
	s.d.	3.4463	2.4078	3.9356
6. Asking or giving information with all interlocutors (n=100)	M	9.7900	15.9600	13.3000
	s.d.	3.9275	2.4204	4.2201

In the fifth and sixth rows are mean scores and standard deviations used for the problem of whether domain has an effect on language used in a particular speech situation. The mean scores in the fifth row were derived from the speech situation "casually conversing" with all interlocutors in each domain. For instance, the mean score for the school domain was derived from "casually conversing" with professors, school administrators, schoolmates, and rank-and-file personnel. In the same way, the mean scores in the sixth row were derived from the speech situation of "asking or giving information" with all interlocutors in each domain.

Table 2 shows the mean scores and standard deviations obtained for language used with varying role-relationships. Mean scores and standard deviations in the first row are derived from the four interlocutors in the home each assumed to have a different role-relationship with the speaker. In the second row are mean scores and standard deviations from varying interlocutors in the school and in the third row, from the different interlocutors in social gatherings.

Table 3 shows the mean scores and standard deviations obtained for language used in the different speech situations. For determining whether a particular speech situation signals a different language behavior, mean scores for different speech situations with a single interlocutor in a single domain were compared. It was deemed adequate for our purposes to consider only some of the interlocutors. Varying group levels were selected: for the home, the siblings; for the school rank-and-file personnel; and for the domain of social gatherings, older people such as hosts or hostesses.

Table 2. Mean scores and standard deviations obtained for language used with different role-relationships

| | | Role-Relationships* | | | |
		1	2	3	4
1. Home ($n=97$)	M	16.9743	15.0412	22.2268	8.7731
	s.d.	7.9948	8.4924	6.6511	4.9168
2. School ($n=100$)	M	30.0600	30.8400	21.1800	22.8900
	s.d.	5.3100	6.4011	6.7191	7.8471
3. Social gatherings ($n=98$)	M	27.0816	21.2346	20.0102	22.0918
	s.d.	6.8103	8.7712	7.3241	9.2240

* Figures heading the four columns indicate: (1) parents, professors, older people; (2) older relatives, school administrators, particular of special boyfriend or girlfriend; (3) siblings, schoolmates, friends; and (4) household helpers, rank-and-file, strangers.

Table 3. Mean scores and standard deviations obtained for language used in different speech situations

| | Situation/interlocutor | | | | | |
| | Home/siblings | | School rank-and-file | | Social gatherings/ older people | |
	M	s.d.	M	s.d.	M	s.d.
1. Casually conversing	3.1052	0.8394	3.3030	1.1051	3.9081	1.0621
2. Asking a favor	3.3263	1.0800	3.3535	1.2816	4.000	1.1693
3. Asking or giving information	3.5473	1.0835	3.5151	1.1578	3.9693	1.1198
4. Giving a command	3.1368	1.2192	3.3030	1.3442	3.6122	1.5025
5. Complimenting	3.5473	1.1027	3.3535	1.3050	4.1020	1.0250
6. Persuading	2.9578	1.2132	3.2424	1.1983	3.7346	1.1740
7. Arguing	3.0736	1.2915	3.3030	1.1586	3.7857	1.2142

These results were then subjected to t-tests. Analysis of variance was first considered before t-tests were to be applied but for our purposes, the available computer could not handle the problem. We then resorted to comparing only two means at a time.

Data Analysis

Table 4 presents the results of t-tests on the differences between means obtained for language used in the domains of the home, the school, and social gatherings. The results indicate that the reported language used in the three domains as a whole differ significantly at the 0.01 level for a two-tailed test (Nos. 1–3). The subjects speak more Filipino than English at home, speak more English than Filipino in the school, and speak English and Filipino equally in social gatherings.

Table 4.   T-values of the differences between means obtained for language used in the domains of home, school, and social gatherings

Means compared	t
1. Home and school	14.5509*
2. Home and social gatherings	8.0384*
3. School and social gatherings	4.5817*
4. Parents and professors	13.3018*
5. Parents and older people in social gatherings	9.5377*
6. Professors and older people in social gatherings	3.2856*
7. Siblings and schoolmates	0.8151
8. Siblings and friends in social gatherings	1.9057
9. Schoolmates and friends in social gatherings	1.1122
10. Household helpers and rank-and-file personnel	15.2838*
11. Household helpers and strangers	13.0901*
12. Rank-and-file personnel and strangers	0.5459
13. Conversing casually in the home and conversing casually in school	16.4574*
14. Conversing casually in the home and conversing casually in social gatherings	9.0372*
15. Conversing casually in the school and conversing casually in social gatherings	4.7464*
16. Asking or giving information at home and asking or giving information in school	13.3810*
17. Asking or giving information at home and asking or giving information in social gatherings	6.0905*
18. Asking or giving information in school and asking or giving information in social gatherings	5.4690*

* $P < 0.01$.

The language used with interlocutors with role-relationships above the peer group level is also significantly related to domain difference. The t-values indicate that the differences between the means of reported language used with these interlocutors are significant at the 0.01 level (Nos. 4–6). With parents more Filipino is used than English, with professors English is almost always used, and with older people in social gatherings more English is used than Filipino.

With interlocutors whose role-relationships are of the peer group level, there is no significant difference in language used at the 0.01 level or at the 0.05 level (Nos. 7–9). In other words, when speaking to brothers or sisters, friends, or schoolmates, domain has no effect on language used. The subjects use Filipino and English equally.

For interlocutors with role-relationships below the peer group level, it is only the language used with household helpers that differs significantly at the 0.01 level from the language used with the others (Nos. 10–12). With household helpers, Filipino is used almost always, while English and Filipino are equally used with rank-and-file personnel and strangers at social gatherings.

Domain has a significant effect on language used in certain speech situations. Differences in language used are all significant at the 0.01 level (Nos. 13–16), although the variance between the language used at home and the other domain is wider than the variance between school and social gatherings. In casual conversation, more Filipino is used than English in the home, more English is used than Filipino in the school, whereas English and Filipino are equally used in social gatherings. The same holds true in asking or giving information.

Table 5 presents the results of t-tests on the differences between the means obtained for language used with interlocutors associated only with the home domain. There is no significant difference between the languages used with parents and older relatives. This is not surprising since both are above the peer group level. In all other instances, however, the role-relationship at home, i.e. above peer group level, peer group level, and below peer group level role-relationship, signals a different language behavior. The mean differences are all significant at the 0.01 level with siblings and household helpers having the widest difference. With parents and older relatives, more Filipino is used than English, although the subjects tend to speak more Filipino with older relatives. With siblings and friends, Filipino and English are equally used, and with household helpers Filipino is almost always used.

Table 5.   T-values of the differences between means obtained for language used with different role-relationships in the home

Means compared	t
1. Parents and older relatives	1.6366
2. Parents and siblings	4.9701*
3. Parents and household helpers	8.6618*
4. Older relatives and siblings	6.5609*
5. Older relatives and household helpers	6.2913*
6. Siblings and household helpers	16.0220*

* $P < 0.01$.

Table 6 presents the results of t-tests on the differences between the means obtained for language used with interlocutors associated with the school domain. The t-values indicate that there is no significant difference between the language used with professors and school administrators. There is no significant difference in the language used with schoolmates and rank-and-file personnel. There are only two distinctions then made in the domain of the school. One group consists of professors and school administrators, and the other group consists of schoolmates and rank-and-file personnel. The language used with each group varies significantly at the 0.01 level. With the first group, English is almost always used although the subjects tend to use more English with school administrators, and with the second group, English and Filipino are equally used.

Table 6. T-values of the differences between means obtained for language used with different role-relationships associated with the school

Means compared	t
1. Professors and school administrators	0.9379
2. Professors and schoolmates	10.3701*
3. Professors and rank-and-file personnel	7.5680*
4. School administrators and schoolmates	10.4106*
5. School administrators and rank-and-file personnel	7.8510*
6. Schoolmates and rank-and-file personnel	1.6553

* P<0.01.

Table 7 presents the results of t-tests on the differences between the means obtained for language used with interlocutors associated with the domain of social gatherings. Only older people (hosts or hostesses, etc.) signal a significant difference in language used. The language used with older people varies significantly at the 0.01 level from the language used with all other interlocutors. With older people, more English is used than Filipino, while English and Filipino are equally used with all other interlocutors in this domain.

Table 7   T-values of the differences between means obtained for language used with different role-relationships associated with social gatherings

Means compared	t
1. Older people and special boyfriend or girlfriend	5.2130*
2. Older people and friends	7.3059*
3. Older people and strangers	4.3086*
4. Special boyfriend or girlfriend and friends	1.0608
5. Special boyfriend or girlfriend and strangers	0.6667
6. Friends and strangers	1.7496

* P <0.01.

Tables 8, 9 and 10 present the t-values of the differences between the means obtained for language used in different speech situations in the home, the school, and social gatherings. In the domain of the school with rank-and-file personnel as interlocutors, the results indicate that a change in speech situation does not signal a significant corresponding change in language behavior. English and Filipino are reported to be equally used in all situations. In the domain of social gatherings, with older people as interlocutors, only the speech situation of giving a command signals a significant change in language spoken and this is at the 0.05 level. In giving a command, subjects tend to use Filipino and English equally and in all other speech situations they use more English than Filipino. In the domain of the home, with siblings as interlocutors the language used in the speech situations of asking or giving information and complimenting differ significantly at the 0.01 level from that used in casually conversing, arguing, or persuading. In the former, more English is used than Filipino, while in the latter English and Filipino are equally used although the tendency is towards Filipino as compared to asking a favor and giving a command where English and Filipino are also equally used but with a tendency towards English. Other speech situations that differ significantly except at the 0.05 level are asking a favor and persuading (where the tendency in the former is towards English and in the latter, towards Filipino), asking or giving information and giving a command (where the tendency in the former is towards English and in the latter towards Filipino), and complimenting and giving a command (where the tendency in the former is towards English and in the latter towards Filipino).

Table 8. T-values of the differences between means obtained for language used in different speech situations in the home domain

Means compared	t
1. Casually conversing and asking a favor	1.5680
2. Casually conversing and asking or giving information	3.1511*
3. Casually conversing and giving a command	0.2084*
4. Casually conversing and complimenting	3.1199*
5. Casually conversing and persuading	0.9768
6. Casually conversing and arguing	0.2003
7. Asking a favor and asking or giving information	1.4040
8. Asking a favor and giving a command	1.1306
9. Asking a favor and complimenting	1.3925
10. Asking a favor and persuading	2.2065**
11. Asking a favor and arguing	1.4590
12. Asking or giving information and giving a command	2.4580**
13. Asking or giving information and complimenting	0.000
14. Asking or giving information and persuading	3.5426*
15. Asking or giving information and arguing	2.7444*
16. Giving a command and complimenting	2.4405**
17. Giving a command and persuading	1.0170
18. Giving a command and arguing	0.3474
19. Complimenting and persuading	3.5173*
20. Complimenting and arguing	2.7271*
21. Persuading and arguing	0.6387

* P <0.01.
** P <0.05.

Table 9. T-values of the differences between means obtained for language used in different speech situations in the school domain

Means compared	t
1. Casually conversing and asking a favor	0.2975
2. Casually conversing and asking or giving information	1.3206
3. Casually conversing and giving a command	0.0000
4. Casually conversing and complimenting	0.2941
5. Casually conversing and persuading	0.3701
6. Casually conversing and arguing	0.0000
7. Asking a favor and asking or giving information	0.6241
8. Asking a favor and giving a command	0.9330
9. Asking a favor and complimenting	0.2712
10. Asking a favor and persuading	0.0000
11. Asking a favor and arguing	0.6312
12. Asking or giving information and giving a command	0.2915
13. Asking or giving information and complimenting	1.1915
14. Asking or giving information and persuading	0.2882
15. Asking or giving information and arguing	0.9223
16. Giving a command and complimenting	1.6300
17. Giving a command and persuading	1.2909
18. Giving a command and arguing	0.2684
19. Complimenting and persuading	0.3351
20. Complimenting and arguing	0.0000
21. Persuading and arguing	0.3622

Table 10. T-values of the differences between means obtained for language used in different speech situations in social gatherings

Means compared	t
1. Casually conversing and asking a favor	0.5708
2. Casually conversing and asking or giving	0.1492
3. Casually conversing and giving a command	1.5934
4. Casually conversing and complimenting	1.3022
5. Casually conversing and persuading	1.0870
6. Casually conversing and arguing	0.7523
7. Asking a favor and asking or giving information	0.1883
8. Asking a favor and giving a command	2.0197*
9. Asking a favor and complimenting	0.6505
10. Asking a favor and persuading	1.5892
11. Asking a favor and arguing	1.2605
12. Asking or giving information and giving a command	1.8904
13. Asking or giving information and complimenting	0.8678
14. Asking or giving information and persuading	1.4363
15. Asking or giving information and arguing	1.1033
16. Giving a command and complimenting	2.6692
17. Giving a command and persuading	0.6365
18. Giving a command and arguing	2.3386*
19. Complimenting and persuading	1.9731
20. Complimenting and arguing	0.8902
21. Persuading and arguing	0.3002

* $P < 0.05$

SUMMARY

This experiment was designed to determine factors affecting the amount of English and Filipino used by first-year college students at the Ateneo de Manila University, Saint Theresa's College, and the University of Santo Tomas, i.e. students coming from the upper middleclass and middleclass sections of the Philippines, and studying at colleges in the greater Manila area both better known and considered to be academically better. The results obtained suggest that the amount of English and Filipino used varies significantly with domain as a whole. The use of more Filipino than English is reported for the domain of the home, more English than Filipino for the domain of the school, and equal use of Filipino and English for the domain of social gatherings. This variance in language used is particularly apparent in speech situations such as casually conversing and asking or giving information that naturally exist in all domains.

Domain, however, does not always have an effect on language used. When interlocutors are of a role-relationship above the peer group level, language used varies. In the domain of the home more Filipino is used than English, in the domain of the school, English is used almost always and in the domain of social gatherings, a tendency towards Filipino exists although, still, more English is used than Filipino. When interlocutors are of the peer group level, domain has no significant effect on language used. Filipino and English are equally used. When interlocutors are of a role-relationship below the peer group level, Filipino is used almost always in the home domain and in the other domains English and Filipino are equally used. These differences in language usage are therefore as much a result of interlocutors as of domain.

The effects of role-relationships were further systematically studied by holding constant the domain and the speech situations and varying the interlocutors. For the domain of the home, the three group levels of above peer, peer, and below peer signal a corresponding change in language used. For the domain of the school only two distinctions are made. One group consists of professors and school administrators, with whom almost always English is spoken, and the other group consists of schoolmates and rank-and-file personnel, with whom English and Filipino are equally used. In the domain of social gatherings, two distinctions are also made. One group consists of older people with whom more English is used than Filipino while the other group consists of all others with whom English and Filipino are equally used.

Speech situations do not seem to have much effect on language used. In the domain of the school, speech situations do not have any significant effect at all. In the domain of social gatherings, it is only the speech situation of giving a command that significantly signals a change in language used. It is possible that this is a result of interlocutor than giving a command per se. It is unusual to give a command to an older person such as a host or hostess in a social gathering, hence the subjects might have felt a need to change the language they were reported to be using from English to Filipino which is more normally used in other speech situations. In the domain of the home, the language used in the speech situations of asking or giving information and complimenting differ significantly from that used in other speech situations in that a tendency towards English is exhibited. Perhaps this is due not to the speech situations per se but to the interlocutors with whom the speech situations are associated. It is more likely that subjects ask or give information and compliment interlocutors of peer group level, thus the tendency towards English. The speech situation of persuading, which differs significantly from these two speech situations, is perhaps more associated with parents, hence the tendency towards Filipino.

REFERENCES

ALATIS, J. E., *editor*
1970   Bilingualism and language contact: anthropological, linguistic and sociological aspects. Georgetown University Monograph on Language and Linguistics 23:1–24.
ARDENER, E., *editor*
1971   Social anthropology and language. London: Tavistock.
BAUTISTA, L., G. CHAN-YAP, A. HIDALGO, A. PATERNO, I. RIEGO DE DIOS
1971   "The language orientation of the Filipino bilingual in terms of fluency, dominance, and usage." Unpublished manuscript. Ateneo de Manila University.
BERNSTEIN, B.
1965   "A sociolinguistic approach to social learning," in *Penguin Survey of the social sciences*. Edited by J. Gould, 144–168. Harmondsworth: Penguin.
BOTHA, E.
1970   The effect of language on values expressed by bilinguals. *Journal of Social Psychology* 80 (2), 1943–145.
BRIGHT, W., *editor*
1966   Sociolinguistics. The Hague: Mouton.
BURLING, R.
1970   Man's many voices: language in its cultural context. New York: Holt, Rinehart and Winston.
CAPELL, A.
1966   Studies in sociolinguistics. The Hague: Mouton.
COOPER, R., L. GREENFIELD
1969a   Word frequency estimation as a measure of degree of bilingualism. *Modern Language Journal* 53:163–166.
1969b   Language use in a bilingual community. *Modern Language Journal* 53: 164–172.

DIL, A., *editor*
1971   *Language structure and language use: essays by Charles A. Ferguson.*
Stanford: Stanford University Press.
1972   *Language, psychology and culture: essays by Wallace Lambert.* Stanford: Stanford University Press.
EDELMAN, M.
1969   Contextualization of school children's bilingualism. *Modern Language Journal* 53:172–182.
ERVIN-TRIPP, S.
1964   An analysis of the interaction of language, topic, and listener. *American Anthropologist* 66 (6):Part 2, 86–102.
1969   "Sociolinguistics," in *Advances in the sociology of language*, volume one. Edited by J. A. Fishman. The Hague: Mouton.
FISCHER, J. L.
1964   "Linguistic and social interaction in two communities," in *The ethnography of communication.* Edited by J. J. Gumperz and D. Hymes, 175–176. Menasha, Wisconsin: American Anthropological Association.
FISHMAN, J. A.
1964   Language maintenance and language shift as a field of inquiry. *Linguistics* 9:32–70.
1966   *Language loyalty in the United States.* The Hague: Mouton.
FISHMAN, J. A., *editor*
1968a   *Bilingualism in the barrio.* Final Report, Contract No. OEC 1-7-062817-0297. Washington, D.C.: Office of Education.
1968b   *Readings in the sociology of language.* The Hague: Mouton.
1971   *Advances in the sociology of language.* The Hague: Mouton.
FISHMAN, J. A., L. GREENFIELD
1970   Situational measures of normative language views in relation to person, place and topic among Puerto Rican bilinguals. *Anthropos* 65: 602–618.
GOODENOUGH, W. H.
1965   "Rethinking 'status' and 'role': towards a general model of the cultural organization of social relationships," in *The relevance of models for social anthropology.* Edited by M. Banton, 1–24. London: Tavistock.
GUMPERZ, J. J.
1964   Linguistic and social interaction in two communities. *American Anthropologist* 66 (6): Part 2, 37–53.
1971   *Language in social groups.* Stanford: Stanford University Press.
GUMPERZ, J. J., D. HYMES, *editors*
1972   *Directions in sociolinguistics.* New York: Holt, Rinehart and Winston.
HOWELL, R. W.
1965   Linguistic status markers in Korea. *The Kroeber Anthropological Society Papers* 55:91–97.
HYMES, D.
1964   "Introduction: Towards ethnographies of communication," in *The ethnography of communication.* Edited by J. J. Gumperz and D. Hymes, 1–34. Special publication of American Anthropologist 66, Part 2.
1967   Models of the interaction of language and social setting. *Journal of Social Issues* 23:8–28.
1971   *On communicative competence.* Philadelphia: University of Pennsylvania Press.

HASSELMO, N.
1961 *American-Swedish: A study in bilingualism.* Unpublished doctoral dissertation. Department of Linguistics, Harvard University.
LABOV, W.
1966 The effect of social mobility on linguistic behavior. *Sociological Inquiry* 36:186–203.
1968 "The reflection of social processes in linguistic structures," in *Readings in the Sociology of Language.* Edited by J. A. Fishman, 240–251. The Hague: Mouton.
LAMBERT, W. E.
1967 A social psychology of bilingualism. *Journal of Social Issues* 23: 91–109.
LIEBERSON, S., editor
1966 Explorations in sociolinguistics. *Sociological Inquiry* 36 (2).
MACKEY, W.
1966 The measurement of bilingual behavior. *The Canadian Psychologist.* 75–92.
1968 *Bilingualism as a world problem.* Montreal: Harvest House.
MacNAMARA, J.
1967 The bilingual's linguistic performance — A psychological overview. *Journal of Social Issues* 23:58–77.
MANGULABNAN, L. A.
1971 *Bilingual usage and need — Affiliation imagery among Filipino college students.* Unpublished manuscript. Ateneo de Manila University.
PASCASIO, E. M.
1972 The language behavior profile of selected Filipino bilinguals. Preprint: *Proceedings of the XIth International Congress of Linguists.* Bologna, Italy. August 28–September 2, 1972.
PRIDE, J.
1971 *The social meaning of language.* London: Oxford University Press.
ROSALES, C., P. SANTOS, E. SORIANO, C. ZARAGOZA
1971 "Language usage patterns correlated with language preference of college Filipino bilinguals." Unpublished manuscript. Ateneo de Manila University.
RUBIN, J.
1968 "Bilingual usage in Paraguay," *Readings in the sociology of language.* Edited by J. A. Fishman, 512–530. The Hague: Mouton.
RUBIN, J., B. H. JERNUUD, editors
1971 *Can language be planned?* An East-West Center Book. Honolulu: The University Press of Hawaii.
TANNER, N.
1967 Speech society among the Indonesian elite: A case study of a multilingual society. *Anthropological Linguistics* 9 (3): 15–40.
TUCKER, G. R.
1968 *Profile of a Filipino bilingual.* Paper presented at the National Conference on Language Teaching, Manila.
WHITELEY, W. F. editor
1971 *Language use and social change.* London: Oxford University Press.
WOLFRAM, W. A.
1969 *Linguistic correlates of social stratification in the speech of Detroit Negroes.* Washington, D.C.: Center for Applied Linguistics.

Correlational Sociolinguistics and the Ethnography of Communication

JACQUELINE LINDENFELD

The study of linguistic variation is still a wide-open field, which makes it both an exciting and a difficult area of investigation. For those of us who are interested in examining linguistic variation in its social context, there are particularly acute problems regarding the choice of a framework, the discovery of significant nonlinguistic variables, and the selection of appropriate methods of analysis. In the present paper I will suggest that the best solution to these problems might lie in the combined use of two prominent models which have sometimes been depicted as irreconcilable, namely, the ethnography of communication and correlational sociolinguistics.

The basic difference between these two approaches has been summed up as follows: "[Correlational sociolinguistics] attempts to explain co-variation in language structure and social structure from a correlational point of view [whereas the ethnography of communication] looks at the two structures as being in themselves so inextricably interrelated as to require not separate but integrated study as a unitary phenomenon" (Grimshaw 1971:97). While such a statement gives a true picture of their differing outlooks, it hides some important points of contact between the two models. We will see that each of them could profit from the insights of the other and that at a certain stage in the analysis they must come together if we are to achieve a precise description of linguistic variation in its social context. Let us first examine some of the characteristics, merits and shortcomings of each approach.

In correlational sociolinguistics, to begin with the more language-centered and less inclusive model, one expects to find a regular and statistically significant pattern of co-variation between certain linguistic variables and some independently chosen social variables. The analysis is based on a large quantity of data usually collected in a complex urban setting. An excellent example is Labov's well-known study of English in New York City in which five phonological variables are shown to co-vary with the speakers' socioeconomic class, age, ethnic identity, etc. (Labov 1966). Another example is Bernstein's analysis of syntactic structure (elaborated and restricted codes) in relation to social class in Great Britain (see, for example, Bernstein 1964). The main criticism which can be addressed to this type of sociolinguistic research is that its scope is rather limited. Each study amounts to the demonstration of relationships between a small number of specific linguistic variables and social variables. Also, anthropologically-oriented researchers should be concerned about its tendency to rely primarily on pre-established social categories. Labov's hints as to the likely importance of more fluid social phenomena, such as "in-groupness," need to be followed by empirical verification in various types of communities. On the whole, despite its remarkably precise methods of data collection and analysis, the work of correlational sociolinguists must be seen as suffering from its restrictive framework and leaving unanswered "a number of basic questions concerning the nature of the relationship of linguistic to social facts" (Gumperz 1972:13). One particular shortcoming in this respect lies in the fact that, as pointed out by Gumperz, "there seems to be almost no correlation between the linguistic distinctness of relevant variables and the social information they carry," which he proposes to remedy by "a more basic enquiry into the nature of communicative processes, an enquiry which extends the notion of linguistic competence to enquire into the nature of communicative competence and the sociolinguistic rules which enable us to use and produce appropriate speech" (1972:14).

The ethnography of the communication model thus heralded by Gumperz is definitely much more inclusive and open-ended than correlational sociolinguistics (for various presentations of the model by its main instigator, see Hymes 1962, 1964, 1972). It aims at the description of communicative patterns in particular speech communities and ultimately at a comparative picture of "communicative economies" in numerous societies. As indicated by its name, it starts from a resolutely ethnographic point of view: the first step consists in observing a speech community in natural communicative situations in order to isolate culturally significant speech events. These emic units are then analyzed in terms of their components (such as participants, code, etc.) and functions, following which the interaction of those elements is to be carefully examined. Obviously, there are many advantages to the use of such a model for the study of linguistic variation. First of all, its broad framework allows the inclusion of any kind of communicative behavior, thus putting language in perspective. Second, the fact that it focuses on interactional behavior, as observed in spontaneous "happenings," makes it particularly valuable to researchers who are interested in examining linguistic variation in its natural environment. Finally, its strongly emic slant opens new avenues for the discovery of nonlinguistic factors of linguistic variation which may have gone totally unnoticed so far.

On the other hand, there are very serious criticisms to be leveled against such an ambitious model. It seems practically impossible, at least for the time being, to undertake as extensive a study of a speech community as suggested by Hymes and still hope to go beyond a superficial level of observation and description. The investigation of the multiple relationships existing between various speech components appears as a particularly formidable task. It is therefore no wonder that so few researchers have attempted to use Hymes' theoretical framework in an empirical fashion. The existing ethnographies of communication exhibit a great lack of details in all but a few areas. As a student of linguistic variation I am particularly struck by the almost total lack of attention paid to the linguistic code (see, for example, Hymes 1966; Hogan 1967; Crumrine 1968; Sherzer 1970). Granted that the emphasis in Hymes' model is deliberately on the FUNCTIONS of language rather than on its structure, it remains that the linguistic code is probably the most important speech component to be examined in relation to others, since differential uses of speech will almost always result in linguistic variation. Another fault of the ethnography of communication in its present state is the fact that its advocates have never been explicit as to the exact methods to be used for an account of all possible relations between the sub-units of a given speech event. If we are to take Sherzer's analysis of Abipon ways of speaking as an example (and it should be noted that Hymes chose this particular piece of research to illustrate a recent theoretical discussion of his model; see Hymes 1972), it appears that the analytical methods needed for this task still need much refinement indeed. Sherzer's study contains a "lexicon" of the speech components present in each of the communicative events examined ("shaman's retribution," "girls' puberty rite," etc.) as well as a sketchy syntagmatic analysis in which he shows some co-occurrence and sequencing patterns found to occur among those speech components. However, the description falls short of telling us what exact relationships exist between them in terms of interaction. Obviously, this is partly a result of the lack of details regarding some of the components. Thus the linguistic code is laconically defined as "the Abipon language." But even in the case of those components which are given somewhat more attention, we are left in the dark as to ways of indicating their influence upon one another.

Should we conclude that the ethnography of communication is not an appropriate model for students of linguistic variation? Certainly not. It has too many positive features, especially its open-endedness and flexibility, for the sociolinguist who is interested in pushing the frontiers of the field as far as possible. It can also help the anthropologically-oriented researcher correct some of the built-in biases of correlational sociolinguistics mentioned earlier. We can best account for linguistic variation if we observe it *in situ*, as part of larger communicative events, and from an emic point of view. We should take very serious notice of the influence of "interactionist" sociologists such as Goffman on the ethnography of communication model, which Gumperz sums up as follows:

Noting that most individuals in everyday situations have considerable freedom in choosing which of several role-relationships to enact, interactionists deny the parallel between social and physical measurement. They point out that information on social categories is obtainable only through language and that sociological measurement therefore always involves both the informant's and the investigator's perception of the categories that are being measured . . . Just as the meaning of words is always affected by context, social categories must be interpreted in terms of situational constraints (Gumperz 1972:15).

This more intuitive way of looking into the social meaning of language definitely makes Hymes' model very attractive, and I would be willing to predict that its framework as well as some of its concepts will play an increasingly important role in the study of linguistic variation in the years to come. However, the adoption of a format based on the ethnography-of-communication model should not preclude the use of certain correlational sociolinguistics methods which have proved their worth in the last few years. We saw earlier that the most neglected area in Hymes' model is the examination of precise interaction patterns between various speech components in a given speech event. It seems obvious that, despite the difference in wording, correlational sociolinguistics has much to offer in this particular area, since it specializes in the description of co-variation patterns between various linguistic and nonlinguistic phenomena. We should, therefore, not be reluctant to use its methods of analysis within the framework of the ethnography of communication, provided that we only use linguistic and nonlinguistic variables discovered at the emic level. Such a combination of the two approaches would allow us to avail ourselves of the insights of each of them while avoiding their respective limitations or shortcomings.

   It may be interesting to consider briefly the opinions of several leading researchers in the field regarding the possibility of combining correlational sociolinguistics and the ethnography of communication. Hymes describes his own model as a particular approach to the study of language in its social context which takes a very broad view of language:

Speech, INCLUDING LINGUISTIC STRUCTURE AS A MAJOR, but not a sole RESOURCE, mediates between persons and their situations. Ordinary linguistic structure, a constituent of the organization of speaking, cannot suffice as a starting point from which to discover that organization. One must begin from speaking as a mode of action, not from language as an unmotivated mechanism (Hymes 1971:67; emphasis added).

This statement could very well be interpreted to imply that one should adopt the framework of the ethnography of communication, without necessarily rejecting the precise methods developed by correlational sociolinguists, to examine linguistic structure in detail in relation to nonlinguistic phenomena. Labov, on the other hand, seems to consider the two approaches as complementary only at a very general level, which would preclude using them both in one and the same study: he draws a hard line between them because he views the ethnography of communication as a purely FUNCTIONAL type of study concerned "with the details of language in actual use" and therefore "complementary with the study of linguistic structure" (Labov 1971:153). As for Fishman, he takes a position which can definitely be taken as a sign of encouragement for the building of a model which would combine Hymes' and Labov's approaches:

Rather than emphasize the ethnography of communication as an end in and of itself the sociology of language would hope to utilize the ethnography of communication, as it would utilize sociolinguistics and social science more generally, in order to more fully explain variation in societally patterned behaviors pertaining to language maintenance and language shift, language nationalism and language planning, etc. (Fishman 1971:9).

The question remains, however, as to the PRACTICAL possibility of combining the ethnography of communication and correlational sociolinguistics. Fortunately, one can point to such a study as Ervin-Tripp's examination of the interaction of three components, namely, the linguistic code, the topic and the listener, in the speech of some Japanese bilinguals whom she observed firsthand. We find in it a very interesting combination of concepts and methods borrowed from both approaches. The general framework is clearly that of the ethnography of communication: "The first step in the experimental study of Japanese-American speech in terms of the topic-audience-language correlations was an ethnographic description of their covariance, based on informant interviews" (Ervin-Tripp 1964:94). Following a description of those three speech components and an informal account of their interaction as determined through the participants' own reports, the author switches to a tighter analysis of data obtained through word associations, sentence completions, semantic differentials, problem stories and Thematic Apperception Tests. The covariation patterns of each two of the three components considered are then examined in a manner which is very strongly reminiscent of correlational sociolinguistics. In the first correlational task, the linguistic code (here defined as Japanese versus English) is found definitely to influence content: the bilingual subjects used in the experiment tended to express Japanese values when speaking Japanese, English values when speaking English. In the second correlational task, the listener (Japanese versus

132 JACQUELINE LINDENFELD

American) is found to influence the linguistic code of those same bilinguals to the extent that "with the Japanese listener, there was much
more disruption of English syntax, more intrusion of Japanese words, and
briefer speech" (Ervin-Tripp 1964:96). As for the third type of interaction examined, namely, that of topic and linguistic code, it turns out to be
more complex than expected and requires that the listener also be taken
into account, thus revealing the kind of intricate web which Hymes'
model prepares us to find instead of the one-to-one correspondences of
correlational sociolinguistics.

In spite of its brevity Ervin-Tripp's study stands as a good example of
the combined use of correlational sociolinguistics and the ethnography of
communication. One important lesson to be drawn from it is that we
should not feel compelled to cover as much in one study as each approach
would on its own. Rather we must direct our efforts to a judicious use of
the better features of each of them. I now firmly believe that correlational
sociolinguistics does not and cannot give a completely realistic picture
of the very complex relations between linguistic and nonlinguistic
phenomena. We must go beyond the restrictive format of studies in which
the categories are preselected.[1] With the framework suggested by Hymes,
which can be reduced to reasonable proportions if we focus on a small
number of speech events in any one study, we will be much more likely to
discover the truly significant relationships existing between the various
speech components. With the help of methods imitated (but not taken
directly) from correlational sociolinguistics we will then at a second stage
be able to confirm the hypothesized relationships by testing them on
larger samples, and thus gradually reach towards ethnosociolinguistic
universals.

REFERENCES

BERNSTEIN, B.
    1964   "Elaborated and restricted codes: their social origins and some conse-
            quences," in The ethnography of communication. Edited by J. Gumperz
            and D. Hymes. American Anthropologist 66 (6, 2):55–69.
CRUMRINE, L.
    1968   An ethnography of Mayo speaking. Anthropological Linguistics 10
            (2):19–31.
ERVIN-TRIPP, S.
    1964   "An analysis of the interaction of language, topic and listener," in The
            ethnography of communication. Edited by J. Gumperz and D. Hymes.
            American Anthropologist 66 (6, 2):86–102.

---

[1] It should be noted that these criticisms apply to some of my own studies such as one in
which I showed the amount of syntactic complexity in the speech of French speakers to
correlate with their socioeconomic status and the degree of formality of the situation
(Lindenfeld 1969).

FISHMAN, J.
   1971   "Preface," in *Advances in the sociology of language*. Edited by J.
          Fishman. The Hague: Mouton.
GRIMSHAW, A.
   1971   "Sociolinguistics," in *Advances in the sociology of language*. Edited by
          J. Fishman. The Hague: Mouton.
GUMPERZ, J.
   1972   "Introduction," in *Directions in sociolinguistics: the ethnography of
          communication*. Edited by J. J. Gumperz and Dell Hymes. New York:
          Holt, Rinehart and Winston.
HOGAN, SISTER HELEN MARIE
   1967   "An ethnography of communication among the Ashanti." Unpublished
          M.A. dissertation, Department of Anthropology, University of Penn-
          sylvania.
HYMES, D.
   1962   "The ethnography of speaking," in *Anthropology and human behavior*.
          Edited by T. Gladwin and W. C. Sturtevant. Anthropological Society of
          Washington, Washington D.C.
   1964   "Introduction: towards ethnographies of communication," in *The eth-
          nography of communication*. Edited by J. Gumperz and D. Hymes.
          American Anthropologist 66 (6, 2):1–34.
   1966   "Two types of linguistic relativity," in *Sociolinguistics*. Edited by W.
          Bright. The Hague: Mouton.
   1971   "Sociolinguistics and the ethnography of speaking," in *Social anthro-
          pology and language*. Edited by E. Ardener. London: Tavistock.
   1972   "Models of the interaction of language and social life," in *Directions in
          sociolinguistics*. Edited by J. Gumperz and D. Hymes. New York: Holt,
          Rinehart and Winston.
LABOV, W.
   1966   *The social stratification of English in New York City*. Washington, D.C.:
          Center for Applied Linguistics.
   1971   "The study of language in its social context," in *Advance in the soci-
          ology of language*. Edited by J. Fishman. The Hague: Mouton.
LINDENFELD, J.
   1969   The social conditioning of syntactic variation in French. *American
          Anthropologist* 71 (5):890–898.
SHERZER, J.
   1970   La parole chez les Abipone. *L'Homme* 10:42–76.

SECTION THREE

Survey Techniques

Sociological Aspects of Black English Dialects in the United States

R. B. SMITH

The past decade has seen an important revolution in dialectology in the United States with the development of techniques in empirical research to reveal patterns in the complexities of language behavior and interaction, and to permit us to abstract certain sociolinguistic principles from these patterns, to corroborate others discovered elsewhere. Traditional dialect geography had, it is true, become exhausted in its continued reliance on techniques of fieldwork and analysis appropriate to a population more geographically settled, more socially stratified, than American society has been in the last forty years or so. Thus its failure to sort out and make sense of the bewildering complexities of language variation in modern American cities. Even Kurath's innovative "levels of cultivation" categories of informant selection (Kurath 1939:44), developed specifically for the American dialect situation, not only seem primitive and inadequate now, but starkly reveal the idealized picture of American society held at that time.

It is principally to William Labov that American dialectology owes its rejuvenation, with his sampling procedures adopted from sociological research, his careful monitoring (in questions put to informants) of context to control style of response, and his pre-selection of linguistic variables in the analysis (Labov 1963, 1966a). He was thus the first to bring some system to the baffling inconsistencies of the "linguistic community" of New York City, where individual behavior was "studded with oscillations and contradiction" (1966a:6). Several important studies followed Labov's example, notably the Detroit studies of Shuy, Wolfram, and Riley (1967) and Wolfram (1969), where sampling was sophisticated and careful, questions (some of which were, it is true, more traditional) monitored to coordinate context with style, and the analysis characterized by the correlation of language data with social categories.

None of these studies was designed to facilitate the elicitation of new linguistic data. (Neither, it might be argued, were the work sheets for the *Linguistic atlas of the United States and Canada* [Davis, McDavid, and McDavid 1969] though their very massiveness made them more hospitable to unanticipated new data.) These new analyses quite deliberately restricted themselves to a very few pre-selected variables, the goal being a discovery not simply of specific language patterns but also of some principles of sociolinguistic behavior underlying those patterns which emerged. (See Labov [1969:19–38] for an enumeration and discussion of a few of these principles.)

An important piece of corollary sociolinguistic research was completed by Tucker and Lambert (1969) in Tougaloo, Mississippi, where, using skillfully designed indirect questions, they asked Negro and white listeners to rank speakers of various American dialects. The resultant pattern of preference, on the part of the Negroes, for the virtually non-regional Network Standard is, though interesting, not surprisingly similar to Labov's discovery of linguistic self-denigration on the part of the New Yorkers, and it may provide indirect evidence that the United States is, as a whole, in some sense a "linguistic community."

Out of these studies have implicitly come, at least for the United States (the Black community included), a number of sociolinguistic projections based on patterns revealed by these studies and the principles conjectured, often explicitly, to underlie these patterns. Some important ones are as follows:

a. The range of dialect variation should continue to show congruence with the social status of the speaker and with his degree of upward social mobility. More specifically, as Labov has shown (1966b), the wider ranges of patterned language variation should continue to be more typical of the lower-middle, socially-upward-mobile classes, with the higher styles exhibiting some "crossover pattern," such hypercorrect behavior providing an index of "linguistic insecurity."

b. The style/context gradations of specific dialect features should remain congruent with each other to provide an accurate index of social class. The validity of Labov's question-monitoring technique of interviewing is of course dependent on the maintenance of this congruence; one now quite intuitively rejects Kenyon's distinction (1948) between CULTURAL LEVELS and FUNCTIONAL VARIETIES, since it seems indisputable that a low style of language is correlative with a casual, spontaneous context, and vice versa (Labov 1969:22).

c. The status-ranking value of any given dialect form should remain fairly stable over time if it is to retain its usefulness as a socially important linguistic index. Thus for Martha's Vineyard, the variation in two diphthongs is carefully traced over several generations among a number of ethnic groups (Labov 1963), but the social significance of any particular

realization of these diphthongs must have remained quite stable throughout this period. The sound change itself was achieved not by linguistic
innovation but by population movements away from the island and
upward and downward movements of populations in the social scale, the
sounds themselves serving as an index of either island or of mainland
orientation.

Ferguson (1959) notes that one of the characteristics of diglossia —
though admittedly it involves a more discrete and systematic ranking of
dialect forms than is found in the United States — is its persistence "over
several centuries," in some cases "well over a thousand years," despite
"communicative tensions which arise in the diglossia situation"
(1959:332). Fischer's "sociosymbolic variants" (1958), such as the phonetic realizations of English *-ing*, "[do] not necessarily remain the same
generation after generation," but the principle (perhaps the only) change
which it undergoes is the erosion of the threshold of the higher form as
more and more speakers adopt it until "its sociosymbolic load is reduced
and eventually vanishes" (1958:56).

d. Those dialect forms characteristic of groups receiving a high ranking,
in subject reaction tests, will tend to be emulated by the ranking population (at least in the higher styles); those characteristic of low-ranking
groups will tend to be shunned. This is indeed the principle which charges
these studies with much of their importance. Dillard (1972) interprets the
Mississippi Negro preference for "Network Standard" English, "insofar
as linguistic evidence may be interpreted in the matter," as signaling
"hope for integration on a truly national scale" (1972:281).

One other, more popularly held notion about the dynamics OF social
dialects (though perhaps more normative than empirical) which, though
it does not necessarily clash with better substantiated and more tenable
principles, is often at variance with them in the projections that they
underlie, is as follows:

e. Bidialectalism commonly develops (or ought to) among speakers of
lower ranked dialects, the burden of learning a new dialect falling (quite
rightly) upon those who would reap the advantage of possessing a social
marker of the class or classes above; and a kind of diglossic competence is
of course expected of all bidialectals. (DIGLOSSIA in this context meaning
— as redefined by Dillard [1972:301] — simply a restriction of the roles,
or domains, of each dialect, the specialization of each dialect's functions.)
This is not only the traditional position in American education but also
the position of many, perhaps most, American dialectologists today
(Fasold and Shuy 1970:xiii), who conceive of their role in education as at
least partly the facilitation of the teacher's job of developing a "biloquial-
ism" among urban black students.

From the evidence we are receiving from members of the black community in the United States, it now seems that these projections are either

premature and wrong, or they do not take some complex variables into account and are hence simplistic. What seems to be happening now is as follows:

a. Though I know of no direct evidence to substantiate the claim, it is impressionistically clear that a very great range of language variation among Negroes, perhaps the greatest range (at least as far as phonological markers are concerned) occurs in those speakers who would be considered by most indices to claim membership in the upper middle class. Just the public language of a number of people could be presented as evidence: Ralph Abernathy and Jesse Jackson come especially to mind. (Exempt from the claim would be those blacks who, though any social index would certainly group them in this class, and though they consider themselves to be black, may be among those 20 percent or so who do not speak black English [Dillard 1972:229] such as perhaps Senator Edward Brooke, or Representative Yvonne Braithwaite.)

Hypercorrect linguistic behavior may, in addition, be in a downward as well as in an upward direction, from the perspective of socioeconomic status (Mitchell-Kernan 1971), thus complicating the notion of "linguistic insecurity." Not only may a speaker "select to encode his relationship to a hearer by monitoring in one direction or another" (1971:74) — that is, toward Standard English or toward Black English — but there also exists the phenomenon of "hyper Black English monitoring," which embodies "the idea of . . . deviation but not the variants which ordinarily obtain" (p. 76).

b. The congruence of H-L style (or variety) of language with formal-spontaneous speech context is often turned topsy-turvy by modern blacks. Though a congruence can usually be assumed to obtain, there is a high incidence of dialect markers normally associated with spontaneous, or casual, speech which simply cannot be assumed to be characteristic of "out-of-awareness" contexts.

There is the added problem for the linguist of interpreting language use and of determining level of style — using criteria other than simple "context." Arthur points out that Black English and Standard English "are more similar at the formal end of the stylistic continuum than at the informal end" (1971:165), but the fit can be merely approximate since the two systems have different traditions and different uses for these styles. Abrahams (1972) notes that a High variety of Black English occurs in the West Indies which is close to, but not identical with, oratorical or highly formal, Standard English; the use of this style, called "talking sweet," has a context, however, which is unique to Black English. That a closeness of linguistic details does obtain between these two varieties of English in their High styles is pointed out by Dillard, where "fanciness [in Fancy Talk] is partially correlated with standardness, but not perfectly" (1972:251).

c. It is highly probable that a few dialect markers have reversed their ranking values in some contexts through an assertion of black ethnic identity and/or solidarity, together with a rejection of the dominant white Standard linguistic value system. Dillard remarks that the phenomenon is most apparent in the use of ethnic slang "by those Blacks whose English is most Standard" (1972:241ff.). This process at the lexical level has also been discussed by Holt, though she sets it in the context of a very conscious "promotion of an ideology" (1971:43), the term "Black" itself having recently undergone such an inversion. Although this kind of evidence for a general reversal of dialect markers may seem linguistically trivial because the process is "under the conscious control of the user" (Dillard 1972:242), it may yet be a hint of a more general out-of-awareness process, given the language sensitivity of the black community.

d. The assumption that high-ranking dialect markers signal an automatic emulation by the ranker (and its converse) is clearly wrong. Most sociolinguists concede that the recognition of linguistic norms is often at variance with language behavior. In fact, it is the general concurrence in specific norms, not the patterned behavior, which defines New York City, according to Labov (1966b:62), as a "linguistic community." To point more specifically at the Tougaloo experiment and the conclusions which Dillard draws from it, Labov states that "relatively few speakers are directly influenced by the speech patterns heard on radio and television" (1966b:74, Note 25).

e. It is generally conceded that complete oral bidialectalism among American blacks is quite rare (cf. Labov 1969:36) for a number of reasons: its linguistic difficulty; the complexity of the speaker–listener relationship and its effect on the choice of level of language; and the motivational and identity problems which are so crucial in using (or even learning) a new language variety (Haugen 1965:125). When true bidialectalism is attested, it is often characterized as "quasi-bidialectalism" (Dillard 1972:209); the rarity of a "clearly bidialectal" American Negro is often attributed to his extraordinary linguistic background (1972:209). Of that fairly large Negro middle class which "manipulates standard English with confidence" (1972:210), most cannot be said to be truly bidialectal at all, since they probably do not speak Black English, or do so on rare occasions and in very limited contexts. Even if it is the case that bidialectalism among American blacks is more common than Labov and Dillard suggests (and we have Stewart's testimony that it may be [1971:48]), it exists virtually exclusively among the middle and upper-middle classes, since bidialectalism has always occured most readily not among the upward mobile classes but among speakers "who have their status assured" (Dillard 1972:208). Among American blacks, it is the Lower Language, then, not the Higher, which is the most easily learned and the most readily used.

To conclude that American Black English does not participate in the linguistic community that is American English would be quite wrong. Black informants have been included in almost every sociolinguistic survey, and their presence has not skewed the resultant patterns perceptibly. But it would also be right to conclude that some important information about Black English would be obscured if we did not approach this dialect as if it uniquely preserved something of its homogeneity and maintained some distance and independence from other American dialects, regional and social. Both history and certain social peculiarities of the black community in American society support this view. What has developed and appears to be continuing to develop in the United States is a retention among blacks of a homogeneity of language and something of an aloofness from Standard English influence in all of its stylistic gradations, and perhaps even some independence in its status-ranking indices — this in spite of a great deal of recent mobility among blacks, mobility both geographic and socioeconomic.

Labov has admitted that "objective socioeconomic position and social mobility may not be accurate indexes of [Negro] participation in the cultural norms of middleclass society" (1966b:70). Most sociolinguistic reasoning is still pervaded by the assumption that America is an open society; we now surely recognize that there exist in America, however much we deplore the fact, groups with severely limited opportunities for mobility. And for these groups, "linguistic behavior must be analyzed along other dimensions" (Labov 1966b:75). For blacks, that behavior doubtless reflects the tensions between the American ideal of full participation in the norms of middleclass society for all, and the American reality of a severely restricted participation for them.

REFERENCES

ABRAHAMS, ROGER D.
   1972   The training of the man of works in talking sweet. *Language in Society* 1(1):15–29.
ARTHUR, BRADFORD
   1971   The interaction of dialect and style in urban American English. *Language Learning* 21(2):161–173.
DAVIS, ALVA L., RAVEN I. McDAVID, JR., VIRGINIA G. McDAVID, *editors*
   1969   *A compilation of the work sheets of the Linguistic Atlas of the United States and Canada and associated projects* (second edition). Chicago: University of Chicago Press.
DILLARD, J. L.
   1972   *Black English*. New York: Random House.
FASOLD, RALPH W., ROGER W. SHUY, *editors*
   1970   *Teaching standard English in the inner city*. Washington, D.C.: Center for Applied Linguistics.

FERGUSON, CHARLES A.
 1959 Diglossia. *Word* 15:325–340.
FISCHER, JOHN L.
 1958 Influences on the choice of a linguistic variant. *Word* 14:47–56.
HAUGEN, EINAR
 1965 "Bilingualism and bidialectalism," in *Social dialects and language learning.* Edited by Roger W. Shuy, 124–126. Champaign, Illinois: National Council of Teachers of English.
HOLT, GRACE SIMS
 1971 "Inversion" in Black communication. *Florida FL Reporter* 9(1, 2):41, 43, 55.
KENYON, JOHN S.
 1948 Cultural levels and functional varieties of English. *College English* 10:31–36.
KURATH, HANS
 1939 *Handbook of the linguistic geography of New England.* Washington D.C.: American Council of Learned Societies.
LABOV, WILLIAM
 1963 The social motivation of a sound change. *Word* 19:273–309.
 1966a *The social stratification of English in New York City.* Washington, D.C.: Center for Applied Linguistics.
 1966b The effect of social mobility on linguistic behavior. *Sociological Inquiry* 36(2):58–75.
 1969 *The study of nonstandard English.* Champaign, Illinois: National Council of Teachers of English.
MITCHELL-KERNAN, CLAUDIA I.
 1971 *Language behavior in a Black urban community.* Monograph 2, Language Behavior Research Laboratory, University of California, Berkeley.
SHUY, ROGER W., WALTER A. WOLFRAM, WILLIAM K. RILEY
 1967 "Linguistic correlates of social stratification in Detroit speech." Mimeographed manuscript, Michigan State University, USOE Cooperative Research Project 6–1347.
STEWART, WILLIAM A.
 1971 Observations (1966) on the problems of defining Negro dialect. *Florida FL Reporter* 9(1, 2):47–49, 57.
TUCKER, G. RICHARD, WALLACE E. LAMBERT
 1969 White and Negro listeners' reactions to various American-English dialects. *Social Forces* 47(4):463–468.
WOLFRAM, WALTER A.
 1969 *A sociolinguistic description of Detroit speech.* Washington, D.C.: Center for Applied Linguistics.

Communication in Culture Spaces

AKIRA YAMAMOTO

1. SCOPE OF SOCIOLINGUISTICS

A typical sociolinguistic image embraces, in principle at least, every aspect of the structure and use of language that relates to its social and cultural function (Lyons 1970:287). A sociolinguistic text lists:
a. Perspective on sociolinguistics:
    Communication in animals and in men
    Linguistics and psychology
    The ethnography of speaking.
The attempt seems to be to establish an interdisciplinary study of language — semiotics, psychology, sociology, anthropology and other fields.
b. Language in social strata and sectors:
    Some sociological determinants of perception
    The reflection of social processes in linguistic structures
    Literacy as a factor in language change.
Here the sociolinguists' interest is to find some linguistic variables which they can correlate with social stratification. Many of Labov's works will belong here.
c. Language reflections of sociocultural organization:
    The decline of German dialects
    The urbanization of the Guarani language
    Types of linguistic communities.
d. Multilingualism:
    A study of the roles of attitudes and motivation in second language learning
    Explorations in the social psychology of language choice
    Bilingual usage in Paraguay.

The last three mentioned above (b, c, and d) seem to constitute the core area in the field of sociolinguistics. Sociolinguists claim that it is primarily through the use of language that people communicate with each other, and that in order to communicate with each other people must share some common social context. Giglioli puts it as follows: speech becomes understandable only in connection with social interaction (1972:13). This, in turn, means that speech will function to point out a certain particular social interaction. In short, then, sociolinguistics is an indexical study of language.

Fishman suggests that the term "sociology of language" is preferable to sociolinguistics, because the assumption of the people in this field is that society is broader than language and therefore provides the context in which all language behavior must ultimately be viewed (1968:6). Fishman further suggests that the sociology of language tries to answer questions in three areas (1972:46–47):

1. Who speaks (or writes) what language (or what language variety) to whom and when and to what end? This subfield in the sociology of language, called by Fishman "descriptive" sociology of language, attempts to disclose the general pattern of language use in a speech community.

2. What accounts for differential changes in the social organization of language use and behavior toward language? This part of the sociology of language is, according to Fishman, dynamic sociology of language which is, therefore, concerned with the patterns and causes of change in the organization of language use.

3. The third part of the sociology of language deals with those wider topics ordinarily treated in the field of applied linguistics: language teaching, the creation or revision of writing systems, language policy decision and language planning. This subfield is more or less the warehouse of sociolinguistic material, methods and techniques.

2. STUDIES IN LANGUAGE AND SOCIETY

Specifically, we may say that the sociolinguists' concern has been to find linguistic variables — phonological, morphological, sporadically syntactic and rarely semantic — and to correlate them with social significances, i.e., social stratification which is determined by socioeconomic, ethnic, and sexual factors.

Thus Wolfram (1969) attempts to describe the speech phenomenon formulating five factors which determine the linguistic variables. To Wolfram, a linguistic variable is determined by the interaction of the following factors: (1) ethnic isolation, (2) socioeconomic status, (3) sex, (4) age and (5) topic of discourse. Labov has published many articles throughout the 1960s: "The social motivation of a sound change" (1963), "Phonological correlates of social stratification" (1964), The social stratification of English in New York City (1966), "The effect of social mobility on linguistic behavior" (1967), and many others whose purpose has been to discover certain linguistic variables within the already defined socioeconomic boundaries. Labov, however, finds that social dialects are not always as clearcut as any sociological survey of stratification may suggest. Very often, he acknowledges, social dialects are an unbroken continuum from one social stratum to another.

3. CULTURE SPACES AND SOCIOLINGUISTICS

Ponsioen defines society as an overall structure embracing unifunctional, multifunctional and territorial social units, imbuing them with a feeling of belonging (1969:15). However, society as such is not experienced by the individual in his daily life. The concept of culture spaces includes such a Ponsioenian statement as part of its definition. The parts which should be specially stressed in the concept of culture spaces are "physical space" or territoriality at a given moment and moreover, the fact that one or more culture spaces are being experienced by individuals in their daily life. It is possible, and probably the case, that one sees at one glance the universe of interaction of individuals in a physical space at a given time. Therefore it will not be hard to construct types of culture spaces, as Voegelin suggests, from the point of view of language use:
a. linguistically homogeneous culture spaces;
b. linguistically heterogeneous culture spaces;
c. culture spaces which are willing to borrow from other culture spaces;
d. creative or innovative culture spaces;
e. mixtures of (c) and (d);
f. others.
When looked at differently, we may find that some culture spaces exclude verbal communication, some other culture spaces exclude visual communication, and still others auditory communication, and so on. Still another point of view will enable us to say that some culture spaces may have a set of rigid selectional restrictions for their membership and some a lax one.

It is important to clarify what kind of criterion or criteria are used for culture space typology. When sociolinguists study the correlation between linguistic variables and social stratification, they seem to be treating different types of stratification as if a single type. When Wolff (1959) discusses his mutual intelligibility, he assumes that it is predictable from the result of contrastive structural analysis. However, he is not clear what kind of speech acts his structural analysis is based on. Local economic and power relationships may result in an intelligibility problem; so may feelings of ethnic self-sufficiency. Consequently the whole situation becomes unpredictable, contrary to what Wolff expects.

Labov (1967) reports that people's choice of language is influenced not only in respect of economic, educational and other observable mobility, but also in respect of subject's evaluations of the desirability or correctness of various pronunciations. He states that people in the same age-group show remarkably similar evaluation; so do people of the same mobility type such as the lower middleclass upward mobility type. When we take social stratification into our analysis of speech, it necessarily complicates the description and very often produces statements such as "verbal behavior in all or in most important respects cannot be predicted" or "the language cannot properly be regarded as a structured integrated system" (Labov 1964:188).

In speaking about the study of stratification in Western societies, Ponsioen suggests dividing societies into three levels (1969:140–142): (i) the macro level, where we apply the image of articulation of society in upper, middle and lower strata; (ii) the meso level, where stratification is based on jobs and, as Ponsioen points out, society presents itself as a ladder which a person can climb up or down; and (iii) the micro level, where stratification is found between individuals and, interestingly enough, people who are stratified as belonging to the same stratum according to (i) and (ii) may be restratified by skin colors, verbal behavior, the way they raise children, religious behavior and so on.

Ponsioen further suggests another three-way typology that will help clarify the above stratification (1969:143–146): (a) feudal type, (b) functional type and (c) conflicting type. By the feudal type of stratification, Ponsioen means that which contains two strata — a society proper or elite, and a nonsociety or the masses. In this, the masses or the culturally poor are never allowed to climb up to the level of a society proper. Thus, status in this pattern is neither ascribed nor achieved, but it is God-given by blood or by ennoblement. The functional type of stratification is that of functions or of roles. People who occupy these roles in the organization are accordingly stratified. Very often, it is believed that education is one of the means to climb up to higher stratum. The conflict type is marked by opposition of interests in obtaining control over society.

The term stratification can stand for such varied types and levels that it becomes obvious that the use of the concept for linguistic variable identification will result in extracomplication, ambiguity, confusion or other problems unless sociolinguists clearly define their use of the term.

Thus Fishman suggests (1966) that the following three basic categories be decided in analyzing verbal behavior:

a. Place at the forefront of analysis the concept of "domain" — occasions on which one language is habitually employed rather than another.

b. Resolve domains primarily into constituent "role relations."

c. Seek out correlations between (a) and (b) and choice of language.

Similarly, Uhlenbeck states that every sentence needs to be interpreted in the light of various extralinguistic data: (1) the situation in which the sentence is spoken, (2) the preceding sentences if any, (3) the hearer's knowledge of the speaker and (4) the topics which might be discussed with him (1963:11).

Hymes (1964b) proposes in a much more inclusive framework that the components of communicative events are: (1) and (2) participants, (3) channels available, (4) shared codes, (5) the settings, (6) the forms of messages, (7) topics and comments, and (8) the events themselves.

4. METHODOLOGY

Given such guidelines or frameworks, we will still face methodological problems as Labov points out (1971). In investigating verbal behavior, we want to observe how people talk when they are not being observed, but a problem which Labov calls the "observer's paradox" usually results.

In an interview situation, we will get only formal, rather unnatural responses from the informants, so we may try to collect only those data generated in the margins of the interview situations. But this will be rather unsystematic though we may get useful sentences sporadically. Labov suggests that a more effective method would be to go beyond the individual interview and deal with whole families and natural peer groups (1971:462). Most of the syntactic forms and/or semantic categories do not occur often enough in ordinary conversation to be subjected to quantificative analysis. So Labov suggests setting up the conditions under which such forms are used. This may be closest to the concept of culture spaces among frameworks proposed by sociolinguists, but investigators will still face the "observer's paradox." The goal, however, will be effectively achieved if we know which culture space we are dealing with. Conversation textbooks show us good examples:

AT TABLE: breakfast, Japanese style

lunch, Japanese style

dinner, Western style (before-dinner drink, dinner, desert, after-dinner drink)

tea, at a friend's house

tea, at a restaurant.

TRANSPORTATION: on the streetcar, to the conductor

on the bus, to the bus-girl

Ginza, Tokyo, traffic congestion.

Specification of culture spaces enables us to delimit the selection of styles of speech and choice of topics, to say the least. In a more practical fieldwork situation, it is next to impossible nowadays to go to a completely unknown places. We will often find some kind of documentation about the people we are to deal with. Therefore we may be able, at least, to expect what kind of culture spaces we may find though we may also end up with a completely new list of culture spaces in a given culture. We may be able to nail down which culture space(s) we are interested in investigating. When we want to get linguistic data, we may ask questions specifying WHERE and WHEN, and, in that space, who is talking to whom, how and about what.

5. COMMUNICATION IN A CULTURE RUBRIC *BURAKU*

The following discussion deals with a *buraku*, i.e., a barrio or hamlet, as a culture rubric which consists of a set of culture spaces.

5.1. *The* buraku

The *buraku* under the present study is situated in the west part of the Honshu, Japan. It is unique in that no family is a farmer, although its surrounding *buraku*s are mainly farmers. It should be noted, however, that this *buraku* is not different from those surrounding it in that all the members of the *buraku* are considered to be a congenial group — members of one family, so to speak — and the *buraku*'s territory is clearly definable. Cornell describes such a situation neatly (1956:175):

All through life there are reminders that one is part of the *buraku*. In relations with outsiders the sense of belonging to one locale is especially acute. This feeling takes root from the fact that at school the children clean their classrooms by *buraku* groups and, in the young people's association of the *mura* [village], individuals participate with their *buraku* fellows in events such as dancing at Bon and the annual school field meet.

Cornell goes on to explain what happens in adulthood:

In adulthood, one is often called by his family name qualified by the home place name as far as the edge of the *mura*, since otherwise it may be difficult to determine which family of the same surname in the area is meant. Or outsiders may simply address him as "the gentleman from Matsunagi" when more explicit identification is unnecessary or his name is unknown.

Our *buraku* consists of twelve households, each of which is briefly described below.

1. A, a¹: small factory owner, president of PTA. He is addressed not by

---

¹   The capital letter is used for the last name, and the small letter for the first name. The capital letter and the small letter (e.g. A,a) stands for a head of the family, i.e. an adult male householder.

his name but by his hereditary position *oyakata*. His wife is called not by her name but by *okaQ-tsan*.[2]

2. B, b: store-keeper, a representative of proteges of Tutelary Deity and an elected chairman of the *buraku* assembly, whose position is called *sewayaku*. He is called by his last name *B-san* [Mr. B], and his wife is called not by her name, but by *okaQ-tsan*.

3. C, c: teacher (junior high school) who joined the *buraku* some time ago. He is addressed not by his name but as *šenšee* [teacher], and his wife not by her name but by *oku-san*.[3]

4. D, d: policeman who was transferred to this *buraku* from another town some time ago. He is in charge of a wider area including many *burakus* but lives in this particular *buraku*. He is addressed not by his name but as *dan-san*[4] and his wife is addressed as *oku-san*.

5. E, e: railroad station master who was transferred to the station which happened to be in this *buraku* and became a member of it some time ago. He is addressed as *eki-tyoo-san* [Mr. Station Master], and his wife as *oku-san*.

6. F, f: store-keeper. He is addressed by his first name *f-san*. His wife is addressed by her first name.

7. G, g: clerk at Public Health Center. He is addressed by his first name *g-san*, and his wife by her first name.

8. H, h: store-keeper. He is addressed by his first name *h-san*, and his wife by her first name.

9. I, i: engineer at the railroad company. He is addressed by his first name *i-san* and his wife by her first name.

10. J, j: construction worker. He is addressed by his first name *j-san* and his wife by her first name.

11. K, k: day-laborer. He is addressed by his first name *k-san* and his wife by her first name.

12. L, l: no work. He is addressed by his first name *l-san* and his wife by her first name.

From what we have described above, we immediately notice that we can tentatively classify twelve households into three status groups.[5]

---

[2] The expression *okaQ-tsan* is used to address a married woman and is a dialectal expression.

[3] The expression *oku-san* is also used to address a married woman and is a standard Japanese expression. People feel differently toward *okaQ-tsan* and *oku-san*, something traditional and something new respectively.

[4] The expression *dan-san* means "honorable Sir," and people in this *buraku* use the term to medical doctors and to police officers.

[5] Comprehensive description is given in Nakane (1970). Status structure in Japan can be found especially in Chapter II, section 2 "The fundamental structure of vertical organization": 40–62.

1. Group A: Households (1) and (2). The householders are *oya-kata* and *sewayaku*, the leaders of the *buraku*. Their wives are addressed as *okaQ-tsan*.
2. Group B: Households (3), (4) and (5). The householders are not native of the *buraku*, but became members later. They are addressed by their professions, *dan-san* being a synonym of "Mr. Policeman." Their wives are addressed as *oku-san*.
3. Group C: Households (6) through (12). The householders are native to the *buraku* and they are addressed by their first names. Their wives are addressed also by their first names.

5.2.   *Verbal Behavior in the* Buraku

In this section we will observe the verbal behavior of the male adult members of the *buraku* and the relevant semantic features in verbal communication among them.

CULTURE SPACE: at the entrance of the hearer's home in the early evening.
SPEAKER: *f-san*, a constituent of Group C goes to the members of the *buraku* to ask for some help.

5.2.1.   *f-san* AND A MEMBER OF GROUP A

f-san	*tego-si-te*	*mora-e-n*	*mon*	*des-i*	*da-ra*	*ka*
	help-do	receivea honorable favorof- possible- not (humble)	NOM	copula- polite (non- past)	copula- supposi- tive	Q

(Could you possibly help me?)

GROUP A:	*tego-si-te*	*yaa-zi*
	help-do	giveafavor toinferior- will (non- polite)

(I will help you.)

a. When *f-san* talks to a member of Group A, he must at least include in his sentence the following semantic features:

+honorific, −pejorative, +humble, +polite

b. When a member of Group A talks to *f-san*, he includes the following semantic features in his sentence:

−honorific, +perjorative, −humble, −polite

5.2.2. *f-san* AND A MEMBER OF GROUP B

f-san: tego-si-te   mora-e-n   mon   da-ra   ka

help-do   receivea   NOM   copula-   Q
          honorable   supposi-
          favorof-   tive (non-
          possible-not   polite)
          (polite)
(Can you give me some help?)

GROUP B: tego-si-te   agee-zi   ne

help-do   giveafavor   SM(polite)
          tosuperior-
          will (non-
          polite)
(I will give you some help.)

a. *f-san* to a member of Group B:

+/−honorific, −pejorative, −humble, +polite

b. Group B to *f-san*:

+honorific, −pejorative,
−humble, +polite

5.2.3. *f-san* AND A MEMBER OF GROUP C

f-san: tego-si-te   gos-e   ya

help-do   receivea   SM (non-polite)
          favorfrom
          equal/in-
          ferior-
          command
(Give me some help.)

GROUP C: *tego-si-te   yaa-zi*

help-do   giveafavor
toequal/in-
ferior-will
(non-polite)
(I will help you.)

a. *f-san* to a member of Group c:

−honorific, +pejorative
−humble, −polite

b. Group c to *f-san:*

−honorific, +pejorative, −humble, −polite

5.2.4.   *dan-san*, A CONSTITUENT OF GROUP B, AND A MEMBER OF GROUP A

dan-san:	*tego-si-te*	*mora-e-n*	*mon*	*des-i*	*da-ra*	*ka*
	help-do	receivea honorable favorof- possible- not (humble)	NOM	copula- polite (non- past)	copula- supposi- tive	Q

(Could you possibly help me?)

GROUP A: *tego-si-te   agee-zi*

help-do   giveafavor
tosuperior-
will (non-
polite)
(I will give you some help.)

a. *dan-san* to a member of Group A:

+honorific, −pejorative, +humble, +polite

b. Group a to *dan-san:*

−honorific, −pejorative,
−humble, −polite

5.2.5. *dan-san* AND *eki-tyoo-san*, BOTH OF WHOM ARE CONSTITUENTS OF GROUP B:

dan-san: tego-si-te   mora-e-n   mon   da-ra   ka

help-do   receivea   NOM   copula-   Q
          honorable   supposi-
          favorof-   tive (non-
          possible-   polite)
          not (polite)

(Can you give me some help?)

eki-tyoo-san:tego-si-te   age-mahyo

help-do   geveafavorto
          superior-will
          (polite)

(I will give you some help.)

a. and b. Among the members of Group B:

+honorific, −pejorative, −humble, +polite

5.2.6. *oyakata* AND *sewayaku*, BOTH OF WHOM CONSTITUTE GROUP A:

oyakata: tego-si-te   gosi   da   wa   ne

help-do   receivea   copula   SM   SM(polite)
          favorfrom (non-
          equal/in- polite)
          ferior

(Give me some help.)

sewayaku: tego-si-te   age-mahyo

help-do   giveafavorto
          superior-will
          (polite)

(I will give you some help.)

a. *oyakata* to *sewayaku*:

+/−honorific, −pejorative, −humble, +polite

b. *sewayaku* to *oyakata*:

+honorific, −pejorative, −humble, +polite

The above description of the relationships among the members of the *buraku* is shown in Figure 1.

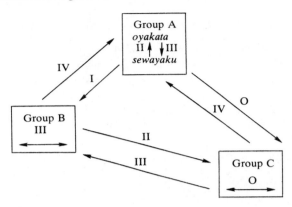

Figure 1.   Relationships among *buraku* members
Key: O = +pejorative, (when [+pejorative], [−honorific] and [−humble] are redundant)
       −polite
     I = +/−honorific, −pejorative,
       −humble, −polite
    II = +honorific, (when [+honorific], [−pejorative] is redundant)
       −humble, +polite
   III = +/−honorific, −humble, +polite
   IV = +honorific, +humble, +polite

6.   A MODEL OF A GRAMMAR

We may now present in Figure 2 our tentative model of a grammar which can incorporate those semantic features discussed in the previous section and those semantic features constant in the speech community — *buraku*.

In the model, we find that the speaker and the hearer (i.e., participants in the activity) are variables, while the space (i.e., where and when), persons permitted to enter the space, the context under the node utterance and other nodes are constant. One of the features under the space is "non-formal" (and the manner of the activity is marked the same in this case), which simply means neither formal nor informal. If it is formal, the time may be the same but the place will not be "at the entrance" of the hearer's home, but in the guest room of the hearer's home, the *buraku*'s meeting house, or some member's guest room where a special meeting is being held. If the space is marked with the feature "informal," the place may be "on the street," or some such public place where anyone can enter and participate in the activity. In the latter case, the linguistic context may be null, i.e., the speaker may abruptly ask for help without even going

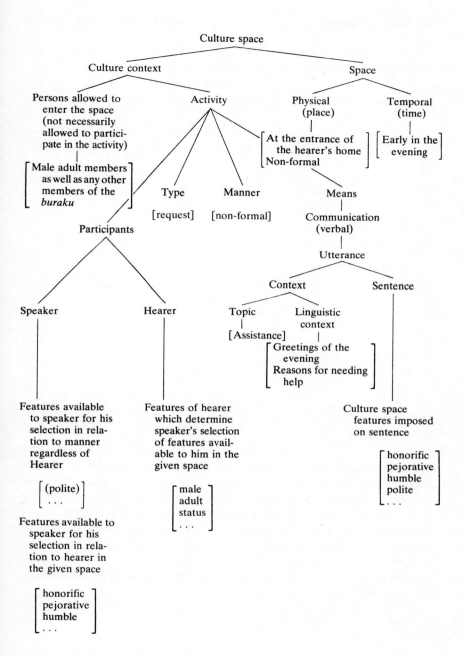

Figure 2.   Tentative model of a grammar

through the ritualistic greetings and explaining the reasons why he needs help.

In the following tables, we will show briefly the relationships of the variables — the social relationships between the speaker and the hearer.

Table 1. Intra-group relations and semantic features derived from them

	Speaker	Hearer	Semantic features			
			Honorific	Pejorative	Humble	Polite
(1)	oyakata	sewayaku	+/−	−	−	+
	sewayaku	oyakata	+	−	−	+
(2)		Group b	+	−	−	+
(3)		Group c	−	+	−	−

Table 2. Inter-group relations and semantic features derived from them.

	Speaker	Hearer	Semantic features			
			Honorific	Pejorative	Humble	Polite
(1)	Group a	Group b	+/−	−	−	−
	Group b	Group a	+	−	+	+
(2)	Group a	Group c	−	+	−	−
	Group c	Group a	+	−	+	+
(3)	Group b	Group c	+	−	−	+
	Group c	Group b	+/−	−	−	+

7. SUMMARY

In the previous section, we have tried to show but just one example of culture spaces in the *buraku* — a "non-formal" culture space where the speaker's selection of semantic features such as honorificness, pejorativeness, humbleness and politeness is determined by the hearer's status. In many informal spaces, it is the age of the hearer in relation to that of the speaker that is the determinant of the speaker's selection of semantic features. In other informal spaces, it is the occupation of the hearer that triggers the selection of the features. Thus different culture spaces impose different selectional restrictions.

We propose the concept of culture spaces as a tentative frame of reference for the study of language in use.

Concept of Culture Spaces: A Proposal

A. ASSUMPTION. Human beings are *homo societicus*, i.e., no human being lives alone segregated from his fellow human beings. Thus combined, human beings constitute a synergy, i.e., a society.

Culture is standardized behavior based on relations of real interconnectedness between people.[6]

B. COROLLARIES

1. When two or more individuals carry out some kind of activity together, they share some physical space on this earth.

2. Since the group is an existent, it occupies one space at a given time.

3. As human beings form dynamic groups, they share many spaces with the same and/or different human beings.

4. Individuals develop a sense of belonging to certain spaces.

5. The space, in turn, comes to be identified as cognitive reality which requires appropriate membership.

6. Membership requirements in general consist of such factors as: (a) sex, (b) age, (c) ethnicity, (d) occupation, (e) status and (f) others. (A space may ignore some of the above, all of the above or none of the above.)

7. The space which provides a place where a social life takes place, therefore, imposes some restrictions on WHAT activity or activities are to be carried out in it.

8. The space may also impose HOW activity or activities are to be carried out.

C. SOME MORE COROLLARIES

1. In leading a group activity, individuals communicate with each other.

2. Hence, a space may impose WHAT communication DEVICE(S) is to be used — media.

3. A space may impose WHAT is to be communicated (or rather what is NOT to be communicated) — contents.

4. A space may impose HOW communication is to be carried out — manner.

5. A space may impose TO WHOM communication is to be directed FROM WHOM.

D. DEFINITION OF CULTURE SPACES. We define such physio-temporal spaces in which individuals are experiencing their daily life as "culture spaces."

---

[6] In assuming thus, we are intentionally excluding spaces occupied by one individual, e.g. one's office space, the bedroom where one is sleeping, etc.

That is, a culture space is a dynamic, composite and particular physical space where *actual* human activities take place at a given time.[7]

REFERENCES

ARDENER, EDWIN, *editor*
1971 *Social anthropology and language.* London: Tavistock.
CARROLL, J. B., *editor*
1956 *Language, thought, and reality: selected writings of Benjamin L. Whorf.* Cambridge, Mass.: The M.I.T. Press.
CARSWELL, E. A., RAGNER ROMMETVEIT, *editors*
1971 *Social contexts of messages.* London: Academic Press.
CORNELL, JOHN B.
1956 Matsunagi: a Japanese mountain community. *Two Japanese villages: Center for Japanese Studies Occasional Papers* 5. University of Michigan.
DILL, ANWAR S., *editor*
1971 *Language structure and language use: essays by Charles A. Ferguson.* Stanford: Stanford University Press.
1971 *Language in social groups: essays by John J. Gumperz.* Stanford: Stanford University Press.
FASOLD, RALPH W.
1969 Tense and the form *be* in black English. *Language* 45:763–776.
1970 Two models of socially significant linguistic variation. *Language* 46:551–563.
FISHMAN, JOSHUA A.
1966 "Language maintenance and language shift as a field of inquiry," in *Language loyalty in the United States.* Edited by J. A. Fishman, 424–458. The Hague: Mouton.
1972 "The sociology of language," in *Language and social context.* Edited by Pier Paolo Giglioli, 45–58. Harmondsworth: Penguin.
FISHMAN, JOSHUA A., *editor*
1968 *Readings in the sociology of language.* The Hague: Mouton.
GIGLIOLI, PIER PAOLO, *editor*
1972 *Language and social context.* London: Penguin.
HOUSTON, SUSAN H.
1969 A sociolinguistic consideration of the black English of children in northern Florida. *Language* 45:599–607.
HYMES, D., *editor*
1964a *Language in culture and society.* New York: Harper and Row.
1964b Introduction: toward ethnographies of communication. *American Anthropologist* 66 (6), part 2: 1–35.
LABOV, WILLIAM
1963 The social motivation of a sound change. *Word* 19:273–309.
1964 Phonological correlates of social stratification. *American Anthropologist* 66:164–176.
1966 *The social stratification of English in New York City.* Washington, D.C.: Center for Applied Linguistics.

[7] We have avoided in our definition the specification that all culture spaces must be occupied by two or more individuals. We may, thus, be able to recapture all culture spaces including those which are occupied by single individuals.

1967   "The effect of social mobility on linguistic behavior," in *Explorations in sociolinguistics* (part II of *IJAL* 33, no. 4). Edited by Stanley Lieberson. Bloomington, Indiana: Indiana University.
1969   Contraction, deletion, and inherent variability of the English copula. *Language* 45:715–762.
1971   "Methodology," in *A survey of linguistic science*. Edited by William Orr Dingwall, 413–497. Maryland: University of Maryland.
LYONS, JOHN, *editor*
1970   *New horizons in linguistics*. Harmondsworth: Penguin.
NAKANE, CHIE
1970   *Japanese society*. Berkeley, Calif.: University of California Press.
PONSIOEN, J. A.
1969   *The analysis of social change reconsidered: a sociological study*. (Third printing, revised and enlarged edition.) The Hague: Mouton.
SMITH, ALFRED G., *editor*
1966   *Communication and culture*. New York: Holt, Rinehard and Winston.
UHLENBECK, E. M.
1963   An appraisal of transformational theory. *Lingua* 12:1–18.
VOEGELIN, C. F., Z. A. HARRIS
1951   Methods for determining intelligibility among dialects of national languages. *Proceedings of the American Philosophical Society* 95: 322–329.
VOEGELIN, C. F., F. M. VOEGELIN
1972   "Dependence of selectional restriction on cultural spaces." Paper for Einar Haugen Festschrift.
VOEGELIN, C. F., F. M. VOEGELIN, LAVERNE MASAYESVA HEANNE
1972   "Hopi semantic and lexical categories." Paper presented at the 1972 Meeting of AAA at Toronto.
WEINREICH, URIEL
1952   SABESDIKERLOSN in Yiddish: a problem of linguistic affinity. *Word* 8:360–377.
WOLFF, H.
1959   Intelligibility and inter-ethnic attitudes. *Anthropological Linguistics* 1:34–41.
WOLFRAM, W.
1969   *Linguistic correlates of social stratification in the speech of Detroit Negroes*. Unpublished M.A. thesis, Hartford Seminary Foundation.
YAMAMOTO, AKIRA
1971   "Toward the formulation of a context grammar." Unpublished paper.
1972   "Cultural spaces in a grammar of language." Paper presented at the Southern Anthropological Society Meeting, Columbia, Missouri.

Sociolinguistic Variation and Semantic Structure: The Case of Tamil kaRi

FRANKLIN C. SOUTHWORTH

In a recently-concluded study of semantic structure in several Indian languages, which focussed on food terminology among other categories, the Tamil word *kaRi* attracted attention because of its multiple meanings.[1] The word occurs in the project data in the following meanings:
1. 'meat' (edible animal flesh)
2. 'vegetable; vegetable dish'
3. 'side dish' (any food preparation served alongside of rice, etc.).[2]
Though this may appear to be a typical case of multiple meaning, it is of interest sociolinguistically because of the possibility of predicting its probable meaning according to the social context in which it is used.

The study on which this article is based, entitled "South Asian Semantic Structures," was sponsored by the National Science Foundation, whose assistance is hereby gratefully acknowledged. Thanks are due to Mr. R. Balakrishnan of Annamalai University, who collected and transcribed most of the Tamil data; to Mr. J. Chandramohan of Madras City, who collected data from Madras and Chingleput District; and to Dr. M. Shanmugam Pillai, who generously provided additional data and gave valuable advice.

[1] The languages involved in the study are Tamil, Hindi–Urdu, Marathi, Indian English and Malayalam. The data consists primarily of conversations on various subjects (agriculture, food, work, and related topics), which were tape-recorded and transcribed.
[2] The *Tamil Lexicon* gives the following meanings: (1) chewing, eating by biting; (2) vegetables, raw or boiled; (3) meat, raw or boiled; (4) pepper. (The last meaning appears in early Tamil texts.) The following entries should also be noted: *kaRi-kkaay* 'pepper'; *kaRi¹-ttal* v. tr. 'to chew; to eat by biting or nibbling' *kaRi²-ttal* v. intr. cf. kaar-; *kaar³-ttal* 'to be pungent, acrid, hot to the taste'.
Burrow and Emeneau provide the following:
1170. Ta. *kaRi* (-*pp*-, -*tt*-) to chew, eat by biting or nibbling; n. chewing, eating by biting; . . . Te. *kaRacu* to bite, gnaw
1171. Ta. *kaRi* vegetables (raw or boiled) . . . *kari* (-*pp*-, -*tt*-) to season (as curries with ghee or oil and spices). Ma. *kaRi* hot condiments, meats, vegetables. Ka. *kaRi* vegetables of any kind (raw or boiled), curry. Koḍ. *kari* curry.
Gundert gives: *kaRi* hot condiments; meats, vegetables . . . *pacca-kaRi* vegetables . . . *kaRi-kaayi* plantains for cari.

Part of the study consisted of brief interviews with a sample of villagers belonging to different social groups. This procedure was carried out in three villages in Chingleput District of Tamilnadu. In these interviews, informants were asked to describe their routine eating habits. When certain terms (including *kaRi*) occurred in the informants' speech, they were asked to define them. Table 1 gives the meanings used for *kaRi* by members of different caste groupings in one village. As the table shows, speakers are clearly divided into three groups by their usage of this word.

Table 1.   Meanings of *kaRi* in different caste groupings

	Brahmins (7 speakers)	Intermediate (14 speakers)	Harijan (5 speakers)
kaRi = (1) (a) meat (all)*	0	0	5
(b) beef (when unmodified)	0	0	1
(c) meat (except beef)	0	7	0
(d) mutton only	0	4	0
(2) meat; vegetable	1**	3	0
(3) vegetable	2**(Iyer)	0	0
(4) NOT USED	4** (Iyengar)	0	0

* Includes all meats available locally: beef, mutton, chicken, pork, duck, pigeon, and occasional wild animals.
** Four village Brahmins (all Iyengars) claimed that they do not use this term in their houses. For a vegetable dish, they use the term *kaRamatu*. One Iyengar, a doctor from elsewhere stationed in local Primary Health Center, gave meaning (2).

The meaning 'side dish' occurs primarily among speakers from the extreme south of Tamilnadu (Kanyakumari District). (This seems to be a result of the earlier political situation, this region having been part of the former Travancore State before 1956. This meaning is substantially the same as the meaning of Malayalam *kaRi*.)[3] In this region, the usual term for 'meat' is *eRacci*, as in Malayalam. The terms *maRa-kaRi* [literally "tree-*kaRi*"] and *kaay-kaRi* are used in this region for 'vegetables' (uncooked), whereas *kuuttu-kaRi* denotes a vegetable preparation; *kozampu* denotes a liquid preparation (either vegetable or meat) which is usually served with the rice rather than alongside of it.[4] Some speakers use *kaRi* only to refer to liquid dishes; the term *parippu-kaRi* ("dal-*kaRi*" = "sambar") also points to this meaning.[5]

[3]   As used in modern spoken Malayalam (author's own observations).
[4]   Information provided by Dr. M. Shanmugam Pillai, Mr. R. Balakrishnan, who are both from Nagercoil area, as well as from conversational materials recorded by R. Balakrishnan in Kanyakumari District.
[5]   The meaning 'liquid dish' and the term *parippu-kaRi* are given by Mr. R. Balakrishnan as his own usage. The latter term is also known in Malabar (author's own observation).

In other parts of Tamilnadu, we find a pattern similar to that of the village mentioned in Table 1.[6] Here, the term *kaRi* is apparently used by the majority of speakers to mean 'meat', whereas those belonging to the traditionally vegetarian castes use the term primarily in the meaning "vegetable" or (for some speakers) "vegetable dish." (As noted above, some Iyengars claim to avoid using this term altogether.) Members of the latter castes use *maamisam* or *eRacci* (occasionally also *pulaal* or *maṭṭan*) to denote 'meat'. Members of non-vegetarian castes use either *kaay* or (less often) *kaRi-kaay* to denote 'vegetables', and appear to lack a general term for 'vegetable dish' (though a number of terms occur denoting specific types of dishes, e.g. *kuuṭṭu* 'thick vegetable preparation', *poriyal* 'fried vegetable preparation', etc.). No general term corresponding to southern *kaRi* 'side dish' appears in our data for any group in this region.

It would be possible to regard each of the variants mentioned as a distinct "dialect" of Tamil, and to describe the above facts in the arrangement shown in Table 2.[7]

Table 2.   Variant meanings in three Tamil "dialects"

		"Dialect" I (southern)	"Dialect" II (northern non-veg.)	"Dialect" III (northern veg.)
'meat'	=	eRacci	kaRi	maamisam, eRacci
'vegetable'	=	maRa-kaRi	kaay, kaRi-kaay	kaay-kaRi
'veg. dish'	=	kuuṭṭu-kaRi	? (kuuṭṭu, poriyal, etc.)	kaRi, kaRamatu
'liquid dish'	=	kozampu	kozampu	kozampu
'side dish'	=	kaRi	?	?
etc.......		.....	.....	.....

Such a description would also make it possible to predict the meanings of certain combinations of terms (e.g. *aaṭṭu-kaRi* = 'mutton curry' in "dialect" I, but 'goat meat' (cooked or uncooked) in "dialect" II; 'meat curry' = *eRacci-kaRi* in "dialect" I, but *kaRi-kozampu* in "dialect" II).

[6]   Conversational data was collected from Madras City, Annamalainagar, and rural parts of Chingleput, South Arcot, Kanyakumari, and Tirunelveli Districts. In addition, informants from Tanjore and Madurai Districts have provided information about their local usage.
[7]   Strictly speaking, each of these "dialects" should be divided into two subtypes according to the data already available. "Dialect" I includes the subtype mentioned above (see Note 5) in which *kaRi* = 'liquid dish'; "dialect" II includes a (low caste) variant in which *kaRi* = 'beef'; and "dialect" III contains two variants: (1) *kaRi* = 'vegetable' (raw or cooked); (2) *kaRi* = 'vegetable dish'.

It is important to note here that the above division into distinct "dialects" on a regional and caste basis refers only to the traditional domestic usage of Tamil speakers. Outside the home, the different "dialects" interact. Following are some specific examples of interaction with regard to the different meanings of this word:

1. A young Harijan man living in Madras City reported that, as a schoolboy, he once asked a Brahmin schoolmate what he was eating for his midday meal. The Brahmin boy replied, *kattri-kaay-kaRi*, which the Harijan boy interpreted as 'brinjal (*kattri-kaay*) and meat'. Knowing that the Brahmin boy did not eat meat, he was puzzled, and said, "How can you take *kaRi*?" to which the response was, "One should not use *kaRi* for that — one should say *pulaal*, *maamisam*, or *eRacci*." (Our informant also stated that these are words that he does not use in normal conversation but has learned mainly from books.) After that, he understood that the word *kaRi* is used differently by others.

2. In a conversation about food involving speakers from several different regions, a speaker from Kanyakumari used *kaRi* to mean 'vegetable' one time, and 'meat' another time. The response he received made it clear that it was understood both times.

3. A colleague from Kanyakumari District states that, although he originally used *kaRi* for 'side dish' and *eRacci* for 'meat'; he changed his usage as a result of living in other parts of Tamilnadu. He now uses *kaRi* for 'meat' and avoids *eRacci* (perhaps because of some pejorative connotations attached to this word outside of Kanyakumari). For 'side dish' he uses *kuuttu*, though this does not necessarily apply to meat dishes.[8]

4. An Iyengar Brahmin doctor (mentioned above in connection with Table 1) stated that *kaRi* is an unusual word, in that it can mean either 'meat' or 'vegetable.' Since village Brahmins invariably reported using *kaRi* to mean 'vegetable' only (or claimed to avoid using the word entirely), it is reasonable to suppose that this multiple meaning originated through contact with members of other (traditionally non-vegetarian) castes.

5. Three mess-servers employed in the vegetarian mess of a large university used *kaRi* in the sense of 'vegetables.' Though belonging to a traditionally non-vegetarian caste, they also used other terms (such as *saatam* 'rice') which are considered to be characteristic of vegetarian castes (see Ramanujan 1968). The presumption is that this usage may have resulted from the context of their employment (possibly also from their desire to impress the interviewer).

---

[8]   M. Shanmugam Pillai, personal communication. (The author takes responsibility for any errors or misinterpretations.)

DISCUSSION

For the purpose of linguistic description, it may be worthwhile to attempt to display the information given above in a dictionary entry format. The following description of *kaRi* attempts to present the different meanings in a hierarchical arrangement, the least marked (i.e. the least contextually restricted) coming first. In this format, the number 1 occurring at any position implies that there is a more marked meaning following: thus, 2 is more marked than 1, 1.2 is more marked than 1.1, etc. As noted, the contextual restrictions apply to social, regional, or linguistic contexts. The meaning given in the first line of the description is (implicitly) present in all contexts; the additional qualifications listed in the following items are added respectively to give the restricted meanings.

	Meaning	Componential analysis
kaRi = 0	'principal food item eaten with rice (or other cereal)'	$\left[\begin{array}{l} + \text{ FOOD} \\ + \text{ PRINCIPAL ITEM} \\ - \text{ CEREAL} \end{array}\right]$
1.1	'meat' (edible animal flesh)	$\left[\begin{array}{l} + \text{ FLESH} \\ \pm \text{ COOKED} \end{array}\right]$
1.2	[domestic usage] 'any animal flesh traditionally eaten by the group'	$\left[\begin{array}{l} + \text{ GROUP} - \\ \text{RESTRICTED} \end{array}\right]$
2	[in collocations] 'vegetable' — cf. *kaay-kaRi, kaRi-kaay*	$\left[\begin{array}{l} + \text{ VEGETABLE} \\ \pm \text{ COOKED} \end{array}\right]$
3.1	[Brahmin or other vegetarian caste, domestic context] 'vegetable'	$\left[\begin{array}{l} + \text{ VEGETABLE} \\ \pm \text{ COOKED} \end{array}\right]$
3.2	[avoided by Iyengar Brahmins] — cf. *kaRamatu*	$\left[\begin{array}{l} \\ + \text{ TABOO} \end{array}\right]$
4.1	[southern] 'prepared dish consisting of meat/vegetable and condiments, eaten as a side dish (liquid, semi-liquid, or dry)'	$\left[\begin{array}{l} + \text{ COOKED} \\ \pm \text{ LIQUID} \end{array}\right]$
4.2	[some southern groups] 'liquid side dish'	$\left[\begin{array}{l} + \text{ COOKED} \\ + \text{ LIQUID} \end{array}\right]$

This description is tentative, for two reasons: first, because the data are not complete for the whole of Tamilnadu (since our geographical distribution is inadequate), and secondly, because the study of other similar examples will probably lead to improvements in the format. Nevertheless, this description clearly contains information which is not present either in the usual dictionary definitions, or in descriptions of individual "dialects" such as those given in Table 2. The dictionary definition gives meanings without any indication of restrictions correlating with social context (see examples in Note 2). The individual "dialect" descriptions indicate the structural relationships of terms. This last type of information is not shown in the description given above, but on the other hand this description does give an overall view which is missing from the "dialect" descriptions. This overall view makes clear the following points:

1. All the meanings given here contain a common core of shared meanings, namely those given in the first line of the description.[9]

2. This common meaning is restricted contextually, in conformity with the eating habits of the group under discussion. Thus, in domestic usage, *kaRi* means 'vegetable' to vegetarians, and 'meat' to non-vegetarians, except in the extreme south, which (along with Kerala) has generalized it in the meaning 'side dish'. In those groups which use *kaRi* in the sense of 'meat', it refers normally to those types of animal flesh considered edible by the individual using the term. Thus, several Harijans stated (in one case without being asked) that *kaRi* in their usage usually refers to beef, whereas members of other castes specifically excluded beef, at least when talking about their own food. On the other hand, our data includes cases of such terms as *yaane-kaRi* 'elephant meat' and *paampu-kaRi* 'snake meat', which occurred in discussions of eating habits in other parts of the world. In this case, then, the effect of social context is similar to that of linguistic context (as in the case of *kaay-kaRi, maRa-kaRi,* which are apparently understood by most Tamil speakers to refer to vegetables).

3. The multiple meanings which appear in the dictionary definition (Note 2), then, are largely in complementary distribution — regionally, socially, and temporally. Thus, in any particular context only one meaning will normally occur. In fact, all individuals who were observed to use the term *kaRi* in more than one of the three main meanings mentioned at the beginning of this article can be accounted for in terms of contact between different "dialects." This is clear with regard to the five instances of interaction presented above, and seems highly likely in the case of those speakers giving meaning (2) in Table 1 ('meat; vegetable'). The only people to give this response were (a) a Brahmin doctor, who clearly had opportunities to hear the domestic usage of other castes (or the usage of fellow students in college and medical school), and (b) three members

---

[9] It is not clear, without additional knowledge of the history of this word, whether the general meaning represents an earlier historical stage. The verb *kaRi* 'bite, chew' (obsolete in Tamil, but still in use in Malayalam) suggests the possibility that the earlier meaning was 'something to chew (along with rice, ragi, etc.).' The early occurrence of *kaRi* 'pepper' suggests the related possibility that *kaRi* is 'the biting one'; cf. the related meanings given in Note 2, as well as Tamil *kaaram* 'pungent taste, chili', and Malayalam *kaaram* 'salt, salt taste'.

of the Naicker caste, who have regular contact with village Brahmins. In fact, of all the three groups in this village, the only one with regular opportunities to observe the household activities of another would be those of intermediate castes who work in or near the houses of Brahmins. Thus, village Brahmins and Harijans are likely to remain unaware of the domestic usage of other castes.

On the other hand, it is also clear that speakers do not "learn" the usage of others in the sense of internalizing that usage. Rather, it would seem that others' usage is added to one's own to create a more complex structure. Thus, instances of "dialect" interaction like those presented above give rise to particular "idiolectal" structures such as the following:

1. educated Harijan living in Madras City:
   kaRi = (1) meat;
              (2) [speaking to vegetarians] vegetable, vegetable dish
2. Kanyakumari speaker in northern Tamilnadu:
   kaRi = (1) side dish;
              (2) vegetable;
              (3) meat
3. Brahmin doctor:
   kaRi = (1) vegetable, vegetable dish;
              (2) [in non-Brahmin or mixed groups] meat

CONCLUSIONS

The above discussion indicates the presence of three levels at which semantic structure can be said to exist:

1. The speech community level — at this most abstract level, the relationship between different meanings and different contexts (social, regional, and linguistic) appear most clearly. In the case of *kaRi*, the only meaning which can be said to be characteristic of the speech community as a whole is that given in the first line of the above description (see Discussion). This meaning exists only implicitly in the individual "dialects." On the other hand, this implicit meaning appears to have persisted over time. Therefore, this is the level of description at which history and description are most clearly relevant to each other.

2. The "dialect" level (see Table 2) — at this level, as de Saussure put it, *"tout se tient"*; i.e. everything holds together because of the way in which terms are opposed to each other. The words "dialect" and "idiolect" have been given in inverted commas in this paper because we wish to deny the implication of discreteness which is often imputed to these concepts. One of the main points which this paper has tried to make is that a great deal is lost when the description is limited to these supposedly isolable entities. This is not to say that individual dialects are not

worth describing, but simply that they are often, in some respects, unintelligible fragments of a larger whole.

3. The "idiolect" level — the structures resulting from an individual's experience with speakers of other "dialects." Given certain information about the cultural context of such interaction (e.g. the fact that only members of certain castes have occasion to hear members of other castes discussing food), most of these structures are probably predictable on the basis of those existing on levels (1) and (2). (The detailed study of such structures is possibly of interest in the study of group interaction in a society.) On the other hand, both (1) and (2) need to be described in order to present the full picture of semantic structure.

Traditional lexicographical definitions are usually on level (1). When they consist (as they often do) of mere lists of meanings, they are not particularly informative about linguistic usage. An implication of cases like the one presented here is that cases of multiple meaning deserve careful scrutiny to see if they may possibly conceal complementation of meanings. A further implication is that descriptivists need to take care to be clear about which level of structure they are trying to describe.

REFERENCES

BURROW, T., M. B. EMENEAU
    1961   *A Dravidian etymological dictionary.* Oxford: Oxford University Press.
DE SAUSSURE, F.
    1949   *Cours de linguistique generale.* Paris: Payot.
GUNDERT, (REV.) H.
    1962   *A Malayalam and English dictionary* (second edition). Kottayam (Kerala): Sahitya Co-operative Society. (Originally published 1872.)
RAMANUJAN, A. K.
    1968   "The structure of variation: a study in caste dialects," in *Structure and change in Indian society.* Edited by M. Singer and B. S. Cohn. Chicago: Aldine.
Tamil Lexicon 1924–1939
    1962ff.   Published under the authority of the University of Madras. Mylapore (Madras): The Madras Law Journal Press.

Perspectives on Sociolinguistics in India

P. B. PANDIT

The number and variety of languages in India have been a subject of major interest since the beginning of linguistic studies in the nineteenth century. During the great phase of the genetic classification of the languages of the world, the languages of India provided ample material for the comparativist. There are numerous languages of the Indo-European, Dravidian, Tibeto-Burman and Austro-Asiatic families spoken in India; moreover, no language of the Dravidian family is spoken outside the Indian subcontinent.

Sir George Grierson's monumental survey (1967), undertaken in the last decade of the nineteenth century and completed in 1927, encompasses all the language families represented in India and gives samples, descriptions and vocabularies of selected items of the numerous languages surveyed; it records a total of 179 languages and 544 dialects.

This vast collection became a veritable language museum; much work of grouping and subgrouping of the language families in India has been done on the basis of evidence available from the survey. Detailed studies, especially of the individual Indo-Aryan and Dravidian languages, have been published. At the same time, reciprocal influences from one language family to another have also been noticed; these consist of borrowings of lexical items and phonological and syntactic patterns.

A large number of loanwords in Sanskrit have been identified as having come from Dravidian or Munda sources. These borrowings suggested the existence of language contacts in the earlier stages of the linguistic history of India; borrowings in the grammatical systems of these languages have also been noted (Bloch 1932; Emeneau 1956).

This diffusion and convergence of linguistic traits in the subcontinent has been correctly interpreted by Emeneau as evidence for considering India as a linguistic area. Studies in typology with reference to the languages in India (Ramanujan 1968; Andronov 1964) also support this view of India as a linguistic area. The concept of linguistic area was mainly a corrective to the exclusive concern of the comparativist in establishing language families; the linguistic area concept is an addition to the perspective of the comparativist and helps him identify and account for more complex cases of language change.

Along with the diversity and variety of the languages of India, the complexity of its communication networks was also noted by the authors of early gazetteers and by Grierson. That people of different social strata have different modes of expression and different styles of speech is not a peculiarly Indian phenomenon but these shrewd observers, who were also administrators, noticed that the contours of these differences were significantly different in India. Grierson has observed:

The literary or Government language of any tract is widely different from the language actually spoken by the people. In some cases this is only a question of dialect, but in others the polite language learned by Europeans and by natives who wish to converse with Europeans is totally distinct both in origin and in construction from that used by the same natives in their homes . . . Nowhere in Hindustan is the language of the village the same as the language of the court and of the school. This is true to a certain extent all over the world, but in India the difference between the two languages is peculiarly great . . . (Mitra 1969:125).

These writers were not concerned with problems of language standardization or of literacy, nor were they concerned with studying the patterns of communication in a multilingual country; nevertheless, their characterization of the linguistic situation in India is meaningful in the light of the current sociolinguistic studies in India.

Language identity, i.e. mother-tongue identity in a multilingual country, is expressed as a concomitant part of simply asserting one's identity with a caste group, a religious group, a regional group and/or any other tangible group in the community; the language label thus becomes an index of loyalty; language labels cannot be directly related to formal features of language structure.

One of the major problems in the census operations in India was to identify the large number of language labels recorded by census enumerators in terms of formally identifiable groups and subgroups of languages. The census superintendents knew that this was not an easy task and they also noticed that caste labels of dialects do not necessarily mean different dialects but they are tags of one's identity. J. S. Bains, in his *General report on the census of India 1891,* observed under the section "The Distribution of the Population According to Mother Tongue":

The instructions issued regarding language ran as follows: "Enter here the language ordinarily spoken in the household of the parents, whether it be that of the place of enumeration or not."

The question put to those enumerated was no doubt simple enough but even to the most optimistic Superintendent of Census, this is no reason for expecting a straight answer. In accordance with the general tendency noted in the introductory portion of this chapter, the first impulse, in many cases, is to return the name of the caste as that of the language. For example, the potter gives "potterish," the tanner "tannerish" or the weaver "weaverish," as his mother tongue, especially if he be either a member of a large caste or a stranger to the locality where he is being enumerated (Mitra 1969:310).

These early observers were cautious, they were also sensitive to the complexity of the situation; they understood that this exclusiveness was nominal rather than substantive. The sociolinguistic work of the last two decades, unfortunately, did not build on these insights. The subjective exclusiveness of the castes concerned has so thoroughly misled the objective social sciences that the change and fluidity of the situation are missed in a static photographic (behaviorist?) view of our empiricism.

The sociolinguists were no exception to this general hazard and hence the enigma of the Indian social situation. In such a context, the linguistic studies followed the surface responses rather than taking a clue from the complexity of behavior to explore the underlying network with its correspondences in the economic, political and even technological changes in an organic, functioning society. The study of "language in society" thus took a path full of pitfalls and only now have we learned enough to see the pitfalls so that in the new perspective they can be avoided.

The three major areas of sociolinguistic studies in the 1950s and the 1960s have been: the "caste" dialects, bilingualism, and the standard and colloquial varieties.

THE CASTE DIALECTS

The caste became a focus of the early work in the study of social dialects in India in the 1950s. Fieldwork on caste dialects in northern India as well as southern India was focused on identifying linguistic correlates of the caste groups in Indian society. In his fieldwork at Khalapur, Gumperz (1958) distinguished different linguistic groups in the village on the basis of phonological speech differences, which matched with the hierarchies of the touchable castes and the untouchable castes.

This striking fit of speech variations and caste hierarchy in a north Indian village led to a series of similar studies of caste dialects. Bright (1960a) compared two Kannada dialects of Bangalore District: the Brahmin dialect and the non-Brahmin dialect of the Okkaliga community. Bright (1960b) proceeded further to inquire into the correlation between the amount of linguistic change manifested in a dialect and the social status of the people who speak it; in other words, "in what caste dialects are the more archaic features to be found?"

A comparison between the Brahmin and Okkaliga (non-Brahmin) dialect of Kannada showed that the Brahmin Kannada is conservative in a less conscious type of change i.e. in phonology and morphology, while it is innovative in a more conscious type of change, i.e. in borrowing and semantic extensions. Bright has considered literacy of the Brahmin as a possible factor in the retention of archaisms.

He supports this observation by comparing the situation of the Brahmin and non-Brahmin dialects in Tulu. Tulu is located to the west of the Kannada-speaking area; it does not have a writing system; literacy among Tulu exists only for their second language, i.e. Sanskrit, Kannada and English. Brahmin and non-Brahmin dialects of Tulu show phonemic change in approximately equal degree; this supports the hypothesis that although "conscious" linguistic change comes largely from higher social strata, "unconscious" change is natural in all strata where the literacy factor does not intervene.

McCormack (1960:79–91) observed three dialects of conversational Kannada in Dharwar and the adjoining districts of Belgaum and Bijapur, corresponding to three social classes, the Brahmin, the non-Brahmin and the Harijan. McCormack, for the first time in the study of social dialects in India, quantified his data. He gave the recognition scores and in these scores the Brahmins were correctly identified by two panels of school teachers and college students.

While the Brahmins were correctly identified, the backward-class speakers were "almost never correctly identified." The reason for this state of affairs was that some urbanized backward-class speakers, when they speak to members of other social classes, borrow elements from the speech of the upper classes. McCormack's study brings out the sharp ranking of differences between the Brahmins and non-Brahmins.

In his study of Tamil dialects, Ramanujan (1968) has also brought out this major dichotomy between the Brahmin and the non-Brahmin speech, the high and the low, in Tamil. He has observed that the dialect differences are used as expressions of social identity; he has made an interesting observation that many of the non-Brahmin forms are constantly used in Brahmin homes when one is angry with a child or when one is ironic or pejorative.

Ramanujan has also mentioned that besides the Brahmin/non-Brahmin contrasts in speech, there are other contrasts such as urban/rural, educated/uneducated, Hindu/Muslim, but he has not taken them into consideration, as no exact information was available on such matters. Ramanujan has noticed that both the dialects, the Iyengar (Brahmin) and the Mudaliyar (non-Brahmin), do innovate, but in different directions: the Brahmin toward differentiation and the non-Brahmin toward generalization of paradigmatic patterns.

These studies indicate that caste is an important parameter in the structure of variation; it provides a convenient pigeonhole in assigning speech differences to the high and the low in the society. But in what way does a "caste dialect" differ from a social dialect? In their pioneering essay (1960) Ferguson and Gumperz observed:

> The total range of speech diversity within a speech community, i.e. the actual language distance between all the varieties found there, is a function of the density of intergroup communication. In societies like our modern American one where social class is fluid and mass communication media are highly developed and shared by most, we would expect the range of variation to be relatively small. Differences would most frequently appear on the level of phonetics or the lexicon but rarely affect the fundamental phonological or morphological structure of the language. In Asia, however, where communication is severely limited by ritual restrictions we would expect these differences to be much greater (1960:9–10).

The assumption that differences — variations — are symptomatic of barriers in communication cannot be sustained. There is no evidence to show that verbal communication is restricted across caste boundaries in a village community or an urban community. Pandit (1969a) has suggested that variation may be interpreted as functional, i.e. it may facilitate communication: if a Brahmin can maintain his social distance by the choice of a variant in his speech, he could have no hesitation in talking with a non-Brahmin; his speech carries sufficient social identification and he is in no danger of losing his caste while talking to a non-Brahmin.

Speech variation is the result of verbal interaction, it is symptomatic of communication rather than of its absence. Variation is functional, and the social dialects need not be considered as symptomatic of barriers in intergroup communication. Ramanujan (1968:471) has rightly observed "The dialect differences appear to be used as expressions of social identity"; they are not results of social isolation. Caste, moreover, is not the only parameter; Pandit (1969a:207–228) has shown in his study of parameters of variation, that high caste/low caste, literate/ illiterate, rural/urban are also relevant factors in understanding the speech variation. Gumperz in a later essay (1969b) has also accepted the position:

> ... caste per se is not sufficient to explain the facts of language distribution, for the anthropological definition of caste as an endogamous group does not account for the linguistic findings. Frequency of contact similarly fails as an explanation since the most divergent group, the sweepers, work in upper-caste homes from sun-up to sundown, and serve as carriers of gossip from one household to another. Only a more detailed analysis of social interaction provides an answer.

BILINGUALISM

A characteristic feature of the Indian linguistic situation is its grassroots bilingualism and multilingualism. Speakers of different languages and dialects live side by side and maintain their divergent speech habits. This situation of stable bilingualism is different, say, from the bilingual situation of immigrant populations in Europe and America, where the second generation of immigrant populations give up their mother tongues and accept and adopt the dominant language of the host country.

In India, on the contrary, a second-generation speaker of Gujarati or Kannada outside his native state maintains his language no matter in what part of India he has settled down; he uses Gujarati or Kannada in domestic settings and uses the colloquial form of the local language in other settings. This is true of all the major languages of India; languages are maintained by second- or third-generation speakers — even beyond three generations.

An Indian is not compelled to give up his food habits, dress habits or speech habits to become acceptable and to feel secure in alien surroundings in the Indian context. Perhaps some underlying homogeneity allows him to exhibit heterogeneity at the surface. As a result of such language maintenance, each state (linguistic state!) in India is a multilingual mosaic. The study of speech variation and social stratification in such stable multilingual contexts assumes different dimensions; choice of language also becomes an important variable.

The notion of a dominant standard language is relatively new in the Indian situation; different languages occupy different roles in the routines of a town dweller in India. The linguistic profile of a citizen of Bombay, if his mother tongue is Gujarati, could be as follows. The Gujarati businessman is likely to speak a Kathiawari dialect (of peninsular Gujarat) in his domestic settings (the enterprising Kathiawaris settled in Bombay even before the turn of the century). Marathi being the local language and the language of the vendors, he will use colloquial Marathi in the local market where he goes out every morning to buy vegetables.

He will use a form of lingua franca Hindustani at the suburban railway station, where he catches his daily 9:35 local to Bombay city. Hindustani is used in all non-elite pan-Indian contexts and the railway platform is a pan-Indian setting (one does not speak in Hindustani to an airstewardess, because, though it is a pan-Indian setting, it is an elite context!).

When he reaches his place of business (and if he is a spice merchant), he will use Kacchi, because it is the language of the spice trade; in the evening, he may see a film, which, again, is a pan-Indian context where standard colloquial Hindustani is used; he may read a newspaper in standard colloquial Gujarati, and if he is educated (at least up to higher secondary standard), he may also see an English film, listen to the cricket commentary on radio in English, and (if he can afford it!) send his children to an English medium school.

Of the four Indo-Aryan languages he uses in his daily routine, it is possible that he has formally studied only one, his mother tongue, at the school; other languages are acquired in the contexts of situation; his "knowledge" of these languages is limited to colloquial use in these contexts. Such situations have brought about a great convergence of language use at the colloquial level.

Multilingualism does not create a barrier in communication; one does not have to "give up" one's language in such a situation. Instead of considering language maintenance as a major problem for investigation, the Indian sociolinguist may ask the question, why do people give up languages?

THE STANDARD AND THE COLLOQUIAL

There is one situation in which languages are given up: with the development of a dominant language. A dominant language can be defined as one whose speakers do not have to learn or use other languages in different contexts. In a large tract of northern India, from Rajasthan to Bihar, a culture language, Hindi, has been superimposed on a variety of different colloquial languages spoken in this region. Hindi has become the dominant language in this region. It is the language of the school and the administration; with the spread of education and literacy, second-generation speakers of local varieties on which Hindi has been superimposed are giving up their local varieties.

There is a similar situation regarding the languages of the backward tribes in rural India. These are some of the nonliterary Indo-Aryan and Dravidian languages and most of the languages of the Austric and Tibeto-Burman families. Speakers of these languages are economically and socially backward. The local literary language exerts the pressure of a dominant language on most of these varieties. With the spread of literacy and education, there are greater chances of the adoption of the dominant language by the second generation of the educated in the tribal population.

The development of standard languages and dominant languages and the problems arising out of such situations require greater attention on the part of students of sociolinguistics in India. The region of northern India where Hindi is the culture language also happens to be the region having the highest rate of illiteracy in the country. One could hazard the guess that the distance between the school language and the home language may be the main cause of a large number of school dropouts. New literates in this situation also lapse into illiteracy because the chances of maintaining a school language in rural settings are meager. There is no reinforcement from the environment because the local variety is quite different from the superposed variety.

The distance between the standard and the colloquial varieties of Indian languages has been discussed in a number of studies. These studies describe various types of diglossic situations (Ferguson and Gumperz 1960). The distance between the ceremonial and the casual, the formal and the informal, may be related to the assertion of the Sanskritic tradition through the process of standardization. In some parts of south India, in the Tamil-speaking regions, antagonism to this tradition is equally prominently noticeable as contributing to the same process from the other end. This development of the emerging standards adds a new dimension to the understanding of speech variation and social stratification; one has to inquire how the norms and the behavior of different social groups impinge on speech variation.

Stable bilingual contexts account for a number of "mixed languages" in India: languages such as Malvi (contiguous to Gujarati and Rajasthani), Khandeshi (contiguous to Marathi and Gujarati, Halbi (contiguous to Marathi, Chattisgarhi and Oriya), and many others have been recorded as mixed languages, but information regarding the patterns of their uses in different social contexts is not available.

Gumperz and Wilson (1971) have shown that in bilingual contexts even if the two languages are quite diverse in their standard varieties, the two languages develop a word-to-word translatability, e.g. Marathi (Indo-Aryan) and Kannada (Dravidian) spoken in bilingual areas have developed such translatability at the colloquial level.

Similarly, Pandit (1972:1–46) has drawn attention to a bilingual situation in Tamilnadu: all speakers of Saurashtri in Tamilnadu are bilingual. They speak Saurashtri in domestic settings and Tamil in all other settings; a very significant convergence of the rules of syntax of colloquial Tamil and Saurashtri has taken place in this situation.

Language maintenance in multilingual communities provides ample evidence that language distance is not absolute but is a function of intensity of contact and social context. In the case of Tamil-Saurashtri bilingualism, it was noted that a native speaker of Tamil was able to understand and speak Saurashtri within the short period of six weeks, while a native speaker of Gujarati (historically related to the Saurashtri) could not achieve comparable proficiency even after six months of fieldwork in Saurashtri; this supplies further evidence to the amount of grammatical convergence that takes place in such contact situations.

The bilingual's grammar is comparable to the diglossic situation where two languages, instead of two styles of one language, participate in a dominant–dominated relationship in a stable bilingual situation. In the bilingual's grammar, the choice of language, rather than the choice of style, is the significant variable.

Saurashtri has a Tamil grammar and an Indo-Aryan lexicon, a situation which can be identified by the conventional label of a "creole," but this would be a creole without a pidgin! The common belief regarding the genesis of pidgin as a halfway meeting of the civilized and the barbarian is too imaginative to be true. Moreover, the notion that creole "fills out a pidgin" also requires some scrutiny in view of such cases of Saurashtri as a creole without a pidgin.

Pidgin and creole are merely labels of contact situations rather than labels of language types. Investigation of different types of bilingual and multilingual situations and study of the so-called "mixed languages" in India provides a better understanding of the process of creolization.

MOTHER TONGUE AND NATIVE SPEECH

The census operations in monolingual countries (or even those with one dominant language) and in multilingual countries collect and classify census data under the rubric of mother tongue, but these data are not easily comparable. In a monolingual country, "mother tongue" may simply reflect language usage, while in a multilingual country, "mother tongue" is intimately related to the identity of the speaker.

The question of mother tongue in a multilingual country is not of form but of function. Consider the situation in northern India during the last two decades: the region from Bihar to Rajasthan, including the states of Bihar, Uttar Pradesh, Himachal Pradesh, Haryana, Madhya Pradesh and Rajasthan, where Hindi as the superposed variety is the language of the school and the administration. The three major languages in Bihar are Magahi, Maithili, and Bhojpuri, which are not, from the point of view of linguistic relationship, "dialects" of Hindi, though the dominant language in Bihar is Hindi. An educated speaker who speaks Magahi at home likes or chooses to return Hindi rather than Magahi as his mother tongue. He emphasizes his identity with Hindi rather than with the Bengali of the neighboring state of West Bengal. At the same time, subregional interests have come to the forefront within certain regions which are under the umbrella of Hindi, and these prompt the native educated speaker to identify himself with the local variety rather than with the superposed variety. Thus, an educated Maithili-speaker may return Maithili rather than Hindi as his mother tongue. Means of mass communication and modes of political propaganda have reached not only the educated and the literate but also the uneducated and the illiterate, so this distinction of the literate and the illiterate and the educated and the uneducated may not be very relevant now; language identity has assumed a symbolic significance. There is one more dimension to the relations between the superposed variety and the local varieties. Here, the superposed variety has two styles: Hindi and Urdu. Hindi style emphasizes the relation with the Sanskritic literary tradition and with the Sanskritic writing system, and Urdu cherishes its relation with the Perso-Arabic literary tradition and the Perso-Arabic writing system. A speaker of any local variety in this northern zone thus makes one more choice of his overall identity either with Hindi or with Urdu, quite unperturbed by what his local variety is like. Language use and language identity have to be interpreted in the context of such situations.

Punjab offers another interesting situation of changing identities. During the British period, Urdu was the superposed variety in the northern part of the subcontinent from Peshawar to Delhi. The local varieties were Dardic dialects, Dogri, various Pahari dialects such as Kului, Mandiali (spoken in the new state of Himachal Pradesh, Mandiali is now called Himachali), Panjabi, and Bangru (spoken in the state of Haryana, now called Haryanvi). Urdu was the language of education and elegance, and the Perso-Arabic script was the preferred writing system for all sections of the population which consisted of the Jats, Hindus, Muslims, and Sikhs. The Sanskritic writing system and the *gurumukhi* writing system were restricted in use — limited to the Hindu and Sikh religious ritual. After the partition, the identity of Sikhs as a group found its expression in the extended use of Panjabi language and *gurumukhi* writing system (notice that while other Indo-Aryan languages were introduced as courses of study in the universities of India in the 1930s, Panjabi was introduced as a course of study at the M.A. level as late as the 1950s, i.e. after the partition). At the same time the Panjabi-speaking Hindus of the north (in the state of Panjab of the British period) and the Bangru-speaking Jats of Haryana, accentuating their differences from the Sikhs, have identified themselves with the speakers of Hindi. The census returns in these regions, during the last one hundred years, provide ample evidence of this choice of a "mother tongue" according to the changing loyalties of the speakers.

Similar situations are found in various multilingual and bilingual areas in India; speakers of Kannada–Konkani–Marathi and Tulu, speakers of Gujarati–Kacchi and Malvi–Rajasthani–Gujarati, exercise their choices of a "mother tongue" with reference to their identity rather than with reference to the patterns of language use. The same is true of tribal areas dominated by one or the other languages of administration and authority. Khubchandani (1972a) has proposed a very useful distinction between "mother tongue" and "native speech," as follows:

native speech: the first speech acquired by the child (claiming some bearing on "intuitive" competence) mother tongue: an individual's regard for a language as his own (guided by one's allegiance to a particular "tradition").

There is an interesting consequence of this identification. Various standard languages as idealized "mother tongues" are distinctly kept apart, each drawing on a different literary tradition (e.g. standard literary Hindi draws its vocabulary from the Sanskrit tradition, standard literary Urdu from the Persian tradition), while the colloquial varieties at the local levels maintain the speech continuum. The identity pressures demand a discrete demarcation of loyalties, a clear declaration of we and they, while the communication at colloquial levels results in convergence of speech patterns.

There has been a monolingual stereotype at the back of the early sociolinguistic studies of the Indian situation; multilingualism has been considered as a deviation and a barrier in communication. Multilingual countries in fact have long traditions of communication across languages. Study of speech in multilingual countries will not only be a contribution to sociolinguistics but it would, by its feedback effects, deepen our understanding of the so-called monolingual situations, the archetype of theorizing. Language is the unit of study for a linguist, but it is a very plastic and malleable part of society, and hence it is a variable among many other variables that make up a social and cultural complex.

REFERENCES

ANDRONOV, M.
1964   On the typological similarity of New Indo-Aryan and Dravidian. *Indian Linguistics* 25:119–126.
BLOCH, JULES
1932   Une tournure dravidienne en marathe. *Bulletin de Societe Linguistique de Paris* 33:299–306.
BRIGHT, WILLIAM
1960a   "Linguistic change in some Indian caste dialects," in *Linguistic diversity in south Asia*. Edited by Charles A. Ferguson and John J. Gumperz. Supplement to *International Journal of American Linguistics* 26(3): 19–26.
1960b Social dialect and language history. *Current Anthropology* 1:424–425.
EMENEAU, MURRAY
1956   India as a linguistic area. *Language* 32:3–16.
FERGUSON, CHARLES A., JOHN J. GUMPERZ, *editors*
1960   *Linguistic diversity in South Asia*. Supplement to *International Journal of American Linguistics* 26(3).
GRIERSON, GEORGE ABRAHAM
1967   *Linguistic survey of India,* eleven volumes. Delhi. (Originally published 1927).

GUMPERZ, JOHN J.
1958 Dialect differences and social stratification in a North Indian village. *American Anthropologist* 60:668–682.
1964 "Hindi–Punjabi codeswitching in Delhi," in *Proceedings of the 9th International Congress of Linguists*. Edited by Horace G. Lunt, 1115–1124. The Hague: Mouton.
1964 "Linguistic and social interaction in two communities," in *Ethnography of communication*. Edited by John J. Gumperz and Dell Hymes. *American Anthropologist* 66(6):part 2, 137–153.
1969a "How can we describe and measure the behavior of bilingual groups" in *Description and measurement of bilingualism*. Edited by L. G. Kelly, 241–284. Toronto: University of Toronto Press.
1969b "Sociolinguistics in South Asia," in *Current Trends in Linguistics, Linguistics in South Asia*, volume five. Edited by Thomas A. Sebeok, 597–606. The Hague: Mouton.

GUMPERZ, JOHN J., ROBERT WILSON
1971 "Convergence and creolisation: a case from Indo-Aryan/Dravidian border in India," in *Pidginisation and creolisation*. Edited by Dell H. Hymes, 151–167. London: Cambridge University Press.

KHUBCHANDANI, LACHMAN
1972a Concept of mother-tongue (mimeo). Indian Institute of Advanced Study, Simla.
1972b Language factor in census (mimeo). Indian Institute of Advanced Study, Simla.

MITRA A.
1969 *Inquiries into the spoken languages of India*. Census of India 1961, volume one, part XI-C(i). Language Monographs 1.

McCORMACK, WILLIAM
1960 "Social dialects in Dharwar," in *Linguistic diversity in South Asia*. Edited by Charles A. Ferguson and John J. Gumperz. Supplement to *International Journal of American Linguistics*. 26(3):79–91.

PANDIT, P. B.
1963 Sanskritic clusters and caste dialects. *Indian Linguistics* 24:70–79.
1969a "Parameters of speech variation in an Indian community," in *Language and society in India*. Transactions of Indian Institute of Advanced Study, volume eight, 207–229.
1969b Comments on J. J. Gumperz's paper (1969a:255–256) "How can we describe and measure the behaviour of bilingual groups?" in *Description and measurement of bilingualism*.
1972 *India as a sociolinguistic area*. Poona: University of Poona.

RAMANUJAN, A. K.
1968 "The structure of variation: a study in caste dialects," in *Structure and change in Indian society*. Edited by M. Singer and B. S. Cohn, 461–474. Chicago: Aldine.

A Demographic Typology for Hindi, Urdu, Panjabi Speakers in South Asia

LACHMAN M. KHUBCHANDANI

Language returns of multilingual societies can be characterized as "icebergs"; much more is hidden than revealed through the sum of individuals' declarations. In a plural society like India — where a community is intricately segmented by religion, caste, status, occupational strata, age, sex, etc. — the interlanguage boundaries have remained fluid in many regions. Until a few decades ago, one's mother-tongue group was not generally a very important criterion in distinguishing oneself from others sharply. This fluidity of language is revealed through the patterns of speech behavior operating across language boundaries. Such communities are not much conscious of the speech characteristics which bind them to one language or the other. People do not associate speech labels precisely with grammatical or pronunciation stereotypes, and standardization and other propriety controls in verbal behavior generally tend to be loose. Consequently, it is often difficult to determine whether a particular discourse belongs to language A or language B.

The notion of "language" is not the same to a speaker as to a linguist. For a speaker, language is an acquired cultural trait. To him, it is more of symbolic significance in identifying himself with a group than its purely formal criteria, which are the *a priori* considerations for a linguist in determining whether a particular speech can find its place within the orbit of a known language or it is altogether a separate language. In linguistic and educational jargon, the term "mother tongue" and "native speech" are often used indistinguishably, which leads to some indeterminacy when applied in different contexts. The term NATIVE SPEECH can be distinguished as the FIRST speech acquired in infancy, through which the child gets socialized. It claims some bearing on "intuitive" competence, and potentially it can be individually identifiable. The term MOTHER TONGUE is mainly categorized by one's allegiance to a particular "tradition," and it is societally identifiable. In the ingroup/outgroup dichotomy, a language which a group or an individual regard as their OWN is accepted as their mother tongue (Khubchandani 1972). In this respect, "language" can be regarded as close to "mother tongue." It represents an institutional reality, being space-and-time-bound to a specific society or culture. A society may have certain overt cultural traits, the interpretation of which does not cause much ambiguity in a particular group, region or country, as a result of implicit social awareness or explicit standardization efforts; e.g. identity of standard languages in Europe. Lack of standardization or overtness of a particular trait leads to fluidity in interpreting abstract attributes — the selection of which is largely based on various prestige factors, reference group pressures and the sociopolitical climate. Response to such attributes may be a product of subjective evaluation conditioned by the degree of awareness in a group with which the claimant desires to be affiliated: e.g. mother tongue in plural societies in the Indian context.

Identification through a particular LANGUAGE LABEL is very much a matter of social awareness on the part of an individual. It is a categorically determined abstract attribute, not necessarily having an exact parallel with structural characteristics in one's speech matrix. It is the most visible mark of differentiation and of collective cohesion. A common language label gives a sense of common feeling, as in the case of other subjective traits such as customs, traditions, faith, nationality. In a simple monolingual situation or in a well-formalized speech group, mother tongue returns may run parallel to prevailing native speech patterns. Whereas, in a complex pluralistic society, or also where speech conventions are relatively less stabilized, seeking an exact parallel between the two may be quite misleading.

Language statistics are often differently interpreted by authorities and pressure groups in many multilingual countries. Indian Census enumeration of the last few decades bears the traces of excitement experienced in multilingual societies over the language issue — particularly during the post-war phase of de-colonization, during which Asia and Africa became keenly aware of their linguistic needs in a modern world. In this context, India has been regarded as a "sociolinguistic giant" (Ferguson 1966) which poses a great challenge to the agencies concerned with social planning. An inevitable measure of fluidity in mother-tongue returns is noticed in certain regions in India and Pakistan. One finds the language question in every decennial census, beginning from 1881, giving rise to various doubts and misinterpretations in the minds of people of different regions, and also intriguing the British administrators who were "alien" to relatively fluid segmentation patterns in language behavior of Indian society. Fluctuations in language returns of the North-Central region in India reveal that speaker's declarations are not necessarily conditioned by their native speech, but are guided mainly by the trends of social identification at a particular juncture of time.

In the 1912 Census, Gait reports (1913:319–320) three-fold difficulties in language enumeration, particularly concerning the North-Central region:

1. The Aryan languages of India have no hard and fast boundaries between them.

2. The want of precision by the people themselves in describing the dialects spoken by them.

Over a large part of Upper India the only general term in use is Hindi — the language of Hind — a comprehensive word which includes at least three distinct languages, Western Hindi, Eastern Hindi and Bihari . . . Lahnda in NWFP[North Western Frontier Province] is commonly regarded as a form of Panjabi, but it is quite distinct from that language.

3. Political considerations:

[These] have given more trouble than heretofore. . . . Amongst many educated Hindus, there is a tendency to belittle the great differences which actually exist between the different parts of the Empire; and it is sometimes alleged that there is practically only one language spoken throughout northern India. . . . On the other hand, Muhammadans often declare that Urdu, the Persianized form of Hindo-stani is the language, not only of their co-religionists, but also of a large number of Hindus in the north of India.

Regarding the 1931 Census, Hutton also expresses the difficulty of distinguishing various dialects of Hindustani, classified by Grierson as different languages. He comments: ". . . generally speaking one dialect fades into another by indistinct and gradual changes so that it is very difficult to draw a hard and fast line" (1933:355–356).

A sense of annoyance on the part of the British administration concerning Indian language fluidity finds expression in Gait's Census Report (1913) thus:

[In the United Provinces,] as in 1901, there were undoubtedly steps taken to cause the returns of language to be falsified: complaints were common that on one side the Hindu enumerators were recording Hindi whether the persons enumerated Hindi or not, and on the other side that Muhammadan enumerators were acting in the same way with regard to Urdu. . . . Although the great majority of Census Officers honestly did their best to describe accurately the languages of the people enumerated by them, it sometimes happened that the entries in the schedules were vitiated by this political bias. . . . It is not too much to say that the figures as they stand are evidence only of the strength or weakness of the agitation in particular districts. Simply because they refused to define their terms before they argued, or rather because they would not take the trouble to understand the terms as used by the census authorities, the controversialists, who were really quarrelling about the respective merits of certain styles as vehicles of instruction, succeeded in utterly falsifying a set of important statistics relating to something entirely different (p. 320).

Hutton (1933) also echoes the same handicap:

The distinction between Eastern and Western Hindi in the Central Provinces and Central India, and between Lahnda and Panjabi in the Punjab was more than the census enumerators could grasp. As for the enumerated, each of course very properly considers his Hindi to be the true Hindi and is not prepared to qualify it by an adjective of locality implying that it is merely a dialect. Too much precision must not therefore be expected of figures representing the use of Eastern and Western Hindi and of Lahnda and Panjabi, as it was necessary in the course of compilation to assign large numbers of speakers of Hindi, and similarly of Panjabi, more or less arbitrarily to one or the other group according to locality, since the returns were inevitably unqualified.

In the case of the spoken language admittedly the use of terms Urdu and Hindi do give rise to embittered controversy between two schools which are generally speaking co-terminous with Hinduism and Islam in religion. In point of practice it is impossible to define any boundaries between Urdu and Hindi as spoken, since the difference consists merely in a preference for a Persian or for a Sanskrit vocabulary, and as an illiterate man uses only the language of common speech it is generally the bias of the enumerator which would determine the category of his return. As far as spoken language goes therefore it was decided, as in 1921, to use the term Hindustani only in the return for the United provinces and with the omission of the script of literacy the use of the term Urdu disappeared. This disappearance caused some searching of heart among Muslims who did not realise that the reason for omitting the term Urdu was that no general record of the script was being made at the Census (pp. 355–356).

It is evident that the British insistence on clearcut categorization and monistic "instant," frequently vacillating decisions concerning languages and scripts — often arbitrarily just to bring some order into the "chaotic" diversity, or at times for serving imperial interests (distributing favors or prejudices to different interest groups through language concessions or constraints) — gave rise to a good deal of suspicion in the minds of people regarding language returns in the Census.

VACILLATING RETURNS

In such a fluid situation one comes across the cases where the speakers testify to different names for the same language at different times. An outstanding example is Khari Boli. Not even mentioned in the 1951 Census, in 1961 almost six million speakers from Rajasthan state reported Khari Boli as their mother tongue, thus foresaking their previous declarations of "Hindi proper." On the other hand, declarations of Braj Bhaka (a dialect of Hindi) speakers in Uttar Pradesh and Rajasthan States show phenomenal decline in preference for "Hindi proper." In the Swai Madhopur district in Rajasthan, 40,558 Braj Bhakha speakers reported in the 1951 Census are reduced to a mere 1,101 speakers in 1961. As seen in Table 1, a breakdown of mother-tongue declarations classified under Hindi in four Rajasthan districts shows this to be characteristic.

Table 1. Hindi speakers in four districts of Rajasthan during 1951–1961

Districts	Total speakers of Hindi		Increase (%)	Mother tongues classified under Hindi (with number of speakers)
Bharatpur	1951	597,868		Hindi 523,582, Braj B 74,286
	1961	1,086,842	81.8	Khari B 917,074, Hindi 124,080, Braj B 45,688
Swai Madhopur	1951	480,573		Hindi 440,015, Braj B 40,558
	1961	809,213	68.4	Khari B 808,112, Braj B 1,101
Ajmer	1951	133,773		Hindi 124,841, Braj B 8,932
	1961	276,764	106.7	Khari B 207,636, Hindi 68,918, Bharatpuri 119, Braj B 69, Kankari 16, Deswali 6
Bikaner	1951	16,372		Hindi 16,198, Braj B 174
	1961	36,960	131.2	Khari B 34,021, Hindi 2,795, Deswali 93, Kankari 26, Braj B 25

One may conveniently interpret from these figures that the Braj Bhakha dialect is becoming extinct and being replaced by standard Hindi, also known as Khari Boli. However, in many districts of Uttar Pradesh and Rajasthan, one notices that speakers continue to use Braj Bhakha grammatical patterns in day-to-day communication. It seems that many Braj speakers now prefer to report their mother tongue as simply "Hindi" without signifying their specific dialect. Those speaking a variety of standard Hindi, however, show the tendency to be specific by declaring their mother tongue "Khari Boli" — presumably in order to distinguish themselves from the Braj speakers, who seem to prefer the umbrella term "Hindi."

In many such instances oscillation in mother-tongue declarations reveals a shift in social identification under changed circumstances. Change in language label does not necessarily signify change in speech habits. This displacement in language label is interpreted by demographers (Bose 1969) as "linguistic displacement," which gives the impression that the use of one language is being abandoned in favor of another. The term "Hindustani/Hindostani" was very current in pre-Independence India, representing colloquial Urdu or colloquial Hindi. The 1951 and 1961 Census declarations reveal the rapid pace of decline in the number of speakers claiming Hindustani in most of the Indian states. Comparison of

the figures of Hindustani, Urdu and Hindi from the 1931, 1951 and 1961
Censuses records the oscillatory trends shown in Table 2 (no language
Census was conducted in 1941 due to World War II).

Table 2.   Claims of Hindustani, Urdu and Hindi mother-tongue speakers in certain Indian
states during 1931–1961

State/Mother tongue	1931 thousands	1951 thousands	Variation 1931–51 (%)	1961 thousands	Variation 1951–61 (%)
Uttar Pradesh:					
Hindustani	46,456	6,743	−86.4	101	−98.5
Urdu ⎫	grouped with	4,300	−	7,892	+83.5
Hindi ⎭	Hindustani	50,454	−	62,443	+23.8
Madhya Pradesh:					
Hindustani	4,990	59	−98.8	1.1	−98.2
Urdu	752	368	−51.0	740	+100.1
Hindi	2,869	19,876	+592.9	21,686	+9.1
Andhra Pradesh:					
Hindustani	754	529	−29.8	0.3	−99.99
Urdu	742	1,600	+115.7	2,554	+59.6
Hindi	31	107	+246.7	136	+27.3
Tamilnadu (Madras):					
Hindustani	393	69	−82.4	0.6	−99.1
Urdu	−	427	−	616	+44.2
Hindi	11	65	+505.8	39	−40.1
Mysore (Karnataka):					
Hindustani	404	740	+83.2	12	−98.3
Urdu	−	878	−	2,035	+131.9
Hindi	32	72	+125.0	82	+13.3
Jammu and Kashmir:					
Hindustani	1.1	92	+8,243.4	0.006	−99.99

These figures reveal virtual extinction of Hindustani, mostly in favor of
Urdu. The only exceptions are the 1951 returns of Uttar Pradesh and
Madhya Pradesh states, which show a sharp rise in Hindi at the expense
of Hindustani. As per the 1961 returns, the total populations of Hindustani in the country is reduced to a bare 122 thousands. Presumably the
partition of the country in 1947 into India and Pakistan was taken by the
masses as a verdict against the concept of Hindustani as a bridge between
Sanskritic Hindi and Persianized Urdu. In this respect, the census figures
indirectly reveal the IDEAL STANDARD of mother tongue cherished by the
group or by an individual not visible in choice of grammatical and lexical
patterns and pronunciation habits.

IDENTITY PRESSURES AMONG BILINGUAL GROUPS

In actual multilingual (and multidialectal) societies we often come across speech groups which are completely bilingual (or bidialectal) and have virtual native control over more than one language (or dialect). Shift in mother-tongue declarations from one language to another in successive censuses, depending on social and political climate, seems to be a frequent feature among such speech groups in India.

In Bihar state, the 1961 returns of the Bihari group of languages, chiefly Bhojpuri, Maithili and Magahi, show phenomenal increases, from 112 thousands in 1951 to 16.4 million in 1961; an increase of 14,611 percent during the decade! In 1951, Hindi and Bihari populations in Bihar State were 81.0 percent and 0.3 percent respectively. However, the 1961 Census reports these populations as 44.3 percent and 35.4 percent respectively; the Hindi population recording a decrease of 34.6 percent during the decade. This is primarily due to the re-emergence of various Bihari languages as distinct from the previously affiliated Hindi group and also to speakers of these languages asserting their distinct identity from one another within the state. The returns of the 1951 and 1961 Censuses from Bihar State in Table 3 testify to the abnormal increase in three main Bihari languages.

Table 3. Speakers claiming main Bihari languages in Bihar during 1951–1961

Languages	1951 claims thousands	1961 claims thousands	variation % 1951–1961
Bhojpuri	1.9	7,842.7	412,341
Maithili	97.7	4,982.6	5,101
Magadhi/Magahi	3.7	2,818.5	75,603

Saharsa district in Bihar returned only 5,418 Maithili speakers in 1951, whereas, the 1961 returns show 1.1 million Maithili speakers in the same district (a rise of over 20,000 percent!). Similar trends, though less dramatic, are noticed among Chhatisgarhi speakers in Madhya Pradesh as well. Durg district in Madhya Pradesh returned only 369,295 Chhatisgarhi speakers in 1951, a figure which in 1961 increased to 1,515,536 (a rise of 310 percent).

There are no cross-tabulations of language data by religion. But one clearly notices Muslims having much closer ties with Urdu than other religious groups. As the Muslim population is mostly scattered throughout the country, so is Urdu. A large proportion of Muslims in many regions tend to have bilingual control over respective language of the region (Telugu, Kannada, Marathi, etc.) and Urdu. During 1951–1961 the Muslim population in the country increased by 25.6 percent, whereas the Urdu-speaking population shows an increase of 68.7 percent. The consolidation of Urdu in almost all states (see Table 2 and 4) is primarily due to the preference of bilingual Muslims for RELIGIOUS identity at the expense of REGIONAL identity. Table 4 shows tabulation variations in the percentages of Muslims and Urdu-speakers to the total population in some of the prominent Indian states during 1951–1961.

Though the proportion of Muslims shows a slight decline to total population in a few states (such as Gujarat, Andhra Pradesh, Mysore) during the decade, ranging between −0.4 and −0.2 percent, the proportion of Urdu mother-tongue speakers to total population in all states registers a considerable rise, ranging between 4.1 and 0.4 percent. The most spectacular shift in favor of Urdu is noticed in Mysore, a Dravidian state, where, despite the proportion of Muslims registering a slight decrease (−0.2 percent) in comparison to the 1951 composition of the population, the proportion of Urdu-speakers records the maximum rise (4.1 percent). In Uttar Pradesh as well, the linguistic composition of population has shifted in favor of Urdu during the decade: with a net rise of 3.9 percent in the total composition of the state, the proportion of Urdu mother-tongue speakers increased from 6.8 percent in 1951 to 10.7 percent in 1961.

Considering the sociocultural situation of the Muslim pockets spread throughout the country, one does not find any evidence of genuine language displacement in daily life, i.e. the abandoning of any regional or minority language in favor of Urdu. Hence these astounding increases in the claims of Urdu mother-tongue speakers in almost all Indian states can be regarded as the assertion by bilingual Muslims of cultural solidarity through Urdu, with the relegation of respective regional languages to subsidiary language status in their subjective evaluation of competence (Weinreich et al. 1968) in reaction to the post-Independence situation in the country.

DIGLOSSIC COMPLEMENTATION

The North-Central region, known as the *"Hindi-Urdu-Panjabi (HUP) region,"* comprising about 46 percent of the total population of India, is typical of the "melting pot" situation, in which NATIVE SPEECH distinctions are undermined in a preference for wider group affiliations. There is a superposed homogeneity in communication patterns in the entire HUP region, with varying degrees of DIGLOSSIC COMPLEMENTATION among many speech varieties. VERBAL REPERTOIRE in a community is hierarchically structured, with many speech varieties enjoying different status/privileges according to overt identity pressures.

A large population of 123 million reported Hindi (proper) as its mother tongue in the 1961 census, though many members speak markedly different variations or altogether different languages for primary

Table 4. Percentages of Muslims and Urdu-speakers to total population in various Indian states during 1951–1961

State	Regional language	1951		1961		Variation during 1951–61	
		Muslims	Urdu-speakers	Muslims	Urdu-speakers	Muslims	Urdu-speakers
Uttar Pradesh	Hindi	14.3	6.8	14.6	10.7	+ 0.3	+ 3.9
Bihar	Hindi	11.3	6.8	12.5	8.9	+ 1.2	+ 2.1
Mysore	Kannada	10.1	4.5	9.9	8.6	– 0.2	+ 4.1
Gujarat	Gujarati	8.9	2.4	8.5	2.9	– 0.4	+ 0.5
Andhra Pradesh	Telugu	7.8	5.2	7.6	7.1	– 0.2	+ 1.9
Maharashtra	Marathi	7.6	6.5	7.7	6.9	+ 0.1	+ 0.4
Delhi	Hindi	5.7	not available	5.9	5.8	+ 0.2	—
Punjab	Hindi-Panjabi	1.8	”	1.9	1.3	+ 0.1	—

communication. These heterogeneous speech groups claiming Hindi as mother tongue can be classified into the following five broad categories (Khubchandani 1972):

1. Those bilingual speakers belonging to the North-Central region (characterized as the "Fluid Zone") who retain their regional or caste dialects of Western Hindi or altogether different regional languages (such as Pahari, Lahnda, Panjabi, Rajasthani, Awadhi, Chhatisgarhi, Bihari) for informal communication with their speech group, but prefer to use

Khari Boli (standard Hindi) for formalized communication. In this diglossia situation, these speakers think of a more PRESTIGIOUS ROLE for Khari
Boli, in contrast to the CASUAL USE of their native speech. They regard
their native speech habits as mere substandard variations of the ALL-
POWERFUL standard Hindi.

2. Those bilinguals who reserve their native speech varieties (as stated
above) merely for communication with elders in DEFERENT–INTIMATE
speech events, but use more and more Khari Boli in other situations
within their speech group. These speakers associate Khari Boli with
URBANITY and MODERNITY, and their actual native speech with RURALITY
and ORTHODOXY.

3. Those bilinguals who use their native speech varieties (as stated
above) for ORAL communication (informal as well as formal) but regard
Khari Boli in Devanagari script as the fit vehicle for WRITTEN purposes
(education, literature, administration, etc.) within their speech group.
The expression of solidarity among Hindus of the "Fluid Zone" through
KHARI BOLI IN DEVANAGARI SCRIPT (Hindi) in response to the similar feeling
among Muslims (primarily among urban and aristocratic classes) expressed through KHARI BOLI IN PERSO-ARABIC SCRIPT (Urdu) has been a
major factor in this trend (Khubchandani 1968).

4. Those monolinguals (mostly rural) speaking regional vernaculars or
languages other than Khari Boli but testifying to HINDI as their mother
tongue because they regard themselves as part of the GREAT "Hindi
tradition."

5. Those belonging to the narrow Khari Boli region around Delhi who
do not natively speak any other dialect or language, and those belonging
to various urban and semi-urban centers of the "Fluid zone" who have not
acquired sufficient control over the language of their region — due to the
genuine displacement of local or subregional dialect or language in their
thrust for urbanity, modernity, or solidarity realized through Khari Boli.

FLUID ZONE

In such fluid situations individuals' Census declarations are made out of
the conviction that their mother tongue is part of a particular "tradition."
These reveal an individual's allegiance and esteem for a particular language, sometimes even in contradiction to his actual speech habits. Language emotions of the speakers of the Fluid Zone are characterized by a
constant shift in language allegiance, as revealed in the oscillating
mother-tongue Census returns of Hindi, Urdu, Panjabi, Kashmiri and
various vernaculars of this vast area, e.g. Lahnda, Dogri, Pahari, Rajasthani, Marwari, Awadhi, Chhatisgarhi, Braj Bhasha, Bhojpuri, Maithili,
and Magahi. Language interest during the post-Independence period has

also served to heighten consciousness and strengthen loyalties among speakers. Hindi, Urdu and Panjabi, as evidenced by the polarization of their literary trends and writing systems (Devanagari, Perso-Arabic and Gurumukhi scripts, respectively) and their official recognition dominate the entire Fluid Zone in India as well as the Panjabi-, Lahnda- and Pashto-speaking areas in Pakistan. Hindi, apart from being the official language of six states and two union territories in the North-Central region, is also the declared official language of India. Urdu is the state language of Jammu and Kashmir in the North-Central region, and is also the declared official language of Pakistan. Panjabi is the state language of newly formed Panjab state in the North-Central region. Two unilingual states, Panjab and Haryana, were formed in 1966 by bifurcating the erstwhile bilingual state — the Punjab — with Panjabi and Hindi as state languages.

On the basis of the communication patterns prevailing among different speech groups and the identificational characteristics attached to their languages, this entire region, divided between two nations — India and Pakistan — is treated as a unified communication region and labelled the "Hindi-Urdu-Panjabi (HUP) Region" or simply the "Broad Hindustani Region" (Khubchandani 1969). Until recently, Kashmiri (a Dardic language) and Pashto (an Iranian language) enjoyed only vernacular status in their own regions, namely, Jammu and Kashmir, and North-West Frontier Province (NWFP), respectively. Both languages remained submerged under Urdu for the purposes of wider group communication. But now they show the signs of asserting their separate linguistic identity, to begin with, in the fields of education and literature. Pashto in Afghanistan also remained under the domination of the Persian language for a long time. But now it claims independent identity as the official language of that country.

In the Panjabi region, on the Indian as well as the Pakistani side, mother-tongue Census returns seem to be tied up with religious affiliation. At the expense of slight statistical inaccuracy, one can say that the Sikhs in the region generally tend to report Panjabi as their mother tongue, and the Hindus show preference for Hindi, and the Muslims for Urdu, although one does not notice any sharp distinction in the speech these three religious groups actually use for primary communication. We have already discussed the abandoning of the Punjab (and also of Delhi and Himachal Pradesh) tabulations in 1951, owing to the emotionally-charged atmosphere on the language issue in these states at that time. But language returns in the Punjab (India) and neighboring states can broadly be interpreted as:

1. Those natively speaking Panjabi, Lahnda, Pashto, Dogri, Rajasthani, Bangru, Hariani, Khari Boli, and neighboring vernaculars, who regard PANJABI IN GURUMUKHI SCRIPT as a FIT VEHICLE FOR FORMAL COM-

MUNICATION (particularly in the fields of education and administration) declare PANJABI as their mother tongue, irrespective of the language or dialect they actually speak at home.

2. Similarly, those who regard HINDI IN DEVANAGARI SCRIPT suitable for such purposes declare HINDI as their mother tongue.

3. Those who regard URDU IN PERSO-ARABIC SCRIPT suitable for such purposes declare URDU as their mother tongue (mostly in the urban centers of the Panjabi, Lahnda and Pashto regions in Pakistan).

The actual number of Lahnda (mainly Multani) speakers is much more than the 9,000 shown in the 1961 Census and their speech enjoys high prestige in society at the spoken level. But, generally speaking, three religiocultural groups align themselves with three different traditions, namely Panjabi, Hindi, and Urdu.

REFERENCES

BOSE, ASHISH
    1969   "Some aspects of linguistic demography of India," in *Proceedings of the Seminar, Language and Society of India (1967)*. Edited by A. Podar, 37–51. Simla: Indian Institute of Advanced Study.
FERGUSON, CHARLES A.
    1966   "National sociolinguistic profile formulas," in *Sociolinguistics*. Edited by W. Bright. The Hague: Mouton.
GAIT, E. A.
    1913   *Census of India: 1911,* volume one, India. Part one, Report. Calcutta: Government of India.
GRIERSON, GEORGE A.
    1927   *Linguistic survey of India.* Classified list. Calcutta.
HUTTON, J. H.
    1933   *Census of India: 1931*, volume one, India. Part one, Report, 348–376. New Delhi: Government of India.
KHUBCHANDANI, LACHMAN M.
    1968   "Hindi-Urdu-Hindustani." Zagreb: Zagreb Linguistic Circle.
    1969   "Functional importance of Hindi and English," in *Proceedings of the Seminar, Language and Society of India (1967)*. Edited by A. Podar, 178–189. Simla: Indian Institute of Advanced Study.
    1972   "Mother tongue in multilingual societies. An interpretation of Indian Census returns," in *Economic and sociocultural dimensions of regionalisation*. Census Centenary Monograph 7. Edited by A. Chandra Sekhar. New Delhi: The Registrar General of India.
MITRA, ASHOK
    1964   *Census of India: 1961*, volume one, India. Part II-C (ii), Language table. New Delhi: Government of India.
WEINREICH, U., W. LABOV, M. HERZOG
    1968   "Empirical foundations for a theory of language change," in *Directions for historical linguistics*. Edited by W. P. Lehmann and Y. Malkiel. Austin: University of Texas Press.

Social Mobility and Specialization in Language Use

GRACE JOLLY

Among the Nyisi of India's Arunachal Pradesh, skill in language use is highly valued. According to the oral tradition, individual social mobility is possible and desirable and the Nyisi cite both traditional and contemporary examples in support of this. In a rapidly changing society, their specializations are also changing; operational knowledge of many languages, for example, is replacing the operational knowledge of many diatypic or dialectal varieties of the same language. But skill in language use remains an important Nyisi requirement for social success, while play with language and talk about talk are continuing sources of their interest and pleasure.

The data for this paper were collected among male students from the Subansiri Division of Arunachal Pradesh, then the North East Frontier Agency, who attended a school in North Lakhimpur, Assam, between 1957 and 1963.[1] The Nyisi language and people are frequently called Dafla or Daphla in earlier accounts. My decision to use their own name for themselves and their language instead of using the pejorative earlier name is in line, I believe, with the Government of India's current practice. The language has been classified as a member of the North Assam group of Tibeto-Burman languages (Grierson 1909:584). Besides Subansiri,

---

[1] The Nysis do not account for a person's age in years but the language indicates for males five stages between birth and full maturity: *ko hojung* 'baby'; *hemi ko* 'toddler'; *nyaga ko* 'boy [literally, man child]'; *ya.pa* 'pubescent youth'; *ya.pa palo* 'youth of full growth and strength'. Most of the subjects of the study were *ya.pa* with a few *nyaga ko* and still fewer *ya.pa palo*. Because this work was done among young males it is limited and partial. There is only the male opinion about verbal behavior of girls and women and nothing about infancy or early childhood. But, because the work was done over a period of five years and by someone who was ostensibly filling an innocuous role, that of a teacher of English as a second language, there were numerous opportunities to observe completely unstaged communication events. Unless otherwise noted, the data are all from my own field notes.

the Nyisi live in the Kameng Division and in a number of villages on the plains of Assam bordering these two divisions.

SOCIAL MOBILITY IN TRADITIONAL NYISI SOCIETY

The Nyisi practice shifting cultivation supplemented by food-gathering in one of the least hospitable parts of eastern Arunachal Pradesh (Elwin 1960:5–6, 15–16). The household of the extended family is the central unit of the society; the family is patrilineal and patrilocal, and the preferred norm is polygynous. In the long Nyisi house, a man may live with his wives, his brothers and their wives, his sons and their wives, and the unmarried children. But there is no common purse or single authority. Each woman grows crops which provide food for herself and her own children, and, in turn, for her husband and his guests. While men cooperate in hunting, fishing, and clearing land, each raises domestic animals and engages in trade entirely on his own behalf. In his activities each man can count on the help of his immediate household and, to a lesser degree, his clan members, sometimes on his wife's household and clan members as well. The extent to which he receives support will depend, however, upon his individual status as a man of wealth and prestige as well as upon the wealth, size, and prestige of his clan relative to the clan with which he may be dealing.

Freedom, individual initiative, and independence are valued qualities and the Nyisi are frequently characterized as highly individualistic entrepreneurs (Shukla 1969:87–88). Their great ones are those who have amassed wealth in the form of moveable property: livestock, particularly the semidomesticated *Bos frontalis*; Tibetan valuables such as swords, woolens, turquoise and silver jewelry; the plates and bells, again of probable Tibetan origin, which they call the plates and bells of the gods; and the prized Assamese *eri* silk. They also take many wives and, while women are by no means chattels, they do constitute at the same time a means of production and a conspicuous display of wealth. Nyisi eschatology reflects the concern with wealth and family. In their land of the dead, the rich are still rich and the poor still poor while those who have never accumulated together enough property to marry and have children are permanently consigned to a noisy and hopeless limbo.

Of course, those who already belong to prosperous, powerful households make marriage alliances with other equally powerful ones; those men who already have property exchange it for wives for themselves and their sons, and these women, in turn, produce wealth in food, cloth, and, most important, children: sons who "build the clan" and daughters who earn bridewealth for their family of origin.

Yet the wealthy do not always remain wealthy and the poor need not stay poor. The value in the culture of individual initiative and of wealth-getting is attested verbally. The tradition persists that anyone can do anything. Proverbs, folktales, and current examples are frequently cited to prove that orphaned children, destitute young couples, and even slaves can get wealth and rise to positions of prestige and power by their work and their wits, and their verbal skills. "Keep chickens," runs the advice to a young boy. "Trade chickens for goats, goats for pigs, pigs for *methan*, and *methan* for a wife. Build your clan."

Verbal skills are, of course, a requisite for the barter in which the young boy is encouraged to engage and for many of the other activities charac-teristic of the successful adult male. While the young Nyisi who is hand-some, well-dressed, and active is admired and frequently designated a "jungle chicken," the mature man, to be respected must also be a "wise speaker," must have "the shaman's Adam's apple." Hence, to judge wisely of the speech of others and to speak well himself are important goals for the Nyisi youth. Each communicative event appears to have a double function: to achieve its immediate goal and to serve as a practice session for the future.

THE SKILLFUL USE OF WORDS

The importance which is given to speech can vary greatly not only between literate and preliterate societies (Garvin and Mathiot 1960) but from one preliterate society to another. Consider, for example, the elab-orate concern of the Burundi (Albert 1972) with speech and education for speaking, compared to the relative disinterest in speech and the lack of formal education for it among the Gbeya (Samarin 1969). When a complete description is available for the Nyisi, they will probably rank near the Burundi.

The Nyisi are frequently described as taciturn by neighboring groups.[2] This reputation is incongruous to one who has had an opportunity to know them well but perhaps it derives from their absence of phatic expression on entering or leaving a house or on meeting someone on the road as well as from the existence of clearly-defined rules about who may speak to whom and where, and about what (Hymes 1964:387; Nida 1964:52). In some communicative events, the use of silence can be as important as the use of speech (Basso 1972:67–86). While young males may sometimes be called upon to speak in the presence of their elders, they are to be hesitant and precede their statements with apologies about

[2]   As late as 1958 an Assamese primer contained the line *dafola okora,* which I take to mean 'Daflas speak badly'. The term *okora* generally means 'stupid' but there is a second meaning which describes the speech of tribal people, presumably speaking Assamese as a second language.

their own lack of verbal skills. Similarly, the not-so-great do not speak out in the presence of the great. A proverb is used with devastating effect when a young or inexperienced person speaks out of turn in a meeting. It runs, "I waited with my bow and arrow for the deer to come out. Deer didn't come out; dog came out."[3] As for a person who constantly gossips and goes about discussing the affairs of others, one says: "Leaving his mother's corpse unburied, he goes about to other men's funerals."

Women, especially young women, are expected to speak little.[4] It is held that the causes of quarrels between men, households, and clans are two: the spread of disease whether by neglect of quarantine or by malignant spells, and the idle and careless talk of women who go from household to household and repeat what they hear. However, women may be called upon as witnesses in litigation and the power of a head wife in her own household, not only over her co-wives and their children but over her husband as well, is something to be reckoned with. An irate wife may, for example, go out onto her veranda and give a recital of her husband's shortcomings to the whole village, something he does not easily live down.

Depending on sex and age, there are sharp differences in adaptation to dialect variation and in attitudes to it. Dialectal and diatypic varieties (Gregory 1966; Halliday et al. 1970) of the Nyisi language are viewed with considerable sophistication by the young men. They could often locate a visitor's village and always his general area by hearing him speak. The speech of some villages and clans was said to be beautiful and that of others "lazy" and "slow." Certainly the Nyisi area presents extraordinary dialectal complexity. Elwin's description (1960) of the uncompromising terrain gives the geographical rationale for the classic situation of speech communities separated from one another by areas of low density of communication.

Elwin (1960:6) writes: "For centuries, the real ruler of the tribal people has been Environment; it has shaped their bodies, directed their art, forced Babel on their tongues . . ."

Grierson (1909:568, 584) chose to ignore as relatively minor the linguistic differences among the Nyisi and between them and their neighboring tribes. He concluded correctly that at least some of the different names for the languages and people were of plain's origin and failed to reflect the hill people's own views of themselves and of their relationships with their neighbors. He treated the tribes commonly called Abor, Miri,

---

[3]   Cf. the Assamese, "At Indra's council a sparrow chirped."
[4]   The tradition perhaps expresses a fervent wish that it were so. Male comments when hearing a Nyisi woman speaking loudly or angrily are something like: "She is after all a Nyisi; as the men are so are the women." Their own women's speech behavior is sometimes compared with that of the women of other groups. Of the Mundaris: "If only our women were as quiet and gentle as their women are!" Of the Ahoms: "They may be better educated than our women but who could endure their constant talk?"

and Dafla as one and their language as one. "Abor-Miri and Dafla are Assamese names for a tribe which inhabits the mountains between the Assam Valley and Tibet. ... The Abor-Miris and the Daflas speak dialects which are so closely related that they can justly be considered as one and the same form of speech."

Among the three tribes Grierson grouped together, contiguous communilects are always mutually intelligible. For example, Nyisi (Dafla) speakers who call themselves and their language *Lel* and who live in the lower part of the Subansiri Division appear to communicate easily with those who call themselves and their language Gallong Adi (Abor) and who live toward the east in the Siang Division. On the other hand, Nyisi-speakers from the Assamese plains below the Kameng Division, who call themselves and their language *Yano,* have been observed to have great difficulty in communicating with Nyisi from the central Subansiri, whom they call *Tagin.* In the last example, the *Yano* speakers were girls of twelve or fourteen and the *Tagin*-speakers were young adult males. Apparently the men could understand the girls' speech but the girls could not understand what was said to them. They were observed in angry tears, thinking they were being teased. Most Nyisi men do travel and gain familiarity with several dialects while girls and women have less opportunity for such experience.

Similar differences in sophistication about dialectal variation between young children and adults are illustrated frequently. One example is the experience of a small child who came to school from the northern section of the Subansiri Division near Tibet. Among the young adults were a couple of virtuosos who could entertain a group by mimicking dialectal varieties of Nyisi speech and asking their audience to guess the geographical provenance. They considered this child a valuable specimen because his dialect was new to them. He had an /f/ in his consonant inventory where they had an /x/ and he used many forms which contrasted systematically with their own. They encouraged him to talk, usually understood, and successfully monitored their own speech for him.

His reception was very different in the children's hostel where he had to live. Convinced that the *aya ko* 'upper child' talked too slowly, the other children drawled whatever they said to him, greeted his speech with laughter and frequently failed to understand him altogether. After two weeks of this treatment, he picked up his belongings, went to the young adults' hostel, and announced his intention of moving in. To his consternation, the usually tolerant young men greeted his speech with shouts of laughter. In his nervous attempt to be very correct in a socially difficult situation, he had said 'I have immigrated,' using a lexical item which is heard only in very restricted literary genres in which shamans recite the great migrations of the tribe. For a very small boy to use it in describing his trip across the school compound with his mosquito net, blanket, and extra shirt was too much for his new hostel mates' gravity. His instruction in diatypic varieties began forthwith.

Among students, formal instruction in speaking included direct criticism and correction with insistence on the repetition of the correct form. Compliments were paid following a well executed narrative or song and there was special attention and approbation for the child who demonstrated originality and speed in puns, repartee, boasting, and insult. Older students viewed their stay in the boarding school as a period of linguistic deprivation as far as their own language was concerned since, while they instructed those less experienced than themselves, they had no one to instruct them. The Nyisi adults who visited the compound to meet a relative or to find an interpreter to guide them through the local bazaar frequently found themselves made captive for an evening and required to tell stories, sing songs, or simply talk and answer questions.[5]

A boy has the right to expect and even to demand instruction and correction in his speech from his father or his uncles. One young man involved in ligitation over some Tibetan valuables which had been stolen from him as a child went to his maternal uncle's house several days before the case was to begin in order to receive instruction about how to handle his testimony. Before going, he prepared a song of over eighty lines in which he stated his plight, repeatedly addressing his uncle as "wise speaker" and "shaman's Adam's apple" and referring to himself in metaphors of helplessness, weakness, and speechlessness.

It is in litigation that the double function of communicative events among Nyisi students is most obvious. The settlement of their quarrels frequently took hours and days. The protagonists would state their cases with all the care and restraint of which they were capable, calling on their witnesses to support them. Older students offered advice and attempted the reconciliation. The dramatic oratory appeared to be verbal overkill, functioning less for the case in question and more as a practice run for future litigations.

Storytelling sessions provide both practice and pleasure. These range from the recounting, by students of any age, of events which may have occurred in their home village, through explanatory and cautionary tales ("What Makes the Earthquake," "How Tigers Came to Be") to the myths depicting the acts of supernatural creatures and ancestors. All stories may require special constraints on the phonology. For example, the speech of crows has velar fricatives instead of velar stops and *Bor*

---

[5]   The students had once composed new words for a traditional tune. A Nyisi visitor heard them singing it, sat them all down and "taught" them the traditional words again, making them sing them over several times until he was satisfied with their performance. None of them gave any indication that they already knew what they were being taught and when it was over they thanked him for taking a concern with their education.

Pacha, the stupid member of the trickster duo, "speaks badly" in a number of ways.

Myths are presented only by older students and the myth is recognized as representative of a literary genre whose organization and presentation is subject to special constraints (Taber 1966:69–70). The non-Nyisi listener is warned that this sort of story is not to be repeated casually to strangers. One notes a special lexis, including a formulaic opening and closure and higher level connectives. None of the ellipsis recorded for casual texts and certain songs seems permitted. The event itself displays some of the features of a graduate seminar. The performer protects himself with a few caveats at the beginning; at the end, the listeners participate with him in a discussion of the performance and compare the effectiveness of his version with others they have heard.

Riddling, the quoting of proverbs, and singing, like storytelling, serve to educate for the future as well as to entertain and establish status in the present. Of the eleven varieties of song text described by one informant, five were recorded and four glossed. The *bemin* "little songs" were sung by all; *buya* and *gumba* "songs for great occasions" were sung or led by experienced singers; *bajum* were long solos composed for personal occasions, again by the experienced; one *id* "song of origins" was recorded by a shaman but remained unglossed, the lexis being either so archaic or so highly stylized that no student would undertake the task. All the song texts are characterized by constraints operating on all strata of the language and differing from one literary variety to the other (Gleason 1967:25).

In Nyisi society there are three types of specialist who display a skill in language use superior to that required in all respected adult males. These are the shaman, the mediator, and the maker.

Chief among the repositories of tribal memory are the shamans. "Some of our old men carry around a thousand years of history in their heads," say the young Nyisi. They are called upon to recite it on certain occasions and stories are told of enormous feats when a man may sing and recite for four or five days at a stretch with only brief periods of rest. Although the Nyisi understand contagion, they appear to have few natural ways of dealing with illness. Therefore they depend heavily on the shaman to contact the supernatural in identifying and curing disease as well as in predicting the future. Shaman are called *nyub* as are metalworkers (Shukla 1969:34). Like these craftsmen, the shaman is invited to the house where his services are needed and, if successful, sent away loaded with gifts of cloth, beads, and meat. Shamans are of three grades: the *nijik nyub* treat ordinary diseases and take omens; the *but nyub* perform sacrifices and treat more serious illness; the great *nyoki nyub* go into trance and perform extraordinary cures. Shamans are assisted at times by *bu*, small boys who, among other things, sing responses during the antiphonal chants. The *bu* is a child who displays aptitude in singing and memorizing ritual and who has had certain characteristic dreams. Like the great one he may assist, the tools of his craft are memorized texts and rituals. The unsuccessful shaman is a joke; the successful one is much sought after and may become very wealthy.

Besides the shaman the *gindung* [mediator, lawyer-*cum*-diplomat] is a specialist in language. Before the extension of civil administration to the area, the Nyisi system of justice resembled nothing so much as international warfare. Humane treatment of prisoners and safe conduct for intermediaries was the rule; beyond that, a man might do what he dared (von Fürer Haimendorf 1962:279–309). When a blood feud seemed beyond resolution by other means, the mediator would be called. He arranged safe conduct for the leaders and organized the meeting in which participants would use their most impressive oratory in stating their cases. Small bamboo tallies would be arranged in rows on the ground to record each point made in enumerating grievances and losses. After days of discussion, a settlement would be reached and the traditional fines agreed on and assessed. Oaths and ordeals might also be used in determining guilt but usually as a last resort after oratory and the examination of witnesses had failed. The mediator, like the shaman, to be successful, had mastered a great deal of text to which he could refer in his reasoning and in giving his judgments.

In an area where the struggle for a living is so strenuous there seems little creative energy to spare for the carving, weaving, and dancing which is found so richly in less difficult parts of Arunachal Pradesh. But there is a special place for the makers, the poets and singers. Among the Nyisi, as among many Amerindian tribes, musical specialization is part of the specialization of the shaman. But the singing and making of songs is not his prerogative alone. There is also a specialization among lay people based on skill and on "individual differences in musical ability. In most cultures a few people are acknowledged to be the best singers" (Nettl 1966:11). Women and even children, as well as men, may be recognized as makers. On one occasion, a young boy was permitted to enroll in the school very late at the strong insistence of an older student who was a gifted singer and composer. His argument was that the youngster held promise of being a singer and, since he himself would graduate the following year, the school would need a replacement. Good singers were not found behind every bush and a school without one was quite unthinkable.

THE NEW SPECIALISTS

As modern India extended government services into Arunachal Pradesh in the form of courts, schools, hospitals, roads, and a military presence, a new specialist became necessary. The *kotoki* "interpreter (Assamese)" was needed to mediate between the Hindi-speaking official and the Nyisi community. Again, skill in language use is the requirement for office, in this case, bilingualism or multilingualism.

Some adult Nyisi speak Tani, a related Tibeto-Burman language spoken by a people who occupy a fertile valley in the heart of the Subansiri Division and with whom the Nyisi have a long tradition of contact. Others speak a pidginized version of Assamese which has been used for centuries in trading contacts with the plains. Some students enrolled in the school already knew these two languages; those who did not learned them quickly. In the Middle School, students gained a near-native proficiency in Assamese which was the language of instruction, a control of the Hindi standard adequate for use in many formal situations, and enough English to serve for the sort of noncommunication useful in distancing others and establishing status. Progress in learning Assamese and Hindi was particularly rapid and Nyisi students often stood high in their classes or completed more than one grade in a year. As students became bilingual or multilingual one began to observe in communication events that apparently easy translatability, facile codeswitching and structural similarity of expressions which has so frequently been noted for Indian languages, even those which are genetically members of different language groups (Emeneau 1956; Gumperz 1962, 1969).

The tradition of the lost books is reported for several hill peoples in India and Burma. It is firmly believed among Nyisi school boys. In the beginning, runs the story, the gods gave all men letters. The plains people wrote theirs on bark; the hill people kept theirs on skins. In time of famine the unfortunate hill people were forced to eat their skins. This is why the people of the plains have a more advanced technology than do the people of the hills. When trying to adapt the Assamese or Hindi or English script to write something in their own language, students were frequently heard to exclaim: "Oh my poor people! Why did you eat the books?"

Writing is considered one of the great gifts of the Indian civilization, something of the same order as peace and roads. Songs are composed which extoll the marvels of the marks on paper by which the *sahab,* twenty days distance from his colleague, can say, "My friend has just told me thus and so." The getting and sending of postcards and letters is not simply a means of long-distance communication but a mark of status as well. Hindi and English are considered more prestigious than is Assamese so older students are frequently called upon to address postcards in one of those languages for younger students who have not yet learned their scripts.

Students did not aspire to use their new language skills in order to work as interpreters, people about whom they felt ambivalent. It was necessary to give a grudging admiration for these new functionaries were certainly powerful and newly rich. But criticism was constantly heard of their abuse of power and of the time they spent keeping their suddenly overextended households in order. Those students who had enrolled in school well after puberty and who had already assumed adult responsibilities at home planned to stay only a few years, just long enough to acquire the minimal degree of bilingualism and literacy to enable them to deal directly with representatives of the outside and not be victimized by unscrupulous go-betweens. Students who started school younger had more time before family pressure required them to return home to work and marry. Also, orphans or those from poor families who could help them little in getting established found themselves in an enviable position, able to continue to study without undue pressure from relatives as long as they earned the passing grades which assured them of their stipends. Some were able to complete highschool and a baccalaureate or graduate degree. These, returning to their own language area in the Government service, made the interpreter in their post obsolete, combining his prestige and that of the formerly non-Nyisi official in one person.

In traditional society success was measured in conspicuously displayed property, hospitality, and a multiplicity of wives and offspring. The control of many varieties of Nyisi was one of the paths to this success. The interpreters defined success in the traditional way and gained it by their bilingualism. Educated young Nyisi officers define success differently, relating to the larger Indian society as well as to their own. For them, polygyny and large families are less appropriate and a civil servant's salary scarcely constitutes wealth in the old terms. However, many who could not otherwise have achieved it have a good measure of security and prestige. They have done it by giving attention to language, becoming multilingual and literate, following, though in a new way, one of the firmly established precepts of their traditional society.

REFERENCES

ALBERT, ETHEL M.
   1972   "Culture patterning of speech behavior in Burundi," in *Directions in sociolinguistics: the ethnography of communication*. Edited by John J. Gumperz and Dell Hymes, 72–105. New York: Holt, Rinehart and Winston.
BASSO, K. J.
   1972   "'To give up words': silence in Western Apache culture," in *Language and social context*. Edited by Pier Paolo Giglioli, 67–86. Harmondsworth: Penguin.
ELWIN, VERRIER
   1960   *A philosophy of NEFA*. Shillong, Assam, India: J. N. Chowdhury.
EMENEAU, M. B.
   1956   India as a linguistic area. *Language* 32:3–16.

FÜRER HAIMENDORF, CHRISTOPH VON
1962   "Moral concepts in three Himalayan societies," in *Indian Anthropology.* Edited by T. N. Madan and Gopala Sarana. Bombay: Asia Publishing House.
GARVIN, PAUL. MADELEINE MATHIOT
1960   "The urbanization of the Guarani language: a problem in language and culture," in *Men in cultures.* Edited by A. F. C. Wallace, 783–790. Philadelphia: University of Pennsylvania Press.
GLEASON, H. A., JR.
1967   "Probings into no-man's land: the marches of linguistics, semantics, stylistics." Unpublished lecture given at Bowdoin College, Conference on Linguistics and English Stylistics, May 4.
GREGORY, MICHAEL J.
1966   Aspects of varieties differentiation. *Journal of Linguistics* 3:177–198. 3:177–198.
GRIERSON, GEORGE A.
1909   *Linguistic survey of India,* volume three, part 1, General introduction, specimens of the Tibetan dialects, the Himalayan dialects, and the North Assam group. Calcutta: Superintendent of Government Printing, India.
GUMPERZ, JOHN J.
1962   Types of linguistic communities. *Anthropological Linguistics* 4(1):28–40.
1969   "Communication in multilingual societies," in *Cognitive anthropology.* Edited by S. Tyler, 435–439. New York: Holt, Rinehart and Winston.
HALLIDAY, M. A. K., ANGUS McINTOSH, PETER STREVENS
1970   "The users and uses of language," in *Readings in the sociology of language.* Edited by Joshua A. Fishman, 139–168. The Hague: Mouton.
HYMES, DELL, *editor*
1964   *Language in culture and society.* New York: Harper and Row.
NETTL, BRUNO
1966   *Music in primitive culture.* Cambridge, Mass.: Harvard University Press.
NIDA, EUGENE A.
1964   *Toward a science of translating.* Leiden: E. J. Brill.
SAMARIN, WILLIAM J.
1969   *The art of Gbeya insults. International Journal of American Linguistics* 35(4):323–329.
SHUKLA, BRAHMA KUMAR
1969   *The Daflas.* Shillong, Assam: North-East Frontier Agency.
TABER, CHARLES R.
1966   *The structure of Sango narrative.* Hartford, Conn.: Hartford Studies in Linguistics.

Modal and Modish Pronunciations: Some Sex Differences in Speech

LEWIS LEVINE and HARRY J. CROCKETT, JR.

This paper summarizes some explorations of a variable not previously given attention in sociolinguistic studies — "mode score" — and of the social psychological attribute the variable is intended to represent — "linguistic conformity." Our results show that linguistic conformity, thus measured, is related to the sex of the speaker, as well as to other characteristics. Our discussion presents reasons for regarding the sex:mode score relation as the most powerful of the set; further discussion in this paper concerns the consonance of that finding with previous work concerning the relationship of one's susceptibility to contemporary linguistic influence to one's sex. Specifically, we have sought to link the facts that men tend to be linguistically more conformist than women while women tend to be more responsive to contemporary linguistic influence than men.

In many previously published quantitative survey studies of intracommunity speech variation, by ourselves (e.g. Levine and Crockett 1966; Crockett and Levine 1967) and by others (e.g. Labov 1966; Anshen 1969; Shuy, Wolfram and Riley 1969) extensive use has been made of variables which characterize the frequency or the intensity or both with which individuals pronounce certain sounds or combinations of sounds in particular sets of words. Scores, expressing percentages of employment of one or another phonological feature, comprise the principal set of such variables. Data obtained in various eliciting situations in such studies have been used to develop associations between the pronunciation scores and measures of the social and demographic characteristics of the speakers, etc. Discussion and explanation of the associations found have invoked social and psychological concepts; in general, one may fairly say that much such research has sought to develop and answer the questions: "What do most people sound like, who talks like whom, to what extent, and why?" It occurred to us that the nature of the linguistic variables employed, given also the nature of survey research, permits only somewhat indirect and diffuse answers to the second of these questions and, in so doing, also makes rather difficult the invocation and postulation of potentially relevant social psychological and quasi-social psychological concepts in the course of answering the fourth question. We thought that a fairly direct measure might be had of linguistic "groupiness" if people were also studied by propensity to pronounce words like their fellows, in addition to being studied by propensity to utter certain sounds, or to employ certain sound features. This paper thus suggests that one may study linguistic conformity, for example, in some ordinary sense of that term, "tapping it" in a reasonable way by measuring the extent to which individuals pronounce words in ways frequently employed by other individuals. Specifically, we study here individuals' tendencies to be members of modal pronunciation groups.

For this study, thirty individuals were selected on a stratified basis — taking account of age, sex, and education — from a sample of 275 individuals who in turn comprised a random sample of the residents of a North Carolina Piedmont community.[1] We considered the ways in which each of the thirty people pronounced a set of sixty-seven words, words which, likewise, were selected on a stratified basis — taking account of structure of main syllable — from a set of over 600 words used in the larger study. We report here on the pronunciations of the main — most heavily stressed — vowels of polysyllabic words and the only vowels of monosyllables. For each word, the various pronunciations found to have been used for the main (or only) vowel were tabulated;[2] in fifty-six cases, a modal or "most frequent" pronunciation was observed. Such words, their respective modes, and those individuals whose pronunciations were modal, are the primary focus of interest in this paper. We eliminated words for which "ties" appeared between top ranked pronunciation alternants and we eliminated words for which the frequency of the modal pronunciation was low and for which there was much scatter of choices among the other pronunciation alternants. For example, in one of its occurrences, 'water' had the modal vowel [ɒ], with an *n* of 14, while the second most frequent vowel was [à], with an *n* of 4; that occurrence of

---

[1]   For details about the community, the sampling, the modes of eliciting and transcription, reliability, etc., see Levine and Crockett (1966) and Crockett and Levine (1967).

[2]   Full details of transcription, etc., are given in the references cited in the preceding footnote; it may be noted here, however, that interviews were taped, and tape recordings transcribed by trained persons using a "check-off" system by which the transcriber selected the precoded transcription judged closest to the pronunciation heard. The phonetic detail recognized in the checkoff system was quite fine: depending on the word, each syllable segment studied was represented by a set of from fifteen to 100 alternative transcriptions (in a multicolumn array based on the I.P.A.). Of course, the checked-off pronunciation alternants are what have been tabulated.

'water' was included. By way of contrast, one instance of 'four' had a two-way tie for top-ranked choice, with an n of 4, and a three-way tie for second choice, with an n of 3; that word instance was not included, although at least one other instance of 'four' was included among the select group of fifty-six. For the fifty-six words forming the basis for this report — the "clear mode" words — the mean of the frequency of pronunciation of the modal vowels, the mean mode, is 10.9, with a standard deviation of 3.4; the values of the modes themselves range from 6 to 23 over the set of words.

As indicated above, we sought to study the range of differences among individual tendencies to contribute to modal pronunciations — to ask whether some individuals are relatively highly "conformist" in pronunciation while others show such behavior less frequently, if at all. We also sought to determine some social and demographic attributes of linguistic conformity. As a first step, "mode scores" were computed for each respondent, by dividing 100 times the number of words for which his or her pronunciation was one of those making up the mode by the number of the set of fifty-six "clear mode" words to which she or he responded. For the purpose of computing these scores, no distinction was made here between words elicited in one or the other of the two eliciting situations we employed, namely, the SENTENCE LIST or WORD LIST situations. Thus computed, respondents' mode scores ranged from 16 to 68, with a mean, for the sample, of 39.0 and a standard deviation of 11.8. The median mode score was 38.5.

Reference was made just above to the two eliciting techniques,[3] the SENTENCE LIST and the WORD LIST. Data previously reported from this community and data from other studies support the belief that differences between the pronunciation patterns manifested in each situation parallel and indicate significant differences between informal and formal speech. In the present paper, by combining instances from each list, we ignore such differences; the following are the reasons why we feel it reasonable to do so. First, although the interaction of formality and conformity may be — indeed, surely is — different for different people, we do not wish to undertake the study of such phenomena at this time and have simply excerpted from our larger data collection a number of words from each situation, namely, thirty-four SENTENCE LIST words and twenty-two WORD LIST words, which, although ad hoc from the point of view of the interaction of formality and conformity, is a constant for all individuals

---

[3] Data were elicited in two ways: respondents were asked to read sentences with blanks in them and to fill in the blanks; words in whose pronunciations we were interested were (a) not those supplied as fillers and (b) hopefully were thus disguised. By contrast, we also had each respondent read a set of words on a word list. Previous work, cited in the second paragraph of this paper, has demonstrated that people respond as if to differences in formality of eliciting situation.

studied. Thus, what we wanted to do, which was to study the mode score analogue of conformity without regard to situational effects, we did do. Second, scores such as R-score, Ing-score, our Epsilon and Open O scores (Labov's EH and OH) (Labov 1966) which are separately computed by situation, are each measures of the frequency or the intensity or both of the use of particular specified consonantal or vocalic categories. Mode scores are measures of linguistic "groupiness" and, since they are computed without regard to any particular phonological category, THE MODE SCORES AND THE INDIVIDUAL PHONOLOGICAL TENDENCY SCORES ARE LOGICALLY INDEPENDENT OF EACH OTHER. It should be obvious to the reader that, for each word, the phonological characteristics of the modal vowel itself are relevant to an individual's mode score only by virtue of whether or not she or he contributed such a pronunciation to the modal pool; the nature of that pronunciation is in no way at issue. And so not only are the mode scores independent of other variable scores, mode scores are also independent of the computations of intersituational score differences, computations whose results are taken to be measures of degrees of attachment to norms, of responses to formality, etc. By way of spelling that point out, consider the following. If a given word appears on both the SENTENCE LIST and the WORD LIST, the modal vowel may be the same on the two lists or different. If there are different modal vowels the difference may be such that the word list modal vowel represents a departure from the SENTENCE LIST modal vowel in the direction of some prestige norm (e.g. [æ:] rather than [ɛyə] in 'bad'), or the difference may not be in the direction of a prestige norm. In the first case, a speaker who contributed to both modal vowels — i.e. who, with respect to the two word instances has a high mode score — also has an intersituational score difference whose sign and numerical value would indicate that increased formality of situation is linked to increased influence of a prestige norm. For him, there would be an empirical connection between high mode score and attachment to norm. In the second case, a speaker who contributed to both modal pronunciations would have a high mode score but an intersituational score difference showing the converse. The reader may easily imagine further situations, e.g. the case of words appearing on both lists whose modal vowels are the same on both lists. This situation would be one with a similar result to the second above but from a different cause; high mode scores would turn out to be not associated or negatively associated with attachment to prestige norms. Our second point, then, is this: although formality of eliciting situation may indeed be a variable which discriminates among people and groups of people with regard to their manifestations of conformity, there is no reason to suspect that formality will work upon our measure of conformity as it works on our measures of pronunciation, because of the independence of the two measures. It is therefore unnecessary to explore that area as a check upon one's work; it is a separate subject of empirical investigation, to be undertaken or not as one wishes.

Although we are not presenting the mode scores of respondents computed separately for WORD LIST data and for SENTENCE LIST data, some observations may be made concerning differences between the modal vowels of the 34 SENTENCE LIST and the 22 WORD LIST words. When we compare modal pronunciations in the two situations we find the following: 21 of the 56 words discussed in this report are on both the SENTENCE LIST and the WORD LIST; of the 21, 12 have the same modal vowels in both situations while for the remaining 9, some pronunciation difference exists. In six of these nine cases, the differences are such that one can say that the WORD LIST modal vowels represent slower or more emphatic pronunciations of corresponding vowels appearing in the SENTENCE LIST situation, e.g. for 'that', [æ] versus [æ˙]; for 'want', [ɔ] versus [ɔw]. For those twelve cases where the modal vowels of words appearing on both lists are the same, seven are cases where the frequency of the WORD LIST mode was higher than the frequency of the SENTENCE LIST mode while four are cases where that order is reversed (frequencies equal in the remaining case). Of the nine cases for which the modal vowels are not the same, eight show smaller WORD LIST frequencies than the corresponding SENTENCE LIST frequencies; however, when one adds the frequencies of the "slow," "emphatic" WORD LIST modal vowels to the frequencies of the appropriate "normal" vowels and compares the sums thus obtained to the frequencies of the SENTENCE LIST modal vowels, one finds, as above, that the WORD LIST frequencies are greater than the SENTENCE LIST frequencies. Thus, although we do not find extensive intersituational differences of vowel quality of the nuclei of modal vowels of corresponding words, quantitative *cum* qualitative inspection does in a new way confirm the notion that intersituational differences which do appear among modal vowels are functions of formality.

RESULTS

Let us begin by considering the relationships between mode score and sex, social class and age.

A relation seems to exist between mode score and sex of respondent. The mean mode score for the sample is 39.0 (median = 38.5, s.d. = 11.8); for men the mean is 43.6 and for women it is 35.0. Table 1 shows frequencies of respondents by sex and by score range; the table shows that women are overrepresented in the low score group and men are overrepresented in the high score group. Table 2 shows frequencies of respondents by educational level and by score range; the table shows that individuals whose formal education ranges from no schooling at all to

Table 1.   Sex of respondent and mode score range

	Men	Women	Totals
Mode score above median	10	5	15
Mode score below median	4	11	15
Totals	14	16	30

$\chi^2=4.8$; $P<0.05$
Median mode score = 38.5

entrance into high-school without graduation therefrom are overrepresented in the high mode score range while individuals whose formal education includes at least graduation from high-school are overrepresented in the low score group. For this table, P is between 0.05 and 1.0, nearer the former than the latter. One must ask whether the two results

Table 2.   Educational level of respondent and mode score range

	Educational level		
	None to high school	High school graduate or above	Totals
Mode score above median	11	4	15
Mode score below median	6	9	15
Totals	17	13	30

$\chi^2=3.40$; $0.05<P<1.0$ ($=0.6$ est.)

are independent; accordingly, Table 3, parts (a) and (b), presents the distributions of individuals by sex and by score range, controlling on education. The table shows that for people of relatively low degree of formal education, the sex:mode score relation holds while for people of relatively high education it does not. Other tabulations (not shown here) reveal, likewise, that the education:mode score relation holds for men but not for women. Thus, in general, high mode scores are associated with men, and this effect is particularly clear among the lower educational groups. To the extent that the sex:mode score and educational level:mode score relations are not independent, a decision must be reached as to whether one rather than the other can be regarded as primary and, if so, which. However, the relevant discussion will be postponed for a few paragraphs during which we will briefly and qualitatively summarize the interactions of mode scores and social variables other than education. First, we report that the occupational category:mode score tabulations confirm the patterns noted above, i.e. over-all, respondents in families headed by blue-collar workers have higher mode scores than respondents in families headed by white-collar work-ers. Further inspections of occupational data and of sex-by-occupational data show some interesting although not statistically significant facts.

Table 3. Sex of respondent and mode score range, by educational level

	Men	Women	Totals
(a) *No schooling through some high school*			
Mode score			
above median	8	3	11
Mode score			
below median	1	5	6
Totals	9	8	17

$\chi^2 = 5.00; P < 0.05$

	Men	Women	Totals
(b) *High school graduate and above*			
Mode score			
above median	2	2	4
Mode score			
below median	3	6	9
Totals	5	8	13

n.s.

First, the sharpest white-collar:blue-collar distinction, without regard to sex, may be observed if one simply compares the "professional" plus "student" plus "general clerical" group to the "semiskilled worker" plus "unskilled worker" group, i.e. if one omits from the white-collar:blue-collar tabulation the eleven "business" and "skilled worker" respon-dents. Both sets of people are interesting. The "business" males all have mode scores above the median and in this manifest the blue-collar rather than the white-collar trend. The "skilled workers" are evenly distributed among the two mode score groups and, thus, in a sense are intermediate between the white-collar and blue-collar groups. After the fact, neither of these observations seem surprising; two intuitively and ethnographically reasonable propositions may be offered. One is that small businessmen in a small southern town may tend to identify with the local working class rather than with a white-collar class; the other is that workers who achieve the dignity of the skilled worker category either themselves identify AWAY from a narrowly conceived local working-class norm or marry women who do. This last possibility arises because of the fact that married women respondents are classified occupationally according to their husbands' occupations. In any case, without regard to the observations just made, the sex:mode score relation holds better for respondents of blue-collar families than for those from white-collar families; thus, the education:sex:mode score picture is repeated. Data on mobility and on status consistency reveal that these too may be relevant independent variables. White-collar people who are high in mode scores, and who in that respect resemble the majority of blue-collar people, are categorically stable with respect to occupation over a generation while of upwardly mobile people, most have low mode scores. Further, of the twenty-two people whose occupations and education are consistent or only moderately inconsistent, fourteen have high mode scores, while of the six people whose occupations and education are highly inconsistent, ALL have low mode scores. If consistency is controlled, the sex:mode score relation is sharper for the "consistent plus moderately inconsistent" group than for the "highly inconsistent" group.

One more nonlinguistic variable will be briefly considered: age. Over the entire age range, i.e. from ca. 20 to 73 years, there is no overall age:mode score relation; the mean age of persons whose scores are above the median is 44.0 as against 43.2 for those whose scores are below the median. When men and women are considered separately, no age relation emerges; however, when respondents are grouped into three categories, "young," "middle-aged," and "old," the sex:mode score relation appears among the nineteen respondents of the middle-aged group. Eight of the nine men have scores above the median while nine of the ten women have scores below the median.

In summary, mode scores seem to be related to sex in that men tend to have higher mode scores than women; mode scores are related to social class in that (a) people with less education tend to have higher mode scores than people with more education, (b) blue-collar workers have higher mode scores than white-collar workers, with some interesting anomalies, (c) people showing occupational stability have higher mode scores than people showing mobility, particularly upward mobility. None of the second set of findings are wholly independent of the first; and, finally, although no overall age:mode score relation exists, the sex:mode score relation holds sharply for middle-aged people.

Two choices exist at this point. Either the sex:mode score relation can be regarded as the outcome of the demography of our group interacting with a general "social class":mode score relation and a truncated age relation or, contrarily, all of these can be seen as at least in part the outcome of demography plus an overriding sex:mode score relation. We choose the latter alternative, for a simple but powerful reason. For all people, for all words, 609 pronunciations are in one or another modal category (out of the total number of pronunciations — some 1680). Slightly over 50 percent of these modal pronunciations can definitely be assigned to the category "national standard vowel," e.g. [ày] in 'pipe' rather than, e.g. [æ] or [ɑ]; and some 29 percent can definitely be assigned to the category "Southeast coastal norm," e.g. [ɔw] in 'avoid' rather than [ɔy], or [∧w] in 'want' rather than [å]. The remaining 22 percent are also standard forms but forms whose regional provenience is in some doubt. Note that NONE of the modal vowel categories, for any of the words, are dialectally odd forms from the point of view of regional norms; moreover, this is so in spite of the rather fine level of detail to which our transcribers worked. The modal pronunciations are clearly not accidentally cumulating idiosyncratic pronunciations but are pronunciations under the control of relatively unambiguous established standards. Now it makes no sense whatever to assume that education lowers mode scores where mode scores reflect conformity to what is, in effect, the SUM of national and regional speech norms. Education might be imagined, in some circumstances, to affect choices of national over regional norms, but not their joint probability of occurrence. And so we cannot interpret the sex:mode score relation as secondary to the education:mode score plus education:demography relations. We must select the other alternative, and consider the sex:mode score relation as the fact, to be added to other data in the literature on sex differences in speech, and to require explanation.

Our previous work (Crockett and Levine 1967) showed that women are more susceptible than men to contemporary influences affecting speech pronunciation. We find some confirmation of this susceptibility in our study of modal vowels. Table 4 shows that women's responses tend to be overrepresented among the "national norm" responses while men's responses tend to be overrepresented among the "regional responses" although it happens to be the case in this community that no overall difference exists between men and women with regard to place of early socialization. Women, then, are more susceptible to contemporary influence than men but show less conformity — have lower mode scores — than men. Two factors suggest themselves; either or both may underlie these male–female differences. First, one may imagine that a lifetime's practice in adjustment to contemporary influences by itself militates

Table 4.   Frequencies of modal responses by norm category and sex of respondent

Sex of respondent	Modal Vowel			
	National norm	Southeast Coastal norm	Other norm	Totals
Men	139(46%)	103(59%)	77(59%)	319(53%)
Women	161(54%)	73(41%)	54(41%)	288(47%)
Totals	300	176	131	607

against what we have called conformity, since contemporary influences change. That is, the entire set of women, under a matrix of contemporary influences over a span of years, are less likely to constitute a homogeneous speech group than are men and, hence, are thereby less likely to contribute to what becomes modes than are men. More specifically, what we imagine here is that the response of no individual, man or woman, to contemporary influence will be instantaneous and continuous. The results of a process of uneven and intermittent response to contemporary influence of a group of people, cumulated over years, where the people are of different ages — i.e. have been responsive for different numbers of years — will be "scatter" or varieties of performance. To the extent that women are more responsive than men, to that extent the performances of the group of women will show more scatter than the performances of the group of men. Together with this possibility, or, in place of it, is the following. Susceptibility to contemporary influences may yield an internal state, in each woman (as well as in each man, but more so for women than men and for more women than men) of multivalence about linguistic norms so that, at any moment, there exists in the habit structure several speech models, unequally or ambiguously valued but nevertheless present. Hence, it may be imagined that the odds are that a woman will be less consistent in pronunciation than a man. If one is less consistent in pronunciation, other things being equal, one is less likely to utter a pronunciation which, on a given occasion, will become a modal pronunciation. Both hypotheses involve some notion such as "scatter"; according to both, women as a group are more likely to evince it than are men as a group. (Such scatter of course need have no effect on the direct quantitative pronunciation variables such as R-score, etc.) The first hypothesis does not make a point of assuming norm competition within each individual; the second does, and predicts inconsistency as a by-product. In either case, more scatter is predicted of women than men and the mode score difference is explained by pointing out that with greater scatter the probability of women's being the group that in fact makes the modal pronunciations modal is lower than that for men. Note that the statistics which have suggested that these differences in probability exist are of course those of Table 1.

Now it is of no importance to this paper to argue the independence or nonindependence of these two possible explanations, or, even, their exhaustiveness. Some theorizing was necessary to link the work showing the greater susceptibility of women to contemporary linguistic norms to the work presented here suggesting the lower conformity — as measured by mode scores — of women. What is important now is to turn to the data, to see what may be gleaned about scatter and consistency. Table 5 shows some results of a study of pronunciation consistency. For the three pairs of words shown, pronunciations of the larger sample of 275 respondents were studied for the repeated use of all possible vowel transcriptions. An instance of a "consistent pronunciation" was the use of the same alternant by an individual for each of the words of the word pair. Consistent pronunciations were then categorized as either "standard vowel" or "nonstandard vowel." Here, "standard" means any standard, be it national, coastal or other (thus, for Table 5, this category is the conceptual SUM of all the categories of Table 4), while "nonstandard" refers to a consistent pronunciation which either contains elements from several norms or is in some other way deviant. Note that for each of the three

Table 5.   Sex and vowel consistency in pronunciation of three word pairs, for "standard" versus "nonstandard" vowels

Word pair		Number of consistent pronunciations		
		For standard vowel	For nonstandard vowel	Totals
"I," "tried"	Men	22	19	41
	Women	15	31	46
	Totals	37	50	87
"nigh," "I"	Men	17	4	21
	Women	11	3	14
	Totals	28	7	35
"night," "night"	Men	52	9	61
	Women	48	25	73
	Totals	100	34	134

pairs presented here, men show more consistencies in the pronunciation of any vowel recognized as standard than do women; women, in two of the three cases, show more nonstandard consistencies. Note, further, that although there are more instances of consistent pronunciations by women (46 + 14 + 73 = 133) than by men (41 + 21 + 61 = 123), the PROPORTION of consistent pronunciations by women, 133/256 or 52 percent is less than the proportion of women in the sample of 275 respondents, which is 56 percent. Women, then, do appear, at least from these data, to be somewhat less consistent than men. More important, perhaps, since both theses discussed above involved a notion such as scatter, is the following. Since our system of coding transcriptions recognizes more kinds of nonstandard pronunciations than kinds of standard pronunciations, the vowel pronunciation consistency of men is over a narrower range of alternants than that of women and, hence, by extension, the nature of men's consistency, over the data summarized by Table 5, is such that they are more likely to contribute to modes than women. The reader may recall here that the data summarized by Table 1 also suggest and the data summarized by Table 4 also strongly suggest the sex difference with respect to scatter. Table 4, for example, shows that 607 of the 609 pronunciations (spoken by the individuals in the sample of thirty) which are modal are pronunciations which may be assigned to one or another norm; men produced 53 percent of these modal pronunciations although men comprise 47 percent of the individuals in the subsample. Since, for each word, there is only one modal pronunciation out of the many pronunciations recognized by our transcription code, and since women outnumber men, it is highly likely that women pronounced words, during our interviews, in a greater variety of ways than did men. It would seem that women are modish and men are modal.

To summarize. We have shown that relationships, which are partially independent of each other, exist respectively between mode scores and sex of respondent, educational level, occupational category and status consistency. We argued that to the extent that these relationships are not independent, the mode score:sex relationship is paramount; our argument made reference to the fact that virtually all of the pronunciations uttered most frequently by our respondents were national or regional standard pronunciations. We compared the thus-justified relation between mode score and sex of respondent to the results of work by the present authors in the same community and to work by others which indicates that women are more susceptible to contemporary linguistic influences than men — i.e. are more subject than men to normative influences which impinge upon them as adults. We suggested two hypotheses to link the two results and presented data relevant to the hypotheses.

We conclude now in three steps. First, we offer our belief that the processes we have called women's relatively great responsiveness or susceptibility to external norm pressure and men's relatively great conformity are processes which generate complementary statistics — such at any event is the spirit in which we presented the hypotheses linking the two processes. Second, we suggest that the loose and general concept, "conformity," which the variable "mode score" is an attempt to tap, refers specifically to a response to the social pressure exerted concretely and immediately by peers, people of approximately coequal status and in frequent and salient contact, while "susceptibility to contemporary influence," as measured by intersituational score differences, the friend's influence test, etc., refers specifically to a linguistic response to the more general, wider provenience, harder to pin down social pressure that gives form, plausibility and necessity to the individual's looking beyond his or her immediate situation. If this suggestion has merit, it is interesting to wonder if other evidence can be found to support the proposition that men, at least in the community studied, respond to localized pressures while women respond to those more widely cast. Further, we could at least dimly see why education too should militate against high mode scores at least to the extent that education does in fact broaden one's horizons. Now let us return to susceptibility for a moment. We have allowed the susceptibility or responsiveness of women to contemporary influence to be seen as a "cause" of their relatively inconsistent use of standard forms and we guessed that involved therewith was some ambivalence about alternative ideas about pronunciation either coexisting or competing in the mind. We now ask if it is not conceivable that some more general and deeper ambivalence, on the part of women, either in Southern communities or more generally, might not be represented by linguistic ambivalence as it would be by other behavioral traits.

Third, and finally, we point out that sociolinguistic data, such as those presented here on mode scores and consistency, as well as those presented elsewhere pointing to relationships — simple and curvilinear — between linguistic variables and social status, mobility, age, sex, all indicate as powerfully and as clearly as can be the fact that language is used by people constantly and powerfully as an expressive device, as a device for covert and indirect communication as well as for direct, overt propositional communication. Teleology becomes no one but if one is to be teleological perhaps therein lies a reason for the preservation, by every language, of so many alternate ways of saying the same thing. In any case, the raw material of alternation comes from the processes of historical change, yet the frequency of use of an alternant, the degree of acceptance and hence the degree of completion of a particular process of historical change, appears to be in part a function of the social structures of communities of speakers and of the social psychological games played by these speakers. (Are local exceptions to Grimm's law of linguistic, sociological or "random" causation?).

Our major point here is this. Given the universality, for expressive communication both on the part of speaker and listener, of the use of different frequencies of employment of alternative forms, we must recognize that if adult, adolescent and perhaps even pre-adolescent speakers of a language are to be regarded as "knowing their language," they must know, in some sense, an enormous stock of statistical information. Most linguists today accept, with more or less simplification, Chomsky's "Cartesian" view of first language acquisition as it applies to the ideal entity studied by today's grammarians and phonologists. We suggest here that the mass of statistical data which must be known in some form or other by a native speaker — the "competence of the native speaker as subject of sociolinguistic study" — is perhaps in no real way less voluminous, is in no substantial way more likely to have been presented in "trial and error" form, and is acquired not very many years later than, respectively, are the data, the mode of first exposure, and the date of first "command," of grammatical and phonological competence. In short we suggest that if the challenge presented to the native speaker by the task of learning to utilize expressively the local and the large scale patterns of speech variation impinging upon him is in fact as great as it seems to us to be, then perhaps native speakers have some prior faculty for selecting whatever is the sociolinguistic analogue of the rules of a grammar, just as it is thought that they do in the case of grammar and phonology. Of course we do not imply that the information itself, the "competence," is such that it can best be described by any system of rewrite rules.

REFERENCES

ANSHEN, FRANK S.
  1969   "Speech variation among Negroes in a small southern community." Unpublished Ph.D. dissertation, New York University.
CROCKETT, HARRY J., JR., LEWIS LEVINE
  1967   Friends' influences on speech. *Sociological Inquiry* 37:109–128.
LABOV, WILLIAM
  1966   *The social stratification of English in New York City.* Washington, D.C.: Center for Applied Linguistics.
LEVINE, LEWIS, HARRY J. CROCKETT, JR.
  1966   Speech variation in a Piedmont community: postvocalic *r*. *Sociological Inquiry* 36:204–226.
SHUY, ROGER W., WALTER A. WOLFRAM, WILLIAM RILEY
  1969   *Methods for the analysis of social dialect.* Washington, D.C.: Center for Applied Linguistics.

The Effects of Marital Status and Age on Sex Differences in Language Style

DIANA WORTMAN WARSHAY

It is the purpose here to examine the possible relevance of marital status and age to sex differences in language style. The paper uses the data of an earlier study by the writer (Warshay 1969) which examined several correlates of sex differences in language style. In that study, marital status was not used as a factor, while age was used only as a control variable. The present analysis was prompted by the fact that a number of the predictions held only for the comparisons between older males and females and not for comparisons between younger males and females.

Below, the background of the earlier study will be described. Then, the results of the present analysis focusing on marital status and age will be given within the context of the variables and results of the earlier study.

BACKGROUND

Sex differences in language behavior were related to the general behavioral styles expected of men and women in American society. These generalized behavioral styles were derived from descriptions given by such writers as Douvan and Adelson (1966), Kagan (1964), Kluckhohn (1955), and Williams (1960).

The male style requires an active, aggressive, instrumental approach with emphasis on the individual, personal achievements, and a future time orientation with a delay of immediate gratification. The female style emphasizes emotionality, passivity, receptivity, concern for and service to others with a concomitant submergence of self and vicarious enjoyment of others' achievements. These behavioral styles were titled instrumental, for the male, and affective, for the female.

The elements of the instrumental and the affective language style were construed as attached to sex as a social status (i.e. a social position) rather than to role (i.e. the ongoing behavior in a specific social situation).

Hence, instead of speech gathered in specific interactions (situational roles), written language samples in a relatively interaction-free situation were deemed more desirable. A setting that left the respondent relatively anonymous was used — large university classes at the start of the academic year. Also, an instrument was devised which would serve as a minimal constant stimulus. This unstructured instrument, the Important Events Test, directed the respondent to "please write down all the events in the past important to you." Such an anonymous and private mode of obtaining language samples was considered more likely to tap the subject's generalized statuses than the subject's situationally more specific role behaviors.

The subjects in the earlier study were 263 middleclass, white, native-born students at a large urban midwestern American state university. They wrote of an aggregate total of 3,311 events. The sample was divided according to sex and to age (under twenty years and twenty years and older) and comparisons were made between the sexes of the same age groupings.

VARIABLES AND RESULTS

For the present analysis, six subjects were omitted from the original sample of 263 (thus reducing the sample size to 257 subjects with an aggregate total of 3,220 events). One of the omitted subjects was the only married female in the younger age category (under twenty years old) in the entire sample; there were no younger married males. The five others omitted were all married and thirty years and older, four females and one male; there were no unmarried subjects in the thirty and over age range. The shortened sample of 257 subjects therefore formed six marital status–age–sex categories. These are: married older females ($n = 15$), married older males ($n = 8$), unmarried older females ($n = 47$), unmarried older males ($n = 51$), unmarried younger females ($n = 104$), and unmarried younger males ($n = 32$). As there are no married younger female or married younger male categories in the present analysis, all comparisons using married subjects are therefore using only older subjects (i.e. there can be no second order partialing because of the lack of younger married subjects). Comparisons were made using Students' t where means were involved and chi square for the remaining variables. The level of statistical significance was set at $P < 0.10$, two-tailed. Finally, where comparisons are made in terms of two values of a variable (e.g. married versus unmarried), other variables (e.g. male versus female) are controlled.

The variables which were most significant for the male instrumental and female affective language styles were: (1) form of reference to events: verb:noun ratio, (2) social psychological location of events, (3) involvement in events, (4) reference to others, and (5) fluency. These will be discussed in turn, below, and the results from the earlier study and the present analysis compared. For each variable, the order will be as follows: first, a description and discussion of the variable; next, a comparison of results for sex differences between the earlier study and the present one; then, the results for marital status; then, the results for age; and, finally, a brief summary of the results for that variable.

Form of Reference to Events: Verb:Noun Ratio

Verbs have been considered a more active mode of description than nouns (Wells 1960:217). Moreover, Morris relates the use of a verb form to the manipulatory stage of action and a noun form to the consummatory stage (Morris 1964:23). Referring to events more in verb forms (e.g. "graduated," "graduating") would thus apply to the male status in American society, whereas noun forms (e.g. "graduation") would apply to the female status.

In the earlier study, males had a significantly higher verb:noun ratio than females. In the present analysis the sex difference still holds, but only for the unmarried (see Item 1, Tables 1 and 2). For the married, the results were not statistically significant although in the expected direction.

Comparisons between the married and unmarried categories were significant, with the unmarried having higher verb:noun ratios than the married.

Age comparisons yielded significant results only for the females, the younger showing a higher verb:noun ratio than the older. For the males, the older have a slightly higher, and insignificant, verb:noun ratio than the younger.

Apparently, marriage depresses the verb:noun ratio for both sexes whereas age depresses this ratio only for females.

Social Psychological Location of Events

Events were classified according to their social psychological location in relation to the subject. Events were located in (a) the PERSONAL SPHERE, in (b) the subject's INTERACTING COMMUNITY, or considered (c) REMOVED. PERSONAL SPHERE events were about the subject's own experiences (e.g. "graduating from high school"). INTERACTING COMMUNITY events were about people with whom the subject could engage in social relations or groups to which he/she belonged (e.g. "my sister's graduation," "school won the football championship"). REMOVED events are those generally known as matters of historical record or otherwise available to all, i.e. "removed" from both the personal sphere and interacting community of the subject (e.g. "Kennedy's assassination," "a beautiful spring day," "the creation of the earth"). The emphasis on individualistic achievement for males was the basis for expecting them to write a higher proportion than females of PERSONAL SPHERE events. The complementary prediction, for females to write a higher proportion of INTERACTING COMMUNITY events, was based upon the collateral orientation of females. No theoretical basis was seen for sex differences for REMOVED events. This appears to be a highly idiosyncratic variable similar to a type of global statement made on projective tests of self-concept (McPartland 1965:11).

In the earlier study, only older males had a higher proportion (than older females) of PERSONAL SPHERE events. Further, only the females had a higher proportion (than older males) of INTERACTING COMMUNITY events. In the present analysis, as in the earlier one, the sex differences are significant, but only for the older (see Items 2a and 2b, Tables 1 and 2).

Table 1.   Important-events test results by sex–marital-status–age category

Item	Females			Males		
	Married older ($n = 15$)	Unmarried older ($n = 47$)	Unmarried younger ($n = 104$)	Married older ($n = 8$)	Unmarried older ($n = 51$)	Unmarried younger ($n = 32$)
1. Form of reference to events: verb:noun ratio						
	0.8	1.6	2.0	1.1	2.9	2.7
2. Social psychological location of events						
a. Personal sphere events (percent of total events)						
	77.8	84.3	88.4	87.7	94.9	88.5
b. Interacting community events (percent of total events)						
	15.3	11.9	9.5	6.8	3.1	6.8
3. Involvement in events (percent of total events)						
	77.8	81.7	83.3	84.9	91.8	84.8
4. Reference to others						
a. Number of others (mean number)						
	7.0	9.2	9.2	4.8	5.9	5.0
b. Positional reference to others (percent of total others)						
	71.4	82.2	75.3	76.3	76.1	74.9
5. Fluency						
a. Number of events (mean number)						
	9.2	14.0	13.5	9.1	10.7	9.2
b. Number of words (mean number)						
	79.5	100.7	98.5	52.6	91.7	71.9

Here, whether married or unmarried are compared, males refer to a higher proportion of PERSONAL SPHERE events than do females, and the females refer to a higher proportion of INTERACTING COMMUNITY events.

Comparisons based on marital status were significant for both sexes, the married writing of a smaller proportion of PERSONAL SPHERE events and a greater proportion of INTERACTING COMMUNITY events than the unmarried.

Age comparisons showed significant sex differences. The older males referred to a higher proportion of PERSONAL SPHERE events and to a lower proportion of INTERACTING COMMUNITY events than did younger males. For the females this distribution was reversed in that the younger females referred to more PERSONAL SPHERE events and to fewer INTERACTING COMMUNITY events than did the older females.

Marriage, thus, reduces the proportion of PERSONAL SPHERE references and increases references to the INTERACTING COMMUNITY — for both sexes.

Table 2. Significant comparisons on important-events test for marital status-age-sex categories

Item	Marital status comparisons		Age comparisons		Sex comparisons		
	Older females Married vs unmarried	Older males Married vs unmarried	Unmarried females Older vs younger	Unmarried males Older vs younger	Married older Females vs males	Unmarried older Females vs males	Unmarried younger Females vs males
1. Form of reference to events: verb:noun ratio	*	*	*	n.s.	n.s.	*	*
2. Social psychological location of events a. Personal sphere event	*	*	*	*	*	*	*
b. Interacting community events	n.s.	n.s.	*	*	*	*	n.s.
3. Involvement in events	n.s.	*	n.s.	*	n.s.	*	n.s.
4. Reference to others a. Number of others (means)	*	n.s.	n.s.	*	*	*	*
b. Positional reference to others	*	n.s.	*	n.s.	n.s.	*	n.s.
5. Fluency a. Number of events (means)	*	n.s.	n.s.	*	n.s.	*	*
b. Number of words (means)	*	*	n.s.	n.s.	*	n.s.	n.s.

$*P<0.10$, two-tailed test. Comparisons were made using Students t for means and chi square (d.f. = 1) for all others.

Age, however, varies in its influence on the sexes. Increased age increases PERSONAL SPHERE references and decreases INTERACTING COMMUNITY references for males. For females, the influence is reversed. In other words, age may exaggerate existing tendencies.

Involvement in the Events

Signifying, through verbal means, one's involvement in an event can be seen as a way of asserting one's achievement or of claiming participation where there had been none (as in INTERACTING COMMUNITY events). Statements such as "I graduated" or "when I heard of Kennedy's assassination" signify INVOLVEMENT whereas "graduated" or "Kennedy's assassination" do not. Males were expected to have a higher proportion of signified INVOLVEMENT in their events than were females given the aggressiveness and individualism associated with the male.

In the earlier study, significantly greater INVOLVEMENT in event references was displayed only by the older males (when compared to the older females). The present analysis agrees with these results. Further, the only significant differences in INVOLVEMENT references occur in those comparisons using the unmarried older males. Specifically, unmarried older males showed significantly greater INVOLVEMENT in their events than did unmarried older females, married older males, or unmarried younger males (see Item 3, Tables 1 and 2).

Marriage apparently reduces INVOLVEMENT for males, and age increases it. For females, there are no significant differences, marriage, and age both slightly reducing INVOLVEMENT.

Reference to Others

The number of OTHERS referred to as well as the mode of reference to them should reflect whether individualism and instrumentality, or collaterality and affectivity, dominate. A collateral orientation, emphasizing group affiliations and goals, should dispose a subject to mention more OTHERS than the having of an individualistic orientation with its emphasis on personal achievement. Moreover, since collaterality emphasizes kin relations and ascribed roles, OTHERS should more likely be referred to in terms of their structural relations to the referred, i.e. by their positional titles (e.g. "teacher," "sister"). Females, therefore, were expected to refer to more OTHERS than were males and to use more positional titles in their references.

In the earlier study, females referred to a greater number of OTHERS than did males and did so more in positional terms. In the present analysis, females also referred to significantly more OTHERS than did males, this being true regardless of marital status or age category (see Item 4a, Tables 1 and 2). However, only the older females (compared to the older males) referred to significantly more OTHERS by their positional titles. For the younger categories, the results were insignificant, but in the same direction (see Item 4b, Tables 1 and 2).

Married females, compared to unmarried, referred to significantly fewer OTHERS. For the males, there was an insignificant trend in the same direction. In regard to mode of reference to OTHERS, married females referred to significantly more OTHERS by their positional titles than did unmarried females, while for males there was no difference in mode of reference.

The age comparisons showed no differences for the females, but the older males referred to significantly more OTHERS than the younger males. Younger females referred to significantly more of their OTHERS by positional title than did older females. For the males, there was an insignificant trend in the same direction as the females' differences.

Marriage apparently acts to individualize females at least in decreasing their references to OTHERS whereas the results are less clear for age.

Fluency

FLUENCY, traditionally and empirically, has been considered a feminine attribute (cf. Jespersen 1938:16–17 and Oetzel's summary of a number of studies in Gallagher 1964:370). In the earlier study, FLUENCY was seen to be a form of non-instrumental consummatory behavior. Males, who are rewarded for their individualistic achievements in American society, were thus expected to be less fluent than the affectively-directed females.

The earlier study found females more fluent than males, as measured by both number of events and number of words. The present analysis shows females generally more fluent than males (see Items 5a and 5b, Tables 1 and 2). Unmarried females wrote of significantly more events than did unmarried males and wrote more words as well, although the latter difference was not significant. For the married males and females, the difference in number of events is insignificant, but the difference in number of words is not, the females writing more.

Unmarried females wrote of significantly more events and wrote more words than married females. Unmarried males wrote of more events (not significant) and wrote more words (significant) than did the married.

Older males wrote significantly more events and (insignificantly) more words than younger males. For females, age differences in number of events and words are very slight and insignificant.

The general picture appears to be that higher FLUENCY is associated with femaleness, age, and an unmarried existence.

SUMMARY AND CONCLUSION

In a re-analysis of the data of an earlier study of sex differences in language style, this study focused on such differences from the viewpoint of the effects of two additional variables, marital status and age. The data had previously been gathered in the form of events important to members of a large university student sample. Using six marital status–age–sex categories, variation in language style was examined in terms of five variables that refer to the above events. The main findings were:

1. Referring to the events in verb, more than in noun, form, shown to be characteristic of males in the earlier study, declined for the married of both sexes and with age for females.

2. Both the earlier study and the current analysis showed older males tending (more than older females) to locate events in their PERSONAL SPHERE and less in their INTERACTING COMMUNITY. The current analysis showed marriage related to a lowered rate of reference to the PERSONAL SPHERE for both sexes. Age, however, tended to increase pre-existing orientations, i.e. older males were even more oriented to the PERSONAL SPHERE than younger males and older females were more oriented to the INTERACTING COMMUNITY than younger females.

3. Signifying verbal involvement in the events, associated more with older males (than with older females) in the earlier study, was related in this analysis largely to unmarried older males.

4. Reference to OTHERS in the events was characteristic more of females, the current analysis verifying this and indicating that older females were more likely to refer to OTHERS in positional terms than were older males. Marriage for females, however, was associated with a decrease in references to OTHERS.

5. FLUENCY was clearly more characteristic of females than of males in both the earlier study and the more controlled current analysis, as measured by numbers of both events and words. Being married was related to lower EVENT and WORD FLUENCY for females and to lower WORD FLUENCY for males. Age seemed to increase EVENT FLUENCY for males.

Considering the above, it appears that sex status and marital status account for variation in language style in a similar way while age only increases already existing tendencies. Being married has an effect similar to being female in that both are related to affectivity in language style; therefore, remaining unmarried and masculinity are both related to an instrumental language style. Age, however, appears to increase instrumentality and affectivity where they already predominate.

REFERENCES

DOUVAN, E., J. ADELSON
1966   *The adolescent experience*. New York: Wiley.
GALLAGHER, J. J.
1964   "Productive thinking," in *Review of child development research* 1. Edited by M. L. Hoffman and L. W. Hoffman. New York: Russell Sage Foundation.
JESPERSEN, O.
1938   *Growth and structure of the English language* (ninth edition). Garden City, New York: Doubleday-Anchor.
KAGAN, J.
1964   "Acquisition and significance of sex typing and sex role identity," in *Review of child development research* 1. Edited by M. L. Hoffman and L. W. Hoffman, 137–168. New York: Russell Sage Foundation.
KLUCKHOHN, F.
1955   "Dominant and variant value orientations," in *Personality in nature, society and culture* (second edition). Edited by C. Kluckhohn and H. A. Murray, 342–357. New York: Knopf.
McPARTLAND, T. S.
1965   *Manual for the twenty-statements problem* (revised May, 1965). Kansas City, Missouri: Department of Research, Greater Kansas City Mental Health Foundation.
MORRIS, C. W.
1964   *Signification and significance*. Cambridge, Mass.: M.I.T. Press.
WARSHAY, D. W.
1969   "Instrumental and affective language styles in sex status." Unpublished Ph.D. dissertation, Ohio State University, Columbus.
WELLS, R.
1960   "Nominal and verbal style," in *Style in language*. Edited by T. A. Sebeok, 213–220. Cambridge, Mass.: M.I.T. Press.
WILLIAMS, R. M., JR.
1960   *American society* (second edition, revised). New York: Knopf.

Sampling, Elicitation, and Interpretation: Orléans and Elsewhere

JOHN ROSS

> Ce que dit le sujet doit toujours être référé
> aux conditions dans lesquelles il le dit: ce
> qui est pertinent, ce n'est donc pas tant le
> "contenu" de l'interview qu'un dirigeant
> d'entreprise accorde au sociologue, que la
> confrontation du discours qu'il lui tient PAR
> RAPPORT À CE QU'IL DIT ET FAIT PAR AILLEURS,
> c'est-à-dire, par rapport à d'autres rôles dis-
> cursifs dont les effets peuvent être saisis
> AILLEURS, PLUS la description de la pratique
> effectuée par le sujet, comme représentant
> d'une place dans le champ des pratiques, par
> le discours scientifique de la sociologie.
> (PÊCHEUX 1969:111)

When we move from the study of *la langue* to that of *la parole*, we find that the choice of syntax and lexis will be governed in any given case by a network of constraints determined by the hierarchical relationship between speaker and interlocutor (in terms of age, sex, education, profession, etc.) and the purpose of the utterance (please, persuade, order, etc.). In other terms, actualized language must be related to the immediate and wider contexts in which it is used. The language used by speaker A in situations X and Y can be characterized and contrasted, as can A's language with that of speaker B in the same situations; the degree of convergence or divergence between the two sets of language is a significant index to the role of language as a social parameter, as will be the discovery whether A and B do or do not possess the same number of variants.

An extreme, well-documented example of definable speaker relationships dictating the choice of linguistic forms is that of contemporary Indonesia, where indeed the *langue* competence in sophisticated circles comprises more than one language (Tanner 1967); the reverse is illustrated by the Subanum drinking culture in the Philippines, described by Frake (1964), in which individual status is determined directly by continued proficiency in manipulating certain linguistic skills.

The study of the whole language aims at a totally comprehensive model of the language and all its resources; the study of language in use, of *la parole*, must aim at defining what subset of the available phonetic, phonological, syntactic, and lexical material is available to a given group of speakers, and how far the individual's choice is governed by his relationship with the language medium and with his singular or plural audience (Gregory 1967). It may emerge that different groups will use different linguistic subsets in the same situation; and it has been demonstrated, at least for British English, that not all speakers are aware of possible situation-adaptive choices (Bernstein 1971). In short, when we pass from *la langue* to *la parole*, we move from linguistics to sociolinguistics.

ORLÉANS STUDY: PRESENTATION AND PREPARATION

The recent Franco-British research project known as the Orléans Study (*Etude Sociolinguistique sur Orléans*) stands firmly in the field of sociolinguistics because, whatever its shortcomings, it set out to explore (even more, to facilitate further exploration of) two hitherto neglected aspects of the French language: the syntax of spoken French and its sociolinguistic variants. Two main types of variation were envisaged: on one hand, variations in the *langue* available to, or at least predominantly used by, different social groups, and on the other, the degree and nature of variation in the language used by members of these groups in varying situations. These aims were nothing if not ambitious, and the Orléans Study cannot hope to provide comprehensive data all along both these dimensions, particularly where codeswitching is concerned. However, it may be that the study's relative failures will prove more useful to future research, particularly outside the field of French, than will its successes.

Any hypothesis must be preceded by an intuition based on a body of randomly acquired experience. As Gumperz, quoting Hymes, points out: "Naturalistic observation and random sampling of speech must therefore be preceded by 'ethnographies of communication' (Hymes 1964), that is, by unstructured observation not tied down to any rigid experimental design." In the case of the Orléans Study, the prehypothetical stages of this sequence were provided by the lives and professional experience of the research team. The hypothesis itself assumed the existence of sociologically significant codes and a correspondence between alternative codes and definable societal parameters. Further, it was assumed that codes and variants can be identified and contrasted descriptively, and correlated with extralinguistic factors residing in the situation and/or in the speaker's own background.

It is worth pointing out that these intuitions apply equally well to English and French. However, whereas the role of English English as a social and sociological index has long been recognized and more or less generously documented, the same cannot be said for French. Social variants and the judgments based on them have been known to exist in France for centuries: we may prefer to set aside Rutebeuf's thirteenth-century apologies for his French on the grounds that this was a case of regional, not primarily intrasociety variation, but the mid-seventeenth-century satirical dialogues *Les Mazarinades* provide spectacular examples of the indecision and hypercorrection later documented by Labov as a lower-middleclass phenomenon. For instance, in the eighth dialogue Jeannin exclaims: *"Odian non, a cause de la guarre tu baballe raison, baille li balle, la guerre ly pu."* Understandably, faced with such an utterance, Pierrot/Piarrot contents himself with sociolinguistic comment: *"Tu vera ou tu vara"* (Rosset 1911).

Despite such historical examples (multiplied in literary sources, particularly in turn-of-the-century realist authors like Bruant, Métenier and Rosny, and more recent writers, mainly Céline and Queneau), little systematic work, apart from dialect studies, has been done on nonnormative descriptions of French (cf. Agnel 1855; Koschwitz 1893; Nisard 1872; Bauche 1920) and, indeed, in nonlinguistic circles there is still a tendency towards a folklore denying the existence of socially conditioned or status-indicative variants of French. It may well be true that the difference between standard French (one form of Parisian) and socially or regionally marked forms is not so sharp — or, to those on the wrong side of the vowel-shift, lethal — as was the case until recently for RP (Received Pronunciation — nonregional standard English) versus "The Rest." Nonetheless, the tradition of "one France, one French," even allowing for situational/stylistic distinctions between *le langage soutenu* and *le langage familier*, seems unreasonable and can be refuted on endless anecdotal grounds, such as middleclass parental reprimands to children: *"on ne dit pas pareil que!"* (this is in fact a frequently used construction, and whereas among children it may be attributed partly to the role of analogy in language acquisition, it is also used by a great many adults — though by no means in all milieux). Whether this traditional belief in a monolithic language reflects an ideological image of society or collective attitudes towards the language, it would seem an interesting topic to pursue (and attempts have been made in the Orléans Study to elicit information about such attitudes).

For one reason and another, then, we know less than we might about contemporary spoken French. It was a consciousness of this lack that led, through common teaching and research interests, to the formation of the Franco-British team which prepared and carried out, with financial backing from the Department of Education and Science and considerable help and goodwill from French officials and private organizations, the Orléans Study (for a full account of the organization and implementation of the project, see Biggs and Blanc [1971]). From the outset, work was conceived in a sociolinguistic perspective, and attempted, in particular through the recruitment of a linguistically-oriented sociologist, to maintain rigorous standards in what for the team was the less familiar task of defining and dealing with sociological data.

In concrete terms, the aim of the study was to collect a representative selection of samples of spoken French, taken within a single urban community, to provide accurately identified, documented raw material for two purposes: the analytical study of varieties of contemporary spoken French, and the provision of authentic extract material for use in teaching French language and culture in secondary and higher education. Equal weighting was given throughout to these two aims, which fortunately turned out to be complementary as far as recordings are concerned. The incidence of sociolinguistics on the theory and practice of language teaching has yet to be worked out fully, but it appears undeniable that the new discipline has a valid contribution to make, already at the obvious, superficial level of the choice of models for imitation and the need for an awareness of the existence of variants.

Consequently, pedagogical and sociological criteria counted equally in the choice of a speech community. Orléans was chosen from a long list of starters for a variety of reasons. By French standards it is a relatively large town (ca. 150,000 inhabitants), apparently predestined for the role of a French Middletown by virtue of being the administrative center of the Loiret, a *département* frequently taken in polls as the "middle of France" from which to predict electoral behavior. The town has a historic core surrounded by high-density municipal housing developments and suburbs of small houses set in gardens; to the south, a satellite town is being built, with a new university, decentralized industry, and administrative office complexes. There is some old-established industry and much post-war industrial expansion. As a *préfecture* and future regional capital, Orléans has a full range of administrative, educational and cultural institutions. Despite Joan of Arc, the town's history is not so overwhelming as to have created a *ville-musée* and, in terms of language, Orléans has no particular reputation, whether for "pure" French or for regional idiosyncracies. In short: a complete French urban community with no disproportionately marked characteristic.

CONTACT, SAMPLING AND ELICITATION

Fieldwork in Orléans was carried out intermittently (i.e. during British university vacations) between 1968 and 1970. The first visit was devoted to making contact with key individuals in the fields of industry, commerce, education, social agencies, etc., explaining the broad aims of the project, and requesting advice. This operation yielded a body of hand-picked, often self-selecting informants who were interviewed to provide a stylized but realistic portrait of the town and its activities. Each interview in the "Portrait" set was individually researched and conducted on an open-ended basis to elicit maximum content information about the interviewee's activities, explanations of the structure and working of institutions, etc. In each case background information on the informant was collected.

The second, indeed, the largest single set of interviews came from a cross-section of the population. A random sample of 1:100 was provided by the INSEE (*Institut National de Statistique et d'Etudes Economiques*) from the registers of the preceding census; people under sixteen and over seventy were not selected, nor were those who had not been educated within the French system, in order to limit our sample to mother-tongue speakers of French belonging to the active population. Batch by batch, potential informants were contacted by a circular letter setting out the aims of the project in general terms (but omitting all reference, overt or implied, to language) and requesting cooperation. Later, a second letter announced that a team member would call in the following week to answer questions and, hopefully, arrange an appointment for an interview. After allowing for changes of address, refusals and other wastage, and the occasional ad hoc adjustment to avoid, for instance, a chance predominance of bakers in a given INSEE category, the "Sample" set comprised 150 interviews. Unlike the "Portrait" interviews, which were tailor-made for each informant, these were conducted on the the basis of a set of standard questionnaires always administered in full, although as a matter of policy extra topics introduced by the informants were always pursued.

Both "Portrait" and "Sample" materials were elicited through face-to-face interviews, although sometimes the interviewer was accompanied by a technician or by a new interviewer, and occasionally informants tended to be chaperoned by mothers or daughters. The locale was invariably chosen by the informant, and was usually his own home or office; this seemed the most desirable location for interviews, particularly with non-public figures, as the home setting bolstered confidence; the consequent occasional sacrifice in acoustic quality was more than offset by the gain in spontaneity.

As far as possible, interviewers were assigned informants so that each category included one recording between peers in sex and age. Interviewing technique was defined very loosely, the main considerations being to create a relaxed, conversational atmosphere and keep the interviewer's interventions to the absolute minimum, the latter to avoid introducing random linguistic stimuli.

The first questionnaire comprised a series of open-ended questions designed to elicit the maximum amount of speech from informants on four main themes: work, leisure, education, and political and social life. The questions were framed to ensure that each subject had at least the opportunity of running the gamut of French syntax, e.g. by projection into the future, the past, the hypothetical or the might-have-been, and by varying the purposive aspect of discourse, mainly between description (objects, events and processes), explanation, and opinion. For each theme questions were divided into a *tronc commun*, administered to every informant, and a *branche*, used when it was clear that the topic had not been exhausted. This questionnaire aimed at creating a general parity of content; as the situation was invariably that of the face-to-face interview, these recordings were intended to illustrate variations in language, in a consultative situation, across the class spectrum.

The second questionnaire, designed by the French sociologist Bernard Vernier, consisted of a series of closed questions relating to cultural habits, the use of language, and the attitudes of informants towards language as a whole, its manifestations, criteria of correctness, etc. Responses to this questionnaire were always recorded, unlike the third, providing a rapid, closed checklist bearing on the informants' educational and cultural experience and family backgrounds. The information here was designed to provide background data on informants for use in identifying and classifying them. (The texts of the open and closed questionnaires are given in this article as an Appendix.)

A third set of recordings was obtained thanks to the goodwill and cooperation of the *Centre Médico-Psycho-Pédagogique,* (CMPP) a counseling center for the parents of children with educational problems. This yielded a set of recordings with roughly constant content: parents discussing their children's problems with a trained social worker. Apart from the intrinsic linguistic interest of the material, the CMPP set provides a useful control corpus to gauge how far linguistic behavior may have been distorted by the use of the standard interview format in the Sample set; in a sense the CMPP recordings reverse the polarity of the interview situation in that, whereas the Sample informants were contacted by the team and granted interviews, the CMPP informants contacted the social worker and solicited the consultation.

A set of unstructured recordings was obtained with the aid of some informants from the INSEE sample who agreed to arrange recordings in the absence of team members: these often took the form of meals with family or friends, or recordings made at the place of work. The intention, obviously, was to obtain evidence of the individual's linguistic performance in non-interview situations with varied status relationships and numbers of participants. Technical problems and the relatively small and varied numbers of recordings obtained in this way make it impossible to envisage conclusive findings about codeswitching. There are, however, enough tapes to check again whether the interview format projected the main corpus of recordings onto a level of uncharacteristic formality (although in view of the average length of interviews — ca. sixty minutes — this seems unlikely) and to give a first idea of the range of variant situations to be explored in the future and their relative feasibility.

Further recordings of overtly public uses of language, in the form of lectures, lecture-discussions and round tables, introduce the variables of the number and proportional roles of participants — in generally acoustically favorable indoor settings. The corpus is completed by a series of short telephone conversations with earlier informants (dealing with non-confidential matters) and a set of hidden-microphone recordings of unknown informants in public places — shopkeepers, ticket clerks, etc. — being asked for information, instructions, or commodities, including a very successful set in which a team member tours bakers' shops in search of, as it happened, unobtainable and largely unknown matzos.

The final tally of recordings was approximately 500, representing more or less 4,500,000 words. Clearly, immediate complete transcription is out of the question. Consequently, sample recordings chosen to cover the range of INSEE categories and those incorporated in the Study's own provisional system, have been transcribed wholly or in part. A semi-orthographic system was adopted in the interests of legibility; it discards all punctuation, which would have prejudged too many linguistic questions, but incorporates indications of liaison, elision, and sound lengthening. Intonation is not indicated: in view of the multiplicity of notation systems, it was judged more efficient to leave this to later individual researchers. Given also that non-studio recordings can seldom if ever be transcribed with absolute accuracy, the transcripts are intended as working documents, to be checked against the tape before use, then edited, and, depending on the intended use, punctuated or otherwise annotated. To simplify access to the corpus, a fully crossreferenced catalog of recordings, including anonymized data on informants and content summaries, as well as descriptive information about the actual recordings, has been scheduled for completion in early summer 1973 (*Etude sociolinguistique sur Orléans* 1974).

INTERPRETATION: LINGUISTIC AND SOCIOLOGICAL MODELS

When linguistic data are collected, they have to be analysed — in terms of what linguistic model? And when the data must also be related to the society of its origin, we need a model accommodating the various societal parameters that interact with language. In the case of the Orléans Study, with its preoccupation with the spoken word, the absence of a comprehensive linguistic model is not the handicap it might at first appear; on the contrary, one of the longterm aims of the Study is to produce, or contribute to the production of, a model of the syntax of the spoken language. It is fair to say, as Raymond Queneau has been saying for over thirty years, that there are two French languages, which we can characterize without too much exaggeration as static and dynamic: written and spoken French. Inevitably, descriptions of French have long been dominated by the written, conventionally "correct" forms of the language; work on the spoken language, sparked off by the publications of the *Français Fondamental* team (though it should be pointed out that their informants were by and large hand-picked to provide a pedagogically acceptable corpus) is now emerging (notably from Roulet, 1969; Lamerand, 1970), but we are still a long way from a comprehensive model capable of defining and contrasting the differential syntax of spoken French. At the present stage, the best solution seems to be eclecticism, drawing on existing models but keeping them firmly in their place as a *morale provisoire*, to be used only until spoken syntax has been more fully formulated.

More crucial, however, is the choice or, indeed, the construction, of a scale of non-linguistic criteria to be used not only in classifying informants and their speech, but in choosing them right from the outset. In the case of the Orléans Study, the only data available were those of INSEE, the organization responsible for population censuses and as its title indicates, the collection of economic information in France. The INSEE system classifies the population according to professional status, the professions or professional grades being ranged in a hierarchy according to a conflation of salary and the length of training required plus, all else being equal, the numbers of employees controlled or the numbers of superiors in the internal hierarchy. In terms of its own brief, this scale functions admirably, but it has several marked inadequacies for our purposes. For instance, the "miscellaneous" category contains groups as diverse as armed forces personnel, priests, and students; educational backgrounds and linguistic behavior seem unlikely to be homogeneous throughout this category. Married housewives, somewhat tactlessly labelled as "*sans activité*," are ranked with their husbands; this makes no allowance for hypergamy, nor for the role the mother apparently plays in determining social mobility, let alone for the changing role of women in modern France.

Even the informant's occupation, taken purely in terms of status, seems an insufficiently sharp index. The nature of the occupation should also be taken into account: relatively low-status occupations (whether graded according to a conventional/financial hierarchy or in terms of the education and training required) such as waiter or receptionist, may entail considerable contact with the public, and interact with linguistic performance to an extent that need not apply in the case of some high-status occupations (e.g. an industrialist leading an isolated professional life with assistants and secretaries to do his talking and writing).

Moreover, we can only guess at the self-image of various occupations: a step towards this missing knowledge would be provided by a prestige scale ranking professions or social categories in the order of subjective evaluations obtained within the society. Unfortunately, French society is one of the many for which such a prestige scale has yet to be developed.

From the INSEE data, we learn the age at which studies were ended; however, we should also take into account the type of education or training undergone, for obvious reasons. We should also bear in mind the family educational background and, so far as it can be gauged, lifestyle, particularly in terms of cultural pursuits.

We can guess at the missing data; we may deduce it from other data; better still, if the aims of our study are fully formulated, we can without too much difficulty extend our survey to elicit the missing information. As far as possible, this was the procedure adopted for the Orléans study, by administering a closed "background" questionnaire to all Sample informants and most of the rest, and by running a special questionnaire, for the Sample, devoted entirely to uses of and attitudes towards language. Even the anodyne warm-up questions (How long have you lived in Orléans? Oh? Where were you before? Do you like it here?) served to establish the subject's provenance and provide indices of integration into (or rejection of) the local community, all for eventual correlation with linguistic indices.

This material was collected with a view to supplement the INSEE data in order to modify the socioprofessional scale and ultimately produce a new scale relevant to sociocultural and, in particular, sociolinguistic inquiry. As a first step, a sociocultural scale, commissioned from Alix Mullineaux of Birkbeck College, London, weights INSEE data with indices of education and family background. One should not lay too much stress on this aspect of the study at this stage because, although fully professional sociological expertise was called on throughout, the construction of classification systems was not conceived originally as a major part of the project; consequently, only limited resources could be devoted to it. Nonetheless, the first model of the sociocultural scale provides surprisingly close correlations with even the first small-scale linguistic investigations (cf. Ross 1972); it is to be hoped that continuing work on the scale and on the language data will produce a fully valid model and indicate the key criteria to be adopted in dealing with other communities. At this point it might be as well to summarize the activities of the Orléans Study to date. Contact was made with (a) institutionally and (b) statistically representative samples of the population, from whom the team obtained fairly lengthy samples of speech and enough background data to produce a profile of each informant. Existing and specially collected data have been conflated to produce a new sociocultural scale on which to grade informants, and the material has been identified and classified in order to make it available to interested individuals and institutions including, first and foremost, those team members working on the first pedagogical applications of Orléans material.

CRITIQUE

What are the main practical problems faced in a collection operation of this kind, and do they lead to shortcoming in the corpus? Can any lessons be drawn for field work recording and sampling in the future?

The first, constant dilemma in recording speech is the need to choose between acoustic quality and spontaneity. The recording studio is the ideal acoustic environment, of course; it is also the setting in which people are most likely to feel ill at ease. We conclude therefore that *in situ* recording is preferable. At no point in the Orléans recording schedule was there any mention of informants showing microphone nerves. From the tapes themselves, one has the impression that any initial stiltedness corresponded more to the first few minutes with a total stranger — and a foreigner at that — than to any inhibitions caused by the presence of a tape recorder. Despite ambient noise and often bizarre livingroom acoustics, no interview was undecipherable, so that while most recordings are not appropriate for phonetic analysis (spectrography, for instance, is totally ruled out), most can be used as teaching material and all are suitable for the study of syntax or discourse analysis.

This is less frequently the case with recordings of more than one informant, mainly because of simultaneous utterances (when married couples were recorded, the amount of this type of jamming was depressingly high). Again, the choice must be made between spontaneity and decipherability. Control, however discreet, by a "chairman" inevitably excludes free interaction between participants. Nor is complex technology a solution: multitrack recordings entail obtrusive apparatus and individual microphones — all right in a sedentary situation, but useless if one aims at recording the more dynamic aspects of language in a group situation. Moreover, apart from the ethical questions raised by such aids as radiomicrophones (illegal in many countries, anyway) and economic constraints, it seems worth remarking that most documented cases of sustained, technically sophisticated recording have been effected with small children or graduate students: groups which are relatively ill-placed to refuse to cooperate. There is, unfortunately, a limit to the demands a researcher can make on an informant's time and goodwill.

In view of this consideration, the "stylistic follow-through" aspect of the original Orléans program was perhaps unduly ambitious. Most contrastive studies published so far have tended to describe more or less isolated small groups on a basis of direct observation over a considerable period of time, and to study the divergence and interaction between group vernacular and the standard language. Unfortunately, we can hardly expect even twenty busy adults to adjust their private and professional lives to allow for a complete range of recordings, particularly when, as in the case of the Orléans Study, there was insufficient time for researchers to have any but the most superficial contacts with informants.

It would seem that the situational dimension can be studied satisfactorily only on a small scale by following groups and individuals over a fairly long period — to avoid research becoming an imposition and exhausting informants' patience. However, it may be that the presence of a comprehensive cross-section of recordings in one or two constant situations might provide a framework in which to locate stylistically varied recordings that otherwise would have to be classed as "oddments."

With recordings of public speech, on the other hand, there is no such problem, whether the microphone is hidden, as on shopping expeditions, or visible, as in a public lecture, where microphones are normal equipment in any case. Moreover, the public context of such samples eliminates any ethical objections. Recording from telephone is, however, a more delicate matter. In the Orléans Study the solution adopted was to exercise restraint and record only calls with non-confidential content.

... AND ELSEWHERE?

What basically is the relevance of the Orléans Study's experience to comparable future work, particularly in differently structured societies? How, for instance, could the Orléans Study relate to the study of, say, a non-literate nomadic community in the upper Amazon? At first sight the connection might appear tenuous, in that the present work was carried out in an urban community in a modern, industrialized, occidental society with little regional divergence, whether administrative, educational, or linguistic. The researchers involved had considerable prior knowledge of the language, the culture, and the institutional framework, aided by the fact that, like all Western societies, French society is lavishly documented, both in sociological inquiry and in administrative and statistical data on the population. How, then, could a study of this type be carried out in a society in which everything must be worked out from scratch?

More easily than one might think. As it turned out, the wealth of existing information served mainly as a short-cut, in the initial stages, to locate and contact informants. Admittedly, the INSEE scale provided a first identification of informants in terms of their socioprofessional position in the community, but only in the short term. Random sampling techniques enabled the team to obtain interviews from a large body of the population in a single standardized situation; in a smaller community such procedures would be less necessary. No pre-existing sociological tools contributed to charting variations in situation; these depend more on direct sociological observation set in a linguistic perspective.

The essential, then, is not the availability of existing institutional apparatus (e.g. a census organization); this can be no more than a tool, and whereas any tool is often better than nothing, tools designed for one job are rarely suitable for another, and it is unlikely that, for instance, a census system will incorporate sufficient parameters, or the right ones, for a full portrait of a society and its language to emerge. We have, in fact, to draw all our own maps, and this is almost always going to entail redrawing and supplementing existing ones.

What does this mean in the field? The choice of informants will depend on the progress of the overall picture of the society; as new information is gleaned, new categories will emerge and, consequently, another set of informants to add to the sample. The collection of linguistic data need not, however, wait until the society's profile is complete: insofar as information is obtained by verbal interrogation and explanation, a first corpus of recordings could be accumulated, to be related later to the overall picture. More conventional elicitation might do worse than follow the broad lines of the Orléans questionnaires, by balancing content questions so that they elicit linguistic forms (and vice versa), always assuming an adequate knowledge of the society, though it is worth remembering that many of the Orléans open questions elicited explanations of aspects of French society, such as the electoral system.

Interpretation of the data and correlation with societal parameters imply the existence of an informant-classification grid appropriate for incorporating linguistic behavior fully into the description of the society. Communities such as the Subanum — surely every sociolinguist's dream — are bound to be rare; however, we no longer need to argue that the use(s) of language and the individual's place within society are intimately related, and that if we come down to a chicken-and-egg perplexity, language is more likely to be the chicken. There may well also be more than an indirect relationship between language and social structures (here, language will probably be the egg).

CONCLUSION

The study of language in its social context is properly the concern of specialists from at least two descriptive disciplines — linguistics and sociology — if we are to have the appropriate linguistic and societal models to produce accurate interpretations of linguistic data. The study of institutional structures, power hierarchies, kinship networks, etc., can surely be paralleled by linguistic inquiry, so that the two operations are simultaneous and complementary. Moreover, in the framework of a general study of this nature, it should be possible to give adequate coverage to the two main variables of descriptive sociolinguistics: one, social status, computed to allow for education, power, prestige, age, and any other parameters relevant to the particular society, informants being studied in a constant situation; the other, variations in the language employed by individuals or small groups when the situation and media relationship change.

The picture presented here is one of cooperation between sociologically-oriented linguistics and linguistically inclined sociology; where actual data are concerned, it seems wiser to draw on the experience of established disciplines. Coordination and integration of linguistic and sociological fieldwork from the earliest planning stages surely constitute the only reliable basis for the emergence of a science of sociolinguistics with a problematic, a rigor, and a praxis of its own. The most satisfactory solution therefore seems to be a return to the underlying principles of the Bloomfield/Sapir or Firth/Malinowski dyads, once more to integrate the study of language into the study of the corresponding society.

APPENDIX: THE STANDARD QUESTIONNAIRES USED WITH THE RANDOM SAMPLE INFORMANTS

1. QUESTIONNAIRE OUVERT: designed to elicit spontaneous speech along four main general content themes.
Questions préliminaires (posées à tous les témoins)
1. Depuis combien de temps habitez-vous Orléans?
2. Qu'est-ce qui vous a amené à vivre à Orléans?
3. Est-ce que vous vous plaisez à Orléans? Pourquoi (pas)?
4. Est-ce que vous comptez rester à Orléans? Pourquoi (pas)?
TRAVAIL — TRONC COMMUN: (questions posées à tous les témoins)
T 1. Qu'est-ce que vous faites comme travail?
    — en quoi est-ce que ça consiste/c'est quoi au juste?
T 2. Est-ce que vous voulez bien me décrire une journée de travail?

T 3. Qu'est-ce qui compte le plus dans votre travail?
— qu'est-ce qui vous plaît, ou vous déplaît dans votre travail?
T 4. Si vous n'étiez pas . . . qu'est-ce que vous aimeriez faire?
T 5. De plus en plus de femmes mariées travaillent aujourd'hui. Et vous
personnellement, est-ce que vous êtes pour ou contre? Pourquoi (pas)?
TRAVAIL — BRANCHE (questions posées aux témoins semblant suscep-
tibles de développer le thème)
   T 6. Et votre femme, est-ce qu'elle travaille aussi? Pourquoi
      (pas)?
   T 7. Et vos enfants, que font-ils?/métier?
   T 8. Est-ce que vous aimeriez qu'ils fassent autre chose? *ou* qu'est-ce
      que vous aimeriez qu'ils fassent (quand ils seront grands)?
   T 9. Avec qui parlez-vous au cours de votre travail?
   T10. De quoi est-ce que vous parlez?
   T11. Etes-vous satisfait de vos conditions de travail? Pourquoi (pas)?
   T12. Qu'est-ce que vous aimeriez voir changer?
   T13. Est-ce que vous avez déjà fait grève? Quand ça?
   T14. Comment ça a commencé/vous pouvez me racontez ce qui s'est
      passé?
   T15. Est-ce que vous avez obtenu satisfaction?
   T16. Etes-vous syndiqué/membre d'une organisation professionnelle?
      Pourquoi (pas)?
   T17. Quel est votre syndicat/association?
   T18. Est-ce que vous êtes actif dans votre syndicat/association? Pour-
      quoi (pas)?
LOISIRS — TRONC COMMUN
L 1. Qu'est-ce que vous faites de votre temps libre — soirées, weekend?
L 2. Comment avez-vous passé dimanche dernier?
L 3. Que ferez-vous pendant les vacances d'été?
L 4. Si vous aviez deux heures de temps libre supplémentaires par jour, que
feriez-vous de ce temps libre?
   LOISIRS — BRANCHE
   L 5. Est-ce que vous avez une voiture?
   L 6. Qu'est-ce que vous avez comme voiture?/
      ça vous gêne de ne pas avoir de voiture?
   L 7. Pourquoi avez-vous choisi ce modèle?
   L 8. Vous vous en servez tous les jours? ou quand?
ENSEIGNEMENT — TRONC COMMUN
E 1. A votre avis, qu'est-ce qu'on devrait apprendre surtout aux enfants à
l'école? Pourquoi?
E 2. Qu'est-ce que vous pensez du latin à l'école?
E 3. Dans quelle matières aimeriez-vous que vos enfants soient forts? (est-il
bon qu'un enfant soit fort?)
E 4. Qu'est-ce qui fait que les enfants réussissent ou ne réussissent pas à
l'école?
E 5. Jusqu'à quel âge est-ce qu'il faudrait que les enfants continuent leurs
études? Pourquoi?
E 6. Est-ce que c'est la même chose pour les garçons et les filles?
   ENSEIGNEMENT — BRANCHE
   E 7. Quelles différences y a-t-il entre les lycées, les C.E.G. et les C.E.S.?
      Et entre les élèves?
   E 8. Est-ce que l'enseignement a beaucoup changé depuis que vous avez
      terminé vos études/étiez à l'école?

E 9. Comment est-ce qu'on fait le choix entre l'école publique et l'école libre?

E10. Comment a-t-on choisi dans votre cas personnel?

E11. Qu'est-ce qui (vous) ferait accepter d'envoyer vos/des enfants à l'école publique/libre (=le contraire du choix déjà déclaré).

E12. Etes-vous favorable à la participation des élèves aux conseil d'administration des écoles?

E13. D'après vous, qu'est-ce qu'il faudrait changer dans l'enseignement actuel?

POLITIQUE/CLASSE — TRONIC COMMUN

P 1. Pour revenir à la ville d'Orléans, est-ce que, d'après vous, on fait assez pour les habitants d'Orléans?

P 2. Nous avons dit ON; mais ON, ça représente qui, pour vous?

P 3. Est-ce qu'il y a d'autres personnes qui comptent, qui ont de l'influence?

P 4. On a beaucoup parlé des évènements de mai dernier. Moi, je n'étais pas en France à l'époque. Est-ce que vous pourriez m'expliquer ce qui s'est passé?

— Pourquoi? A votre avis, comment est-ce qu'on peut expliquer ces évènements?

POLITIQUE/CLASSE — BRANCHE

P 5. Lorsque vous votez pour un député, qu'est-ce que vous attendez de lui?

P 6. Dans les élections nationales, pourquoi est-ce qu'il y a deux tours?

P 7. Comment est-ce qu'on décides on vote, la seconde fois?

P 8. Quelle est la différence, pensez-vous, entre la Droite et la Gauche?

P 9. Est-ce que les différences entre les classes sociales sont très marquées à Orléans?

P10. A quoi est-ce qu'on reconnaît? le . . . (reprendre le vocabulaire
un . . . utilisé par le témoin)
les . . .

P11. Est-ce qu'on peut passer d'une classe à l'autre? Comment?

p12. Est-ce que les différences entre les classes ont tendance a augmenter ou a diminuer? Pourquoi (pas)?

2. QUESTIONNAIRE FERME: designed to elicit informant data to supplement INSEE information.

1. Age et lieu de naissance.

2. Sexe.

3. Etat-civil.

4. Nombre d'enfants.

5. Date d'arrivée à Orléans.

6. Profession.

7. Nationalité d'origine du conjoint . . . père . . . mère . . .

8. Renseignements sur les membres de la famille (morts ou vivants) ayant terminé leurs études:

Relation avec enquêté (grand-père maternel, grand-père paternel, père, mère, conjoint, frères, soeurs . . . enfants . . .)

Age de la personne, diplôme obtenu, nombre d'années d'études, profession.

9. Enfants en cours d'études: sexe, âge, types d'études et d'établissement.

10. Y a-t-il des membres de la famille qui ont fait, font ou feront (a) du latin (b) du grec?

11. Y a-t-il des membres de la famille qui ont fait, font ou feront leurs études dans un établissement privé/(libre): enseignement primaire/secondaire/supérieur?
12. Niveau d'instruction du témoin: diplôme le plus élevé.
13. Nombre d'années d'études (témoin).
14. Avez-vous étudié le latin? le grec?
15. Type d'études et conditions de scolarité (témoin) primaire — secondaire — supérieur — privé/public — établissement — diplôme préparé — interne/externe — lieu.
16. Ecoutez-vous la radio? nombre d'heures par semaine/jour? Votre chaîne préférée? vos émissions préférées (en noter les trois premières).
17. Regardez-vous la télévision? nombre d'heures par semaine/jour? Chaîne préférée? Emissions préférées (v. 16).
18. Est-ce que vous allez au cinéma? Fréquence? Films préférés?
19. A votre avis la radio, la télévision et le cinéma sont-ils des instruments de culture: RADIO? TV? CINEMA?
20. Est-ce que vous faites de la photographie? Nobre de films dans l'année? Genre de photos préféré?
21. Est-ce que vous faites de la peinture? Est-ce que vous aimez regarder des tableaux? Peintres préférés? Fréquence des visites au musée et aux expositions hors musée.
22. Vous aimez la musique? Compositeurs préférés (type de musique) Est-ce que vous possedez un électrophone/tournedisque? Est-ce que vous allez au concert? Fréquence?
23. Vous allez au théâtre? Auteurs préférés? Nombre de pièces dans une année?
24. Quels sont les titres des périodiques, journaux, revues de toute sorte que vous lisez régulièrement?
25. Nombre de livres lus dans une année. Genres préférés? Nombre de livres possédés.
26. Y a-t-il un parti politique qui représente bien vos opinions? Où vous classez-vous politiquement?

REFERENCES

AGNEL, EMILE
   1855   *Observations sur la prononciation et le langage rustiques des environs de Paris*. Paris.
BAUCHE, HENRI
   1920   *Le langage populaire, grammaire, syntaxe et dictionnaire du Français, tel qu'on le parle dans le peuple de Paris, avec tous les termes d'argot usuel*. Paris.
BERNSTEIN, BASIL
   1971   *Class, codes and control*. (Bernstein's collected papers 1958–1971, with an extensive biographical and theoretical introduction). London: Routledge and Kegan Paul.
BIGGS, PATRICIA, MICHEL BLANC
   1971   L'Enquête socio-linguistique sur le Français parlé à Orléans. *Le Français dans le Monde* 85:16–25.
Etude sociolinguistique sur Orléans
   1974   Catalogue des enregistrements compiled by Joanna Lonergan with Jack

Kay and John Ross. Colchester: Orléans Archive, University of Essex Department of Language and Linguistics.

FRAKE, C. O.
1964 How to ask for a drink in Subanum. *American Anthropologist* 66:6 part 2:127–132.

GREGORY, MICHAEL
1967 Aspects of varieties differentiation. *Journal of Linguistics* 3:2.

GUMPERZ, J. J.
1970 *Sociolinguistics and communication in small groups*. Working Paper 33. Berkeley, Calif.: Language Behavior Research Laboratory.

HYMES, DELL
1964 *Language in culture and society*. New York: Harper and Row.

KOSCHWITZ, EDWARD
1893 *Les parlers parisiens, anthologie phonétique*. Paris.

LAMERAND, RAYMOND
1970 *Syntaxe transformationnelle des propositions hypothétiques du français parlé*. Brussels: AIMAV.

NISARD, CHARLES
1872 *Etude sur le langage populaire de Paris et sa banlieue*. Paris: Franck.

PÊCHEUX, MICHEL
1969 *Analyse automatique du discours*. Paris: Dunod.

ROSS, JOHN
1972 Enquête sociolinguistique et description syntaxique. Paper delivered to the Third International Congress of Applied Linguistics, Copenhagen.

ROSSET, THEODORE
1911 *Les origines de la prononciation moderne étudiées au XVIIe siècle*. Paris.

ROULET, EDDY
1969 *Syntaxe de la proposition nucléaire en français parlé: étude tagmémique et transformationnelle*. Brussels: AIMAV.

TANNER, N.
1967 Speech and society among the Indonesian élite: a case study of a multilingual community. *Anthropological Linguistics* 9:15–39.

Social Differences in White Speech

RAVEN I. McDAVID, JR.

I. This paper summarizes the information available about social differences in the language of whites who are speakers of English, principally but not exclusively in the United States. It is based on identifiable utterances of identifiable informants; the evidence is available to other scholars who may wish to refute or replicate the findings. Essentially the evidence consists of: (1) published surveys, such as Joseph Wright's *English dialect grammar* (1905) and *English dialect dictionary* (1898–1905), Harold Orton's *Survey of English dialects* (1962–1971), Hans Kurath's *Linguistic atlas of New England* (1939–1943), and Harold Allen's *Linguistic atlas of the Upper Midwest* (1973–1976); (2) the accessible if yet unpublished materials of the Linguistic Atlas of the Middle and South Atlantic States, the Linguistic Atlas of the North-Central States, and related collections; (3) independent investigations such as Harold Paddock's thesis (1966) on the speech of Carbonear, Newfoundland; (4) derivative studies based on systematic investigations, notably the regional linguistic surveys in North America.[1]

---

[1] The insistence on observed field data, rather than intuition, is based on repeated observations of experienced fieldworkers that informants have the human quality of suscep-tibility to self-bamboozlement, especially when a linguistic form seems to be a social marker. In the South, informants of some education have often denied the existence in Caucasoid speech of forms that are widely distributed in the region and that they even use themselves. Nor should one take too seriously sentences self-generated in an effort to test grammatical-ity. Students of American Indian languages will recall Sapir's attempt to ascertain the existence of a certain verb form. Suggesting it to the informant he asked, "Can you say it?" "Yes." "What does it mean?" "It don't mean nothing."

For my own part, I remember that when Charles C. Fries suggested, early in 1952, that three-object sentences (with indirect object, direct object, and object complement) might simply not occur in English, I vainly tried to produce a counter example. However, a year later, in a telephone conversation I caught myself saying, "We've elected *us Ike president*, and now we're stuck with him."

II. This paper is deliberately restricted to reporting on Caucasoids who are native speakers of English in English-speaking communities, contrary to the emphasis of American sociolinguistics in the past decade. Mission-oriented and at least partially sponsored by educational administrators, most of that research is concerned with the language of blacks and Spanish-speakers in Northern and Western cities; almost no attention is given to the speech of the largest disadvantaged group, the native whites, or to previous regional surveys.[2] Since most of the investigators were Northerners, there was almost no attention to regional differences in educated speech. Furthermore, most of these investigators have not only avoided reference to upperclass speech, even in the North, but have set up research designs that exclude speakers of upperclass varieties of English.[3] As a result there has been a disproportionate attention to so-called "Black English," though it has not been defined, and though its existence has been challenged, especially by linguistically sophisticated Southerners of African descent.[4] As a Southern Caucasoid I do not feel that I should meddle in these matters. I am prepared to recognize a de facto Black English in Chicago, if not in Charleston, much as we can recognize a separate Ukrainian Language in North America if not necessarily in Europe. I concede to my more brilliant colleague James H. Sledd the role of Ralph Nader to the Black English industry.

III. In evaluating social differences in language we have moved a considerable distance from the polar opposition between "correct" and "incorrect."[5] We now recognize that the status of any linguistic form involves a complicated set of interlocking dimensions: the medium (speech or writing), the degree of formality, the relationship between the speaker and the auditor, the attitudes of both parties, the identification of the speaker with his community or parts of it.[6] Even more important are the dimen-

---

[2]   A notable exception to the neglect of the speech of poor whites is the work of Lawrence M. Davis with Appalachian migrants and their descendants in Chicago's Uptown, on the North Side (Davis 1971).
    Shuy, Wolfram and Riley (1968) and Wolfram (1969) made no use of the collections for. the Linguistic Atlas of the North-Central States, which included a dozen interviews from Detroit and its environs.
[3]   E.g. Labov (1966), Shuy, Wolfram and Riley (1968). The only intensive investigation of American upperclass metropolitan speech, and how it differs from the upper middleclass, is Uskup (1974).
[4]   E.g. Williamson (1967, 1970). A black Southerner, teaching in a Southern metropolitan area, Miss Williamson — with the aid of her students — is in a unique position for observing Southern informal speech of both races and all classes; perhaps for that very reason her work is rarely cited and almost never taken seriously by the magnates of the sociolinguistics industry.
[5]   Joos (1962a, 1962b); Allen (1964).
[6]   Labov (1972). Observers differ in what they consider the community norm. Labov apparently takes as his the adolescent street gangs; without any less sympathy for the individual, other observers, such as David W. Maurer (Mencken 1963: ch. 11), might well consider such groups parasitic.

sions of history, geography and social position; geographic or social isolation from cultural foci is likely to prosper the retention of archaisms and inhibit the spread of local innovations.[7]

IV. There are, finally, two complications resulting from the world-wide dissemination of English (that such complications would be multiplied enormously if the varieties in India, Pakistan, Bangladesh, Nigeria, the Phillipines and the West Indies were included is sufficient justification for limiting the scope of this paper).

At least in North America, where we have the largest amount of comparable evidence, it is impossible to trace any regional or local variety of English to any single regional dialect in the British Isles. Even in the educated speech of the Atlantic Seaboard, which has been influenced by educated London English since the beginnings of settlement, no community follows London practice in every detail.

Second is the problem of determining the standard against which other varieties are to be judged. Although class distinctions in the British Isles have become somewhat abraded with the simultaneous development of the Welfare State and new concentrations of wealth and power, Received Standard is still the prevailing model, with some concessions to Scots in the Northern Kingdom (an independent Irish standard seems as remote as unification of the island). In smaller units of the Commonwealth, such as the Falklands or Tristan da Cunha, where no substantial local elite has arisen, Received Standard is perforce still the approved model. In Australia, Canada, and New Zealand, however, its preeminence is less generally conceded, though in each country there is a vocal minority ("Brits" the Canadians call them, in humorous disparagement) who consider it the only legitimate mode of speaking.[8] Counterparts of the "Brits" also exist in various neighborhoods, communities and occupations in the United States — including some proper Charlestonians (South Carolina) who still openly bemoan the success of the American Revolution.

Competition with Received Standard varies from country to country. Little is known about varieties of educated New Zealand speech; in Australia there are supposedly no significant regional variants, except possibly in Tasmania; in Canada, as in the United States, there are marked geographical differences, and local standards have

---

[7]   R. McDavid (1967). The archaisms and innovations in question may be of various origins, including aboriginal or immigrant languages.
[8]   Orkin (1970) sets up an opposition between "standard English" and "General American," with Canadian usage somewhere nervously in the middle. By "standard English" Orkin apparently means the upper reaches of Received Standard, confined to the English hereditary landed aristocracy. Orkin shows little familiarity with the diversity of educated speech in the United States (R. McDavid 1969).

been recognized and encouraged by the Canadian Broadcasting Corporation.

The situation in the United States is fluid. Each major colonial center developed its own prestigious speechways, more or less independent of the others. Though some of these have lost their luster or have been engulfed in metropolitan agglomerations, others have persisted and new ones have arisen as the nation moved westwards. Since no one can fairly claim superiority, it would seem logical that all the local varieties of educated American English should be recognized as equal. But in Orwellian terms, some are apparently more equal than others. During the presidency of Lyndon Johnson, for instance, it was common practice for Easterners to deride foreign policy as discussed in a "cornpone accent," and at the opening of the Watergate hearing it was piously observed that Southern senators could not possibly conduct an adequate investigation. On the other hand, Albert H. Marckwardt reported from Kentucky a contrast felt between the coldness of John F. Kennedy's speech and the human warmth of Lyndon Johnson's. Since other varieties from the Atlantic Seaboard, notably those of eastern New England, were suspect in the American heartland for being too much like British English, there arose the myth of a "General American" — a myth that now survives despite the demonstration that regional varieties exist in the Middle West. Under other labels — such as "network English" and "consensus English" — it has received much favorable comment from sociolinguists, particularly those wishing to provide what they considered a standard to those unfortunate enough to be poor and to speak in Southern accents. Informally, I had personally noticed only one genuine speaker of "network English," Richard Nixon, though the pulpit style of Billy Graham came close to qualifying before events of 1973 made him revert toward his native North Carolinian. However, that "network English" exists became dramatically evident as the media displayed the accents of Kalmbach, Strachan, Segretti, Chapin, Haldeman and Ehrlichman.[9] Perhaps a side benefit of Watergate will be a distrust of homogenized speech and greater respect for those who reveal their regional origins as they talk. It seems apparent that Jimmy Carter has become a particular beneficiary of that attitude.

V. An ideal model for describing social and regional differences in speech would follow Austin (1972) and include all the phenomena of communication — proxemics, haptics, kinesics, suprasegmentals, phonology, morphology, syntax and vocabulary.[10] But in our imperfect world

9   The term *Watergate English*, apparently coined by Aitken Pyles, appeared in the Chicago *Sun–Times*, August 19, 1973.
10   For these terms and others, see Austin (1972).

we are far from achieving this model. Systematic work in proxemics, haptics, kinesics and paralanguage is at best a quarter-century old; the most comprehensive study of one communication situation — *The natural history of an interview* (McQuown 1970) — took fifteen years to complete. We have no generally accepted notation, and almost no comparative studies in depth. Of course we can make certain general statements, principally of an anecdotal order. As the Watergate hearings progressed, my manual and facial gestures were frequently compared to those of Senator Ervin; and years ago the entomologist Henry Townes, a sometime neighbor of mine, had remarked that some of these manual gestures are apparently restricted to the Carolina uplands. But more specific statements are few.

For suprasegmentals there is also little comparative work. Despite suggestions in Pike (1945), there has been little questioning of the notions of four levels of pitch, let alone descriptions of how such levels function in particular varieties of English. For stress we have little more to go on; for the transitional and terminal phenomena, grouped together in Trager and Smith (1951) as "junctures," we have much less. Again, we can make impressionistic and anecdotal statements; for instance, the difference between highest and lowest pitches, between strongest and weakest stresses, seems to be greater in Received Standard and in Southern and South Midland American than in Great Lakes American — and these impressions may be dramatically confirmed, as in a 1957 confrontation between Joos and Sledd (in Trageremic terms Sledd's *nón + sênse* was interpreted by Joos as *nón | sénse*; my speech follows Sledd's). But the details are still to be worked out. By way of exception is the placement of primary stress in particular words, which is to be discussed along with other matters of phonemic incidence.

Systematic treatments of English syntax are rare. A decade and a half of transformational rule-writing has produced nothing more waterproof than we had before; in fact, the transformationalist's disparagement of data has discouraged objective comparative work. Some comparative work has been done by sociolinguists, but largely with selected items. The treatment here is similarly restricted, though the body of comparable data is somewhat larger and better controlled.

Attempts to structure the lexicon have so far been futile; even such heroic operations as Cassidy's *Dictionary of American regional English* touch only a part of it. So far as the social significance of vocabulary items is concerned, there seem to be two conclusions: (1) the better educated tend to use national terms rather than regional ones — *mantel(piece)* rather than *fireboard, cottage cheese* rather than *curd(s)*; (2) on the other hand, upperclass speakers strongly identified with a community will use the regional or local term with those they consider their social peers, while the newly risen and other peripherals, those concerned with external norms, will avoid local terms, using them rarely and often denying their existence.[11]

Our observations then are restricted:

1. Phonology:[12]
   A. Differences in the system of phonemes.
   B. Differences in the phonetic shape of the phonemes.
   C. Differences in the incidence of the phonemes.
2. Morphology:[13]
   A. Differences in the system of inflections.
   B. Differences in the phonemic structure of inflections.
   C. Differences in the incidence of inflections.
3. Syntax: Selected Features

We will also dismiss the medium of writing from our discussion. Within the English-speaking world, standard writing is highly uniform, differing only in vocabulary, a few local spelling conventions (e.g. *center* and *centre, labor* and *labour*), and an occasional principal part of a verb. For the United States, and probably by implication elsewhere, the differences between standard and nonstandard were pretty well covered by Fries (1940). A generation later we need only add a few amendments:[14]

1. The population of educational institutions at all levels has swollen tremendously. It is still possible for an inmate, almost anywhere, to get something like a good education, but this is rarely inevitable. Ill-prepared for the new constituencies that began flooding the schools in the 1920's, the educational bureaucracy has taken refuge behind such clichés as social promotion, life adjustment, peer group identity and recognition of life styles, to the disparagement of academic values. Today, even a college diploma is no guarantee of a mastery of reading, writing, and ciphering — the traditional curriculum of the elementary schools.[15]

2. Although misspellings have heretofore normally reflected confusion between the sound system of the writer and the conventions of

---

[11]   My first cues as to the effects of racial segregation on language behavior came from vocabulary checklists distributed to students at the University of Illinois in the spring of 1950. Almost without exception, blacks native to Chicago used the Southern terms *crocus sack, croker sack* to designate a burlap bag, rather than one of the more common Middle Western terms, such as *gunny sack.*

[12]   This analysis follows Kurath-McDavid (1961).

[13]   A full treatment of morphology would also include bases and derivational suffixes; regrettably, comparable evidence is scarce.

[14]   Fries's evidence is of World War I vintage — letters to the U.S. Government about personal problems, which would probably put the writers on their best linguistic behavior.

[15]   There is no need to rehearse the statistical horrors, including the fact that in some urban school systems the average high school inmate performs at least two years below the normal expectations of his grade. Demands for the same kind (if not degree) of accountability demanded of baseball managers and football coaches have generally been brushed aside or disparaged as reactionary, as have been attempts to enrich the elementary curriculum with larger doses of elementary subject matter. *Subject matter*, in fact, is a dirty word to many of our most advanced educational theorists.

English orthography, new word-recognition schools of reading instruction have produced new kinds of misspellings, based on confusion of the visual shapes of words. And the disparagement of rote-learning by "liberals" and "conservatives" alike has reduced the emphasis on spelling that might correct misspellings, of whatever origin. The fact that, in the past, large numbers of speakers of English, of various sociolinguistic status and dialect backgrounds, have mastered the conventions of the written mode — reading and spelling alike — suggests that a part of the problem may be a failure of will on the part of the schools.

VI

1 A. Socially significant differences in the system of phonemes are few:
a. The absence of an /h/ phoneme, as in many of the folk dialects of Southern England. Vestiges of this absence occur in other lands, including Cornish settlements in the American Middle West.
b. Lack of a contrast between /θ,ð/ and /f,v; t,d; s,z/: *thin, fin, tin, sin; then, Venn, den, Zen.*[16] In various forms, the loss of this contrast is manifest in urban proletarians of English or Irish origin, to say nothing of many blacks and speakers with various foreign-language backgrounds.
c. Lack of a contrast between /v/ and /w/: *vile, wile.* Traditionally associated with Cockney, it also appears in the folk speech of the South Atlantic States, but does not seem to be systematic there.
d. Lack of contrast between /ɔi/ and /ɜ/: *oil, earl.*[17] This feature, like the up-gliding dipthong [ɜɪ] for /ɜ/, seems to be of North American origin, since it is not found in any dialect records in the British Isles. It is traditionally associated with lowerclass New York speech, but is far less common than it used to be.[18]
e. Preservation of the contrasts between reflexes of Middle English /æ:/ as in *male* and /æi/ as in *mail*. This feature is most common in folk speech of Southern England, if not limited to it (Kurath and Lowman 1970).

[16] For many Southern cultivated speakers, especially males, /θ/ and /ð/ often become /t/ and /d/ in informal conversation with their peers.
[17] Folklore would have New Yorkers reversing the incidence of the phonemes, giving *earl boiner* instead of *oil burner*; this is a characteristic reaction when a speaker lacks a contrast that exists in a hearer's speech. At one time the lack of contrast even appeared in the usage of some upperclass New Yorkers.
[18] The up-gliding diphthong in *bird* and the like is also found in some varieties of Southern speech; however, the contrast with *Boyd* seems to be maintained in the South, and the up-gliding diphthong in *bird* is without social significance.
As for other neutralizations: however exotic they may seem to those who lack them, there is only regional significance (and that sometimes declining) in the lack of contrast between *pin* and *pen*, between *cot* and *caught*, between *horse* and *hoarse*.

1B. Differences in the phonic quality of the phonemes. These are usually of local significance.

a. The centralized beginning of long vowels and diphthongs is associated in Britain with Cockney, lowerclass London speech. In Australia, however, it is hardly stigmatized at all; "Broad Australian," of which highly centralized beginnings are characteristic, is simply one variety of standard Australian, and to many ears sounds more masculine than the "cultivated" or "modified" alternatives, more or less influenced by Received Standard (Mitchell and Delbridge 1965).

b. Raised and lengthened varieties of /æ/ and /ɔ/, often with in-glides, are associated with semi-educated speakers in American cities of the Middle Atlantic Seaboard, and a few urban areas of the Middle West.

c. Dentalization of the alveolar consonants /t,d,n,s,z,r,l/ is especially associated with the semicultivated of New York City. It may ultimately be due to foreign-language backgrounds.

d. Raised beginnings of /au/ and backed beginnings of /ai/ occur in various communities, but are more likely to provoke amiable humor than social stigmatization. The monophthongization of Southern /ai/ is often misinterpreted (and even mis-heard) in other regions, but carries no social significance at present.[19]

1C. Since phonemic incidence typically involves single words, representative examples will suffice.

a. Omission of weak-stressed syllables before the primary stress: 'fessor for professor, 'merican for American, 'sho-unce for insurance (Fisher and R. McDavid 1973).

b. Generalization of the Germanic pattern of initial stress to words of Romance derivation: ró-mance, pó-lice, ée-ficiency.[20]

c. Heavy stress on what are normally weak-stressed final syllables, perhaps reflecting older patterns in borrowings from Romance: presidént, elemént.[21]

d. Such isolated words as Italian with initial /ái-/ April with final/-áil/. Those pronunciations are generally oldfashioned, and may once have been standard, such as bal-cóny instead of the present bál-cony. The pronunciation/ài + tǽ|jən/ by Carter became a minor campaign issue in 1976.

---

[19]   At one time, monophthongal /ai/ before voiceless consonants was considered nonstandard in the South (except for the Charleston region, Southerners generally had it finally and before voiced consonants), but the broadening of economic and educational opportunities has removed the stigma.

[20]   For some of these words, the stress may vary with position in the phrase or sentence, e.g. hotél but hótèl swítchbòard.

[21]   Such syllables were stressed in Chaucer's verse.

2A. Systematic features of inflection.

a. Some nonstandard dialects, notably in Newfoundland, formally distinguish a present, with zero inflection (*I think, he think*) and a timeless non-past (*I thinks, he thinks*). It is possible that this aspectual difference occurs in some varieties of Irish English.[22]

b. A number of nonstandard dialects have either preserved the older distinction between singular and plural in the second person pronoun, as in the west country of England, or have developed new second person plurals. In the United States one finds /jɪz/ in urban communities (less often in rural), *you-uns* in the South Midland, and *mongst-ye* on Chesapeake Bay. The distinction also appears in standard informal Southern and South Midland *you-all*.

c. The *-ing* of the present participle, the *-d/-ed* of the preterite and the past participle, may be lacking; speakers are rarely consistent.

2B. Differences in the shape of the morphemes.

a. In pronouns:

i. The generalization of the /-n/ of *mine* for other absolute genitives: *ourn, yourn, hisn, hern, theirn*. Absolute *its* is so rare that I hope I may be pardoned for not having found **itsn*.

ii. Levelling of the pattern of the compound reflexive-intensives, so that *hisself, theirself, theirselves* replace *himself, themselves*.

b. In adjectives:

i. Inflectional rather than periphrastic comparison of participles and long adjectives: *lovinger, beautifullest*.

ii. Double comparison of adjectives: *more prettier, most ugliest*.

c. There are divergent shapes of the plural morpheme for nouns, usually in the direction of regularity: *oxes, houses* (with /-s-/). Several nouns have been regularized in standard usage, or at least regular forms appear alongside traditional irregular ones. Since the Walt Disney movie, *dwarfs* has been common in American usage.[23]

d. Verbs.

i. Occasional survival, notably in Southern England, of historical /-θ/ in the third singular present: *he rideth*.

ii. Variant forms in the past tense and the past participle. These

---

[22] In the United States, an aspectual difference in the use of the copula has been noted in the speech of many urban blacks: no copula in the present, *be/bees* in the non-past. But there is nothing like the systematic difference in the entire body of verbs as reported in Paddock (1966).

[23] Nonstandard speakers often have disyllabic plurals of nouns in /-sp/, /-st/, /-sk/, sometimes with the final stop lost, sometimes with it retained. A clear regional patterning in England is shown in the evidence in Orton (1962–1971), as well as in the records from Southern England in the Archives of the Linguistic Atlas. See R. and V. McDavid (1978).

may be survivals of older forms, such as *clumb* or *clome* for the regular form *climbed*. On the other hand, they may be regularizations not yet accepted as standard, such as *blowed, drawed,* for *blew, drew* (Atwood 1953; V. McDavid 1956; Mencken 1963).[24]

2C. Incidence of inflections. Most nonstandard varieties of English distribute inflections somewhat differently than the standard, though the inflectional categories seem to be present. At least in the United States, no community or speaker is fully consistent.

    a. Nouns sometimes lack the plural inflection (*two boy*) or the genitive (*Mr. Brown hat*).[25]

    b. Verbs may lack the third singular /−s/ inflection or generalize it for all person–number forms: *he do, we does*. Mixed usage is very common.[26]

    c. The present of the verb *to be* may vacillate among *am, is, are,* and *be*, with certain alternations especially frequent in particular communities.

    d. The preterite of *to be* may vary between *was* and *were*. Mixed usage is common.[27]

3. Syntax. Most of the socially significant features of syntax involve verb forms; they are most significant in formal styles of discourse, especially in writing. Many of them occur in cultivated informal speech in some regions or communities.

    A. Omission of the auxiliary *have* in statements, especially in the third singular, before past participles.

    B. Omission of the copula *to be*, especially the third singular *is*, in statements before adjectives, predicate nominatives, present participles, past participles.

    C. *For to* and *for* as infinitive markers.

---

[24]   The use of *-in* instead of *-ing* in the present participle is a matter of region and style, and does not necessarily have social significance. In fact, it is often deliberately used by upperclass speakers (especially the British landed aristocracy and their analogues in the American South) in conversation with their peers.

[25]   Zero plurals of nouns of measure — *two mile, three ton, five year, six foot, ten pound* — are widespread, and may even occur in formal writing (*two mile* on Michigan highway signs, *load three ton* on a sign on the University of Chicago campus (R. and V. McDavid 1964). For what the information is worth, many uninflected plurals, of various categories of nouns, have been observed in the campaign speeches of Governor George C. Wallace of Alabama.

[26]   The zero third person is common in the South of England, with the disappearance of older /-θ/. Generalized *-s* has been characteristic of northern British usage since 1300, as evident in the *Cursor Mundi*. That many speakers of American English say *he do* but *they thinks* probably reflects the facts of dialect mixture rather than any hypercorrection.

[27]   Some writers in eighteenth-century England used *you was* as a singular and *you were* as a plural.

D. *Ain't* and *hain't* (the latter being more stigmatized) as negative forms of *have/has* and *am/is/are*.[28]

E. Multiple negation, which may be mere double negatives like *he ain't done nothing*, or structures as complicated as *there ain't nobody never makes no pound cake no more.*

The inventory is probably incomplete, since regional surveys have been undertaken for only small parts of the English-speaking world, and intensive surveys of particular communities are even rarer.[29] But the evidence in hand suggests that a description of present-day English is bound to be complicated, and that within the body of Caucasoid Anglophonic discourse there is much to be explored before scholars can justifiably dichotomize on the basis of race or ethnic antecedents.

REFERENCES

ALLEN, HAROLD B.
  1964   "Linguistics and usage," introduction in *Readings in applied English linguistics* (second edition). Edited by Harold B. Allen, 271–274. New York: Appleton-Century-Crofts.
  1973–1976   *Linguistic atlas of the Upper Midwest,* three volumes. Minneapolis: University of Minnesota Press.
ATWOOD, E. BAGBY
  1953   *A survey of verb forms in the eastern United States.* Ann Arbor: University of Michigan Press.
AUSTIN, WILLIAM M.
  1972   *The behavioral components of a two-way conversation: Studies in linguistics in honor of Raven I. McDavid, Jr.* Edited by Lawrence M. Davis, 231–237. University, Alabama: University of Alabama Press.
BAUBKUS, LUTZ, WOLFGANG VIEREK
  1973   Recent American studies in sociolinguistics. *Archivum linguisticum* 4:103–111.
DAVIS, LAWRENCE M.
  1971   *A study of Appalachian speech in an urban setting.* Final report: Project 0–E–142. Washington: U.S. Department of Health, Education and Welfare.
FISHER, LAWRENCE E., RAVEN I. McDAVID, JR.
  1973   Aphaeresis in New England. *American Speech* 48:246–249.

---

[28] *Hain't* is always considered more oldfashioned or rustic than *ain't* (Atwood 1953; V. McDavid 1956; Mencken 1963). An ill-conceived press release about the 1961 *Webster's Third New International Dictionary* evoked such a hurricane of hostility (R. McDavid 1971) that James Sledd (1964:473) observed sardonically that apparently any redblooded American would prefer incest to *ain't.* However, there is solid evidence that *ain't* is often used informally by *upperclass* speakers among their peers, chiefly but not exclusively in the American South.

[29] As Kurath pointed out (1968), the orderly development of sociolinguistics would have started with stable small communities in the middle of clearly defined dialect areas, rather than with megalopolitan agglomerations.

FRIES, CHARLES C.
1940   *American English grammar*. New York: Appleton-Century-Crofts.
JOOS, MARTIN
1962a The five clocks. *International Journal of American Linguistics* 28:p. 2.
1962b Homeostasis in English usage. *College Composition and Communication* 13:18–22.
KURATH, HANS
1968   The investigation of urban speech. Publication of the American Dialect Society 49:3–12.
KURATH, HANS, *et al.*
1939   *Handbook of the linguistic geography of New England*. Providence, Rhode Island: American Council of Learned Societies. (Second edition, revised, 1973. New York: AMS Press.)
1939–1943   *Linguistic atlas of New England,* three volumes, bound as six. Providence, Rhode Island: American Council of Learned Societies. (Reprinted 1972, three volumes. New York: AMS Press.)
KURATH, HANS, GUY S. LOWMAN, JR.
1970   The dialect structure of southern England: phonological evidence. Publication of the American Dialect Society 54.
KURATH, HANS, RAVEN I. McDAVID, JR.
1961   *The pronunciation of English in the Atlantic States*. Ann Arbor: University of Michigan Press.
LABOV, WILLIAM
1966   *The social stratification of English in New York City*. Washington: Center for Applied Linguistics.
1972   *Language in the inner city: studies in the black English vernacular*. Philadelphia: University of Pennsylvania Press.
McDAVID, RAVEN I., JR.
1967   Historical, regional and social variation. *Journal of English Linguistics* 1:25–40.
1969   Review of *Speaking Canadian English*, by Mark M. Orkin. *American Speech* 46:287–289.
1971   False scents and cold trails: the pre-publication criticism of the Merriam *Third*. *Journal of English Linguistics* 5:101–121.
McDAVID, RAVEN I., JR., VIRGINIA G. McDAVID
1964   *Plurals of nouns of measure in the United States. Studies in languages and linguistics in honor of Charles C. Fries*. Edited by Albert H. Marckwardt, 271–301. Ann Arbor: The English Language Institute, University of Michigan.
1978   *Intuitive rules and factual evidence*: /−sp, −st, −sk/ *plus* {−Z}. *Linguistic and literary studies in honor of Archibald A. Hill*, volume two. Edited by M. A. Jazayery *et al.*, 73–90. The Hague: Mouton.
McDAVID, VIRGINIA G.
1956   "Verb forms in the North-Central States and Upper Midwest." Unpublished Ph.D. dissertation, University of Minnesota.
McQUOWN, NORMAN A.
1970   *The natural history of an interview. Manuscripts in Cultural Anthropology 15*. Chicago: The Joseph Regenstein Library, University of Chicago.
MENCKEN, H. L.
1963   *The American language* (one-volume abridged edition with new material). Edited by Raven I. McDavid, Jr., with the assistance of David W. Maurer. New York: Alfred A. Knopf.

MITCHELL, A. G., ARTHUR DELBRIDGE
1965   *The speech of Australian adolescents*. Sydney: Angus and Robertson.
ORKIN, MARK M.
1970   *Speaking Canadian English*. Toronto: General Publishing Company.
ORTON, HAROLD, *et al.*
1962–1971   *Survey of English dialects*. Introduction; four volumes, each in three parts. Leeds: E. J. Arnold and Son.
PADDOCK, HAROLD
1966   "A dialect survey of Carbonear, Newfoundland." Unpublished thesis, Memorial University of Newfoundland.
PIKE, KENNETH L.
1945   *The intonation of American English*. Ann Arbor: University of Michigan Press.
SHUY, ROGER, WALTER A. WOLFRAM, WILLIAM K. RILEY
1968   *Field procedures in an urban language study*. Washington: Center for Applied Linguistics.
SLEDD, JAMES H.
1964   Review of *A linguistic introduction to the history of English* by Morton Bloomfield and Leonard Newmark. *Language* 40:465–483.
TRAGER, GEORGE L., HENRY LEE SMITH, JR.
1951   *An outline of English structure*. Studies in Linguistics, Occasional Paper 3.
USKUP, FRANCES L.
1974   "Social markers in urban speech: a study of Chicago elites." Unpublished Ph.D. dissertation, Illinois Institute of Technology.
WILLIAMSON, JUANITA V.
1967   *A phonological and morphological study of the speech of the Negro of Memphis, Tennessee*. Publication of the American Dialect Society 50.
1970   Selected features of speech: black and white. *College Language Association Journal* 13:419–433.
WOLFRAM, WALTER A.
1969   *A sociolinguistic description of Detroit Negro speech*. Washington: Center for Applied Linguistics.
WRIGHT, JOSEPH
1898–1905   *The English dialect dictionary*, six volumes. Oxford: Henry Frowde.
1905   *The English dialect grammar*. Oxford: Henry Frowde.

Language Choice and Socialization in a Multilingual Community: Language Use Among Primary School Teachers in Ghana

JEAN URE

Socialization we will take to refer to the acquisition of socially recognized behavioral norms. This can refer to different kinds of behavior and in particular to behavior of which language is a part. Socialization is developmental, the product of repeated interactions, and may be a two-way process: the mutual influence between teacher and class is a case in point. The present study, however, is not a time–depth study, but rather seeks patterns of language behavior within a community at a specified time. The assumption is that where these patterns are marked and regular, they will continue to be so, and that continued exposure to regularities provides conditions of acquisition and modification of language behavior. Socialization is not conceived of here as exclusively a process by which senior members of a society impose patterns of behavior on juniors: the question of the dynamics of a developmental process and the relation in theoretical terms between the concepts of development and norm are not touched upon here. Without going further into these problems it is still possible, however, to focus upon those aspects of social behavior, and in particular regularities in the choice of language, when junior members of the community interact with senior ones. Here we seek to distinguish regular patterns of choice from a bilingual or multilingual language repertory in interactions between primary school teachers in Ghana and their contacts, in whatever capacity, with interlocutors below a certain age.

All primary school teachers in Ghana are at least bilingual, having as a minimum both their mother tongue and English, the national official language of the country ("state language" — Ellis 1971), the language in which they acquired their teacher's certificates and in which the major part of their teaching is carried out. In addition, most teachers have also acquired some knowledge of at least one other Ghanaian language. There are more than forty languages in Ghana, and with or without schooling there is a considerable amount of bilingualism arising out of contact situations. All primary school pupils who go beyond the first year can also be expected to be at least minimally bilingual between the mother tongue and English.

Data for this study are provided by the language diaries of a number of primary school teachers and education officers from different parts of Ghana. The language diary as a method of sociolinguistic investigation has been more fully described elsewhere (Ure 1972; Forson 1968). Briefly, it consists of a diary in which the events of the day are recorded, like any diary, with an additional column in which the language used is also recorded. To provide help in interpreting the diaries, the diarists also make a list, on a form provided, of all interlocutors encountered in the course of the day, with details such as estimated age, estimated mother tongue, degree of acquaintanceship, etc. An example of an extract from one diary with its list of interlocutors is provided as an Appendix. The present data, which were drawn from the materials of the Language Diary Project at Legon, consist of diaries covering 286 days, half being working and half free days. Cards were made for all events involving participants under the age of twenty, and these were then sorted to find how far choice of language was regularly associated with types of situation.

The diaries examined were collected on three rather different occasions and represent three rather different sets of circumstances. For this reason they were in the first place sorted separately. To begin with we will take the set that has been most useful to our present purpose: a set of ninety-five diaries from teachers from all parts of Ghana, recording two normal days under normal working conditions. These diaries were collected in 1970 and are referred to as set C. Set B is a larger set of 154 diaries, including diaries kept by the diarists of set C, collected from a residential refresher course at Winneba the previous year. Working and free days follow an abnormal pattern here, and encounters with young people are much fewer and different in kind; diarists had in the main no contact with family or pupils and were restricted to chance encounters, friends' children, newspaper boys and other youthful street vendors. The last set to be considered here, with thirty-seven diaries, was the first to be collected and contains some of the features of both B and C. The diarists first kept a record of a day's work at a non-residential course, then of a free day at home and finally of a normal day's teaching in school; some diarists recorded more than one day of a kind. All encounters with all juniors listed in these diaries have been extracted and indexed. Where the juniors' ages were noted this information has been used to obtain average ages for the young interlocutors. These figures suggest something of the difference between the three sets of diaries: set C, with normal home and working conditions, gives an average age of twelve and one-half; set A, part normal, part exceptional, has thirteen years; and set B, the residential course, has fourteen years as average age.

One question immediately arises: how far do the diaries give a fair picture of the full range of the teachers' contacts with juniors? Each diary covers about a page, single or double sided, of foolscap in handwriting of varying sizes, usually listing between twenty and thirty events. Clearly quite a lot must get left out — strikingly so in the case of the parents who say good morning to one son and good night to three. What does the sample offered in the diary represent? We must take it that the events recorded are those that are perceived as significant. And this applies not only to the selection of individual events for notation, but to the proportions in which different types of events are recollected, for perception and memory are aided by the set of stereotypes and role expectations of the culture to which the diarist belongs. That a selection principle of this kind operates when diaries are kept (and in other forms of reporting of events), whatever the culture within which the reporting takes place, is a hypothesis that has been impossible to test within the framework of the present research. For the time being it is enough to recognize that there is likely to be a selection principle in operation, and that, if there is, it may operate to facilitate the first stages in our investigation by bringing out dominant patterns of language behavior in an intensified form.

In addition to the selective principle that chooses what to include and what to pass over, there is a further factor that enables diarists to condense their account of the day's happenings: different types of event are treated with different degrees of detail. Interactions with individuals tend to be more carefully treated in these diaries than interactions with groups or as a member of a group: lessons and church services, both well represented in the diaries, are cases in point. For purposes of the present research, it has been decided to exclude references to lessons where there is no reference to individual interaction. Thus routine entries, naming the subject of a lesson and the form, and naming, for language choice, the official and predictable medium of instruction, are left out. This principle excludes the following:

8:45 A.M. Teaching children in class	English
11:00 A.M. Religious lesson time with the school	English

and also:

11:45 A.M. Vernacular story and drama	Akan

but it includes:

10:30 A.M. Sending a child to Ankamu for chalk	English
11:30 A.M. Talking to the bell boy about the school bell	English
1:15 P.M. Advised two truants to go to school	Efutu

In cases like that of the two truants, if the diarist lists details of age, name, mother tongue, etc., for the two truants separately, with the implication that two sets of factors bore upon the language choice, two cards are made and the event counts as a double one. If the truants are listed without separate details, or no details are given, it is treated as a single choice and only one index card is made and counted when the cards are sorted.

The first stage in sorting the cards was to isolate those cases where there was in fact no choice of language, where the interlocutors were, or were estimated to be, unilingual, so the only possibility of communication was with another speaker of their mother tongue. In set C there were twenty-six such cases. Of these, twelve were relations, eleven servants and nine schoolchildren, while only three were strangers. These categories, as implied by the figures, are not all mutually exclusive; a number of the interlocutors at most stages in the sorting belong to the first three categories at once. The average age of this first "no choice" category is below that of group C interlocutors in general: ten and one-half years, with six of the children being of preschool age, five years or below. Set A has only four such unilingual interlocutors, average age six and one-half. Similarly, in set B there are four, with an average age of six: two babies, one newsvendor and a local child of whom some teachers ask the way and whom they guess to be unilingual. (Not included in any category, though he belongs more nearly to this than to subsequent ones, is our one and only newborn baby, lulled to sleep by his father's Akan lullabies.)

There is another "no choice" category: where the interlocutor has two or more languages of which only one is known to the diarist. One might expect to find fairly numerous examples of English here, both because of its roles as language of education and as state language, and also because it is frequently quoted as having the function of an external koine. In fact out of the 285 interactions listed for set C, English occurs with only four interlocutors (five interactions) as a "no choice" language: two interactions in school, once in the North of Ghana, to a parent who has brought his child to school for enrollment, and once to a school messenger, and also once to a little francophone brother and sister. In set B, out of forty-five interlocutors and forty-seven recorded interactions, we have four interlocutors with whom there is no choice but English, three newsvendors and a bar boy, two illiterate and one with minimum estimated literacy, all with only "broken" English. This gives a total of nine out of 433 interactions and eight out of 158 interlocutors with English as a "no choice" language. Altogether, however, English is used quite frequently, accounting for 21.5 percent of the events in C, 35.5 percent of the events in A and 45 percent of all events in residential course B. In all but the nine interactions cited above, however, there were at least two common languages available and English was therefore used as a matter of choice. It is the criteria for this choice that are now a major part of our subject matter.

Before considering the various choice categories, it should be noted that in all the diaries analyzed there are no cases reported of failure to communicate at all for lack of a common language. This may be explained by the selective process referred to above — that failures did occur but were dismissed as not significant. However, it seems entirely possible, considering the teachers' range of language skills, that failures were very few. Teachers from group C, on the evidence of languages *actually used* during the two days at home and two at Winneba, master on the average 2.9 languages each (see Table 1), and it seems almost certain that some will have further competence that the four days' experience did not bring out.

The first of the choice categories is that in which two bilingual participants who share the same mother tongue and at least one other, choose to use the mother tongue. This is the section where the largest number of events are recorded, with a number of relatively frequent interactions

Table 1. Languages used by teachers of Group C in the course of four days at home and at Winneba

Language	Number of speakers in Group C		Number of speakers in Ghana (1960 census)
	As *first* language	As *second* language	
I			
Akan (Twi-Fante)	23	15	2,657,020
Ewe	10	6	876,230
Ga	2	4	236,210
II			
Adangbe	0	2	237,440
Akpafu	1	0	5,370
Dagaare	2	0	201,680
Dagbani	1	3	217,640
Efutu	2	0	33,870
Frafra	0	1	138,370
Gonja	1	0	62,700
Kassem	0	1	37,030
Krobo	0	3	(an Adangbe dialect)
Kyerepong	1	0	33,780
Lelemi (Buem)	1	0	14,900
Mampruli	1	0	58,710
Nzema	0	1	178,120
Siwu (Lolobi)	1	0	2,860
Wali	0	1	47,200
		Total population	6,726,820
III			
French	0	2	
Hausa	0	3	
Yoruba	1	0	

I.   Ghanaian languages examined at 'O' level.
II. Other Ghanaian languages.
III. External languages.

of the same dyad: in set C we have fifty-six such interlocutors and 110 events. These contrast with thirteen instances of dyads sharing a mother tongue but using the other language. In both cases interactions of parents and children predominate. We may compare the range of use of the two languages in parent–child interactions. Using the same mother tongue we have thirty parent–child dyads with sixty-eight language events recorded. Using the other tongue we have nine parent–child dyads with eleven language events. The range of use of English is simply described, as all but two of the language events represent orders or instructions. The two exceptions are a child back from boarding school twice discussing her studies with her father in English. In the mother tongue orders are also given — twenty out of sixty-eight events — but there are also nine discussions and mealtime conversations, eleven greetings, three occasions of collaboration and help between adults and juniors, six occasions of practical care of younger ones, and three each for religion, recreation and carrying messages. A similar range of language use occurs in sets A and B in this category, though the events are less numerous.

These two choice categories, either mother tongue or other tongue, need to be considered in conjunction with a third category: shared mother tongue and other language, alternating language use. The separation of these three categories is in fact a procedural device for convenience of sorting since it seems probable that we would find that all such pairs, sharing two languages, would alternate if we had enough data. In set C this category contains those dyads that interact most frequently of all: twelve interlocutors with forty-eight recorded events, twenty-six in the Ghanaian language and twenty-one in English. All interlocutors are offspring or wards of the diarists. Here nine requests or orders and also one request from child to parent are given in the mother tongue. Eleven requests and orders are given in English. There are twelve discussions and conversations at table in the mother tongue, including one discussion of school work; in English the parents give seven extra lessons or help with homework at home. Set A has nine events in the mother tongue: conversation (three occasions) and playing (two occasions), as well as four errands. These alternate with six events in English: four errands, one help with study and one practical. The B set, residential, do not see any children frequently enough to provide evidence of alternation.

A summary of the range of use of the mother tongue and English in "no choice" situations and also in those situations where they stand in a choice relation is given in Table 2:(i) and (ii). This table includes all the classes of interlocutor sharing the same mother tongue with the diarist — friends, pupils, colleagues and one instance of a tribal meeting (classified under "social") involving some young students. With none of these classes of interlocutor are interactions frequent enough to allow alternation.

Next we have the categories in which there are two shared languages, but not a common mother tongue. These are subdivided: those where the local language is given preference and those where English is selected. We have the same total number of interlocutors making each choice, if we take groups C, A and B together, but the number of interactions is rather higher for the local language, which seems to be preferred for more prolonged interactions and repeated contacts. The details of the figures for this category are, in the case of the local language: group C, twelve dyads with eighteen events; group A, five dyads with nine events; group B, six dyads with seven events; total, twenty-three dyads with thirty-four events. In the case of English we have in group C seven dyads with nine events; in A two dyads with four events; in B fourteen dyads with fifteen events; total, twenty-three dyads with twenty-eight events.

A summary of the range of use of a common local language (other than a shared mother tongue) and English in those situations where they stand in a choice relation is given in Table 2:(iii).

The data provided by the language diaries is not always full enough to be classified according to the foregoing categories; sometimes details of mother tongue or of second language are missing, or occasionally details of the nature of the interaction (e.g., entries like "with Mr. Oppong" or "at school"). Such cards were, in the first place, classified together under the heading "Data Lacking," and nine out of the 433 contributed no more to the total findings of our investigations than to the frequency figures for the languages concerned. The great majority in this category, however, consisted of entries for interactions with pupils, and for these events a further heading, "school," was set up. Added to these were thirteen cards from group C, two from B and three from A in which the diarists were acting in their roles as teachers. All interactions but one in this category (a home visit to sick children) took place on the school premises. In nearly all of these cases, whether or not explicitly stated, the alternatives were a local language and some form of simple English, however imperfectly mastered. (The diaries were kept toward the end of the school year, so that there will have been few absolute beginners.) Just one little girl — a seven-year-old Mampruli-speaker — is claimed to have known no English. The figures for language use in school are brought together in Table 2:(iv). It will be noted that all kinds of language use reported for English, the official language of instruction, are parallelled for the Ghanaian language, the choice of English being three or four times more frequent — five times in the case of discussions. The actual teaching is excluded from our count, but if it had been included the figures would have been similar because the mother tongue is used in the vernacular language lessons and in some scripture lessons, as well as more generally before the use of English is established. Thus, with reservations about the

Table 2. Range of bilingual language use

	Action			Personal interaction				Values				Institutionalized activity					Total
	Cooperation	Practical arrangements	Orders and errands	Enquiries	Messages	Discussion/conversation	Meals in common	Social encounters, visits	Greetings	Behavior — reprimands, advice, etc.	Feelings — comfort, congratulations, etc.	Requests by children	Study at home	Storytelling	Recreation	Religion	
(i) No choice:																	
Ghanaian language	–	5	17	2	3	8	2	–	11	2	–	3	–	–	2	–	55
English	–	4	1	–	–	2	–	–	–	–	–	–	–	–	–	–	7
(ii) Same mother tongue or English:																	
Ghanaian language	5	21	67	10	3	30	9	2	21	6	1	1	2	–	4	6	188
English	–	7	26	3	2	6	–	–	2	1	–	–	8	1	–	–	56

																	Total
(iii) Common Ghanaian language or English:																	
Ghanaian language	5	7	10	—	4	3	—	—	2	—	—	—	—	—	—	—	26
English	—	13	5	2	—	1	—	—	—	—	—	—	—	—	—	—	21
Total excluding school:																	
Ghanaian language	5	33	94	12	10	41	11	2	34	8	1	4	2	—	6	6	269
English	—	24	32	5	2	9	—	—	2	1	—	—	8	1	—	—	84
(iv) School:																	
Ghanaian language	—	2	6	1	—	4	—	—	1	2	—	—	—	—	—	—	16
English	—	5	19	1	—	22	—	—	3	5	—	—	—	—	—	—	55
Total including school																	
Ghanaian language	5	35	100	13	10	45	11	2	35	10	1	4	2	—	6	6	285
English	—	29	51	6	2	31	—	—	5	6	—	—	8	1	—	—	139
																	424

language of certain subject lessons, we find that the whole range of language use in school is one of coordinate bilingualism.

The sorting of the cards is now completed: the categories for sorting have covered all the data — 424 events, plus nine with data lacking. Before considering the range of use of the languages concerned, we will consider the question raised at the outset: how far is the information provided by the diary a reliable sample? This question poses itself most clearly in the case of the age range of the interlocutors. If the information is reliable, as both home and school are equally represented, we might expect the full age range of juniors to occur in our diaries fairly evenly distributed — this would give eight juniors on an average for each year of age. (On the other hand, we can have no reason for expecting to find *frequency* of interaction evenly distributed.) However, in the whole list of interlocutors under the age of twenty we have only one under the age of one, one one-year-old, two two-year-olds and three three-year-olds: seven interlocutors instead of the predicted thirty-two, with only eleven events to represent the preliminary stage of language socializ- ation — socialization into the acquisition of the mother tongue. Yet it seems certain that there must have been more children, and that the children must have had rather more language contact with their diarist parents than is recorded here. Some evidence of this can be obtained from the diaries themselves. For instance, we can deduce the presence of two babies from the conversations of two young married couples discussing their baby-minders, though there is no direct reference to the baby itself. More strikingly, during the 286 days recorded in the diaries we have three child-naming ceremonies, one congratulatory visit to a colleague's newly delivered wife, and one visit of condolences on the death of a four- month-old baby. It seems reasonable to conclude that the use of language with the function of primary speech socialization is one of the functions that tends to get passed by in the selective process referred to above — though not completely so. The eleven cases of interaction that we do have recorded, few as they are, show a fairly wide range of language function: playing, singing, practical care, feeding, comforting, scolding and greeting. So it would seem in this instance, despite the operations of the selective memory, that we have been able to extract the relevant information concerning language use from our data, as well as a certain indication of language attitude.

It would be interesting to follow up this study, after further validation, with a comparative one on the relative effort in different communities and subcommunities, to promote the infant's primary acquisition of the mother tongue. One might, for example, form the hypothesis that in a traditionally bilingual society more importance is given to extensive passive exposure in language acquisition: it has been suggested to me by a native Siwu speaker that it is by long periods of quiet listening on market days that Ewe is acquired (before it is encountered at school) by native Siwu-speaking children. For testing of this hypothesis, however, further research is required (in this connection see Kaye 1962).

It is also interesting to note that among the primary teachers and education officers who have contributed diaries there appear to be no cases of parents and guardians attempting to introduce English into the home as a "second mother tongue," let alone as a replacement for the mother tongue, as is reported to happen among elite families in the cities. Our findings, which we will now discuss in fuller detail, show English as having its own place in the home with a limited range of functions.

When the data for the language diary pilot project were first sorted (Ure 1972), a set of categories based on the culture-specific classification according to "institutional domain" was used (Ure and Ellis 1972): the relevant domains were domestic, education, shopping, transport, sport and recreation, religion, broadcast medium and written medium. This pilot study dealt with half our data for set A — 442 events including all interlocutors. Not all of these categories are equally relevant to juniors: only domestic, education and shopping are at all frequent. DOMESTIC is a major category with our present data, accounting for almost all the events in (i), no choice, and (ii), same mother tongue, as well as some in (iii). Altogether this category accounts for about three-quarters of the total. Four-fifths of these events were in the mother tongue. In (i) and (ii) we have twenty-seven orders and errands in English, twenty-six of which are to sons, daughters or junior near relations, confirming a tendency reported in the earlier study for parents to switch language when they switch roles from the exercise of care to the exercise of an authority that requires domestic services. These orders represent nearly half the English language events in (i) and (ii), though only a quarter of the total orders given. The sixty-seven orders and errands given to bilingual interlocutors in the mother tongue in (ii) are evenly distributed between relations and servants. Other domestic uses of language are all predominantly Ghanaian and bear out the findings of the pilot study, in which the Ghanaian language accounted for 78 percent of all choices.

EDUCATION is here accounted for by the events in the "school" category plus ten cases of study at home. Total figures are eighteen Ghanaian language and sixty-three English — 22 percent Ghanaian language. This is a lower proportion than in the pilot study, which accounted for interactions with adults as well as with juniors.

SHOPPING was a category in our pilot study giving 82 percent Ghanaian language — all cases of local people shopping locally from street vendors and also from a certain proportion of adult skilled craftsmen — tailors, bakers, etc., where, in several cases, some conversation on the subject of their trade appears to have accompanied the transaction. In the present study, however, we have equal frequency of Ghanaian language and

English: twenty-three events, eleven Ghanaian language and twelve English. Seventeen of the purchases were by teachers on the residential course, strangers to the town, buying newspapers and snacks from young street vendors. These events are classified under the heading "practical arrangement," and the category of shopping accounts for ten of the twenty practical arrangements in Table 2:(iii), the section classifying the occasions on which a common language is chosen when the mother tongue is not available.

SPORT AND RECREATION, 86 percent in the pilot study, gives us six cases of juniors and adults enjoying games together, always in a Ghanaian language.

RELIGION, 56 percent in the pilot study, also has Ghanaian language only, at church. There is no record of adults supervising their children's bedtime prayers, though prayers at bedtime are very regularly recorded by adult diarists and may be in either language.

TRANSPORT gives us two bus journeys with a little girl in which the local language was spoken. In the pilot study we have 94 percent local language on public transport.

BROADCASTING and the reading of BOOKS AND NEWSPAPERS are not mentioned by the diarists in connection with their junior interlocutors. But because the young people will have had some opportunity to hear and see what their elders at home have seen and heard, we may count our findings on adult listening and reading as contributing to the young people's range of bilingual language experience. Broadcasting takes place in both English and the major Ghanaian languages; English is listened to most frequently (90 percent — relatable to the proportions of time allocated to the different languages by the Ghana Broadcasting Corporation), but the programs heard show the same range of use — mainly news and popular music — for English and the Ghanaian languages. All newspapers and all books reported, apart from some school text books and one devotional work in Ewe, are in English.[1]

[1] Apart from books used in class, there is not even indirect evidence in our diaries of children reading or being read to (in adult diaries such as these, this evidence would take the form of records of book buying, requests for books, or discussions of private reading). Books are in too short supply in the country and reading is too infrequent a habit for it to be likely, even with a very large number of diaries or with diaries kept by children themselves, to find adequate information about the range of written registers available. For those considering possible applications of a study of language use such as the present one, it would be useful to have a description of the potential range of use of the written medium to set against our finding for spoken language use. But methods other than the language diary must be used to obtain this information for theoretical reasons, as well as for the practical considerations of the relative infrequency of reading. The diary is a record of dyadic interactions, in which speakers and addressees are brought together and interact at a given point in time and space. Literary utterances are not thus dyadic in character, addressees are many and various, and the interaction is rarely two-way and is not bounded in time and space. A description of the range of potential use of spoken registers can be derived from a sufficiently large sample of actual events; a description of the range of potential use

The final system of classification groups the events according to type of situation, first using a set of categories to group the situations actually encountered, categories derived from the diarists' own accounts of the events, and therefore culture-specific in their application. These are then grouped in more general categories, such as would be relevant in cross-cultural studies. Examples of the first set are greetings, conversation and meals: "Greeted X," "Conversation with children playing *oware*," "Had lunch with Y." The more general classification has four classes: action, personal interaction, values, and institutionalized activity.

The first of these, ACTION, corresponds in principle to Malinowski's language-in-action: activity, of which language is only a part, that has its effect on the physical disposition of things (and sometimes of people) in the immediate situation. Under this heading we have first *cooperation* between adults and children, activities in which adult and junior have the same or comparable roles, such as weeding the garden or helping in the house; then, *practical* activities in which the participants have distinct roles, such as cutting someone's hair, buying and selling, etc; next, activities in which there are hyperordinate and subordinate roles such as giving children orders or sending on errands. Altogether we have 24 percent English in "action" situations where there is a choice of language. In the first category, cooperation, only the mother tongue is used; in the second and the third both language options are drawn upon (we have already discussed the role of English in trading, one of the "practical" functions of language, and of English as a register for the exercise of authority within the literate family). It is the first of these three types of situation, cooperation, that is the most interesting from the point of view of language socialization.

In the section headed Cooperation we have situations in which children are being socialized, through language, into a series of specific motor

---

of written registers may have to be derived from an inventory of writings that have been produced, but are still in the preliminary stages or in arrested stages of diffusion. Recent bibliographical studies are helpful here. Books are known to exist in the Akan- and Ewe-speaking communities that reach few, if any, of their potential addressees (for Akan, see Sutherland 1969; for Ewe, see Duthie 1972). Duthie has analyzed the range of registers represented in 262 Ewe publications and has found books on a wide range of topics (some with a degree of specialization and others more general) and a wide range of functions (entertainment, formal and informal education, administrative, etc.). Seventy-seven of these books are specifically for children, and others are suitable for adults or children. This list is not exhaustive, for Duthie's research is still going on. Few of these books, however, as Duthie points out, are readily available. A study of the availability of books in Akan, Ewe and Ga suitable for schoolchildren, with a bibliography of books currently in print, has been made by Sutherland (1969), and problems of distribution of publications are further discussed by Otoo of the Bureau of Ghana Languages (Otoo 1969).

From the foregoing it would appear that there is considerable potential in the registers of literature for children in the Ghanaian languages; although the degree of specialization is never very high, the variety of types of subject matter and of different social functions of text give a register range that is, relatively speaking, quite a wide one.

skills and socially productive skills (the acquisition of the relevant know-how) and a series of social relations involving a balance of subordinate and coordinate role relationships with adults in the capacity of learners and collaborators. (For an example see the specimen diary, 4:55 P.M.) Such relationships, skills and uses of language are all presupposed by contemporary educational policies involving integrated syllabus and discovery methods, and in a multilingual society the facts of language use outside school in such situations will clearly be most relevant to the educational planner. In fact, the proportion of these events to the total *action* language uses in "choice" situations outside school is low: 3 percent. This figure may in itself prove significant; figures from other communities are needed to assess its real importance. But also, because it is so low, the figures for language choice are a great deal less reliable than those for the other categories. A more extensive survey would be desirable. If this were carried out and if the findings bore out the preference for the mother tongue shown by the present research, this would argue strongly in support of the present movement among educationalists in Ghana toward the extended use of the Ghanaian languages (Chinebuah 1970) in subject teaching (as distinct from just the "vernacular" lessons) and, even more, for the use of the Ghanaian languages where an integrated approach is used.

The second general heading in our classification of situation types is that of PERSONAL INTERACTION, in which the use of language is itself an activity affecting the mental disposition of the participants in the language event, whether this is a matter of information, or good will, or merely a social introduction, or other types of interpersonal communion, cognitive or affective. For this type of language event use of English in "choice" situations outside school is 14 percent. In our data we have, first, *enquiries* and *messages*, both predominantly, though not exclusively, in the Ghanaian language; of these one message and three enquiries concerned school affairs. *Discussions* outside school show the same preference. Under this heading we include the frequent diary entries using this word, also "chat," "conversation" and "talked to." It probably covers a fairly wide range of types of interchange, from desultory talk on a wide range of topics to serious consideration of particular problems, but there is not enough evidence to attempt a breakdown into different kinds of interchange. In our "discussions" in choice situations outside school there is a marked preference for the Ghanaian language: thirty-three occasions out of forty. The discussions using English were nearly all with pupils, and presumably the language choice was conditioned by the teacher–pupil relationship — the encounters took place outside school, some on the way there or back, or at a football match after school hours. There is also one case where school as topic of conversation appears to condition the language choice: a schoolgirl daughter, returned from boarding school, narrates her experiences to her teacher father. The proportion of English used in discussion and conversation is considerably greater if we take events at school into consideration as well. In the pilot investigation discussions took place between adults in both languages in and out of school. A classification according to topic showed almost complete coordinate bilingualism: all topics mentioned occurred in both languages, with the exception of personal matters, where only the Ghanaian language was used. The more intimate interpersonal encounters, *meals in common* and *social visits*, select only the Ghanaian language; *greetings* use the Ghanaian language predominantly, but not exclusively. Altogether we find, in personal relations, a factor that accounts for two-thirds of the English language choices is the existence of a role relationship between the two participants deriving from the educational domain, whether that of teacher–pupil, education officer–office boy, or teacher–pupil–teacher. The existence of such a relationship is sufficiently powerful on occasion to affect language choice even when the participants are no longer interacting within the framework of the educational domain.

The next section, VALUES, is one of the most important for socialization; it includes a range of situations in which language functions to communicate or reinforce the community's system of social and moral values. This may be language used to direct behavior by such means as *reprimands*, *advice*, or *encouragement*; assisting in the internalization of these values by such means as emotional adjustment, *comforting*, or *congratulating*; or finally, and particularly relevant to the present topic, testing by children of the system of social values that they have assimilated by asking permission from adults for various activities. In these value situations the figure for English in choice situations outside school is minimal: one in fourteen choices. Adding the figures for school the proportion for English jumps from 7 percent to 28.5 percent — figures which, however, have less significance than most of those for the preceding sections because of the small number of events. With this section, as with the action-cooperation section, further data are desirable.

The final section, INSTITUTIONALIZED ACTIVITIES, deals with social activities that are overtly rule-governed. Of these, study at home and religion each belong to a wider social domain that has already been discussed. Recreation includes football, *oware* [a traditional game with counters and a "board" consisting of hollow receptacles] and ludo. In all of these, a Ghanaian language is used. There is one single case of a storytelling session in English; this may be evidence to confirm the fears of some traditionalists, that storytelling is in fact dying out, at least in homes where there is literacy, electric light, or a radio, or perhaps storytelling, as far as these diaries are concerned, is one of the situation types that suffer from selective memories. Certainly, from the author's own experience, talented storytellers are still to be found in the community at large and are of all ages (cf. Crowley 1971), though their talents are likely to be more exploited in the less literate homes (Kaye 1962).

CONCLUSION

There is a very high degree of bilingualism among Ghanaian juniors in the social milieu of primary teachers. The few unilingual children tend to be very young.

The range of language usage to which our diaries show juniors to be exposed and in which they are seen to participate is one of compound bilingualism between the Ghanaian languages and English. There are virtually no areas of language use, according to our classification, in which the Ghanaian languages are not sometimes used; the English language skills all duplicate skills in the mother tongue.

This language experience is, however, in some respects limited. In particular, virtually no opportunities are reported for the development of fantasy and the imagination, as represented by stories either told or read. The only stories reported were told in English, half an hour only in 286 days and one event only; it is the one skill in English that is not duplicated in a Ghanaian language. Reading for pleasure is reported by adults, but always in English (existing literature in the Ghanaian languages is known from other sources not to be readily accessible). There is evidence too in the diaries of opportunities for the young people to extend their mental horizons by reading — opportunities that do not appear to be taken up. Children are reported as selling and fetching newspapers, but not reading them. Since books and newspapers are known to be within their reach, the two most obvious explanations for these restrictions on intellectual experience are: (1) that storytelling and reading take place, but are either disregarded by selective memory, or (less likely because the reading matter belongs to the adults) that factual and imaginative reading takes place without the adults' cognizance and (2) the fact that the printed books and newspapers are available in English only may serve as a disincentive.

Two areas of language experience that are crucial in the linguistic socialization of the young person take place only or mainly in the Ghanaian language, according to the evidence of diaries — the acquisition and practice of skills through cooperation with adults and the acquisition and testing of a system of social and ethical values. The proportion of events of these two types appears to be very low and provides a striking contrast with the very high proportion of orders and errands, for example. The explanation here may be that language contact with adults in such situations is indeed as restricted as it appears to be.

The alternative explanation makes use of the selective memory hypothesis: all types of event where only the Ghanaian language is used are likely to be underrepresented in the diaries, as these are kept in English. Even if this is so, one may doubt whether the frequency of such types of event would prove to be very considerable, though one may be prepared to find present figures multiplied several times over. It would be desirable to test this hypothesis with a number of diaries collected in the main Ghanaian languages; this is clearly indicated as a follow-up of the present investigations.

The regular use of the Ghanaian language for these key functions of linguistic socialization is linked with the regular use of the Ghanaian language in the domestic social domain, to the virtual exclusion of English except in special circumstances — a use which in our data extends beyond the activities and social relationships within the organizational framework of domestic affairs to meals in common, visiting (where the social relation is purely a personal one) and discussions of topics of purely personal interest.

The other social domain that regularly conditions language choice where juniors are concerned is education though there are frequent exceptions: there are no categories of language function at school except for formal lessons, which are excluded from our data, in which the Ghanaian language is not sometimes used.

Apart from the categories of language function in which only the Ghanaian language is chosen and which have been discussed above, all categories of events show coordinate bilingualism, drawing on both languages, though not in the same proportions. The reason for the choice of language must thus be sought not in the type of event but in the particular circumstances of the language situation. In the case of all language events taking place outside school, the Ghanaian language is the unmarked member of the pair and reasons need to be sought for the choice of English. In the case of language use in school, English is the unmarked language and reasons need to be sought for the use of the mother tongue.

Outside school we have found English used on about 50 percent of the occasions of giving orders to intimates and have suggested that this represents a distancing device, either because of its function as the language of school (which is how it is likely to be perceived by the children who learn it there) or as the general language of external administrative authority, not otherwise represented in our data of language use involving juniors. (It also occurs in similar proportions as the language of commerce.) Outside school we have found English used in interaction with teachers and educational personnel, even outside the framework of the educational domain, and in discussing educational topics. These findings account for the majority of cases of use of English outside school.

Inside school the Ghanaian language may be used for errands and practical activities not directly related to educational activities and when the interaction may be presumed to be based on neighborly rather than professional role-relationships such as sending a child for sardines or borrowing a ruler in class. In the classroom the progress of a lesson may be interrupted for an explanation in the mother tongue; a few such explanations are recorded in the diary and classified under "discussion." An analysis of recordings obtained in the classroom shows that such explanations are fairly regular occurrences in the primary school.

The present study is an exploratory one, and any conclusions can only be tentative and subject to further investigation. On the basis of the evidence before us it would appear that a complementary relation exists between the Ghanaian languages and English as the languages of socialization at home and at school, and that this has the effects of a marked compartmentalization of experience and of the mental processing of experience, as well as a tendency for the teacher's professional role to dominate in a high proportion of his interpersonal social contacts. This adds up to a pattern of "strong classification and strong frames" such as in Bernstein's education typology characterizes his "collection code" (Bernstein 1971). This appears to relate directly to the policy for language in education operating in 1970 when the data were collected. It was not a state of affairs satisfactory to many teachers (cf. Birnie and Ansre 1969, passim; Ure 1968; Abbiw 1967), and new policies are now being initiated (as proposed in the Education Review Committee Report 1967, cf. Chinebuah 1970).

APPENDIX 1:
SHEET TO ACCOMPANY DIARY OF LANGUAGE USE RESEARCH PROJECT
C/O DEPARTMENT OF LINGUISTICS, UNIVERSITY OF GHANA, LEGON

Name: Abu I
Date: 30-6-70
    L/A Primary School
Place(s): Village near Tamale

Name or other designation	Sex	Age (Approx.) 20, 25, 30	Profession or occupation	First language(s)	Other language(s) including English and "broken English"	Literacy (none, medium, good)	Personal relationship with you (brother, old friend, recent friend, acquaintance, etc.)	Reference to language diary (time or "event number")
Yourself	M	30	Teacher	Dagbani	English	good		
Kassim	M	30	Electrician	Gonja	English	good	Stranger	2:25
Wife	F	20	Housewife	Dagbani	–	none	wife	5:50

APPENDIX 2: SPECIMEN LANGUAGE DIARY (EXTRACT)

Name: Abu
Postal Address: L/A Primary School
near Tamale
Office reference number

First Language: Dagbani
Date: 30/6/70   Working day
(Cross out which does not apply)

Time hours:mins.	Place	Language events	Language(s) used
1:25	School	Arrived in the school. A child reported that he was charged 2½p. for selling biscuits. Normal school and classroom activities began.	Dagbani
		C. K. Kassim brought his child for enrolment in class one for next academic year.	English
4:05		I left the school. Greeted and responded to people on the way. I told a 3½-year-old boy not to hold the back tyre of my bicycle on the way.	Dagbani
4:10		I arrived and responded to welcome greetings from my house inmates.	
4:30	Village	Two B-Middle School girls called in my house and the conversation was centred around the discharge of my junior brother who was currently in the hospital.	Hausa
4:55	"	Children who helped me in my backyard garden asked and were permitted to dig for crickets after I had ordered them to send out fowls from the garden. Conversation between the children and me ensued until we left the place.	
5:50	"	My wife was ordered to serve me with water for bath.	Dagbani

REFERENCES

ABBIW, D.
1967   The aim and the need for the teaching of the mother tongue in the primary school. *Ghana Teachers' Journal* 4.
BERNSTEIN, BASIL
1971   "On the classification and framing of educational knowledge," in *Knowledge and control*. Edited by M. Young. New York: Collier-MacMillan.

BIRNIE, J. R., G. ANSRE, *editors*
1969   *The study of Ghanaian languages*. Legon: Ghana Publishing Corporation.
CHINEBUAH, I. K.
1970   The Education Review Report on the study of Ghanaian languages. *Ghana Journal of Education* 1(2):22–45.
CROWLEY, DANIEL J.
1971   *Folklore research in Africa*. Accra: Ghana Universities Press.
DUTHIE, ALAN
1972   Ewe language publications. Paper for the Tenth West African Languages Congress. Legon: Mimeo.
EDUCATION REVIEW COMMITTEE
1967   *Report*. Accra: State Publishing Corporation.
ELLIS, JEFFREY
1971   *Linguistics in a multilingual society*. Accra: Ghana Universities Press.
FORSON, BARNABAS
1968   "Description of language situations . . . representing a bilingual register range (Akan varieties and English)." Unpublished M.A. thesis, Legon.
KAYE, BARRINGTON
1962   *Bringing up children in Ghana*. London: Allen and Unwin.
OTOO, S. K.
1969   "The Bureau of Ghana Languages — its operations and difficulties," in *The Study of Ghanaian languages*. Edited by J. R. Birnie and G. Ansre, 43–45. Legon: Ghana Publishing Corporation.
SUTHERLAND, EFUA
1969   "Textbooks for the study of Ghanaian languages," in *The Study of Ghanaian languages*. Edited by J. R. Birnie and G. Ansre, 24–42. Legon: Ghana Publishing Corporation.
URE, JEAN
1968   The mother tongue and the other tongue. *Ghana Teachers' Journal* 4:38–55.
1969   "The teaching of language in use in a multilingual society: a proposal for a Bridge Course," in *The study of Ghanaian languages*. Edited by J. R. Birnie and G. Ansre, 61–72. Legon: Ghana Publishing Corporation.
1972   "Eine Untersuchung des Sprachgebrauchs in Ghana. Die "Sprach-tagebücher" von Grundschullehrern," in *Zur Soziologie der Sprache*. Edited by Rolf Kjolseth and Fritz Sack, 136–156. Opladen: West-deutscher Verlag.
URE, JEAN, JEFFREY ELLIS
1977   "Register in descriptive linguistics and linguistic sociology," in *Issues in sociolinguistics*. Edited by Oscar Uribe-Villegas. The Hague: Mouton.

The research described in this paper was undertaken as part of *The Language Diary Project: the range of language use among primary school teachers in Ghana*, supported by a grant from the Social Science Research Council of Great Britain.

Relational Bilingualism:
A Socioeducational Approach to
Studying Multilingualism Among
Mexican-Americans

JACOB ORNSTEIN

SOME PRELIMINARY NOTIONS

Much scholarly attention has understandably been devoted to problems of defining, measuring and describing bilingualism. By now the volume of literature on the topic is staggering to say the least, and it may be perhaps cynical to say that the point of diminishing returns may have been reached as regards the ultimate implications of an ultra-minute dissection of the surface isolates of the phenomenon. This could indeed lead to an ultimate superstructure capable of collapsing of its own weightiness and unwieldiness.

At the latest "summit" on the subject, the 1967 International Conference on the Description and Measurement of Bilingualism, held at the University of Moncton, in Canada, serious doubts were expressed regarding the very notion of measuring bilingualism in the first place. E. C. Malherbe, (Kelly 1969:50), a respected scholar from South Africa, affirmed:

It is doubtful whether bilingualism PER SE can be measured apart from the situation in which it is to FUNCTION in the social context in which a particular individual operates linguistically. The only practical line of approach to this complicated problem which I can suggest is to assess "bilingualism" IN TERMS OF

Appreciation is expressed for research support which has led to this and related studies from The Research Institute of the University of Texas at El Paso, the Hogg Foundation for Mental Health, the University of Texas at Austin and the Spencer Foundation, Chicago. Acknowledgement should be made as well of a number of constructive suggestions from various colleagues, as well as of the contribution of Miss Ellen Müller, Coronado High School, El Paso, Mr. Arturo Piñón, El Paso Public Schools, and Mr. Alfonso Márquez, a senior at this university, in acting as a panel of independent judges to evaluate language performance of our linguistic subsample. Whatever the weaknesses of this study may be, however, they are solely attributable to the author.

CERTAIN SOCIAL AND OCCUPATIONAL DEMANDS OF A PRACTICAL NATURE in a particular society. Here again the criterion is to be "bilingualism for what." PURPOSE AND FUNCTION are the main determinants.

A Dutch colleague, Berthe Siertsema (Kelly 1969:155), even went so far as to declare that:

As long as the different intonational features can alter the entire meaning of one and the same "phatic" utterance, can even change it into its opposite as in irony or sarcasm, what sense is there in measuring phatic material only (supposing all the time that this would indeed be possible)? Had not we better drop the whole idea of "measuring" in the study of bilingualism?

Developments in sociolinguistics, or the very development of this specialty, bid fair to effect fundamental changes of emphasis. Fishman (1972:250–255, 302) submits the notion of a "microsociolinguistic" approach to "societal bilingualism," in which the focus is on the domains of bilingual interaction. Gumperz (1964) studies language both by "small groups" and the "language community," wherein each individual is in possession of a certain number of different codes or styles, amounting to his "linguistic repertoire" (1967). Likewise Labov (1970) emphasizes peer-group affiliation as a function of the varying styles of language used, insisting strongly upon the inalienable interrelation of language and society. In the concept of "language and ecology" advanced by Haugen (1971), multilingualism is viewed as one of the possibilities wherever linguistic diversity occurs.

The foregoing may suggest that the author totally rejects the entire body of research and writing on bilingualism, and the refinements in thinking about it which have been developed. Quite the contrary. He regards as basic and precious the contributions made by such well-known pioneers as Weinreich, Von Rafler, Pavlovitch, Ruke-Dravina, Mackey, Leopold, and a considerable number of others (as well as those mentioned elsewhere in this paper). Nevertheless, he is convinced that examination of bilingualism, let us say, by tests of reaction time and other psycholinguistic measures, in more or less artificial contexts, may have given us its total potential yield by now. At the same time, new developments in "ethnomethodology" and the study of "ordinary behavior" by such a sociologist as Goffman (1972), and Jakobovits (1971), a psycholinguist, coupled with linguistic insights from "discourse analysis" may be more rewarding.

This may be the time to start shifting the emphasis radically from the linguistic to the societal one, without, of course, throwing out the baby with the bath water. The general focus would then have to be on the bilingual/bicultural individual and how he exists and functions within society, and the "small groups" to which he belongs. The issues that occur are manifold. What are the possible relationships of this state of bilingualism to other personal characteristics as well as to the so-called social variables of a "dependent" type? How do bilinguals fare, and perform and compete in the various domains of living crucial to them, by comparison with monolinguals? How do bilinguals and bidialectals measure up against monolinguals in the education arena where vocational success or failure is conditioned? Are these issues by now perhaps not more important than Ivory Tower exercises which appear to have little implication for real life?

Although there are those who would split hairs over terminology almost endlessly, we are assuming biculturalism to be an analog both of bilingualism and bidialectalism, despite the fact that certain exceptions obviously can occur. It is true, of course, that there are varying degrees of identification with the respective culture associated with a language or language variety. Yet even those who react against their native culture and life style, and attempt to assimilate to the "mainstream" one, remain differentiated until total assimilation may occur. Hence it seems to us that the description of Haugen (1973) of a bilingual as one who is not a monolingual ought to suffice. That bilingual or bidialectal (in the sense sometimes of not controlling a standard mainstream language or variety) is then *ipso facto* bicultural, it would appear. By the same token, a similar dichotomy may be assumed between the respective analogs of "bicultural" and "monocultural."

Accordingly the writer submits an approach in which bilingualism/biculturalism is viewed against the social contexts in which the individual functions. For want of a better term we may call this "relative" or, perhaps even better, "relational bilingualism," posited within the framework of the notion of "functional bilingualism." Here again we are extending the basic concept of "functional" as ordinarily used among linguists to cover both the linguistic and the societal axes. Hence attention is paid not only to the facts about his ability to perform in the various language varieties he possesses, but also to how this, coupled with his bicultural status, may relate to the roles played by him in society, by comparison with a "homogeneous" monolingual/monocultural (or monodialectal/monocultural).

At this juncture let us define our notion of "relative" or "relational" bilingualism as a construct based on the possible relationships of the bilingual/bicultural state to other societal variables, be they demographic, sociological, psychological, educational, or the like. In our project of Southwest Studies on Southwest Bilingualism, for example, we are interested in how linguistic and cultural factors may relate to age, sex, socioeconomic status, residence, attitudes to the respective Anglo and Mexican-American subcultures and life styles, career aspirations, ethnic militancy and the Brown Power movements, and perhaps most importantly, educational performance and goals. As will be seen in our description of the Project, our approach is "microcosmic," surveying as it does a cross-section of the undergraduate enrollment of the University of Texas at El Paso, apparently the most highly bilingual/bicultural senior college in the fifty states. This means that well over one-third of the entire enrollment is, in effect, Mexican-American, and in varying degrees bilingual and bicultural.

There is easy enough access, it is believed, to the scholarly and popular literature of bilingualism that the writer feels no compulsion to summarize it here, and may assume it as a given among colleagues of common interest. Among the very best surveys of the subject are those of Haugen which in our opinion deserve reading or re-reading by all workers in this area (1956, 1973), as well as Weinreich (1953, 1956) and, of course, Kelly (1969). Hence the remainder of this paper will merely concentrate on the University of Texas at El Paso sociolinguistic project as a basis for applying the concept of "relational bilingualism/biculturalism." No claims of excellence are, however, made, and those inclined to replicate the techniques of our El Paso "model" are admonished that the workers involved in it are fully aware of its imperfections and limitations. Perhaps, however, its greatest strength may be in its intention to extend the parameters of bilingual/bicultural research, which has, in our view, perpetuated the undersirable bias of focusing either on bilinguals or bidialectals who are either very distant from the "mainstream" of their national societies, in the United States or abroad, or part of the "culture of poverty."

As a result increasingly are we here in El Paso becoming aware that at least some of the cherished notions regarding differentiations between monolinguals and multiculturals are presumptions not necessarily vindicated by empirical research. Hence, many of our findings are necessarily in the category of substantiations of null hypothesis type, where no visible relationship can be seen to exist. Obviously further replication is needed in other localities of the U.S. Southwest and among other ethnic groups both here and in other countries.

Finally, whatever the defects of our "model," it ought to be said that the members of our Project "team" have been genuinely motivated to come to grips with our own "sociolinguistic situation." In this day of civil rights drives, wars on poverty and efforts at the remediation of disadvantaged school learners, anthropologists and other social scientists, no less than linguists, have at least become "aware" of the crying desiderata in our backyard, on a par at least with more exotic and remote sites thousands of miles distant.

DESCRIPTION OF A BROADGAUGE INTERDISCIPLINARY SOCIOLINGUISTIC SURVEY

In 1969, after some preliminary groundwork the year before, an informal interdisciplinary sociolinguistic "team" at the University of Texas–El Paso decided to undertake a random, stratified sample survey of the entire fulltime undergraduate student body. Sixteen subgroups were established, consisting of Mexican-Americans versus Anglos (at this school, virtually all who are not Chicanos), and further divided into categories according to sex, and year of college. Although involving others from time to time, the nucleus of the "team" was constituted by Paul W. Goodman, Department of Sociology; Bonnie S. Brooks and Gary Brooks, School of Education; William Russell, Department of Modern Languages; and the writer. During the academic year 1970–1971 we completed a sampling of approximately 5 percent of the undergraduate enrollment, amounting to 301 subjects.

The team had devised a "Sociolinguistic background questionnaire: A measurement instrument for the study of bilingualism (Brooks, Brooks, Goodman and Ornstein 1972), now copyrighted and revised. It consists of 106 items including demographic questions, as well as others relating to self-evaluation of Spanish and English competence, relative usage of the languages in various domains of living, language loyalty, and attitudes to the Anglo versus Mexican-American subcultures. A rating scale for socioeconomic status, based on a modification of the Hollingshead and Duncan systems was devised by Goodman (1970).

All subjects also completed the *College and University Environment Scales* (CUES), devised by Pace et al. (1969) for the Educational Testing Services. This consisted of 160 true–false items, in which respondents reacted to their perceptions of their college environment. Results available from administration at other institutions make possible the comparison of findings with similar and dissimilar schools elsewhere.

A subsample of 10 percent of the overall sample was taken of bilingual students for elicitation, in order to assess their performance in both languages. As was natural, part of their output was in a highly interferential mixed variety of Spanish, or what Haugen has termed a "bilingual dialect" (1969:72, 370–371) or "contactual dialect" (1971), and which Els Oksaar of Hamburg University, at the First International Symposium on Language Acquisition, held September, 1972 in Florence, referred to as "L³" or "Language 3."

A complete analysis of the results of the CUES test has already been performed by Murray (1972), comparing differences in reactions by Anglos and Chicanos along the dimensions of: (1) Practicality, (2) Propriety, (3) Community, (4) Awareness, and (5) Scholarship. While this may sound, to some extent, abstract and farfetched, the fact is that the instrument gives some insight into the "climate or environment" of an institution, and how students perceive and relate to it. Murray found that in our 301-student sample, sex differences played a greater role than ethnic ones. Only in the scholarship dimension was an ethnic difference manifested in that Chicano students, although presumably stemming from a culture in which authority and learning are generally more actively "respected," rated the seriousness and scope of this University's scholarly thrust significantly lower than did the Anglos.

ALL subjects, then, completed the *Sociolinguistic Background Questionnaire* and the CUES instrument, but only our "language subsample" also underwent linguistic elicitation. A written questionnaire constituted an optional Part B of the background instrument. In Spanish and English respectively, this included instructions to subjects regarding choice of topics for essays, intended to reflect elementary, intermediate and advanced control of each language. Elementary topics comprised such topics as "A typical day in my life," intermediate ones, such themes as "Life in Mexico versus the United States," while advanced themes were intended to bring them up to their highest level of abstraction, conceptualization, or better, the linguistic realization of same, with such choices as "Religion as a Force in Life," "Machismo or Male Preeminence in Latin Societies," "The Brown Power Movement," and the like. A means of control of the relative written fluency was represented by our requirement that identical themes had to be chosen in the two languages.

Coupled with the above was an open-ended interview in which peer bilingual investigators again attempted to bring the students to their highest level of competence. Ordinarily several subjects were interviewed together, which seemed to favor more relaxed verbal interaction. As is well-known by now, "visceral" issues were generally those which elicited the most uninhibited language behavior, with such issues as "Machismo among Mexican-Americans" or the future of the Brown Power Movement almost certain to draw fire. No restrictions were placed on codeswitching, and indeed, as the majority had undergone most or all of their formal schooling in English, realization of abstract concepts triggered a great deal of Spanish–English switching, while some subjects were unable to go beyond the elementary everyday level in either speaking or writing Spanish. Only one subject rated below intermediate level in both Spanish and English for writing and speaking alike.

Regarding the writing tasks, we feel that our attention to this aspect of language performance provides a dimension ordinarily lacking in American sociolinguistic field research, perhaps because of the heavy weight still felt of the Bloomfieldian structuralist stricture (under the influence, presumably, of campstool anthropologist–linguists like Boas) that "Language is speech." Our view is that, without minimizing the central importance of oral vernaculars in the speech communities of the world, reading and writing skills are important aspects of communication skills in advanced technological societies such as ours. The British "school" of Bernstein (1961) and Lawton (1968), particularly the latter, nevertheless do include written compositions in their elicitation battery focusing upon realization of a "restricted" versus an "elaborated code."

As for our oral interviews, these lasted from twenty minutes to a full hour, since some subjects appear more inherently communicative than others. Each subject's output was rated by a panel of three independent bilingual judges thoroughly familiar with the Southwest as a sociolinguistic area. Our rating scale was somewhat inspired by the one employed in the Department of State's Foreign Service Institute, and in our case we employed ascending numbers going from (1) No functional knowledge through (2) Elementary, (3) Intermediate, (4) Advanced, to (5) Educated Native (fractions were, for better or worse, also employed). Separate scores were assigned for speaking and understanding, simply designated as the oral skill as well as writing. An overall performance score for each language was also given. Thus far, we have based ratings pretty much on performance in standard (Mexican) Spanish so that a considerable number of nonstandard items in a subject's output served to lower his rating. At later stages in our research we envision rating subject's performance in the Southwest Spanish or English variety or dialect, if indeed they do not control a standard one. Appropriate designation and explanations to this effect would, then, have to be made.

It will be seen that no explicit reading task was utilized, although it is possible, we feel, to extrapolate calculus-wise a reading score particularly from the writing performance, and in part from the oral performance. The fact is that intermediate reading is a given since the bilingual subjects had all graduated at least in the upper half of their class; nevertheless, they would probably perform at a lower level in Spanish reading, since their formal schooling had been almost exclusively in English, with only two to four years of Spanish as a school subject for the majority. Moreover, the fit between the writing system and speech is close enough that reading can be accomplished almost without training. Admittedly, problems of lexical and conceptual nature would automatically impede high scores, despite a great deal of potential cognate transfer through the commonly shared abstract vocabulary of Greek–Latin origin.

The socioeconomic rating scale was devised by Paul W. Goodman (one of our original "team" members), of our Sociology Department, who combined features from two other well-known scales. He reversed the Hollingshead values for amount of education and added an eighth value, while simplifying Duncan's occupational indices to an eight-point scale, adding up both numerical values for the result. It should be explained that El Paso and certain other parts of the Southwest find ethnic groups living much less in homogeneous enclaves or ghettoes, hence the validity of residency as a factor was questionable. This is not to suggest that our Southwest is a Utopia, but this fact did emerge in the sociological part of our study. Moreover, Goodman explains his methodology in full in Goodman (1970).

Returning to purely language issues for the present, the ratings of our subsample; known as the V-series, may be viewed in Table 1.

It may be seen from our chart that Spanish performance was considerably weaker overall for our sample than was English. Nevertheless, scores for both languages were clustered at above the intermediate level, and namely between 3.0 and 3.9. The main reason for this is that here in the Southwest, particularly in the El Paso region, English performs communication functions in formal domains, while Spanish corresponds to

Table 1.   V-series language performance ratings (n = 30)

Subject No.	Spanish Oral	Written	English Oral	Written
1	2.7	2.0	3.7	3.8
2	2.8	2.6	3.8	3.8
3	3.7	3.0	3.7	4.0
4	3.0	3.0	4.0	4.0
5	2.7	2.7	3.7	3.5
6	2.2	1.8	3.2	2.2
7	4.0	3.8	4.0	3.8
8	2.3	2.2	3.8	3.5
9	3.5	3.3	3.8	4.0
10	3.0	2.8	3.7	3.7
11	3.7	3.5	4.0	3.7
12	2.2	2.3	3.8	3.8
13	3.0	3.0	4.0	4.0
14	3.5	3.5	4.0	3.7
15	2.0	2.0	3.7	3.7
16	3.5	2.7	3.8	3.7
17	2.8	2.7	4.0	3.8
18	3.8	3.8	4.0	4.5
19	3.8	3.2	4.2	4.0
20	4.0	3.0	4.2	4.2
21	4.0	3.5	4.4	4.2
22	3.8	3.2	4.0	3.7
23	3.2	2.5	3.8	3.8
24	3.0	2.7	3.5	3.8
25	4.3	3.3	4.2	4.2
26	2.7	2.5	3.8	3.8
27	4.5	4.0	3.8	3.0
28	2.5	3.2	3.2	3.5
29	3.8	2.7	4.5	3.8
30	3.8	3.0	3.2	3.2

Key: 1 = No functional knowledge
2 = Elementary
3 = Intermediate
4 = Advanced
5 = Educated native

informal ones, serving very much as a vernacular. This is often the distributive and complementary relationship in areas of stable bilingualism.

A better understanding of the language performance results may be had by consulting the analysis in Table 2. In it one may see that, as fractions were used in the ratings, cut-off points between the categories are sometimes sharp, and at other times gradual.

As can be seen, Table 2 indicates approximately one-third of sample with LESS ability in Spanish oral and written performance than in English performance. One-half of the sample have performed at intermediate or higher level in Spanish, whereas two-thirds have achieved at least intermediate ranking or better in English (nine of these scoring 3.8).

Table 2. V-series (*n* = 30)

Scale	Spanish Oral	Written	English Oral	Written
Part A. Distribution of oral and written scores				
1.0–1.9	–	1	–	–
2.0–2.9	10	13	–	1
3.0–3.9	15	15	17	20
4.0–4.9	–	–	–	–
5.0	5	1	13	9
Part B. Distribution of combined scores				
1.0–1.9	–	–	–	–
2.0–2.9	13	13	1	1
3.0–3.9	16	16	21	21
4.0–4.9	–	–	–	–
5.0	1	1	8	8

The high English performance ratings from 3.0 to 5.0 are most likely due to the fact that English is overwhelmingly the language of instruction in schools and for use in formal domains.

These thirty bilinguals of the subsample are quite a homogeneous group, linguistically speaking, yet only one subject performed at the elementary level in BOTH English and Spanish.

Further observations on the performance of the V-series sample may be consulted in Müller-Brooks (1972), and in Ornstein (1975a, 1976).

Aside from performance ratings which will be elaborated upon in future writings, it should be pointed out that a large quantity of usable data has been assembled in the course of this project, which begs for further exploitation. This includes additional series, from other types and subjects, comprising tapes, compositions and background data. There is need for carrying out specialized sociolinguistic studies along the lines of Labov's "variable model." Readers are referred to several inventories of Southwest Spanish and English phonological and grammatical variants potentially utilizable as sociolinguistic variables (Ornstein 1971b:27–28, 1972).

Quite frankly, the lack of a sufficient number of linguists ready and willing to undertake various phases of analysis at this very school has compelled us to seek outside "consultants," who are completing various specialized studies on the basis of portions of the elicited corpus sent to them. These include: Jerry Craddock, University of California, Berkeley, concerned with dialectology and lexicon; David Foster, Arizona State University, Tempe; Robert Phillips, Miami University, Oxford, Ohio, phonology; Fritz Hensey, University of Texas, Austin, grammar and syntax; and others. A small task force on error analysis in Spanish and English is headed by William Russell and Ana María Márquez of the Modern Language Department. Their findings to date were discussed at the first Workshop on Southwest Area Linguistics, sponsored by our Cross-Cultural Southwest Ethnic Study Center, April 6–8, 1972, at this university. This resulted in the first collection of papers on Southwest Spanish, edited by J. Donald Bowen and the writer, which also contain other essays, including at least one on the Northern New Mexico–Southern Colorado dialect of Southwest Spanish (Bowen and Ornstein 1976).

It should be observed that, from the linguistic point of view, attempts are being made to describe Southwest Spanish in both its standard and nonstandard dimensions. Our elicited corpus contains rich evidence of the functioning of the extensive codeswitching common to bilinguals in such areas of stable bilingualism as ours. It may turn out to be most desirable, it occurs to us at this point, to posit a third dimensional V^3 or "Variety 3" along the lines, as we have mentioned, of Haugen's "bilingual" or "contactual dialect," or Oksaar's L^3 or "Language 3." This would have the advantage, through positing a sort of independent linguistic entity, of de-emphasizing linguistic interference as a possible explanation of phenomena thus explainable, as well as invoking "weak control" of one of the language pair, or attributing new creations to the mere fact of language contact which appears to generate all sorts of structures which are *sui generis* in nature. Haugen (1973) and Gumperz (1967:50) concur in affirming that language contact creates its own norms of "correctness."

Along with this, the general performance of our subjects led us to question seriously the implication inherent in the notion of compound bilingualism that two language systems are so merged that the individual may be hampered in communicating in either one. Although for the U.S. Southwest the problem of linguistic disadvantagedness — particularly in English — is an urgent issue, we are tempted to hypothesize that societal factors may play a greater role in bilingual communicative handicaps.

Moreover, it appears to us that relational bilingualism, focusing at it intends on the functionality of multilingualism more than upon its nature, ought to be particularly apt for dealing with this elusive "third dimension" or "V^3," as we would like to rewrite it. For one thing, it would be less likely to base analyses of bilingual output on the traditional clash of two standard language systems, and the expectation of wholly predictable interference phenomena. Rather would it willingly accept a nonstandard variety which, despite its usual lack of prestige, is an important component of the communication network of any bilingual speech community. A series of papers prepared by the writer touches upon such issues (Ornstein 1970, 1971a, 1971b, 1972, 1975a, 1975b, 1976), although on many problems of Southwestern multilingualism, the surface has barely been scratched in undertaking studies which seek to cope realistically with nonstandard as well as standard language varieties in this linguistic area.

SOME FINDINGS AND PROMISING RELATIONSHIPS

As is not uncommon in the amount of data already gleaned in both the overall sample of 301 subjects, as well as the subsample of thirty bilinguals, analysis lags far behind collection. One of our greatest interests of course was in seeking out and discovering meaningful relationships between linguistic and socioeducational variables. By now we can at least show how the subjects of the V-series sample ranked comparatively in combined Spanish, as well as English, language performance, together with their standing in the principal U.S. measures of educational performance. The latter comprise: high school rank; outcomes in the mathematical and verbal portions respectively of the standardized Scholastic Aptitude Test; and grade point average, representing the cumulative total marks received in courses thus far. Attention is invited to Table 3, consisting of a comparison of Language Performance and Educational Achievement Indices. Although much discussion would be possible, no more can be done within our scope than to indicate the mean and standard deviations in appropriate places.

One of the most interesting findings, just to give a single example from the above, was that social class did not relate strongly with language performance in our sampling. The members of our research team have suggested that this may be due to the fact that, by and large, although there were differences of socioeconomic status ranging from Upper Lower to Lower Upper, there is a communality in the Mexican-American subculture here that makes for homogeneity. Another explanation probably is that the sample is biased in favor of individuals aspiring to upward mobility, already screened at a number of points in the educational ladder, and undoubtedly more effective in communication skills (particularly English) than the majority of their peers.

Table 3. Language performance and educational achievement indices V-series (n = 30)

Subject No.	Sex	Age	SES	CL	H.S. rank	SAT math	SAT verbal	G.P.A.	Combined Span. perf.	Combined Eng. perf.
1	F	19	3	1	1	507	584	3.4	2.4	3.8
2	F	19	2	1	1	383	448	1.9	2.7	3.8
3	M	18	1	1	1	389	472	2.6	3.4	3.9
4	F	21	2	4	1	478	600	3.3	3.0	4.0
5	M	21	3	4	1	496	525	2.1	2.7	3.6
6	M	22	2	1	–	289	237	1.0	2.0	2.7
7	F	22	2	4	2	261	346	2.7	3.9	3.9
8	M	20	2	4	1	627	665	3.0	2.3	3.7
9	F	21	3	2	–	–	–	–	3.4	3.9
10	F	19	–	1	1	564	474	2.9	2.9	3.7
11	M	22	2	4	3	407	366	2.9	3.6	3.9
12	F	20	4	3	3	452	436	2.2	2.3	3.8
13	M	21	3	4	1	577	587	4.0	3.0	4.0
14	F	24	2	4	1	507	448	2.8	3.5	3.9
15	F	19	4	3	1	357	383	3.4	2.0	3.7
16	F	19	3	2	1	430	359	3.1	3.1	3.8
17	F	19	4	3	1	–	–	3.3	2.8	3.9
18	F	19	4	2	1	473	572	3.0	3.8	4.3
19	F	20	1	3	3	448	497	2.6	3.5	4.1
20	F	25	2	3	2	447	346	2.5	3.5	4.2
21	M	21	1	2	1	–	–	2.6	3.8	4.3
22	M	21	1	3	1	414	369	2.0	3.5	3.9
23	M	21	2	4	2	505	368	3.1	2.9	3.8
24	M	26	1	2	1	474	442	1.8	2.9	3.7
25	F	21	2	4	1	497	396	3.0	3.8	4.2
26	M	24	2	4	–	488	515	2.4	2.6	3.8
27	M	20	4	1	2	–	–	2.3	4.3	3.4
28	M	20	3	2	2	353	361	2.3	2.9	3.3
29	F	18	4	1	2	358	335	1.7	3.2	4.2
30	M	21	1	2	2	335	342	1.7	3.4	3.2
Mean	1.5	20.7	2.2	2.7	1.5	442.2	441.3	2.6	3.1	3.8
s.d.	±0.5	±1.95	±1.0	±1.1	±.685	±14.2	±14.2	±3.0	±3.1	±2.0

Key:

Dashes (–) represent information not available

CL=Class: year of college

SES=Socioeconomic status

1=Lower-lower

2=Upper-lower

3=Lower-middle

4=Upper-middle

5=Lower-upper

H.S.=High school rank

H.S. Rank:

1=First quarter

2=Second quarter

3=Third quarter

SAT=Scholastic Aptitude Test

G.P.A.=Grade Point Average

Span. perf=Oral and written Spanish ratings combined (see Scale below)

Eng. perf=Oral and written English ratings combined (see Scale below)

s.d.=Standard deviation

Language Performance Scale:

1=No functional knowledge

2=Elementary

3=Intermediate

4=Advanced

5=Educated native

Moreover, in accordance with the aims of our "relative bilingualism" approach, we have attempted to go beyond the ten variables represented in Table 3, and have made bold to investigate a much larger number. In order to do this our team examined the Sociolinguistic Background Questionnaire, and posited sixty-eight variables, with Pearson product-movement correlations on thirty of them. All variables could not be considered for this type of analysis because of the manner in which the coding and card-punching was performed.

Table 4 is therefore a "correlational matrix" in which only those correlations significant at the 0.05 level of confidence are listed.

Obviously, the very proportions of this "correlational matrix" are mind-boggling and not conducive to easy analysis, so that it is only presented here to help convey how we are in practice going about the work of performing a broadgauge socioeducational descriptive study of our sample. The basic task of our team at this point is to exploit the possibilities present in this set of relationships, which are basically of three types: (1) Intralinguistic variables, (2) Correlations between linguistic and socioeducational factors, (3) Correlations between purely socioeducational variables. The third type, it ought to be added, are mostly to be found outside the V-series subsample, and indeed within the overall sampling of 301 undergraduate Mexican-American and Anglo subjects. In order to do justice even to the intralinguistic factors, however, it is necessary to pursue further our ongoing task in which specialists analyze and discuss in depth the outcome of our hypotheses in the light of statistical significance and accepted social science research techniques. This is, however, not all. Beyond statistics and neat rows of columns with their impressive apparatus, it is necessary to discover and interpret their implications for Southwestern educational socio-linguistics.

For the present, it will have to suffice to make some rather general remarks about a few of the findings reflected in the matrix. At this juncture it seems clear that they will vary in usefulness according to the particular specialties of both of both academicians and persons involved in social intervention programs among Chicanos. For example, particularly language and communication specialists and educators in close contact with bilinguals/biculturals ought to be interested in such items as the following:

1. Written English performance is very highly related to grade point average (GPA), or overall academic achievement.

2. Combined (overall) Spanish performance has a significant positive correlation with combined English performance; nevertheless, it does not correlate with written English skill (merely a part of overall performance).

3. Written English skill has a positive relationship with the Verbal

portion of the Scholastic Aptitude Test (SAT), the most widely employed American college entrance instrument.

4. Self-evaluation of Spanish skills relates positively with actual performance, but self-evaluation of English skills does not relate significantly to the latter.

5. High school Spanish courses showed no correlation with performance in Spanish on our test, whereas the taking of such courses at the college level had a strong relationship with performance in the written Spanish skill.

Moreover, social scientists from quite a range of disciplines, both inside and outside the academic environment, ought to find interesting and useful such findings from our sample as the following:

1. Attitudes of loyalty to Spanish and English languages appeared to have no significant relation to performance in either.

2. Attitudes of loyalty to Mexican-American and Anglo cultures respectively appeared to have no meaningful correlation with performance in either Spanish or English.

3. A greater amount of use of Spanish in "mainstream" contacts (that is, in work, school and formal domains) correlates positively with acknowledgement of adjustment problems to the dominant Anglo culture.

4. No relationship appeared to exist between attribution of the importance of English skills and actual performance in English.

5. The higher the level of father's education, the greater the likelihood that Spanish would be the predominant language in the bilingual's home and peer-group domains.

6. Pro-militant attitudes were positively related to acknowledgment of adjustment problems to the Anglo "mainstream" but showed no correlations with linguistic performance.

7. Number of siblings appeared unrelated to educational achievement, despite expectations that monetary pressures would have some negative effect, through the heavy burden of outside work.

Again here, article-length studies are possible on almost any of the above points. These have begun to be undertaken. Pertinent discussion in some detail is already available in Goodman and Renner's "Social factors and language in the southwest" (1978), Goodman and Brooks (1974) and Müller-Brooks' "Interviewing Mexican-American bilinguals: An open-ended pattern" (1972), and in further papers available through our Center.[1]

We will only say here that among the most interesting hypotheses were those that failed to vindicate themselves, in our sample at least. Obvi-

---

[1] Individuals interested in the papers available through our Center, a number of which are relevant to the theme of the present paper, may request current lists from: The Librarian, The Cross-Cultural Southwest Ethnic Study Center, Box 13, The University of Texas at El Paso, 79968, U.S.A.

Table 4. Correlation matrix–V-series and total Spanish surname or bilingual ($n = 100$ or $100+$)

Variable	Father's education	Mother's education	Social Class	Work use of Spanish	Home use of Spanish	Environment use of Spanish	Pre-college use of Spanish	College use of Spanish	Church use of Spanish	Recreation use of Spanish	No. Siblings
Father's education											
Mother's education	+										
Social Class	+	+									
Work use of Spanish	o	o									
Home use of Spanish	+	+	+	+							
Environment use of Spanish	o	o	o	o	+						
Pre-college use of Spanish	o	o	o	o	+						
College use of Spanish	o	o	o	o	+		+				
Church use of Spanish	o	o	o	+	+		+	+			
Recreation use of Spanish							+	+	+		
No. Siblings	−	−				−		−			
Adjustment problems						+		+			
Attitude towards militancy											
Difficulty of college Spanish								−			
Lang. preference						+		+			
English fluency (self-evaluation)				+	−						
Spanish fluency (self-evaluation)			−	+				−	−	−	
Importance of English											
Total Score – Language Usage				+		+	+	+	+	+	
High School Rank*											
GPA*											
SAT-Math*				o	o	o		o	o	o	
SAT-Verbal*				o	o	o		o	o	o	
Spanish Perf. Combined Score				o	o	−		−	−	o	
English Perf.* Combined Score				o	o	o		o	o	o	
Oral Spanish* Score						−		−			
Written* Spanish* Score				o	−	−		−	−	o	
Oral English Score*				+	o	o		o	o		
Written* English Score				o	o	o		o	o		

Similarity of College Spanish

	Lang. preference	English fluency (self-evaluation)	Spanish fluency (self-evaluation)	Importance of English	Total Score –Language Usage	High School Rank*	GPA*	SAT-Math*	SAT-Verbal*	Spanish Perf. Combined Score	English Perf.* Combined Score	Oral Spanish* Score	Written* Spanish* Score	Oral English Score*	Written* English Score
Lang. preference															
English fluency (self-evaluation)															
Spanish fluency (self-evaluation)															
Importance of English															
Total Score –Language Usage															
High School Rank*															
GPA*															
SAT-Math*															
SAT-Verbal*															
Spanish Perf. Combined Score															
English Perf.* Combined Score															
Oral Spanish* Score															
Written* Spanish* Score															
Oral English Score*															
Written* English Score															

*$n=30$ (otherwise n is 100 or greater)
Key: + = Positive relationship significant at 0.05 level
– = Inverse relationship significant at 0.05 level
0 = No relationship at 0.05 level

ously, correlational studies such as ours could easily contribute to breaking down some long-held and cherished beliefs about bilinguals/biculturals in our society, or at least to making distinctions between differing types of bilinguals. For example, contrary to the findings of Grebler, Moore and Guzmán (1970) in a somewhat related study of Los Angeles Chicanos, we found, as noted, no significance between language loyalty to Spanish and English and performance in either. Perhaps even more surprising than this was that, in our sample at least, social class was not found to be positively related with language performance — an outcome also at variance with the general findings in Los Angeles of Grebler and associates. What makes this all the more intriguing is that, in a common-sense way, we know that families assimilating to Anglo life styles tend to try to reduce or eliminate use of Spanish altogether, endeavoring often to realize English in a hypercorrect manner, without a trace of linguistic interference (particularly intonational patterns from Mexican Spanish).

A possible explanation of the above is that, at least in the El Paso milieu, socioeconomic status of the home in which the bilingual is reared is secondary to the appropriateness of English and Spanish in the various domains of living. In our situation of stable bilingualism here, after years of coexistence the relative distributive roles of the two languages are highly circumscribed, with codeswitching involved in patterns which still beg for more adequate description. Perhaps also a great deal of leveling has occurred, because of the relative homogeneity of the sample, with the majority of subjects from Upper Lower and Lower Middle socioeconomic status. Possibly more importantly than this, they are an elite group because of having graduated in the upper half of their high school classes, have survived through all selection processes along the educational ladder up to college, and have a common aspiration toward upward mobility.

Furthermore it is hoped that through this broadgauge relational approach it may be possible to help reduce the negative orientation so common in research among culturally-differentiated populations, with a strong bias in favor of the most deprived populations in our society. While there is no denying the powerful association between nonstandard language, poor scholastic results, and lower socioeconomic status, it is equally unscientific to omit from consideration average and high achievers among such minority groups as Mexican-Americans, blacks, and Native Americans. Again here, our data reveals that a considerable number of our subjects, although stemming from a "culture of poverty," demonstrate academic achievement equal to or superior to their Anglo peers. This of course requires further and systematic analysis.

All this has powerful implications for educators and others involved with the so-called minority groups, and faced by a perplexing spectrum of problems. Not the least of these is the charge that most standardized tests are "culturally unfair" except to affluent middleclass "mainstream" groups. Another is the growing revolt against monolithic school performance norms for minority and mainstream groups alike. Still another is the controversy over remediation of nonstandard, stigmatized language varieties, coupled with demands that vernaculars such as Black English and Southwest Spanish be accorded some legitimate place in the school context.

Accordingly, a concern with the alleged inequities stemming from culturolinguistic factors is rapidly spreading throughout industry and government as well as the school environment, as evidenced by the burgeoning number of court cases. Consequently, if differentiated norms are indeed in the offing in a nation supposedly dedicated to cultural pluralism, then perhaps the kinds of correlations presented in this study are partially thrown into a cocked hat. Possibly, on the other hand, one needs to begin thinking in terms of dual sets of norms, and namely an interethnic group one, as well as an intragroup set.

Finally, it occurs to us that if our correlational measures, although gross in many ways, could be replicated in many other bilingual contexts, many of our folk beliefs about multilingualism might be demolished. Our approach, in sum, is one seeking its strength in the combined resources of interdisciplinary research, and by that same token in as much replication as possible in similar and dissimilar environments. It is thus that the correlational matrices might assume ever greater significance.

REFERENCES

BERNSTEIN, BASIL
  1961 "Social class and linguistic development: a theory of social learning," in *Education, economy and society.* Edited by A. H. Halsey, Jean Flood and C. Arnold Anderson. Glencoe, Ill.: Free Press.
BOWEN, J. DONALD, JACOB ORNSTEIN, *editors*
  1976 *Studies in Southwest Spanish.* Rowley, Mass.: Newbury House Publishers.
BROOKS, BONNIE S., GARY D. BROOKS, PAUL W. GOODMAN, JACOB ORNSTEIN
  1972 *Sociolinguistic background questionnaire: A measurement instrument for the study of bilingualism.* (Revised) El Paso: Cross-Cultural Southwest Ethnic Study Center, University of Texas at El Paso.
FISHMAN, JOSHUA A.
  1972 "The sociology of language; an inter-disciplinary social science approach to language in society," in *Advances in the sociology of language.* Edited by Joshua Fishman. The Hague: Mouton.
GOFFMAN, ERVING
  1972 *Relations in public: Microstudies in public order.* New York: Basic Books.
GOODMAN, PAUL W.
  1970 A comparison of Spanish-surnamed and Anglo college students. Paper

presented at the Rocky Mountain Social Science Association, Annual Meeting. Boulder, Colo.

GOODMAN, PAUL, BONNIE S. BROOKS
1974   A comparison of Anglo and Mexican-American students attending the same university. *Kansas Journal of Sociology* 10:(Fall)181–203.

GOODMAN, PAUL W., KARTHRYN RENNER
1978   "Social factors and language in the Southwest," in *Problems in applied educational sociolinguistics: Readings in language and cultural problems of U.S. ethnic groups.* Edited by Glenn G. Gilbert and Jacob Ornstein. Rowley, Mass.: Newbury House.

GREBLER, LEO, JOAN MOORE, RALPH GUZMÁN
1970   *The Mexican-American people: the nation's second largest minority.* New York: Free Press.

GUMPERZ, JOHN J.
1964   "Linguistic and social interaction in two communities," in *The ethnography of communication.* Edited by John J. Gumperz and Dell Hymes. *American Anthropologist,* 66 (6) Part 2:137–153.
1967   "On the linguistic markers of bilingual communication," in *Bilingualism in the modern world.* Edited by John MacNamara. *Journal of Social Issues* 23:48–57.

HAUGEN, EINAR
1956   *Bilingualism in the Americas: a bibliography and research guide.* University: University of Alabama Press.
1969   *The Norwegian language in America: a study in bilingual behavior* (second edition). Bloomington: Indiana University Press.
1971   The ecology of language. *Linguistic Reporter* Supplement 25:(Winter)19–26.
1973   "Bilingualism, language contact and immigrant languages in the U. S.: a research report," in *Current Trends in Linguistics X,* part one. Edited by Thomas Sebeok, 505–591. The Hague: Mouton.

JAKOBOVITS, LEON A.
1971   Preliminaries to the psychology of ordinary language. Typescript. (To appear in *Revolution in psychological theory.* Edited by W. A. Brewer and L. A. Jakobovits.)

KELLY, L., *editor*
1969   *The description and measurement of bilingualism.* Toronto: University of Toronto Press.

LABOV, WILLIAM A.
1970   The study of language in its social context. *Studium Generale* 23:30–87.

LAWTON, DENIS
1968   *Social class, language and education.* New York: Schocken Books.

MALHERBE, E. C.
1969   "Discussion," in *The description and measurement of bilingualism.* Edited by L. Kelly. Toronto: University of Toronto Press.

MÜLLER-BROOKS, ELLEN
1972   "Interviewing Mexican-American bilinguals: an open-ended pattern." Paper presented at the First Workshop on Southwest Area Linguistics, Southwest Ethnic Study Center, University of Texas at El Paso, April 6–8.

MURRAY, WAYNE
1972   "Ethnic and sex differences as related to perceptions of a university environment." Unpublished Ph.D. dissertation. Las Cruces: New Mexico State University.

ORNSTEIN, JACOB

1970   "Sociolinguistics and new perspectives in the study of Southwest Span-
        ish," in *Studies in language and linguistics 1969–1970*. Edited by R. W.
        Ewton, Jr. and Jacob Ornstein, 127–184. El Paso: Texas Western Press.

1971a   "Language varieties along the U. S.–Mexican border," in *Applications
        of linguistics. Selected papers from the second International Congress of
        Applied Linguistics*. Edited by G. E. Perren and J. L. M. Trim, Cam-
        bridge: Cambridge University Press.

1971b   Sociolinguistic research on language diversity in the American South-
        west and its educational implications. *Modern Language Journal*
        55:223–229.

1972   Toward a classification of Southwest Spanish nonstandard variants.
        Linguistics 94 (December).

1975a   "Sociolinguistics and the study of Spanish and English language var-
        ieties and their use in the U.S. Southwest," in *Three essays on linguistic
        diversity in the Spanish-speaking world*. Edited by Jacob Ornstein,
        10–45. The Hague: Mouton.

1975b   *A sociolinguistic study of Mexican-American and Anglo students in a
        border university*. Border State Symposium Series 3. Edited by Will
        Kennedy. San Diego, Calif.: San Diego State University, Institute of
        Public and Urban Affairs Press.

1976   A cross-disciplinary sociolinguistic investigation of Mexican-American
        bilinguals/biculturals. *La Linguistique* 12:131–145.

PACE, C. ROBERT, *et al.*

1969   *College and university environment scales (CUES, form x-2)*. Princeton,
        N.J.: Educational Testing Service.

SIERTSEMA, BERTHE

1969   "Discussion," in *The description and measurement of bilingualism*.
        Edited by L. Kelly. Toronto: University of Toronto Press.

WEINREICH, URIEL

1953   *Languages in contact*. New York: Linguistic Circle of New York.

1956   Research frontiers in bilingualism studies. *Proceedings of the Eighth
        International Congress of Linguists*. Oslo, Norway, 786–797.

SECTION FOUR

Language and Cultural Identity

The Future of the Oppressed Languages in the Andes

XAVIER ALBÓ

1. INTRODUCTION

This work refers to the problem of Quechua and Aymara, distinct and major languages in Peru and Bolivia yet low in prestige.[1] Those zones in which these languages and Spanish coexist, that is, in the greater part of the central and southern range of Peru, the entire plain and almost all the valleys of Bolivia, are my major concern. However, primarily Spanish zones, as in the tropics and on the coast, many of them national political linguistics centers and recipients of Quechua and Aymara migrations, are

The present work has benefited much from the collaboration given by Sr. Gamaniel Arroyo of the Ministry of Education of Peru and of Doctors Cerron and Parker of the Plan for Linguistic Support of the University of San Marcos in Lima and of the discussions held in Bolivia with the personnel of the National Department of Adult Education of the Ministry of Education, of the National Institute of Cultural Investigation for Popular Education (INDICEP, Oruro), the Center of Investigation and Promotion of Rural Affairs (CIPCA), and with the historiographer Dr. Barnadas.
[1] According to the latest completed census data the population of Bolivia was distributed in 1950 (Bolivia 1955), according to the mother tongue, into Spaniards (36 percent), Quechuas (36 percent) and Aymaras (25 percent) — totalling three million (the 1972 estimations are close to five million; see Note 18 for most recent figures). In Peru the census of 1961 (Peru 1966) distributes its ten millions (estimated fifteen million in 1972) of inhabitants into monolingual Spaniards (60 percent), Quechuas (35 percent), of which two-thirds speak the Ayachuchano and Cuzqueno dialects, and the other third central dialects unintelligible to the former, and 4 percent Aymara. In Bolivia the problem is more extensive but also simpler. In the south of Peru the problem presents the same characteristics. In 1958 Schaedel (1967) estimated that in the eight provinces of the south of Peru, with a total population of 2.8 million, there were 12 percent monolingual Spaniards and 54 percent monolingual Quechua or Aymaras, the rest being bilingual, generally of native origin. On the national level the problem is less extensive and more complex, as the fragmentation of the Quechua dialects is greater up to the point of obstructing mutual intelligibility. This aspect has been treated by Torero (1964, 1970, 1972), Parker (1963, 1972a) and Escobar (1972b).

also touched upon. The considered situation has its parallel in various provinces of the Equatorial range (especially from Imbabura to Chimborazo), with the difference that there Quechua has an even lower prestige than in Peru or Bolivia. But, because of the lack of sufficient data, I will have to overlook Equador here. Although the empirical illustrations come only from the Andes region, the problem is up to a certain point the same as in other places in which similar dual structures exist, with minority groups dominating majorities of different culture.[2]

The situation of other ethnic groups in the jungle and in a few enclaves of the high plateaus, e.g. the Uru of Bolivia and the Jaqaru of Peru, are not considered here as their problems are different. The greater part of these miniscule groups are rapidly becoming extinct and it is very clear that, despite the best intentions and efforts of missionaries, academic groups, or others, they are condemned to assimilate themselves into the overwhelmingly powerful majorities arrayed around them.

2. THE CONCEPT OF OPPRESSED LANGUAGES

The languages of which we are referring are usually called native, autochthonous, vernacular, indigenous, etc. But these adjectives do not sufficiently express the social dimensions which mold their peculiarities.[3] Greek, after all, is the indigenous language of Greece. Moreover, in certain traditionally Spanish zones of the Andes Spanish is actually the native tongue while Quechua is the foreign tongue of the immigrant groups. Or, if we do not accept this criterion, we should also not accept that Quechua be called "native" in so many regions of Argentina, Bolivia, Equador and also Peru; it was either introduced in these regions by the Inca only a few years before the colonization, or perhaps later by the missionaries, under full Spanish rule.

Another group of concepts elaborated by sociolinguistics, e.g. languages of low prestige, unofficial, substandard, with a low functional specialization, etc., brings us closer to the problem of languages such as Quechua and Aymara. These sociolinguistic concepts are still limited to the phenomenological sphere. They simply describe some social qualities of certain languages as opposed to those of others (of greater prestige,

---

[2]   But only up to a certain point. For example, within the continent, Paraguay offers quite a few similarities but the oppression of the Guaraní is not as great (Rubin 1968) thanks especially to the fact that during colonization, besides the situations such as we describe in this work, there was the unusual case of the Jesuit *Reducciones* [autonomous communities of Christian Indians] where the Guaraní did not undergo the same social oppression (Meliá 1969, 1971). In Guatemala and in several Mexican states the situation is more complicated than in the Andes because of the great number of native languages.
[3]   In spite of the fact that UNESCO (1953) defines the vernacular tongue in terms of social and political domination.

etc.) which coexist within the same social structure. What they do not do is establish even a causal explanation meant to get to the root of why some languages are subordinate. For this reason I suggest here that these languages be characterized as oppressed languages.

In sociology, especially of the Third World where social contradictions are more violent, it is common to organize the analysis of society on the basis of a division between a group or dominating class and the dominated, and also between an oppressor-group and an oppressed, the groupings inspired more or less remotely by Marxism. From this practice have also arisen concepts derived from other disciplines, such as, for example, the "pedagogy of the oppressed" (Freire 1970). By analogy — and in line with what has already been suggested by Meliá (1971) for the Guaraní — the use of the term "oppressed language" may enable a better understanding of the peculiarities of many languages which are ordinarily characterized on a purely historical basis as "indigenous," or more superficially, as "of low prestige."

In fact, thanks to particular historical circumstances, human groups of a certain language and culture have come to be dominated by groups of various other languages and cultures, both sharing the same asymmetrical social global structure. These historical circumstances may involve migrations, as happens with so many ethnic groups in the United States. At other times they may involve the arbitrary manner in which national boundaries are formed, as has been the case in many new African states. The clearest cases, however, are those of conquests, with their resulting paradox that the conquered are at the same time the most established groups in the country and become major sectors of it. This is the case of the populations of the Andes.

After conquest, it gradually came about that the culture of the conquered Andine groups, although preserving its independence in many aspects, lost its radical independence — above all on the political level — and little by little lost many other characteristics too. Economic, social, religious, expressive and axiological structures, in spite of notorious peculiarities, became reinterpreted in the light of the function of the new situation of domination in which they circumscribed. For example, the symbolism of the Andine feast day may have reinforced the system of oppression, demonstrating within a festive atmosphere in a village of mestizos the renewal of foreign authority. A dual asymmetrical structure then arises, characterized not only by cultural duplicity between the dominating minority group and the dominated majority but also and primarily by mutual and unequal dependence between both groups. The culture of the dominated group ceases to be a culture and in reality is reduced to a subculture. It continues to have many autonomizing compensations, which, echoing Lewis (1961, 1969), will allow us to legitimately speak of a "native subculture of poverty," giving it a certain continuity which is often indirectly encouraged by the dominating group. However, the inequality of power which characterizes this situation impoverishes the subculture more and more and slowly paralyzes its creative dynamism. This is what Ribeiro (1970) calls "deculturalization." In most cases it develops its retreating and conservative mechanisms of defense. At certain moments revitalizing native uprisings can occur, with more expressive goals than the recovery of effectiveness. But on the whole, particularly with the coming of industrialization in the dominating sector and unless the composition of forces in the basic dual structure changes, the destiny of the native impoverished subculture will continue heading toward sclerosis, will continue impoverishing itself by functioning in relation to the dominating structure, and finally will be reduced to simple characterization as the lowest social class within a "more modern" national society. Because of this Greaves (1972; cf. Stavenhagen 1965) can already doubt the validity of the model of dual culture in the region of the Andes, suggesting as an alternative the convenience of a model of classes. It is debatable if we have arrived yet at this stage of the process, particularly in the Andean Sierra and the Altiplano. But without doubt it is this process which leads to this outcome. It seems sufficient at the moment to speak of an oppressed subculture and of a pressure which, throughout the ages, not only oppresses, but even kills, unless — I repeat — unless the composition of the forces in the matrix structure changes. Obviously there are also limits in "zones of refuge" (Aguirre 1967) where sociocultural independence is better maintained and the dominating minority group also mixes more with the dominated majority class. But these counter-examples do not have a comparable volume, nor do they set forth processes such as the ones indicated here. Cases such as that of the conquered Greeks culturally influencing the Roman dominator are not encountered in Bolivia and Peru.

Within this wider framework, the cultural element of "language" undergoes a similar process, but with peculiarities worthy of note. Thanks to its own intricate internal structure, the native language maintains its independence on a level higher than that of other cultural elements. There is no question of its reduction to a "sublanguage" or "dialect" of the dominating language; Quechua and Aymara continue to be languages in the full sense of the word. But the impoverishing and internally atrophying process is also at work. The dynamics of the change itself of the whole language, occurring within the context of an oppressive dependence, acquire a clear directional extralinguistic sense: the language is no longer ruled so much by linguistic laws of internal change (although this element is also present), but by the necessity above all of yielding more and more to the language of the dominating group and thereby gradually acquiring new elements of its structure, first on the level of vocabulary, later also on the levels of phonology and grammar. This situation may be prolonged over centuries. Thus the native languages remain alive in large sectors of the population, but with diminished vitality. They are oppressed languages. In limited cases, throughout a phase of bilingualism in which the dominated group acquires as a second language that of the dominating group, the native language of the oppressed may be lost and only traces remain in dialectical variants of Spanish which reflect the native substratum. Also here one can come up against examples of greater resistance in "zones of refuge" (and in the more dense nuclei, centers of cultural tradition, such as Cuzco and Tiwanaku) and of rapprochements of the dominating language toward the dominated. But these also do not reach the same volume nor do they have the same consequences.

We have insinuated that the dominating social group can indirectly encourage the partial independence and subsequent continuity of the native impoverished subculture; this is owing to the fact of its interest in maintaining the privileges and status quo which the dual structure guarantees. Also on this level the peculiarities of the language factor play an important role, thanks to their greater independence. In an extreme situation of rigid dualism the global society would have a bilingualism consistent in reality with a double monolingualism: on the one hand, the dominating minority which only speaks Spanish, and on the other, the dominated majority which only speaks its native language (various ones the length of the Andes), the intermediaries which unfold in both languages being relatively scarce. In this ideal model the double monolingualism accomplishes the optimum function of social distinguisher and maintainer of the system. On one hand, the language becomes an identifier, and, in certain cases, a very effective social discriminator, which, like a calling card, ensures, in whatever circumstance, the social classification of anyone: the language cannot be changed so easily as the dress; and the "accent" even less. On the other hand, the language is not only a social identifier; it also blocks and eliminates the possibility of transition in cutting communication between those of different language groups and obliges those of the same sociocultural group to communicate verbally only among themselves, reducing the contacts between groups to a few stereotyped cliques which assure the rigidity and permanence of the system. Social oppression in the dual society produces double monolingualism and this in turn guarantees the persistence of the dual society. The oppressed language becomes in turn oppressive.

3. DIMENSIONS OF LANGUAGE OPPRESSION IN THE ANDES

The present situation in the Andes, in some regions more than in others, and even more than has been characterized, shows itself to be a double monolingualism because of the dual asymmetrical oppressing structure. At the same time the increase of bilingual speakers, particularly of Quechua and Aymara origin, who learn Spanish, shows on the one hand a greater flexibility in what previously was rigid dualism, and on the other, may foreshadow the step towards the "modern society" of classes in which, as the end result of the process, the oppressed cultures and languages are forced to yield to the developing impetus of the dominating framework.

Let us begin with the historical dimension since colonial times, which here we can only sketch. At first sight it is surprisingly at odds with, but ultimately confirms, the outline presented in previous paragraphs. As Ricard (1961) has effectively documented, the official linguistic policy of Spain in America was always one of reserving public life for the Spanish-speaking class; it decreed repeatedly that once and for all the Indians must by Hispanicized. Nevertheless, in general, this policy proved ineffective and the Indians continued being monolingual in their language. I would add that such a policy would necessarily HAVE to prove ineffective, because the inherent dualism of the asymmetrical structure — which the Spanish-Creole elite basically never wanted to touch — demanded it. Thus a systematic divorce between word and reality was produced, analogous to one which existed always between the laws of the Indians and Indian practice. Independence did not change things, but rather worsened the paradox, particularly in the last century in which *latifundismo* [large landownership] dominated. The enthusiasm for "modernizing" (Hispanicizing) the Indian in the press or in parliament was redoubled, while at the same time neolatifundist robbery transformed cultural communities into estates, therefore reinforcing the dual structure and making it impossible for these enthusiasms to be effective. Only in the last decades have changes in the social structure been observed which brought with them an increase of bilingualism, of the Hispanicizing process, and at the same time, something of an increase in the prestige of Quechua and Aymara. All this is owing primarily to the presence of new factors such as land reform and the industrializing process on the coast, which will be further developed.

At present, the oppressive situation and the processes of change appear to be in unequal distribution of functions for each language in the various spheres of activity. Figure 1 synthesizes this fact.[4]

The figure refers only to the regions in which there is a Quechua or Aymara majority. But even here there is a clear functional discrimination. If there had not been socio-language oppression, the dividing line

---

[4] For a broader discussion of this point in Cochabamba see Albó (1969, 1970, 1974). Here I limit myself to preserving a synthetic, macrosocial vision based especially on Bolivia. What I here call spheres of activity is similar to, without being identical to, that which Fishman calls DOMAINS.

Language

A

Spheres of activity

1. Technico-professional world
2. Official world
3. Institutions of mutual
   relations:

   socialization in schools

   written means of
   communication

   oral means of
   communication

   politics

   commercial networks

4. Expressive world (religious,
   artistic, folklore)

5. Traditional rural world

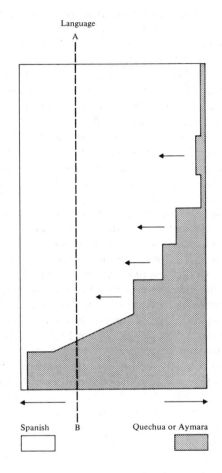

Spanish   B   Quechua or Aymara

Figure 1. Functional distribution of languages in the bilingual zones of the Andes (estimate)

would coincide in any sphere with line AB, because in such regions approximately seventy percent of the population is Quechua or Aymara. But it is not so. So in the distribution of speakers of one or the other language as in the selection of one or the other language in the case of bilingualism, it is understood that, outside of the sphere of rural tradition, Spanish should be prevalent. And in the case of the technico-professional world and of the official world it is understood that Quechua and Aymara are to be practically excluded.

The apparent exception, or rather ambiguity, of that which is called the expressive world, in reality confirms what has already been said. Turner (1969) pointed out that, if we want to emphasize the emotive communitary pole (as opposed to the structural or *Gesellschaft*), it is easier to choose symbols derived from the more oppressed or marginal sector of society — a fact which I can confirm also in the selection of the language spoken in the study of the Valley of Cochabamba (Albó 1970).

Within this keynote, the recent advances of the oppressed languages in the sphere of institutions for mutual relations are significant. A few years ago the use of Spanish in radio broadcasting or in the political world was as imperative as it remains today in the technico-professional world. Only in the school system, and correlatively in the world of the press, are the oppressed languages still almost completely absent, although the new plan for bilingual education in Peru (see below) and several timid attempts of the press in Quechua and Aymara in Bolivia,[5] show signs that there may be some change in the near future. But up to now these recent developments only smooth over the situation without changing it.

In the light of this crushing and even barring of Quechua and Aymara in certain functional sectors, we can better understand the concrete form in which these languages remain atrophied.

In the first place even their idiomatic internal structure has atrophied. The main symptom is the growing impoverishment of vocabulary,[6] particularly in semantic areas related to the spheres in which Quechua and Aymara are outlawed. Impoverishment may be followed by the disappearance of ancient words (e.g. the terminology of relationship), or by the absence of neologisms in the face of new technical advances (e.g. *radio*), or often by the formation of pairs of words in which one word is of native origin and connotes the traditional semantic area and the other word is a borrowing from the Spanish which means the modern semantic area — which is generally more socially prestigious. For example, in Quechua a traditional kitchen would be *q'uncha,* but a modern one would be *cocina* and in Aymara the paternal father-in-law would be *awkchi* while a maternal one would be *suegro.* Or the native numerals would be maintained to count the flock, but Spanish borrowings would be used to tell the

---

[5]   There was in 1972 a monthly Quechua–Spanish periodical in Cochabamba and another Aymara–Spanish one in La Paz, both orientated towards the education of the peasant. The latter has an edition of 5,000 copies. In a daily Cochabamba newspaper I have also seen some advertisements in Quechua.

[6]   There is also a certain amount of atrophy in the phonological and grammatical spheres. For example, in the Quechua of Cochabamba the phonological series of the glottal and aspirate occlusive, typical of Bolivian Quechua but absent in Spanish, occupies the lowest place in the list of frequency of phonemes of Lastra (1965) and there is evidence that traits such as these, and other grammatical points such as the object-verb order or the density of modal verb suffixes, lessen in frequency of use as the social level of the speaker rises (Albó 1970:228–253, 309–376). But in general in these spheres it is not so much a question of impoverishment. The native structures of phonological and grammatical order are not so easily lost. Rather they alternate with those acquired from the dominating Spanish language. Likewise, for the new speakers of Spanish what is most characteristic of their substandard dialects of Spanish is the phonology and grammatical constructions inherited from the mother or substratum tongue.

time or dates. If we try to quantify this lexical impoverishment we find that in the corpus used by Stark (1972) in Chuquisaca, a third of the dictionary words are Spanish borrowings, and in the corpus used by Lastra (1968) in Cochabamba, more than half are borrowings. If, instead of using vocabulary lists, we base our studies on the frequency with which the borrowings are repeated in the text, we have figures collected in a sample of twenty Quechua-speakers of a graduated social scale in rural Cochabamba (Albó 1970:359): the frequency of Spanish borrowings grows according to the topic; fear of spirits (11 percent), production of corn liquor (12 percent), agriculture (24 percent), other rural experiences (33 percent), politics (41 percent), modern medicine (48 percent). This impoverishment may reach a point in which the use of the native language becomes almost impossible for certain topics, as in explaining the functioning of a tractor, for example, or for typical abstract conceptualizations of the academic world. Because of this we speak of primitive languages as only apt for dealing with the very concrete, overlooking the fact that such languages lack the mechanisms to form abstract terms or neologisms adapted to new technological advances. They can be formed; the Germans did so in the time of Luther and the Indonesians are doing so at present. But, simply, the present conformation of the social structure does not give primitive languages a chance to develop these internal potentials.

One paralinguistic aspect of the atrophy of the oppressed languages is lack of coordination or control of the attempts to reduce them to a uniform writing. In the popular conception there are many who think that it is a question of "dialects" so primitive that they are not even suitable to be written. In general, chaos reigns. Parker (1972b) has been able to say that perhaps there are more alphabets than authors, since several use various ones. The invading oppression of Spanish has obliged the more accepted alphabets up to now, almost irrevocably, to ignore the very contrastive systems of the Quechua and Aymara phonology and to distort them in order to adapt incongruously the contrasts — and the inconsistencies — of the Spanish alphabet because it is the dominating one. Several linguists who write, not for their colleagues, but for the public, have had to yield to the force of the extralinguistic factors, abandoning the most logical in order to come close to the Spanish.[7] If these languages were not outlawed from the schools, and thus from the literary and academic world, it would be easier to suggest, little by little, the necessity of effectively making their writing uniform. Success at this would become

[7] Such is the case of the Biblical societies which have left a phonemic alphabet suggested by Pike as similar to the Spanish alphabet, especially in the publications of the Center of Alphabetization and Aymara Literature (CALA) in La Paz. The sociolinguistic complexity of the problem of the alphabet and its relations with Spanish has been treated in Albó (1970:150–159).

a relatively secondary matter under the linguistically distorting but socially integrating tutelage of the Spanish system.

On an extralinguistic level the atrophy already takes the form of public fear of the use of one's own language — one of the clearer windows of the personality — thanks to a symbolic power which identifies the language with less prestigious members of society. The school is one of the principal instruments for fostering this atrophy. On the one hand, with its constant discouragement of the vernacular in the class or in public acts before the community, it is effective in creating the feeling of shame and public loss of prestige in using one's own tongue. On the other hand, it is ineffective in forming a coordinated bilingualism which might succeed in handling the mother tongue and the official Spanish language with equal skill. In the majority of cases the school only forms subordinate bilingualism which hastily defends itself in a substandard Spanish dialect of as low a prestige as the native tongue. In this way the oppressed continue to need their mother tongue as an expressive medium of their personality, while in their relations with the public world its use remains diminished if not totally annihilated. Those who place themselves in the perspective of the established order would say that the reason for the resulting frustration is "because they do not know Spanish well." Those who place themselves on the subversive platform would say that the reason is "because the established disorder does not want to accept their language."

4. COUNTERCURRENTS AND RECENT STRUCTURAL CHANGES

As a counterpoint to all that has been said up to now we should point out which groups have attempted to create a place for Quechua and Aymara and which factors have smoothed or altered the rigidity of the traditional structure. For the first we will be guided by the documented bibliography of Rivet (1951–1956).

The pioneers are the missionaries. In the first decades of colonization many missionaries of Peru proclaimed the evangelization of the Indian in Spanish and also in Latin, either through indolence or to avoid any possible heretical formulations of the holy doctrine. But at the end of the sixteenth and the beginning of the seventeenth centuries a noticeable flowering of religious and linguistic works in Quechua and Aymara occurred (Albó 1966:402–404). In 1625, a primer in Quechua–Spanish in 6000 copies is mentioned. We must come to the nineteenth century to find followers to this precursor. There is a pause of almost two centuries with only the appearance of sporadic works, many of them new editions, dedicated almost exclusively to religious ends and to two subsidiary fields: practical linguistics, for training new missionaries, and on a much smaller scale, drama, also with evangelizing ends.[8] The pragmatic character of this movement is marked by its theme and also by the growing concentration on the "general" or open languages (lingua franca), particularly Quechua and to a lesser extent Aymara.[9] Little by little, partly because of missionary policy, the innumerable local languages which thrived at the beginning of colonization were yielding before Quechua, which even extended to new regions beyond the old frontiers. With this sub-unifying process through the diffusion of a common language of low prestige, the double monolingualism of the dual structure remained more evident.

The second flowering comes in the nineteenth century, above all in relation to romanticism. The block of production continues being of a religious character, now complete with the contributions of Biblical societies, and others of a linguistic character, already secularized. But the novelty is that in this century poetry, songs and tales begin to be published in Quechua and Aymara. Also at the beginning of the nineteenth century arise the interminable proposals and counterproposals for an alphabet and, already on a commercial level, innumerable trilingual pamphlets with the "most common words." Within the romantic thrust should be placed the first educational and political writings in the native language. It is notable that, in spite of its assertive independent tone, the pan-Andine rebellion of Tupac Amaru has not left any mark in the bibliography of Rivet, except for the mention of the linking of this leader and Curate Valdés, compiler of the famous Quechua tragedy, *Ollantay,* presented before Tupac Amaru in his general quarters (Lewin 1967:238, 513–514). And, in opposition, in spite of the Hispanicizing impetus of the Independence, some of its proclamations were the first political documents translated into Quechua. Nevertheless, in these and later translations of political documents into Quechua or Aymara, they are the efforts of individuals who want to show off without attempting seriously the politicization of the Indians. More realistic were the efforts of such educators as Curate Beltrán in Oruro, or, in this century, Doctor Nuñez Butrón, from Juliaca, editor of the periodical *Runa Soncco.* But these are mere grains of sand on the shore.

[8] It becomes difficult to reduce the facts of Rivet to statistics because of the lack of dates and the great amounts of material, which includes many works with only linguistic allusions. Limiting ourselves to the religious and linguistic material with many fragments in Quechua or Aymara, we have the following approximate figures for groups of years:
1532–1580: 2 religious (1Q and 1Ay) and 2 linguistic (Q)
1581–1650: 38 religious (24Q and 14Ay) and 23 linguistic (17Q and 6Ay)
1651–1800: 32 religious (24Q and 8Ay) and 23 linguistic (17Q and 6Ay)
The last period, in spite of containing more than double the period of time, has less production with relation to the second period. In concrete terms, during 1650–1750 only six works can be attributed with certainty to that era. In Equador the entire process is dephased, the first productions corresponding to the second half of the eighteenth century.
[9] One speaks of the third general language, Puquina, only in the first decades.

A third surge, antedating Rivet, is attributed directly to the international linguistic community and, more indirectly, to the increase of programs of national or international aid in the field, together with the socioeconomical rise of the peasant. For all this, in the last few years the quantity and quality of studies in Quecha and Aymara has sharply increased, the techniques of their learning in specialized institutions of good quality has improved[10] and new projects of bilingual promotion[11] and the circulation of literature in the native language[12] have been born.

Partly as a result of the academic surge and partly as a result of political changes, new focuses in educational politics have formed lately which take the oppressed languages more into account. Up to 1973, action had not gone beyond the planning stage in Peru, and, in Bolivia, not even beyond the good wishes of some secondary branch office of the Ministry of Education and of some private institutions. Thanks perhaps to a major governmental decision and to greater support from academic institutions, the plans which were being formulated in Peru have been gaining in precision, although there were still, in 1973, serious ambiguities. For example, on the one hand, drastic changes such as the obligation to teach a native language as a second language in high schools were announced, and the creativity of the oppressed groups in their own language was encouraged. But on the other hand, this effort at Hispanicization seems only to use native languages in its initial stages[13] and there are not even educational means — such as the elaboration of texts and the preparation

---

[10]   Such as the *"Plan de Fomento Linguistico"* of the University of San Marco in Lima and the Maryknoll Institute of Languages in Cochabamba. There are more than twenty centers in Peru and Bolivia where Quechua and, to a lesser extent, Aymara are taught. Outside of South America Aymara is also taught at one university and Quechua at more than a dozen, many of them having prepared fine pedagogical materials. For more details see the *Andean Linguistics Newsletter.*

[11]   Particularly the project of Ayacucho (Burns 1968a, 1968b and 1970) and others, more recent, also born in the shadow of the Summer Institute of Linguistics. Aside from the forest groups, in 1970 the effort reached five provinces, thirty-nine teachers and 1,500 students of Ayacucho. In Bolivia it reached, up until 1973, 3,000 literate Aymaras in a variable number of schools of two provinces and a considerably smaller number of Quechua children in Cochabamba. Between 1967 and 1973 23,000 primers were distributed in Aymara, in Cochabamba, 1,000 in Quechua (data provided by the Summer Institute of Linguistics at La Paz.)

[12]   Particularly the Center of Alphabetization and Aymara Literature (CALA) in La Paz, affiliated with the Summer Institute of Linguistics, which has published more than fifty pamphlets particularly of a religious kind. Among these a hymnal and a bilingual pamphlet have already reached a global edition of 30,000 copies a year. Two other religious Catholic Aymara publications have in two years reached circulations of 50,000 and 80,000 copies, very high figures in the Bolivian context. But the production of the natives themselves is even smaller for natives outside of the religious context.

[13]   Moreover, we are passing from the bilingual plan (alphabetization in the mother tongue followed by alphabetization in Spanish together with teaching of Spanish) to the oral plan (oral teaching of Spanish with the mother tongue as a medium of instruction followed by alphabetization in Spanish) through which the native will continue being incapable of writing in his own language. See the criticism of Pozzi-Escot (1972) of the bilingual method.

of teachers — which permit the execution of more developed revolutionary means.[14]

These have been the main countercurrents at the level of planning and personal enthusiasm. But on the level of effectiveness the main impacts towards a new situation have rather come from changes in socioeconomic factors, such as have been suggested above. The industrialization in cities, in the mines and on the mechanized plantations has stimulated migrations above all to Lima and the Peruvian coast, and with it, Hispanicization.[15] But other processes are stimulating at the same time a greater Hispanicization and a greater prestige of the oppressed languages. Some of these processes, such as the colonization by Quecha- and Aymara-speakers in the tropics, are also expanding their linguistic frontiers. The two most influential factors have been perhaps land reform (particularly the Bolivian, much earlier than the Peruvian) and the coming of the transistor radio. At the root of land reform the rigid dualist set-up has been broken to a large extent; reform has overcome the social, economic and political status of the peasant, has increased social as well as geographic mobility, has made the rural commerce network more dense and has opened schools throughout the countryside.[16] As a result of all this the rural population has discovered the possibility and functionality of Spanish bilingualism, and, at the same time, it no longer feels such shame in using its language in a new context. As for the transistor radio, its popularization in the 1960s has brought broadcasting to the most distant dwelling, originating another process, also of a double effect. On the one hand, Spanish is now heard daily everywhere, and on the other, the development agencies, the curates, the politicians, merchants, artists, etc., have realized that through radio they have the entire countryside at hand, and have begun to diffuse their messages in Quechua and Aymara, contributing thus indirectly to a reevaluation of their importance.[17]

The present situation, as a result of these recent changes, can not be

[14]   The most basic documents on Peruvian linguistic policy are Peru (1972a, 1972b, and 1972c) and number 7 of the periodical *Educacion*, a monograph on the subject. See also the summary of Parker (1972a). In this atmosphere were also born other studies such as those of Escobar (1972a, 1972b). For the more timid efforts of Bolivia, see INDICEP (1971) and *Centro Pedagogico Portales* (1972).

[15]   It would be interesting to conduct a study which would establish what socioeconomic factors have influenced so effectively the Hispanicization of the Peruvian coast, with priority given to the industrializing and migration processes of today.

[16]   In Peru the proliferation of rural teaching partly predates land reform. In Bolivia the great push came a little after the reform. Before there were only isolated efforts, primarily in the border zone with Peru, around the nucleus of Warisata (La Paz) and in the nuclei of Vacas and Ucureña in Cochabamba. In all these cases Hispanicization was pursued at all costs.

[17]   In La Paz in 1972 there were twenty radio stations of which the majority did some broadcasting in Aymara and the bigger ones also in Quechua. Four of them, of which three are commercial and almost completely urban, broadcast almost all day exclusively in Aymara.

even vaguely estimated. In Bolivia we have only the census of 1950, before land reform.[18] In Peru we can count the comparative figures of the censuses of 1940 and 1961 which already reflect something of the migration to the coast. These show for the whole country (Parker 1972a) an increase from 47 percent to 60 percent of monolingual Spaniards, a relatively stable figure of bilinguals (from 17 percent to 19 percent) and a clear reduction in the percentage of monolingual natives (35 percent to 20 percent). But if we limit ourselves to the mountain regions of the greater indigenous concentration, particularly in the south of the country, there are no great changes. Based on the census of 1961, Quechua or Aymara would continue being the mother tongue of the great majority of the population in several provinces such as Ayacucho (93 percent), Apurimac (95 percent), Cuzco (89 percent) and Puno (94 percent). It is a question therefore of changes which have taken place primarily on the coast, the great pole of industrialization and immigration.

5. THE DILEMMA AND THE PLANNING OF THE FUTURE

The panorama of light and shadows presented here until now does not allow us to forsee with any precision the course which the future will take. The changes in most industrialized sectors, particularly on the Peruvian coast, suggests that, as industrialization advances, the Andes will be Hispanicized. But everywhere this advance still seems very distant in many regions and in others, as in the Aymara world around La Paz, in spite of the close influence of that city, movements which are reevaluating the native languages are arising.

To all this is added the existence of a double radical option with relation to the oppressed languages: accelerate their extinction or revitalize them. In principle, the question of whether one learns Spanish or not should be on the margin of this dilemma, but more often Hispanicization coincides

---

[18] Preliminary data from the 1976 National Census give the following figures:

	Regular language at home 1950	1976	Monolinguals 1976	Bilinguals Spanish plus native language(s) 1976
Spanish	36.0	53.7	37.2	
Quecha	36.5	26.8	14.6	
Aymara	24.6	18.6	7.4	40.5
Other native languages	2.9	0.9	0.3	

In the city of La Paz only 2.3 percent of males and 5.5 percent of females are Aymara monolinguals, but 13.7 percent of the families speak Aymara regularly at home and 52.8 percent of males and 50.4 percent of females know Spanish and also one (or more) native language, presumably Aymara (Addendum, 1978).

with the accelerating option of extinction. Those who advocate Hispanicization and extinction believe that their opponents, with their "romanticism" want to maintain a status quo, even involuntarily, which would impede progress. At the same time those who want to reevaluate the native languages believe the others are maintaining a status quo in imposing their dominating ethnocentrism, and, in this way, are perpetuating the oppressive situation in which the native populations find themselves.

To progress in the midst of these dialectics, it is convenient to present sketchily the main arguments which are usually wielded in favor of one or the other alternative and weigh the value of each one, thus arriving at a formulation which is perhaps complex, but more balanced and attainable. In discussions on the topic, emotional factors usually abound and never fully explain all the arguments, by which we may easily suppose that the contrary option completely excludes one's own option. Thus it is necessary to make a careful and calm distinction if we wish to advance.

The main arguments which favor at least the partial extinction of the oppressed languages (or Hispanicization) are:

1. Given the established order, it is always easier to maintain it than to change it. The proposals should thus arise from the stability of the present.

2. Economically the cost a radical transformation of the system would require is excessive. Concretely, the evaluation of the vernacular tongues and the preparation of material in three (or more) languages in place of one implies a multiplication of efforts which does not justify the possible advantages of the means (cf. Bowers 1968).

3. National and Latin American integration demands a common language for general communication. On the national level, in Bolivia, as well as in all Peru, only Spanish can fulfill this function — thanks to the growing number of Spanish monolinguals and the multiplicity of native languages and dialects which are not understandable among themselves. On the continental level this fact is even more evident. Moreover, the vehicle-language of integration should be assured of a vast written production, multifaceted and on every level.

4. With the maintenance and even more with the development of the native languages in face of Spanish, national division (vertical) is favored and, if these are various languages, they stimulate unnecessary and counterproductive cultural (horizontal) conflicts among groups which, because they are weak, should be more united.

5. With the maintenance of the primitive or atrophied native languages, in the final analysis a certain harm is done to those that we claim to favor, as their full entrance into the national modern system is blocked or at least delayed.

6. Those same peasants are the first to want to forget their language

and pass into Spanish or to at least desire this step for their children, so that they will not have to suffer the same as their parents.

The main arguments which favor at least the partial vitalization of the oppressed languages are:

7. The present situation clearly implies an injustice in denying the native population its full right to the use of its own language without socially discriminatory effects.

8. It is indispensible for the self-development of the native groups that they first become themselves, find their group identity and self-confidence. Only then will they become self-dynamic and able to participate actively in the progress of the country. In the other manner at the most they will be developed, but they will remain mere passive recipients and not participants. If at the moment some of them think only of Hispanicization, it is precisely because the present structure has made them lose their identity and only permits them social achievement through alienation.

9. To communicate a message effectively we must use the language and signs of those who are to receive it. At the same time, this same criterion of methodology should be used for the integration of present native populations into the life of the country, either on educational, political, commercial or other levels.

10. The roots of the Andine identity are in Quechua and Aymara. The national symbology should be inspired from this source, and one of the most powerful Andine symbols is the language.

11. In fact, the country is constituted of various cultural groups which could be called nationalities (Ovando 1961). Given this fact, integration is only valid with harmonic respect among these groups. Only thus would it be possible to establish the foundations for a Bolivian, Peruvian or continental unity. But if the language is not included in this process, the doors are closed from the beginning, as the loss of the language is the death of the village.

12. The native languages are as perfect and as fully capable as the modern ones. Their outlawing is based on the false belief that they are inadequate as vehicles of progress. The premise being false, the conclusion is also.

Not all the arguments deduced by one or the other side have the same force and implications. Moreover, according to the underlying conceptions, some would give subjectively more force to specific reasons and not see the others. Concretely speaking, there are arguments which are counterbalanced by others. For example, 4 and 6 versus 8 and 11; 1 versus 7; 12 versus 5. Argument 4 on the production of divisions may be strong in its vertical dimension to those who have harmonic functionalist vision (although even argument 11 of the opposite side may have force). On the other side, to a Marxist, the same vertical division would appear to demonstrate the fundamental contradiction which the dialectic of the struggle between classes places in the way of progress. Nevertheless, this same Marxist will accept the force of the same argument 4, in its horizontal dimension, because for him these cultural divisions among the exploited disfigure the fundamental contradiction and underline others in a counterproductive form.[19] On the other hand, arguments 10 and 11 will seem strong to those who have been made familiar with them and have lived the whole problem of the minority "nationalities" of so many European countries. Arguments such as these have been used since the last century by Irish, Czechs, Flemish and Catalans. In my opinion, there is a basis of truth in them, especially in 11, and they reflect emotive forces which can be very influential at times. Nevertheless, if they become absolute they do not sufficiently allow for the dynamic and changing character of the cultures, and, within them, of the languages. Synchronically, the cultural model is necessary for the survival of the individual and of the group, but diachronically, the elements of these cultures change constantly, particularly with the coexistence of other factors such as migrations, contacts and interchanges between cultures and new technical conditioning which invalidate the previously crystallized solutions in a culture. In spite of the strong cohesive value, language, just as religion, is not free from this agitation and it would be *a priori* to say that it is untouchable. All things considered, it is clear that there are sufficiently weighty reasons supporting each side so that it is impossible to think of a simple solution consisting of choosing either extreme and rejecting the other. Granted that there are also various underlying conceptions, one cannot place oneself in an absolutely neutral situation of the passive observer. To maintain oneself in a scientific nirvana is unscientific because beneath the illusion of neutrality the conditionings which doubtless are present in this ivory tower are not explained. A way of ferreting out these conditioning conceptions is to present a plan for the future involving choices and decisions.

In a plan it should be clear what is the goal and what are the steps so that this goal may be effectively achieved. In the final instance the goal is not so much the perpetuation or the isolation of determined cultural or linguistic forms, but rather that those individuals and groups which presently live and express themselves (in an atrophied form, due to the structural oppression) through determined cultural and linguistic patterns come to live and express their internal potentialities in a fully adequate manner. That is to say, the goal is the person and the group of persons, rather than the culture of the language.[20] The achievement of

---

[19] It is interesting in this regard to recall the criticism that a young Marxist of Indian extraction (Reinaga 1972) establishes against traditional Andean Marxism, because it eliminates "Indian" cultures dogmatically in its statements copied from industrial Europe.
[20] Sometimes I have the impression that some of the anthropologists who speak against ethnocide and opt for the isolated maintenance of determined cultures do so less in the

this goal through the promotion and development of the dominated native element, or of the dominating foreign element, depends partly on the conception which one has of development and promotion. As for myself, I believe that it is more probable to achieve the stated goal if from the beginning one is stimulating that which the development of the internal potentialities of the presently-oppressed groups supposes. But the choice of the one or the other road also depends irremediably on the means at hand. To propose an objective and be determined to achieve it by utopic or inadequate means is the same as not seriously wanting the objective, with all the practical and ethical implications which such a rejection entails.

In the light of these premises and arguments which, in my opinion, are no more solid in favor of one or the other option, the following opposed criteria arise: As for the goal of full personal realization of the oppressed groups, neither argument 8 (for vitalization), nor argument 3 (for Hispanicization) can be avoided. As for the effective means to attain the goal, neither argument 9 (for vitalization), or the necessity of communicating to each one on his own terms, nor argument 2 (for extinction) on the economic improbability of the multilingual intentions on a grand scale, can be avoided. In summing up what has been said, it seems that implementation of the goal demands two general principles:

a. The language (and other cultural elements) of the major oppressed sector should be realized and promoted to assure the initial effectiveness of the message and to create self-confidence and consciousness of group, thus awakening the creative action and the active participation of the said sector in the totality.

b. The Spanish language of the dominating groups should also be encouraged so that the oppressed sector manages the language completely because (given present social and economic conditions and the difficulty in changing them) this is the only possible way the said sector can now acquire the technical and academic capacity necessary for a dialogue on an equal basis with the dominating group and stop being the marginal and oppressed sector in the innumerable processes of national and continental integration.

The second part has, without doubt, a flavor of fatalism and of impotence before the inevitable. If we consider the historical perspective we should accept the enslaving eminence of those integrating movements. Nevertheless, I neither affirm nor negate the fact that the final result shall be the extinction of the oppressed native languages with full Hispanicization of the groups which speak it today. This depends on the level to which

---

interests of an absolute cultural relativism or through humanism, but rather because deep inside they fear being deprived of "subjects" of study in their field. Once someone characterized a certain ethnologist of this type as an entomologist.

the means here suggested succeed in attaining a language balance of powers. If they do not succeed, industrialization will probably sooner or later lead to extinction; but if a certain balance is achieved and if moreover the interested groups decide it, it is possible that evaluation of the native languages will lead to a pluralism which will be comparable, to a certain point, to that in certain European countries.

At the beginning of the use of (a) there are no other difficulties than those imposed by the social and particularly the economic limitations already alluded to. For example, in the beginning, the production of literature (particularly expressive) in native languages should not be excluded, nor the teaching of those languages with second-language methods in the secondary schools and universities. But limitations exist. As for the level of execution, together with the policy of appropriation of funds to implement more ambitious goals, priority should be given to the most economically advantageous means. In contrast, in the implementation of (b), there is a difficulty. The Hispanicizing policy is that which has already been adopted by all concerned bodies, including the pioneers of bilingual education and the architects of the new educational plans of the Peruvian government.[21] Also on this level, there is enough ground to cover in the development of effective techniques for teaching a well-assimilated standard Spanish. For this, the actual grammatical perspective must be put aside and we must insist more on oral and written practice. But the most imminent risk is that the effort made in (b) will drown any initiative in the effort to implement (a). So that this conflict will not arise, the oppressed languages should no longer be outlawed in education, for example, but should rather, within reason, be encouraged. And, in general, to attain the equilibrium of language powers, the accent should be more on (a).

To conclude, I will limit myself to underlining a point which I consider very important and profitable, but on which the existing renovating projects insist very little. It is a question of a more systematic use of the oppressed languages in the means of social communication, especially broadcasting, not so much to "give advice" from top to bottom, but rather so that these means may be converted into a vehicle of expression for the same Quechuas and Aymaras in their own language without even the

---

[21] I have already mentioned the ambiguities of the Bilingual Educational Plan of Peru. See note 13. The Summer Institute of Linguistics with its affiliated institutions for bilingual education and its publications has not seriously tackled the problem discussed here of establishing the identity of the group and the participative creativity of the native oppressed groups. At the most the Institute will say that "in the Hispanicization of Quechua-speakers one should not claim to transfer in a rapid step that which is 'basically intransferable in its essence'" (Burns 1970). The team of INDICEP in Bolivia is the one which has gone the farthest in its revitalizing plans. We may also recall that its founder is French-Canadian. But, in spite of the evident progress, his formulations do not sufficiently consider the global socioeconomic context nor the dynamic aspects of the culture, particularly in a situation of cultural contact and dependence.

obstacle of illiteracy. Probably by this path, together with parallel means on educational levels and on a more basic level, in the economic spheres, there will be an acceleration of a more massive sort towards the reevaluation of the oppressed languages and it will be possible to encourage the creativity, now in a state of lethargy, of its speakers. Problems such as the production of literature or the unification of the alphabet, which sometimes cut off or sterilize discussions, will be resolved more easily if this previous basis exists.

REFERENCES

AGUIRRE BELTRAN, GONZALO
    1967   *Regiones de Refugio*. Mexico: Institute Indigenista Interamericano.
ALBÓ, XAVIER
    1966   Jesuitas y cultural indigenas: Peru 1568–1606. *América Indígena* 26:249–308, 395–445.
    1969   Sociolingüística de los valles de Cochabamba, Bolivia. Paper read at the Fifth Symposium of PILEI, Sao Paolo, Brazil (published in the Acts).
    1970   *Social constraints on Cochabamba Quechua*. Latin American Studies Program Dissertation Series 19. Ithaca, N.Y.: Cornell University.
    1974   *Los mil rostros del quecha*. Lima: Instituto de Estudios Peruanos.
Andean Linguistics Newsletter
    1969   Published by Louisa Stark (University of Wisconsin) and Gary Parker (University of San Marcos, Lima).
BOLIVIA: DIRECCION GENERAL DE ESTADISTICA
    1955   *Census of 1950*. La Paz: Argote.
BOWERS, JOHN
    1968   "Language problems and literacy," in *Language problems in developing nations*. Edited by J. Fishman *et al.*, 381–401. New York: Wiley.
BURNS, DONALD
    1968a   Niños de la Sierra peruana estudian en Quechua para saber español. Paper presented at the Congress of Indigenists in Mexico.
    1968b   "Bilingual education in the Andes of Peru," in *Language problems in developing nations*. Edited by J. Fishman *et al.*, 403–414. New York: Wiley.
    1970   La castellanización de la población no hispano-hablante en el Perú: meta y metodología. Paper presented at the 39th International Congress of Americanists in Lima.
CENTRO PEDAGOGICO PORTALES
    1972   Informative bulletins for the First Congress of National Languages, Cochabamba, February, 1973.
Educación
    1972   Number 7 dedicated to bilingual education. Periodical for teachers published by the Ministry of Education of Peru.
ESCOBAR, ALBERTO
    1972a   *Lenguaje y discriminacion social en America Latina*. Lima: Milla Batres.
    1972b   *El reto de multilinguismo en el Perú*. Lima: Institute of Peruvian Studies.

FISHMAN, JOSHUA A.
1968 "The relationship between micro- and macro-sociolinguistics in the study of who speaks what language to whom and when," in *Bilingualism in the barrio*. Edited by J. Fishman *et al.*, 1000–1028. Washington, D.C.: Office of Education.

FREIRE, PAULO
1970 *Pedagogía del oprimido*. Montevideo: Tierra Nueva.

GREAVES, THOMAS C.
1972 Pursuing cultural pluralism in the Andes. *Plural Societies* (Summer) 33–49.

INDICEP
1971 Seminar on the planning of alphabetization and adult education for 1972. Conclusions.

LASTRA, YOLANDA
1965 Segmented phonemes of Quechua of Cochabamba. *Thesaurus: Boletin del Instituto Caro y Cuervo* 20:48–62.
1968 *Cochabamba Quechua syntax*. Janua Linguarum Series Practica 40. The Hague: Mouton.

LEWIN, BOLESLAO
1967 *La rebelión de Túpac Amaru y los orígenes de la Independencia de Hispanoamérica*. Buenos Aires: SELA.

LEWIS, OSCAR
1961 *Anthropologica de la pobreza*. Mexico: Fondo de Cultura Economica. (Original English edition 1959: *Five families*. New York: Basic Books.)
1969 *La vida*. Mexico: Mortiz. (Original English edition 1965: New York: Random House.)

MELIÁ, BARTOMEU
1969 *La création d'un language chrétien dans les réductions des Guaraní au Paraguay*, two volumes. Strasbourg.
1971 *El guaraní dominante y dominado*. *Acción: Revista Paraguaya de Reflexion y Dialogo* 11:21–26.

OVANDO, JORGE
1961 *Sobre el problema nacional y colonial de Bolivia*. Cochabamba: Canelas.

PARKER, GARY J.
1963 La clasificación genética de los dialectos quechuas. *Revista del Museo Nacional* (Lima) 32:241–252.
1972a Notes on the linguistic situation and language planning in Peru. To be published at the 23rd Georgetown Round Table on Language and Linguistics.
1972b Sugerencias para un alfabeto general del quechua. Center of Investigation of Applied Linguistics, work document 13. University of San Marcos.

PERU: DIRECCION NACIONAL DE ESTADISTICA Y CENSOS
1966 *VI Censo nacional de publación*. Lima.

PERU: MINISTERIO DE EDUCACION
1972a National seminar of bilingual education. Preliminary bulletin.
1972b *Primer seminario de educación bilingüe*. Some suggestions and motions.
1972c National policy on bilingual education.

POZZI-ESCOT, INES
1972 "El uso de la lengua vernacula en la educacion," in *Primer Seminario*

Nacional de Educacion Bilingüe. Edited by the Ministry of Education of Peru, 43–54. *Education* 7.

REINAGA, RAMIRO
1972   *Ideología y raza en América Latina.* Mexico: private edition.

RIBEIRO, DARCY
1970   The culture-historical configurations of the American peoples. *Current Anthropology* 11:403–434.

RICARD, R.
1961   Le problém de l'enseignement du castillan aux Indiens d'Amérique durant la période coloniale. *Bulletin de la Faculté des Lettres de Strasbourg* 39:281–296.

RIVET, PAUL, GEORGES CREQUI-MONTFORT
1951–1956   *Bibliographie des langues aymará et kičua,* four volumes. Paris: Institut d'Ethnologie.

RUBIN, JOAN
1968   *National Bilingualism in Paraguay.* Janua Linguarum Series Practica 60. The Hague: Mouton.

SCHAEDEL, RICHARD P.
1967   *La demografía y los recursos humanos del Sur del Perú.* Mexico: Interamerican Indigenist Institute.

STARK, LOUISA
1972   *Sucre Quechua.* Madison: University of Wisconsin.

STAVENHAGEN, RODOLFO
1965   Siete tesis equivocados sobre América Latina. *Política Exterior Independiente* (Rio de Janeiro) 1.

TORERO, ALFREDO
1964   Los dialectos quechuas. *Anales Científicos de la Universidad Nacional Agraria* 2:446–478.
1970   Lingüística e historia de la sociedad andina. *Anales Cientificas de la Universidad Nacional Agraria* 8:231–264.
1972   "Grupos lingüísticos y variaciones dialectales," in *Primer Seminario Nacional de Educacion Bilingüe.* Edited by the Ministry of Education of Peru, 3–12.

TURNER, VICTOR
1969   *The ritual process: structure and antistructure.* Chicago: Aldine.

UNESCO
1953   *El uso de las lenguas vernáculas en la educación.* Paris.

A Comparative Study of Language Contact: The Influence of Demographic Factors in Wales and the Soviet Union

E. GLYN LEWIS

1. THE NEED FOR COMPARATIVE STUDIES OF CONTACT

Until comparatively recently, in spite of the contribution of Weinreich (1953) and with the exception of Haugen's study (1956) of the Americas and the work of Fishman (1966, 1971), little attempt has been made to institute comparative studies of societal bilingualism or even to identify the bases on which such studies might be mounted with any degree of confidence. This should not be taken to imply that detailed analyses of bilingualism in a single country or in more limited localities are not important. Indeed, one reason for the danger that derives from the lack of comparative studies is the excellence of many descriptive studies of limited compass. The more exhaustive such studies are, the greater the likelihood that some isolated aspect may be seized upon as comparable to some isolated aspects in the description of another situation. Nevertheless, it is not so much the discrete points of similarity which are relevant but the pattern of the variables. Significance lies in the parallelism of the interplay of factors. It is more than possible that the methodology of descriptive individual studies needs to be reviewed. A new paradigm is required if the descriptive studies are to rise to a new level of theoretical interest, and this paradigm will need to take into account the methodology of comparative studies.

One of the principal intentions of comparative studies should be to facilitate and improve the description of individual cases by identifying general factors. This enables the student to realize better the significance of what may be unique or eccentric in a particular case. The identification of general characteristics is a prerequisite to the formulation of a typology of societal as well as individual bilingualism. And it is the tendency to extrapolate from too restricted an analysis of a single situation or from an analysis undertaken without the possibility of comparison in mind that has made the hitherto proposed typologies of bilingualism somewhat unsatisfactory. If social and especially educational policy and planning in bilingual countries are to be soundly based and effective, it is necessary that they should not be the results of unwarranted conclusions arising from the use of non-comparable and therefore irrelevant data. One important safeguard against such dangers is the discovery of principles which enable us to evaluate relevance, and this can come only from a sound methodology of comparative studies of languages in contact. This will need to include historical or diachronic as well as contemporaneous or synchronic studies of contact — the rise and fall of linguistic empires, for instance, as well as the mapping of contemporary complexes. To that extent and in a way that is not equally true of linguistic studies of the more "pure" kind, diachronic and synchronic comparisons have to be undertaken together even when the aim of the study is to map a contemporary situation. The distinction between what may be called the dynamics and statics of bilingualism is not categorical, but it is both useful and proper.

2. PRIMARY FACTORS

2.1. *Geography*

The factors which promote societal bilingualism may be primary or secondary. The former category includes all the conditions which go to produce contact of language of whatever kind, and these may be economic, demographic, or simply physical. The latter, secondary category consists of conditions which do not bring about but, rather, influence the specific characteristics of bilingualism in any particular case, and these are more especially ideological, religious, and educational. It is to be expected that the primary variables should be more frequently shared by several countries and that the nature of their operation should be similar in those cases. On the other hand, the secondary variables will vary between different countries, though there are general features in the operation of secondary factors, too. Herman Paul (1960) was among the first serious linguists to consider the primary variables, though his generalizations are apt to be sweeping, and he does not seek to exemplify them. He writes:

The most frequent cause of bilingualism is of course the situation of a community upon the confines of two linguistic areas and it occurs in a greater or lesser degree according to the activity or the intercourse between them. Again it may be due to journeys and the temporary residence of individuals in foreign countries; it may become more marked where individuals permanently migrate from one country to another, and still more where large masses of population are permanently transplanted by conquest and by colonization.

These factors continue to operate today, but the relative importance of one or the other of them has changed enormously during the last half century.

2.2. *Economic Factors*

2.2.1. "PROFESSIONAL" MIGRATION. In the main, attention has been focussed hitherto on the geographical contiguity of linguistic groups, but currently there are far more opportunities for the contact of even large groups of different nationalities than those provided by the sharing of boundaries. The most powerful agencies for establishing contact nowadays are economic, and the different levels of economic conditions exert reciprocal influences. The highly developed areas pull and the less developed areas push the inhabitants into different kinds of migration, but the demographic composition of the migrant group is usually similar in all countries. They are usually young male adults, and even when they are married they tend not to be accompanied by their wives or families for some time. Usually they are unmarried (Thomas 1938). Sometimes migration is highly selective in the sense that only particular skills or kinds of skills may be involved. This is exemplified in the "brain drain" of doctors, for instance, from the Indian subcontinent to Britain. Selectivity has been a long-standing characteristic of migration, and it has fairly predictable consequences for the native tongue of the migrant and to a lesser extent for the language of the host country. From the earliest times, Greek craftsmen, for instance, penetrated Roman society, and Roman nobles brought in specialists like the Greek teachers, who had an enormous influence on the diffusion of the Greek language among the young. Celtic craftsmen during the La Tène period, when Celtic civilization was most exciting, settled in several parts of southern Europe, so that there was constant intercourse between Greek traders and the Celts, with consequences for the Gallo-Roman dialects of the area (Whatmough 1970). The Alpine ranges ceased to be a barrier to the Celtic craftsmen, who set up permanent market places in Switzerland and even farther south. The pre-Italic dialects bear witness to this contact (Whatmough 1933). Trade and commerce are also the reason for the spread of Greek in Islam, and for the development of Greek and Russian bilingualism which was sometimes a pronounced feature of Byzantine history (Baynes and Moss 1961:356). However, this kind of fairly individualized contact does not rank high among the causes of societal bilingualism. It was not until the Greeks actually colonized parts of the western Mediterranean, at Messalia and in southern Italy, for instance, that Greek entered into significant contact with the local languages to produce mass bilingualism in certain areas.

Whatever importance these individualized forms of economic activity may have had in ensuring language contact in the past, they are almost insignificant at present. Where skilled migrants are concerned, educational facilities have ensured that they usually know the language of the country to which they are destined before they leave. Those who do not know the local language are usually employed as teachers of their skill to those who know the language of the teacher. The impact of "craft or professional bilingualism" is negligible. Even where larger scale commerce and trade are concerned, the influence has been diminished by the almost general employment of two or three major world languages as contact media, so that the diversity of language contact evidenced in history by the development of commerce is now discouraged. This is true even within a multinational state, whether it is the Soviet Union, or India, or one of the African states for instance. Trade and commerce within the Soviet Union, between republics, is very largely conducted in the lingua franca, Russian — a condition induced not only by the spread of the Russian language but also by the degree of centralized control of trade between Soviet republics. So far as external international commerce is concerned, the Soviet Union is conforming very much to the pattern of other states. Over 40 percent of the students who are learning a foreign language at school (and language is a compulsory component of all secondary curricula) are learning English; and this is done, it is acknowledged, for the purpose of encouraging trade and commerce not necessarily with native speakers of English, but also with English speakers in Africa and other areas where the English language is current. In Wales, trade and commerce does not enter significantly into the causes of contact mainly because other causes have made its contribution irrelevant.

2.2.2. INDUSTRY.   Of far greater importance as an economic variable is the development of large-scale industry which, if it is to have a significant linguistic influence has to be "labor intensive" in character and very rapid in its incidence. Unless these two conditions are fulfilled so as to provide for sufficient saturation of speakers of a new language, the labor requirements of the new industry are likely to be met by the local population or by migration from the neighboring and usually uniform linguistic area. The current industrialization of the Republic of Ireland is having little effect linguistically even in the more Irish-speaking areas, partly because of the educational policy of the government in ensuring the maintenance of this language, but mainly because the industry is capital rather than labor intensive, and its development is phased so as to take account of the availability of local labor. This was not the case in Wales. There, industrialization was based on the introduction of heavy extractive industries requiring large numbers of unskilled labor. When the process was relatively modest, the demands of even new industry were met by movement, very often seasonal, from the surrounding districts, so that there was only a dialectal problem of communication. After the 1840s this supply was soon exhausted, and the long-distance English migration into Monmouthshire and Glamorgan became the most prominent feature of the demographic scene in England and Wales for the rest of the century. Within about fifty years, from about 1825 to 1875, the foundations on which the Welsh language had continued to survive were almost completely eroded. In 1825 it could still be claimed that about 70 percent of the population of the whole of Wales spoke Welsh and more than 35 percent of the whole population were monolingual Welsh. This was in spite of the long history of political domination, centuries of conquest, the presence of an alien Church, and a system of education (where it existed) which was antipathetic to all things Welsh. With the coming of large-scale industry, by 1891 (when language censuses were first instituted) the proportion of speakers of Welsh had declined to 51 percent, and the proportion of those who were monolingual to 29 percent. In 1961 the figures were 26 percent and 0.7 percent.[1]

A similar situation is occurring in the Soviet Union without as yet having quite the same catastrophic effect. There has always been extensive bilingualism in the Soviet Union in all its republics and involving all Soviet languages. This has been largely fortuitous, unplanned bilingualism, arising from the geographical contact of peoples. It is represented for the first time in the 1970 Census (*Izvestiya*, April 17, 1971), and reveals, for instance, 6.0 percent non-Russian bilingualism in Armenia, 2.3 percent in Kirgizia, and among the Daghestan nationalities an average of 8.9 percent, with the Lezgin highest among the separate nations with 22.3 percent. Supervening on this traditional type of language contact, usually involving localized languages and dialects, there is a very rapid increase of planned language contact and Russian-based bilingualism (*Izvestiya*, April 17, 1971). In the case of Armenia this amounts to 30.1 percent; among the Kirgiz it is 19.1 percent, and among the peoples of Daghestan it is as high as 41.7 percent, with the Nogai as high as 68.5 percent. Some proportion of this Russian-related bilingualism is rapidly making traditional, historical language contact less significant.

The springing up of new industrial centres, the discovery and exploitation of material wealth, the cultivation of virgin lands and the development of all types of communication systems needed by these processes intensify the mobility of the population and contacts between nations (Rogachev and Sverdlin 1963:15).

Partly because the developments are so rapid and so voracious of manpower, the local population are frequently unable and even more reluc-

[1] Unless otherwise stated, the population statistics, general and linguistic, in respect of Wales, are derived from the relevant Official Census Tables for England and Wales.

tant to abandon their traditional way of life in rural surroundings to work in massive new industries. Long-distance migration fills the gap, and new, usually Russian- and Ukrainian-based language contacts are created.

The Kazakh Republic is a good example of how these new industrial factors operate. Even before World War II there had been some immigration into the republic, but during that war Kazakhstan became the arsenal of the Soviet Union to which industrial plants were transferred from the West. In Tadzhikstan similar large-scale industrial projects were inaugurated, such as those of the Nurek GES and the Dushanbe Combine. Among the Kazakhs, over 41 percent use Russian as a second language. It is not surprising that the contacts among languages are far more complex. The proportion of Kazakhs living in the Republic has declined from 56 percent in 1926 to 32.4 percent in 1970, while the proportion of Russians has increased from 20 percent to 42.8 percent, and the other ethnic groups from 10 percent to 18 percent. Among the Tadzhiks, 15.4 percent of the native population use Russian as a second language but the contact situation is usually even more complex in that republic. For instance, at the Nurek plant to which we have referred, over half the work force is Russian and only 27.8 percent Tadzhik, the remaining 20 percent consisting of Ukrainians, Belorussians, Tatars, Mordvins, Uzbeks, and smaller representations among ten other nationalities. The position of the native Tadzhiks is even more precarious in the Dushanbe plant, where the Russians account for over 55 percent of the work force and the Tadzhiks only 15.2 percent, with representations of other nationalities of an order similar to the Nurek plant (Perevedentsev 1966).

3.   MIGRATION

In Wales and in the Soviet Union rapid and labor intensive industrialization is the most prominent factor in producing new type language contacts, partly because it involves migration over long distances, thus introducing new language communities, and partly because it produces urbanization which ensures that the new populations mix. Migration is usually characterized by certain invariant features in respect to age, sex, and marital status, and the impact of these characteristics on the language complex of a particular locality is predictable. This is borne out by the evidence from the Soviet Union involving large masses of population and scores of different languages. In Kazakhstan there was a total net gain of 920,000 from migration constituting nearly 40 percent of the total population increase. In Estonia the total increase was 62,000, of which 28,000 (45 percent) were the residue of migrations over the same period. Nevertheless, even massive migration serves only to produce increased contact opportunities and does not submerge the language of the native populations, and this from the standpoint of long-term language contact and bilingualism is as important as the original contact. Thus, though the 40 percent of the population of Kazakhstan was migrant, the decline in the level of language maintenance has been quite small. In 1970 98 percent of the Kazakhs still claimed the national language as their native tongue, a drop of only 1.6 percent in nearly fifty years. In Estonia, during the period 1959 to 1970 the proportion of Estonians who claimed Estonian as their native tongue rose from 95.2 percent to 95.5 percent, in spite of considerable migration (*Izvestiya*, April 17, 1971).

Migration has been induced by various means — punitive national deportation, student direction, family resettlement, and individual voluntary recruitment. To a considerable degree the movement is planned, and agencies are created not only to organize the recruitment but also to feed the available labor to the place where it is required according to planning needs (Zaionchovskaia, Perevedentsev 1964:178). Such state planning is characteristic of the Union of South Africa, also, but whereas in that republic the possibility of language contact arising from movement of labor is neutralized by the segregation of the immigrants or seasonal workers, in the Soviet Union there is complete freedom of contact and very little if any racial or national prejudice (Arutiunian 1968) save as concerns the Jews. This again is a new feature of Soviet contact situations. In the past, Slav migrants though they would tend to move to Central Asian cities, would be located in new settlements on the borders of the old Muslim cities. This is no longer the case, and there is complete intermixture with profound consequences for the contact of Russian speakers in particular, with speakers of other languages. This is exemplified, too, in the Sakhalin area of Siberia, where the population increased from 100,000 in 1939 to 650,000 in 1959 — slightly under twenty years, in fact. This involves 520,000 new settlers arriving in the main within a period of eight years (1946–1954). Consequently the labor forces in many of the industrial projects were seldom more than 3 percent native born, and often more than ten nationalities might be represented (*Voprosy trudovykh resursov v rayonakh Sibiri* 1961:157).

This is parallel to what happened in Glamorgan, South Wales. Between 1851 and 1901, while the population of England and Wales as a whole rose by only 80 percent, the increase in Glamorgan was over six times that figure. The numbers involved in this increase in Glamorgan were 1,210,000, over half a million of whom were immigrants. In the period 1851–1871 Glamorgan was second only to London and its surrounding counties in the level of its immigration. From 1871–1881 the rate was higher in Glamorgan than anywhere else in Britain, and of this movement into Glamorgan 57 percent was from English areas. Between 1871 and 1911 Glamorgan recruited 67 percent of its 116,000 miners and iron workers from the English border counties. Consequently, between 1861 and 1911 the number of non-native-born inhabitants of Glamorgan increased to 390,000, and this represented only the residue of over 430,000, over 55 percent of them monolingual English. (Friedlander and Roshier 1966) As a result, the Welsh language in Glamorgan declined. In the 1850s before the full force of migration became apparent, Glamorgan was predominantly Welsh-speaking, more so in the upland and highland areas where industrialization first occurred. Figures of over 65 percent Welsh language maintenance have been given for even the most Anglicized areas, and as high as 98 percent in the upper reaches of the valleys, with a high incidence of Welsh monolingualism. In 1891 when the first official figures became available, the overall percentage of Welsh had fallen to 51 percent, representing 3.5 percent of the total national Welsh-speaking population. In 1961 the intensity of Welsh speech in Glamorgan had declined to 17 percent, although, because of the parallel decline of the language elsewhere in Wales and the immense increase in the total population of Glamorgan, its share of the national total of Welsh had risen. Though Glamorgan had previously lost only 30 percent of its Welshness in well over eight centuries of English political domination, the subsequent loss within one eighth of that time, a century of industrialization, was over 60 percent. That the fate of the Welsh language in the most industrialized area of the country was not more unfortunate is due partly to the fact that industrialization began in the strongest Welsh-speaking areas, the hills, and was fed initially by migrants from other Welsh-speaking areas. This is the first short-distance migrant phase. The second phase, however, is that of predominant English labor supply and long-distance migration, which was massive and exploited over a short period. The English saturation was far above the "threshold level" required to maintain the status of the local language. The first phase gave the Welsh language an opportunity to adapt to change: the second phase was too intense and rapid to allow of the English being assimilated. This fact was stressed by the "Commission of Enquiry into Industrial Unrest" (1917). Until 1895:

... the inhabitants, in many respects showed a marked capacity for stamping their own impress on all newcomers, and communicating to them a large measure of all their own characteristics; of more recent years the process of assimilation had been unable to keep pace with the continuing influx of immigrants.

4.   URBANIZATION

If rapid industrialization requires immigration, very often over long distances, the effect of immigration is mediated through urban development. Of course, for the creation or perpetuation of language contact it is not necessary to have urbanization even, in these days of immensely improved systems of communication. Perhaps one of the best illustrations of this fact is the situation in the central North West Amazon straddling the Brazilian–Colombian border, where within a population of barely 10,000, twenty-five linguistic groups are involved and every individual knows three or four or more languages (Sorensen 1967). Here it is the comparative inaccessibility that has promoted the maintenance of the several languages in contact. The same phenomenon is witnessed in the Soviet Union, too. For instance, Daghestan represents over thirty different nationalities and linguistic groups, and this is not the result of recent population movement. What migration has done there is to superimpose a new level of ethnic and linguistic heterogeneity upon a complex historical situation. Consequently, all schools in Daghestan receive children from between five and twenty-five nationalities. School 7 in the Krasnodar district is attended by children from twelve linguistic groups. The same kind of traditional linguistic contact situation obtains in the Ferghana Valley of Tadzhikstan, for instance.

Nevertheless, urbanization has always been one of the main mediators of linguistic change, and especially of the erosion of the maintenance of local languages. For instance, though the Roman Emperors did very little to encourage the adoption of Latin by the conquered peoples, it was their policy to encourage the foundation or extension of towns and cities. The recreational, educational, and commercial facilities offered in the towns meant the promotion of Latin. Administration and the organization of everyday affairs from the towns brought the rural hinterland under the Latin influence, and the language irradiated from those centers. Consequently, the towns ensured the contact of languages within limited social environments and the diffusion of opportunities for contact over a comparatively wide area as well. This was especially true of the urban centers of Asia Minor, where several local languages — Lycian, Lydian, Galatian, Cappadocian, etc. — were brought into contact with each other and with Greek in the towns; but the lingua franca was able to irradicate from the centers to the frequently hardly accessible rural surroundings. African urban centers are probably among the best instances of this influence of urbanization upon language contact at present. It is reported, for instance, that in Madina, the urban settlement ten miles north of the University of Ghana Legon, the residents speak over eighty different languages. The majority, over 70 percent, claim to be able to speak at least three languages, and only 4 percent claim competence in only one language (Berry 1971).

The extent of urbanization and of its influence on the maintenance of local languages in the Soviet Union is very considerable. In the intercensal period 1959 to 1970 the number of urban settlers increased by thirty-six millions (36 percent), while the rural population decreased by 3,100,000 (2.8 percent). Two-thirds of the new urban population come from the immediate rural areas, so that during the first phase of industrialization, as in Wales, short-distance migrants tended to support the local language within the urban area, but at the same time they were exposed to increasing risk from the need to employ a lingua franca because of the very large number of intrusive languages, including Russian, which might be spoken in any one town. For instance, Tashkent has nearly trebled its size since 1926. Alma-Ata is ten times the size it was in 1926 and Dushanbe has grown from being a small town of 5,000 to a large city of over 250,000. Frunze had added 180,000 to its population in thirty years and Chimkent has grown by over 120,000. It is also noteworthy that the larger cities have grown more rapidly than the smaller or the medium-size cities, and this means that the dependence on long-distance migration, great even in the medium cities, is very much more pronounced, with consequently greater linguistic complexity in the composition of the populations. In 1959 the indigenous population of Frunze amounted to no more than 17 percent of the total, while 68 percent were Russian or Russianized immigrants and the remaining 15 percent were made up of five other significantly large linguistic groups. The ratio of indigenous to immigrant populations in Alma-Ata was even more adverse, in that only 13 percent of the population was indigenous and over 75 percent was Russian, the remaining 12 percent consisting of seven other nationalities. In Daghestan in 1824 only three nationalities were represented in Derbent; now there are forty-seven.

In Wales the growth of towns and cities and their association with rapid industrialization has meant the polarization of the Welsh-speaking rural and the Anglicized urban areas. Five of the thirteen counties of Wales identify themselves as predominantly rural and agricultural. In 1891 the proportion of the total population who were Welsh-speaking in these five counties was an average of 90 percent, while the predominantly industrial urban areas of Glamorgan and Monmouthshire had percentages of 51 and 70. In 1961, though the intensity of Welsh in the rural areas had declined from the 90 percent or 95 percent of 1891 to 68 percent and 75 percent in 1961, the reduction was nothing like as great as in the urban areas. For instance, it declined from 51 percent to 17 percent in Glamorgan, and from 20 percent to 3 percent in Monmouthshire. The polarization between rural and urban areas is reflected by a similar polarization within both rural and urban counties, though it is more extreme in the latter. For instance, in 1901 the urban and rural intensity indices for Anglesey were 85 percent and 93 percent, respectively; for Brecon they were 20 percent and 87 percent, and for Caernarvon 80 percent and 96 percent. The same kind of disparity between urban and rural proportions of Welsh has occurred ever since, and one county, Merionethshire, where in 1901 the intensity of Welsh was greater in the urban than in the rural areas, has now reversed that position, so that all the rural areas in the predominantly rural counties are far more intensely Welsh than the urban areas. In the industrial counties the disparity between the intensity of Welsh in the rural and the urban areas has increased considerably. In Carmarthenshire the difference rose from 17.5 percent to 33 percent; and in Glamorgan it rose from 20 percent to 25 percent. These increases in the difference between the rural and urban intensity of Welsh are reflected in all the other counties.

At the same time, while the intensity of Welsh is greater in the rural areas, the urban areas contain a far greater proportion of the total number of Welsh speakers simply because the urban population is far more dense. This simple fact, however, is full of significance for the maintenance of the language and for attitudes towards the language. The rationale or the justification for the maintenance of Welsh is no longer the same as when the great majority of the Welsh-speaking population lived a rural life and associated the language with a traditional folk culture. As shown in Table 1, an investigation of attitude among school-age children and young adults, three groups of each age category having been selected according to the intensity of Welsh in their areas, revealed that attitude varied not only in intensity, whether favorable or unfavorable, but according to the reasons given for the choice of attitude.[2] In all areas and types of schools, as the students grow older, the attitude becomes increasingly less favorable to Welsh and increasingly favorable to English. In the areas where English is generally favored (Category C), the disparity between Welsh and English attitudes increases. In areas where Welsh is generally favored (Categories A and B), the disparity decreases to the extent that at 14+ there is an attitudinal switch from Welsh to English.

Table 1. Mean scores of attitude to Welsh and English on Thurstone tests according to age and linguistic area

| | Type of linguistic area | | | | | |
| | A — 68–81% Welsh | | B — 48–55% Welsh | | C — 3–26% Welsh | |
Ages	Welsh	English	Welsh	English	Welsh	English
10+	3.97	5.87	4.22	5.66	5.39	5.06
12+	4.26	5.45	4.78	5.16	5.50	4.82
14+	4.86	4.81	5.16	4.92	5.92	4.58

An analysis of the data on which Table 1 is based reveals that in nearly half the sample population, and particularly in Categories A and B schools, the distribution of "attitude to Welsh" responses is either highly favorable, or highly unfavorable to the language, with a correspondingly

[2] Languages Research Project (Schools Council for England and Wales) at the University of Wales, Swansea.

very limited number of neutral responses. In Figure 1, the curve of the distribution shows a peak covering the mean scores 3 to 4.5, and a secondary peak covering the mean of 7.3. The distribution of the scores for English is almost unimodal in all types of school, and the percentages of the scores falling within the neutral range are usually much higher than they are for Welsh.

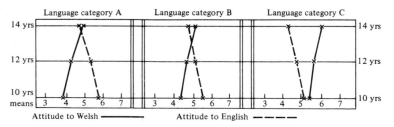

Figure 1.   Change of attitude to Welsh and English according to age and type of area.

A content analysis of the attitudes to the two languages was also made, as in Figure 2, from which it becomes evident that the choice of favored response varies consistently with the area from which the subjects were drawn. For instance, where the percentage responses of students in the English-speaking area to Item 3 of the English scale ("English should be taught all over the world") was in the range 40–60 percent (varying according to age), the percentage response in the Welsh-speaking schools was in the range 23–33 percent. Item 8 in the same list ("English is a beautiful language") produced a range of 40–60 percent in the English-speaking area and 21 percent in the Welsh area. It is not unlikely that attitude to the two languages, and especially Welsh, is a function of the linguistic character of the locality, and that individual variance within localities is limited. The more thoroughly Welsh the area, the more favorable is the attitude to Welsh and the less favorable to English.

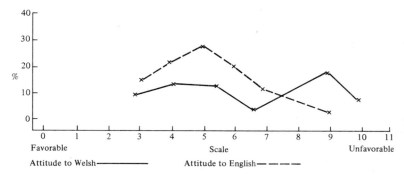

Figure 2.   Frequency distribution of attitude scores.

However, the attitude to Welsh, even if it is favorable, is different in the urban and rural areas. The traditional view has been that the rural areas are the main conservative agents of ethnic features, especially language. This remains true statistically, in the sense that the proportion of native language communication contacts is likely to be greater than the proportion of second language contacts (the intensity factor favors the native language). But even statistically, an increasing proportion of the total of the speakers of even local languages live in urban surroundings. This fact has to be taken in conjunction with another tendency. Urbanization does not simply change the statistical structure of the population. The greater social mobility of urban residents and the greater range and frequency of informational contacts make for greater social awareness in towns and cities; and where the speakers of the native language are a minority, for a far greater ethnic awareness — an intensification of their feeling for the language in particular. This, again, tends to produce polarization, since they are conscious of isolation.

Immigration has produced polarization of attitudes for other reasons. Because of its identification with industrialization and urbanization, immigration has brought about in the first place a discontinuity in the geographic spread of Welsh in Wales, and of a large number of Soviet languages. This, in turn, has initiated two further changes — a structural change where group boundaries are broken down in the industrial areas, and a substantive change whereby the group norms themselves tend to be abandoned. Furthermore, though group boundaries tend to remain intact in rural areas, the tendency of substantive changes in the towns and cities is to spread into the surrounding areas, and because the towns are centers of higher education and administration, to spread the influence of such changes well beyond the radius of physical or geographical contact. The net result of these changes, whether confined to urban centers or diffused more generally, is to polarize individual attitude to the native language as between group attachment — a feeling of loyalty on the one hand, and on the other a realistic–personal assessment of the immediate value of the language. This division within the individual's attachment to language is exemplified by an analysis of the favored language in different domains of use.

5. OTHER FORMS OF MIGRATION

5.1. *Temporary Evacuation*

Industrial immigration is not the only form of population movement which has helped to induce new forms of language contact, either in the Soviet Union or Wales, or, for that matter, in earlier centuries and in

344   E. GLYN LEWIS

other countries. For instance, the Yakut nation, which has occupied the basin of the River Lena and the Aldan and Kalyma river areas for a very long time, once inhabited the south Siberian steppes, as its language reveals (Okladnikov 1968). Encapsulated in the vocabulary of Yakut are remains of the contact with Mongol and Buryat languages, and with peoples inhabiting Asia, Iran, and China. Theirs has been the history of a long migration of the whole people. The movement of the Celts across western Europe and to the south, and ultimately outside the continent to Britain, is another instance with comparable indications of language contact and periods of bilingualism. However, such total national migrations though vastly important, are relatively infrequent, and they are unlikely to be significant in the creation of any future pattern of language contact.

On a smaller scale, the temporary group movement has interesting implications. The evacuation of families and of young school-age children during World War II had a severe though limited adverse effect on the maintenance of Welsh. Some schools which had previously been exclusively Welsh changed almost overnight when large numbers of monolingual English children arrived for protection from air attack. In many instances the character of the schools was changed, and though it is more than probable that the arrival of monolingual English children only accelerated the process of language shift, it is nevertheless the case that the evacuation brought forward that shift by as much as a complete generation. The case is similar in the Soviet Union. Between June, 1941, and February, 1942, nearly ten and a half million people were moved into the Volga, Urals, Western and Eastern Siberian oblasts (six million) and Kazakhstan, Central Asia, and Transcaucasia (three and a half million). Although in theory the migration was temporary, and in fact large numbers did actually return to their original localities, equally large numbers remained. Although the maximum impact was temporary, three years after the end of the war, for instance, in Irkutsk, 15 percent of the evacuees remained.

5.2.   Military Presence

The presence of the army, either as a consequence of military conquest and occupation, or for reasons of international security in areas where no aggression is intended, or in those which are more or less permanent international training areas, is another demographic factor affecting language. Prior to the industrialization of South Wales, the most important factor promoting the English language had been military conquest by the early Normans. The coastal strip in North and South Wales is pockmarked with Norman castles which safeguarded the administrative power of the English and formed the bases of English civil power in later centuries. These "English boroughs" were equivalent to the *cannibae* of the Roman Empire. In classical times some of the towns of the middle east, such as Thyateria, were created from colonies of soldiers to whom holdings were granted from state lands (Magie 1950). Military occupation of whatever kind operates in a variety of ways. For instance, the creation of a multinational army requires the use of a lingua franca so that whatever the native languages of the recruits may be they are soon bilingual on the basis of the acquisition of a new and dominant language. This is the case in Yugoslavia, where all military units are multinational and the Serbian language comes to be regarded as a lingua franca. The result is that the influence of that language on the other languages constituting the complex in Yugoslavia is enormously increased (Magner 1967). The Soviet Union has pursued the same policy since 1930: ethnic groups are fragmented, and though very occasionally exceptions may be made, as in the case of Armenia in a period of political discontent, recruits from a large variety of different language communities complete their military service together. The Communist Youth Organization (Komsomol) functions in a similar fashion. It has been used to recruit immigrants, especially to the Soviet Far East, which has come to be called Komsomol Territory. This organization, too, ensures multinational groupings with the same consequences for language. However short the period of service may be, it facilitates the breakdown of language loyalty. Of course, the lingua franca employed by the military need not be the language of the conquerors. The Incas decided on the local Quechua as the common language in the military and totalitarian administration of the country, and the Catholic Church took over that lingua franca as a going concern, thus ensuring the survival of that language as a dominant element in a complex of language contacts (Toynbee 1953:523).

5.3. *Deportation*

Sometimes a significant contribution is made to a societal bilingualism by punitive group movement (directed, not as in the case of refugees), as well as by the deportation of nationalities. Lithuania in 1948, Latvia between 1949 and 1951, and Estonia in 1949 saw the deportation of groups estimated at over half a million people. Elsewhere, however, whole nationalities and ethnic–linguistic groups have been deported over vast distances. In 1941 the deportation of the Volga Germans was decreed, and of these the number in Soviet Asia was estimated at one time to be one million, located in the Altai, in Kazakhstan, and in the Novosibirsk and the Omsk oblasts. Between 1942 and 1944, Kalmyks (134 thousand), Karachai (75 thousand), Chechens and Ingushi (500 thousand), and Balkars (42 thousand) were deported to North Kazakh-stan and Kirgizia, the Karachai mainly to areas between Dzhambul, and the Balkars to the Kirgiz border. The Kalmyks were also deported to Kazakhstan and Kirgizia (Roof 1960). Chechen and Ingushi often inter-mixed with the indigenous population of the deportation areas, for instance, those beyond Frunze and in the Petropavlovsk regions. These reception areas undoubtedly felt the influence of the deportees. After the political thaw, broadcast talks in the Ingush language and publication by the Kirgiz State Publishing house of works by Balkar and Karachai writers were announced. The Germans, too, received some attention, in spite of their deportation, and a newspaper in their language appeared in the Altai Territory and some German programs were broadcast from Alma-Ata.

5.4. *Slavery*

Too little is known of the influence on language of punitive or enforced migration, whether this involves the segregation of the immigrants or not. For example, slavery is an important component of such movements, and though we have some studies of the impact of slavery on the economy of various countries, we have, so far as I know, no study of the linguistic consequences. Yet the influence of Greek slaves in Roman households or as teachers was effective in creating a considerable degree of bilingualism in Rome, so that Quintilian rationalized the teaching of a second lan-guage on its incidence; and Cicero, though he approved of the Greek influence, was anxious about its impact on the mother tongue of a young Roman child. Slavery, it has been suggested, may account for a good deal of the influence of non-Indo-European Asian languages on Greek dialects (Atkinson 1952:14). The number of Thracian slaves in Lauricum in Xenophon's time was greater than the whole population of the smaller Greek city states. In the Athens of the fourth century, ten thousand slaves were employed in domestic service (half of the slave population), but they were also employed in secretarial posts, as banking employees, and as commercial agents, where very often their native tongues would be useful and because of which they were both able and encouraged to maintain them. They were drawn from numerous nationalities. In Hellenistic times Rhodes had a very large multinational slave population consisting of Lydians, Phrygians, Cilicians, Cappadocians, Galatians, Syrians, and Armenians. The Greek slave trade at all times embraced Italy, Illyria, Armenia, Palestine, Egypt, and even Ethiopia. The Romans added Ligurian territories, Sardinia, Spain, and Gaul, as well as Germany, to the slave-trade areas. The Augustan wars in Spain, Germany, the Alpine area, Illyricum and Panonia put large numbers on the slave market. The

Celtic element in this trade, though recognized, has probably been greatly underestimated. Intermarriage involving slaves produced temporary bilingualism in large numbers of families. It cannot be but that such a widespread practice involving such enormous numbers, sometimes concentrated in small city environs, had considerable influence on language contact, especially on attitude to contact, and therefore to the promotion of individual and societal bilingualism.

6. SIZE AND DISTRIBUTION OF POPULATIONS

6.1. *Size of Linguistic Group*

Thus it is that we find exemplified in the Soviet Union and to a lesser extent in Wales three types of linguistically significant movement of large numbers of people: permanent displacement of a nation; permanent displacement of a relatively small portion of a nation or of a number of nations, creating enclaves in the host areas; and infiltration of numbers of individuals such as skilled workers and slaves. All three types may work simultaneously and their relative importance may be difficult to disentangle, but they have produced important changes in the status of languages in the Soviet Union and Wales, as they have done in other countries down through history. But motivation for movement and the type of movement involved are not the only variables which relate to the demographic aspects of language contact. For instance the size and distribution of the different language groups involved are also important considerations. It is to be expected, for example, that Yugoslavia, a country of approximately twenty million people, with a considerable number of different language communities, should have high levels of bilingualism, since the size of these communities and their even distribution make contact inevitable. It has ten nationalities each numbering more than 100,000, and even more different language groups, ranging from 1,000 (Austrians) to 86,000 (Slovaks). Consequently, each of its six republics is linguistically heterogenous (Magner 1967). The situation in the Soviet Union is vastly more complex. The Census of 1970 was conducted on the basis of the recognition of 122 nationalities, twenty-three of them with more than a million people, but some, like the various peoples of the North, with fewer than a thousand (Yukagirs have 600). Furthermore, the fifteen constituent Union republics are themselves extremely heterogenous linguistically. At present the Russian Republic has representatives of sixty nationalities, and even an autonomous republic within the Russian Republic like Daghestan contains fourteen linguistic groups, each more than 5,000 strong. Kazakhstan has seventeen nationalities with populations of more than 15,000; and one administrative district (oblast), namely Dzhambul, which is typical of many others, is inhabited by twelve different language groups each with over 5,000 representatives. The city of Moscow in 1970 consisted of seven million Russians and eight other nationalities with over 8,000 each, together with very large numbers of significantly-sized but smaller communities. The importance of the size of these minority groups in areas like Kazakhstan or Tadzhikstan is apparent when it is seen that the smaller nationalities, irrespective of their rate of out- or in-migration, tend to be less retentive of their native languages than the larger ones. The latter, even if we exclude the Russians, who are disinclined not only to shift language loyalty but even to learn a second native Soviet language, all have very high levels of language maintenance (*Izvestiya*, April 17, 1971). For instance, Azerbaijanis had a higher level in 1970 (98.2 percent) than in 1959 (96.7 percent). The same is true of Armenians, 89.9 percent in 1959 and 91.4 percent in 1970. Those who have declined in the last intercensus decade, like the Kazakhs, show only a very slight diminution — 98.4 percent to 98 percent, or, as in the case of the Georgians, a slightly larger fall, from 98.6 percent to 93.4 percent.

The nationalities in the middle ranges, those of a quarter to half a million, seem to be able to hold their own much as the larger nationalities do. For instance, Bashkir, the largest of the middle group, has increased since 1926, moving from 53.8 percent to 66.2 percent in 1970. The degree of language maintenance among Avars fell by 2.1 percent between 1926 and 1970. Chechens have declined by 1 percent. Of the intermediate nationalities, the average erosion of language maintenance is approximately 3 percent over forty years, the greatest decline occurring among the Ossetes (9.3 percent) and Lezgins (3.5 percent). Dargins have continued to retain a relatively high level of language maintenance. Among the others, between 1926 and 1970 Buryats have had a loss of 5.5 percent and Yakuts a loss of 3.4 percent. The smaller nationalities, irrespective of the proportion of their populations dispersed outside their home republics, tend to be less retentive than the larger or the intermediate nationalities. Those which are under greatest pressure, the Mansi, for instance, (4,500) have a considerable decline from a maintenance level of 88.9 percent in 1926 to 59.8 percent in 1959 and to 52.5 percent in 1970. Similarly, the Nivkh (4,400) had an enormously increased rate of linguistic assimilation — from 3 percent to 24 percent between 1926 and 1959, increasing to 50.5 percent in 1970. Others among the small nations, like the Tats (17,000) and Evenki (25,000) also declined, from 86.6 percent to 72 percent between 1926 and 1970 in the case of the former, and in the latter case from 63 percent to 55 percent between 1926 and 1959 and to 51 percent in 1970. The very small nations, those not much exceeding a thousand, like Itelmen (35 percent) and Yukagir (46 percent) have at present very low levels of maintenance.

Size, we can conclude, irrespective of the operation of other factors is important in facilitating or obstructing the maintenance of a national language. Though Wales is not subject to the kind of multinational pressures experienced in any one republic in the Soviet Union, it, too, exemplifies the importance of this variable. For instance, the thirteen counties of Wales could be identified in 1891 as belonging to one or another of three categories according to the size of the Welsh-speaking population. Five had proportions of Welsh language maintenance in excess of 90 percent. Four counties ranged between 51 percent and 68 percent, and four ranged between 10 percent and 50 percent. Between 1891 and 1961 each group behaved consistently, in the sense that the rate of decline of each group was fairly uniform as between members of that group, and each group maintained the same kind of differential with each of the other groups as it appeared to have in 1891. In other words, the rate of decline bore a consistent relation, both within and between the groups, to the size of the Welsh language group at the beginning of the period under review. This was independent of the operation of other variables such as the rate of outward migration from the Welsh-speaking counties, or the rate of in-migration in the third group, i.e. the most Anglicized. Thus, the first group, the most Welsh, declined from a range of 90 percent — 95 percent Welsh language maintenance in 1891 to a range of 70 percent — 75 percent eighty years later. The second group declined from a range of 51 percent — 68 percent to a range of 20 percent — 35 percent, and the smallest Welsh group declined from a range of 10 percent — 50 percent to a range of 3 percent — 17 percent.

6.2. *Difference Between Stable and Migrant Populations*

Whatever the rate of decline of language maintenance within a stable population, there is a far greater loss among the migrants. This proposition does not need emphasizing since it is well illustrated in North America and elsewhere. But in those cases the population on the move was effectively isolated from contact with their origins. It is interesting to note that the same result holds equally in a small nation like Wales where the emigrants to England are nowhere beyond 200 miles of their native villages and towns, as well as in a vast complex like the Soviet Union where, though the distances are greater, the immigrant populations are still within the same political system, and the opportunities for communication within that system are fairly uniform. Precise figures for the status of Welsh outside Wales cannot be ascertained because the official census for England and Wales does not provide for the enumeration of those who claim Welshness outside Wales. In the Soviet Union, however, precise figures are available. For instance, while the level of maintenance among all Russians in 1970 was 99.8 percent, it is 96 percent among Russian emigrants. This figure is exceptionally high simply because of the reluctance and the lack of pressure on Russians anywhere in the Soviet Union even to become acquainted with a second language. With other nationalities the story is very different. Among Ukrainians there is a difference of 36 percent between language maintenance among the stable and the emigrant populations. Among the two groups of Georgians the difference is 25 percent, and among Armenians 12 percent. The same is true of the smaller nationalities. For instance, among the Lezgin the difference is 24 percent, among the Ossetes it is 37 percent, and among the Karachai 30 percent. The difference is least among the group of Central Asian nationalities whose migrant populations are largely interchangeable, in other words dispersed within the Central Asian complex. For instance, the difference between stable and migrant Uzbek populations is only 1 percent (98.4 percent and 97.4 percent), among the Kazakhs the difference is between 98.4 percent and 95.6 percent, and among Azerbaijhanis between 97.6 percent and 95.2 percent. The disparity among Turkmen is 6.9 percent, among Tadzhiks 3.5 percent and among Kirgiz 5.4 percent. It appears possible, therefore, that even among migrant populations the rate of decline in language maintenance is affected by the possibility that the area within which migration occurs is culturally homogenous, or by the fact that the languages spoken within the area of movement, though different in many ways, belong to the same family, as is often the case in the Central Asian Republics.

So far we have discussed the demographic factors involved in language shift as if language contact or greater opportunities for such contact inevitably lead to language shift, but this is not the case. For instance, hardly any changes have occurred in the relative position of the languages spoken in Switzerland since 1850 (Mayer 1956). From that date onwards, roughly 70 percent of the population have been German-speaking, and a little above 20 percent French-speaking, slightly more than 5 percent Italian-speaking, and even the very small Romansh community have remained relatively stable at 1 percent. The same is true of the Daghestanis of the Soviet Union. Though they are small nationalities and have a very long history of contact, both among themselves and with Russian and Georgian, the percentage of those claiming the national languages as their mother tongues is nowhere lower than 89.8 percent (Nogai), and in the case of most of them, well over 95 percent. Where contact leads to shift, in the Soviet Union the reasons have to be sought in new economic factors. A comparison of the position of the languages spoken in the Siberian lands, where the level of language maintenance is down to an average of 50 percent, will support this contention, since there are some most spectacular economic developments occurring. The same thing is true of Wales. Before the demographic factors which we have noted began to operate, and while the economy was still very largely traditional, the Welsh language was stable and at a relatively high survival level. The decisive factor facilitating language shift has been a revolutionary change in economic conditions, and this still operates adversely. As Haugen (1950) pointed out in another context, "Language pressure is only a special form of social pressure," and we have to analyze the latter to be able to understand the former.

7.   REINFORCEMENT OF MIGRATION

It has to be stressed that there are very many subordinate variables to be considered, even if we limit our analysis to population movement. For instance, no movement of population other than the total migration of a nation like that of the Yakut or the Celts is likely to have an appreciable influence on the local languages unless the immigrant population is continuously reinforced. This is exemplified, for instance, in the history of Latin and Greek influence. The Romanization of Britain proved to be superficial because there was never a sufficiently large reinforcement additional to the original group. The Romans replaced rather than reinforced. The same is true of the Romanization and Hellenization of parts of Asia Minor and Egypt. First, the Roman enclaves yielded to Greek influence because they were isolated from their source. Then the main native stock of Greek-occupied colonies were able to remain native in speech and to cope with the original Greek penetration because the settlers were not sufficiently reinforced. The need for constant reinforcement is exemplified by various ethnic and linguistic groups within the United States. In Arizona and California, in spite of favorable conditions, the speakers of Spanish were never able to do more than make a superficial impression on the linguistic and cultural situation. The present position of Spanish is due almost entirely to continuous reinforcement of the language by Spanish-speaking Mexican immigrants. The same is true elsewhere in the United States because of the constant flow of Puerto Ricans or other Spanish-speaking groups, like the Cubans in Miami. In New England, the French language is rapidly being forsaken because of the lack of physical reinforcement, and in spite of the prestige of that language and other kinds of what might be called ideological support from France; and it is recognized even within the French-speaking community as a foreign language. The high degree of language shift in Wales was ensured not simply by the size of the original immigrant flow from England into South Wales, but even more by the constant reinforcement of those immigrants even at a time when Welsh industry was in recession and thousands of native speakers of Welsh were emigrating to the United States and Australia. This is true also of the Soviet Union, where the

Russian language is very differently placed from Georgian or Armenian, for example. The availability of inexhaustible Russian reinforcements has been crucial, even when the original balance in a multinational industrial complex has been not greatly in favor of Russian.

8. DIFFERENTIAL GROWTH RATES

Apart from the forms of reinforcement we have discussed, there is another demographic factor which serves to reinforce (or to neutralize in some cases) the effect of the flow of immigrants, namely a differential natural growth rate. It is possible for considerable numbers to switch their language and to assimilate linguistically with another group and yet for their original language group to maintain itself and even to expand. This has been the case in Montreal. There, ethnic fertility differentials have been shown to be unfavorable to English. In the last two decades the advantage gained by English is due to French switching of language loyalty. Conversely, the French language is able to compensate for losses because ethnic fertility is very favorable to that language (Lieberson 1965). The case is somewhat similar in Switzerland. In recent decades the German language has been gaining slightly on the French because of the considerable fertility differentials which exist between the French and Germans of Switzerland. This tendency for increasing German predominance is not evenly spread, however, since there has been considerable internal migration between populations of the French-speaking cantons which have their own fertility differential — Geneva, Neuchâtel, and Vaud having lower birth rates than the other French cantons, Fribourg and Valais (Mayer 1956).

It is this factor which has helped to ensure that non-Russian languages in areas of considerable Russian immigration have been able to maintain and in some cases to increase the percentage of the population claiming the local language. The birth rate is especially low among European Soviet populations. In 1967 the reproduction index for the Baltic republics was less than 1. In Latvia the birth rate was as low as 1.4 percent and the natural growth rate 0.34 percent. In certain areas of northwest Russia the population was declining. The muslims of the Central Asian republics have, on the contrary, very high rates of fertility — 3.7 percent on the average, with Tadzhiks, for instance, being near the mean at 3.73 percent, two and a half times greater than Russians. Furthermore, the birth rates in the rural areas, the main areas of language conservation, have been consistently higher than the rates in the urban areas. In 1926 they were 4.6 percent and 3.4 percent, respectively, and in 1964 they were 2.2 percent and 1.7 percent, respectively. Partly because of these considerations, the natural population growth rates have been six or seven times greater in the areas of immigration, and this difference has tended to increase with time.

In Wales the differential growth rate has, contrary to the examples we have given of other countries, militated against the survival of the Welsh language. The decline of Welsh in rural Wales cannot be attributed entirely to depopulation. The rate of natural growth has almost invariably been unfavorable. The rate for England and Wales as a whole from 1951 to 1961 was 4.5 percent and for Wales alone 3.4 percent. During the same period the rate in some of the most conservative of the Welsh-speaking areas was only 0.4 percent. In two of the most thoroughly Welsh-speaking counties deaths exceeded births. The decline in some of these counties has been greater than the rate of out-migration by between 6.6 percent in some counties and 14.8 percent. Although this loss by decline in natural growth can be distinguished from decline by migration, the cause for the former is, in fact, very largely prior out-migration from the rural areas and in-migration to the urban. Migrants are not likely to be a truly representative sample of the total population, and this is especially true of the age of migrants, among whom there is always an excess of adolescents and young adults. In 1911, for instance, 22 percent of the migrants into Glamorgan from Somerset were under twenty-four; 22 percent between the ages of twenty-five and thirty-four; and 21 percent between thirty-five and forty-four. This is typical of the immigrants from other English areas, and it is a reflex of the pattern of rural emigration. In consequence of the age distribution of inward migrants into the industrial areas and of outward migrants from the Welsh-speaking rural areas, the proportion of marriageable young people fell in the rural areas and rose in the urban. As a result, the proportion of young children up to the age of fourteen and of young adults between fifteen and twenty-four in the rural counties is well below the average for the whole of Wales. Glamorgan, with 23 percent adolescents and young adults, is well above the average of 13 percent. The differential fertility rates of rural and urban areas, together with the consequent disproportion between the number of children and old people in these areas (both attributable to population-movement patterns), have contributed greatly to the decline of the Welsh language. Bilingualism in Wales is progressively a characteristic of increasing age — in the rural areas there are far more old people than young, so that the reservoir of conservation is becoming shallower. In the urban areas the proportion of the young is very much higher, but they do not represent the element necessary to conserve the language. They are, in the nature of things, too heavily and too early exposed to English influences. Between 1901 and 1970 there has occurred an age polarization in respect of support for the Welsh language which reflects the rural/urban polarization.

9. THE FAMILY

Though intermarriage may be conducive to language contact even within a demographically stable society, it is more often a factor which reinforces the influence of population movement. Whether it does or not depends on the system of marriage, or the family organization which is regarded as obligatory. In the extended polygamous family, for instance, such as that of many of the African tribes, there are not one but several families, each clustering round one of several wives, with their own native or tribal languages. The same is true of the tribes of the northwest Amazon. Because of exogamy, a child's mother represents a different tribe and a different linguistic group from the father's. A woman invariably uses the language of the father when talking directly with her children. But she is usually not the only woman from her tribe in the longhouse, and there are in all probability groups of other women from other tribes and language groups as well. During the day there is a good deal of conversation, the women talking in their original languages but able to follow very easily the purport of the general talk (Sorenson 1967).

In developed countries, and especially those within a Western family organization pattern, intermarriage is usually the result of migration. Whatever the direction of the influence of such new contacts, whether to favor the indigenous or the intrusive tongue, bilingualism is the predictable result. For instance, during the Parthian occupation of Mesopotamia there was extensive intermarriage between the Greek settlers and the native population, a process which is illustrated by documents from Europus which show that in the first and second centuries the names of the men were normally Greek but those of their wives and daughters Aramaic or Iranian (Jones 1937). Mesopotamia became a thoroughly bilingual settlement. The dominant language and sentiment was Greek, but the population became increasingly orientalized. Then again, Cyrene was a great Greek city where all the original settlers had taken Lybian wives. Miletus was as Greek as Cyrene, but there, too, Carian blood intermingled with Greek and the two languages existed side by side (Tarn 1938). So it is in the Soviet Union.

Before the Revolution, it is true, marriages between different nationalities, even within the Muslim faith, were extremely limited in such areas as the Caucusus, Central Asia, and particularly Turkestan. This has changed over the last few years. It has been stated, for instance, that the diffusion of the Azerbaijzhan language among the Tats is promoted by mixed marriage. Similarly, the use of the Circassian language was undoubtedly promoted by the Circassian women who married into Abazin families and taught their children Circassian. The tendency of these two groups to intermarry has accelerated, so that they represent the highest percentage of mixed marriages in the Caucusus — 24.6 percent

Circassian males and 26 percent females enter into mixed marriages, the percentages of Abazins being 36 percent males and 25 percent females. Of these mixed marriages, well over half of the Circassians marry Abazins, and well over two-thirds of the Abazins marry Circassians. (Smirnova 1967:140) In the cities, because of the increased opportunities for national contacts, the rate of intermarriage increases rapidly. In Ashkabad, of the 381 marriages registered in 1920, eighty-one (21 percent) were contracted between different nationals. By 1940 the proportion had increased to 31 percent and the number to 400. The same process can be exemplified in the city of Tashkent, where intermarriage between Russians, Uzbeks, Tatars, Ukrainians, Jews, Armenians, Kazakhs, Tadzhiks, Mordvins, Belorussians, Azerbaijzhanis, Bashkirs, Chuvash, or Poles increased from 19 percent to 22 percent between 1926 and 1963. The rate was four times higher in the new suburbs of Tashkent than in the old city (Khanazarov 1963).

The language of the offspring of these marriages depends upon several factors, but principally upon the prestige of one or other of the languages. For instance, an analysis of marriages and the language consequences for children in the city of Karasuk, the center of an ancient culture in Novosibirskaya oblast, showed that parents who were both of Ukrainian origin and claimed that language as their mother tongue brought up their children to regard Russian as their first language. It is not surprising, therefore, that parents of mixed Ukrainian and Russian stock induced a language shift in their children (Perevedentsev 1966). In Tashkent 79 percent of the mixed marriages where Russian was already the language of one of the partners resulted in that language becoming the normal means of communication with the children.

In Wales it is difficult now to speak of Welsh or English stock, and intermarriage has to be interpreted in purely linguistic terms. The total number of pupils who come from homes where both parents are Welsh-speaking has declined from 66,200 to 53,700, a difference of 19 percent from 1952 to 1972. On the other hand, there has been a rise from 1,500 to 1,800 (20 percent) in the number of homes where the father alone speaks Welsh, and from 2,200 to 2,700 (20 percent) in the number where the mother alone speaks the language. The total number of pupils between five and fifteen registered in the schools in 1961 was 329,400, and in 1971 389, 500. Thus, there were in 1961 over 215,00 (65 percent) who came from homes where neither parent spoke Welsh, and this figure had increased to 285,000 (73 percent) in 1971. It appears that the increase in the proportion of homes where neither parent speaks Welsh is roughly the same as the loss in the number where both parents speak the language, and this combination of losses is disconcerting. The loss, amounting to 13 percent between 1961 and 1971 in the homes where both parents spoke the language, is greater than the gains in the "one Welsh parent" homes.

To aggravate this loss, the linguistically homogenous maintain the Welsh language among the children far more effectively than mixed language families. For instance, in 1971 81 percent of the children (75.5 percent in 1961) in the homes with two Welsh parents were considered to have Welsh as their mother tongue on entry in school, compared with 19 percent and 24.5 percent of the children in homes with one Welsh parent. Furthermore, the shift from Welsh to English as a first language, which occurs as the children grow older, is 10 percent in the families where both parents speak Welsh, but nearly three times that percentage in the "father–Welsh" homes (26 percent) and twice as great in the "mother–Welsh" homes (21 percent). There is a considerable difference between mixed families according to whether it is the father or the mother who speaks Welsh. In 1961 the shift toward English with age was 8 percent greater in "father–only Welsh" homes than in "mother–only Welsh" homes. If we take into account all age groups, the proportion of children from "father–only Welsh" homes who maintain Welsh as their first language was 6.1 percent and 6.9 percent in 1961 and 1971, respectively, while the percentages for children in "mother–only Welsh" homes were 10.5 percent and 11.7 percent (Lewis, current research).

10. CONCLUSION

I have attempted to make in this paper a tentative comparison of the operation of a very few of the more significant variables, the primary factors, conducing to language contact. These factors have been considered mainly but not exclusively in the contexts of two very disparate countries, Wales and the Soviet Union. At the same time, the current operation of these factors has been compared with their historical operation in other countries. It is hoped both to elaborate the analysis of the current situation in Wales, as has been attempted for the Soviet Union (Lewis 1972), and to expand the historical dimension of the comparison as well. In this way it may be possible to advance somewhat the theoretical stance of students of language contact or of societal bilingualism, and to place that phenomenon in a truer perspective. At the same time, the secondary variables, which have not been discussed here, need to be considered. These secondary factors, and especially education, social ideology, and philosophy, together with the actual operation of a political policy, do not bring about contact so much as they influence the nature of the contact when it emerges and the attitude of the populations to it.

REFERENCES

ARUTIUNIAN, IV.V.
1968   Opyt sotsialno-etnicheskogo isseldovaniya po materialam Tatarskoi ASSR. *Sovetskaya etnografia* 4:3–13.

ATKINSON, B. F. C.
1952   *The Greek language*. London: Faber and Faber.

BAYNES, E., R. MOSS, editors
1961   *Byzantium: an introduction to East Roman civilization*. London: Oxford University Press.

BERRY, J.
1971   "The Madina project," in *Language use and social change*. Edited by W. H. Whiteley. London: for the International African Institute by Oxford University Press.

COMMISSION OF ENQUIRY
1917   Commission of Enquiry into Industrial Unrest. London: H.M.S.O.

FISHMAN, J. A., editor
1966   *Language loyalty in the United States*. The Hague: Mouton.
1971   *Bilingualism in the Barrio*. Research Center for Language Science Monograph. Bloomington, Indiana.

FRIEDLANDER, D., P. ROSHIER
1966   Internal migration in England and Wales. *Population Studies* 20.

HAUGEN, E.
1950   Problem of bilingualism. *Lingua* 11(3):271–290.
1956   *Bilingualism in the Americas*. University, Alabama: University of Alabama Press.

JONES, A. H. M.
1937   *The cities of the Eastern Roman province*. Oxford: The Clarendon Press.

KHANAZAROV, K.
1963   *Sblizheniye natsii i natsionalnykh yazykov v SSSR*. Tashkent.

LEWIS, E. G.
1972   *Multilingualism in the Soviet Union: aspects of language policy and its implementation*. The Hague: Mouton.

LIEBERSON, S.
1965   Bilingualism in Montreal: a demographic analysis. *American Journal of Sociology* 70.

MAGIE, D.
1950   *Roman rule in Asia Minor*. Princeton, New Jersey: Princeton University Press.

MAGNER, T. F.
1967   Language and nationalism in Yugoslavia. *Canadian Slavic Studies* 1(3):333–347.

MAYER, K.
1956   "Cultural pluralism and linguistic equilibrium in Switzerland," in *Demographic analysis: selected readings*. Edited by J. J. Spengler and O. Duncan. Glencoe, Illinois: Free Press.

OKLADNIKOV, A. P.
1968   *Yakutia — before its incorporation*. Montreal: Arctic Institute of North American Publication 8.

PAUL, HERMANN
1960   *Prinzipien der Sprache Geschichte* (sixth edition). Darmstadt: Wissenschaftliche Buchgesellschaft.

PEREVEDENTSEV, VIKTOR IVANOVICH
1966   *Migratsya naseleniya i trudovye problemy Sibiri*. Novosibirsk.
QUINTILIANUS, MARCUS FABIUS
1938   "Selected passages from the *Institutio Oratoria*," in *Quintilian on education*. Translated by William M. Smail. Oxford: The Clarendon Press.
ROGACHEV, V. I., M. SVERDLIN
1963   Sovetskaya narodnovaya istoricheskaya obshchnost lyudei. *Kommunist* 9:11–20.
ROOF, M. K.
1960   Recent trends in Soviet migration. *R.E.M.P. Bulletin* 8(1):1–18.
SMIRNOVA, Y. S.
1967   Natsionalno smeshannye braki v narodov karachayevocherkessi. *Sovetskaia etnografiya* 4.
SORENSEN, A. P.
1967   Multilingualism in the North West Amazon. *American Anthropologist* 69:670–684.
TARN, W. W.
1938   *The Greeks in Bactria and India*. London: Cambridge University Press.
THOMAS, D. S.
1938   *Research memorandum on migration differentials*. New York: Social Science Research Council.
TOYNBEE, A.
1935   *A study of history*, volume five. London: Oxford University Press.
Voprosy trudovykh
1961   *Voprosy trudovykh resursov v Rayonakh Sibiri*. Novosibirsk.
WEINREICH, URIEL
1953   *Languages in contact: findings and problems*. New York: Linguistic Circle of New York.
WHATMOUGH, J.
1933   *Pre-Italic dialects of Italy*. Cambridge: Harvard University Press.
1970   *The dialects of ancient Gaul*. Cambridge: Harvard University Press.
ZAIONCHOVSKAIA, Z. H., V. I. PEREVEDENTSEV
1964   *Sovremennaya migratsiya naseleniya krasnoyarskogo kraya*. Novosibirsk.

Linguistic Contacts and Elements of Ethnic Identification

M. GUBOGLO

The growing differentiation of scientific knowledge has brought forth a number of complicated theoretical and methodological problems in the field of ethnography. Of particular importance is the solution of problems pertaining to different fields of science; this will eliminate some "blank spots" that have remained only because, being in the sphere of several sciences at once, they nonetheless cannot be solved by the traditional methods of any of these sciences. A mechanical combination of such methods is not effective enough to determine the sphere of a new field of knowledge that has emerged on the borderline between some well-established branches of science. An exact determination of the sphere of ethnolinguistics, the chief task of which is the study of a wide range of problems that combine into the highly diffuse subject of "language and ethnos," depends on a number of factors. The decisive role goes to the investigation of objects within the scope of the field itself. In turn, the effort to determine the borderline of the field is, like any other type of classification, conducive to further investigation.

Scholars from different countries have not yet evolved a uniform and exact concept of the subject of ethnolinguistics. This was most vividly reflected in the work of the ethnolinguistics section at the VIIth International Congress of Anthropological and Ethnographical Sciences. The great diversity of subjects discussed by the section was in itself an indication of the fluctuating structure of ethnolinguistics at its present stage. The presence of ethnography and linguistics with their firmly established traditions makes it extremely difficult to distinguish works that are strictly within the scope of ethnolinguistics. It is quite easy, however, to draw a line between the ethnographic and linguistic reports delivered at the Congress.

A similarity between the Soviet and American trends in ethnolinguistics, as regards the definition of its subject, lies in the fact that linguistic material is largely analyzed with reference to ethnogenetic problems, i.e. ethnic problems pertaining to the past. In most cases, the basic object of investigation is the vocabulary. Sometimes other structural units of the language are studied, but speech and oratory are altogether left out of consideration. The difference between the Soviet and American approaches is that American ethnolinguists confine themselves to studies of language that have no written expression. Their Soviet counterparts, on the contrary, study all the languages of our planet; their work is based upon the idea of a close link between the development of languages and extralinguistic factors. This work covers languages without a written equivalent, languages that have only recently acquired it, and those with a long-standing written tradition. This has resulted in a substantial expansion of the scope of research and has led to the necessity of distinguishing, apart from ethnolinguistics, such fields as sociolinguistics, psycholinguistics, and some other related ("hybrid") fields. That, in turn, calls for a more precise definition of their subjects. The intensive work on the problems of language policy, language construction, and the functional development of the languages of the Soviet nations has led to the point where, being totally preoccupied with language and its social functions, scholars are no longer paying attention to individual speech conduct.

Meanwhile, studies in variations of speech conduct of individuals, social groups, and whole ethnoses under conditions of lively ethnic contacts are of particular importance for multinational Soviet society, which is becoming increasingly bilingual. The significance of these studies becomes strikingly apparent in light of the fact that international contacts are maintained in this country at different levels ranging from ethnic situations in the constituent Soviet republics to such a microsocial unit as the family. The basic problems of contemporary ethnolinguistics include the dependence of speech conduct upon factors that are external to the language and the speaker, the typology and mechanism of speech conduct, the relation between speech conduct and an individual's adherence to elements of his people's or other people's culture, and the dependence of speech conduct upon national values and orientations of an individual. These problems are being tackled as part of studies in socioethnic and ethnolinguistic processes which have been gaining in scope over the past years.

The present report is an attempt to review some results of Soviet ethnosociological research that includes some ethnolinguistic problems.

As the primary ethnic determinant, a language is a subsystem of the ethnos system. Within the ethnos system, it is placed on the same horizontal line as other ethnic determinants: ethnic self-consciousness, material and spiritual culture, traditions, customs, etc. An original combination of ethnic determinants (elements of the ethnos) accounts for the unique nature of each ethnic community. Each element of the ethnos has multiple functions, the integrating function being one of the most important. An individual recognizes his or her ethnic affinity with reference to a number of elements typical of the ethnos, including the language: therefore, the structure of ethnic consciousness may be represented as a hierarchy of elements of ethnic identification. An analysis of an individual's ties with his ethnic community, with reference to specific elements of the ethnos, can, in our opinion, reveal the functional load of each element of the ethnos. With this approach, conscious identification of an individual with his ethnos (for instance, with reference to the language, origin, historical destiny, etc.) is represented by elements of ethnic identification.

Unlike ethnic self-consciousness, which structurally is a simpler notion meaning an automatic (spontaneous) identification of an individual with his ethnic community, ethnic consciousness is a kind of multiple (multistage) identification with the same ethnos. These ideas evolve in every person; first, on the basis of a realistic recognition that the elements of the ethnos in question are only typical of the given ethnic community and not any other one, and, second, because of the understanding that the individual himself is a bearer of elements of the given ethnos. Ethnic consciousness can be SIMPLE and COMPLEX in form. If an individual identifies himself with only one ethnic community with reference to the bulk of its characteristic elements, this type of ethnic consciousness may be defined as simple (or homogeneous). If an individual identifies himself with one ethnos with reference to a number of elements, and with another ethnos with reference to one or several other elements, this type of ethnic consciousness is referred to as complex (or heterogeneous or mixed).

The interviewing of different population groups in the Udmurt Autonomous Soviet Socialist Republic (Vasil'eba, Pimenov and Khristolyubova 1970) has revealed an uneven functional loading of the same elements of ethnic identification in the structure of ethnic consciousness among rural and urban dwellers. The rural dwellers' ties with their Udmurt ethnos are reflected, first and foremost, in their speaking the Udmurt language. The subsequent steps in the hierarchy of ethnic consciousness are folk rituals and customs, then the material culture (food, clothing, homes, etc.), with ethnic self-consciousness occupying only the fourth place. Among the urban Udmurts, the language is a vivid and, apparently, integrating determinant, as compared to the rest of the identification elements. Like the rural Udmurts, the urban Udmurts regard their language as the main factor by which they identify themselves with the Udmurt nation. Yet here the similarity ends. The second element, as regards the ties of the urban Udmurts with the Udmurt ethnic community, is their ethnic self-consciousness; the third is the professional layer of spiritual culture (as is known, this emerged only in Soviet times and at present is rapidly growing); and the fourth is the folklore layer of traditional spiritual culture.

In the Udmurt ethnos, the same element of ethnic identification plays a different role in urban and rural environments. The difference between the language and the national rituals which, respectively, rank first and second in the structure of ethnic consciousness of the countryfolk, amounts to 28 percent. In the city, the difference between the first and second elements (the language and ethnic self-consciousness) is less, amounting to 17 percent.

The leading role of the language, which is the primary intra-ethnic integrator among the rural section of the Udmurt ethnos, stems in particular from the fact that in the countryside the language is part and parcel of the Udmurt national culture. In the city, on the other hand, the system of national culture includes spiritual values produced with the help not only of the Udmurt language, but of other languages as well, e.g. with the help of a language which serves as a means of international communication.

Urbanization creates certain prerequisites for shifting the focus of ethnic orientations from traditional forms of culture to modern forms expressed in the professional culture; it also enhances the role of subjective factors. In the ethnic consciousness of some interviewed rural dwellers of the Moldavian Soviet Socialist Republic, ethnic identification elements were distributed as follows: (1) the language, (2) the realization of ethnic identity (ethnic consciousness), (3) spiritual culture (music, dancing, folklore), and (4) folk festivals. An interview with some urban intellectuals revealed the following distribution: first the realization of their ethnic identification (the integrating function of ethnic self-consciousness) and, second, spiritual culture. In contrast to the rural dwellers, the language ranked third (as opposed to first). Thus, socio-professional status causes marked changes in the structure of ethnic consciousness. Hence, the same elements of the ethnos have different functional loads in rural and urban environments. For a Moldavian villager, the most obvious factor identifying him with his Moldavian community is his language; for a city dweller, it is the realization of his ethnic identity. Apparently, in the countryside objective features (elements) of the ethnos are more frequently and more extensively combined with their subjective realization.

The integrating function of elements of the ethnos manifests itself in different ways in different ethnic environments. The hierarchies of ethnic identification elements of two nations existing in their single-nationality environments would be, in all probability, closer to each other than the hierarchy of those elements of two groups of one nationality found in different types of ethnic environments.

Social factors change the functional load of elements of the ethnos, whereas the ethnic environment changes ethnic identification elements themselves. There is a situation, however, in which ethnic consciousness remains sufficiently stable. A relative weakening of the role of language as a factor uniting members of an ethnic community is compensated for by the enhanced role of the other elements. The situation is totally different, however, when, influencing the formation of ethnic consciousness as objective factors, there are elements related to genetically heterogeneous ethnoses.

Let us consider some examples. The greatest interest in national Karelian songs, dances, music, and wedding ceremonies is shown for the most part by those rural dwellers in Karelia (Klement'ev 1971) who have retained their native Karelian language. The presence of an element of another nationality (another language) in the ethnic consciousness of the Karelian countryfolk shows that the state of other elements of the Karelian ethnic community is dependent upon that factor. Of the Karelian countryfolk whose native tongue is Karelian, 9.9 percent prefer Karelian folk songs; 14.8 percent prefer Karelian folk music; 16.4 percent show a preference for Karelian folk dancing; and 27.1 percent prefer the folk wedding ritual. A comparison of national orientations of the said Karelians with those whose native tongue is that of another nationality, indicates that the abandonment of the Karelian language is accompanied by a loss of interest in the folk wedding ceremony. As has been shown by questionnaires, the internal monolithic unity and the stability of the Karelian ethnos are maintained by a series of factors with reference to which every Karelian recognizes himself as a Karelian. All of these elements of ethnic identification may be divided into two groups. The most important factors include the nationality of one's parents, the Karelian language, the presence of relations or friends who are Karelian by nationality and, finally, the notion of "the homeland." Weaker factors include the national customs, the Karelian material culture, folk songs and dances, and least of all national literature and the arts. The professional layer of the Karelians' spiritual culture is not yet as highly developed and widespread as non-professional folk culture. Therefore, the abandonment of the native Karelian language makes the strongest impact upon the deepest cultural layer; with the Karelian countryfolk, in particular, this is shown by the weakening or loss of interest in the national wedding ceremony.

In Udmurtia, 33 percent of the city dwellers and 46.3 percent of the villagers have spoken in favor of the traditional Udmurt childbirth ritual, whereas the respective figures for those whose native language is not Udmurt are 13.4 percent and 21.2 percent. Both the attitude toward elements of traditional culture and the knowledge of these elements have proven to depend upon whether the function of the intra-ethnic integrator is performed by the Udmurt or a non-Udmurt language. The adherence to or, on the contrary, the lack of interest in elements of national culture is only one facet of man's national orientation and reflects the significance of one or another element of culture as a factor of intra-ethnic integration.

In today's Karelia, the lack of interest of the countryfolk in the traditional forms of culture results from language processes. The growing numbers of bilingual persons and the continuous spreading of the Russian language (which, with some groups of Karelians, is an effective means of promoting not only international, but also intra-national relations) intensify the integrating function of the native language or substitute another language for it, and influence primarily the elements of the ethnos that are related to spiritual culture. In other words, language assimilation finds its closest correlation in assimilation processes in the sphere of spiritual culture.

The weakening of intra-ethnic ties among both urban and rural populations depends upon a number of factors, the primary one being the stability of the integrating function of the language. This means that the language as an element of ethnic identification with the integrating function plays an important role inside the ethnos as a link between its separate systems, and is at the same time a significant factor in the general stability of the ethnos as an independent system. There is more than a one-way relation between the language and other elements of the ethnos. In some cases, the weakening of the integrating function of the language is compensated for by the strengthening of the same function of other elements of the ethnos, so that the entire system of ethnic consciousness remains intact. In other cases, the weakening of the integrating function of the language results in the growing indifference of an individual to the rest of the ethnic identification elements and, via this intermediary stage (the de-ethnization), initiates the process of ethnic assimilation.

REFERENCES

ARUTJUNJAN, JU. V.
  1971   *Sotsial'naja struktura sel'skogo naselenija SSSR* [The social structure of the rural population of the USSR]. Moscow.
AVRORIN, V. A.
  1970   Opyt izuchenija funktsional'nogo vzaimodejstvija jazykov u narodov Sibiri [The experience of the study of the functional interaction of languages among the peoples of Siberia]. *Voprosy jazykoznanija* 1:33–34.
BROMLEJ, JU. V.
  1971   K voprosu ob ob"edtivnykh osnovanijakh etnicheskogo samosoznanija [On the question of the objective bases of ethnic consciousness]. *Vsesojuznaja nauchnaja sessija, posvjashchennaja itogam polevykh*

— *arkheologicheskikh i etnograficheskikh issledovanij v 1970 g. (Tezisy dokladov sessionnykh i plenarnykh zasedanij)*, 12–15, Tbilisi.

CHISTOV, K. V.
1972   Etnicheskaja obshchnost', etnicheskoe coznanie i nekotorye problemy dukhovnoj kul'tury [The ethnic community, ethnic consciousness and some problems of spiritual culture]. *Sovetskaja etnografija* 3.

DESHERIEV, JU. D.
1966   *Zadonomernosti razvitija i vzaimodejstvija jazykov v sovetskom obshchestve* [Norms of development and the interaction of language in Soviet society]. Moscow.

DROBIZHEVA, L. M.
1971   Sotsial'no-kul'turnye osobennosti lichnosti i natsional'nye ustanovki (Po materialam issledovanij v Tatarskoj ASSR) [The sociocultural characteristics of personality and national aims (based on research in the Tatar A.S.S.R.)]. *Sovetskaja etnografija* 3:3–15.

GUBOGLO, M. N.
1972   Sotsial'no-etnicheskie posledstvija dvujazychija [Socioethnic consequences of bilingualism]. *Sovetskaja etnografija* 2:26–36.

KLEMENT'EV, E. I.
1971   Jazykovye protsessy v Karelii (Po materialam konkretno sotsiologicheskogo issledovanija karel'skogo sel'skogo naselenija) [Linguistic processes in Karelia (based on materials of a specific sociological investigation of the Karelian rural population)]. *Sovetskaja etnografija* 6:38–44.

KOZLOV, V. I.
1969   *Dinamika chislennosti narodov* [The dynamics of enumeration of peoples]. Moscow.

LEONT'EV, A. A.
1969   *Jazyk, rech', rechevaja dejatel'nost'* [Language, speech and speech activity]. Moscow.
1970   *Trudy VII Mezhdunarodnogo kongressa arkheologii i etnografii* [Transactions of the VIIth International Congress of Archaeology and Ethnography] 5. Moscow.

VASIL'EBA, E. K., V. V. PIMENOV, L. C. KHRISTOLJUBOVA
1970   Sovremennye etnokul'turnye protsessy v udmurtii (Programma i metodika issledo vanija) [Contemporary ethnocultural processes in Udmurtia (Program and methodology of investigation)]. *Sovetskaja etnografija* 2.

Region, Religion, and Language: Parameters of Identity in the Process of Acculturation

MAHADEV L. APTE

Anthropological studies of the phenomenon known as acculturation or culture contact generally entail many prerequisites and subsequent analyses of its several relevant features (Beals 1953; Herskovits 1938; Redfield et al. 1936). Among the prerequisites are the ethnographies of the two or more societies which come in contact, and the duration and nature of such contact; for instance, is the contact between two societies of equal status, or is one society dominant; is the contact due to geographical contiguity or to migration, etc. Analyses may focus on such aspects as the following: (1) changes that may occur in the observable cultural traits of the populations in contact: for example, changes in clothing, diet, marriage patterns, agricultural and other occupational techniques, ceremonial behavior, family structure, child rearing, etc.; (2) attitudes of the members of each society toward such material changes: their acceptance of, or indifference or resistance to them; and (3) consistency or discrepancy between objective changes and subjective ethnic identity.

The aim of this paper is to describe briefly an extended culture contact situation resulting from the migration of one community to a different linguistic region and to analyze the ethnic identity problems faced by its members.

Although a single criterion for a distinct collective identity, such as language, may be available to the members of a minority community, other criteria may be equally influential. Often the choice of a particular criterion or the different priorities given to various criteria is the result of socially relevant factors (Barth 1969:15) and motivations of the minority

Fieldwork on which this paper is based was done in the state of Tamilnadu in south India from September 1971 to July 1972. I am grateful to the American Institute of Indian Studies for a Senior Research Fellowship which enabled me to undertake the research.

community members. In populations which are already stratified, culture contact over an extended period may develop into congruence of codes and values, if structural parallels exist by way of ascribed social status of various groups within the two populations. In such cases, change in ethnic identity from one group to its structural counterpart is conceivable.

In the South Asian region there exists a caste and/or *varṇa* structure which can be considered a special case of a stratified polyethnic system. Migrants from one region to another may therefore find it convenient to acquire the sociocultural identity of structurally parallel caste or *varṇa* groups in the dominant population in the new region.

The main thesis of this paper is that, in the South Asian context, groups with high ascribed social status, namely Brahmans, easily adapt to the regional identity because they can readily associate themselves with the Sanskritic Great Tradition[1] shared by most regions in South Asia. Similar opportunities are available to groups with low ascribed social status only if comparable groups exist in the dominant population. If, however, the structural parallels do not exist, or if a group is desirous of upward social mobility and seeks the goal of higher social ranking, then the factors emphasized in ethnic identity may be an affiliation to a broader reference group outside the new region and a continuation of religious practices emanating from the original home region. Thus the available criterion of language for the retention of a distinct identity for a whole community may be superseded by other criteria such as religion, region, or *varṇa* status.

BACKGROUND

The community under discussion is that of the Marathi-speakers (also Mahrattas) in the state of Tamilnadu in south India, which consists of about 50,000 people. Marathi, an Indo-Aryan language, is spoken by approximately forty-one million people in the state of Maharashtra on the west coast of India. Tamiḷ, the official language of the state of Tamilnadu, belongs to the Dravidian language family and is spoken by approximately thirty-seven million people.

The present-day Marathi-speakers in Tamilnadu are in most cases descendants of Marathi-speakers who immigrated approximately 200 years ago. The initial migration into Tamilnadu was due to the establish-

---

[1]   Starting with Redfield (1955), anthropologists who have worked in South Asia have generally recognized two distinct traditions. These are known as Great Tradition and Little Tradition. The former generally refers to existing Sanskritic literature consisting of religious scriptures and other works on philosophy, law, polity, literary criticism, and epistemology in general; and to the pan-Indian religious ideology and practices emanating from this literature. The latter refers to localized innovations and interpretations of the great body of Sanskritic religious and secular literature.

ment of a small Maharashtrian principality in Tanjore District toward the end of the seventeenth century. The Maratha kings ruled Tanjore District and some of the surrounding areas for about 150 years. There were later migrations of Marathi-speakers during the nineteenth century. Although Marathi-speakers are scattered all over Tamilnadu in small numbers, they are primarily concentrated in four districts, the largest group being in the city of Madras.

There are three major caste groups among the Marathi-speakers in Tamilnadu: Deshastha Brahmans, who were closely connected with the Tanjore kings as administrators and priests; tailors, who appear to be later migrants; and Marathas,[2] who are Kshatriyas [warriors] and were the ruling caste of the Tanjore kingdom. The Brahmans, although still living in large numbers in the city of Tanjore, are now concentrated in the city of Madras. Their migration from Tanjore District to the urban center of Madras began about seventy years ago. The tailors have spread all over Tamilnadu and have sizable groups in many major cities. A large number of them live in the city of Madras. Except for a few scattered families who are related to the former Tanjore kings and still live in Tanjore City and the surrounding areas, the Marathas are mostly concentrated in the northern part of Tamilnadu and are primarily agriculturists. They also have a sizable population in the city of Madras.

LINGUISTIC PROFILE OF THE COMMUNITY

Members of the Marathi-speaking community still use their native language, but it is generally restricted to the home and to interaction with the immediate and extended family. The preferred second language is Tamil, the state language of administration. Most members of the community speak Tamil with native fluency and seem quite at home conversing with Tamil-speakers in all types of social interaction. Thus the community is clearly bilingual, although the individual members are aware that they can be identified as a separate linguistic group. The objective criterion of separate language usage is sufficient to distinguish the Marathi-speakers as a separate community from the rest of the Tamil population (Vreeland 1958:86) and this seems reinforced by the subjective criterion, namely the awareness of their distinct linguistic identity on the part of the Marathi-speakers. This is also substantiated by the fact that since the taking of census began in 1891, the number of Marathi-speakers has not altered in any substantial way.

[2]   Everywhere in India except in the state of Maharashtra, all Marathi-speakers are known as *Marathas* or *Mahrattas,* irrespective of their sociocultural background, including caste. Within Maharashtra, however, the term is used only to refer to a caste group with Kshatriya status.

SEPARATE GROUP IDENTITIES WITHIN THE COMMUNITY

Although the objective criterion of language exists to separate the Marathi-speakers as a community distinct from the dominant population, the separate group identities within the community seem much more influential and dominant than the common identity. These collective identities are based on caste status, socioeconomic conditions, distinct historical and sociocultural traditions, and religious ideologies. The three caste groups in the community appear isolated from each other; each has its own formal organizations, and there is very little contact and communication among them (Apte 1974). Each group seems motivated in a different direction and appears to respond differently to the existing sociocultural, political, and economic conditions. Marathas as a caste group are not relevant to this discussion. Judging by their sociocultural and historical background, however, they show characteristics similar to those of tailors rather than of Brahmans. Thus the major distinction appears to be between Brahmans and non-Brahmans. Each of these groups exhibits different trends of ethnic identity, as reflected in their attitudes and actions discussed below.

Brahmans

Brahmans as a group within the Marathi-speaking community in Tamilnadu are the most advanced in terms of education, prestige, jobs, and income. As late as the 1930s many of them owned land and had influential positions in the social structure of villages, primarily in Tanjore District. Even today many are absentee landlords and have ancestral houses and property there. Their efforts to organize themselves as a community and especially to help their group members get higher education go back to the beginning of this century. In 1912 an educational fund was established to give financial support to young Brahman boys and girls for higher education. The association has thrived through the years and now has substantial endowment funds. The majority of the Brahmans interviewed had finished school and many of them have college degrees. This educational level has been achieved not only by the younger generations but also by the previous two generations.

In terms of economic conditions, the Brahman group seems much better off than its non-Brahman counterpart. Brahmans hold the highest percentage of white-collar and professional jobs and also have a higher average income than the tailors or the Marathas. Many of them hold high administrative positions in private firms and in state and central government offices. The number of Brahmans who are engineers, doctors, lawyers, and college or university professors is also quite high in comparison to the numbers of tailors or Marathas holding such jobs. Available sources indicate that the situation was the same in the 1930s.[3] Thus it is obvious that Brahmans as a group are socioeconomically more advanced than tailors.

Until recently, the Brahman group in the Tamiḷ population enjoyed a long period as a political and cultural elite. This was due, to a considerable extent, to their religious domination of the rest of the population, to their superior position as the inheritors of the Great Tradition of Hinduism, and also to their favorable attitude toward Western education (Béteille 1969:66–67, 165; Hardgrave 1966:213). The Marathi-speaking Brahmans shared in this elite status and the advantages which accrued from it. The Marathi Brahman group has a great deal in common with its counterpart in the Tamiḷ population, the Tamiḷ Brahmans, with whom they share a number of rituals, religious rites, and extensive philosophical and classical literary knowledge, all part of the Great Tradition of Hinduism. They practice a number of religious restrictions similar to those followed by Tamiḷ Brahmans, reflecting their common beliefs in pollution and purity. The divisions between Marathi Brahmans are closely linked to those between Tamiḷ Brahmans, and are based primarily on religious and philosophical interpretations of Vedic texts. The two major religious sects among Tamiḷ Brahmans are that of the Smarthas [worshipers of Shiva and believers in *advaita* philosophy] and that of the Shri Vaishnavas [worshipers of Vishnu] (Béteille 1969:71). The Marathi Brahmans follow the same two sects, although the majority of them appear to be Smarthas and the distinction does not exist to the same rigid degree. More Brahmans in the Marathi-speaking community in Tamilnadu know the Devanagari script than non-Brahmans, not because they read Marathi literature but because they read Sanskrit religious scriptures.[4]

In recent years the social, political, and economic domination by the Brahmans in Tamilnadu has suffered a considerable setback because of the development of non-Brahman political forces, especially those in the Dravida Munnetra Kazhagam Party which now controls the state legislature. As a result, the Brahman community generally feels discriminated against with regard to higher education and jobs in government services (Béteille 1969:164–168). The Marathi Brahmans share this feeling with the Tamil Brahmans and complain about the deliberate discrimination against them and the lack of opportunities in various fields, even for qualified persons. Thus the Marathi Brahmans seem to identify them-

---

[3]   The economic inquiry undertaken by Rao and Rao (1937) included observation of family size, education, type of occupation, income, housing, and food consumption among Brahmans and non-Brahmans in the Marathi-speaking community in Madras. The conclusion of the inquiry was that Brahmans as a group were socioeconomically much better off than non-Brahmans.
[4]   Both Marathi and Sanskrit are written in the Devanagari script.

selves more with Brahmans in south India and to have little affinity with the Maharashtrians in Maharashtra.

Tailors

The tailors as a group appear to be more evenly distributed throughout Tamilnadu than the Brahmans, although they too are concentrated in large numbers in the four northern districts including Madras. They are more recent arrivals than the Brahmans. Most of them started their migration to the south with the British army camps approximately 150 years ago.

The majority of the tailors continue their traditional occupation, either in their own tailoring shops or working for others. Those who are not tailors are in related businesses, such as cloth selling or buying. The level of education among the tailors is low, and they fall into a much lower income group than the Brahmans. Very few of them hold whitecollar jobs and even fewer are in any high-status professions. No caste group comparable to the Marathi tailors exist in the dominant Tamil population. (Their only competitors are the Muslim tailors.)

The tailors are organized into formal associations in almost all towns in which they live in substantial numbers.[5] The goals of all tailor organizations appear primarily to be caste solidarity and high *varṇa* identity. The usual pattern of such organizations is to form a committee of active members of the community to collect funds, and to help the community members in whatever way possible. Most of the tailors' associations in various towns own buildings specially constructed so that they can be rented out for marriages and other special ceremonies. These buildings are provided without charge to community members for religious or other functions but are rented to those outside the community. Often such buildings are the primary source of income for the associations.

The tailors seem to desire a high *varṇa* identity. Because of their traditional occupation they are included in the third category of *vaishya* of the classical fourfold *varṇa* division. They claim Kshatriya status, however, by calling themselves Bhavasara Kshatriyas. They have myths which suggest that originally the tailors were Kshatriyas [warriors]; but in order to survive during a mass destruction of the Kshatriyas by a Brahman in ancient times, they concealed their Kshatriya identity and pretended to be dyers and tailors, as advised by a goddess. They have imitated many of the religious and cultural practices of the upper *varṇa*s. Thus their efforts seem to be directed toward a broader and higher *varṇa*

---

[5] Tailors are concentrated in large numbers in the following cities and towns of Tamilnadu: Coimbatore, Kumbhakonam, Madurai, Salem, Tirupattur, Vellore, and Walajah Pet. There are voluntary associations of tailors in all of them.

identity and the status associated with it. All associations of this kind in Tamilnadu are known as Bhavasara Kshatriya Associations.

The organizational pattern among the tailors in Tamilnadu is a microcosm of similar but large-scale activities undertaken by the tailors and dyers in all parts of south, west, and north India. These groups started their organizational attempts at the national level as early as 1911, when the first all-India Conference of the Bhavasara Kshatriyas was held in Dharwar in Mysore State. Since then the tradition of holding such conferences has continued, the last one having been held in Poona, Maharashtra in December 1972. The main office of the all-India organization known as Akhil Bharatiya Bhavasara Kshatriva Mahasabha [All-India Bhavasara Kshatriya Association] is located in Bombay. Histories of the Bhavasara Kshatriyas have been written in which elaborate origin myths are told and their claims to Kshatriya status are justified. The primary emphasis of the national organization is to encourage caste organization in various parts of the country and to encourage self-help among caste members toward better socioeconomic and educational status. The prominent members of the communities in different parts of India have built temples and hostels for students and have undertaken other similar activities for the benefit of the tailor communities. A monthly caste newsletter called *Bhavasar Jyoti* is published from Poona, Maharashtra.

The religious ideology and behavior of the tailors connect them closely to their original home region of Maharashtra. Tailors are worshipers of Panduranga or Viṭṭhal, a deity associated with an old and popular religious sect in Maharashtra, the *Vārkarī* sect (Deleury 1960). This particular sect still survives and has a large following all over Maharashtra. One of the important marks of affiliation with this sect is the semiannual pilgrimage to Pandharpur, where the oldest temple to the deity is located. From the thirteenth to the sixteenth century, a number of Marathi saints composed devotional songs in praise of the deity, and these are still popular among Marathi-speakers both within and outside Maharashtra. One of these saints, Namdev, was a tailor. He is one of the most popular saints and is said to have traveled as far north as Punjab to spread the worship of Panduranga and the philosophy of his religious sect. The tailors in Tamilnadu seem closely associated with this religious sect partly because of Namdev. In many Tamiḷ cities and towns with a large tailor community, temples to Panduranga have been built and are usually under the control of the local community associations.[6] In many others, there exist active *bhajan* [devotional song] groups which meet every week to sing the devotional songs in praise of Panduranga composed by Namdev and his contemporaries.

Thus the tailor community appears to retain its regional religious

[6] There are Panduranga temples in Coimbatore, Kumbhakonam, Madras, Vellore, and other cities in Tamilnadu.

identity which has a reference point outside Tamilnadu. At the same time the tailors are interested in upward social mobility for their whole caste group and have attempted to achieve it by claiming a higher *varṇa* status, as described earlier.

CONCLUSIONS

These rather brief descriptions of the two groups within the Marathi-speaking community in Tamilnadu clearly suggest that language, although retained by the community members in the home environment even after an absence from the homeland of more than one hundred years, does not play a significant role in creating a conscious ethnic identity for the entire community. Instead, each group appears to have a distinct focus of self-identity and emphasizes different criteria for it. The Brahmans lean toward their counterparts in the dominant population for ideological reasons and also because of common bonds at the economic, educational, and sociocultural levels. The tailors emphasize the *varṇa* identity within the framework of pan-Indian social structure, and their regional affiliation to their homeland in terms of their religious behavior. There is very little communication and interaction between Brahmans and tailors. Each group is thus self-perpetuating and uninterested in relating itself to any other status group within the minority community objectively identified as such. This conclusion is further supported by the existence of separate voluntary associations for each group, separate residential areas,[7] and separate modes of religious, occupational, and educational behavior.

The primary *raison d'être* for these different groups thus appears to be the socially ascribed status, which determines the nature of self-identity and motivation for either assimilation into or distinctness from the dominant population of Tamilnadu. The primary parameters of identity in this culture contact situation appear to be caste, religion, and region rather than language, although language is the main objective criterion distinguishing this community from the dominant population.

REFERENCES

APTE, MAHADEV L.
    1974   "Voluntary associations and problems of fusion and fission in a minor-
            ity community in south India." *Journal of Voluntary Action Research*
            3(1):43–48.

[7] In the city of Madras, Brahmans are primarily concentrated in such areas as Mylapore and Triplicane. The tailors, however, are scattered through all parts including some suburban areas.

BARTH, E., *editor*
1969   *Ethnic groups and boundaries.* Boston: Little, Brown.
BEALS, RALPH
1953   "Acculturation," in *Anthropology today.* Edited by A. L. Kroeber, 621–641. Chicago: University of Chicago Press.
BÉTEILLE, A.
1969   *Castes: old and new.* Bombay: Asia Publishing House.
DELEURY, G. A.
1960   *The cult of Vithoba.* Poona, India: Deccan College.
HARDGRAVE, R. L.
1966   "Religion, politics, and the DMK," in *South Asian politics and religion.* Edited by Donald E. Smith, 213–234. Princeton, N.J.: Princeton University Press.
HERSKOVITS, M. J.
1938   *Acculturation: the study of culture contact.* New York: J. J. Augustin.
RAO, T. RAMCHANDRA, B. R. DHONDU RAO
1937   "South Indian Maharashtrians," in *South Indian Maharashtrians,* Silver Jubilee Souvenir. Edited by N. R. Kedari Rao. Madras: Mahratta Educational Fund.
REDFIELD, R.
1955   The social organization of tradition. *The Far Eastern Quarterly* 15(1):13–21.
REDFIELD, R., R. LINTON, M. J. HERSKOVITS
1936   Outline for the study of acculturation. *American Anthropologist,* new series 38:149–152.
VREELAND, H. H.
1958   "The concept of ethnic groups as related to whole societies," in *Report of the ninth annual round table meeting on linguistics and language study.* Edited by W. M. Austin, 81–88. Georgetown Monograph Series on Languages and Linguistics 11. Washington, D.C.: Georgetown University Press.

Sociopsychological Bases of Language Choice and Use: The Case of Swahili Vernaculars and English in Kenya

JOSEPH MUTHIANI

Kenya, with its Europeans, most of whom speak English and Indian and generally communicate with non-Indians either in Swahili or English, added to its over forty ethnic and, therefore, linguistic groups, is an interesting arena for the study of an individual's choice of language in various situations. In this paper, the term "ethnic group" will be used when referring to any group whose members are culturally related or have the same or comparable national origin; e.g. the Europeans.

The history of Kenya has produced a complicated linguistic situation in functional terms. One can speak of VERNACULARS; meaning the languages of specific small ethnic groups, developed in various cultures to meet special needs (Molnos 1969:54). Vernaculars are not usually used to non-members of given ethnic groups. One can talk about MOTHER TONGUES, which are first languages for individuals, handed down from their mothers. For instance, a Luo person in an urban area may be taught Luo by his Luo-speaking mother (a mother tongue), but grow up speaking Swahili as his vernacular, because it is the language of his urban community, substituting his ethnic group. In another case, one can specify LINGUA FRANCAS, sometimes defined as languages which are habitually used between groups of people whose mother tongues (or vernaculars) are different (Heine 1960:15). Although a lingua franca is supposed to be a person's second language, occasionally, and in the case of Kenya, it can even be one's mother tongue, depending on the parties engaged in a conversation.

Obviously, Swahili is used in Kenya as a major lingua franca, initially spreading from the coast into the mainland among the Bantu-speaking ethnic groups (Harries 1966:224–229). In its creation, as Brain suggests on the basis of recent studies of marriage patterns on the coast, Arab men married African women whose offspring, although claiming the ethnic identity of their fathers, would speak the languages of their mothers (Brain 1969:4). In that situation, a language with a Bantu structure developed as a medium of communication. Heine suggests that on the basis of differing linguistic traditions between people of the northern and southern coastal ranges of Swahili, the language originated on the northern Kenya coast, sometime between A.D. 700 and A.D. 800. It was then spread by economic expansion and the rise and growth of Islam, among other factors (Heine 1960:82–83).

With the presence of Swahili-speaking traders in the interior of the country, Swahili became established as an important lingua franca with the various trading centers acting as its dissemination points (Polomé 1967:12), although there were geographical, cultural and historical factors upsetting its chances for a rapid spread (Brain 1969:71). The establishment of colonial rule in East Africa had immense repercussions with linguistic consequences. In the work of governing and developing the colonies, new types of communication and linguistic patterns were developed.

Since, at the initiation of colonialism in East Africa, Swahili was already used widely as a lingua franca, the Germans adopted it, along with German, as an official language in their Tanganyika possession. Since the Germans' African assistants had to be educated in Swahili, the prestige of the language among Africans has risen ever since. Indirectly, this policy raised the status of Islam, because a great number of the Africans educated in Swahili were Muslims. Also, the Germans boosted the status of Swahili by transcribing it into Latin script from the previous Arabic script, the former being better suited to express certain elements of the language (Brain 1969:9). The Germans' deliberation was advantageous, not only in Tanganyika, but also in Kenya.

When missionaries first came to East Africa, they found Swahili invaluable to their work (Heine 1960:92–94). They used it frequently since it was already a lingua franca of several areas they traveled to to establish mission stations. In the struggle between Christian and Muslim missionaries for larger numbers of converts, the use of the language was intensified. A story is told about how one missionary's Swahili porter would convert other porters to Islam behind his employer's back by virtue of the porters' ability to use Swahili (Brain 1969:10). Such occurrences caused the Christian missionaries to distrust Swahili because of its association with Islam (Heine 1960:91), but its use even among Africans themselves still increased. Eventually, Christian missionaries tended to use vernaculars instead, thus elevating their status also. Considering the fact that religious organizations largely controlled and supported the education system in the colonies, it is easy to see how powerful the effect of their preference for vernaculars could be. The curricula put emphasis on vernaculars as the medium of instruction for primary schools and on

English for secondary schools (all the early secondary schools were run by missionaries), and this practice played a major role in shaping the linguistic situation of Kenya.

We now come to the situation whereby the Africans in Kenya were exposed to English and Swahili away from home, and to their vernaculars in small linguistically homogeneous groups and at home. But the use of Swahili had the most favorable chance to become dominant, thanks to the increased population that came with the building of the railway from the coast to Uganda. Swahili rapidly became the language of the railway workers and the medium of communication between employers and employees. Thus, by the beginning of the colonial period, Africans in Kenya began to be gradually pulled in two different linguistic directions — Swahili and English.

The colonial administration encouraged the immigration of European settlers to the colony. These Europeans, though coming from various countries of Europe were considered as, and formed, one ethnic group. At the same time, the Asians, most of whom were Indians, and most of whom had discovered the importance of Swahili while laborers in railway construction, formed another ethnic group as they became specialized as a merchant class. Of necessity, these new ethnic groups generated a dialect of Swahili, later to be known as *Kisetla,* because of its intensive use by the European settlers who, unlike the Indians who were becoming something like middleclass merchants and, in practice, the middlemen between Africans and Europeans, lacked direct contact with African vernaculars.

It is sometimes suggested that *Kisetla* may have been encouraged by a pattern in which European children, in contact with Swahili-speaking nursemaids during their infancy, learned a form of "babytalk" Swahili. Separated from their nursemaids before learning advanced Swahili, these children grew up thinking the Swahili they spoke was the real thing (Brain 1969:13). I disagree with this theory on the grounds that *Kisetla* was formed by European settlers as a functional communication tool. In this case, it was the mature European settlers, not their children, who needed to communicate. Having no time to learn the standard rules of the structure of the language, their linguistic interaction with the other groups forced them to use different rules so long as they were able to be understood. Anyone who can speak "standard Swahili" could use these rules and produce perfect *Kisetla.* For instance (the examples are not inclusive):

I.   For the present tense, just use the verb stem:
/*Yeye fanya kazi sana*/
instead of /*Yeye anafanya . . .*/ 'He works hard'.
/*Karibu fika*/ for /*Karibu Kufika*/ 'almost arriving'.

II.   Future Tense → Present Tense + Adverb of Time.
      Past Tense → Present Tense + Adverb of Time.
      /Mimi fanya kazi kesho/ 'I will work tomorrow'.
      /Mimi fanya kazi jana/ 'I worked yesterday'.
III. Simple Subjunctives → Uninflected Verb Stem:
      /Kwenda pika chakula/ for /Kwenda ukapike chakula/
      'Go [and] cook food'.
IV.   Negative → No + Verb Stem:
      /Hapana simama hapa/ for /Usisimame hapa/ 'Don't stand here'.
V.   Direct Object → Verb Stem + Personal Pronoun:
      /Mimi piga wewe/ for /nitakupiga/ 'I'll strike you'.
VI.   All Class Concords → N-Class Morphemes (Markers):
      /mtu hii/ for /mtu huyu/ 'this person'
      /matunda kubwa/ for /matunda makubwa/ 'large fruits'
VII. Grammar Translation is alright:
      a. [WH] Questions → [WH] at Subject Position.
         /Maduka yako wapi/ → /Wapi maduka/ 'Where are the stores?'
         /Waanza lini/ → /Lini waanza/ 'When do you start?'
         /Wewe ni nani/ → /Nani wewe/ 'Who are you?'
         /Unafanya nini/ → /Nini unafanya/ 'What are you doing?'
      b. Impersonal Verb to have:
         i. use the locative -ko (English uses the verb to be for this)
         ii. introduce the sentences with the -ko forms.
         /Kuna daraja/ → /Iko da raja/ 'Is there a bridge?'
         /Kuna dijiji/ → /Kiko kijiji/ 'Is there a village?'
         /Kuna mji mkubwa/ → /Uko mji mkubwa/ 'Is there a city
         (large town)?'

Phonologically

I.   Avoid Nasals:
     a. by dropping them;
        e.g. /watu wanne/ → /watu wane/ 'four people';
     b. by supplying a vowel (usually u) after the nasal;
        /mji/ → /muji/ 'town/city' /mut/ → /mutu/ 'person'
        Thus /mtu hii/ (above) is actually /mutu hii/.
II. Use some English stress:
     /walákini/ → /wálakini/ 'nevertheless'
     /tafádhali/ → /tafádhali/ 'please'
     /lázima/ → /lázima/ 'must' or 'necessary'.

Some aspects of *Kisetla* have been incorporated into colloquial, but standard, Swahili. One hears a lot of standard Swahili speakers saying /tafádhali/, /walákini/, etc. However, this seems to fit a psychological explanation that such speakers are "educated" Africans who subconsciously try to imitate members of their social status, some of whom are Europeans. This confirms the theory that the process of KISETLANIZATION was the work of Africans responding to adult Europeans in the same manner as the latter spoke to them. The process was more pronounced where communication was between a European and an African of very low status. The latter, who may have been a good Swahili-speaking African, would at first be surprised by the Europeans' deviant linguistic forms, but, because of his low status, he was in no position to correct the Europeans (Brain 1969:13). Unwilling to embarrass the Europeans by using the standard forms in his reply, he would use the new style.[1]

However, because many of the European settlers came from South Africa where they had farmed what the Africans considered their own land, there was some resentment of some of their language forms among the Africans. All South African Europeans were considered *Kaburu*, a term which essentially means "the Boer." To an African, the name *"Kaburu"* has negative connotations, such as "naughtily conceited," "rude," and "sneering." Africans saw *Kaburus* as purposely refusing to learn standard Swahili because they considered such an action as lowering their status to the level of the Africans. Their lack of perception and recognition of some aspects of African culture aggravated this feeling.

For instance, consider: */Kuja hapa boi/* 'Come here boy!' */Kwenda lete bunduki/* 'Go, bring the gun!' */Kuja/* and */Kwenda/* are common verbs used in commands. The word */boi/* corrupted from /boy/ was used to refer to African servants, most of whom would not be called "boys" in their African cultural setting since they were circumcised mature men. Consequently, *kwenda* was, for a long time, considered rude in an imperative sentence. Up to now, *kuja*, as an imperative verb, has not yet been considered proper in a normal communication. Instead, *njoo*, which cannot be inflected into any other forms, replaces it.

The scope of the effect of particular language forms is dependent on the number of people who use them. Here, we find a confirmation of this rule. Because of the intensive use of imperative forms by all Europeans, even non-*Kaburu*, the Africans came to conceive them as one and the same group. This is indicated by the saying, *"Hakuna tofauti baina ya Mzungu na Kaburu"* [there is no difference between a European and a Boer] — voiced whenever an African complains about the misdeeds of a certain European.

The colonial, and even post-colonial, language policy has had a tremendous effect on language use in Kenya. Since education is the critical differential for development and subsequent cultural change, it is through

---

[1] Of course, some Africans would favor the European style, if they did not know the standard form.

education that the knowledge and skills of the Western World were passed to Kenyans in the process of modernization (Lepage 1964:4–13). The British provided the link between Kenyans and the Western World. As a result, English became the medium through which the skills for development were, and still are, learned and used. It is the language of the high-paying jobs which require formal education. Because of this association with gainful employment, knowledge of English as a symbol of education gives an African, at least symbolically, a high status (Molnos 1969:13).

Swahili, on the contrary, seems to be associated with less educated people who mainly work as laborers. It is largely considered as the language of the "masses" and the medium of politics (Whiteley 1969:114). For instance, /Harambee/ [a calling cry to do something together] was formerly associated only with lower status people, or the laborer class. After its adoption as a national motto and incorporation onto the coat of arms of the Republic of Kenya, its connotation became ameliorated. Another word that followed the same process is /Wananchi/ [fellow countrymen]. Before its adoption into politics, it meant "a native" (with contemptuous connotations). By personal experience I have found that many Africans who can speak English but have low-status jobs (e.g. auto mechanics and farm workers) would rather speak Swahili than English. This is their usual practice with the lower status people they are always in contact with.

So, as an index of the structuring of social relations, language use in Kenya may be used to predict social behaviors between members of different ethnic and task groups, with very limited exceptions. These behaviors, says Fishman (1967:4) are largely based on status and role expectations. We are warned that the ". . . more extreme forms of social stratification would tend to generate 'restricted' codes in its low-status groups, and . . . any educational system controlled by the high-status groups, will be designed to preserve the *status quo*" (Whiteley 1970:88). In Kenya, this situation resulted in the evolution of three major communication functions — in-group language, out-group language, and the language of specialized information. The crystallization of these patterns structured the symbolic bases for language choice for intragroup and intergroup relations.

With the highest probability, one can predict that an African who knows English would use it with a European stranger even without any knowledge as to whether the European understands it. An African would be likely to approach an African stranger in Swahili, but if they both know English and they are both acquainted, they would use English, so long as they do not normally speak the same vernacular. Likewise, Asians would use their ethnic languages among themselves, Swahili to Africans, and English to Europeans. Europeans also would use their various languages among themselves, English to the Asians and Africans who know English, and Swahili to those who look as if they do not understand English (low-status category) — e.g. in transactions such as shopping.

The above observations tend to support the theory that language choice is influenced by the role and status of the individual in relation to that of the other participants in a speech event. "A status, as distinct from the individual who may occupy it, is simply a collection of rights and duties. . . . A role represents the dynamic aspects of a status" (Linton, 1936:113). The sociological theory which maintains that every member of the society represents a number of role-sets and status-sets calls for the theory of THE DEFINITION OF THE SITUATION, which simply means the stage of examination and deliberation preliminary to any self-determined act of behavior (Coser and Rosenberg 1968:233). To illustrate this: an educated African in Kenya, say a civil servant, will write his work reports in English, use Swahili at public meetings, and speak his vernacular with his family. Thus, each situation is defined in a way that calls for the choice of its functional language.

Having given a summary of the process by which three major ethnic groups were formed — African, Asians and Europeans — and the three major language patterns — vernaculars, Swahili and English — let me now give a few general propositions concerning inter-ethnic language choice and use. I will try, also, to show how empirical observations back these propositions and how the language choices and uses are linked with sociopsychological phenomena. This is just an attempt, since I am no expert in any of these fields. English and Swahili will be treated here as lingua francas and the local or intra-ethnic lingua francas, like *Gunjarati* and African and European vernaculars, will be ignored.

Proposition 1

Although vernaculars are typical of intra-ethnic group communication, patterns of social stratification may force an individual to use lingua francas for members of his own ethnic group.

OBSERVATIONS. Within their own families and with members of their own ethnic groups, members of each ethnic group use their vernaculars. But, it is important to recognize that any speaker may control several languages (at least three) or portions of them ". . . and change from one to another for situational reasons" (Fishman 1970:280). Thus, in official hours, most people in Kenya will tend to use English; for shopping in the city center they may use Swahili. This may be done by members of the same ethnic group with the same vernacular. In this context, the choice and use of English can be predicted with the highest probability. Swahili will be used if the identity of the business man/woman is obscure.

Proposition 2

Lingua francas are used for communication across ethnic lines.

OBSERVATIONS. Swahili is used as a lingua franca intensively between Africans and Asians but if an African and an Asian meet a European, it will be highly probable that they will switch to English if they intend to include him in the discussion. The reverse is also predictable — an African and a European will switch from English to Swahili if they want to include an Indian in their discussion. Here the two parties are assuming that the third party does not understand English. Should their assumption be wrong, they will then switch back to English, very often, because the third party will respond in English, probably to show them he is also educated (remember, English is a symbol of education). Thus, it is apparent that different speech systems or codes create for their speakers different orders of relevance and relations. "The experience of the speakers may be then transformed by what is made significant or relevant by different speech systems" (Gumperz and Hymes 1972:473).

Proposition 3

Lingua francas tend to be adopted after prolonged contact between the groups involved.

OBSERVATIONS. We have seen how Swahili was adopted by coastal peoples after their long contact with Asian and also African traders. As it came upland, the choice became between it and English, depending on which one a person had most contact with. This confirms the notion that dynamics of language behavior depend on sociocultural dynamics of particular multilingual speech communities at particular periods in their history. Here, "the emphasis is on the individual choosing among alternative modes of behaviour in accordance with linguistic social constraints" (Fishman 1967:280). It takes time to choose a lingua franca as an alternative for one's own vernacular. In the case of Kenya, one's linguistic behavior is ascribed by virtue of his belonging to a certain social group which has a long history in its structuring.

Thus, where the relationship between the persons has been previously structured and a particular language used by them, it is difficult to pass over to a new

language. The language has become an intrinsic part of the structural relationship.
. . . (Fishman 1967:503).

Proposition 4

The larger the group in a speech community, the less its resistance towards accepting a new language.

OBSERVATIONS. "The psychological basis of the established social norms, such as stereotypes, conventions, customs and values, is the formation of common frames of reference as a product of the contact of the individuals" (Sherif 1966:106). To establish a desirable group frame of reference for the uses of English and Swahili in various situations in Kenya, a large number of people was necessary to convince people that their stereotypes were practical and proper. Language is a group produce with ". . . natural and conventional signs which make up the communication system for the group" (Hall 1970:98). Without large units of each ethnic group in Kenya with desirable attitudes, the use of Swahili and English as lingua francas could have been difficult. The Europeans would rather use English, because it is "the language of the (colonizing) master." The Asians would rather use Swahili, because most of them are businessmen and have no time for the kind of education that makes one capable of handling English. The Africans would resent English because it is a "colonial language" and Swahili because of its associations with the slave-trading Arabs. To placate this situation, large units using these lingua francas mushroomed convincing members of their ethnic groups that the new language behaviors were acceptable.

Proposition 5

Establishments of definite functional roles for different languages in a society tend to create a stable multilingualism.

OBSERVATIONS. Since the monopoly of access to languages of specified information can be viewed as a retention of class privilege by elites, those in Kenya who have access to English, which is the language of specified information in the sense that it is the language of higher education, tend to stabilize this role — either functionally or symbolically. At the same time, Swahili is the language of wider communication in the country and its role is indispensible. This raises the probability of many Kenyans, especially Africans and Asians being trilingual. The individual's choice of one language over the others will always depend on his definition of the situation.

Proposition 6

The status or prestige imparted by a language to the participants in a speech event is an important factor in language choice.

OBSERVATIONS.   With the notion that social acts have intended and unintended functions, the consequence of an act may be the consequence intended or it may be one which was not intended. In empirical terms, when Africans and Asians in Kenya use English as "the language of education," they subconsciously raise their status or assume the prestige of the educated elite. Conversely, when Kenya Europeans use Swahili to the Africans and Asians they do not know, they assume that the latter belong to the lower, semi-educated and less-prestigious status. Should the Africans or Asians understand English, they would use it right away, thus showing that they do not belong to that symbolically lower class. The three levels of actions are applicable here (Dewey and Bantley 1949): (1) Reaction — where things are viewed as acting under their own powers, (2) Interaction — where thing is balanced against thing, and (3) Transaction — where all phases of action are dealt with as a unit.

Proposition 7

Conceptual advantages in the use of a particular language influence the individual's choice of a functional language.

OBSERVATIONS.   It has already been stated that language behaviors among the three ethnic groups in Kenya are ascribed in the sense that the individual has no choice but to observe the norms already established when the status and role he fills were established. So, the structured groups consist not only of differentiated parts, but also of internal and external relations of the members of these various groups. From this point of view, a member's location in the social structure is of great importance. It is not possible for an individual to find all locations satisfying. However, "If he is satisfied with his location, he may make great effort to maintain it and resist anything that might bring about a change in the structure of the group" (Cartwright and Zandler 1953:79). Thus, the satisfying advantages of language use in Kenya perpetuate the already structured patterns, causing constraints to any possible deviation of behavior.

So goes the story of language use in Kenya. The foregoing is but a sketchy explanation of the patterns and bases by which the three ethnic groups choose Swahili over English, and vice versa, for functional communication. It is not hard to explain why a person has to speak a lingua franca — if it is the only way to communicate, he will be forced by the situation to attempt the little he thinks he knows even to the point of pidginizing the lingua franca. Or, after several repeated occasions, the languages of both parties may be pidginized to eventually form a lingua franca. However, when there is more than one lingua franca and the parties in a speech event may understand all of them (at least some of their forms), then we may need a psychological explanation as to why one is chosen over another. Without a practical field research one may push things where they do not belong. This is very apparent with things psychological; this is why it was thought best to correlate psychological probabilities with observable and explainable sociological behavior patterns. Table 1 summarizes the predictability of the Kenyan language situation.

Table 1. Predicting language choice in Kenya

Lower ⟶ Lower			
	African	*Indian*	*European*
African	Swahili/ Vernacular	Swahili	Swahili*
Indian	Swahili	Vernacular**	Swahili
European	Swahili	Swahili	English

Lower ⟶ High			
	African	*Indian*	*European*
African	Swahili	Swahili	Swahili
Indian	Swahili	Vernacular	Swahili
European	English	English	English

High ⟶ Lower			
	African	*Indian*	*European*
African	Swahili/ Vernacular	Swahili	English
Indian	Swahili	Vernacular	English
European	Swahili	Swahili	English

High ⟶ High			
	African	*Indian*	*European*
African	English	English	English
Indian	English	English/ Vernacular	English
European	English	English	English

* e.g. A lower-status African approaching a lower-status African will very likely use Swahili or an African vernacular; for a lower-status Indian he will use Swahili; for a lower-status European he will use Swahili.
** e.g. *Ego* will use a vernacular of his ethnic group if the identity of *Alter* is known to him, or if *Alter* responds in a given vernacular.

REFERENCES

BRAIN, JAMES
1969   "Basic structures of Swahili," part 2. Syracuse University.
CARTWRIGHT, D., A. ZANDER, *editors*
1953   *Group dynamics*. New York: Harper and Row.
COSER, LEWIS, BERNARD ROSENBERG, *editors*
1968   *Sociological theory*. New York: MacMillan.
DEWEY, JOHN, ARTHUR BANTLEY
1949   *Knowing and the known*. Boston: The Beacon Press.
FISHMAN, JOSHUA
1967   *Language problems of developing nations*. Oxford: Oxford University Press.
1970   *Readings in the sociology of language*. The Hague: Mouton.
GUMPERZ, JOHN, DELL HYMES, *editors*
1972   *Directions in sociolinguistics*. New York: Holt, Rinehart and Winston.
HALL, D. M.
1970   *Dynamics of group action*. Danville, Illinois: Interstate Printers and Publishers.
HARRIES, LYNDON
1966   "Swahili in modern Africa." Paper presented at a Conference on the Language Problems of Developing Nations, at Airlie House, Va., November.
HEINE, BERN
1960   *Status and use of African lingua francas*. Munich: Weltforum.
LEPAGE, R. B.
1964   *The national language question*. Oxford: Oxford University Press.
LINTON, R.
1936   *The study of man*. New York: Appleton-Century, 1936.
MOLNOS, ANGELA
1969   *Language problems in Africa*. East African Research Centre, Circular 2.
POLOMÉ, EDGAR
1967   *Swahili language handbook*. Washington, D.C.: Center for Applied Linguistics.
SHERIF, MUZAFER
1966   *The psychology of social norms*. New York: Harper and Row.
WHITELEY, WILFRED
1969   *Swahili, the rise of a national language*. London: Methuen.
WHITELEY, WILFRED, *editor*
1970   *Language use and social change*. Oxford: Oxford University Press.

Cree–English Bilingualism in Northern Alberta

REGNA DARNELL

Much of the population of the present-day world is bilingual, yet linguists have, for the most part, continued to assume that a language is a language is a language, etc., whether it is spoken as a first language, an only language, a second language, or one of several languages. When serious attention has been given to the multiple language competence of bilingual and multilingual speakers (e.g. Weinreich 1966), attention has tended to be restricted to linguistic interference between two idealized language systems. Factors of social environment and language use, in such a view, are secondary and can be classified blandly as "extralinguistic."

The perspective of anthropology and other social sciences has, in contrast, the advantage of dealing with social reality in interaction with linguistic systems to show what real people are up to when they speak to each other in one or more languages. It is this social–functional context which constitutes perhaps the most important contribution of linguistic anthropology to linguistic theory at the present time. The assumption of the social scientist, in contrast to that of the linguist, is that language use is a socially adaptive process whereby members of human societies interact with one another and among themselves. To speak a language thus means not only to know its formal structures and produce grammatical sentences but also to use such grammatical utterances in socially appropriate ways.

Two Cree Language Development Workshops were held in the Province of Alberta, Canada, in June and August of 1972, sponsored by the Department of Indian Affairs and Northern Development. I am grateful for the opportunity to have participated in these workshops in the dubious capacity of non-native speaker with training in anthropology and linguistics. I would particularly like to thank Roseanna Houle, Margaret Makosis, Maggie Dion, and Frances Thompson for their help and patience. Barbara Burnaby read the original draft of this paper. A. L. Vanek shared in the research and provided feedback at all stages. Financial support for my own fieldwork has come from the Boreal Institute of the University of Alberta.

In recent years, precedents for such a view of bilingualism and language function have developed in several disciplines, including linguistics per se. Chomsky has set for linguistics a goal of reflecting in linguistic description the knowledge that speakers of a language must have to produce grammatical utterances. This "knowledge" has, however, been understood as knowledge of linguistic rules (without reference to knowledge of one or more additional languages). Anthropologists have been among those to reformulate this goal to include the wider knowledge speakers must have to use their language, for example, in the concept of "communicative competence" as elaborated by Hymes. From such a perspective, it is the language USE which is foremost and the language STRUCTURE which is EMPLOYED to bring about socially meaningful ends.

This paper will describe a single case in which bilingual speakers of Cree and English in northern Alberta have attempted to examine their own bilingual situation in order to encourage language maintenance among young Indians. Although none of the individuals involved are trained linguists, they ARE the experts on their situation and are highly motivated to make their own knowledge explicit so that it can be effectively transmitted to the next generation. Because there is little educational material written in Cree and there are few Cree people with formal teaching credentials, the individuals who wish to develop teaching programs in their language have to draw upon their own knowledge to prepare materials and implement their use in classrooms. The author of this paper has been fortunate to participate in such a project. An examination of the way in which native speakers of Cree went about constructing language materials will be used here to illustrate the kind of linguistic knowledge which speakers CAN abstract from their own experiences in speaking two languages if there is a compelling reason to seek such generalization.

Native peoples throughout Alberta, and North America generally, have turned progressively more attention to the formal teaching of their languages in recent years as pressure from the majority culture has increased. One important goal of the proposed American Indian Cultural Center in Edmonton, Alberta, is the attainment by students of fluency in both English and Indian languages; this is seen as a prerequisite of educational upgrading in an English-based curriculum. Much of the recent impetus toward language teaching comes from the so-called pan-Indian movement, in which native peoples from many tribes and geographical areas are becoming aware of shared problems of linguistic and cultural retention. Many Indian leaders have returned to their own tribes and reservations with a new determination that being Indian is important in today's world. Like the shared symbols of buffalo hunting and Plains headdress, the continued viability of native languages has become a crucial part of remaining Indian.

The Province of Alberta has forty-two bands and eight official languages, a mosaic of linguistic diversity which makes the Canadian problem of French versus English seem simple. In several of these languages, extensive programs are now underway to teach the languages and prepare educational materials in them. The remainder of this paper will deal with the efforts made by the Cree (the largest group of native language speakers in northern Alberta) to carry out such a program.

The Cree Language Development Workshops were explicitly organized to provide materials which could be used throughout the Province of Alberta, although there is considerable dialect divergence in the included area (still within Plains Cree). This required a spirit of compromise among the delegates from diverse reserves. In linguistic terms, it meant settling on the dialect of central Alberta as a standard form. In social terms, it meant that materials should be adaptable for use with children who spoke no Cree at all as well as those who spoke only Cree. The magnitude of the task was clearly recognized from the outset. In an effort to represent the accumulated knowledge of the Cree about their language, the teachers participating in the workshop stressed the need to invite Indian leaders, particularly old men, to come and work with the group. The old men knew Cree as it was spoken in the old days,[1] and the teachers, most of whom were younger and more fully bilingual, wanted to ensure that they would be teaching the "proper" Cree.

Another concern of the group was for Provincial government recognition of the native language skills of Cree teachers. The workshops were conceived as formal training in Cree and in teaching methods; as a result, the teachers wanted recognition that they were specialists. The trend in Alberta is toward such recognition, although it is a slow process. Many of the present Cree instructors are still formally classified as teacher aids, although they take full responsibility for language classes. Recent amendment of the Alberta School Act to allow for instruction in any language where facilities, teaching materials, and qualified staff are available encourages projects such as the one described here.

In making their decisions the participants drew eloquently on their own bilingual experience to search for solutions to the educational problems of their children. Most of the participants were middle-aged ladies who had attended mission schools; they are Cree-dominant bilinguals (dominance based on relative fluency in the two languages and on switching to Cree in informal social contexts). Descriptions by these ladies of their early education in English schools are strikingly similar. Oral English was

[1] I have elsewhere (Darnell 1971:159–160) referred to this old-style language as "traditional Cree," contrasting it with informal or "Anglicized" Cree. Certainly it is the elders who are the recognized authorities on Cree language and it is THEIR knowledge which speakers of all generations are eager to see passed on to their children. Many of these less authoritative speakers will, of course, themselves become elders.

never taught, and reading and writing were taught by memory. Indian
students learned to read long passages without understanding what they
read. Teachers did not speak Cree and could not, therefore, use contrastive examples from Cree to ensure understanding of English. Most of the
students learned their English at home, where the English spoken was a
local form divergent in many respects from the standard English of the
classroom. For many individuals with this kind of educational background, standard English remains a fossil throughout life.

Because the teaching of English was formal and mechanical, many
Cree-dominant bilinguals almost totally lack intuition for the productive
processes of English. For example, the forms "work," "workable," and
"worse" will all be seen as unrelated, that is, as separate lexical items; that
"workable" is derived from "work" and that other English words are
treated in the same manner is not perceived. This phenomenon is particularly interesting in light of the fact that Cree, a so-called polysynthetic
language, constructs new words in this form much more frequently than
does English.

Many native speakers find Cree morphology transparent. For example,
the following are Cree compound nouns:

Tōtōs	'breast'
-*Apoy*	'liquid'
Tōtōsāpoy	'milk'
Tōtōsāpopimiy	'butter'
-*pimiy*	'grease'
Tōtōsāpopimihkan	'margarine'
-*khan*	'fake, artificial'

In explaining these forms to me, one native speaker of Cree split the
syllables incorrectly to correspond to the morhpology, i.e. *tō-tōs-apoy*
rather than *tō-tō-sa-poy*. These would, of course, normally be pronounced according to the syllables, following the CV–CV . . . structure
normal to Cree (consonant clusters are always CVC–CVC), but in
explaining the word, the morphology was seen as paramount.[2] However,
when the same native speaker was pressed concerning morphological
productivity IN ENGLISH, the result was a feeling that English structure
does not allow for that sort of thing. Apparently one of the things a Cree
speaker has to learn in order to speak English is that words are isolated
units whose form does NOT change. This may then be overgeneralized to
obscure perception of instances in which English operates in the fashion
associated with Cree.

The same tendency toward compartmentalization of linguistic patterns

---

[2]   Compare Sapir's Southern Paiute example (1949:49–50) used by him to postulate a
notion of "psychological reality" which could outweigh linguistic structure in perception of
the analyst *cum* native speaker.

is found in the assignment of stress. For example, in English there is a difference between "black bird" and "blackbird" which is generally described by linguists in terms of juncture. Many Cree compounds are formed similarly. However, several native speakers of Cree consistently fail to distinguish between these two forms in English, although two separate Cree words are necessary to translate them:

kaskitew piēsīs	'black bird'
chachakayos	'blackbird'

Stress is apparently not felt to be a feature of meaning in English. Native speakers of Cree seem to generalize that English words have a set stress pattern and that Cree words reassign stress in the surface structure depending on inflection; for example, in the imperative, the underlined syllable receives stress:

a-pik	'you [plural] sit down'
a-pī-tan	'let us sit down'
mītsōk	'you [plural] eat'
mītsotān	'let us eat'

Thus, when English DOES use stress to distinguish between two forms, native speakers of Cree tend to hear the forms as homologous.

In devising teaching materials, the ladies, themselves Cree-dominant bilinguals, had to think in terms of children for whom Cree would often be a second language. They were unanimous in recognizing a need for materials graded in difficulty so that children could follow them easily while knowing little Cree. In implementation, however, this required some index of degree of difficulty. The most obvious criterion was length of word, which was understood to mean number of syllables; morphological transparency did not seem to affect perception of a long word as difficult.

In line with the aim of introducing simple material first, the conference participants decided to prepare a basic word-list of fifty items to be used with preschool children. The assumption was that whole sentences were too long to remember and that simple lexicon was the place to start. The word-list included simple commands, everyday objects, and the numbers from one to five.

Suggestions for reading material for primary school children were, however, more interesting. In spite of the agreement that length of a word should be the major criterion for difficulty, a number of long words were included in the storybook prepared by the group as a whole. Other words, though of equal length, were rejected as being hard and more appropriate for older children. In this case, cultural value outweighed linguistic form in determining what was difficult to learn. The words which were considered easy were words used in normal conversational Cree. The words rejected as difficult were words more appropriate to formal Cree narrative, many of them archaic and not known even to all adult speakers of the language. All of the teachers realized that, whatever might be the ultimate aim of fluency in traditional Cree, teaching must start with basic informal speech. Appropriateness to formal narrative would cause a word to be classified as "too hard" even if it was very short, indicating that speech style was more important than sheer length in deciding what to use in elementary materials.

Perhaps the most crucial decision which had to be made by the workshops was regarding a standard orthography. Because the materials were to be used throughout Alberta Province, the decision was to use both syllabics and roman orthography. In some areas of the province, Cree syllabics are felt to be undesirable because of their association with missionaries; elsewhere, Cree is not Cree unless it is written in syllabics. Individual variation in children's fluency also encouraged the group to use a roman orthography in addition to the syllabics.

All of the workshop participants were concerned about maintaining the purity of the Cree language in spite of extensive contact with English. However, there were three major strategies within this concern:

1. Cree words should be pronounced in their full form, without contraction of any syllables;
2. Lexical borrowings from English should be avoided;
3. Missionaries and other emissaries of the white society should not be permitted to discourage Cree people from continuing to use their own language.

All three of these aims inclined the group toward placing its stress on syllabics rather than on some adaptation of the English alphabet.

It is, however, in the full pronunciation of Cree words that syllabic orthography most particularly provides a means to ensure "correct" speech. The Cree spoken in northern Alberta has a late phonetic rule in rapid speech which reduces high unstressed vowels. For example:

kinistohten chi?[3] 'Do you speak Cree?' (careful speech)
kinstohten chi? 'Do you speak Cree?' (rapid speech)

In some instances the dropping of such a vowel causes stress to be reassigned in the word or sentence. For example:[4]

Māmiskochikātew kakinōtinitohk. 'It tells of the rebellion' (careful speech)
Māmskochkātew kakinōtntohk. 'It tells of the rebellion' (rapid speech)

In the second form, two syllables are reduced to consonant clusters in the

---

[3] The /h/ is a phonetic preaspiration of the stop in the next syllable.
[4] This sentence is taken from materials prepared by Anne Anderson of Edmonton.

first word and two more in the second (in the second word, the /n/ becomes syllabic). The underlined syllables show the effect on stress. Many Cree speakers are aware of differences in pronunciation depending on speed of utterance and can repeat words at different speeds without confusion.

The Cree teachers were unanimous that syllabic writing would encourage continued writing of the reduced vowels as the "proper" way to write Cree. They were not concerned about pronunciation but felt that the spelling should reflect the full (noncontracted) forms. Thus, syllabic writing constitutes a relatively abstract phonological representation. It is not simply a phonetic writing system; what is written is very often not pronounced. Many of the mistakes made by primary school children learning to read and write syllabics indicate that they have not learned to spell words at this more abstract level but are simply writing what they hear in their own speech.

Vowel reduction, of course, vastly increases the number of incomplete syllables written by the children. Children learning to write syllabics do not hear the reduced vowels and do not feel any need for them to round out the syllabic structure normal to Cree. They are also, of course, influenced by the English alphabet, which uses the letter rather than the syllables as its basic unit. Children in school have already learned the alphabet and find it easier to learn a new writing system if they can simply equate a letter with a syllabic symbol. This is possible only with the final symbols, so they are learned more quickly than the full syllable units (consonant plus vowel), which are the basic units for the Cree syllabic orthography.

Adults concerned with writing Cree also make mistakes which reflect the linguistic intuition behind their syllabic writing. For example, there is a tendency toward hypercorrection in which syllables are filled out where they should not be:

*pāsikisigan for pāskisigan 'gun'

In this lexical item, /s/ SHOULD be written as a syllable final rather than as a reduced vowel of the syllable /si/. Yet individuals who have written the Cree language extensively will often overgeneralize and expand a syllable which actually does not have the reduced vowel. Some words, of course, do have natural syllables which use these final markers, for example, *mispon* 'it is snowing'. These are unusual if not irregular forms and only practice can show the non-native speaker which include reduced vowels and which do not. Moreover, Cree speakers in English frequently syllabify ENGLISH words to conform to a CV–CV structure. For example, Father Le Calvez of the Beaver Lake Mission at Lac La Biche records a persistent mispronunciation of the English name "Flora" as "*Pe-lo-na.*" That is, /f/ does not exist and a vowel insertion is necessary to make it a full syllable. The /l/ is non-native to Plains Cree, but is known from many proper names; /lo/ is a full syllable. The /r/ is absent in the dialect and becomes /n/; /na/ is a full syllable.

The syllabic writing system is also abstract in that it provides a geometrical representation of the form of the language. Each consonant is represented by a shape which is rotated through four planes, each of which represents a vowel. Four is the sacred number of Cree tradition and the writing system reflects a four-way symmetry which is in keeping with the cultural symbolism. The psychological reality of the vowel system, then, is as follows in (a):

(a)

In articulatory terms, however, the reality is less symmetrical (b), and in terms of phonetic realization (c), a fifth vowel is necessary which is not present in the syllabic orthography at all.

(b)   (c)

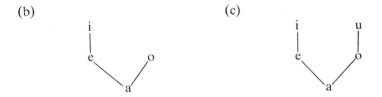

The fifth vowel /u/ is subject to considerable dialect variation and is not consistently distinguished from /o/. However, the syllabic orthography does provide a means for writing /u/, through redefining it as /iw/. The /w/ is not a consonant with a syllabic representation of its own; rather it is represented by a dot after the syllabic. A /w/ after the syllable is represented by a small circle. This need to write /u/ occurs infrequently and does not seem to mar the symmetricality of the syllabic system for its users.

The problem of the fifth vowel is additionally complicated for the linguist in that some dialects of Plains Cree as spoken in Alberta have a tendency to raise front vowels:

Again the system is symmetrical, although the raising of /o/ to /u/ is represented in the orthography only in extreme cases. It is interesting to note, however, that one of the major inconsistencies in syllabic spelling is between /i/ and /e/, part of this being the result of raising in certain dialects and in the speech of certain individuals within communities.

The participants in the workshop decided to make two major changes in the traditional manner of writing syllabics which they felt were necessary if the writing was to represent the spoken language unambiguously. Diacritics were introduced by group concensus to represent vowel length and /h/. They are correct that both are meaningful in their language. However, the group also realized that too many diacritical marks were confusing and hard for children to remember. A number of individuals favored using the diacritics only where ambiguity would otherwise result; the explicit logic was that in other cases native speakers would know and produce the correct form automatically. The decision to use diacritics in all environments was made after discussion demonstrating that, at least in some parts of Alberta, many Cree children were NOT native speakers of Cree. Therefore they would need cues to pronunciation which a speaker with the native intuition of a first language would not require.

The question of length arose because of the existence of a number of minimal pairs, for example:

mimōsom   'my moose'
mimosōm   'my grandfather'
sakāhikan   'nail'
sākahikan   'lake'

Students' questions about the difference between these led teachers to search for a way of indicating the difference that all native speakers of Cree heard between the two words. The decision was to mark length with /¨/ above the syllabic.

The question of length was complicated, however, by the symmetrical character of the syllabic writing system as a whole. Several members of the workshops insisted that some syllables were always long, e.g. /wi/ and /mi/; others suggested that /e/ was never long. Because of these difficulties, several people felt that length should not be marked in the orthography at all, again because native speakers did not make mistakes in this anyway. (From a linguistic point of view, however, a symmetrical treatment is possible, with long and short forms occurring with each syllable and vowel.)

The second inadequacy of the syllabic system to be taken up was the representation of /h/. In some words /h/ is clearly syllabic, e.g. *oho* meaning 'owl'. In this case, a geometrical representation of /h/ seems called for. But not all /h/'s are syllabic. Particularly common is a preaspiration of stops after a long vowel, which is a meaningful distinction in

Cree, e.g. the suffixes /-ak/ and /-ahk/ are not equivalent. Because of these two kinds of /h/, the group decided that a diacritical mark, / ''/, should be used before the syllable in question. The preaspirated forms were hard for native speakers to hear and were recorded inconsistently, with some feeling that any native speaker would know this too. Some phonetic /h/'s were not recorded at all because they have no meaning. For example:

Wihtna (h) itwa.   'Say it slowly'.

In these cases the /h/ is simply a reflex of the need to get from one vowel to another. The CV–CV structure encourages the insertion of some consonant, in this case /h/. It is never heard by native speakers.

The final problem of orthography comes with the so-called "English version" of the syllabics. The workshops agreed early on that the syllabic orthography should be the basis for the roman orthography so that Cree students could move from one to the other. The English version remained entirely secondary in terms of discussion but it did force the consideration of the question of voiced and voiceless stops, which indicated an implicit contrastive analysis with English made by at least some Cree speakers. English, of course, has six stops:

p   t   k
b   d   g

Cree has all of these phonetically, but needs to represent only one for each pair in the orthography. The alternation of /k/ and /g/ is the most common in Cree and generally follows a rule that word-initial and word-final forms are pronounced /k/ and the word-medial form is pronounced /g/. For example:

peyak   'one'
peyagwan   'just the same'.

This rule seems to cause no difficulty in roman orthography. Both the syllabic and the syllable-final marker are recorded as /k/, the voiceless form which is obviously perceived as basic. There is also no problem with /p/ and /b/, although both are present; the /b/ is actually quite rare, particularly in some local dialects, and there is no question of writing it.

However, the English equivalent for the /t/ and /d/ pair became the major source of potential disagreement in initial discussions by the Cree teachers. Several individuals prefer to use /d/ in all syllabic positions. The major reason is that the Cree /t/ is quite different from the English one and students make the frequent mistake of using the English form, which is aspirated and alveopalatal. The Cree form is apicodental and unaspirated. Native speakers point out that children know not to use an English /d/ but may be confused with /t/ because it is different in Cree and English. All participants realized that the usual Cree sound was intermediate between the two English sounds, but disagreed on how to represent it. In syllabics, of course, the problem does not arise because /t/ and /d/ are merged.

There were a number of objections, however, to the use of /d/ from other members of the group. The /d/ is a fairly rare sound in Cree and the occurrences are partially dependent on the dialect of Plains Cree; e.g.:

Namoya nantaw. 'I'm not bad' alternates with *Namoya nandaw.*

Individual speakers are, however, consistent in their forms for a given lexical item.

Another objection was the inconsistency of representing the syllabic /t/ as /d/, while retaining /t/ as a representation for the final syllable marker. This was reasonable to the group favoring /d/ because of the greater aspiration in the syllable-final /t/, which bought it closer to the English /t/.

A final reason for preference of /d/ was implicit in all discussion: the similarity of /t/ and /th/. Plains Cree does not have /th/ and native speakers have extreme difficulty with the English combination /th/. For example, to the question "how do you say three trees in Cree?" a perfectly reasonable response is "nine" (i.e. three times three is nine). Many bilingual speakers, especially if their written English is poor, assume that these are homologous. Reliance on /d/ as an orthographic convention, fully realizing that it isn't "really" an English /d/, seems to many Cree-dominant bilinguals the way to avoid the entire problem. For this group, there was no contradiction between this and the choice of the voiceless form for the other two stops.

In spite of the linguist's obvious preference for an orthographic /t/, the sophistication of contrastive analysis involved in the choice of /d/ is remarkable, and the sort of phenomenon generally ignored in linguistic descriptions by outside analysts. The motivation to teach Cree children with as little conflict as possible is clearly reflected in the orthographic choices.

A final problem of the orthographic representation of Cree in the roman alphabet is that of /ch/. The English /ch/ is considerably more harsh than the Cree equivalent; moreover, the Cree sound alternates according to dialect and lexical item with /s/. Many native speakers feel that the /j/ of English and/or French is a more appropriate representation of the Cree sound (most of the missionaries in northern Alberta were French and many Cree people still speak French more fluently than English). The group favoring /j/ also points out it has the advantage of being a single orthographic symbol. However, the matter is confusing. The English name "Joe" tends to be pronounced "*Choe*" in line with the assertion made above. But the French "*Jesus*" comes out as "*Sesus*", taking power away from the equation of /ch/ and /j/. Again, of course, the difficulty does not arise in syllabics, which simply incorporate the Cree range of sounds in a single symbol.

In sum, then, the knowledge of linguistically naive native speakers about their own language can be abstracted by them for a practical and socially motivated purpose in a way which may incidentally increase a linguist's analytical understanding of Cree. The orthographic choices, for example, clarify the nature of the syllable as a word-building unit in Cree and provide evidence for the speakers' perception operating in the speech of Cree-dominant bilinguals. The practicality of such insights as applied to language teaching for native people is virtually unassailable because the teachers devising the materials have firsthand experience and understanding of a situation they too have faced. They are articulate and goal-directed in their programs in a way which must be incorporated in the knowledge of linguists if linguistic description is ever truly to reflect the way native speakers organize their knowledge to attain social goals.

REFERENCES

DARNELL, REGNA
  1971   "The bilingual speech community: A Cree example," in *Linguistic diversity in Canadian society*. Edited by Regna Darnell, 155–172. Edmonton, Canada, and Champaign, U.S.A.: Linguistic Research, Inc.
SAPIR, EDWARD
  1949   "The psychological reality of phonemes," in *Selected writings of Edward Sapir in language, culture, and personality*. Edited by David G. Mandelbaum, 46–60. Berkeley and Los Angeles: University of California Press.
WEINREICH, URIEL
  1966   *Languages in contact* (fourth edition). London, The Hague, Paris: Mouton. (Originally published 1953.)

Bilingualism and Language Maintenance in Two Communities in Santa Catarina, Brazil

JÜRGEN HEYE

1. INTRODUCTION

During February and March 1973, under the auspices of the Universidade Federal de Santa Catarina, sociolinguistic fieldwork was conducted in the two neighboring communities of Pomerode and Rio dos Cedros to determine the state of bilingualism and to describe the sociolinguistic stratification of the population. Both towns were selected on the basis of their similar history and their relatively easy accessibility. For the purpose of this investigation a team of fieldworkers under the direction of the author was set up, composed of graduate students in linguistics participating in the VI Brazilian Linguistics Summer Institute. Before beginning to describe the linguistic side of both communities, let us look briefly at their respective developments.

1.1. *Pomerode*

Pomerode was founded in 1870 as the Parish of São Ludgero by German immigrants who had come to the Itajaí valley. They came mostly from Upper and Lower Pomerania in Germany, brought to Santa Catarina through the efforts of Dr. Blumenau. The name "Pomerode" is said to derive from an immigrant named Rohde who had come from Pomerania. The first settlers were all farmers. Throughout the early settlement period

My thanks to all those graduate students who participated in the preparation and execution of this survey during the VI Instituto Brasileiro de Linguistica, and to the local authorities in Pomerode who kindly provided the most important statistical data, much helpful information about the historical development of both Pomerode and Rio dos Cedros, as well as transportation and other assistance.

the function of the Lutheran pastor was of utmost importance for the community. He was the person who organized not only the religious life of the early immigrants but also established the first schools, hospital and other community projects.

Today Pomerode has a population of some 13,000 — more than half of whom live in outlying rural areas. The township, incorporated as such in 1934, comprises a total area of 210 square kilometers. A large segment of the population works the fields, raising a variety of vegetables and cattle. The latter gave rise to the first important industrial enterprises of Pomerode, the establishment of a meat-processing plant. The most significant industry today is the manufacture of chinaware (*Porcelana Schmidt*), which is the largest employer. Pomerode is basically a Lutheran town but, since the surrounding communities are mostly Catholic, there is also a fairly large number of Catholics in Pomerode itself, and is interesting to note that there is no conflict between the two denominations. The physical aspect of Pomerode is a pleasant one; the architecture shows a pronounced German influence, with many houses built in the *"Fachwerk"* style. Situated along the Rio do Testo, the town forms a cross with the principal bridge at its center. Pomerode is serviced regularly by bus from Blumenau, the industrial and commercial center of the region some 40 kilometers to the southeast. Although cars are becoming increasingly numerous, the bicycle is the most common means of transportation in and around town.

1.2. *Rio dos Cedros*

Rio dos Cedros is separated from Pomerode by a small mountain range. Situated in the valley of the Rio dos Cedros, the town has almost the same number of inhabitants as Pomerode (12,000) but the township covers an area almost twice as large, 556 square kilometers. Thus, it is much less densely populated, and it is almost impossible to speak of an urban population there. The absence of any noteworthy industry increases this impression. Rio dos Cedros is an agricultural area par excellence, rice and tobacco being the most important products.

Founded in 1875 by Italian immigrants, the township was incorporated in 1961. The history of its settlers deserves mention here. The efforts of Dr. Blumenau to bring German immigrants to Santa Catarina were stopped in 1870 when Germany entered a state of war with France and would no longer give its citizens permission to leave the country. Dr. Blumenau then approached the Austro-Hungarian authorities in Vienna, asking them to provide him with immigrants so that he could maintain the quotas to which his contract with the Brazilian government obligated him. Vienna encouraged farmers from Southern Tyrol to follow Dr.

Blumenau to Santa Catarina. These immigrants were, of course, speakers of Italian, although they belonged politically to Austria. Thus the vast majority of Italian immigrants to that part of Santa Catarina came from one province, Trento, and many of them settled in Rio dos Cedros. The principal source of income for the population today is rice-growing (production in 1969: 270 tons), followed by tobacco and corn. Most families in Rio dos Cedros still make their own wine, but they rarely sell it.

The influence of the Catholic church in Rio dos Cedros is noteworthy. During the first decades of settlement Rio dos Cedros was part of the Franciscan Brothers' parish of Rodeio. In 1913 the town established its first vicariate, under the Salesians. The cultural influence of the Salesians has been especially strong; they established a seminary and for many years ran the schools in Rio dos Cedros.

A substantial Italian library was set up and much was done to remain in contact with the mainstream of Italian culture. During the *"Estado Novo"* of Getulio Vargas, however, much of the library was burned by government agents and the teaching of Italian (and German) in the schools was forbidden. Today Rio dos Cedros has a kindergarten, a large primary school, and two junior high schools. There is also a small hospital run by Vicentine sisters. Most social activities of the population still center around the church; there are soccer fields and two small restaurants in the town. Rio dos Cedros gives a general impression of rural tranquility; the houses are mostly built of wood, brightly colored, with Italian scenes painted on the windowshades, and neatly kept front yards. The modern church and the Salesian seminary dominate the architectural scene. The town center itself is formed by the intersection of three roads, one leading to Pomerode, the other along the Rio dos Cedros towards Timbò to the south and the third leading into the mountains of Alto Rio dos Cedros. Regular bus service is provided from Blumenau via Timbò. Reaching some of the isolated families often requires a four-wheel-drive vehicle or a horse.

Comparing the towns one notes a much higher level of industrial and commercial activity in Pomerode, and much more agriculture, but almost no cattle, in and around Rio dos Cedros. The historical development of both towns is strikingly similar, though they were settled by speakers of different languages. Along the limits of the townships there are a number of Italian-speaking families on the Pomerode side. The few German-speaking families on the Rio dos Cedros are located on the road to Timbò. We observed little social interaction between families speaking different languages in this border region. Obviously, Pomerode is the more prosperous town, but there is also a certain frustrated ambition of not being able to expand economically; Rio dos Cedros seems to be more content with its agriculturally-based economy. One might also note that none of the abject poverty which marks so much of Brazil is visible in either community. Neither town suffers from unemployment although family income is quite low.[1]

2. OBJECTIVES

2.1. Bilingualism in Pomerode and Rio dos Cedros

The objectives of this investigation centered around bilingualism in Pomerode and Rio dos Cedros. We wanted to obtain comparative data in both communities with respect to the maintenance of an immigrant language, proceeding from the assumption that each group of immigrants arrives in the new country as monolingual speakers. This assumption is obviously true in the case of Pomerode and Rio dos Cedros, but in addition to being monolingual speakers of German and Italian, respectively, each group also brought its own dialect: upper and lower Pomeranian, and the dialect of the Trentino-Alto Adige region. In an investigation of bilingualism, the dialect or dialects of the immigrant groups in question play a subordinate role. Although no particular attempt was made in the present study, it can be shown conclusively that the Italian-speaking group in Rio dos Cedros forms a much more homogeneous linguistic group, i.e. the Trentino dialect is still found among many speakers of "Italian." In Pomerode, the dialect of the original settlers has by now leveled off to a kind of phonologically neutral immigrant German. This can be explained at least partly by the arrival of German-speakers from other dialect areas over the last few decades,[2] contributing substantially to this levelling-off process. From the above it should be understood that "Italian" in Rio dos Cedros means Italian with pronounced phonological and lexical features of the Trentino dialect, and "German" in Pomerode means an almost neutral (i.e. with few traces of the original dialects) immigrant German. One also notes, at least impressionistically, fewer cases of grammatical and lexical interference among Italian speakers in Rio dos Cedros. This type of interference (Oberacker 1972:383–431) as well as a degree of phonological interference is quite frequent among German-speaking descendants of immigrants.[3]

---

[1] No figures are available, but income is estimated between US$ 60 to 100 per month.
[2] There has been very little recent immigration to Pomerode. Exact figures are not available.
[3] Examples:
Mach die Janellen zu, es schuft — 'close the window, it's raining'.

Janellen 'windows'   Port. janela + Germ. fem. pl. suffix -en
schuft 'is raining'   Port. chover + Germ. 3 p. sg. pres. suffix -t.

Hol mir bitte eine Latte blaue Tinte — 'Please get me a can of blue paint.'

Latte 'can'   Port. lata + Germ. fem. sg. suffix -e (but: German Latte 'board')
Tinte 'paint'   Port. tinta + Germ. fem. sg. suffix -e (but: German Tinte 'ink').

But for the present study neither of these aspects was taken into account.

2.2.   Attitudes about Bilingualism

We were also interested in obtaining some indications as to the attitudes which these groups manifest towards their respective immigrant languages and the official national language — Portuguese. We assumed that there exists a correlation between language attitude, as, for example, manifested by the usefulness of the language for the speaker, and the degree to which the immigrant language is maintained by its speakers. Attitudinal manifestations were determined by studying the language functions in various situations, (in the home, in public, etc.) on the one hand, and by observing indirect language behavior on the other.

2.3.   Comparative Language Functions

In relation to language function, we wanted to determine differences in functional use of each immigrant language in each community and compare it with the functional use of Portuguese. For this, we selected the four basic language skills (speaking, reading, writing and understanding), language use in social places (club, work, church) and situations (mealtimes, storytelling, scolding), and with social groups (neighbors, family, authorities, etc.). Thus comparative data was obtained which shows the direction of bilingual development for each group of speakers. In some cases it is possible to observe this movement within one family by studying the responses given over two or three generations, thus determining the generational spread of bilingual development.

2.4.   Immigrant Language Maintenance

A further objective of this study was to investigate the attitudes which speakers manifest toward the maintenance of an immigrant language. We proceeded from the assumption that if no external factors, such as interference from the government, are involved, the immigrant language will be maintained as a functional means of verbal communication if the group of speakers attributes positive values to the immigrant language, i.e. if its speakers see certain advantages in using the language. If the speakers see no such advantages, the immigrant language is likely to disappear sooner.

2.5.   Training and Further Research

Our final objective was to develop a research tool which would allow us to conduct similar investigations, in other parts of Brazil, dealing with immigrant languages.[4] As a corollary, we wanted to introduce Brazilian graduate students to sociolinguistic fieldwork and sociolinguistics in general, an area of linguistics which is still very much in its initial phases.

3.   METHODOLOGY

3.1.   Basic Tools

For this study two basic tools were used to obtain relevant data: a questionnaire in Portuguese and informal interviews, conducted by sociolinguistically trained fieldworkers. A basic questionnaire was developed and tested in a preliminary study with a small group of representative members of each community. Due to the relatively high illiteracy rate in both communities, it was found to be more efficient to have the interviewer fill out the questionnaires. The final questionnaire was constituted of the following parts:

A. PERSONAL DATA (age, education, profession, residency, origin, mother tongue) with fifteen questions;

B. LANGUAGE FUNCTIONS divided into: language skills, language function outside the home (mealtime, singing, storytelling, scolding, etc.) and language function in social groups (friends, neighbors, strangers, authorities), with a total of twenty-two questions.

C. ATTITUDES AND LANGUAGE MAINTENANCE (twelve questions), concerned with the learning of Italian (German) in school, and willingness to cooperate in any effort to maintain the language locally.

The respondents were asked to evaluate the questionnaire itself, and the fieldworkers evaluated the interview and the environment (house) where the interview was conducted. This last question was deemed useful as a further indication of social status of the respondent, together with the other two SES indices, education and profession. The question concerning the interview had a double function: it served to evaluate not only the course of the interview but also the way the interview was conducted by the fieldworker. In post-fieldwork conferences each interviewer was asked to explain why he had given a certain rating to a specific interview.

Although considerable care was taken to phrase the questions in a

---

[4]   Fieldwork was recently begun in Jaraguá do Sul, S.C. under the direction of Prof. Mario Bonatti of the Federal University of Santa Catarina, using the questionnaire and the methodology of the present study to investigate the multilingual situation (Portuguese, German, Italian) in that community.

simple, unambiguous manner, some flaws were noted during the pre-tests, and corrected by each fieldworker.

In one question, emphasis was placed on teaching the children to write in the immigrant language. But illiteracy of the parents made this question irrelevant, as can be seen from the high number of negative answers (see section 4.5.). A similar problem arose in a subsequent question where the respondent was asked which language he would choose if he/she were to "write" his/her life history. "Write" was replaced by "tell" in the final application of the questionnaire. In general it was felt that the questionnaire was adequate but could be condensed and improved for future fieldwork in this area.

3.2. Training of Fieldworkers

In this study graduate students of linguistics with some knowledge and considerable interest in sociolinguistic fieldwork were trained by the author. Preparation included work sessions on such topics as history of German and Italian immigration to Santa Catarina, construction and evaluation of questionnaires, thorough study of sociolinguistic investigations (Labov 1968; Shuy et al. 1968; Heye 1974), and interviewing techniques. Before the actual fieldwork was undertaken, each interviewer was evaluated by the group, and as a result some felt unprepared and withdrew. Those who remained were grouped into workteams, usually one male and one female. In Rio dos Cedros the interviews were conducted by four teams and in Pomerode by six teams, each conducting approximately ten interviews of thirty to forty minutes each. For the work in Pomerode, the teams were arranged so that most had one member with at least a working knowledge of German, since it was found during the preliminary fieldwork that in this town there were quite a few monolingual German speakers. This was not the case in Rio dos Cedros with respect to Italian.

3.3. Selection of the Sample

It was decided that, within the limits of the present study, a random sampling procedure would not be viable. In Rio dos Cedros the sample was selected on the basis of availability and location. No appointments were made for the interview. Each team was assigned to a given area, and this allowed us to cover most areas within the limits of the township. Depending on the number of dwellings in each area, the interviewing team decided on the interval between families selected (e.g. if there were about fifty houses in area B, every fifth house would be interviewed). Due to the absence of a clearly identifiable urban center, no distinction was made between rural and urban dwellings.

In Pomerode the same approach was maintained, but two additional factors had to be taken into account: (1) the urban population in the center of town, and (2) the presence of the chinaware factory, where a number of interviews could be conducted in a short time. This meant the addition of two teams to conduct interviews in the urban center and the *"Porcelana Schmidt."* We therefore obtained a higher number of com- pleted questionnaires for Pomerode (sixty-nine) than for Rio dos Cedros (forty-four). The number of families interviewed in both communities was sixteen; the teams that worked with families were instructed to interview at least two, possibly three, members of different generations in each family. This generational spread permitted close observation of changes in degree of bilingualism, language, function and attitudes within one family and may be taken as an indication of language development of the two groups. Our sample, although not randomly selected, proved to be representative of the population.

3.4. *Problems*

During the actual fieldwork some interviewing teams experienced a number of difficulties which need to be explained, since we believe that they are not specific to the population under study here. The first problem was the frequent apprehension that the interviewers were representatives of a federal government agency investigating the individual and his family. We attempted to counteract this fear by securing permission to conduct fieldwork from the local authorities and by providing each field- work team with a written statement that the survey was not conducted for a federal government agency. The following case may illustrate this point. The Mayor of Rio dos Cedros had kindly assigned his jeep and a driver to provide transportation for the teams interviewing in the outlying and not easily accessible farms. Often it was only after the driver, who normally waited in the car, had introduced the fieldworkers to the family that the interview could be conducted, since the driver was well known to the family. The causes for this fear, at times verging on hostility, must be sought in two different areas: (a) the negative experiences which many immigrants or descendants of immigrants had during the *"Estado Novo"* of Getulio Vargas and during World War II when the Brazilian govern- ment banned the teaching of Italian and German as well as publications in these languages — many of the older informants still remember those days vividly, when many people were harassed and jailed because they were heard speaking Italian or German; (b) a different problem arose in Pomerode, especially in the more rural areas. We knew that there would be a number of monolingual speakers, especially among elderly persons, but we did not know when the teams would encounter them. Thus, it happened on a few occasions that a monolingual Portuguese team attempted, unsuccessfully, to interview a monolingual German speaker. The problem was solved by sending another team with a bilingual speaker to complete the interview.

A total of 120 interviews were planned and only seven could not be completed. This gave us 113 questionnaires with primary data.

4.   RESULTS

The results of the present survey of bilingualism will be given in summary form, highlighting those aspects which to us seem most pertinent. The basic data is given in the form of tables in an appendix.

4.1.   *Social Characteristics of the Sample Population*

In both communities sixteen families were selected and interviewed. In Rio dos Cedros this meant between three and four members of different generations in each family. In Pomerode the average number of family members interviewed was lower, between two and three. In Pomerode we also completed thirty-one questionnaires with respondents outside their house, either at their place of work or in the street. This resulted in a total of sixty-nine interviews in Pomerode and forty-four in Rio dos Cedros. The distribution between sexes was even, 35 male to 34 female in Pomerode and 23 male to 21 female in Rio dos Cedros. In both samples the various age groups were equally well distributed. Our youngest informant was twelve and our oldest, in Rio dos Cedros, ninety-seven years old. In general we interviewed a slightly older group of persons in Rio dos Cedros, i.e. the age group 46–60 years is most heavily represented. In Pomerode the next lower group 31–45 years is proportionally large. No more than one-third of the population has gone beyond primary school. In each community some 20 percent of the sample had not completed primary school. The illiteracy rate in Santa Catarina is one of the lowest in Brazil, but nevertheless there are many people, regardless of their national origin, who cannot read or write. Another point to be made in this regard is that many of the older members of the respective communities received their first schooling in Italian or German. As late as the mid-1930s most immigrant communities hired and paid their own teachers, often from abroad, and instruction was given in the immigrant language. It is not uncommon, therefore, to find persons who can read and write German but are almost illiterate in Portuguese.

In our study this group constitutes not more than 10–12 percent of the sample.

The professional activities of the sample population in both communities can be summarized in five comprehensive categories, excluding housewives and students, which constituted about 40 percent in each sample. The five categories are: (1) unskilled labor — mainly factory workers and farmhands. This group is much more frequently represented in Pomerode than in Rio dos Cedros, where there is no industry and most people who work the land also own it. This is further reflected by the reverse proportion in the following category; (2) skilled labor, including farmers, which dominate in Rio dos Cedros; and the varied skills needed in the manufacture of chinaware, which dominate that category in Pomerode; (3) small business including shopkeepers, tailors, butchers, etc. This category is also more frequently represented in Pomerode (10 percent), due to its more pronounced commercial activities; (4) civil service. In this group were included teachers, policemen and employees such as secretaries, in both government and local industry. This group is evenly represented in both communities (10 and 15 percent); (5) the final category, labeled "other commercial activities," included all those who exercised higher functions in industry and commerce, as in the various managerial positions in the chinaware plant in Pomerode.

We realize that these categories merely represent a first approximation and will have to be revised and refined in subsequent studies. The breakdown of professional activities of the sample does reflect the principal difference between Pomerode and Rio dos Cedros, i.e. the most frequently represented activities in the former were all related to business and industry, and in the latter to agriculture.

To complete the social picture of both communities we included a subjective evaluation of the type of dwelling of each family interviewed. Fieldworkers were instructed to evaluate each house without asking any specific question. We decided on this approach since we found that informants would become more apprehensive if we asked any questions related to the financial status of the family. Each dwelling was judged in terms of three levels in the following way: Level 1: brick or wood construction, electricity and running water, radio, TV and/or refrigerator, well-kept front yard. Level 2: electricity and running water, little furniture, radio, but no TV or refrigerator, front yard not well kept, house needs paint. Level 3: wood or adobe construction, no electricity or running water, no radio, house unpainted, front yard not fenced off from pasture or fields. From these observations we obtained an impressionistic basis as to the financial situation of each family. This information was then added to the indices of education and occupation to arrive at an approximative index of the socioeconomic status of each family. In Rio dos Cedros the average socioeconomic status indices were generally higher than in Pomerode.

4.2. Origin and Length of Residency

We found that almost all members of our sample had lived in the respective towns at least ten years. Although this result was neither aimed at nor expected, it is easily understood, since the population is a relatively stable one. Over half of our informants in Pomerode were born there (58 percent). In Rio dos Cedros about 40 percent of the sample were born locally. As regards the parents of the informants, one notes for Pomerode that most were also born there or in the immediate vicinity, a few came from other towns within the state of Santa Catarina, and only between 12 and 15 percent had immigrated from Germany. The parents of the Rio dos Cedros group are quite evenly distributed between those who were born locally, in the state, and those who had come from Italy. As regards the grandparents of both groups, over 50 percent were born in the "old country" (Germany or Italy). Some 18 percent of our Rio dos Cedros informants indicated that their grandparents were Austrian. This is politically correct (or was, at the time) but linguistically wrong, since they were speakers of Italian, or the Trentino dialect of Italian. One can say, perhaps at the risk of overgeneralizing, but based on our data, that the immigration cycles in Pomerode had begun earlier and were completed earlier as regards the second and third generation; for Rio dos Cedros this does not seem to be the case. It also means that the Italian-speaking group had more men immigrating and then marrying local women whereas the German-speaking immigrant often came alone and then brought his wife from Germany.

4.3. Mother Tongue and Second Language

The term "mother tongue" is defined here as that language which the child learns from his parents at home before he reaches school age. We found that 80 percent of the Pomerode sample gave German as their mother tongue, compared to 75 percent of the Rio dos Cedros group with Italian as the mother tongue. In Pomerode only 10 percent had Portuguese as their first language, whereas the percentage for Rio dos Cedros was twice as high. Those in the remainder of the sample are best described as complete bilinguals since they learned both the immigrant and the national languages simultaneously. On the other hand, 55 percent of both groups learned Portuguese when they started their formal education between the ages of six and fourteen. About 10 percent of each group learned Portuguese between fifteen and twenty-one years of age, mostly at work or during military service; the same number of people learned Portuguese before reaching school age. In Pomerode there were some 15 percent of the sample who learned Portuguese only as adults and, as indicated by further questions during the interview, so imperfectly that they are best considered monolingual speakers of German. This group is made up mostly of older persons living on farms in the more distant areas. We found no monolingual speakers of Italian in Rio dos Cedros.

4.4. Language Function

When investigating language function in these bilingual communities we took two measures into consideration: (1) EQUALITY: the informant uses both immigrant and national language equally. He cannot tell which language he uses more frequently or feels more comfortable in using; (2) DOMINANCE (Weinreich 1964:79–80): the informant uses one language more frequently than the other, he feels more at ease using it. Although varying degrees of dominance can be distinguished, they add little information to the present study.

4.4.1. LANGUAGE SKILLS. These are divided into Speaking, Reading, Writing and Understanding. Again the effects of schooling and illiteracy play an important part in separating Speaking and Understanding from Reading and Writing. For the latter two skills Portuguese dominates, but more so in Rio dos Cedros (52 percent versus 72 percent). Most informants indicated that they spoke and understood Portuguese and German or Portuguese and Italian equally well. Some 30 percent of the sample in Rio dos Cedros claimed that they spoke Italian more and better than Portuguese, as compared to about 25 percent for German in Pomerode. Of the Italian-speaking group 20 percent also indicated that they speak and understand some German. Dominance of German for reading and writing was indicated by 15 percent of the Pomerode sample. The corresponding figure for Italian was 10 percent. Rio dos Cedros ranks neither in the dominance level nor on the equality level, but it is clearly represented, though we have no measure of the degree of multilingualism there. Italian figures only marginally in Pomerode, mostly through intermarriage and work. In general we found equality (Portuguese and German, Portuguese and Italian) for speaking and understanding, dominance of Portuguese for reading and writing. Both samples remain numerically balanced.

4.4.2. LANGUAGE USE AND SOCIAL INTERACTION. We limited our investigation of language use to five settings which can be clearly defined in terms of social interaction. They were: work, clubs, church, sports and shopping. For both samples we found little or no equality between national and immigrant language, but instead dominance of either Portuguese or German. In Rio dos Cedros Portuguese dominates clearly in all settings. Only at work does Italian dominate for some 35 percent of the sample. The situation is almost reversed in Pomerode; for 48 percent of the sample German is the dominant language in church (Lutheran); for some 40 percent that language dominates at work and when shopping. Equality of Portuguese and German in Pomerode was generally less than 15 percent of the sample. Dominance of Portuguese was indicated for the settings of club and sports.

4.4.3.   LANGUAGE USE AT HOME. Here we compared dominance and equality of immigrant and national language in six situations (meals, putting children to bed, prayers, songs, storytelling and scolding). We assumed that these situations would involve much verbal interaction and would therefore yield sufficient comparable data. We found that the results were not markedly different from those obtained for the social interaction settings. Again Portuguese dominates in all six situations for the Italian-speaking group in Rio dos Cedros. Italian language dominance was indicated by about 35 percent for meals, storytelling and scolding. For all other situations percentages below 25 percent were indicated by this sample. In Pomerode the German-speaking group registered Portuguese dominance only for songs and storytelling (about 40 percent); in all other situations German dominates with percentages ranging from 42 percent to 52 percent. Percentages of Portuguese–German equality were low, ranging from 15 percent for storytelling to 66 percent for prayers and from 15 percent for songs to 3 percent for prayers for Portuguese–Italian equality.

4.4.4.   LANGUAGE USE IN RELATION TO GROUPS. The last group of questions in this part concentrated on language use in relation to groups of people. We distinguished five groups: Family, friends, neighbors, authorities and strangers. It was found that Portuguese was the dominant language for speaking to authorities and strangers for 70 to 80 percent of the German speaking sample in Pomerode. The remaining 20 to 30 percent can be accounted for by considering: (a) that some are monolingual speakers of German and (b) that most of the local authorities also speak German. For the Pomerode group German dominates over Portuguese in relation to family and neighbors (about 55 percent); with friends the percentage was balanced between Portuguese dominance and German dominance (35 percent). In Rio dos Cedros there is a similar Portuguese dominance in relation to authorities and strangers (75 percent and 90 percent), but we found no clear Italian dominance for any of the remaining groups, i.e.

friends (35 percent), family (45 percent), neighbors (48 percent). Thus it becomes clear that Italian in Rio dos Cedros is, in terms of use, subordinated to Portuguese, i.e. the national language is in a dominance position in most settings, home situations and social groups. In Pomerode the situation is more complex; Portuguese dominates in some situations, especially outside the immediate home environment, but German dominates in such settings as work and church, at meals, and with children. It seems therefore that the functional value of German is on a comparable level with Portuguese in Pomerode. Italian, on the other hand, has a lower functional value than Portuguese in Rio dos Cedros.

4.5. *Attitudes and Language Maintenance*

Language attitudes are taken to be those feelings and subjective manifestations which the individual has towards his own native language as well as towards other contact languages. Language attitudes may or may not be openly manifested. In cases of immigrant and national language contacts, questions of language attitudes are often intimately related to questions of language maintenance, i.e. the subjective values attributed to one will influence the direction and extent of use of the other. When one looks at language maintenance in the two communities under study, we must exclude one factor which in other situations may be of great importance, that of governmental language planning programs. In Brazil today there are no such programs in relation to immigrant languages.[5] The absence of teaching programs of immigrant languages in the schools is perhaps best attributed to the lack of trained teachers and the shortage of funds rather than to any specific government policy. This does not mean that the local population is opposed to the teaching of German or Italian in school. On the contrary, we found that over 80 percent of the sample in Pomerode would like their children to learn German in school; and most of them (70 percent) would be willing to actively support any efforts in that direction. For the Rio dos Cedros sample the percentages are somewhat lower as regards the teaching of Italian in the schools (68 percent and 62 percent). In Pomerode, 60 percent of the sample was in favor of a German radio or TV program, but in Rio dos Cedros only half of the group expressed interest in Italian language programs. We found that in Pomerode some 90 percent of the sample would teach their children to speak German; in Rio dos Cedros only 75 percent would

---

[5] One of the few remaining German language newspapers published regularly is the *Brasil Post* of São Paulo.

teach their children Italian. Fewer people would teach their children to write the immigrant language, for the obvious reason that few of the parents themselves still read or write German or Italian. With regard to the informants' opinion of the continued use of the immigrant language, about two-thirds of the sample in Pomerode gave a positive answer whereas in Rio dos Cedros over half the sample believes that use of Italian will not continue, but has, in a sense, outlived its usefulness for them regardless of the fact that at the present time it is still widely used. The trend towards Portuguese dominance continues to be shown in the answers to the following questions. Informants were asked to indicate which language they would select to tell their life-history: in Pomerode 61 percent of the sample chose Portuguese and 28 percent German; and in Rio dos Cedros Portuguese was selected by 77 percent and Italian by 21 percent of the sample. As regards the language which the informant personally prefers to speak, it was found that in Pomerode 48 percent prefer to speak Portuguese, 33 percent prefer German, and 14 percent expressed no particular preference. In Rio dos Cedros 68 percent prefer to speak Portuguese, 25 percent prefer Italian and 10 percent had no preference.

It becomes clear that in Rio dos Cedros the deterioration process of the immigrant language is more advanced than in Pomerode. The sample there attached fewer positive values to Italian, indicated a lower extent of use to that language and believe that use of Italian will end there. In Pomerode the trend is similar but not as strongly marked. This direction of language maintenance is also corroborated by the response obtained to the last question of the attitudinal part. Informants were asked about the advantages they saw in speaking German or Italian. We found in Pomerode that 38 percent believe that being able to speak German facilitates communication in that town; 35 percent think it helps them to find employment or move ahead in their jobs; for 12 percent of the sample knowledge of Germans brings no particular advantages. Comparing these figures with those obtained for the sample in Rio dos Cedros for Italian we note that, although some 40 percent believe that knowing and speaking Italian will facilitate communication in that town, about one-third do not see any advantages in being able to use Italian, and it is not considered necessary for employment purposes in Rio dos Cedros. Thus it is shown that less than half of the sample in Rio dos Cedros sees any particular advantage in knowing Italian, but knowledge of German is still considered an advantage by three-quarters of the sample in Pomerode. We also find that, in general, more positive values are attributed to German in Pomerode than to Italian in Rio dos Cedros. The functional value of German is higher than that of Italian, and as regards mainten- ance of immigrant languages in that area of Brazil, there is no doubt that Italian will disappear more rapidly than German. The often negative or indifferent attitudes manifested by the Rio dos Cedros sample towards Italian are taken as an indication of this trend. The present investigation is one of the first attempts to study the immigrant population of Santa Catarina from a sociolinguistic point of view. It is therefore obvious that a number of improvements in methodology and analysis (questionnaire, sampling procedures, statistical analysis) should be made, but we are convinced that the data presented here are significant and representative for the two communities under study.

APPENDIX: SUMMARY OF RESULTS — POMERODE AND RIO DOS CEDROS

Abbreviations: P = Portuguese   Pom. = Pomerode
G = German   RdC. = Rio dos Cedros
I = Italian   Equal. = Equality
Q = Questionnaire   Domin. = Dominance

Number of interviews: 113
Pomerode: 69
Rio dos Cedros: 44

Table I.   Sex and age groups

	Pom.	RdC.
Male (*n*)	35	23
Female (*n*)	34	21
under 20	16	9
21–30	13	4
31–45	22	11
46–60	17	13
over 60	6	7

Table II.   Level of education

	Pom.	RdC.
Incomplete Primary	15	10
Complete Primary	36	23
Complete Secondary	18	11

Table III.   Estimated social status

	Pom.	RdC.
Level 1	26	26
Level 2	16	15
Level 3	15	3

Table IV.   Occupations

	Pom.	RdC.
Housework	16	9
Students	12	8
Unskilled labor	11	1
Skilled labor	6	13
Small business	6	3
Civil service	7	7
Other business	11	3

Table V.   Length of residency

	Pom.	RdC.
Less than 5 years	6	–
5–10 years	3	–
Over 10 years	60	44

Table VI. Origin

	Pom.	RdC.	Vicinity		S. Catarina		Germany		Italy	
			Pom.	RdC.	Pom.	RdC.	Pom.	RdC.	Pom.	RdC.
Informant	40	21	17	13	8	10	4	–	–	–
Father	26	7	20	12	13	11	8	1	1	10
Mother	22	8	25	16	11	12	10	2	1	6
Mat. grandparents	9	1	9	9	15	5	32	6	4	22
Pat. grandparents	13	–	7	7	14	1	28	6	7	25

Table VII. Mother tongue

	Pom.	RdC.
German	54	–
Italian	5	33
Portuguese	8	7
P + G	1	–
P + I	–	4

Table VIII. Age Portuguese was learned

	Pom.	RdC.
under 6 years	7	5
6–14 years	37	24
15–21 years	8	5
over 21 years	11	7

Table IX.   Language skills

	P + G Equal	P + I Equal	P-Domin		G-Domin	I-Domin	Some G
	Pom.	RdC.	Pom.	RdC.	Pom.	RdC.	RdC.
Speaking	29	18	14	13	18	13	6
Writing	13	6	37	34	10	4	3
Reading	17	11	32	30	10	3	4
Understanding	46	41	9	3	6	–	10

Table X.   Language in social interaction

	P + G Equal	P + I Equal	P-Domin		G-Domin	I-Domin	Some G
	Pom.	RdC.	Pom.	RdC.	Pom.	RdC.	RdC.
Work	11	3	28	27	27	14	1
Club	9	7	31	26	17	11	2
Church	8	3	26	32	33	9	1
Sports	5	4	32	27	14	10	1
Stores	10	3	29	30	28	11	3

Table XI. Language at home

| | P + G Equal | P + I Equal | P-Domin | | G-Domin | I-Domin | Some G |
	Pom.	RdC.	Pom.	RdC.	Pom.	RdC.	RdC.
Meals	9	4	18	24	36	16	2
Children to bed	7	3	18	28	31	11	–
Prayers	5	1	27	39	35	4	–
Songs	5	6	30	32	27	6	3
Telling stories	11	1	29	28	23	12	2
Scolding	8	4	22	24	30	16	–

Table XII. Language in social groups

| | P + G Equal | P + I Equal | P-Domin | | G-Domin | I-Domin | Some G |
	Pom.	RdC.	Pom.	RdC.	Pom.	RdC.	RdC.
Family	8	4	19	20	36	20	1
Friends	17	7	24	23	24	14	2
Neighbors	13	3	16	20	37	21	–
Authorities	7	3	48	37	12	4	–
Strangers	3	3	54	39	9	2	–

Table XIII.   Language attitudes

	Yes		No		Indifferent	
	Pom.	RdC.	Pom.	RdC.	Pom.	RdC.
Children learn German or Italian in school?	57	30	8	12	–	2
Would cooperate?	47	27	9	14	7	3
Would like radio/TV program in G/I?	42	25	17	16	5	3
Would cooperate?	29	20	24	17	9	7
Teach child *speak* G/I?	62	32	4	12	–	–
Teach child *write* G/I?	54	16	12	28	–	–
Will G/I continue?	46	18	16	23	4	3

Table XIV.   Language preference

	P + I Equal		Port.		German		Italian		P + G Equal	
	Pom.	RdC.	Pom.	RdC.	Pom.	RdC.	Pom.	RdC.	Pom.	RdC.
Tell life history in	–	–	42	34	19	2	2	10	3	–
Prefer to speak	–	4	33	29	23	1	3	11	10	–

Table XV. Advantages of speaking German/Italian

	Pom. (G)	RdC. (I)
Facilitates communication	27	18
Necessary for work	25	4
Know about G/I culture	9	7
No particular advantages	9	12
No answer	6	3

REFERENCES

ALBERSHEIM, URSULA
1962   *Uma comunidade teuto-brasileira, Jarim*. Sao Paulo: INEP.
BONATTI, MARIO
1968   *"Lingua e cultura italiana em uma comunidade rural de Santa Catarina."*
       Unpublished Ph.D. dissertation. São Paulo: Universidade de São
       Paulo.
FAUSEL, ERICH
1937   Eine deutsch-brasilianische Wortsammlung. *Auslandsdeutsche Volks-
       forschung* 1:308–311.
HEYE, JÜRGEN
1974   Language attitudes and bilingualism in Merano, Italy. *Revista Brasileira
       de Linguistica 1*.
1975   *A sociolinguistic investigation of multilingualism and language attitudes
       in the Canton of Ticino, Switzerland*. The Hague: Mouton.
LABOV, WILLIAM
1968   *The social stratification of English in New York City*. Washington, D.C.:
       Center for Applied Linguistics.
OBERACKER, CARLOS
1972   "Transformações da lìngua alemã no Brasil," in *Homen, cultura e
       sociedade no Brasil*. Edited by Egon Schaden, 383–431. Petropolis:
       Editora Vozes.
SCHADEN, EGON
1972   "Algums problemas e aspectos do folclore teuto-brasileiro," in *Homen,
       cultura e sociedade no Brasil*. Edited by Egon Schaden, 436–450. Pet-
       ropolis: Editora Vozes.
SHUY, ROGER, W. WOLFRAM, W. RILEY
1968   *Field techniques in an urban language study*. Washington, D.C.: Center
       for Applied Linguistics.
WEINREICH, URIEL
1964   *Languages in contact* (second edition). The Hague: Mouton.

Cherokee: A Flourishing or Obsolescing Language?

WILLIAM PULTE

The purpose of this paper is to present the results of a household survey conducted in several Oklahoma Cherokee communities in an attempt to obtain reliable data on the extent to which Cherokee is spoken by children in full-blood families.[1] The data make possible an appraisal of the claims of Wahrhaftig (1970:9–24) regarding the vitality of Cherokee, claims which contrast sharply with the widespread popular belief that Cherokee is "a dying language" no longer being learned by children. In the discussion to follow, the survey results will be examined in some detail and an attempt will be made to explain the fact that Cherokee is more widely spoken in some communities than in others. In conclusion, it will be suggested that the scale proposed by Miller (1972:2), by which languages are ranked according to their vitality, provides a useful framework within which to consider the case of Cherokee provided that certain modifications are made.

There is a widespread belief on the part of Oklahoma whites that Cherokee is no longer spoken by full-blood children. While it is felt that such children may frequently understand the language, it is thought that they rarely speak it. This belief has been challenged by Wahrhaftig (1970:18), who presents statistics showing that a majority of full-blood Cherokees under the age of eighteen speak Cherokee in addition to English. Wahrhaftig's data, gathered systematically, refute the extreme form of the popular view of Cherokee as a language near extinction. It is

This study has been made possible by grant number OEG-6-73-0774-(280) from the United States Office of Education to the Greasy Creek Board of Education, Adair County, Oklahoma.
[1] The term full-blood, as used here, is not to be understood in a biological sense; it is employed in eastern Oklahoma to refer to members of identifiable Indian communities who speak an Indian language.

impossible, however, to make an adequate appraisal of the long-term viability of Cherokee without examining the bilingualism of Cherokee adolescents and children more closely. Before one can assess the likelihood that the present generation of bilingual Cherokee young people will transmit the language to members of the following generation, it is necessary to know to what extent they presently employ Cherokee in interaction with siblings and peers. If it were the case that the younger speakers in Wahrhaftig's sample speak Cherokee primarily with older Cherokees, then the likelihood that Cherokee will continue to be learned by members of subsequent generations would seem slight.

In order to learn more about the nature of bilingualism among young Cherokee-speakers, a survey of all Indian households with at least one child enrolled in the first six grades of four rural schools was undertaken.[2] The schools in question are located at Marble City in Sequoyah County, Greasy Greek in Adair County, and Tenkiller and Lost City in Cherokee County. It should be noted that the Greasy Creek School is attended by children from three Cherokee communities: South Greasy, Greasy Creek, and Rock Fence.[3] The Tenkiller School is attended by children from the Cherokee settlements at Barber and Sugar Mountain, and the Lost City School by children from Fourteen Mile Creek and Spring Creek. The Marble City School is attended by Cherokee children from only one community, that of Marble City itself, which is one of the four communities included in the earlier Wahrhaftig survey. It should also be pointed out that the communities with children attending the Lost City School are geographically contiguous to the Hulbert community surveyed by Wahrhaftig; they are, however, somewhat more rural in nature and therefore more conservative than the Hulbert community. There thus exists a certain degree of comparability between the two surveys. The samples in each case are somewhat different, however, since Wahrhaftig's sample includes persons from all generations, while the present survey is limited to households with children enrolled in elementary school. In addition, the data sought in the two surveys is rather different: while Wahrhaftig was interested in determining the extent to which Cherokee is spoken within a given Cherokee community as a whole, the primary purpose of the study reported here was to learn about the bilingualism of children in families in which Cherokee is actually spoken. While data was gathered for families in which only one parent is a Cherokee-speaker, the primary focus of the present study is upon house-

---

[2]   The four schools included in the survey are the participating schools in the Cherokee Bilingual Education Program, a bilingual education project funded under Title VII of the Elementary and Secondary Education Act and administered by the Greasy Creek Board of Education.
[3]   The existing Cherokee communities have been identified by Wahrhaftig (1968: 512–515).

holds in which both parents are Cherokee-speakers, and in which children regularly hear the language spoken.

The interview schedule which was employed contained questions regarding the parents' knowledge of Cherokee and their use of the language with each other and with their children. Parents were also asked questions about the children's use of Cherokee with siblings and peers as well as with the parents themselves. The interviewer speaks Cherokee and English and employed both languages in conducting the survey.

Table 1 displays data regarding the parents' knowledge of and use of Cherokee. The first item shows the number of household units in which husband and wife both speak Cherokee and the number in which a Cherokee-speaker is married to a non-Cherokee-speaker. In every instance in which only one of the parents speaks Cherokee, the children were found to be monolingual speakers of English. As a result, households of this kind are not included in any subsequent tabulation. The second item in Table 1, dealing only with households in which both parents can speak Cherokee, shows the extent to which Cherokee is used by the husband and wife when speaking to each other. The third item reports which language or languages the parents use when speaking to the children.

Table 1. Parents' use of Cherokee

		Greasy Creek	Lost City	Tenkiller	Marble City
Number of households in which one or both parents are Cherokee speakers	Both:	55	21	21	21
	One:	12	11	12	18
Language of parents with each other	Cherokee:	41	16	17	18
	English:	8	5	4	2
	Both:	3	0	0	1
Language of parents with children	Cherokee:	32	12	11	11
	English:	6	3	5	6
	Both:	3	1	1	1

Examination of Table 1 reveals that almost one-third of the Cherokee-speaking parents surveyed at Marble City are married to non-Cherokee-speakers. At both Lost City and Tenkiller this tendency is also strong, with approximately one-fourth of the Cherokee-speakers interviewed married to non-Cherokee-speakers. At Greasy Creek, however, more than 90 percent of the Cherokee-speaking parents included in the survey are married to Cherokee-speakers. As noted above, in every instance in which only one parent can speak Cherokee the children are monolingual in English. Children from households in which the parents speak English exclusively do not, accordingly, learn Cherokee in the larger context of the extended family.

The second item in Table 1 shows the number of households in which the parents speak predominantly Cherokee, English, or both, with their children. Only those household units are included in this tabulation, and in all subsequent ones, in which both parents can speak Cherokee, since as noted above, children almost universally are monolingual in English when only one parent can speak Cherokee. Examination of the second item reveals that, in those households in which both parents can speak Cherokee, Cherokee is employed as the principal means of communication between husband and wife in a large majority of instances in all four communities.

If one were to have access only to the data summarized thus far, it might seem that Cherokee is extremely vital, since a majority of Cherokee-speakers in each community marry Cherokee-speakers and subsequently employ Cherokee with each other within the home. Examination of the third item in Table 1 shows the position of Cherokee to be weaker than one might expect, however, since a large minority of parents who use Cherokee with each other employ primarily English in speaking to their children. This is the case at Marble City and Tenkiller in approximately one-third of the households, in one-fifth of the households at Lost City, and in less than one-sixth of the households at Greasy Creek. It seems likely that parents who use mostly Cherokee with each other but speak primarily English to their children have made a conscious decision that the children should become English-speakers, not Cherokee-speakers. In several instances the interviewer was told by such parents that the children would need to speak English well in order to acquire satisfactory employment in the larger society and that knowledge of Cherokee could not help their children in later life. The kind of bilingualism just described, in which parents prefer one language when speaking to each other, but use a second language with their children, is an obviously unstable bilingualism which can be expected to result in the complete replacement of the first language by the second. The fact that this sort of bilingualism exists in a large minority of Cherokee households places the continued vitality of the language in doubt.

The data displayed in Table 2 are concerned with the extent to which the children in the households surveyed speak Cherokee. The first item reports on the number of households in which children respond in Cherokee when spoken to in Cherokee.[4] Regardless of the extent to

---

[4]   Local observers, contending that children do not speak Cherokee, at times report that children answer in English when spoken to in Cherokee. For this reason, data regarding how children respond when spoken to in Cherokee was considered important. In the first item of Table 2, the number of households in which children answer in Cherokee is presented for each community, considering all households in which Cherokee is the preferred language of

which parents speak Cherokee to the children, if an appreciable number of children tend to speak only English to the parents, then the position of Cherokee would seem to be weak. The data reveal that this is the case at Marble City, where the children in approximately half the households answer in English when spoken to in Cherokee. In Tenkiller this is the

Table 2. Children's use of Cherokee

		Greasy Creek	Lost City	Tenkiller	Marble City
Considering all those households in which parents prefer Cherokee with each other, in how many do the children respond in Cherokee, English, or both, when spoken to in Cherokee by the parents?	Cherokee: English: Both:	26 7 8	9 4 3	11 5 0	8 2 7
Considering only those households from the above group in which parents prefer Cherokee with their children, do the children respond in Cherokee, English, or both, when spoken to in Cherokee?	Cherokee: English: Both:	25 1 6	8 1 3	7 2 2	8 2 1
Considering all those households in which parents prefer Cherokee with each other, in how many do the children use Cherokee, English, or both, when speaking with each other?	Cherokee: English: Both:	29 8 4	13 3 0	8 6 2	7 11 0

case in one-third of the households, in less than half at Lost City, and in less than one-fourth of the households at Greasy Creek. These figures are somewhat misleading, however, since they include the households in which parents speak primarily English to the children, and one would expect a tendency for these children to lack fluency in Cherokee and to use English even when spoken to in Cherokee. The second item of Table

---

the parents with each other; in a number of such households, English is the preferred language of parents with children. In the second item of Table 2 the same question is asked, considering a subset of the households taken into account in the first item; namely, those in which Cherokee is the preferred language of the parents with the children.

2 is more significant; in this item, only the households in which parents speak primarily Cherokee to the children are taken into account, and the number of households in which the children reply in Cherokee, English, or both, is tabulated. The results show that, in a great majority of instances, children reply in Cherokee when spoken to in Cherokee. The third item of Table 2 shows the number of households in which the parents perceive that the children speak Cherokee more often than English with each other. In all the communities except Marble City, in virtually all the households in which the children are spoken to primarily in Cherokee by the parents, Cherokee is the language used most often by the children in interaction with each other. The figures for Marble City show, however, that the children prefer to speak English to each other in a number of homes in which they are most often spoken to in Cherokee by the parents. Marble City is thus unique: while all the communities contain some households in which parents are bringing about a language shift by speaking English to the children, only at Marble City is there a tendency for children to speak mostly English even though their parents habitually speak to them in Cherokee.

In summary, these data indicate that Cherokee enjoys relatively great vitality at both Greasy Creek and Lost City. At Tenkiller and Marble City, on the other hand, Cherokee seems to be gradually yielding to English. At Greasy Creek, in household units in which both parents can speak Cherokee, the parents speak primarily Cherokee to each other in almost 80 percent of the homes. Furthermore, in over 75 percent of the households in which the parents speak mostly Cherokee with each other, it is also the language spoken most often to the children. In a large majority of the latter households, the children speak mostly Cherokee to each other. A similar situation obtains at Lost City. In both communities, Cherokee is employed primarily by parents with their children in a very large majority of the households in which both parents know the language, and within these latter households, Cherokee is the language spoken most often by the children in interaction with each other in a large majority of instances.

The position of Cherokee at Tenkiller is somewhat less secure. In almost one-third of the households in which the parents speak primarily Cherokee to each other, they prefer to speak English with their children. In those households in which the parents do speak mostly Cherokee with the children, however, the children use primarily Cherokee with each other in all but three instances, and in two of these the parents report that the children speak both Cherokee and English to each other.

At Marble City, as at Tenkiller, approximately one-third of the parents who speak Cherokee to each other prefer to use English with their children. At Marble City, however, unlike Tenkiller, even in those cases in which parents use Cherokee with the children, there is a strong tendency for children to speak English to each other. There are eleven households at Marble City in which the parents use primarily Cherokee with the children, but there are only seven households in which the children speak primarily Cherokee to each other.

It seems appropriate at this point to comment further upon the two principal tendencies apparent in the above data which favor the replacement of Cherokee by English. The first is the tendency of Cherokee-speaking parents to use English with their children; the second is the tendency of children to shift to English despite the fact that their parents habitually speak Cherokee to them.

The first tendency takes two forms. In some households, parents speak primarily English to each other as well as with their children. In other households, parents speak Cherokee to each other but prefer to use English with the children. Parents who speak mostly English with each other are likely to be at least as fluent in English as in Cherokee. In many cases, one or both have attended a boarding school, an experience which strongly favors the shift to English. In each community, however, the number of households in which husband and wife prefer to speak English to each other is relatively small. In a much larger number of households, the parents speak Cherokee to each other, but prefer to use English with the children. Such parents frequently speak English far less fluently than Cherokee; their children, as a result, sometimes speak a peculiarly Cherokee-flavored dialect of English acquired on their parents' model, but have little or no knowledge of Cherokee. The existence of this kind of bilingualism indicates the ambivalence with which Cherokee is regarded by many Cherokees, who attempt to facilitate the learning of English by their children at the expense of Cherokee.

The tendency for children to shift to English despite the fact that their parents use Cherokee with them is apparent at Marble City. Significantly, the incidence of marriages between Cherokee- and non-Cherokee-speakers is also particularly high at Marble City. This results in situations in which a child from a Cherokee-speaking household will be forced to speak English with many members of the extended family. The pressure to use English within this larger context is apparently frequently sufficient to bring about a shift from Cherokee to English on the part of many children from Cherokee-speaking households.

The effects of television and of the school experience upon the children's use of Cherokee seem to be less significant than the two factors just described in favoring the shift to English. Television sets are quite common at both Greasy Creek and Lost City, as well as at Tenkiller and Marble City, and yet Cherokee enjoys much greater vitality in the former communities. In addition, parents were questioned regarding the bilingualism of each of their children immediately before entering school as compared with the present. Only a few parents noted instances in which children spoke primarily Cherokee before entering school, but later switched to English as a result of the school experience. Wahrhaftig (1970:16–17), commenting upon the relatively greater use of English by children at Marble City, notes that:

> In some households in Marble City, there are preschool children who speak fluent English even though English rarely is spoken in the household. Their parents think the learning results from watching television. However, in Bull Hollow there are non-English-speaking children of preschool age who have watched as much television but have learned no English. The children in Marble City have first cousins (second brothers and sisters in Cherokee kin terms) with whom they play who are the children of a white mother and who speak no Cherokee. Evidently children in Marble City learn English from their playmates or at least enough English to make sense of and learn from the English they hear on television. In the absence of direct language learning from English-speaking kin, the children in Bull Hollow do not learn English from television.

At this point one can reasonably raise the question of the future vitality of Cherokee. The prospects for Cherokee being learned by subsequent generations of speakers seem particularly good at Greasy Creek, where Cherokee-speakers tend to marry Cherokee-speakers, and to speak primarily Cherokee with their children. The two factors outlined above which seem to favor replacement of Cherokee by English are not present to an appreciable extent at Greasy Creek: Cherokee-speaking parents do not tend to make a conscious shift from Cherokee to English to hasten their children's acculturation, and there are few exclusively English-speaking household units within the extended family which would tend to favor language shift by children in Cherokee-speaking households.

The situation at Lost City is somewhat comparable, although a higher proportion of Cherokee-speakers marry English monolinguals than at Greasy Creek. While the fact that many children at Greasy Creek and Lost City speak Cherokee with each other is not a sufficient condition for the language to be transmitted to members of the next generation, it would seem to be a necessary one: it is doubtful that children who use mostly English now will speak primarily Cherokee with their children twenty years from now. The best that one can say, then, is that it is likely that Cherokee will be learned by members of the next generation at both Greasy Creek and Lost City.

At both Tenkiller and Marble City, however, to an increasing extent the necessary condition for Cherokee being retained in the future is absent: children in a sizeable proportion of households in both communities use English with each other because their parents speak primarily English to them and consequently deprive them of the opportunity to acquire Cherokee. In addition, at Marble City the inroads which English is making in the extended family further weaken the position of

Cherokee. One can conclude that Cherokee is presently relatively vital at Greasy Creek and Lost City, less vital at Tenkiller, and declining at Marble City.

Miller (1972:2) has suggested that languages can be ranked by their degree of vitality. He proposes that a given language be classified on a four-point scale as flourishing, obsolescing, obsolete, or dead. The last two categories are quite straightforward: a dead language no longer has any speakers, and an obsolete language is one which, although it is remembered by older members of the community, is no longer used as a vehicle for social interaction.

Miller's categories "flourishing" and "obsolescing" are less clearly defined. Using Navajo as an example of a flourishing language, Miller (1972:2) notes that "English is used on almost all occasions as a second language. Children entering school know little or no English, and adults will not use English among themselves." Shoshoni, on the other hand, is considered to be obsolescing. Miller (1972:2) comments that "Shoshoni is still being used as a vehicle for social interaction, but the settings in which it is used are restricted. Not all (and in some cases, none) of the children still learn the language. And if it is being learned, normally English is also being learned at the same time."

Miller's criteria for classifying a language as flourishing or obsolescing might profitably be sharpened somewhat, as consideration of the Cherokee case will show. As stated, his criteria seem to imply that widespread bilingualism within a speech community implies the obsolescence of the minority language, thus precluding the possibility of stable bilingualism.

Miller's "flourishing" category should be revised to include languages which are used exclusively or nearly so in all domains of life, as well as languages which are used predominantly within at least one major domain, but not all. Miller's scale is revised accordingly in Table 3 along the lines just suggested.

Table 3.   Revised language vitality scale

Vital				Non-vital
flourishing: in all domains	flourishing: in at least one domain	obsolescing	obsolete	dead

Returning to the four Cherokee communities reported on above, at Tenkiller and Marble City English seems to be replacing Cherokee as the language of communication between parents and children and as the preferred language of the children with siblings and peers. What is probably the last major domain reserved for Cherokee in these communities is thus becoming an English domain. Cherokee at both Tenkiller and Marble City can therefore be classified as obsolescing.

At Greasy Creek and Lost City, however, one can argue that Cherokee is flourishing, although it is not used in all domains of life. It is likely that a majority of the adults in both communities use English with other adult Cherokees in certain contexts. However, Cherokee can still be considered flourishing in both communities, since it is the preferred language of both parents and children in at least one domain; Cherokee is the language of daily life in a majority of households.

Miller's scale might be further revised to provide for both slowly obsolescing and rapidly obsolescing languages. If this modification were made, then Cherokee at both Tenkiller and Marble City, where Cherokee is the preferred language in a large number of households, might be classified as "slowly obsolescing" while a language which is being learned at the most by only a few children could be termed "rapidly obsolescing." An example of a rapidly obsolescing language is Kiowa, which is apparently no longer being learned by children, but which is still spoken by members of older generations in interaction with each other.

As Miller (1972:1) notes, the degree of vitality of a minority language has educational implications. This is certainly true in the Cherokee case. The popular white view, shared by many educators, that Cherokee is no longer spoken by children has been shown to be an incorrect one. The degree of vitality exhibited by Cherokee in communities like Greasy Creek clearly calls for the educational use of the language in the local schools. Even in communities such as Marble City, where the language seems to be obsolescing slowly, a case can be made for an educational role for Cherokee. In communities of the latter type, of course, the precise nature of this role will be somewhat different from that in communities such as Greasy Creek, in which Cherokee is more flourishing.

REFERENCES

MILLER, WICK R.
1972   Obsolescing languages: the case of the Shoshoni. *Language in American Indian Education* (Winter):2–12.
WAHRHAFTIG, ALBERT
1968   The tribal Cherokee population of eastern Oklahoma. *Current Anthropology* 9:510–519.
1970   *Social and economic characteristics of the Cherokee population of eastern Oklahoma.* Anthropological studies 5. American Anthropological Association.

Chicano Bilingual/Bicultural Education

HENRY TORRES TRUEBA

This paper is not a survey of the existing bilingual/bicultural (b/b) programs organized by or for the Chicanos. It attempts rather to explore the types, scope, problems, and philosophy of Chicano b/b programs based on information gathered from life histories, questionnaires, formal and informal interviews, and active participation in such programs.

INTRODUCTION

The b/b education represents for the Chicano community the single most important effort to change the traditional educational philosophy expressed in standard policies and institutions throughout the country. B/b programs are thus seen by the Chicanos as a major breakthrough in the ethnocentric rigidity of curriculum and the overall school orientation towards a presumed monocultural middle-class American student. Chicanos also see b/b education as an opportunity to build up personal pride, self-identity, and a more meaningful and sensitive school that recognizes the reality of our pluralistic American society. Finally, *La Raza* believes that b/b education ultimately will open the door to full Chicano participation in the socioeconomic opportunities that this country offers.

Two definitions are in order here: Chicano and b/b programs. "Chicano" has been, and still is, a controversial word. I use it here synonymous with Mexican-American, *Hispano, La Raza,* etc. Chicano is a term that has been applied to "radical" Mexican-Americans and, more recently, to all Mexican-Americans. Simmen (1972:56) has defined Chicano as "An American of Mexican descent who attempts through peaceful, reasonable, and responsible means to correct the image of the

Mexican-American and to improve the position of this minority in the American social structure." This definition, although essentially correct, is restrictive. I would define Chicano as "A person of Mexican descent residing permanently in the United States, who perceives his culture as unique, that is, different from the Mexican and the Anglo cultures, and actively works to defend his cultural heritage and his social and civil rights, in order to improve his economic, political, social, and religious life."

We must now define bilingual/bicultural education. B/b education should be distinguished from remedial programs, from programs with English as a second language, and from bilingual programs which exclude the cultural component. The main purpose of the above programs is to facilitate the language change of the monolingual child, that is, from the native tongue of the child to the official language, English. In contrast with these programs, b/b education intends to train the child in two languages without his losing either one and to acquaint the child with a new culture without rejecting his own. The assumption is, contrary to what traditional remedial programs presupposed, that monocultural/monolingual education is an undesirable goal. The goal of b/b education is to enrich the child's human experience with two compatible and alternative languages and cultures. Traditionally, the American educational system has demanded that the culturally different child rapidly assimilate American culture and language, which are conceived as a homogeneous unit. The result, of course, was that the child would gradually see his people, his language, his culture, and himself as undesirable. Therefore, he would be psychologically damaged, divided, and impaired in his learning and intellectual development. B/b programs see the minority child and the Anglo child as being in equal need of enlarging their cultural universe and perceiving each other as acceptable and equally good.

In order to appreciate the scope and types of b/b programs, their underlying philosophy, and their significance for the Chicano, the reader must be reminded of the facts of life which Chicanos must confront, and of which they have become painfully aware.

CHICANO SOCIAL REALITY

1. The Chicano population, now the second largest minority in this country, is calculated to be over five and one-half million, of whom 90 percent live in the southwest, representing at least 12 percent of the total population of this area.

2. The ancestors of the Chicanos arrived in this country as early as 1609, and they settled in what is today Santa Fe. They lived in rural areas

for many years; however, at the present time, over 80 percent of the Chicanos live in metropolitan areas.

3. According to the 1960 census information, 56 percent of the Chicano labor force works in factories, mines, and construction: 19 percent work on farms; 17 percent in professional or clerical jobs; and 8 percent in service occupations.

4. Unemployment for Chicano males is twice the national unemployment rate.

5. Thirty-five percent of all Chicanos in the southwest (1960 census) have a family income of less than $3,000 per year, and in some areas of the country, even the median family income is under $3,000 (Texas, for example).

6. Chicano median education for men and women, twenty-five years old and over, is 7.1 years of completed school (1960 census), compared with 12.1 for the Anglo population. Furthermore, while the Anglos have at least 22 percent with one year or more of college education, Chicanos count on only 6 percent to reach that level of education.

7. Twenty percent of the GI's in the Vietnam frontline were Chicanos, even though the total population of Chicanos represents only 3 percent of the country's total population.

8. More important still is the fact that most Chicanos have experienced in a variety of ways — sometimes overtly, sometimes in a subtle manner — the psychological oppression of being segregated, laughed at, neglected, despised, or abused not only by private individuals in the dominant society, but also by its official authorities and its public institutions. They see Anglo society as a hostile enemy that has used all possible means to undermine Chicano culture and language.

In response to these sad and complex facts of Chicano social life, there is a unanimous and energetic opposition of Chicano educators and students who say loud and clear: "*Ya basta!*" [It's enough!]. Therefore, the Chicanos seek to strengthen their language and culture as a means of restoring personal and group respect, pride, and self-sufficiency.

The full significance of b/b Chicano programs can be appreciated only in this light. It goes beyond the utilitarian and immediate rewards of personal advancement and the advantages of having a school diploma.

TYPES AND SCOPE OF B/B CHICANO EDUCATION

At present, there are two main types of b/b programs: (1) programs for children (either monolingual or quasi-bilingual) during the first years of school from kindergarten to third or fourth grade, and (2) programs for bilingual teachers to train them in b/b education in order that they may effectively work with Chicanitos at all levels of education, from elementary through high school, either as teachers or administrators. The emphasis on Chicano language and culture is essential to both types of programs.

The aim or the scope of these programs is essentially the intellectual emancipation of the Chicano. The main long-range objectives of the first type of b/b programs as expressed by Chicano educators are:

1. To help Chicanitos maintain or create a positive self-image.

2. To provide cultural continuity for the Chicanitos as they move from their environment to the Anglo institution of learning.

3. To develop and maintain pride in their cultural heritage and build a more definite self-identity without losing the benefits of formal education.

4. To develop curricula on the basis of Chicano language and culture whereby the content and the means of communicating knowledge become relevant to the Chicano.

5. To stop and counteract school discrimination against Chicanos.

6. To upgrade the academic achievements of Chicanos.

7. To encourage Chicanos to fully participate in the national life of American society.

The goals of the second type of b/b programs, i.e. those geared to train teachers in b/b education, are complementary to the goals of the first type:

1. To train teachers who can create the proper classroom atmosphere where the Chicanitos can retain and develop a positive self-image.

2. To equip teachers with the knowledge of Chicano culture necessary to build pride in their cultural heritage.

3. To train teachers as agents of change in their respective institutions, stimulating them to make innovations in educational methods, techniques, and curricula.

4. To make teachers the models for incoming Chicano students who aspire to higher education.

As an illustration of the content of the second type of b/b programs and the means of obtaining the proposed goals, I will briefly describe the Mexican-American Education Project (MAEP) of California State University, Sacremento (CSUS), which was started under the tutelage of the anthropology department in the fall of 1968.

MAEP AT CALIFORNIA STATE UNIVERSITY, SACRAMENTO

The MAEP began with an Experienced Teachers Fellowship Program funded by the United States Office of Education. It started with only five experienced Chicano teachers, fourteen Anglos, and one black teacher. At that time CSUS had very few Chicano students and no Chicano faculty members. The program emphasized courses in culture, culture and personality, culture change, poverty, agents of change, and cultures of Mexico. The main objective was to sensitize Anglo teachers to the special needs of Chicano students. Community involvement was encouraged. In the next academic year, 1969–1970, most program participants were experienced Chicano teachers. The program was reorganized to prepare b/b teachers and placed instructional emphasis on educational techniques and curricular innovations. Since then, the MAEP has striven to strike a balance between the rigid M.A. degree requirements, the central course work, the particular needs of students, and involvement in the local Chicano community. Evaluations from faculty and students showed the need for a more flexible organization of the academic activities. In 1971–1972 the MAEP added the "early childhood" component to serve students' interests in the education of Chicano children at the preschool and first grade levels.

As it stands today, the b/b program at CSUS offers an M.A. in Social Sciences with specialization in Chicano Studies, and it requires a minimum of thirty-one semester units distributed as follows: twenty-four units or more in social sciences, of which nine units must be taken at the upper level in an area of concentration (anthropology, criminal justice, economics, geography).

Basic Course Work

First semester

ANTHROPOLOGY: Basic concepts of culture and culture change (6)
HISTORY: Readings in Chicano History (3)
INTERDISCIPLINARY I: Chicano Involvement in Education (3)
EDUCATION: Introduction to Bilingual Education (3)
Second semester
ANTHROPOLOGY: Anthropology and Education (3)
GOVERNMENT, SOCIOLOGY, ECONOMICS: Seminar in Social Sciences (3)
INTERDISCIPLINARY II: Chicano Education, Synthesis and Application (3)
Electives in Social Sciences or Education (3)
THESIS (4)
If a student feels sufficiently prepared in an area required by the present program, he or she may, upon approval by the director, change his or her course work. Furthermore, students are encouraged to take additional courses within the school regulations.

At the end of its fifth year the MAEP has prepared over one hundred b/b teachers with an M.A. in Social Sciences and Chicano Studies, who for the most part have returned to their school districts as teachers, resource persons, administrators, or counselors. Others have been hired by the state Department of Education or by federal b/b programs. A few others have continued their education towards a Ph.D. Much of the success of this program is the result of the leadership coming from the administrative and teaching staff and the intensive interaction of the students, faculty, and the local Chicano community. During the current academic year there are seven Ph.Ds. and four M.A.s teaching from the departments of anthropology, economics, education, history, government, and sociology. Six of these instructors are Chicanos (two of them with Ph.Ds.).

By interviewing the participants during the last two years, I have arrived at the following conclusions which indicate the effectiveness of the program and its fundamental philosophy of education. Thirty-nine Chicano graduate students working for their M.A. in Social Sciences were given questionnaires and interviewed. The results are as follows:

1. In terms of the impact of the MAEP on the life of the participants, 75.6 percent feel that the project made a significant change in their careers because :(a) it made them aware of their social responsibilities and personal capabilities; (b) it gave them the opportunity to obtain a master's degree and helped them to orientate their education towards the Chicano community.

2. When asked about the project's capacity for producing innovative teachers, 91.9 percent of the participants replied that the MAEP had offered them a unique opportunity to design educational programs and techniques that will improve Chicano education.

3. Concerning the selection of project students, 83 percent consider selection practices fair and essentially based on the qualifications of the candidates, i.e. high academic performance and a strong commitment to improve Chicano education.

4. The aspirations of project students go beyond the masters level: 29.7 percent plan to continue towards a doctorate, and 43.2 percent see the project as an initial step in the increase of their own potential, though they are not inclined to continue academically for a doctorate.

5. A majority of these Chicano students (54.1 percent) feel the need to visit as many local schools as possible to assess the situation of Chicano education and to help Chicano students.

6. Most students, however, realize that during this year's training their primary commitment is to their academic work, especially through the use of the library (86.5 percent).

7. In spite of one emphasis on group solidarity, Chicano students feel personally responsible for the outcome of their school training (86.5 percent).

8. Chicano students have two main concerns about their academic performance: (a) the demands that course work and the master's thesis

represent, and (b) the lack of familiarity with proper academic behavior (75.7 percent).

9. The previous concerns are consistent with the three major challenges that many Chicanos (64.8 percent) face in school in order to:

a. adjust to the academic environment, especially when there is a conflict between school and community responsibilities (21.6 percent);

b. have confidence in their own ability, experience, and judgment (27.0 percent);

c. place themselves culturally, educationally and politically (16.2 percent).

10. When asked about the relevancy of MAEP curriculum, 97.3 percent of the participants answer that between 50 and 100 percent of the curriculum is directly applicable to their needs as teachers and administrators in schools with a heavy Chicano population.

11. Nevertheless, some students (21.6 percent) would like to see curricular modifications, and others (35.1 percent) would welcome a cut in extracurricular Chicano meetings, which in their opinion are unproductive.

12. Three out of four students have no serious economic problems during the year of training at the MAEP.

13. According to the project participants, the most important need of the Chicano community is:

a. Educational upgrading via b/b programs (48.6 percent).

b. Political leadership and political power (21.6 percent).

c. Solidarity of *La Raza* (10.8 percent).

d. Ideological leadership and more doctors of philosophy (2.7 percent).

e. Other (16.7 percent).

14. Given the opportunity, 43.2 percent of the students would like to replicate the MAEP elsewhere, while others see themselves directly involved in elementary or high school teaching of Chicanitos (40.5 percent).

15. The ideal job for the project participant would involve direct contact with as many Chicanos as possible and offer opportunities for personal intellectual growth (67.5 percent).

16. The two most important targets of the students during training are: (a) to gain knowledge rapidly, and (b) to show academic ability (67.5 percent). Other targets are the enjoyment of time to read, write, plan, and to make lasting friendships with other Chicanos.

17. Two-thirds of the participants (64.9 percent) were elementary school or high school teachers before joining the MAEP; the remaining either were students or had jobs other than teaching.

18. During early childhood 2.7 percent learned English first and

learned Spanish later (still as children). Nonetheless, the great majority (64.9 percent) learned Spanish first and English later. Only 18.7 percent of the students learned English exclusively during childhood. Finally, 13.5 percent learned English and Spanish at the same time.

19. In spite of the previous findings, and although all project participants are bilinguals to a degree, only 8.1 percent feel more fluent in Spanish than in English, and less than half of them (45.9 percent) feel they speak English as well as the Anglos. Less than one-third of the participants (27.0 percent) think they speak English better than they do Spanish, and only 18.9 percent are aware of having a slight accent in English.

20. In the home, 48.6 percent use both English and Spanish, 29.7 percent use English exclusively, and 16.2 percent use Spanish exclusively.

PROBLEMS OF B/B EDUCATION

The internal and external evaluations of the program at CSUS, and similar programs, also suggest serious problems that b/b education must face. During a major three-day b/b conference in Sacramento, December 8th through 10th, where most b/b Chicano programs were represented, Chicano educators and students expressed their areas of concern with regard to problems extrinsic and intrinsic to the programs.

Extrinsic to the Programs

1. Lack of institutional support at all levels. B/b education is sometimes considered unpatriotic, politically radical, and wasteful. Unstable and meager funding reflects this lack of support.
2. Rigid educational views that curtail curricular flexibility and innovative teaching.
3. Political rivalry among Chicanos and competition for the same meager resources that divides community support.
4. Departmental and school-structured divisions that curtail effective use of personal and material resources.
5. Traditional policies for distribution and use of funds on the part of federal, state, or local agencies.

Intrinsic to the Programs

1. Lack of models of b/b education which could be replicated and lack of information about existing programs.

2. Inadequate conceptualization and justification of particular methodologies, techniques, and curricular innovations of the programs currently operating.

3. Lack of adequate personnel to staff programs, especially personnel proficient in the languages involved.

4. Lack of critical self-evaluation to assess the achievement of proposed goals, the effectiveness of the techniques used, and the reorientation of the program.

5. Conflicting philosophies of education on the part of staff and participants.

Most Chicanos present at the Sacramento conference seemed to recognize that b/b programs have developed too fast in the last five years to have been able to reassess and coordinate their activities. Since cooperative action and coordination are somehow contingent upon the philosophy of education that underlies b/b programs, it is important, at this point, to discuss the two polar positions of Chicano educators.

ANTITHETICAL PHILOSOPHICAL POSITIONS OF CHICANOS

The "Within-the-System" Philosophy of Education

This philosophy insists on the institutionalization of Chicano programs, that they be incorporated into the existing institutions of learning with full status equal to any other educational program. By implication, this philosophy strives to incorporate the Chicano population into the mainstream of American society with rights and obligations equal to those of the Anglos. American society, nevertheless, is seen by these Chicano educators as a pluralistic society that has never been homogeneous and has ignored the educational needs of the minority students. Education would, in their opinion, open the door to social and economic opportunities for the Chicano students. The steps to be followed are: (1) legislative and financial support for the existing b/b programs, (2) an increase in number of the rank and file professional academicians and educators who would be working with Chicano students, serving as models for Chicano students, and acting as middlemen between the educational institutions and the students, and (3) a gradual change from within the system of education to make it more tolerant of cultural differences and more responsive to the needs of Chicanos.

The "Out-of-the-System" Philosophy

The advocates of this philosophy of education do not want to infiltrate the American educational system which they consider rotten and crumbling. They want an entirely different structure, independent from the Anglo system, with its own goals, its own rules, and one in which the control remains in the hands of Chicanos themselves. Since the main assumption is that the Anglo educational system cannot be patched or restored because it is collapsing already, this educational philosophy stresses Chicano self-sufficiency, not competition with the Anglos; Chicano self-determination, not dependence on Anglo sources; Chicano creativeness, not imitation of the Anglos. The meaningfulness of learning that comes from human experience and the values of Chicano culture are to be maximized. They emphasize *carnalismo* [brotherhood] of all Chicanos, whether they are students or faculty, and de-emphasize ritual behavior between teacher and student. These are the major tenets of the "out-of-the-system" philosophy of education:

1. True learning is part of life, based on personal experience, and therefore part of one's own culture, involving the whole human being, his intellect, his heart, his wishes, aspirations, and values. Therefore, learning must capitalize on the student's language, family structure, dietary and dressing patterns, religion, and beliefs.

2. Learning must take place as an exchange of ideas between teacher and student, and among students in a symmetrical relationship where the students' wishes, rights, and intellectual inputs are respected by the teacher and the flow of messages is balanced and meaningful. This symmetrical relationship would discourage the rigidity, dishonesty, and incoherence of instructors that inhibit the student's intellectual growth.

As an example of this "out-of-the-system" philosophy, D.Q.U. (Dewanahwidah-Quetzaltcoatl University), a Chicano-Indian university near Davis, California, has been mentioned by some Chicanos. I am not prepared, however, to evalute this example. But where we draw the line between IN and OUT of the educational system constitutes a controversial issue not yet resolved. What is important here is to note the way in which some Chicanos perceive the Anglo educational system and their contribution to our understanding of that system.

SUMMARY AND FINAL REMARKS

Chicano b/b education is beginning to stand on its own feet, struggling between two opposite philosophies, but strong enough to become a symbol of intellectual freedom and a promise of a better future for the Chicano community. In the view of the Chicano staff and participants, b/b education goes beyond a fair share of the good things of life in American society: it means social recognition, respect, and self-determination. While Chicanos may complain at times that there are more chiefs than Indians, on many other occasions chiefs and Indians iron out their differences and work cooperatively, showing a true *carnalismo* and love for each other. Quietly, the "within-the-system" programs grow and show their fruits, thus giving *La Raza* a new sense of confidence and optimism.

REFERENCE

SIMMEN, EDWARD
    1972   *Pain and promise: the Chicano today.* New York: New American Library.

Helping Africans to Speak for Themselves: The Role of Linguistics

ROBERT G. ARMSTRONG

Formal linguistics is concerned with the whole theory of human speech. As such it deals in an abstract way with universals, and it is neutral to all values and norms except the value of the pursuit of theory itself — a goal which needs no defense at an international scientific congress. A complementary and normative research goal of anthropological linguistics is the application of linguistics and the whole experience of ethnography to the study of high forms of human thought and ideas. This can be done by discovering and recording the peak phenomena of thought and speech in a great variety of societies. These peak phenomena include great works of oral literature, the ideas of serious thinkers on a great variety of topics, and even the subtleties of intimate conversation and of humor. My own experience in this field has been mostly in West Africa, especially Nigeria; and in drawing largely on that experience for this paper, I am sure that what is true of West Africa is relevant to many other places.

A piece (or work) of West African oral literature is typically a synthesis of various activities which are different in kind. It is by definition mainly an oral production; its written form comes later and usually because the originating society has already recognized it as important and worthy of preservation. There is first of all the string of words and sentences that make up the poem, the recitation, the story, the speech, or the words of the song. If the piece is a poem, there is the special set of characteristics that make it so. There is the elaborate series of voice qualifiers that separate it from ordinary conversation. There is often a musical form, with or without a musical accompaniment, in which the piece is embedded. The piece may also be partly expressed in dance. And there may be some kind of play involving masks, a special arrangement of artists or performers and audience, or relation of all to some shrine or altar, the whole being related to other works of art, such as sculpture or mural painting. And there may be special costumes and other use of symbols involved. Full publication of such works involves such different media and kinds of editorial work simultaneously that we may well speak of multidimensional publication.

The forms of speech used are often quite special and intended to signal what Calame-Griaule has called "the poetic intention." The effect of this is to pose a great many grammatical, lexical, and phonological problems to the would-be recorder of oral literature. These problems are so severe that the usual reaction to them has been to publish impressionistic transcriptions and very loose paraphrasing in English or French.

The first dimension of publication must therefore be linguistic mastery of the language of the oral piece. No easy task! We must have a solid grasp of the phonology and morphophonology of the language, so that we may not miss the subtleties of wordplay amidst the often gross dramatic effects of the voice qualifiers. Yoruba and Idoma poets like to play with patterns of assonance and even the identity of sounds so that the identity of sound is contrasted with great differences of meaning and syntax. For example, in the Idoma *alekwū* poetic legend, *"Onugbo mlOkō,"* the line *Īwīya lenyi wīya έ ōō* 'an evil spirit has stirred up the water', the near homonyms *Īwīya* 'evil spirit' and *wīya* 'stir up' are thrown together poetically in a powerful line. They are quite distinct etymologically; and syntactically one is the subject, the other is the predicate head.

Surface structure and deep structure may be played against each other in this way, and a deliberately contrived series of identical or nearly identical syllables may bridge great chasms in the deep structure. For example, the chanted prayers of a traditional Yoruba ironworker, who is a strong member of the syncretistic *aladura* cult (cherubim and seraphim), has the dramatically uttered lines:

Èmi ni mọ mọ́ọ mọ mọ mọ,
'I am the one who will build, build, build'
Èmi ni mọ mọ̀ mọ̀ mọ̀
'I am the one who surely knows, knows, knows.'

These may be analysed thus:

Topicalization Subject Predicate

		Pre-verb,	verb	verb	verb
èmi ni	*mọ*	*mọ́ọ*	*mọ*	*mọ*	*mọ*
I it is (who)	I	Future	build	build	build

Topicalization Subject Predicate

		emphatic	pre-verb	verb	verb	verb
èmi ni	*mọ*	*mọ̀*		*mọ̀*	*mọ̀*	*mọ̀*
I it is (who)	I	surely		know	know	know [repetition for emphasis]

We know the syntax and morphology of this utterance by comparing it with dozens of similar, mostly less poetically marked sentences. We can see the poet's deliberate use of regular but optional vowel harmony when we know that the various words of similar shape have the following alternate forms: *mo* = *mǫ,* 'I'; *máa* = *maa* = *ma* = *mǫ́ǫ* = *mǫǫ* = *mǫ,* a pre-verb showing future action; *mà* = *mǫ̀,* an emphatic pre-verb. He could have said, *mo mà mǫ̀ mǫ̀.*

Similarly, although most West African verse, apart from Hausa and Fulani, is neither metered nor rhymed, this does not mean that we can ignore rhythm and assonance. These are very important indeed; and they must be clearly shown in the writing because it is hard to guess at them in the absence of mechanically repetitive prosodic patterns. We need to know precisely what contractions the poet has used and what vowel and tone sandhi. Without this, the elaborate wordplay found in West African literature is almost sure to elude us. And in the same way, our writing must be sensitive to the elaborately structured parallelisms that are as characteristic of West African verse as of ancient Biblical Hebrew poetry.

So, for example, if we write the following Idoma ancestral mask chant in base-forms that correspond more or less to the deep structure of the syntax, we are still a long, long way from the poetry that grips the Idoma and makes them weep. (The following example is from Armstrong (1969), *"Onugbo mlOkō,"* lines 80–91; high tone is shows by ´, mid-tone by ¯, and low tone is unmarked.)

80. *Ǫtū le wú Onugbo ɔyí ɛ́nɛ́ Okō oo*
    Ikpó ɛ̄nɛ̄ Onugbo pīya nnyā oo
        Eléé Okō gbo oōkwū ɔtɛ́ ī nyɔ ká nū oo.
    Aná Okō le okónu hɛ́,
    Onugbo, ɔyí ɛ́nɛ́ m oo,
85. *Gāā káá! gāā káá!*
    Aná Onugbo nyɛ̄ɛ̄,
        Ólí ɛ̄nɛ̄ Onugbo je ga icō nnyā oo,
    "Okō, Okō ɔyí ɛ́nɛ́ m awɔ bú enyi nnyā á oo!"
    Okō ka ó wɛ ami bú enyi ā nóó!
90. *Okō, Okō ka ó wɛ ami bú enyi ā nóó!*
        Elééé!

Unless we are quite expert in the morphophonemics of the language, we shall completely miss the powerful, driving rhythms of this passage in which the tensions of the story are rising rapidly to a climax. We shall miss the song-like quality of Okō's answers in lines 89–90, and the fact of the repeated *"ko"* syllables and *"o"* assonance.

The morphonological machinery of this language is so complex that it is, in my view, far more economical to write phonemically and tonemically rather than morphophonemically. The above passage written with all the vowel sandhi and tone changes shown as they are pronounced reveals the rhythms and assonances of the line and is immediately understandable to any one who knows the central dialect of Idoma:

80. Ǫtū le wóOnugbo ɔ́nÓkō ɛ́ɛ́ oo.
   Ikpó nōOnugbo pīa nnyā oo,
      Eléé Okō gboōkwɔ́té ī nyɔ́ kúnū oo.
   AnóOkō lokónu hɛ́,
      "Onugbo, ɔ́nɛ́m oo,
85.   Gāā káá! Gāā káá!"
   AnóOnugbo nyɛ̄ɛ̄,
      Ólí nōOnugbo je gicō nnyā oo,
      "Okōō, Okɔ́nɛ́m awɔ́ béenyi nnyā á oo!"
   Okō kó wami béenyi ā nóó!
90. Okō, Okō kó wami béenyi ā nóó!
   Elééé!

80. Anger boiled in the heart of Onugbo,
      brother of Okō.
   Though Onubgo had turned away,
      Eléé, Okō started on his hunt again.
   Then Okō called,
      "Onugbo, my brother,
85.   Come a while! Come a while!"
   Then Onugbo changed,
      Raising his gun,
      "Okō, Okō, my brother it is you
         who muddied that water!"
   Okō said, "It was not I who muddied
      The water!"
90. Okō, Okō said, "It was not I who
      muddied the water!"
   Elééé!

The manner in which West African languages shall best be written is still a matter of keen controversy among the linguists and intellectuals who are involved. One does not have to agree with any particular solution in order to see that there is a problem here requiring careful study in the separate cases of the many and various languages, and that the balance of orthographic considerations may well be different as we pass from one language to another.

The second dimension is the publication of a faithful translation and a full annotation of both the original and the translated texts. By publishing a translation, we commit ourselves publicly to the correctness of the transcription and also to an opinion as to the meaning of the original. We cease to hide our doubts and ignorance behind the proclaimed weird and mysterious beauty of the original, which is apparent only to initiates, or behind the assertion that only true-blue, native-born sons of the xyz soil can possibly understand the poetry of their grandparents. The translation of poetry and other literary forms is of course notoriously difficult, and there is no such thing as perfect translation. Still we cannot avoid trying. No human being can learn more than a tiny fraction of the languages of Africa; and for the literatures of all the rest we must rely on translations. We may be encouraged in this by the words of an anonymous reviewer in *The Times Literary Supplement*:

A translation is one of the most important kinds of commentary on a poem; and in the struggle to know what a poem is and how it works, a poet capable of translating into poetry has far-reaching advantages over academic criticism (Anonymous 1973).

One rule that can be borne in mind is that so far as possible the poetic imagery of the original ought to be translated straight, even at the cost of a certain strangeness. The usual alternative to this is to substitute an English or a French cliché for a difficult metaphor in the original. Not only is the resulting translation remote from the original, but also it is full of clichés. The reader soon begins to wonder how anybody can get excited about such stuff.

In my experience, perhaps 80 percent of the imagery of Yoruba and Idoma poetry can be put into English with enough success to justify the effort. For the last 20 percent, which would sound wholly unpoetic or even ridiculous in translation, one can use a standardized phrase and then explain in a footnote what is happening. For example, in one of his stage directions to his opera titled *"Ọba Kò So,"* Ladipọ (1972:74–75) writes that Tìmì takes out his arrows *". . . ní ìrètí pé òun yíó' ṣe Gbọ̀ọ́nkáà bí ọṣẹ́ ti ń ṣe ojú:."* We translate this as *". . . hoping to teach Gbọ̀ọ́nkáà a lesson he will never forget."* Our footnote explains that the Yoruba actually says, *". . . treat him as soap treats the eyes."*

The modern, high-fidelity, portable tape recorder has added a dimension of its own to the study of oral literature. One really ought not to be satisfied with anything less than a Nagra, expensive as it is. Only with first-rate equipment can one hope to get the full range of the powerful musical qualities of so much of African oral literature, or capture the marvelous subtlety of the voicing of the storytellers, or the unaccompanied chants and incantations, or the talk of the public speakers. And the subtlety of African languages is such that our most experienced native-speaking transcribers must often strain even with a very fine recording. In these matters, the best is none too good.

We are beginning the stereophonic recording of percussion orchestras. This technique opens up wholly new opportunities for the understanding of talking musical instruments in the midst of ensembles, as well as making really gorgeous recordings possible. In Africa we are in one of the great musical and poetic provinces of the world. It is time that we made up our minds to stop being amateurs and to set about organizing, making, and publishing professional recordings of what is here.

The third dimension is therefore the publication of really good recordings of oral literature. All too often, of course, publication begins and ends at this point. There are by now quite a fair number of good-quality records on the market that give a mosaic of bits and pieces of fine performances. We are usually given little more than the titles of these pieces. A published recording, in this sense, should be of the whole work, just as we expect to publish the whole of a European opera or symphony or oratorio, or record a play by Shakespeare, Molière, or T. S. Eliot on records or on published magnetic tapes. Cheap, popular records of favorite bits can, of course, follow this, but must not be the excuse for our avoiding the main task.

It will be obvious to many of you that there is still another side to African oral literature, and that is its visual aspect, the publication of which may be regarded as a fourth dimension. Most African music is connected with dance in some way. The master storytellers deserve to be watched, because they do a great deal of in-place acting as the story proceeds. Much of the poetry of the cults is connected with masks and sacred places. Some of these have their secret aspects that must be respected; but they also have a public side that can be photographed.

For all these reasons, we must also be thinking of the sound film as an important medium of publishing African materials, and this is our fourth dimension. The pioneering work has already been done by such men as Jean Rouch, at the Musée de l'Homme, and by Frank Speed, at the University of Ibadan and the University of Ifẹ. What remains is the work of organizing support for such films on a larger scale and the giving of serious resources to this work.

Does all of this appear utopian? It is not only feasible, it is already being done! The pilot models have been made and have had successful trial runs. I am describing the present, the year 1973, in the study of African oral literature. I have described what we now know very well to be the case: the fact that African oral literature is an integral part of the great arts of West Africa and cannot be separated from them without grave loss. Our program of publication must express this fact. Measured by our previous efforts, the costs of this program are high. Measured by the fact that we are now able to bring to life the work of African universities and schools in a wholly new way, the costs of the tasks ahead are modest indeed. I feel confident that African governments will be willing to pay these costs, once they understand the possibilities of the road ahead. The various programs of Black Studies and Afro-American Studies in the United States have a similar long-term interest in such publication. It is up to us to prepare ourselves to give guidance and content to the work that is crying to be done.

For linguistics itself, the point is that an African language must be studied whole: phonology, morphophonology, morphology, syntax, lexicon, and suprasegmental expressive systems must all be tackled more or less simultaneously. Once we have passed a certain elementary level, the oral literature itself and the needs for its study provide us with a guiding thread for linguistic research that cannot fail to have an effect on the development of theory.

Jean Ure, of the University of Ghana, has suggested a fifth dimension: the placing of works of oral literature in their full social, cultural, historical and, therefore, human contexts. It is only then that they can achieve the full flowering of their meaning. The importance of this may be seen in Ọla Rotimi's recent play, or music-drama, *Ọba Owọnramwẹn*, about the last king of the Benin Empire, who was captured and taken into exile in 1897. The play makes very effective use of the Benin's Edo Cultural Group to do a prologue, an epilogue, and music at important ceremonial points during the play. The epilogue is a lament sung by two almost naked young men while doing a long, slow dance with their hands clasped on top of their heads in the position of mourning. It is sung in the unaccompanied, dissonant organum of this area, musically almost unknown to the rest of the world. In this tradition, two voices sing parallel melodies at a dissonant interval. It is a very powerful style indeed, and in this context — as a lament for the death of a whole society and way of life — the song of the two young men absolutely tears one's heart out. The same lament published or performed in the abstract, with some such title as "Edo Lament," would not have one-tenth the impact that it does coming at the end of Rotimi's play, in the context of defeat and a sea change in the Benin way of life (Rotimi 1974).

I should like to close by giving a number of examples of the sort of oral material that can be gathered in the field with a Nagra tape recorder and produced for publication when there is good control of the language and when the editorial team includes colleagues with linguistic training and native-speaking knowledge of the language. Needless to say among anthropologists, one needs very good relations with the people involved in order to find, collect, and interpret this level of material. One does not quickly find the key people to interview and record. And the interview itself must be conducted with great tact and sensitivity, if traditionally-minded old people are to be drawn out and enabled to speak freely. Such an interview is often best conducted by a trained and understanding colleague who is a member of the community. The portable, high-fidelity tape recorder enables one to study and transcribe what is said in meticulous detail later on.

The first example is from the story of a blind Idoma farmer, who to this day continues to sustain himself by farming, twenty-six years after losing his sight. He describes his initial despair and his early attempt at suicide, which his family frustrated. Then he records what transpires the same night as he lies in bed with his wife (see Appendix 1).

This is not only a poignant human document. It contains the important sociological point that without their father, the daughters cannot be married properly.

The second example is from the long interview with Ode, the professional gravedigger who refuses to speculate on the calendar year when his host's grandmother died and was given the first coffin burial:

Ọ̀ncé: Ó kwú 194. . . . ?
Ode: Ń kɔɔ̄mā lɛ ā gɛɲ́ N wɔ̄cōo-
        gwucéɛkwɔ nɛ u. Ogwucéɛkwɔ nūŋ̄ gwō ipúnū á.

Ọ̀ncé: She died in 194. . . . ?
Ode: I don't speak like that anymore!
        I am a man of tradition. It is in tradition
        that I am immersed.

His description of his procedure during the burial of a "bad death," where the deceased has died of a taboo disease such as tuberculosis, leprosy, elephantiasis, or epilepsy, is a unique personal and ethnographic document (see Appendix 2).

The bad death is a recurrent theme in West African writing. This is the first time it has been described by the man who must bury the corpse. The interview is also a document of one kind of professionalism in a traditional African society: "Since I do this, I am not someone who goes to the farm."

Similarly, the much maligned and caricatured Èṣù concept in Yoruba religion has recently been revealed in an entirely new light by the work of dos Santos and dos Santos (1971). They collected relevant poetic texts from Babalọlá Ifátóògùn, a very learned, traditional divination priest from Iló'bú, near Ibadan. Called "the Devil" or "Satan" by Christians and Moslems and "the god of mischief" or "the Trickster" by anthropologists, Èṣù may now be seen as the messenger of the gods, the god of events, who makes everything happen. Events are morally neutral and can work for us or against us. Without Èṣù everything would stop, and the universe would collapse. From one of Babalọlá Ifátóògùn's chants we know that a fundamental symbol of Èṣù is the spinning, round-pointed snail shell, called òkòtó, which is much used as a top in gambling games. The sacred poem in question in the chant called Orí' ṣírí'ṣí Èṣù 'Various Types of Èṣù,' from the Odù Ogbè Ìrẹ̀tẹ̀, is as follows:

Ó ní Òkòtó
Ó ní Agbegbe lójú
Bẹ́ẹ̀ ló sì ń fi ẹsẹ̀'kan 'ṣoṣooṣo
Pòòyì rànyìn-rànyìn-rànyìn kálẹ̀.

He said, "Òkòtó."
It has a wide hollow top
And thus, with only one leg
It spins around and around on the ground.

The upward spinning spiral of the snail shell is in fact an evocative symbol of "*Eṣù*'s dynamic principle and manner of self-multiplication. *Èṣù* is the one infinitely multiplied" (dos Santos and dos Santos 1971:8, 94, 101). The fact is that more than a century of interviewing Christian and Moslem converts about *Èṣù* has resulted only in caricatures of the concept. A few hours work in a carefully prepared situation with a real *babaláwo* 'divination priest' and a first-class tape recorder plus several weeks of hard work doing a preliminary transcription and translation of the tape, have opened up a whole new chapter in the study of African religion. This work has given us new questions, problems, and perspectives that we will be a long time in exploring.

Another fascinating passage is from the astonishing satirical scene called "*Ọba Ìkà*" 'The Cruel King,' in the late Kọ́lá Ògúnmọ́là's opera, *The Palmwine Drinkard* (Ògúnmọ́là 1972). The solemn entrance of the King is accompanied by a parody of a royal Yoruba praise-song (see Appendix 3).

Finally, there is Tìmì's incantation before the gates of Ẹ̀dẹ̀, with which he brings the people of Ẹ̀dẹ̀ out to welcome him, quiets them down, and persuades them to support him. The "argument" of the incantation is a series of powerfully suggestive metaphors (see Appendix 4).

In the more traditional contexts from which Ladipọ has borrowed them, the metaphoric incantations of the dew and the ocean are used by *egúngún* masks or by market traders to attract a crowd, and by *babaláwos* to attract clients. The term, *àtẹ̀pẹ́* 'that which is trodden and endures' is a secret name for earth. The imagery of the *oló'gbùró* bird is used to quiet down the crowd. The whole incantation is in the form of a typical *Odù* poem from the *Ifá* divination literature — or liturgy. It is in fact a small part of a very long, taboo Ifá chant that cannot be recited without first sacrificing a goat.

I repeat that in recording this level of oral literature, the best is none too good. It is hard, meticulous work to transcribe even the best of tape recordings of such traditional materials, and their translation and interpretation are yet another chapter. But on the other hand, a first-class tape recorder gives a level of fidelity that enables one to analyze short stretches of utterly traditional speech on the sound spectrograph in the laboratory, far from the village where the recording was made.

In this way, traditional people, like Adama and Ode above, can now speak directly into the permanent record, without their words being filtered and censored by interpreters, anthropologists, and other intermediaries. The interpretation of such oral documents is, of course, not easy, but more people, especially Africans, will undertake it as time passes. The millenial orality of African style sets great tasks for the student. But they are very rewarding tasks. The whole method of linguistics and ethnology is needed for the interpretation of such oral texts; but the exercise will contribute importantly to both sciences.

Finally, the publication of really good bilingual literary texts can revolutionize language teaching, especially if they are accompanied by good phonograph or tape recordings; and in some cases even by sound film. The student of an African language can in this way study highly memorable, live utterances in context and within a framework of linguistic theory. And Africans who speak the language of the original work may deepen their knowledge of English (or French) by studying the translations. These procedures open up fresh and important possibilities for nearly all the disciplines in the university to expand their dialogue with the people of the country in which they are working.

In this enterprise, linguistics flexes all its muscles and enters into cooperation with many other disciplines, but with ethnography first of all. In it, linguistics reaches the ultimate expression of its value: the development of human communication on many levels and between all the peoples of the earth.

APPENDIX 1[1]

Céé otú i bī alɔ gwu
tá gbóógbó āa. Bɛ̄ɛ kɛpllóo-
jigwéɛpa kótú āa, ŋ kē kɛlāŋ̀.
Ufi í kē cē llyaŋāŋ̀. Céé
ó labɔ̄ fīm, n yɔ̄ kpɔ́. Ó i
fīm igbɔmpa n yɔ̄ kpɔ́. Anó
i fīm igbɔmɛtá á, anó
kÁdáma! anúŋ kóō hmɾ́h?
Anó kɛlā nāanɔ́ɔ í ka āa
kāmíɔ jāhɔ̄ kāmíɔ pó.
Amíɔ́ lɔ́né nóóóó . . . Abōcē
nnyā ɔ́ɔ ī yáamíɔ āa, ɔ́námíɔ
dúú māa ó héɛgbēcíŋ̀. Qínámíɔ
dúú māa óó támíɔ abɔ̄ŋ̀,
anɔ́ɔ támíɔ ɔkwu gē yɛ á,
anɔ́ɔ kē mɔí ɛtá ɛ́.
Amíɔ ge kwú ɔí ɔ́ɔmā céé ɔ̄cɛ
dúú kúwā ɔ́ɔ gaáá líije kúnū nóó.
Amíɔ ɔ́ɔ í bīuwā gĺlá a.
Qgbɛ ɔ́ɔ kē bīuwā gĺláŋ̀,
Bélo óó kē bīuwā gĺláŋ̀,

Then when night fell, we lay for a while. [Until] about midnight; I didn't speak. Iyaŋā was afraid. Then she slapped me; I stayed still. She slapped me a second time; I stayed still. Then she slapped me a third time and she said, "Ádáma!" Then I said, "Yes?" Then she said that the thing she was going to say, I should listen and I should hear it. That I have no brother . . . [helping me]. That since this sickness had been affecting me, no brother of mine had helped me; that she was the one who had borne three children. If I died, regarding the children none of the men would receive their bridewealth. It was I who would be able to take care of them. Qgbɛ could not take care of them; Bélo could not take care of them. That I knew that in

---

[1] From Ádáma's Story, unpublished. Interviewer and transcriber, Samson Q. Q. Amali. Translated and edited by R. G. Armstrong and Samson Q. Q. Amali.

amíɔ jé kɔɔ . . . Idɔ̄ma amāa
ɔbɔ́nyā ɔ̄ɔ ge kwú ɔyētá née
gē gbɔ̄ɔ . . . gbīinɔ̄lúwā á.
Qyētá ɔ̄ɔ̄māa, aípɔ̄lánɔ̄ɔ óo
kē wenēñcɛ́, cɛ́é anɔ̄ɔ kwúwā
ú kpó, éé kɨla wāamā gɛ nóó.
Ammááá kóocōō anɔ̄ɔ ī gbɔ̄ɔkɔ
lamíɔ. Ęlā nāanɔ̄ɔ ī ka nnyāa,
īkō nāamíɔ pélā kɔ́Qwɔicō gɨlá,
gbɛ́gɛ́ nāamíɔ ī gicɔ́ɔci āa,
kámíɔ̄ hū yíyāmíɔ odéeɲ̀.
Ņ kóō hmm. Ņ kɨla tóohi gɛ nóó.

Idoma here if a woman's husband
dies, she watches over their
compound for three months. After
those three months, since her
children were small, she would take
them away and they would not come
here any more. But please!! She
begged me. The thing she was saying
to me here, if I can hear the word of
God, since I am a church-goer, I
should not do anything to myself. I
said, "Yes." I made no other answer.

APPENDIX 2[2]

Okwū nēe bɔ̄bí ajɛ kídɔ̄ma,
Idɔ̄ma āā anú yɔ̄ bɨlɔ á.
Eko nōokwū ɔ̄ɔ̄mā ge kwú, uwá
lɛhɔ̄ tū jāā gaá fum. Eko né
lɛhɔ̄ tū gaá fum né kokwōbɔ̄bí
ɔ̄ɔ kwú yɔ̄ɔ u, ŋ gaáā ŋnɔ̄ɔlé āa,
ŋ ŋná mllokōpī. Ņ gaáā ŋnɔ̄ɔlé
āa, ŋ ŋná mlleēpōobɔ̄bí-bɔ̄bí,
ēpū ɛyɛ́í nūŋ wolɛcí kúnū āa.
Ņ kɨla nyēē ŋ kwɔ́ŋngbɛ́cí ú, ŋ kwú
kwábɔ̄ amu. Iko nūŋ gaáā nyokwū
ɔ̄ɔ̄māa, ŋ kɨla nyēē, ɛcí nūŋ gé
cē gē lé, ɛ́ nūŋ gé labɔ̄ kwokwū
āa ŋ kwɛ́cí ɔ̄ɔ̄mā ú, n le cē i lé.
N nyēē ŋ kwīkpɛcɔ̄ ú, n lɛcí āa
gwu mlílílílí (kpó),
inɛ́ɛgba nūŋ gē gwɛcí née yɔ̄
bɨlɔ ɔ̄ɔ̄māa, eko gē . . . n nɛcí
ɔ̄ɔ̄mā gwu mlílílílí, okwū nēe kwú
née yɔ̄ bɨlɔ ɔ̄ɔ̄māa ɔ̄cɛ dóodu í
jikwūnū gɛɲ̀. Ǫcɛ nōo likwū
je nāa gē je bɔ̄ɔ eī lígílígí,
ɛcí nūŋ géē bī, ɛcí kún nōo yɔ̄ɔ
nnyāa, ó le nyeī éé anó gɔlé á.
Ę̄ɛɛm n nɛcí hɨla mɨlílílílí,
ācɛnyā kpó! ācɛnyīlɔ dúú í yɛ̄ɛcɛ
gɛɲ̀. É lɔwɛ kpó gwū né i pé tíinu
mɨlí kpó kpɛ́éɱ́ née yɔ̄ bɨlɔ.
Uwá jɔbúgwū wā gém é jɔnyūgwū
wā gém kúuculo kɛ́cí, ācōhīɲ́ māa
gé gbabīije gé i je kwajɛ gɔpám.
Kɛ́cí. Inɛ́ɛgba né lēnēe bá ā yá
mɨlí kpó kpɨlīgīdi, ɔpá nēhɛ́ é kwú

The deaths that are bad in the land of
Idoma, of our home, Idoma, that is it.
When somebody dies that death, they
send a message all the way to me. They
then send a message to me,[and]they say
that somebody has died a bad death;
when I am about to set out from home, I
leave with *okōpī*-medicine. I leave with
sacred sacred ("bad") leaves, various
leaves of which I am the one who has
their medicine. And when I go, I take a
medicine-armlet and put it on my arm
here. When I am going to bury that
corpse, and then, the medicine which I
will break and eat, before I touch the
corpse I take that medicine and I eat it.
After that I take a pebble and cleanse
the medicines completely. When I am
cleansing those medicines, when . . . I
have cleansed those medicines
completely, with respect to the person
who has died like that, nobody weeps
any more for him. A person who weeps
and you have just a little tear on his face,
the medicine which I hold, my medicine
here, he rubs it on his face before he
goes home. Uum, I rub the medicine
completely. All the women! The men
too are no longer outside. They close
the doors when they have gone inside,
everybody, completely, like that. They
bring a cock for me, they bring a hen for
me for the ceremony of the medicines.

---

[2] From *Interview with Ode the Gravedigger*, unpublished. Interviewer and transcriber, Samson Q. Q. Amali. Translated and edited by R. G. Armstrong and Samson Q. Q. Amali.

wā gém, ɔpá nēhέ né kwú wā gém
nēe yɔ̄ bĺlɔ ɔ̄ɔ̄māa, eko né lɔwɛ
gwŭ, ami wɛ ɔ̄cɛ, ami ōfōfōōfŭm
gé jokwŭ ɔ̄ɔ̄mā nyɔ̄ gaáā nyi á.
Ami ōfōōfŭŋ gē kpáajɛ tɔ̄gɔ̄ á.
Tɔɔ, ŋ kɛka héééééééjimōo! ɛka
héééééééjimōo!! a pó gidigidigidi,
É lɔwɛ kpó gwū kpέŕh.
n kwókwū ɔ̄ɔ̄mā ú ŋ kwú
bɔ́tū. N ne bī jāāāāāāāā tíipácí
i yɛ, ŋ kwɔ́ɔ̄ ú tá tɔ́ɔ̄gɔ̄. Okwū
ɔ̄ɔ̄māa, ɔ́gɔgɔ́ kɔ́ɔ̄gɔ̄ ɔ̄ɔ̄māa
né bu āa, ɔ̄ɔ̄mā lɔ̄lɔ́lókwū gɛ
nóo, súgbɔ̄dí kó wokwōōbɔ̄bí.
Ọ̄gɔ̄ né bu āa é hɔ̄gɔ̄ . . . iyɔ̄gɔ̄
ɔ̄ɔ̄māa, iyēnū lé kɔ́gllɔ́. Iyɔ̄gɔ̄
né ī i nyokwū bɔ̄bí iyēnū é hɔ̄ɔ̄
lɔ́gllɔ́. Ṇ kwɔ́ɔ̄ ú jāāā ŋ gaá
kwɔ́ɔ̄ ú nyi. Igbīhi kúm nūŋ gaá
kwɔ́ɔ̄ ú nyi nēe yɔ̄ bĺlɔ ɔ̄ɔ̄māaa . . .
ŋ gāā . . . gāā ódúúdɔ̄lέ nōo yɔ̄
bĺlɔ ɔ̄ɔ̄māa, ŋ kwúufiye ú n
lɛbɛ gwu mĺlílĺlí kpó.
Inu nó yāanú nōo yɔ̄ bɔ́ɔ
āa n lɔ̄lá wɔɔ́ n lɔ́ tɔ̄lá. Iyó
kúnụ̄ mĺlílĺlí kpĺlīgdīī
nēe iyóobɔ̄bí kúnū mílí āa
ó i yɔ̄lá. Eko nūŋ ŋmáabɔ́ɔ gē
wɔ̄lέ n liyē gwā n lɛcí lé
le ŋ́ŋkpēcí ā gwīyē
mílí kpó anúŋ géē wɔ̄lέέ έ
ŋṵ̄ŋ gē gaáā gwu tá
gé lódĺlé klĺ ɔ̄dɔ́ɔ á.
    Ajɛ kĺdɔ̄ma mílí kpó nēe
yɔ́ɔ nnyāa kwɛga dóodu nīĺdɔ̄ma
tέɛgba kwu é kɔdōōbɔ̄bí ɔ́ɔ i yá, okwū
nɔ́ɔ kwú nɔ́ɔ yɔ̄ɔ nnyāā ó okwū
nɔ̄cɛ dóodu (í nyiň) ɛgɛlɛ géé
wēɛgiím iyĺiyĺiyĺí āa. Odúúdáajɛ
kĺdōma nūŋ ī yúkĺlókwōōnyi kwúm á.
Ẹ̄ɛ . . . bégé nūň kēēē yá nnyāa
ŋ wɛ ōcée núň gɛhɔ̄ň.

Some people to start with will give up to
a pound, cash down. For the medicine.
When they have done all these things
completely, they bring me a white cloth.
The white cloth which they brought me
there like that, when they have closed
the doors, I am the person, I alone will
take that corpse to go and bury it. It is
I alone who put earth into the hole. I
say, Ẹka héééééééjimōo! ɛka
héééééééjimōo!! You hear the sound of
running feet. They shut all the doors. I
take that corpse and hold it against my
chest. I hold it all the way until I get to
the bush, I put it into the hole.
Regarding that corpse, that rectangular
hole which they did for it, that one no
longer has a chamber because it is a bad
death. The hole which they dig, they call
the hole . . . the name of that hole is
"trench." The name of the hole which
they dig for a bad corpse, its name is
called "trench." I take him all the way, I
take him to bury. After I have gone and
buried him like that . . . I come to the
very compound like that ((from which
he brought the corpse)), I take a broom
and sweep it completely. The house in
which he lived, I set fire to it and I burn
it. All of his possessions, all his bad
possessions are burned.

When I leave there and come home, I
bathe and eat medicine, using the liquid
medicine to bathe all over completely,
then I will come home before I lie down
or eat anything.
    In all of Idoma Land, like this,
wherever there are people of Idoma
origin, when they say that something
bad has happened, a person who has
died like this, it is a corpse that nobody
will bury, a bicycle will come to my place
sooner or later. It is in all the Land of
Idoma that I do my work of burying
corpses. Since I do this, I am not
someone who goes to the farm.

APPENDIX 3³

Aké'wì:	*Ọba 'oooo!* *Ọba Ìkàààààà!* *Máa wolẹ̀ òòòòòò!*
Ẹmẹ̀wà:	*Ọba 'ooooooo!* *Ọba Ìkàààààà!* *Máa wolẹ̀ òòòò!*
Aké'wì:	*Ó pàdé oníʼjà ní kòròwó 'oo!* *Ọba Ìkàààààà!* *Máa wolẹ̀ ooooooo!*
Ẹmẹ̀wà:	*Ọba 'oooo!* *Ọba Ìkàààà!* *Máa wolẹ̀ ooooo!*
Aké'wi:	*Ó pàdé oníʼjà ní kòròwó!* *Ó namọ ọlọ́mọ ní patia!*
Ẹmẹ̀wà:	*Ọba 'ooooo!* *Ọba Ìkàààààà!* *Máa wolẹ̀ ooooo!*
Aké'wì:	*Adámọlóró àdáàgbàgbé 'oo!* *Ọba Ìkàààààà!* *Máa wolẹ̀ oooooo!*
Ẹmẹ̀wà:	*Ọba 'ooooo!* *Ọba Ìkàààààà!* *Máa wolẹ̀ ooooooo!*
Aké'wì:	*Ìwọ lọba tí í sọ̀rẹ́ mé'jì í dọ̀tá!* *Ìwọ lọba tí í forí omiyeé* *gbáraa wọn!*
Aké'wi àti *Ẹmẹ̀wà:*	*Ọba 'ooooooooo!* *Ọba Ìkàààààà* *Máa wolẹ̀ ooooooo!*

Praise-Singer:	Oh King . . . ! Cruel King. . . . ! You are welcome . . . !
Courtiers:	Oh King. . . . ! Cruel King. . . . ! You are welcome. . . . !
Praise-Singer:	He met his enemy in a dark corner⁴ Cruel King. . . . ! You are welcome. . . . !
Courtiers:	Oh King. . . . ! Cruel King. . . . ! You are welcome. . . . !
Praise-Singer:	He met his adversary in a dark corner! He flogs another's child with a whip!
Courtiers:	Oh King. . . . ! Cruel King. . . . ! You are welcome. . . . !
Praise-Singer:	[The one] who inflicts pain never-to-be- forgotten! Cruel King. . . . ! You are welcome. . . . !
Courtiers:	Oh King . . . ! Cruel King . . . ! You are welcome . . . !
Praise-Singer:	You are the King who makes two friends enemies! You are the King who knocks the heads of kinsmen together!
Praise-Singer and Courtiers:	Oh King. . . . ! Cruel King . . . ! You are welcome. . . . !

³ From Ògúnmọ́là (1972:90–93).
⁴ So as to finish him off.

APPENDIX 4[5]

Tìmì: *Mo wáá dé'lú Ẹ̀dẹ lố'ní*
          'oooooooo!
          Aféfé léléélé ló ní kí ẹ wáá
          fé bá mi.
          Àwọn àfòngìrìyàyàyà náà
          ló ní kí ẹ tò mí wá.
          Ẹrìjé-ní-í-ṣe- baba- Ẹrìjé,
          Ẹrìjè- náà- ní- í- ṣe- baba-
            Ẹrìjì- jéè- jéè,
          Ẹrìjì- jéè- jéè- náà- ní-í-
            ṣe-baba- Ọlásúdẹ,
          Ọlásúdẹ- ní- í- ṣe- baba-
            Àtèpé, [6]
          Ló wá dífá fún Bóló'gbùró-
            bá-pakájà-ilè-gbogbo-
            ẹyẹ-ní-í-pa-késẹ-késẹ!
          Igba abéré!
          Igba atarere!
          Igbaarọ́, igbaarọ̀!
          Igba ẹké ní í fọwọ́ tilé!
          Igba aláàmù náà ní í fọwọ́
            tògiri!
          Kí ẹni gbogbo kí wọn kó
            wáá fọwọ́ tì mí 'oooooo!
          Ó tún di Bóló'gbùró-bá-
            pakájà-ilè-gbogbo-ẹyẹ-a-
            tún-pa-késẹ-késẹ!
          Ọ́ deja tó ló'un ò báabú ṣe!
          (NÍPA AGBÁRA ỌFỌ̀ ÀTI
          OÒGÙN, TÌMÍ PE ÀWỌN
          ARÁ ẸDẸ JỌ)

Ará Ẹdẹ: *Gẹrẹrẹ, àwọn máa kó wọn*
            bò!
          Gẹrẹrẹ!

Tìmí: I have arrived at *Ẹdẹ* town today
        . . . !
        It is the gentle wind which said
        you should blow to me.
        It is spirits of teeming termite
        swarms which said you
        should come to me.
        Air-is-the-Father-of-Dew,
        Dew-is-the-Father-of-showers,
        Showers-are-the-Father-of-the-
        Ocean,
        Ocean-is-the-Father-of-long-
        trodden-Earth,
        Who were the ones who cast Ifá
        for
        When-the-*Oló'gbùró*-song-
        sweeps-the-ground-all-the-
        birds-are-silent.[7]
        Two hundred needles!
        Two hundred alligator peppers!
        Two hundred blacksmith's
        gourds, two hundred
        mud-fish!
        Two hundred rafters support the
        house!
        Two hundred lizards support the
        wall!
        Let everybody support me!
        Again, When-the-*Oló'gbùró*-
        song-sweeps-the-ground-all-
        the-birds-are-silent!
        It is like the fish defying the
        deep![8]
        (BY MEANS OF INCANTATIONS
        AND CHARMS *Tìmì* ASSEMBLES
        Ẹdẹ TOWNSPEOPLE.)

Ẹdẹ TOWNSPEOPLE: Slowly, let the net
        bring them along,
        In a moving throng!

---

[5] From Ladipo, 1972 42–43.

[6] The names of ancient or mythical *babaláwos*, or diviners.

[7] The *Òló'gbùró* bird is a kind of partridge which lives in deep forests beside rivers. It accompanies its spread-wing mating dance with a strange call. I have had to invent a verb phrase "song-sweep" to render the Yoruba *pakájà*, which means 'to throw one's robe over the left shoulder' — a deeply metaphorical use in this context.

[8] I.e., "If you people do not come before me willingly."

REFERENCES

ANONYMOUS
1973 "Homer in silver gilt," review of *To Homer through Pope* by H. A. Mason in *The Times Literary Supplement* 3:696, London, 5 January 1972.
ARMSTRONG, ROBERT G., S. Ọ. Ọ. AMALI
1969 *The ancient music of the Idoma* (phonograph record with text). New York: Asch Mankind Series.
DOS SANTOS, J. E., D. M. DOS SANTOS
1971 *Eṣu Bara Laroye.* Ibadan: Institute of African Studies.
LADIPỌ, DURO
1972 *Ọba Kò So* (bilingual text of opera). Ibadan: Institute of African Studies.
ÒGÚNMỌ́LÀ, KỌ́LÁ
1972 *The Palmwine Drinkard* (bilingual text of opera). Ibadan: Institute of African Studies.

ADDENDUM

A fair number of important publications of African oral and musical literature have appeared during the six years since this paper was written. The main task that lies ahead still is the multimedia publication of an artistic event in which the various "dimensions" are really synchronized, thus permitting the close, comparative study which they deserve. The great possibilities that lie at hand are still little used. The improvement of small cassette recorders has increased the temptation to record African music with less than professional high fidelity.

REFERENCE AND RECORDINGS

LAPIDO, DURO
1973 *Ọba Kò So* (complete recording on phonograph records, matching the published text). Ibadan: Institute of African Studies.
1975 *Ọba Kò So* (complete stereophonic recording on phonograph records). Washington, D.C.: Traditional Music Documentation Project.
ÒGÚNMỌ́LÀ KỌ́LÁ
1974 *The Palmwine Drinkard* (complete recording on phonograph records, matching the published text). Lagos and Ibadan: EMI for Institute of African Studies.
ROTIMI, ỌLA
1974 *Ovonramwen Nogbaisi.* Ibadan: Oxford University Press.

SECTION FIVE

Modernization

A Typology of Language Education in Nigeria

C. M. B. BRANN

The question of language education in a multilingual, pluricultural, and polyethnic federation like that of Nigeria is one of fundamental importance for the development of the country itself. It is so complex that until recently linguists and educationists have shied away from it, the former being more concerned with the analysis and description of major or minor members of families encompassing some 400 distinct languages (Hoffman 1974), the others struggling with general questions of curriculum adaptation and development in the post-Independence phase. Only recently, the repeated calls for education in the mother tongue, movements towards mass literacy in hitherto underdeveloped parts of the country, and debates over furthering one or several national languages or one of several state languages have brought the question of language education to the fore. But if we look for sociolinguistic data, we will find that there is very little information at hand: the number of languages in the country, their use in educational institutions, even their use in the overall educational process, is wide open to speculation. The present preliminary study could not therefore draw upon a body of well-established facts to present a tailormade typology to fit them. Rather, I will attempt, in the light of available information, to provide a framework which will be the basis of practical surveys of the language situation in Nigerian education, somewhat in the manner of the language education surveys that have been successfully accomplished in anglophone East Africa (cf. Prator 1967).

I am much indebted for information and assistance to Dr. R. Stanford, formerly of the Zaria/Jos Institute of Linguistics, as well as to Professors C. Hoffman and K. Williamson formerly of the Department of Linguistics, University of Ibadan.

SURVEY OF SOME PREVIOUS TYPOLOGIES AND THEIR
RELEVANCE TO THE NIGERIAN SITUATION

1. At least a dozen excellent typologies of multilingualism in society have been proposed in the past ten years (since the Brazzaville symposium of 1962), all of which contribute to an understanding of the Nigerian situation, but none of which wholly fit or describe it. Gumperz (1971) points out that with "the ruling groups of many modern Asian and African nations, total bi- or multilingualism is the rule rather than the exception" in terms of the use of the mother tongue and another language (mostly English and French). He distinguishes five types of communities in terms of societal economic development, from the hunter/gatherer to the highly stratified urban society in which the code matrix may include distinct languages (diglossia) as well as varieties of the same language. Within each of these communities, several types of language codes are distinguished. This model could well be applied to particular communities in Nigeria, and to some extent this has been done by Mafeni in his study of Nigerian pidgin (1971).

2. Ferguson (1971b) distinguishes three criteria concerning language usage in a nation: (1) the extent of use in writing; (2) the level of standardization; and (3) the dominance configuration of the languages. These criteria are too bald and westernized to be applicable to the West African situation. They have, moreover, been refined by Ferguson in his "National Sociolinguistic profile formulas" (1971c). Here we have a scale of major, minor, and special languages ranging from a minimum of 25 percent of all speakers in a given population for a major language to 5 percent for a special language. This range does not cover any language in Nigeria except perhaps Hausa (with twelve million native speakers and eight million estimated bilingual speakers; cf. Kirk-Greene 1967). The scale as it stands would have to be adapted for application to the Nigerian situation. Another drawback is the lack of distinction between indigenous and foreign languages (immigrant or resident) and a lack of attention to their symbolic status in the dominance configuration: that is, the importance of a language is not necessarily commensurate with the number of its speakers, as in the case of the role of English in Nigeria or that of Arabic.

3. Stewart (1962) has proposed a typological description which he expanded and refined in 1968, and on which Ferguson (1971b) drew. Here he distinguishes TYPES, FUNCTIONS, and DEGREE of language use, all of which will be used in our subsequent typology of the Nigerian situation: of his seven types, S, C, V, D, A, K, and P, I have retained the first four in the appended typology, the last three not being germane to the Nigerian setting. I have also retained the functions i, e, s, r, and l, have discarded o, p, and g, and have added others specific to language in

education. The measure of the degree of the use of languages in six classes, ranging from class I with 75 percent of the population to class VI with less than 5 percent, was not suitable for Nigeria, and another scale was substituted — but the categories have been maintained.

4. Kloss' typology (1966), though positing ten variables, discusses only the first in detail: types of speech communities, for which he distinguishes a "national core community" of a minimum of 3 percent speakers and three types of speakers: the monolingual, the bilingual, and the multilingual. For a description of Nigerian multilingualism, the limitation of the term "core community" to language groups above 3 percent is far too high: only a dozen of the 400-odd languages in Nigeria can claim so many speakers, and there is no linguistic, educational, or ethnic reason to suppose that less populous languages do not belong to the national core community. But Kloss' other variables could prove valuable for further studies. In his "Notes concerning a language-nation typology" (1968), he classifies types of states in relation to the number of mother tongue speakers of the official language. In the case of English in Nigeria (which is spoken as a native language by practically no one, though here again some research is needed), the type of exoglossic state is defined. In such cases, it is important to make a further distinction between "official" and "national" languages, such as is made in Nigeria, for instance. Though English is the official language of the Federation, it is not termed the national language, this term being reserved to no single language, but to a series of indigenous majority languages. The term "development status" or *Ausbau* of the languages, provides criteria for literacy and standardization. Kloss' legal status of the speech community is similar to Stewart's functional divisions. It is difficult, however, to see how the term "proscribed" or "tolerated" can come under such a category: these have to do with the ACCEPTABILITY of a language, and could be classified under language dominance. Finally, Kloss' numerical division into six classes, starting this time with 90 percent for category I and descending to 3 percent or less for category VI is hardly applicable to any multilingual developing country.

5. While characterizing the present situation and problems of multilingual states quite well, Armstrong (1968) does not offer a classification of these policies or practices.

6. Fishman (1968a) argues that linguistic homogeneity is a prerequisite to economic advance and bases his language-nation types on this. But the division of the Federation of Nigeria into twelve states in 1967 and into nineteen in 1976 was undertaken precisely in order to encourage greater local economic development. Since this has obviously proved successful, an argument opposite to Fishman's could be proposed. The effect on the language situation in Nigeria is interesting: before the division, the linguistico-cultural hegemony of dominant languages dampened local

initiative, while the present conscious development of local languages since the division has enhanced self-development.

But Fishman goes on to say that "more important than the designation of types is the analysis of VARIETIES of language spoken by individuals (cf. Kloss 1966, 1968; Ferguson 1971a, 1971b, 1971c; Stewart 1962). This, to our mind, would be the second step in the process of sociolinguistic analysis and description. In the case of multilingualism in Nigeria, we are still in the first phase of classification.

7. Fishman (1967) also refers to the term Ferguson used in 1959 to distinguish the use of two languages by individuals or society. Applied to the educational situation, that is, teaching in one or more languages, Kloss (1966:10) has coined the terms "monopaidoglossia" and "dipaidoglossia" which we have borrowed and extended in Table 1. Such "in-group" terms may be useful when describing precise forms of polyvalence in societal linguistic processes.

8. Hunt (1966) develops variables based on an analysis of social attitudes both of individuals and of society. It is perhaps in such a scheme as this that Kloss' variables of "tolerance" (1966) (i.e. acceptability of a language) could be accommodated.

9. Fishman (1971) lays down criteria for three types of national language policy decisions, depending on the historical consciousness ("great tradition"), spread, and function of language within a polity. This would mean that national policies would be made on the acceptance, by the comity of nations or by the nation itself, of such a tradition, or absence of traditions. In the case of Nigeria, however — and this may be true of other rapidly industrializing nations — such great traditions may be in the making: historical consciousness is an element that can be consciously created as part of the nation-building process. (Fishman himself has written about this concept of language loyalty, which, according to him, has created the consciousness of nationhood in the United States.) There is much talk at present in Nigeria of "the great cultural tradition," of which the Nigerian was certainly not conscious yesterday. Hence it would be erroneous in a typology of policy-making to limit such "great traditions" to those languages that have been so classified by Western scholarship.

10. Fishman (1968b) points out the widespread condition of diglossia in the new nations of Asia and Africa, both in terms of indigenous languages and between an indigenous and a foreign (international) language of wide communication. In the case of northern Nigeria, he even posits a state of English-Hausa-Arabic triglossia, which will be discussed further on. This is an important dimension, missing in the typologies of Ferguson, Stewart, and others and to which we have given the term of demoglossia (mono-, di-, and poly-).

11. The danger of applying Western yardsticks and terminology to the

African multilingual situation is discussed by Hurel (1970). Yet while criticizing existing typologies, he might have pointed out that many aspects of them are valid for West Africa, *mutatis mutandis*. We welcome his call for the collection of empirical and statistical data on the West African situation.

12. Mackey (1970) comes closest to our present needs. For each of the four spheres of home, school, community, and nation, he offers variables which go a long way toward describing the Nigerian situation, except that there are cases of trilingual schooling, or change overs from one to two or three languages of instruction which are not caught even in his fine mesh. It is, however, the only comprehensive statement on the subject so far, the vast literature on bilingual education having been more concerned with the problems of specific communities than with the overall types.

13. Houis (1971) offers *"critères de classement"* of linguistic societies, distinguishing five variables: sociological, cultural, geographical, ecological, and linguistic. The educational aspect would, presumably, come under the ecological. On his consideration of *"le bilinguisme africano-européen,"* however, he points out that the development of this type of bilingualism is in direct proportion to the educational opportunities offered by the African state, since all post-primary education is either in English or French (excluding the Portuguese-speaking territories), and in the francophone countries most primary education is in French also. He points out the differences between the francophone and anglophone countries as the result of former colonial policy, a variation which is pertinent to our subsequent characterization of primary schooling in Nigeria. The book brings another important contribution to education in multilingual African societies by pointing out (1) that the same vernaculars are taught across the political borders — hence the desirability of cross-frontier collaboration — and (2) that there are fundamental language typologies underlying groups of African languages, which should be taken into account when provisions are made for textbooks for schools of minority ethnic groups. This suggestion may be particularly significant in Nigeria now where some multilingual states are embarking on projects of primers and readers for their primary schools in a number of indigenous local languages (e.g., The Rivers Readers Project as described by Williamson 1976). In our subsequent chart, Appendix 1, this structural relationship between languages has unfortunately not yet been taken into account, owing to lack of information. On the other hand, there are many situations in which closely related languages are not deemed to be mutually intelligible by their speakers for reasons of attitude (acceptability), as noted by H. Wolff for Angas/Sura *vis-à-vis* Hausa (quoted by Kirk-Greene 1967:100). Thus questions of attitude and motivation are important variables in language-planning processes, and are not less so in educational administration.

14. Dil (1973) put forward proposals to balance the cultural claims of national groups with the process of modernization in terms of the number of languages that could reasonably be expected of any member of the community. This could be done by harmonizing (1) local languages, (2) languages of special status and (3) international languages in a "plus or minus two-and-a-half language model." This model is relevant when considering the number of languages that a Nigerian child can be expected to absorb in home, community, and school (cf. UNESCO 1972).

15. Fishman (1972) enlarges the policy description based on the existence or absence of a "great tradition" referred to above. He describes Type A policies: the choice of a "language of wide communication" as the language of instruction, generally imported and rarely the mother tongue of any pupil (e.g. English in Nigeria, French in Senegal). Here bilingual education is in fact restricted to the very beginning of schooling or avoided altogether: the pupil will evolve a personal bilingualism but not through the school (hence the significance of the term dipaidoglossia). Type B policies exist where the administration recognized "an overriding and indigenous integrative principle, but yet provided for local variation under and beneath it or over and above it" (Fishman 1972). We find examples of this in Nigeria, particularly in the north. Type C policy occurs in the presence of several "great traditions." Since pupils will be educated in their respective mother tongues (polypaidoglossia?), the question arises of when they will be able to learn one or several languages of the partners in the polity to facilitate intercommunication; an alternative possibility is an exterior language of wide communication taken over to solve the problem, as with English in India (exopaidoglossia?). This type of policy may arise in Nigeria, where the three major languages, Hausa, Yoruba, and Igbo, are each developing, in different measure, their own mother tongue education. We shall see that in Nigeria all three policy types in fact coexist.

16. Adekunle (1972a) classifies languages into six levels according to their interaction within and across administrative units of district, division, province, state, region, and nation. This division could be of interest for a multilingual study of education, since multilingual Nigerian states such as Kwara, Bendel, and Rivers have adopted "divisions" according to ethnolinguistic units which may have their own language practices. Nigerian languages are also placed in four classes in accordance with degrees of official (though unwritten) recognition. There is unfortunately no mention of diglossia. The place of Nigerian languages in education is seen diachronically in three periods, missionary, colonial, and national, but the breakdown of the use of vernaculars in schools quoted from Oke (1969) is incomplete in respect to the multilingual states. The role of English is discussed, and pidgin, Arabic, French, and Latin are men-

tioned. There is a second classification of standard languages according to Stewart (1962).

In the above typologies, language has been viewed in a single and multiple aspect within different layers of society: the home, the community, the school, and the nation. For what it is worth, and in order to avoid the polyvalence of the term "bilingualism," the system in Table 1 is proposed, the first three groups of which will be applied to the Nigerian situation.

Table 1. Language in society

A.	Home (individual)	A1	Unilingualism unilingual	A2	bilingualism bilingual	A3	multi-lin-gualism multi-lingual
B.	Community	B1	monoglossia monoglot	B2	diglossia diglot	B3	polyglossia polyglot
C.	School	C1	monopaido-glossia	C2	dipaido-glossia	C3	polypaido-glossia
D.	Ethny/nation	D1	monodemo-glossia	D2	didemo-glossia	D3	polydemo-glossia
E.	State	E1	monopolito-glossia	E2	dipolito-glossia	E3	polypolito-glossia

LANGUAGE IN NIGERIA: A TYPOLOGY

Before outlining the appended typology it is important to take account of the present politicosocial dynamics. Since 1900, the year of creation of "Nigeria" as an administrative entity (by Lord Lugard), there has been a clear movement of separation and diffusion. The initial division into two large blocks corresponding to the Muslim north and the Christian south into the Northern and Southern protectorates, with two dominant languages (Hausa and Yoruba) became three groups of provinces, Northern, Western, and Eastern with three dominant languages: Hausa, Yoruba, and Igbo. A further division of the Western Province created four regions, North, West, East, and Mid-West, the latter without a clearly dominant language. Though Edo is the traditional language (group) of the ancient Benin empire, Igbo and Yoruba are spoken, both as mother tongues and as contact languages, in the new region along with other languages (cf. Oke 1972). The latest division in 1976 into nineteen states brought about the enfranchisement of many ethnic languages (not dialects) which until then had been dominated by more prominent languages, thus liberating for development much withheld energy (cf. our argument above on Fishman's thesis [Point 6]). That the development of local language goes *pari passu* with local economic development is very plain to those familiar with the Nigerian scene.

Another generalization of Fishman's was that Christianity brought about the linguistic homogeneity which necessarily precedes economic development. Again in Nigeria the opposite is the case. In the north the domination of Islam through the Hausa–Fulani oligarchy imposed a certain linguistic homogeneity on the multilingual people — together with economic stagnation. On the other hand, the Christian missions, both in the south and later in the north, translated into writing and developed the local languages for educational and proselytizing purposes, through translations of the Scriptures. The list of languages, upon which the present typology is based, is largely taken from those which have been so translated, this being a sign of their educational status. Just as with the European vernaculars of the early Middle Ages, organized educational development has been largely in the hands of religious groups, Christian as well as Muslim, and depended on spoken languages which were reduced to writing.[1] The main difference between the Muslim north and the Christian south is that while in the south the languages of instruction in primary institutions were the various vernaculars plus English, in the north it was a classical Arabic parroted by ear. Thus in the north, Islam did not initially develop indigenous languages, but is now doing so with the translation of the Quran into Hausa.

Of the present nineteen states, twelve can be said to be linguistically homogeneous or monopolitoglot. They are *BC, KD, K, NG, SK* States with Hausa, *LG, OG, ON, OY* States with Yoruba, *AN* and *IM* States with Igbo, and *CR* State with Efik (Ibibio). That does not mean that in these states there are no linguistic minorities, but it means that there is a single majority language furthered by the Ministries of Education. The other seven states are polydemoglot with local languages being developed according to the policies of each State Ministry of Education through and for its primary education system. This politico-linguistic development and situation is illustrated diagrammatically in Figure 1.

Contrasted with this centrifugal trend, which is both historical and actual, there is also a concurrent powerful centripetal tendency, deriving from the nationism so well described by Fishman. Precisely in order to further a consciousness of nationhood, there have been various proposals on the topic of national language, ranging from a single one (Hausa or Yoruba [cf. Banjo 1976], through a tripartite system (Hausa/

---

[1]   The extent to which the missionary enterprise has contributed to the literacy of Africa is often ignored. A very high proportion of its languages were first reduced to writing by missionaries, and in many languages the only literature available, even today, is the Bible and a few Christian books. Until comparatively recent times nearly all schooling was carried out in mission schools and colleges, and most of Africa's leaders had some of their education in such schools (Coldham 1966:ii–iii). Our list taken from this source was supplemented by a list of "Bible Translations 1972" issued by the Institute of Linguistics, Zaria.

Yoruba/Igbo), a quinpartite (Hausa/Yoruba/Igbo/Efik/Edo), and finally to the adoption of nine national languages (as in Ghana under Nkrumah), such as are at present used over the national broadcasting network (Hausa/Yoruba/Igbo/Efik/Edo/Kanuri/Tiv/Fula/Ijo).

In selecting languages for the present typology (see Appendix 1), out of the 400 separate vernaculars, four educational criteria have been applied: (1) Languages used in the community for religious worship (r), or mass media such as newspapers (n) or broadcasting (b); (2) languages used in the schools as languages of instruction (e) or as subjects (s) which are certified (c) at the various educational levels; (3) languages used in the extended community within Nigeria (w), as inter-African languages (a) or between nations (i); and (4) languages learned for educational development for international understanding (i), technological advance (t), or scholarship and learning (l). (Superior numbers indicate levels or degree of use. Thus, "e^1" = a language of instruction at the primary level; "e^2" = secondary level; and "e^3" = tertiary level. "c^1" = certification at the primary level; "c^2" = secondary level; and "c^3" = tertiary level. "r" refers to the degree to which the scriptures have been translated into a particular language, so "r^1" = some use; "r^2" = one testament translated; and "r^3" = the entire Bible translated. The three levels of broadcasting — state, national, and international — are indicated respectively by "b^1," "b^2," and "b^3." Other elements are broken down into numerical degree of diffusion, as listed in the key to Appendix 1.)

Since languages have been chosen for their relevance in education, many preliterate languages have been omitted from our list. This may mean that through the accident of missionary interaction with one group rather than another, some larger language groups are not represented in the educational picture. The figures given for speakers are taken from one or more national censuses or interpretations thereof, especially those of Westermann and Bryan (1970), Kirk-Greene (1967), and Coldham (1966). The disparity between the figures of 1931, 1925, and 1963 censuses calls for attention. At all events, all languages with speakers above 500,000 will have been included in the Appendix 1 chart.

While in most cases the figures for ethnic descent given in the censuses also are those of language spoken, this is not true of the Fulani, many of whom are Hausa unilinguals, others are Hausa–Fula bilinguals, while yet others are Fula unilinguals (the cattle-raising Fulani). Similarly, many other communities of minority languages live in diglossia with a major language of a continuous ethnic group, especially those bordering on Hausa, Yoruba, or Igbo majorities. Thus Kirk-Greene (1967:88) estimates that some 5 million non-Hausa in the north speak Hausa as their second language. In the Mid-Western State, the population in the west uses Yoruba as their second language (cf. Oke 1972) while Igbo is used in the east. In the South Eastern and Rivers states, at least until the late civil

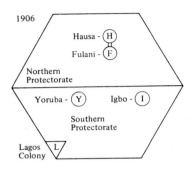

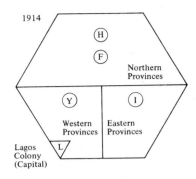

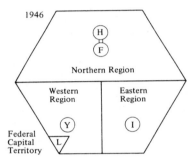

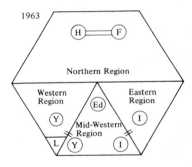

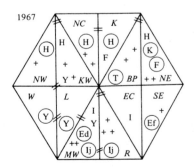

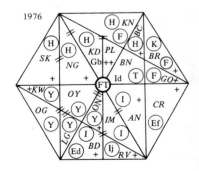

war, some ethnic groups had Igbo as their second languages (cf. Adekunle 1972b:80; Williamson 1972). The question of diglossia of indigenous languages is one which has not yet been studied, although an inquiry into the multilingualism of primary school pupils is being made by the writer.

The Nigerian languages can be classified either according to the number of speakers or the political prestige of the language, as in the case of nine languages chosen for national broadcasts, which are here designated "national languages." Of these, Hausa, Yoruba, and Igbo form a class apart, representing 50 percent of all Nigerian speakers — 30 out of 60 million. All three have a standardized form originally based on the dialect of a particular locality: the Hausa of Kano, the Yoruba of Oyo, and the Igbo of Owerri have become the standards speakers are called upon to conform to for these languages. Moreover, these three languages are spoken outside their indigenous areas as contact languages, and Hausa and Yoruba are spoken by large indigenous Hausa and Yoruba communities as linguae francae in wide parts of West Africa (Heine 1970:138, 151). They are therefore both intergroup languages (w) as well as inter-African languages (a). For Hausa one might even suggest the status of an international language (i), linking Nigeria with Niger as it does on an official plane. Edo, Efik, and Tiv are associated with strong local traditions, while Fula, Kanuri, and Ijo are spoken by scattered communities (in fact, Ijo is regarded by some linguists as constituting four separate languages). A third class would be comprised of languages used over regional broadcasting networks which are generally those directed

---

Figure 1. Politicoglossic anamorphosis of Nigeria
Key:
Languages (Languages indicated are used in the Federal Nigerian Broadcasting Services.)

H = Hausa	T = Tiv
Y = Yoruba	Ef = Efik
I = Igbo	Ed = Edo
F = Fula	Ij = Ijo
K = Kanuri	+++ = multilingual

States 1967–1976	*States 1976*	
BP = Benue Plateau	AN = Anambra	KN = Kano
EC = East-Central	BC = Bauchi	KW = Kwara
K = Kano	BD = Bendel	LG = Lagos
KW = Kwara	BN = Benue	NG = Niger
L = Lagos	BR = Borno	OG = Ogun
MW = Mid-Western	CR = Cross River	ON = Ondo
NC = North-Central	GO = Gongola	OY = Oyo
NE = North-Eastern	IM = Imo	PL = Plateau
NW = North-Western	KD = Kaduna	SK = Sokoto
R = Rivers	FT = Federal Territory	RV = Rivers
SE = South-Eastern		
W = Western		

at groups exceeding 100,000 speakers. A fourth class would comprise the bulk of independent minority languages, while a fifth class would include language varieties in a relationship of dependence to a larger group as subgroups or dialects.

In a class by themselves are English and pidgin. We can see them, in their Nigerian form and function, either as separate languages, or as representing two opposite ends of a language continuum called English, which exists in Nigeria in a state of complementary distribution, the speakers varying both as to their level of education and social code. At the one end of the continuum we have Standard Nigerian English (SNE, as defined by Banjo 1976) and at the other pidgin, both of which can function as Nigerian indigenous languages or "mother tongues" (m), intergroup contact languages (w), and inter-African languages (a), while only English in its standard variety functions as an international language (i). No one has as yet assessed the number of speakers — or understanders — of the different varieties of the continuum. Some studies estimate that 10 percent of the population are speakers of English (cf. Bamgbose 1971), which would bring English numerically to the status of Fula or Kanuri; however, we would hazard a much smaller percentage of standard English speakers. Based on the number of students per year who earn school certificates and who may be said to possess some English in the four language skills, there may be some 500,000 now in the country. (In this figure we exclude the great number of students who leave school at Primary 6 and those leaving at Modern 3 [nine years of schooling], as their English skills are very incomplete.) If, however, we take higher education as our basis of Standard Nigerian English (12 + 3 years), we arrive at a figure of only 80,000 SNE speakers. The figure of 10 percent quoted by some writers would therefore not represent only speakers of SNE, but would include speakers of any form of English on the continuum from standard English to pidgin.

We have suggested that English and pidgin are in a state of complementary distribution. As the only language of government and administration, SNE is the language of national communication without being the national language (unlike in Ghana, where SGE is recognized as the national language), even though it guarantees the linguistic unity of the country. It is used in those situations in which pidgin is not used, and vice versa. SNE is spoken in the towns on formal occasions, in offices, and in stores, but not in the market; it is spoken in formal instruction at school. Pidgin is spoken in the family, even among members of the same language group (e.g. in the Mid-West) as a familiar idiom, between different groups as an intergroup language on friendly occasions, in petty trade, in the market, and even as an informal language of instruction in some primary schools where pupils of different ethnic backgrounds come together, especially in the cities of the Mid-West, the great cities of the south and the *sabongaris* [foreigners' quarters] of the cities of the north. Since pidgin is also the mother tongue of Nigerians born in the *sabongaris* (cf. Mafeni 1971), it is in fact becoming creolized. Similarly SNE is also the mother tongue of some Nigerians born into educated families of mixed Nigerian ethnic origin in cities where a third Nigerian (majority) language is spoken. Since pidgin is still looked upon as an imperfect form of English, it is not formally taught as a subject, has no grammar or primer (other than those written for members of the U.S. Peace Corps!). Since both SNE and pidgin have *droit de cité* in many parts of Nigeria and on various occasions, they should be classified both as Nigerian and as foreign languages.

The case of Arabic is similar, yet different. Though it is the sacred language of millions of Muslims throughout the country, it is used as a contact language by very few, and because of this limited usage, we question Fishman's classification of a Hausa-Arabic-English triglossia in the north; one could rather speak of a triglossia composed of the local language +H +E in the cities of the north, and +p +E in the south. The Shuwa Arabs speak an indigenous nonliterary dialect of Arabic as their mother tongue. As a language of education, the role of Arabic in Nigeria is undergoing a change from a hieratical language to a modern language of international communication such as French. With the present translation of the Quran into Nigerian languages (a start is being made with Hausa and a Yoruba translation has existed since the beginning of the century), its role may change completely within the next fifty years. Like English, Arabic has a privileged cultural position and is therefore not a wholly foreign language.

Other European languages studied in Nigeria at various levels have been included in Appendix 1 to show their societal and educational functions. French, Portuguese, and Spanish, for example, share an inter-African and international function. French is particularly important for international communication with neighboring francophone countries in East Africa (Dahomey, Cameroon, Togo, Niger, Ivory Coast, Senegal, etc.). French (together with English and Arabic) is an official language of the Organisation of African Unity, which was the reason for its massive introduction into the educational system after independence. But whereas in Ghana, Sierra Leone, and Gambia (the other three countries involved in the West African Examinations Council, which is the last surviving pre-Independence intergovernmental organization of anglophone West Africa), French has become a compulsory subject in secondary education. This has not yet been possible in Nigeria because of a shortage of teachers. It may, however, become a reality within the next forty years.

The usefulness of German and Russian for technological study and economic advancement has been emphasized by Ubahakwe (1972), as a result of a questionnaire sent to university departments of languages. According to him, they should be stressed to a greater degree than should French. Latin and Greek, of which only the former has now been listed in university curricula, are a lost cause of European assimilation but have played quite an important role in the early days of the grammar schools and universities in Nigeria (though not such a strong one as in Sierra Leone or Ghana, where they have taken firmer root). Ministries of Education have unanimously advocated their replacement by a modern language — French.

The important question as to which of the Nigerian languages, English, and pidgin are currently spoken as second languages, by what proportion of the population, and by which ethnic speakers, has unfortunately not been included in the census of 1973 — which is a golden opportunity lost. The figures under (d) diglossia in Appendix 1 are therefore sporadic and impressionistic.

There are three spheres of community influence in language education, that of religious worship, of newspapers, and of broadcasts. Of these, religious worship in churches or mosques or traditional ceremonies (e.g. name-givings, marriages, wakes, commemorations) is the most significant educational influence. No research on the incidence of English, Arabic, or Nigerian languages in these areas has as yet been made (although it forms part of the writer's current research). Both in churches and mosques, Nigerian languages and second languages can be mixed into or between sermons, prayers, and songs. Since many vernaculars have their own translation of Scripture, it is likely that services will be held in the language of the local community, or in the major Nigerian language, or in English in the case of a mixed linguistic community. Our rating scale from 1–3 is somewhat superficial (depending on the extent to which Scripture has been translated into the Nigerian language) as an index of the present use of Nigerian languages in religious (Christian) services. But it must not be forgotten that the same vernaculars can likewise be used in the mosques, along with the hieratical Arabic. In the schools, morning prayer at assembly is generally in English, whereas Sunday School would be in the vernacular. Extracurricular religious instruction in the north is both in Arabic and in the vernacular, but the Arabic is usually understood in a general way, rather than comprehended verbatim.

The influence of newspapers in Nigerian homes is minimal, except in the cities, and cannot therefore be said to constitute a major factor in language education at present; this, however, may radically change in the near future with the increasing urbanization and industrialization of Nigerian life. National newspapers are all in English; only in the three major Nigerian languages is there any vernacular material.

More significant in a largely oral society is the impact of Nigerian languages in broadcasting. Nine indigenous languages are regularly broadcast on the federal level, while others are relayed from local stations in each state capital. The radio relays not only Nigerian languages, but also Nigerian English (in all its varieties) and pidgin, the former in formal announcements and talks, the latter especially in comedy or advertising.

The Nigerian Broadcasting Corporation (NBC) serves at three levels, the state, national, and international levels. At the state level we have the languages shown in Table 2.

Table 2. Languages used in Nigerian radio broadcasting at the state level

State	Languages broadcast
Benue Plateau	Kaduna
East Central (Enugu)	Igbo, English
Kano (Kano)	Hausa, English
Kwara (Ilorin)	Bar(i)ba, Idoma, Igala, Igbirra, Kanuri, Nupe, Yoruba
Lagos (Lagos)	English, Yoruba
Mid-Western (Benin)	Edo, Igbo, Ijo, Isoko, Itsekiri, Urhobo
North Central (Kaduna)	Hausa, Idoma, Igala, Igbira, Tiv, Yoruba
North Eastern (Maiduguri)	Fula, Hausa, Kanuri
North Western	Kaduna
Rivers (Port Harcourt)	Kalabari, Kolokuma, Ikwere, Khana
South Eastern (Calabar)	Efik, English
Western	Yoruba, English

At the national level nine languages are used in addition to English: Edo, Efik, Fula, Hausa, Igbo, Ijo, Kanuri, Tiv, and Yoruba, while at the international level only four languages, English, French, Hausa, and Arabic are used.

Language Function in Formal Education

The list of Nigerian languages has been based on those with translations of Scripture, and most of these languages are also used as media of primary instruction in the initial stages, varying from one to six years. This depends on the introduction of English as a medium of instruction, which is generally earlier in the case of minority languages and later in the case of well-established major languages. But as the language of instruction is not necessarily the mother tongue of all, or even most, of the pupils in any one locality, this special problem will be discussed in the typology of language learning situations (see Tables 4–10). Of the three major Nigerian languages, Yoruba has the most advanced program of mother tongue primary education, culminating in the present "Ife project" (Fafunwa 1969; Afolayan 1976). This is at once a realization of several ideals: the ideas of the missionaries of the 19th century (who generally taught in the vernacular); those of the enlightened colonial government advised by the Phelps-Stokes report in the 1927 memorandum on "The place of the vernacular in native education" (United Kingdom Colonial Office 1927); and the post-Independence national cultural aspirations of Nigeria, comprising a rare case of fulfillment of pre-Independence policies. As shown in Williamson's article on the "Rivers Readers Project" (1976), many ethnic minorities in the multilingual states are now following the same trend, but it remains to be seen how far the atomization of vernacular education is practicable and vital. A parallel case in Switzerland is the use of the four independent dialects of Romansh as separate media of instruction in primary schools. The relative roles English and pidgin play as media of instruction in primary schools is the subject of present study: it is likely that all varieties along the continuum hypothesized previously are used by primary teachers, themselves often speakers of imperfect English. Pidgin may also be used as a language of transition between the vernacular and English, a transition which characterizes the continuum.

As a subject of study in primary education (s^1), only the more established vernaculars have hitherto been used, but it is expected that more will be used in coming years. Again the introduction of English as a primary subject varies with each state, division, and even school and class, which is the reason for our proposed sliding scale in Table 3. Pidgin, not having an official position, is not taught as a subject. Arabic has been taught (as s^1) in a vast number of Quranic schools, but parrot-fashion rather than formally. The Ibadan Seminar in 1965 on the teaching of Arabic in Nigeria recommended that it should not be introduced to students until three years before the ending of primary education, that is, in the fourth or fifth years (the north has seven years of primary school compared to six years in the south) (Hunwick 1965:27). French is taught at the primary stage in some elite city schools but no other foreign language is taught at that level.

The certification of vernaculars at the primary stage (c^1) is an important stage in their popular evaluation. Hitherto only the major languages have been so certified, but this may change with time. The main aim of certification has been propagation of English for the purpose of obtaining employment.

At the secondary level the ratio of Nigerian languages to English is reversed when compared to primary education. Officially English alone is the medium of instruction (e^2), although some teachers certainly use the local language unofficially. No investigation of this unofficial use and its quantification has yet been attempted. As teaching subjects (s^2), only four Nigerian languages are officially used which lead to certification (c^2): Hausa, Yoruba, Igbo, and Efik. Ubahakwe (1972) computed the relative percentage in the four language areas taking the four major languages for the December 1970 West African School Certificate. Of the total candidates in schools located in each language area, 24.2 percent took Efik, 42 percent Igbo, 29.8 percent Hausa, and 67.8 percent Yoruba, showing the vitality of the latter. Yoruba has virtually become a compulsory subject for school certificates in the Western State, whereas in the other core states no pressure is brought to bear upon pupils. The percentage of students passing in these languages is, however, remarkably low (around 25 percent), as there are as yet very few trained teachers of Nigerian languages. English is compulsory (s^2) and (c^2) in most schools, giving the basis for our estimate of the number of SNE speakers. This is at present around 45,000 a year, having gradually risen from 5,000 since independence in 1960.

Omitting, for the purposes of this paper, teacher-training levels, we come to forms of higher education in which English is the sole medium of instruction (e^3). As University subjects, most Nigerian languages can be studied at departments of linguistics and Nigerian languages (s^3), but only four (Hausa, Yoruba, Igbo, and Edo) are at present certifiable (c^3) in major degree or diploma courses. This number will increase as universities are founded in all the capital cities in the country (new creations are under way in Jos, Kano, Benin, Calabar, Ilorin, Port Harcourt, etc.). English is taught at degree and postgraduate level at all universities as well as Arabic *cum* Islamic studies. French is taught to degree level at five universities and in secondary position at the university colleges. German is taught to degree level at two universities (Ibadan and Ife) and as ancillary in the others. Portuguese and Spanish are only taught as subsidiary subjects at one university each (Ife and Nsukka respectively), while Russian is taught as a subsidiary subject at the established five. Ubahakwe (1972) has made an evaluation of the most popular languages at university language departments with respect to their contribution to (1) national unity, (2) international understanding, (3) cultural development, and (4) technical development. By combining factors and percentages, he arrives at the following point system: English $6\frac{1}{2}$; Nigerian languages (taken together) 4; German and Russian $3\frac{1}{2}$; French and Arabic 3; Portuguese, Spanish, and Greek $2\frac{1}{2}$; and Latin $1\frac{1}{2}$ (which is a surprising result). Whether it is a valid basis for language-teaching policy is open to argument. These factors are tabulated on our Appendix 1 chart under "t" = technological, "l" = scholarship and learning.

Language and Communication

The fourth, demoglossic group of language factors is tabulated under "w" = intergroup or contact language, "a" = inter-African use and "i" = international use. The three major languages (Hausa, Yoruba, and Igbo) also serve as contact languages in diminishing proportions, with Hausa covering most of the north, Yoruba the Western and Lagos States, and Igbo the East Central and Mid-Western States. (There are other vernaculars that are similarly used, but the extent to which they are used in bilingualism, diglossia, or demoglossia has not been investigated.) The same languages have a similar role as languages of instruction in areas of mixed minority languages (w = e^1). Hausa is used in many schools in the north outside its ethnic centers; Yoruba is used in some schools in the Mid-West in non-Yoruba-speaking areas (for instance, Igara). Ibo was used in the same way before the civil war (cf. Williamson 1976). The extent to which they are used is the object of our current inquiry. English is the most important language in this category:

Of all the heritage left behind in Nigeria by the British at the end of the colonial administration, probably none is more important than the English language. This is now the language of government, business and commerce, education, the mass media, literature, and much internal as well as external communication (Bamgbose 1971:35).

This statement does not, however, qualify what is meant by the term "English," a definition we have hazarded in our above hypothesis. Adekunle (1972b) has shown how English as "w" is in complementary distribution with the Nigerian languages in the usual four language situations: public formal, public informal, private formal, and private informal (1972b:99, 114). To what extent Arabic is a "w" within Nigeria has not been ascertained. It is specifically mentioned by El-Garh (1970), but the extent to which the use of Quranic Arabic engenders phatic communion and can be used as an actual means of communication remains open to question. Pidgin, if we take it as a separate language, plays essentially the role of "w" between speakers of different groups on informal occasions but is mainly limited, like SNE, to towns. Determining the extent to which school children use these languages as compared with the wider community is one objective of current study.

As inter-African languages, several indigenous Nigerian languages have been listed in Appendix 1, notably Hausa, Fula, Yoruba, Kanuri Bariba, Busa, etc. English has the same function between the anglophone countries of West, East, and South Africa, while French has been introduced to overcome the artificial political boundaries that separate Africans from their officially francophone neighbors. Since Nkrumah, and again since the end of the Nigerian civil war, there has been much talk of closer association between West African countries, anglophone and francophone, which will add to, rather than diminish, the importance of English and French as inter-African languages. At this writing the role of Portuguese has not yet been fully realized as there have been very few contacts with the Portuguese-speaking territories of Angola and Mozambique.

The same European languages also serve as international languages in a wider sense, especially English and French. For the position of French in Nigeria, the writer has evaluated a questionnaire to Nigerian administration, finance, commerce, and industry as to the practical utility of French language skills for the next ten years (Brann 1977b), which will aid the planning of teaching French at the various institutions in the country.

MULTILINGUALISM OF THE INDIVIDUAL

As we mentioned previously, it is not possible at the present time to say precisely which languages in Nigeria are spoken by whom in diglossia, and which as third or fourth languages. It has been demonstrated that the mother tongue can be one of four types: (1) a dialect of a larger group of languages like Ibani (dialect of Ijo); (2) a vernacular not yet fully standardized, like Shuwa Arabic, Pidgin, or Abua; (3) a fully standardized vernacular like Efik or Idoma; or (4) it can be English, as in the case of some Nigerian children of mixed ethnic parentage. Or, if we apply the criteria of quantity, a mother tongue can belong to one of six categories of Nigerian languages (cf. Appendix 1). Individual multilingualism depends upon the monoglossia or diglossia of the child's home, the monodemoglossia or didemoglossia of his wider community, and the monopaidoglossia or dipaidoglossia of his school. The actual situation is the object of empirical inquiry which, in view of the large population, can at best be made on a sample basis. For the moment we will have to content ourselves with a logical typology. Half of the Nigerian population are speakers of any one of the three major languages and could therefore theoretically remain unilingual, were it not for their schooling in English. How many of these achieve bilingualism in some variety of Nigerian English is open to investigation. The other half of the population, even though they may increasingly be schooled in their own mother tongue, is likely to learn one or another of the Nigerian contact languages or one of the dominant languages of the nearest large ethnic community, as well as English. If in the north we add Arabic to the languages normally studied by a young pupil, then we have a state of triglossia or tetraglossia, which need not be a special burden as each language will have its own domain. For this reason it would seem difficult to limit the optimum to two-and-a-half languages per person as Dil (1973) maintains. Nor are psycholinguists unanimous as to the dangers or advantages of multilingualism in the overall educational process. In Nigeria there are two main views on language education, one holding that thorough cognition is best achieved in mother-tongue unilingualism, the other that since bilingualism is the educational goal of the country, it might as well be brought about in the *mollia tempora fandi*: this is the school of "straight for English." Added to this exoglossic bilingualism, there is a strong current of opinion that every Nigerian should know another (major) Nigerian language (Nigeria, Educational Research Council 1972).

As a model of variations in the development of individual multilingualism, the present sliding scale of second language inception (Table 3) has been devised from which cases may be drawn for the subsequent models of formal language education.

Table 3.   Sliding scale for multilingual language learning

Case No.	Home (Mother tongue)	Community	School 1	School 2
1.	Language 1 (unilingual)	Language 1 (monoglot)	Language 1	Language 1
2.	L1	L1	L1	L2
3.	L1	L1	L2	L2
4.	L1	L2	L2	L2
5.	L1	L1	L2	L3
6.	L1	L2	L2	L3
7.	L1	L2	L3	L3
8.	L1	L2	L3	L3
9.	L1/2 (bilingual)	L2	L2	L2
10.	L1/2	L2	L2	L3
11.	L1/2	L2	L3	L3
12.	L1/2	L3	L3	L3
13.	L1/2	L3	L3	L4 (dipaido-glossia)
14.	L1/2	L3	L4 (dipaido-glossia)	L4
15.	L1	L1/2 (diglossia)	L2	L2
16.	L1	″	L2	L3
17.	L1	″	L3	L3
18.	L1	″	L3	L4
19.	L1	L2/3	L3	L3
20.	L1	″	L3	L4
21.	L1	″	L4	L4
22.	L1	″	L4	L5

Some Cases: Hypothetical and Real

The columns "Home," "Community," and "School" in Table 3 are relevant both in space and time to a child learning languages. For the home, a unilingual and bilingual position has been hypothesized; for the community, monoglossia as well as diglossia has been suggested; and for the school we have the corresponding position of monopaidoglossia and dipaidoglossia.

CASE 1 is the case of the perfect monoglot. He may belong to a minority language group and may never go to school. He is therefore unable to communicate beyond his immediate community. He may belong to a majority language group and leave primary school with only that language, if the present trend continues. The monoglot will be a well-integrated individual in terms of his community, but he will be unable to move about the country and even less able to communicate on the official level. The case is not as hypothetical as it might seem, as we have met many individuals of this type.

CASE 2 belongs also to a majority language community. At school, he may learn a "w" — i.e. a further Nigerian language — or SNE, depending upon current policy.

CASE 3 belongs to a minority group whose language is not yet taught at primary school; his schooling is therefore in his second language which may be a Nigerian vernacular, Nigerian Standard, or indeed SNE. There have been arguments in favor of starting school with English, if the pupil has to learn another language through instruction in any case; this is the "straight for English" policy. This is the case in multilingual communities in the north and mid-west as well as in Lagos. The question is whether instruction in a foreign language (foreign from the point of view of cultural implications), English, is more difficult for the child than instruction in another Nigerian language in which concept formation would certainly be easier (cf. Fafunwa 1969; Afolayan 1976; Taiwo 1972).

CASE 4 is the case of the child whose home language (mother tongue), is not that of his community — i.e. his home is a kind of enclave. This is not uncommon with Igbo families in the north, civil servants transferred to a different state or part of the same state, etc. In this case, the child has to learn the dialect, the vernacular, or the standard of his community since one will be the language of instruction at the local school.

CASE 5 is the case of the child who goes to school in a language community different from that of his home. He may have to travel some distance to the nearest school outside his community or there may be no school available in his community language or mother tongue, as in the multilingual communities of the Beneu Plateau. He will be instructed in a second Nigerian language and also learn a third, either a Nigerian standard language, Arabic, or English.

CASE 6 is the case in which the child's community language and the language of instruction of his first school years is not his mother tongue. In addition to his home and community languages, he learns either an additional language of wide communication, that is, a further Nigerian standard language, Arabic or English.

CASE 7 is the case in which the community language of a child is not that of his home language, which is perhaps a dialect or minority language. In addition the "e¹" is not the community language, but perhaps a Nigerian standard language like Hausa in one of the northern states. In order not to be overburdened, the child may stay in this language throughout primary school.

CASE 8 refers to the situation in which, in addition to the above case, it is decided to introduce a second language into primary school, either as "s²" or "e²," which may be an additional Nigerian standard language, Arabic, or English.

CASE 9 is based on balanced bilingualism, that is, on the child already using two languages at home. These may be different varieties of the same language group or entirely different Nigerian languages, perhaps a sub-dominant and a dominant language, or a Nigerian language and pidgin. He will be schooled in the dominant language, perhaps a Nigerian standard and he will continue primary schooling in it.

CASE 10 is as above, but a second language of instruction, a Nigerian standard; Arabic, or English is introduced during primary education.

CASE 11 refers to a bilingual child who continues with the dominant language in the community but is schooled in a new Nigerian standard in which he continues throughout primary school.

CASE 12 shows a bilingual child of mixed parentage living in a community speaking a third Nigerian language, perhaps but not necessarily a Nigerian standard. His schooling begins and ends in that third language.

CASE 13 refers to a bilingual child who uses a language of wide communication in his community and school to which is added a fourth language, perhaps a Nigerian standard or English.

CASE 14 refers to the situation of a bilingual child who uses a third language of wide communication in his community, to which is added a further language in school, either a Nigerian standard or English.

CASE 15 refers to a new series concerning unilingual children in a community of diglossia of which their mother tongue may or may not be one. The child of Case 15 is limited to the dominant language of the community, which is carried over to school.

CASE 16 is a similar situation but one more language is added in upper primary or secondary school, either a Nigerian standard, Arabic, or English.

CASE 17 is the case in which the "e¹" is neither of the community languages, but possibly a "w," a Nigerian standard, and is maintained throughout school.

CASE 18 is similar, but an "e²" is added, probably English.

CASE 19 is the hypothetical case of a child living in a diglossic community, neither of which languages is his mother tongue. This would again be the case of a family enclave (e.g. a *sabongari*). At school, he would be instructed in the dominant language of the two community languages (perhaps Hausa), throughout his primary schooling, at which stage he finishes. Like several other examples cited, he would have no contact with English as "e²."

CASE 20 is as above, with a second Nigerian standard or English added to the languages already used.

CASE 21 occurs when the school is removed from the bilingual community, possibly because of distance. The child is taught in an "e¹" which is his fourth language; he continues in this language.

CASE 22 results when a further language, possibly English this time, is added to the above.

These several cases have been spelled out at length in order to show the probable complexity of the multilingual situation in the context of education and the consequent need for a sliding scale of language education. It has been shown that from the point of view of language learning, some children are bound to be more favored than others in regard to the simplicity or complexity of their education. What has to be established empirically is just how much language complexity in education is tolerable and how much is desirable. At the one extreme, the monolithic monoglot does not further communication in a Nigerian regional or national context. At the other extreme, it is suspected that the Nigerian polyglot does not possess a high competence in any of his languages and therefore has a poor conceptual formation as well as being unable to communicate accurately. What we have attempted to point out is that it may not be enough to stop at the limiting of mother-tongue teaching. This solves only the first half of the Nigerian language education problem.

FITTING THE LANGUAGES INTO THE SCHOOL SYLLABUS

Having considered the varieties of language in Nigerian society and some of the variations in their acquisition, we now have to consider some means of accommodating them in the educational system. In doing so, two main criteria must be fulfilled: the personal development of the individual pupil or language group and the needs of present society in its national and international aspirations. From the point of view of individual development, educationists have been unanimous in their opinion that sound intellectual and moral growth depends on an individual feeling at one with his language and tradition — that is, best individual development requires that the individual be taught in his mother tongue. His community may require him to adopt a regional language in addition. In large parts of Nigeria, particularly in the north, the individual is required, in addition to assimilating his home language(s) and traditions, to learn Arabic to be included in the Islamic community. In order to enter public employment or a profession, he will require a knowledge of English at various levels. If he reaches secondary education, he will in addition require an international language. All these have to be accommodated in a school system of two levels of six classes each. This system is foreseen for the country as from 1981 when the thirteenth year (upper sixth) will be incorporated into the university (National Policy on Education 1977).

The difficulty of planning any language syllabus in a multilingual and heterogeneous society like Nigeria is that the social settings of language as well as the individual layers of language learning cannot conveniently be brought under one common scheme of schooling. Centralization of curriculum and timetable — such as is known in Latin countries like France — would be unthinkable in the pluralistic society of Nigeria. In order to accommodate the many variables which we have attempted to show above, we have to look for elements in common to the whole structure around which to build a design. So long as it is agreed to maintain and expand English as the language in common, the school year in which English is introduced as language of instruction (E on our charts), in relation to the mother tongue or dominant Nigerian language, can serve as a matrix for the placement of other variables, that is, the introduction of further Nigerian languages of wide communication as school subjects (s), of Arabic as the special language of Islam (a), of French as the language of external contact (f) or of other international languages for additional contact of learning (i, t, l). An important question concerns the point at which languages of instruction (indicated by capital letters on our charts) and languages as objects of study (i.e. subjects indicated by small letters) should be introduced in relation to one another during the six to seven years of primary school and the five to seven years of secondary school.

Alternatives for Language Teaching in Nigerian Schools

In the first design Table 4, we propose an increment of a new subject language every other year, that is, years 1, 3, 5/7, 9; 2, 4, 6/8; 3, 5/7, 9; 4, 6/8 and 5/7, 9. (Each figure represents the year in which the new language is added; the bar is the transition from primary to secondary school.) This mode has the advantage of a regular and rhythmic increase. The variables in the commencement of English as a language of instruction, in relation to which the model is built up, correspond to actual language policies in the country.

CASE A is the policy called "straight for English" which is practiced in urban areas where English is more often spoken in the homes and the community than anywhere else, in places in the country where there is no common Nigerian language of wider communication, or where there is a

Table 4. Major mother tongue with transition of language of instruction from major standard to English, with biennial language increment

	Infancy 1–5 years	Primary I–III 6–8 years	Primary III–VI 9–11 years	Secondary I–III 12–14 years	Secondary IV–V 15–16 years
M = S (Case A)	E_s^e	$+_a^{s2}$	$+_{\bar{\imath}}^{s2}$	$+_{\bar{\imath}}^{f1}$	$+_{\bar{\imath}}^{f}$
M (Case B)	S_e^e	E_s^e	$+_a^{s2}$	$+_{\bar{\imath}}^{f}$	$+_{\bar{\imath}}^{f}$
M (Case C)	S_e^s	S_e^s	$+_a^{s2}$	$+_{\bar{\imath}}^{s2}$	$+_{\bar{\imath}}^{f}$
M (Case D)	S_e^s	S_e^s	E_s^e	$+_{\bar{\imath}}^{s2}$	$+_{\bar{\imath}}^{f}$
M (Case E)	S_e^s	S_e^s	S_e^s	E_s^e	$+_{\bar{\imath}}^{f}$
M (Case F)	S_e^s	S_e^s	S_e^s	E_s^e	$+_{\bar{\imath}}^{s2}$
M (Case G)	S_e^s	S_e^s	S_e^s	S_e^s	E_s^e

Key to Tables 4–10

M(m) = mother tongue
D(d) = dialect
V(v) = vernacular
S(s) = standard or major language
E(e) = English
A(a) = Arabic
F(f) = French
H(h) = Hausa

Capitals indicate languages of instruction, while lowercase letters indicate subject languages.

+ = language increment.
$\frac{x}{y}$ = choice of languages.
l/t = language of international scholarship or science and technology.
Superior numbers indicate level of study: 1 = primary; 2 = secondary.

resistance against a common Nigerian language. Whether this English is SNE or an idiolect along the English continuum is a subject for investigation. In some places it can also be pidgin. In places where there is a uniform (minor) mother tongue, this can be taught as a subject from the start; in those areas where there is no common mother tongue, a Nigerian standard can be introduced as a subject in the first or third year. Since English is introduced at an early stage, other languages can also follow. There is no reason why in such a case French should not be introduced at the primary stage, followed by other languages at the secondary stage. This is a common practice in countries like the Netherlands where many pupils master English, French, and German in addition to their mother tongue.

CASE B is the custom in some city schools which follow the practice of devoting the first year to the mother tongue. In this model, a Nigerian standard or Arabic could be introduced in the 4th primary year. This would follow the recommendation of the Ibadan 1965 seminar with regard to the introduction of Arabic at a point at which the language of instruction is already well known.

CASE C is also found in cities. CASE D is widely practised by schools throughout the country where English becomes the language of instruction in the fourth year. CASES E and F were proposed as policy by the 1927 memorandum of the Advisory Committee on Education. Case 6 is the Ife Project, in which English is introduced as a subject in the first primary year but not taught as a language of instruction until the first year of secondary school. This would mean that French could only be introduced two years later, a policy which has the approval of some (Evans 1972).

In a second design (see Table 5), we propose a plan in which fewer languages are introduced, with a language increment every three years in a regular rhythm — that is, 1, 4/7, 10; 2, 5/11; 3, 6/9; 4, 7/11; 5/8; 6/9; 7/9.

In a third design (see Table 6), a rapid increase in language training in lower primary school is proposed in accordance with the theory, supported by Penfield and Roberts (1959), of the high language learning capacity of young children. This follows the argument that languages should be learned at a time when the physical and psychological structure of pupils are at their most impressionable and skills are acquired with little effort, rather than the later introduction which requires higher motivation and increased effort — the argument basic to the FLES (Foreign Languages in Elementary Schools) programs throughout the world. This rapid momentum would slow down in the upper school, where language learning becomes a conscious process. The design proposed is 1, 3, 4/7, 9; 2, 4, 5/7, 9; 3, 5, 6/8, 10; 4/6, 7; 5/7, 8; 6, 7, 8; 7, 8, 9.

In a fourth design (see Table 7), we follow the opposite hypothesis of language learning, i.e. that a child must learn one language of instruction

Table 5. Minor mother tongue with transition of language of instruction from minor tongue to English, and triennial language increment

	Infancy 1-5	Primary I-III 6-8	Primary III-VI 9-11	Secondary I-III 12-14	Secondary IV-V 15-16
M = D/V	E_c^m		$+\frac{s}{a}$	$+\frac{f}{s2}$	$+\frac{f}{a}$
M	M_c^m E_m^c		$+\frac{s}{a}$	$+\frac{f}{s2}$	$+\frac{f}{a}$
M	M m M_c^m E_m^c		$+\frac{s}{a}$	$+\frac{f}{s2}$	$+\frac{f}{s2}$
M	M m M_c^m M_c^m	E_m^c	$+\frac{s}{a}$	$+\frac{s}{a}$	
M	M m M_c^m M_c^m	M^m	E_m^c	$+\frac{s}{a}$	
M	M m M_c^m M_c^m	M_c^m	M_c^m	E_m^c	$+\frac{s}{a}$
M	M m M_c^m M_c^m	M_c^m	M_c^m	M_c^m	E_m^c

Table 6. Minor mother tongue but major standard first language of instruction, with transition to English and rapid increments at primary stage

	Infancy 1-5	Primary I-III 6-8	Primary III-VI 9-11	Secondary I-III 12-14	Secondary IV-V 15-16
MT = D/V	E_c^s	$\frac{a}{s2}$	$\frac{a}{s2}$	$\frac{f}{s2}$	$+$
MT	S s	E_s^c $+$	$\frac{a}{s2}$	$\frac{f}{s2}$	$+$
MT	S s	S_c^s E_s^c	$+$		
MT	S s	S_c^s S_c^s	E_s^c	$\frac{f}{s2}$	$+$
MT	S s	S_c^s S_c^s	S_c^s	$\frac{f}{s2}$	
MT	S s	S_c^s S_c^s	S_c^s	$\frac{a}{s2}$	$\frac{a}{s2}$
MT	S s	S_c^s S_c^s	S_c^s	E_s^c $+$	
MT	S s	S_c^s S_c^s	S_c^s	E_s^c	$\frac{f}{s2}$

Table 7. Major mother tongue and major standard for instruction, with transition to dual instruction in English and another language (dipaidoglossic school) and increments mainly in secondary school

	Infancy 1-5	Primary I-III 6-8	Primary III-VI 9-11	Secondary I-III 12-14	Secondary IV-V 15-16
MT = S	ES_s^e +		$\frac{a}{s2}$	$\frac{t}{1}$	
S	S_s^s	ES_s^e +		$\frac{t}{1}$	
S	S_e^s	S_e^s	ES_s^e +	$\frac{t}{s2}$	$\frac{t}{1}$
S	S_e^s	S_e^s	ES_s^e +		$\frac{t}{s2}$
S	S_s^s	S_e^s	S_e^s +	$\frac{a}{s2}$	$\frac{t}{s2}$
S	S_e^s	S_e^s	S_e^s	+	
S	S_e^s	S_e^s	ES_s^e	$\frac{a}{s2}$	f
S	S_e^s	S_e^s	S_e^s	ES_s^e $\frac{a}{s2}$	f

thoroughly before new ones can be added as subjects, and that languages are better added in the upper school as subjects requiring a conscious effort of learning; this theory is held by the psycholinguists of the Russian school like Belyaev and presented in cognitive code-learning theory. The design then would be 1, 4/7, 9; 2, 5/7, 9; 3, 6/8, 9; 4/7, 9; 5/7, 9; 6/8, 10; 7, 8, 11.

A special design (Table 8) would be necessary for the gradual transformation of the Quranic schools which employ Arabic as the language of instruction into elementary schools with English as a language of instruction and Arabic as a subject. (Table 9 illustrates a similar situation except that another northern language would be the medium of instruction, and in addition to English and Arabic, Hausa would be taught as a subject.)

So far we have assumed that English will become the language of instruction at some definite point in the primary school. This transition from one to a second language of instruction is critical:

it is in the change-over from the vernacular or union language, as the medium of instruction, that the greatest practical difficulty arises. The consensus of opinion shows that when a pupil reaches the stage in the elementary school when English is taught, it will take a whole year at least in which progress in the subjects of education must be subordinated to the acquisition of the new medium. Again and again we have evidence of the harmful results from the gradual introduction of what is no more than a smattering of bad English (United Kingdom Colonial Office 1927).

It is this argument that influenced the organizers of the Ife project (1) to begin teaching English as a subject early; (2) to have English taught by specially trained teachers; and (3) to defer the transition to English as a language of instruction until after the mother tongue (here a majority language) and the basic school subjects taught in it have been thoroughly learned.

Another possible solution would be a practice of dipaidoglossia in teaching different subjects — that is, some subjects would continue to be taught in the mother tongue, while others would be taught in English. This possibility has not been shown on our models, but it is well known to the practitioners of bilingual schools and is mentioned in the Memorandum of the Advisory Committee quoted above (United Kingdom Colonial Office 1927).

For the many Nigerian pupils whose mother tongue is not a majority language, however, it will be necessary to learn at least one Nigerian language of wider communication in addition to English. This was the express recommendation of the first National Curriculum Conference in Lagos in 1971 (see Nigeria, Educational Research Council 1972). If a student's mother tongue is a dialect of a larger language group, a pupil may find that his schooling will be in the group vernacular, which he will then have to learn. For the primary school, therefore, the mother tongue,

Table 8.   Hausa medium of instruction with transition to English and introduction of Arabic

	Primary							Secondary					
	1	2	3	4	5	6	7	8	9	10	11	12	13
	E_h^e		+a			$\frac{s2}{f}$						$+\frac{i}{f}$	
	H_e^h	E_h^e		+a			$+\frac{s2}{f}$					$+\frac{i}{f}$	
	H^h	$+^e$	E_h^e		+a			$+\frac{s2}{f}$				$+\frac{i}{f}$	
	H^h	+e		E_h^e		+a			$+\frac{s2}{f}$			$+\frac{i}{f}$	
	H^h	+e	+a		E_h^e			$+\frac{s2}{f}$				$+\frac{i}{f}$	
	H^h	+e		+a		E_h^e		$+\frac{s2}{f}$				$+\frac{i}{f}$	
	H^h	+e			+a		E_h^e		$+\frac{s2}{f}$			$+\frac{i}{f}$	

Table 9. Other northern language as the medium of instruction with transition to English and introduction of Hausa and Arabic

	Primary							Secondary					
	1	2	3	4	5	6	7	8	9	10	11	12	13
	E_m^e	+e	+h	+	+a			+f				+f	
	M_c^m	E_m^c	–	+h	+h	+a		+f				+f	
	M^m	+e	E_m^c	–	+h	+h	+a		+f			+f	
	M^m	+e	+h	E_m^c	–	+h	+a			+f		+f	
	M^m	+e	+h	+h	E_m^c	–	+a	+a	+f			+f	
	M^m	+e	+h	+h	+h	E_m^c	–	+a	+f	+f	+f	+f	
	M^m	+e	+h	+h	+h	+h	E_m^c	–	+a		+f	+f	

English, and another language is needed, while for the secondary school two more languages can be added as subjects, giving the number of languages to be learned by the average Nigerian pupil which are enumerated in Table 10.

Table 10.   Languages needed in formal school education

Primary			Secondary	
L1 (M)	L2	L3	L4	L5
D	V/Ss	Ee	s^2/a	a/f
Vv	Ee	s/a	a/f	f
Ss	Ee	a/s^2	f/a	f/t (1)
Ee/P	s/a	f/a	s^2/f	f/t (1)

Primary = 2(V/S) + 1 (s/a/f);
secondary = 1(E) + 2 (s^2/a/t).
(See Key to Tables 4–10.)

Varieties of Dipaidoglossia in Nigeria

Corresponding to the several languages of instruction that are used in Nigerian schools, there can be varieties of dipaidoglossia, which are likewise found in other parts of Africa, especially in Cameroon.

CASE A refers to the situation in which two languages run in parallel streams which are nevertheless independent of one another. This is the case in the present Ife Project. Each stream is monopaidoglossic: Yoruba is the only language of instruction of one group, while in the same school another control group is taught in English. A similar case is found in the bilingual school in Yaounde, where one stream is in French and the other is English.

CASE B is the case in which different subjects are taught in different languages. This is the case in most Nigerian primary schools during the years of transition from the Nigerian language of instruction to English. First arithmetic is taught in English, then, say, nature study, while history and geography are still taught in the Nigerian language. In a fully "bilingual" school, each subject teacher may have his preference for the language of instruction. In other schools, to more clearly stress the bilingual nature of education, each subject is alternatively taught first in the one and then in the other language, so that pupils grow up as complete bilinguals rather than attaching one language to one field of study and another language to another field.

CASE C is the not-uncommon case in primary schools in linguistic border communities where consecutive interpretation by the primary teacher is used: a statement is first made in the pupil's local vernacular and is then repeated in the standard of the wider community. This is the case in Igara in the Mid-West, where a teacher will say one thing in Igara (related to Igbirra) and then translate it into Yoruba (cf. Oke 1972).

CASE D is the equally common case in which mixed language is used. It is especially common during the time English is being introduced but in many cases is continued throughout primary school. Statements are made in mixed language. This is the way that counting is still taught in most Yoruba schools where numbers are first said in English and then in Yoruba; it is a system inherited from missionary education and was intended to serve as a mnemonic device. We distinguish here of course between the conscious use of mixed language for educational purposes and the unconscious lapses, due to language interference, of teachers.

In the situation found in Nigeria, dipaidoglossia can occur in the following combinations: (1) between two Nigerian languages, generally a minor and major (a vernacular and a standard), (2) between a Nigerian language and pidgin or English, and (3) between a Nigerian language and Arabic (especially in the north). The effect on pupils' cognitive processes as well as their ultimate language skill in either or both languages remains the object of research.

CONCLUSION

Since at the present, our knowledge of what is actually happening in language education in the various multilingual parts of the country, both as to the use of Nigerian languages and their relationship with Arabic and English/pidgin, is imperfect, we can only suggest some general typologies as instruments of possible research. The nature of Nigerian society is too complex to call for a single solution or imposition of a single language. Rather, each ethnic unit deserves a special study of its language in relation to the educational process; something of the sort is being undertaken, in collaboration with educationists, by the Department of Linguistics of the University of Ibadan and the Institute of Linguistics at Zaria (Stanford 1972; Williamson 1976). Such studies should certainly be the combined effort of descriptive linguists, sociolinguists, psycholinguists, and language methodologists, as was the East African survey (Prator 1967). In its complexity, the Nigerian field of language education may be said to represent examples of all possible situations in the world, a polypaidoglossic microcosm. Any investigation, however, should take into account the situations of language education in other parts of the world. The Nigerian educational language planner may not find in this paper a ready-made answer for action, but he may find a methodological hint as to the possibilities of comparison and choice. The aim of the present typology is not to be prescriptive, but indicative.

APPENDIX 1.   LANGUAGE IN EDUCATION AND SOCIETY IN NIGERIA

Key:
CLASS

AE= Adamawa-Eastern	E= (Indo-) European	M= Mande
BC= Benue Congo	GV= Gur-Voltaic	NS= Nilo-Saharan
Ch= Chadic	K= Kwa	S= Semitic
		WA= West Atlantic

TYPES

D= Dialect	V= Vernacular	I= Foreign/International
C= Classical	S= Standard	

LANGUAGES

P= Pidgin	S= Standard (major language)
F= Fula	A= Arabic
H= Hausa	Y= Yoruba
E= English	N= Nigerian English

FUNCTIONS

m= mother tongue	a= inter-African	d= diglossia
n= newspapers	t= science and technology	b= broadcasts
s= subject of education	i= international	e= medium of education
c= certification	l= literature and	w= wider communication
	scholarship	within Nigeria
		r= religion

For r, b, e, s, c, w, a, i, there are 3 levels each, depending upon the degree or level of use. The following quantitative breakdown applies to mother-tongue speakers (m) and second-language speakers (d):

1= up to 100,000 speakers
2= 100,000 to 1,000,000
3= 1,000,000 to 3,000,000
4= 3,000,000 to 5,000,000
5= 5,000,000 to 10,000,000
6= 10,000,000 and above

STATES

BP= Benue Plateau	L= Lagos	NW= North Western
EC= East Central	MW= Mid-Western	R= Rivers
K= Kano	NC= North Central	SE= South Eastern
Kw= Kwara	NE= North Eastern	W= Western
	DAH= Dahomey	CMN= Cameroon

(Note: This classification system is based upon the political division of 1975.)

Notes

LANGUAGES   Opinion on the status of language — as to whether they are dialects of one language, a group, or a cluster — varies and is changing. In selecting 100 languages (94 Nigerian languages and 6 European languages), not all Nigerian languages that make a contribution to the educational process have been covered. (In point of fact, any language in which a child grows up at home contributes to his education.)

CLASSIFICATION   Classification has only been given for the wider family, in order to show the diversity represented in Nigeria. In some cases, classification is not definitive.
NUMBER OF SPEAKERS   No definitive statement exists, since the 1963 census does not always distinguish between ethnicity and language. The present figures are based on estimates of the three linguists mentioned above. Again, little is known about the diglossia of speakers beyond various statements of linguists (e.g. Kirk-Greene 1967) and anthropologists.
LOCALITY   Sometimes individual cities have been identified with a language; at other times divisions have been mentioned. In the case of some major languages, whole states have been included.
TYPOLOGY   Brackets have been used in cases where the situation applies to a small minority of speakers.

Table 1. Language in education and society in Nigeria

Language	Class	Type	Speakers 1,000's m	d	States	Locality		Typology
Abua	BC	V	24		R	Abua		Vmre^{1}s^1
Agatu	K	V (Idoma)	35		BP	Oshigbudu		Vmr^{2}e^{1}s^1
Agwagwune	BC	V	30		SE	Agwagwune		Vmre^{1}s^1
Agbo	BC	V	35		SE	Itigidi		Vme^1
Alago (Arago)	K	V (Idoma)		H	BP	Lafia		Vmdre^1
Angas	Ch	V	136	H$_2$	BP	Kabwir		Vm^{2}dre^{1}s^1
Arabic	S	C	–		All			C^{3}b^{3}e$_1$s$_1$c^{2}e^{2}s^{3}c^3 wa^{3}il
Arabic, Shuwa	S	D (Arabic)	150		NE	Maiduguri		Dm^{2}r
Bachama	Ch	D (Bata)	20	F/H	NE	Adamawa	d	Dmdre^1
Bar(i)ba	GV	V	55		Kw & DAH	Borgu + Ilorin		Vmrbe^{1}wa
Bassa Komo	BC	V	100		Kw	Kabba	d	Vmr^{2}e^{1}s^1
Bekwarra	BC	V	35		SE	Ebeten	d	Vmre^{1}s^1
Bete (Bette-Bendi)	BC	V	17		SE	Obudu	d	Vmre^1
Birom	BC	V	118	H	BP	southern Jos	d	Vm^{2}de^1
Bokyi (Boki)	BC	V	87		SE	southern Ogoja		Vmre^1
Bura	CH	V	175	H$_2$	NE	Biu	d	Vm^{2}de^1

Table I (*continued*)

Language	Class	Type	Speakers 1,000's m	d	States	Locality		Typology
Busa	M	V	100		Kw	Ilorin	+	$Vm^2re^1s^1$
						Borgu	d	
Chawi	BC	V	10		NC	Zangen/d		$Vmre^1$
Dakkarkari	BC	V	70		NW	Zuru		$Vmdre^1$
Dghwede	Ch	V	13	H_2	NE	eastern Gwoza	d	Vme^1
Duka	BC	V	25		NW	Rijau		$Vmre^1$
Edo (group)	K	S	1,000		MW	Benin		$Sm^3r^2nb^2e^1s^1s^2s^3c^3w$
Efik (Ibibio)	BC	S	3,200		SE	Calabar		$Sm^3r^2nb^2e^1s^1s^2c^3s^3w$
Egede (Igede)	K	V	12		BP	Idoma	d	$Vm\ re^1s^1$
Eggon	BC	V	143		BP	Eggon/d		$Vm^2r^2e^1s^1$
Ekajuk	BC	V	15		SE	south western		$Vmr^2e^1s^1$
						Ogoja	d	
Ekpeye	K	V	51		R	Ahoada	d	$Vmre^1s^1$
Eleme	BC	V (Ogoni)	29		R	Okarki		$Vmre^1s^1$
English	E	V/I/S	10 percent of population	P_2	All	Towns		$(V)\ IS\ (m)\ d^4r^3nb^3$ $e^1s^1c^1e^2s^2c^2\hat{c}e^3s^3c^3w^3$ $a^3t^3t^3$
Epie	K	V	16		R	Yenagoa		Vme^1s^1
						Brass		
Etche	K	V	60		R	Ahoada	d	Vme^1s^1
Etsako	K	D (Edo)	120		MW	Auchi		$Dm^2dre^1s^1$
Eza	K	V (Igbo)	180		EC	Abakaliki		Vm^2de^1

Table I (continued)

Language	Class	Type	Speakers 1,000's m	d	States	Locality	Typology
French	E	I	–		–	–	Ib³s²c²s²c²aitl
Fula	WA	S	3,000	H₂	NW, NC NE, K + BP	(West Africa) Adamawa	Sm¹d r²nb²e¹s¹wa³
Ganawuri (Aten)	BC	V	10			south western Jos	Vmre¹ d
Gbari (Gwari)	K	V	344	H₂	NC NW	Kaduna Minna	Vm²dr²e¹s¹ d
German	E	I	–		–	–	I (s²c²) s³c³t¹l²
Glavda	Ch	V	19		NE	eastern Gwoza	Vme¹
Gude	Ch	V	50	H₂	NE	southern Mubi	Vmde¹
Gokana	BC	V (Ogoni)	55		R	Bori	Vmre¹s¹
Hausa	Ch	S	13,000 5,000	(m) (d)	NW, NC, K, NE, BP, Kw	(+ West Africa)	Sm⁶s⁶nb³e¹s¹c¹c²s²c² s³c³w³a³i
Higi	Ch	V	180	H₂	NE + CMN	Michika	Vm²dr²e¹s¹a
Ibani	K	D (Ijo)	27		R	Bonny	Dmde¹s¹
Idoma	K	S	490		BP	Oturkpo	Sm²s²be¹s¹
Igala	K	S	350	Y₂	KW	Idah/Kabba	Sm²s³be¹s¹
Igbirra	K	S	426		MW (MW) KW, BP	Asaba Okenne Koton Karifi	Sm²rbe¹s¹ d
Igbo	K	S	9,200		EC, MW	State Ika	Sm⁵b²e¹s¹s²c²s²c³w²
Ijaw	K	VS	1,100		R, MW	Brass Bomadi	SVm³t¹b²e¹s¹

Table I (*continued*)

Language	Class	Type	Speakers 1,000's m	d	States	Locality	Typology
Ikwere	K	V (Igbo)	260		R	PHarcourt	$Vm^2re^1s^1$
Ikwo	K	V (Igbo)	150		EC	southern Abaka-liki	Dm^2re^1
Iregwe	BC	V	15		BP	western Jos	$Vmre^1$
Ishan	K	D/Edo	200		MW	Ubiaja	$Dm^2e^1s^1$
Isoko	K	S (Urhobo)	200		MW	Oleh	$Sm^2rb^2e^1s^1$
Itsekiri	K	S (Yoruba)	30	P	MW	Warri	$Sm\ drbe^1s^1$
Izi	K	V (Igbo)	200		EC	Abakaliki	Dm^2re^1
Jaba (Jarawan Kogi)	BC	V	60	H_2	NC	Kwoi	$Vmdre^1$
Jarawa	BC	V	59		BP, NE	Pankshin d / Bauchi d	$Vmre^1$
Jibu	BC	D/Jukun	10		NE	eastern Beli	$Dmre^1$
Jukun (group)	BC	V	300		BP, NE	Wukari / Sardauna s	$Vmre^1$
Kaje	BC	V	35		NC	Zonkwa	Vme^1
Kamberri	BC	V	100		NW	western Konta-gora	Vm^2e^1
Kanakuru	Ch	V	20		NE	Shellem	Vme^1
Kanuri	NS	S	2,300		NE, NW CMN	Maiduguri	$Sm^4rb^2e^1s^1wa^2$
Khana	BC	V (Ogoni)	94		R	northern Bori	$Vmrbe^1s^1$
Kilba	Ch	V	88	N	NE	Hong	Vme^1

Table I (*continued*)

Language	Class	Type	Speakers 1,000's m	d	States	Locality	Typology	
Kolokuma	K	D/Ijo	30		R	Odi	Dmrbe¹s¹	
Kukele	BC	V	33		SB	Ogoja	Vmre¹	d
Kuteb	BC	V	26		BP	Takum	Vme¹	
Kalabari	K	D/Ijo	25		R	Buguma	Dmrbe¹s¹	
Latin	E	C	–		–	–	C (r) s²č²s³č²i¹²	
Longuda	AE	V	32	H₂	NE	northern Numan	Vmd	d
Mambila	BC	V	95		NE + CMN	Gembu	Vmre¹	
Margi	Ch	V	135	H₂	NE	Bornu	Vm²dre¹	
Mbembe	BC	V	60		SE	Obubra	Vmre¹	d
Mumuye	AE	V	250		NE	Zina	Vm²dre¹	
Nembe	K	D/Ijo	66		R	Nembe	Dmre¹s¹	
Nupe	K	S	750		Kw, NW	Bida	Sm²r³be¹s¹	d
Ogbah	K	V (Igbo)	10		R	Omoku	Vme¹s¹	
Ogbia	K	V (Igbo)	22		R	Oloibiri	Vme¹s¹	
Ogoni (group) cf. Khana Gokana + Eleme	BC	V	165		R	PHarcourt	Vm²r³be¹s¹	
Okrika	K	D/Ijo	81		R	Okrika	Dme¹s¹	
Ora	K	D/Edo	1	Y	MW	Owan	Dmre¹	d
Pero	Ch	V	20		NE	Filya	Vmre¹	

Table 1 (continued)

Language	Class	Type	Speakers 1,000's m	d	States	Locality		Typology
Pidgin	E	V	10% of the population	$\frac{E}{2}$	All in South and North	All in South cities in MW, ports, *sabon-garis*		$V(m)d^4(r)(b)(e)w^3a^3$
Portuguese	E	I	–			–		$Is^3a^2l^2]$
Rukuba	BC	V	50		BP	Rukuba Jos	d d	$Vmre^1$
Russian	E	I	–			–		$Is^3l^3l^2$
Spanish	E	I	–			–		$Is^3ai^3l]$
Tangale	Ch	V	100		BP	Kaltungo		$Vm^2r^2e^1s^1$
Tera	Ch	V	46		NE	Bornu		$Vmre^1$
Tiv	BC	S	1,500		BP	Gboko, Makurdi		$Sm^3r^3b^2e^1s^1$
Tsamba (Chamba Daka)	AE	V	162	F	NE,BP + CMN	Sardauna	s d	Vm^2re^1a
Tula	AE	V	19		SE	Gombe		Vme^1
Umin (Union)	BC	V	640		SE	Biase		$Vmre^1$
Urhobo	K	S	30		MW	Ughelli	d	$Sm^2r^2be^1s^1$
Waja	AE	V	15		NE	Bauchi		$Vmre^1$
Yache (Akweya)	K	V			SE, BP	Northern		$Vmre^1$
Yakur-	BC	V	100		SE	Ogoja		Vm^2re^1
Yala	K	V	50		SE	Ugep Western		$Vmre^1$
Yergam	BC	V	60		BP	Ogoja Langtang.	d	$Vmre^1$
Yoruba	K	S	11,300	$\frac{H}{2}$	W + L (Kw) (MW)	Western & Lagos States Ilorin, Kabba, Akoko	d	$Sm^6r^3b^2e^1s^1c^1s^2c^2 s^3c^3w^2a$

REFERENCES

ADEKUNLE, M. A.
1972a Multilingualism and language function in Nigeria. *African Studies Review* 15(2):185–207.
1972b "Sociolinguistic problems in English language instruction in Nigeria," in *Sociolinguistics in cross-cultural analysis*. Edited by D. M. Smith and R. W. Shuy, 83–102. Washington, D.C.: Georgetown University Press. (With comments by Dell Hymes on a proposed typology of the relationship of Nigerian languages to English, 107–114.)

AFOLAYAN, A.
1976   The six-year primary project in Nigeria, in *Mother tongue education: the west African experience*. Edited by A. Bamgbose, 113–234. London and Paris: Hodder and UNESCO.

AJOLORE, O.
1971   "Towards a national language policy." Paper presented at a seminar at University of Lagos, Department of English.

ARMSTRONG, R. G.
1968   "Language policies and language practices in West Africa," in *Language problems of developing nations*. Edited by J. A. Fishman et al., 227–236. New York: Wiley.

BAMGBOSE, A.
1971   "The English language in Nigeria," in *The English language in West Africa*. Edited by J. Spencer, 35–48. London: Longman.

BAMGBOSE, A., *editor*
i.p.   *Language in education in Nigeria: proceedings of the 1977 Kaduna symposium*. Lagos: National Language Centre.

BANJO, L. A.
1976   Language policy in Nigeria, in *The Search for national integration in Africa*. Edited by D. Smock and K. Bentsi-Entchill: 206–219. New York: Free Press.

BRANN, C. M. B.
1975a *Language in education and society in Nigeria: a comparative bibliography and research guide*. Quebec, International Center for Research on Bilingualism.
1975b Standardisation des langues et éducation au Nigéria. *African Languages* (London) 1:204–224.
1977a Educational language planning in Nigeria: problems and prospects. *Africa* (Rome) 22 (3):317–336.
1977b The role of language in Nigeria's educational policy: some comments and inferences. *Nigerian Language Teacher* (Lagos) 2:32–38.

COLDHAM, G. E.
1966   *A bibliography of Scriptures in African languages*, two volumes. London: British and Foreign Bible Society.

CSA
1960   *Meeting of specialists on the adaptation of education to African conditions*. CSA Publication 59. Lagos: CSA (Scientific Council for Africa South of the Sahara).

DIL, A.
1973   "Towards a general model of language planning policy," in *Anthropology and language science in educational development*, 55–58. Paris: UNESCO.

EL-GARH, M. S.
1970   *Arabic in Nigeria. Why, when and how to teach it.* Ibadan: University of
       Ibadan, Departments of Arabic and Islamic Studies.
EVANS, H. J. G.
1972   Does everybody need French? *Le Francais au Nigeria.* Journal of the
       Nigerian French Teachers' Association, Ibadan 7(2):18–28.
FAFUNWA, A. B.
1969   The importance of the mother tongue as a medium of instruction.
       Nigeria Magazine 102 (September–November):539–542.
FERGUSON, C. A.
1971a "Diglossia," in *Language structure and language use: selected essays,*
       1–26. Stanford: Stanford University Press.
1971b "The language factor in national development," in *Language structure
       and language use: selected essays,* 51–59. Stanford: Stanford University
       Press.
1971c "National sociolinguistic profile formulas," in *Language structure and
       language use: selected essays,* 157–184. Stanford: Stanford University
       Press.
FISHMAN, J. A.
1967   Bilingualism with and without diglossia: diglossia with and without
       bilingualism. *Journal of Social Issues* 23(2):29–38.
1968a "Some contrasts between linguistically homogeneous and linguistically
       heterogeneous polities," in *Language problems of developing nations,*
       53–68. New York: Wiley.
1968b "Nationality-nationalism and nation-nationism," in *Language prob-
       lems of developing nations,* 39–51. New York: Wiley.
1970   *The politics of bilingual education.* Georgetown University Monograph
       Series on Language and Linguistics 23.
1971   "National languages and languages of wider communication in the
       developing nations," in *Language use and social change.* Edited by W.
       H. Whiteley, 27–56. London: Oxford University Press. (Also in *Lan-
       guage and socio-cultural change: selected essays,* by J. A. Fishman,
       191–223. Stanford: Stanford University Press.)
1972   "Bilingualism and bidialectal education: an attempt at a joint model for
       policy description," in *Language in socio-cultural change: selected essays,*
       by J. A. Fishman, 331–339. Stanford: Stanford University Press.
GUMPERZ, J. J.
1971   "Types of linguistic communities," in *Language in social groups:
       selected essays,* by J. J. Gumperz, 97–113. Stanford: Stanford Univer-
       sity Press. (Also published 1968 in *Readings in the sociology of lan-
       guage.* Edited by J. A. Fishman, 460–472. The Hague: Mouton.)
HEINE, B.
1970   *Status and use of African lingua francas.* Munich: Weltforum Verlag.
HOFFMAN, C.
1976   The languages of Nigeria by language families, in *An index of Nigerian
       languages.* Edited by K. Hansford et al., 169–190. Accra: Summer
       Institute of Linguistics.
HOUIS, M.
1971   *Antropologie linguistique de l'Afrique noire.* Paris: Presses Univer-
       sitaires de France.
HUNT, C. L.
1966   "Language choice in a multilingual society," in *Explorations in
       sociolinguistics.* Edited by S. Lieberson, 112–125. The Hague: Mouton.

HUNWICK, J. O., *editor*
1965   "Report on the seminar on the teaching of Arabic in Nigeria, held at the University of Ibadan 11–15 July, 1965." Ibadan and Kano, Ahmadu Bello University and University of Ibadan.

HUREL, R.
1970   "A note on theoretical models of plurilingualism with special reference to the West African situation." Paper presented at the 7th World Congress of Sociology.

KIRK-GREENE, A. H. M.
1967   The linguistic statistics of Northern Nigeria: a tentative presentation. *A.L.R.* 6:75–101.

KLOSS, H.
1966   "Types of multilingual communities: a discussion of ten variables," in *Explorations in sociolinguistics*. Edited by S. Lieberson, 7–17. The Hague: Mouton.
1968   "Notes concerning a language-nation typology," in *Language problems of developing nations*. Edited by J. A. Fishman, et al., 69–85. New York: Wiley.

MACKEY, W. R.
1970   A typology of bilingual education. *Foreign Language Annals* 3(4):596–608. (Also in *Advances in the sociology of language*, volume two. Edited by J. A. Fishman. The Hague: Mouton.)

MAFENI, B.
1971   "Nigerian pidgin," in *The English language in West Africa*. Edited by J. Spencer, 95–112. London: Longman.

NIGERIA, EDUCATIONAL RESEARCH COUNCIL
1972   *A philosophy for Nigerian education.* Report of the national curriculum conference September 8–12, 1969. Ibadan: Heinemann.

NIGERIAN FEDERAL MINISTRY OF EDUCATION LANGUAGE CENTRE
1972   *Preliminary report on the Language Centre, primary school questionnaire.* Lagos: Language Centre.

OKE, D. O.
1969   The vernacular as a medium of instruction in Nigerian primary schools. *Journal of the Nigerian English Studies Association* 3(1):97–100.
1972   Language choice in the Yoruba-Edo border area. *Odu,* new series, 7:49–67.

PENFIELD, W., L. ROBERTS
1959   "The learning of languages," chapter eleven of *Speech and brain mechanisms.* Princeton, N.J.: Princeton University Press.

PRATOR, C. H.
1967   The survey of language use and language teaching in Eastern Africa. *Linguistic Reporter* 9(8):1–28.

STANFORD, R.
1972   "Vernacular reading materials in primary schools: a report and some observations." Paper presented at the 10th West African Linguistics Congress, Accra, March 1972.

STEWART, W. A.
1962   "An outline of linguistic typology for describing multilingualism," in *Study of the role of second languages in Asia, Africa and Latin America.* Edited by F. A. Rice, 15–25. Washington, D.C.: Center for Applied Linguistics. (Second version 1968 as "A sociolinguistic typology for describing national multilingualism," in *Readings in the sociology of language.* Edited by J. A. Fishman, 531–545. The Hague: Mouton.)

TAIWO, C. O.
1972   *The mother tongue as a means of promoting equal access to education in Nigeria.* ED/WS/307, June 8, 1972. Paris: UNESCO.
UBAHAKWE, E.
1972   "Towards a national language policy in Nigerian education." Paper presented to the 5th conference of the Nigeria English Studies Association, Nsukka, July 1972.
1965   "Criteria for language policy decisions in Nigerian education." Unpublished M.A. thesis, University of California, Los Angeles.
UNITED KINGDOM COLONIAL OFFICE
1927   *The place of the vernacular in native education* (African no. 1110). Advisory Committee on Education. London: HMSO.
1943   *Memorandum on language in African school education.* (African no. 1170). Advisory Committee on Education. London: HMSO.
UNESCO
1972   *The role of linguistics and sociolinguistics in language education and policy.* UNESCO document ED/WS/286, 28th February 1972. Paris.
WESTERMANN, D. H.
1925   Place and function of the vernacular in African education. *International Review of Missions* 14:25–36.
WESTERMANN, D. H., M. A. BRYAN
1970   *Languages of West Africa. Handbook of African languages II* (with supplementary bibliography by D. W. Arnott). London: International African Institute.
WILLIAMSON, K.
1976   The Rivers Readers Project in Nigeria, in *Mother tongue education: the west African experience.* Edited by A. Bamgbose, 135–153. London and Paris: Hodder and UNESCO.

Social and Linguistic Structures of Burundi, a Typical "Unimodal" Country

A. VERDOODT

After having examined the problems presented by bilingualism in Alsace, Lorraine, the Grand Duchy of Luxemburg, and eastern Belgium in an earlier study (see Verdoodt 1968), we thought it quite relevant to continue our work by studying the same issue in another country. And after having accepted a position to teach sociology at the Official University of Bujumbura, we considered it only natural to select Burundi as our object study.

It is now generally accepted that education in both the academic and sociological senses is the most important factor of economic and social development. However, just as development depends on education, education depends on language. This is such an obvious fact that no one seems to pay any special attention to it. Nevertheless we know that every effort of education, be it during or after schooling, entails the use of language. The degree of fluency and understanding in this language is the key to the efficacy of education and therefore to the degree of development. Mathematics, history, or administrative science class material will not be learned if the professor or the student does not have sufficient knowledge of the language in which the subject is taught (see "A Study of Polylingual School Children": 10). This is what we shall try to study in the case of Burundi.

After sections concerning fundamental geographic and economic data and a short description of Burundi's historical and political evolution, we will go somewhat more deeply into an analysis of the linguistic laws and rules apparent in the administration, the education system, the

A preliminary version of this study has been published by the Centre de recherche et d'information socio-politiques (Brussels 1970) and the Centre international de recherche sur le bilinguisme (Quebec 1970). The elaboration upon our preliminary study has met with the approval of both groups.

courts of law and the army. We will conclude with a study of the principal cultural manifestations of these laws in the different languages spoken in Burundi.

We shall now focus on Burundi as one of the countries which have recently acquired their independence. Indeed, these countries do not all have the same ethnolinguistic problems.

In order to use here a distinction made by Fishman (1968) we should consider:

A. "Amodal" countries, i.e. those lacking any sufficient tradition at the national level and which will willingly adopt an international language for all purposes.

B. "Unimodal" countries, i.e. those which do have a great national tradition and which are torn between the desire to respect this particular authenticity on the one hand (namely by maintaining a native language as the national language) and to comply with the demands of modern times on the other (by recognizing an international language as the official language).

C. "Multimodal" countries, i.e. those in which several great traditions are discernible (namely through the retention of numerous indigenous languages) alongside an international language being used as a lingua franca.

Burundi, a central African republic, has 3,000,000 inhabitants, 95 percent of whom speak Kirundi, a fact which undoubtedly makes the country "unimodal." We must also remark that although countries of this sort are relatively numerous in Asia, they are quite rare in Africa. To our knowledge, there are only five besides Burundi: Botswana, Lesotho, Madagascar, Rwanda, and Somalia.

1.   GEOGRAPHIC AND ECONOMIC DATA

The Republic of Burundi is located between the latitudes of 2° 30′ and 4° 30′ South and between the longitudes of 29° and 31° East. It covers an area of 27,834 square kilometers and has approximately 3,000,000 inhabitants.

This country, bordered by Rwanda, Uganda, Tanzania, and the Congo, covers a region of broken high plateaus on the northeastern shore of Lake Tanganyika. The altitude, which in some areas soars above 2,000 meters . . . , decreases toward the northeast. . . . This altitude permits cultivation at different levels and an active way of life, based upon both cattle-raising and agriculture, which explains in part the high population density (seventy-nine inhabitants per square kilometer). The economic resources depend mostly upon the traditional form of cattle-raising. . . . But coffee and cotton are being widely cultivated on the mountain slopes and palms are being grown for their oil near Lake Tanganyika. Fish from the lake and banana trees are two other significant natural resources.

Bujumbura, which is located at the northeast end of the lake, is the capital and principal city of the country (approximately 70,000 inhabitants). The Hamitic (Tutsi) peoples, which are above the Bantu (Hutu) agricultural-ists, form an aristocracy of cattle raisers. There are still some descendants of paleonegritic pygmoid farmers: these are the Batwa.[1]

No one has sufficiently accounted for the many existing racial and social subdivisions, either in research on physical anthropology or in demographic studies. In 1956 the relative proportions were estimated to be 12.39, 86.48, and 1.13 percent for the Tutsi, the Hutu, and the Twa, respectively (D'Hertefelt et al. 1962:120).[2]

At the time of the arrival of the white man at the end of the nineteenth century, Kirundi was the only Bantu language spoken throughout the whole country. There were a few small Swahili-speaking communities along Lake Tanganyika, however. Nowadays in the urban centers there is a certain tendency to use Swahili as the language of commerce. As for Kirundi, it exhibits few social or regional differences. Some claim that they can hear a difference in the language when it is spoken by the Hutu and the Tutsi on one hand and by the Twa on the other. We are also under the impression that the language spoken in the Moso and Imbo regions has some idiosyncrasies, but there are no dialects in the strictest sense of the word (D'Hertefelt et al. 1962:121).

Kirundi is also spoken in Bugufi, which was once a part of Burundi but now belongs to Tanzania. The Barundi have few problems in being understood by people coming from Rwanda, Bushubi, and Buha (west-ern Tanzania) or by quite a few inhabitants of the eastern Congo (Bukavu) and of southern Uganda. This area represents a linguistic bloc of close to 8,000,000 people, of whom 6,000,000 live in Burundi and Rwanda, with close to 2,000,000 in Tanzania, and 300,000 near Bukavu.

The first problem of the Rundi language that we shall discuss is that of its spelling. Upon their arrival in Burundi, white priests introduced the Latin alphabet and the same sort of western orthography for both Kinyarwanda and Kirundi. In 1925, the missionaries in Rwanda insti-tuted a reform which was not applied to Burundi. In 1951, on the suggestion of a Belgian linguist (Meeussen), the provincial commissioner, having consulted the missionaries and priests in Burundi, accepted some changes which made Kirundi and Kinyarwanda more similar to each other, but still distinct languages.

In 1956, Father Rodegem, of the White Fathers of Africa, suggested another change which never received official approval. It was, however, supported by Coupez, another Belgian linguist. We should note that this

---

[1]　*Grand Larousse* on Urundi (Swahili spelling now abandoned).
[2]　See also the more recent articles, which are also more complex, by M. Ndayahoze: "Le tribalisme au Burundi," *Unité et Révolution* (November 23, 1968) 1, 2; "Les origines du tribalisme au Burundi," *Unité et Révolution* (December 24, 1968), 3.

new system met with much resistance. In 1963 Father Ntahokaja proposed a new series of changes to be made, especially in the area of accent marking.

It is to be noted that Protestant publications had for a long time adopted an orthography somewhat similar to that of Kinyarwanda. Today, however, there is evidence of a return to the old spelling of the first missionaries as it was reformed by the provincial commissioner of Burundi in 1951. All in all, it is this orthography which is the most widely used. It does have the inconvenience, however, of not indicating all of the fundamental features of the language.

Recently, the government of Burundi became more acutely aware of the difficulties caused by the lack of a standard orthography. Therefore the Burundi government requested an expert from UNESCO, who in turn brought in an Italian expert from the University of Padua, Professor A. Mioni, to study the situation. After two visits to Burundi, Professor Mioni turned in a report (unpublished) to which we will refer frequently below (see Section 4).

Although Burundi has relative linguistic unity, there do remain some problems: first of all, with the orthography; secondly, with a Swahili substratum; and finally with the necessary use of an international language — in this case, French — for contacts with the rest of the world.

2. POLITICAL AND HISTORICAL DATA

There is not much certainty in what we know of Burundi history. Legend tells us that the drum of the Burundi king (the drum was the symbol of monarchy) is the brother of the drum of the Rwanda kings in that both of them are said to have been cut from the same tree trunk, the stump of which lies on the border between the two countries at Le Petit Kumoso.

Between 1895 and 1899 the Kingdom of Burundi became a German protectorate. This protectorate was firmly established only after a series of developments precipitated by the military. Along with Rwanda and Tanganyika, it was part of German East Africa. Although the German governors practiced a policy of indirect government, supporting both the king and traditional chiefs, German influence was strong enough to make a mark on the cultural and political life of the country. On the one hand, the order introduced by the Germans finally had the effect of strengthening Burundi's internal unity under the leadership of a single *mwami* [king]. And on the other hand, innovations in education have left traces discernible even in the Rundi language itself.[3]

---

[3]   The following are a few examples: *ishule* (from *Schule*), *ihera* (from *Heller* = *centime*), *rurupapura* (from *Papier*), *intofanyi* (from *Kartoffeln*).

In the middle of the war of 1914–1918, Burundi was taken from the Germans by the Belgians. In 1922, however, Bugufi, an area in the northeastern part of the kingdom, was annexed by Tanganyika Territory. The League of Nations entrusted the administration of the Kingdom of Burundi (mandate regime) to Belgium on August 31, 1923, and the United Nations confirmed this protectorship in 1946.

Like the Germans, the Belgian authorities retained the monarchical government in Burundi. The Belgian administration was only indirectly concerned with the organization of the country. Thus a legislative ordinance of October 4, 1943, requires that there be an administration composed of the king, appointed according to custom and invested by the governor, and of chiefs (*chefs*) and assistant chiefs (*sous-chefs*) named by the *mwami* — some invested by the territorial governor, and others by the resident of the country. It should be noted that this country had a distinct juridical character and its own traditions, as opposed to what was the case with the colony of the Belgian Congo.

The United Nations proved to be more concerned with controlling the progressive evolution towards an autonomous or independent regime than the League of Nations ever was. A mission of the Trusteeship Council visited the country every three years so as to keep up-to-date on this evolution. In accordance with this, the Belgian government in 1952 recognized the existence of the *Conseil supérieur* of the country and of the *Conseil de chefferie*, and then created the *Conseil de sous-chefferie* and the *Conseil des territoires* (only the latter was a European creation). In 1956 the first step toward a sounding-out of public opinion was made when an election was proposed. The adult males were to elect the *sous-chefferies* by secret ballot instead of leaving their composition to the desires of the *sous-chef*. In this way it was hoped that by starting at the bottom, the *conseil* would some day attain a composition more truly representative of the population.

In 1959 the *Parti de l'Union et du Progrès National du Burundi* (UPRONA) was founded; its tendencies were nationalistic and monarchistic. On November 10, 1959, the Belgian government took a position before the legislature that an autonomous government should be expected to develop soon in Burundi. From a practical point of view, the most important innovation was to be the transformation of larger *sous-chefferies* in towns or villages under the direction of *bourgmestres* [mayors] and town councils. These town councils would then elect, in great measure, the members of the national *conseil* [council], who, having legislative power, would control local government set up by the *mwami*.

From August 23 to August 31, 1960, a colloquium was held in Brussels concerning the problems and the future of Burundi. The representatives of the protectoral administration, and the members of the provisional commission entrusted with the handling of affairs during the transitional period leading to the establishment of a new regime, as well as delegates from the numerous political parties, met together there. And at the opening meeting, the *mwami* Mwambusta was also present. The preparation of the elections was the subject of primary concern at the time of this meeting. The Rundi delegates made a most important decision when they modified the electoral law to include a "passus" which would prevent the family and the relatives by marriage of the *mwami* — up to those twice-removed — from receiving an electoral mandate.

On November 27, 1960, Prince Louis Rwagasore, standard-bearer of the UPRONA nationalist party, was restricted to his residence because of his political activities. The prince, a son of the *mwami* Mwambusta, was given this order by the resident general.

On April 12, 1961, the Commission of Trusteeship of the United Nations approved by a vote of eighty-three to one (Belgium), with three abstentions (France, Spain, and Portugal), a plan to solve the country's problems. The plan was to provide for direct legislative elections controlled by the United Nations. These general elections, held on September 18, 1961, resulted in a landslide victory for the UPRONA party. Prince Louis Rwagasore, who was no longer under residential surveillance after December 12, 1960, was the biggest winner of these elections, and became prime minister of the government of Burundi. He was later assassinated by a Greek subject, Jean Karageorgis, on October 13, 1961.

A commission of inquiry from the United Nations arrived in Bujumbura on October 29th in order to gather information on the circumstances of Rwagasore's death. The commission was to conclude that the crime was the result of political, family, and personal conflicts (see also Nuwinkware 1962).

Finally, on July 1, 1962, Belgium granted Burundi its independence and the country immediately became a member of the United Nations (D'Hertefelt et al. 1962:238–246).

On November 28, 1966, Colonel Michel Micomvero proclaimed the land a republic. The new regime, although it maintained good relations with the many technical assistants from France and Belgium, as well as with all of the countries belonging to the European Economic Community, began to evidence increased sympathy towards those socialist countries whose leaders could speak French quite fluently. We have noted this cultural phenomenon in reading *Unité et Révolution*, the voice of the party in power (UPRONA), which reports on visits by several groups: a mission of Guinean youths, a delegation of Guinean women (*Unité et Révolution* 4), a North Vietnamese mission (*Unité et Révolution* 17), and finally a mission from Congo-Brazzaville (*Unité et Révolution* 17). All of these missions and delegations visited Burundi and addressed the populace there. A Tanzanian delegation was unable to organize a meeting for the hill-dwelling population because no one in the group spoke either French or Kirundi. The same sort of socialist tendencies that *Unité et Révolution* has discussed regarding foreign affairs are also found in the new domestic policy.

From a cultural point of view we should also note the abolition of the *minerval* [fee paid for education], which was a reinforcement of power by the Ministry of National Education with regard to the autonomy of private schools, and the establishment of the *gong unique* [single gong]. It is because of the latter that work is permitted only from 7 a.m. to 2 p.m., Monday through Friday, in Burundi. The aim of this measure is to insure that members of the UPRONA party will have enough time to hold meetings and devote each Saturday morning to collective work (*Unité et Révolution* 1, 2, 19).[4]

3. JURIDICAL AND ADMINISTRATIVE DATA

The principal text dealing with language usage in Burundi is the Constitution of 1962. The twenty-first article stipulates: "The official languages of Burundi are Kirundi and French." Although this constitution was suspended on July 8, 1966, the stipulation still seems to be in effect. However, the orders in council published in the *Bulletin Officiel du Burundi* (B.O.B.), which were automatically published in both languages in 1962–1963, are now appearing less and less frequently in Kirundi, except for texts concerning agriculture, the issuance of postage stamps, and reports on cotton markets — probably because these texts follow a regular formula. We must note here the lack of a French–Kirundi juridical lexicon, the preparation of which would certainly help the translation service.

Thus the civil servants under statute (approximately 9,000) as well as those under contract (approximately 4,000) need not take any test in the Kirundi language in order to be appointed to their positions. Even future judges need not show proof of their knowledge of this language. The great majority of documents in the ministries are written exclusively in French. There are a few documents in Kirundi, however, especially those dealing with relations among towns or villages, but even in this area the general services use French for the most part to handle these affairs. All

---

[4]   There are some exceptions made for the fields of aeronautics, teaching, health services, etc., and more recently the *gong unique* was done away with, but collective work was maintained on Saturdays. More complete information may be found in: H. P. Cart, "Conception des rapports politiques au Burundi," a paper for the first conference of the University (of East Africa), Social Science Council, held at Makerere College, Kampala, January 3, 1966. Number 378, mimeographed. (It has been published in *Etudes congolaises*, C.R.I.S.P., Brussels, 9(2), 1966.) Also C. Karolero, *Etude de quelques problèmes de commandement dans l'armée du Burundi*, thesis presented for the title of *licencié* in social and military science, Brussels, *Ecole Royale Militaire*, 1967.

the bookkeeping of the towns is done exclusively in French. On the other hand, as for the meetings of the *conseils communaux* [communal councils] (reformed as *assemblées communales consultatives* [advisory communal assemblies] on September 30, 1965), we might note Article 28 of Law Decree 001/767 of September 1, 1965, concerning the organization of town government (B.O.B. 10/65): "The meetings of the communal councils are to be conducted in Kirundi. And the minutes are to be written in Kirundi while the meeting is in session. At the end of the meeting, the minutes are to be approved as read by the councilmen." Our observations show that the town civil servants use Kirundi almost exclusively when dealing with their constituents.

As for the schooling system, let us first refer to the program of the official (state) primary schools. It dates back to October, 1961, but is still in use today. In it we might note a section regarding the French language (there is no such chapter concerning Kirundi):

A noticeable improvement as to the quality of the teachers should provide for a more extensive study of the French language as early as the first year of studies . . . This does not mean . . . doing away with Kirundi. In the beginning Kirundi will play an important role as a link between knowledge about the surrounding world and learning of French. Quite often, the teacher will have to take recourse to the native language to explain to the children what their limited French vocabulary would otherwise prevent them from understanding.

Nevertheless we do feel that the primary skills of reading, spelling, and writing can be taught in French. At the secondary level, French is of prime importance, but a substantial program in Kirundi has been organized so that the children will not be without knowledge of their native language.

One can see that this program implies that the teachers must be very competent in French, and it also permits some freedom as far as the teaching of Kirundi is concerned. In principle, Kirundi is taught as a separate subject of study only from secondary schooling on. There are many exceptions to this last rule, however, for in most of the schools children learn to read in their native language. The same rule applies to the parochial Roman Catholic schools, and these schools are by far the most numerous. In these institutions there is nothing more than an oral French class given the first year and written French is not taught before the second year. All courses are conducted in Kirundi until the third year. At that point, French becomes the language of instruction, although in some schools this change to French is put off until the fourth or even the fifth year, even though such a wait is contrary to the directives set forth during official school inspection.

In the official schools, there are 180 classes in which spoken French is taught as early as the first year and where classes on written French are given in the second year. Moreover, we found some schools in which the official program is being applied as strictly as possible and where everything, even writing, is taught in French from the first year onward. Instruction in Kirundi does not begin until the third year, with classes meeting three times a week. The following schools are involved in the program:

1. At Bujumbura: the section preparatory to the *Athénée* [public secondary school]; the *École d'Application* [prep school] of the *École Normale Primaire de l'État*; and the official primary schools of Buyenzi, of the Asian district, and of the second and fourth districts;

2. The official primary schools of Gitega, Rumonge, Moramvia, Bubanza, Mugera, Mwaro, Rutegama, Muhinga, Kasorwe, Mwakiro, Muramba, Ruigi, Kayongozi, Kigamba, Rubanga, Ngozi, and Songa;

3. Since more often than not the teachers are Burundi nationals, it is quite possible for them to refer to the native language whenever necessary. But when these teachers are not Burundi natives, as at the *École d'Application* [prep school] Stella Matutina in Bujumbura, this recourse is impossible. Thus the children are totally "immersed" in French and are only taught Kirundi after the third year. It is important to note that the students attending this school are the children of high-ranking officials of the capital. These children are thus initiated directly into French without any preliminary training in their native language.

We must also note that in a few private schools, namely those belonging to the Mohammedan Association of Burundi, classes are conducted in Swahili before French is used.

What is the result of having so many different systems? It is quite difficult to say without making an overall study. R. Bastin, Chief Inspector of Secondary Education, has made a study which might answer the question. And C. Michel, Inspector for Primary Education, has commented as follows in a long memorandum (unpublished) concerning "some causes of failure in the first year": ". . . the most important thing is the language spoken at home. And here, as far as the French language is concerned, the children are even worse off, since the family's not speaking French is hardly a positive factor." More than anything else he regrets "the deplorable tradition of assigning . . . first year classes . . . to non-qualified personnel, who do not have sufficient knowledge of the French language."

French is used more frequently than is Kirundi in the intermediate grades in technical and normal schools;[5] and it is the only language used in the advanced grades.

In the secondary schools English is also taught. Greek and Latin are only taught in the last year of the humanities program, except in some

---

[5]   At the *Ecole Normale* in the lower grades, all classes are in French except for the two hours weekly of Kirundi.

small seminaries where these two languages are taught earlier.[6] It is to be noted here that in Bujumbura there are several schools, the Official University — still uncompleted — and in *École Normale Supérieure d'État*, as well as an *École supérieure d'Administration*. Only in the latter two institutions is there a program of Kirundi.

We must note here the Royal Decree 01/96 of September 16, 1962, resulting in the creation of the *Académie de la langue et de la littérature rundi* [Academy of Rundi Language and Literature].

> We, Mwambutsa IV, King of the Barundi,
> To all present and yet to come, greetings.
> Considered the constitution of Burundi;
> Considered the law of July 29, 1962, on the application in Burundi of lawful and legislative acts decreed by the tutelary authority;
> Considered the decree of December 26, 1888, concerning the institutions applicable in Burundi by virtue of ordinance number 33 of December 15, 1927;
> We have decided and we decide:
> ARTICLE 1. A public institution to be known by the name of: *Académie de la langue et de la littérature rundi* has been created, endowed with civil status. Its office is located in Bujumbura.
> ARTICLE 2. The task of this institution is to undertake the study of Rundi literature and language and to promote literary activities. It will also draft both a dictionary and a grammar.
> It will promote the study of Rundi language and literature in the schools. It will supervise the correct usage of Kirundi for the broadcast media and for official publications.
> The *Académie* can oversee the editing and publication of literary and linguistic pieces, organize literary contests, and award prizes to the winners of these contests.
> ARTICLE 3. The *Académie* is composed of twenty members; it can elect honorary members.
> ARTICLE 4. The first twelve members of the *Académie* are called the effective members. Eight other positions . . . are to be filled by joint selection, by the members . . .
> ARTICLE 8. . . . . The steering committee will be changed every three years . . .
> ARTICLE 11. The following acts are subject to the administrative control of the government, exercised by the Minister of National Education by means of a consenting decree . . .
> the establishment of the *Académie's* own internal rules and regulations and the modifications that are later undergone by these rules and regulations.
> organizations of contents . . .
> other acts . . . that the Minister of National Education will have . . . previously approved . . .
> ARTICLE 13. Each year the president of the *Académie* addresses the following items to the President of Parliament and to the Minister of National Education:

[6]   Father J. B. Ntahokaja, president of *Académie rundi*, said in the *Burundi chrétien* 1, No. 7 (1962), that he hoped that: "In the highest level of the humanities it might be useful to consider teaching a second African language to insure good relations with Burundi's neighboring countries. Swahili seems to be the most reasonable language for this purpose." This statement had no repercussions whatsoever. Mioni in his report to UNESCO suggests the same thing for trade and professional schools.

a report on the activities of the *Académie* during the past year;
the figures for past expenditures;
the program planned for the coming year.
Given at Bujumbura, October 16, 1962.
By the King.
Mwambusta IV.
The Minister of Justice,
Nuwinkware, P. Claver.

In Section 4 we will see some rare accomplishments of the Academy.
In the administration of justice, Kirundi is spoken more often than not in the *tribunaux de résidence* (of which there are sixty-one) and in the *tribunaux de province* (of which there are ten, eight being effectively *de province* and two having the competence of a tribunal *de province* at Mwaro and at Rutana). But, even so, the minutes are always taken down in French. And the *tribunaux de première instance* [Courts of First Authority] (of which there are four) as well as in the *Cour d'appel* [Court of Appeals] and the *Cour de cassation* [Court of Final Appeal] (which can act as *Cour Suprême* [Supreme Court]) almost all activities are carried out in French: statements by lawyers, minutes, etc. It is to be noted that the *Code des lois et règlements du Burundi* [Code of the laws and rules pertaining to Burundi], when published, will be written entirely in French. Of course there has existed, since 1963, a *Service de codification* in which officials have been attempting to classify all sorts of national customs, but they have yet to publish their first work. There is even a translation service available to the Barundi, but hardly anyone ever sends it any texts to be translated. Besides, the lack of a glossary of juridical and administrative terms greatly hampers the work of such a service.

In the army, all written documents appear in French: orders, handbooks, correspondence, etc. Officer training is conducted first in Kirundi alone, then in both French and Kirundi, and finally only in French. Soldiers' training is conducted for the most part in Kirundi, unless it is handled by Belgian instructors. But orders are always stated in French. Those that have been issued from headquarters are always in French when they are received by the officers, but are often translated into Kirundi for communication to the troops.

4. SOCIOCULTURAL DATA

It is important to recall here that the German presence in the Burundi area from 1899 to 1916 helped to introduce some aspects of the German language. But what is even more significant is that it brought in many outside elements originating from what is today known as Tanzania. These newcomers generally spoke Kiswahili, which thus became, with the Germans' approval, the lingua franca of Burundi and of all East Africa.

Moreover, the Arab and Indian merchants dealing with the Barundi were much more willing to speak this lingua franca than any other language. This is why the first schools founded by the Germans conducted courses in Kiswahili.

For a long time the subsequent Belgian presence did nothing to change this state of affairs. This was mainly because the merchants stayed where they were established, in the urban centers, where the Burundi aristocracy did not want to live. Besides, law and order were maintained by troops from the Congo who often spoke Kiswahili.[7] To this day there are still many of these Congolese in the Burundi *gendarmerie* and police department who would rather use Kiswahili than Kirundi. And in large urban centers such as Bujumbura, Gitega, Ngozi etc. one often hears Kiswahili. Because of the ethnic and cultural factors that made Bujumbura, today the capital of Burundi, somewhat of an appendage to the Belgian Congo (cf. Baeck 1957), it was at one time debated whether that city should belong to the Congo instead of to Burundi.

The population today is quite different from what it was like ten years ago. Of course "many intellectuals babble in a patois composed of both Kiswahili and French, and the rarely ever speak good Kirundi at home" (Boyayo 1966:6). But they also do not speak Swahili very often.

At the present time, primary and secondary schools include courses in Kirundi within their regular curricula, but one must note that only one-third of the Barundi children are admitted to these schools. The other children generally receive their schooling from catechism classes, which are usually conducted in Kirundi. It should be noted, nevertheless, that with such a meager cultural background these less-educated Barundi prefer to read texts written only in Kirundi (see below), whereas the intellectuals would rather read French texts.

We have also noted the following in Mioni's report (unpublished) to UNESCO:[8]

Often the Barundi, even those who have been to school, read at a faster rate in French than in Kirundi. This, of course, does not mean that their knowledge of Kirundi is not as complete as their knowledge of French. On the contrary, the cause for such a phenomenon is quite different. One must read Kirundi slowly because the orthography neglects certain important aspects of the structure of the language — such as the tones and quality of vowels — and it is not always immediately apparent what is the meaning of a particular word. Thus, one must

---

[7]   The presence of Congolese soldiers can be explained by the following: Belgian political policy entailed sending soldiers to areas unknown to them. We might note that their lingua franca was Lingala.

[8]   Let us hope that the *Académie rundi* finds the specialists and funds necessary to inform themselves about the successful efforts of linguistic standardization carried out in Soviet Asia, Indonesia, Ireland, Israel, Japan, and Turkey. See especially: J. Fishman, *Sociolinguistics* (Rowley, Mass.: Newbury House, 1970); and J. Fishman, C. Ferguson, and J. Das Gupta (editors), *Language problems of the developing nations* (New York: Wiley, 1968).

read the whole sentence and then decide on the meaning of the word by placing it in context (page 9).

This problem is complicated even more when we also consider the numerous alternative orthographic conventions already mentioned above. We shall gladly accept the conclusions reached by Mioni:

To establish a standard orthography, it would be very desirable for the government of Burundi (or, in its name, the Department of National Education and Culture) to organize conferences among scholars and to set up an ad hoc committee. When the new orthography is established, the government would decide that as of a certain date all printed matter would have to conform to the new orthography. At the very least, if a work did not satisfy these regulations, it would not receive government subsidies.

This solution would entail a plan . . . of training all school teachers and typographers. . . . A permanent reviewing committee would have to proofread everything to be published, especially school textbooks. The *Académie nationale de la langue et de la littérature rundi* could be accorded this job. . . . (page 39).

Another problem here is that of the reform of the Kirundi language to fit modern usage. Once again we can cite Mioni:

The problem of reforming the national language is very acute in all countries which have recently acquired their independence, just as it was a problem during the last years of the nineteenth century in the Balkan and Baltic countries. . . . Some authors and scholars who had faith in the resources of these languages made great efforts to create new words to describe modern technical and scientific concepts. Today one can speak of atomic physics or astronautics in Czech, in Romanian, or in Bulgarian (page 45).

In the case of Burundi, it is necessary to find intellectuals who have faith in the potential of their language and who will try to reform it gradually. The density and output of modern means of communication as well as the possibility of there being some administrative planning in this area would make the task much easier to accomplish in Burundi than it was in the Eastern European countries. . . . In our opinion, the *Académie Nationale de la langue et de la littérature rundi* should be entrusted with this work (page 62).

We must emphasize here that the *Académie rundi* has only modest financial means at its disposal. It has, to this day, published only a few mimeographed pamphlets (one grammar and three collections of literature). As regards the creation of the nation's culture, we should comment here upon all the oral literature particular to Burundi. It comprises nine parts, each having different value: stories, tales, and legends which are closely linked to history; fables and proverbs which cover a wide range of moral and philosophical subjects; epic poetry which is martial, pastoral, or hunt-oriented; eclogues, ballads, and songs.

Today, this mass of literature is beginning to be written down.[9] Poetic

[9] For example: F. Rodegem, *Patrimoine culturel rundi* (fourteen mimeographed volumes).

creativity is still very much alive, with independence and the founding of the republic being new sources of inspiration.

We must note the relative scarcity of any creativity of cultural phenomena in French. Thus in the work of J. Jadot, *Les écrivains d'expression française au Congo Belge et au Rwandi-Urundi* (1958), we have found no fictional works composed initially in French by a Murundi. As for scientific literature, we have found in Clement's *Essai de bibliographie du Rwanda-Urundi* (1959) some titles which we shall mention below, in alphabetical order, and to which we shall add some more recent publications:

Barakana, G. L'unification des langues du Rwanda-Urundi, *Civilisations* 1:67–79, 1952.

Boyayo, A. L'importance de la poésie guerrière dans la reconstruction de l'histoire nationale, *Revue nationale de l'éducation au Burundi* 3(5):4–8, 1966.

Burijo, J. Note sur l'orthographe des principaux noms géographiques du Burundi, *Kongo-Overzee* 3–4:224–225, 1957.

Biroli, J. Les civilisations africaines en face du monde occidental, *Servir* 3:130–134, 1954.

Barakana, G. Contactname tussen Zwarten en Blanken, *Nieuw Afrika* 1:5–11, 1949.

Muhirwa, A. Opinions d'un Murundi sur les poisons et l'anthropophagie, *Servir* 4:198–200, 1947, 5:240–248.

Gelders, V. and J. Biroli. Native Political Organization in the Rwanda-Urundi, *Civilisations* 1:125–136, 1954.

Makarakiza, A. *La dialectique des Barundi*. Académie Royale des Sciences coloniales, Brussels, XIX, 1959.

Ntuyahaga, M. Au Burundi. Le départ et la rentrée des vaches, *Grands Lacs* 8:23–32, 1946–1947; translated by J. Nicholson under the title "The Departure and Return of the Cattle in Burundi" and published in *A Selection of African Prose*. Edited by W. Whitely, 141–164. Oxford University Press, 1950.

Ntahokaja, J. B. La musique des Barundi, *Grands Lacs* 64:45–49, 1948–1949.

Ntahokaja, J. B. Proverbes et sentences, *Grands Lacs* 15:13–19, 1948–1949.

We must also add, *Sur les traces de mon père. Jeunesse du Burundi à la découverte des valeurs*, by Michel Kayoya, published in 1968 by the Presses Lavigerie. This book is a unique testimonial of a Murundi who describes, in French, his psychological hardships when confronted with Western culture.

As for publications in Kirundi, they are almost always only religious or scholarly works. They are often translations or adaptations of books in French concerning the same subjects (catechisms, missals, hymnals, books on hygiene, and quite recently, the entire Bible). French school-books are often reworked and reedited as well as translated. However, there are a few books that were initially conceived and written entirely in Kirundi by Barundis, namely the grammars written by Fathers Emile Ngendagende, François Xavier Muteragiranwa, Gabriel Ngeza, and Jean-Baptiste Ntahokaja. We must also note the titles of some short novels such as:

Bandyatuyaga, Terensiyo. *Ishano ritariwe ntirirutswa* [Poison not taken], the story of a happily married couple.

Mpozezi, Johani. *Umugumyabanga* [The faithful wife], 1960, in which a girl who led a clean life during her student days in Europe comes back to the home country and has a good marriage.

There are also some books of a more poetic nature, such as the following:

Horumpende, Father A. *Ndangamir' Indanga* [I lift my eyes to the heights].

Ndigiriye, Father Emile. *Iragi ry iryakera vy-i Burundi ku biti binyakirundi* [What history teaches us about the Barundi].

Makuta, Father L. *Adarangabwami* [Royal way].

Rurayinga, Monseigneur L. *Ukuri gutsinda ikinyoma* [Truth triumphs over wrongdoing].

Mpozenzi, Yohani. *Uwange buva i Muhana. Umugani wa Yohani Rubinia.* [Intelligence comes from contact with others], moral tract against alcoholism, 1960.

Cercle Saint Paul (Burasira, 1960). *Umurya W'I Burundi* [The harp in Burundi], folks and modern songs.

There are also some brochures, including the following:

Bigangara, J. B. *Umwepiskopi wa mbere w'Umurundi amaza imyaka 25 ahawe Ubusaserdoti,* Presses Lavigerie, 1964–1966, 62 pages. (Also published in French under the title: *Le premier évêque Murundi à l'occasion de son jubilée sacerdotal,* 1964–1966, [The first Murundi Bishop on the occasion of his Sacerdotal Jubilee].

Nkura mu mubindi ndagukure mu bantu [You take me from the beer mug and I cast you out from the people], concerning alcoholism (anony-mous).

All of these books are of Catholic inspiration and are published by the Presses Lavigerie at Bujumbura. The books published by the *Centre évangelique du Kitaga* are also translations, with the exception of:

Mbindigiri, Thomas. *Dutanguranumucyo* [Help for new Christians].

Let us mention here the work, financed by UNESCO, by Father J. B. Ntahokaja, president of the *Académie Rundi: Ubuhinga kama* [Tradi-tional art], which contains the Rundi drawings that met with such great success at the African Festival at Dakar in 1965.

Cultural diffusion is promoted by churches (both Roman Catholic and Protestant), libraries, and cultural centers.

We found three bookstores in Bujumbura, one in Gitega, and one in Ngozi, all selling mostly French books. Most of the books at the library of the Official University at Bujumbura and at the cultural centers are also in French, though these institutions may be sponsored by the Belgian, United States, French, or Zaïre embassies.

There is also a public library in Bujumbura, but not many people use it as it is not kept up-to-date. We might mention as well that there is a new Catholic center for documentaries at Gitega, a Protestant center, and the especially important library of the *Centre du coopération au developpement* (CCD). This CCD library was created following a Belgian-Rundi convention, signed in accordance with a bilateral agreement between the two countries. The goal was to improve the training of postmasters and bookkeepers. After this, a second program was developed at the request of Kabugubugu Amédée (Minister of National Education in 1964) to improve the quality of the inspectors, school principals, and teachers. And then even a third program aimed at instilling enthusiasm in workers in the social sector, as well as those who coordinate development, was set up. This last program also handled the small farmers and agriculturalists.

As there are no daily or weekly publications written in Kirundi, it is quite easy to understand why periodicals imported from Belgium or France (or distributed by their embassies) are so popular. Although China no longer has a diplomatic representative in Burundi, Chinese magazines translated into French — as well as other publications — continue to arrive by mail.

We might also note that there are a few newspapers coming from Congo Kinshasa, Rwanda, and Uganda.

There are, however, some magazines published in Burundi, the list of which follows:

Amajambere y'Uhurundi, in Kirundi, published twice weekly by the UPRONA party.

Ben'Urugo, in Kirundi, for the Catholic family movement.

Bulletin de la Banque Nationale, monthly.

Mimeographed diocesan bulletins:

Entre Nous, Gitega diocese (since 1937).

Petit Echo de Ngozi, Ngozi diocese (since 1956).

Ondes du Lac, Bujumbura diocese (since 1960).

La Croix du Sud, Bururi diocese (since 1962).

Bulletin économique et financier, published monthly by the Department of Economic Affairs.

Bulletin mensuel d'information diplomatique, Board of Political Affairs and Information of the Department of Foreign Commerce.

Bulletin Officiel du Burundi, Government Printing Office.

Bulletin de statistique, Rundi Institute of Statistics.

Burakeye [Dawn], in Kirundi, Alliance of Protestant Missions.

Burundi agricole, Department of Agriculture and Farming.
Contacts, mimeographed bulletin from the Gitega Athénée.
Intumwa [Apostle], in Kirundi, Gitega.
Ishirahamwa [Hand in Hand], in Kirundi: J.O.C., Bujumbura.
Mariya Mawa [Mary, our Mother], in Kirundi, magazine of the Légion de Marie [Legion of Mary].
Ntaheba, in Kirundi, for the Chiro [youth movement].
Jeunesse africaine, for the leaders of the Xaveri movement, Bujumbura.
Kosho [Tomorrow], in French: Athénée of Bujumbura.
Kirwi, Collège du Saint-Espirit, Bujumbura; mimeographed.
Ndongozi [The guide], in Kirundi, bimonthly.
La voix de l'U.G.E.R. (Union générale des étudiants de Rumuri), in French; mimeographed.
Revue nationale d'éducation du Burundi, twice yearly, Department of National Education.
Unité et révolution, fortnightly, publication of the UPRONA party.
Théologie et pastorale, three times a year, published by the Conference of Bishops of Rwanda and Burundi.
Que vous en semble?, thrice yearly, published by the Cercle Saint Paul du Grand Séminaire du Bujumbura.
Revue de l'Université Officielle de Rumuri (Bujumbura), thrice yearly.

The most important publication is doubtless *Ngongozi*, which has a circulation of approximately 20,000. It is of Roman Catholic inspiration and appears entirely in Kirundi. It is to be noticed that apart from the publications patronized by the churches, there are only official periodicals, exclusively in French, with the recent exception of *Amajambere* (mentioned above).

The national radio broadcast of the Republic of Burundi, "La Voix de la Révolution," is presented daily in Kirundi, French, and Swahili.

There are five newscasts daily. The time period allotted to Kirundi, French, and Swahili is the same in theory. But in fact, the Swahili allotment is a bit shorter. In addition to the five newscasts in French, there are replays twice daily of the international news of the R.T.B. (*Radio-télévision belge*).

The following are the weekly programs usually broadcast in Kirundi (all are about thirty minutes long): educational, medical, civic, agricultural, and Protestant programs, as well as ones of the Union of Burundi Women, the Union of Burundi Laborers "*République Oyé*," and the Inter-African Co-operative. Short plays are also presented weekly. In contrast, the following other programs are broadcast in French instead: programs for teachers and young people, serials, the "*Match des Incollables*," the "Radio-club," the "*Heure du mystère*" [Mystery hour], the United Nations program, "*Chasse à la solitude*" [Away from solitude], the "Rendez-vous litteraire" [Rendezvous with literature], "*En vedette à*

Paris," the drama program, "*Actualité du monde*," "*Chansons sans frontière*," and "*Quelques anecdotes*." A few programs are broadcast sometimes in French, sometimes in Kirundi: a program on economics, the Armed Forces magazine, the "*Voix de la Révolution*" inquiry, the Roman Catholic program and the "*Voix de la J.R.R. (Jeunesse révolutionnaire Rwagasore*)."

There is also a "*courrier*" [mail-in service] for listeners in Kirundi, French, and Swahili. And at least one program, "*Sports et Rythmes*," is trilingual.

All in all, there is more French than Kirundi and more Kirundi than Swahili.

The "*Voix de la révolution*" is about to undertake a large-scale poll throughout the country to find out what the people would like to hear over the radio. The results will undoubtedly reveal the wishes of the population from both the cultural and linguistic points of view.

There is also a Protestant broadcasting station at Bujumbura. Its programs consist mainly of music, but they also might include conferences on religion in Kirundi, French, English, and Kiswahili.

There are no phonograph records to speak of in Burundi, but thousands of recordings played over the radio are greatly enjoyed, especially by adults. The choice of younger listeners (under twenty-five) tends to be French, English, Congolese, and South American rhythm records.

There are no movie theaters except in Bujumbura and Gitega. However, films loaned by the various embassies are shown in school auditoriums from time to time; they are usually in French.

Plays are given only in schools. As well as the popular comedies of Molière, scenes from everyday life are presented by country thespians.

Currently there is a tendency to stress the use of Kirundi alone in the churches. This has been the case among Protestants for some time, however. And today, the liturgy is in French in few churches besides the Cathedral of Bujumbura; elsewhere, services are conducted in Kirundi. Of course, Latin is still used in some circumstances, but Kiswahili seems to be reserved for churches located in a single parish in Bujumbura, inhabited by Congolese immigrants.

As far as private correspondence is concerned, the language most often used is Kirundi, even among the intellectuals. Some students prefer to use French, however, when writing to close friends.

Administrative correspondence is almost exclusively written in French. Businessmen — especially Arabs and Hindus — speak Swahili. In the factories and private offices (located predominantly in Bujumbura), orders are almost always given in Swahili and French.

The language spoken by Barundi intellectuals is more often than not a mixture of sentences in both French and Kirundi, depending on how easy it is to express oneself on a given subject in either language.

As we have already stated, many people understand Kiswahili in the larger towns. Thus many foreigners who live in these areas learn Kirundi with more difficulty than they do Kiswahili. In the central parts of the country, however, Kirundi is spoken more often.[10] Posters and advertisements are often in Kirundi, except for the official ones in French (street signs, direction markers, etc.). We must note as well that there are also some signs in Kiswahili and even in English (in the Asian quarter).

Speeches addressed to the public are usually given in Kirundi; French is used for conferences of intellectuals or foreigners. In Parliament, the tendency is to speak in Kirundi but to write reports in French. In the *assemblées communales consultatives* [town meetings] all business is carried out in Kirundi.

In conclusion, we should point out that those Barundi who attended schools having a majority of European students fared quite well. In the past, the linguistic situation in Burundi was amenable to this sort of training in French. Students used to be conditioned for it. But this is no longer the case. There are very few French-speaking students currently in Burundi schools. And the consequences are being felt already. Barundi students hardly ever use French outside the classroom; it is easy to understand that the level of competence in the language has decreased significantly. Students are no longer conditioned to learn French as their language of culture and, what is more serious, some no longer feel the need to speak the language correctly as an instrument of communication. A study is being conducted to determine the influence of the Rundi substratum, the national and native language, upon the French superstratum, the official national language. This study is based on an analysis of errors found in papers from the 1966 national examination for admission to secondary schools. The conclusions reached in this study might make possible the elaboration of a special method of teaching correct French in Burundi. And this leads us to question the quality of teaching there. It is essential that at the same time that the schools produce an elite class of administrators, doctors, schoolteachers, etc., they do not draw the great majority of students away from agriculture and farming. And the results of the national examination study will not allow us to jump to the conclusion that the elite, who often obtain teaching positions in higher education, have received really adequate training. Thus we must agree with comments that are still valid today even though made in the 1960s by members of the Fulreac mission (*Fonds de l'Université de Liège de recherche et d'aide au Congo*): ". . . the primary schools fail to fulfill their mission in two ways. They train neither farmers nor elite, and thus educate no one who is really capable of leading the nation" (Bastin 1966).

---

[10]   We estimate that about 50,000 people do not have Kirundi as their mother tongue, but about 500,000 would have some knowledge of Swahili.

Let us conclude by setting up a language chart (see Table 1). The order of symbols (F = French; K = Kirundi; S = Swahili; E = English; LG = Latin-Greek) represents, in Table 1, the frequency of usage of the particular language.

Table 1.   Frequency of language use in Burundi

Medium	Production	Use
Oral literature — fiction	K	K
Written literature — fiction	(K)	FK
Scientific literature	F	FE
Imported periodicals	FS	FS
Domestic periodicals	FK	KF
Radio	FKSE	?
Phonograph records	–	FES
Films	–	F
Churches	K (L)	K (L)
Private correspondence	K (F)	K (F)
Administrative correspondence	F (K)	F (K)
Working language in private enterprise (situated almost exclusively in Bujumbura)	SFK	SFK
Advertisements	KFS	KFS
Official notices	FK	FK
Speeches in Parliament	KF	KF
Speeches in the *assemblées communales* [town meetings]	K	K
Higher education	F (E)	F (E)
Secondary education	FEK (LG)	FEK (LG)
Primary education	FK	FK
Conversation among Barundi	K	K

5. CONCLUSIONS

We have attempted to limit ourselves to a positive study of the facts. Thus we stated in our communication at the Sixth World Meeting of Sociology (see Verdoodt 1966) that, in effect, each state will conceive and organize systems for its citizens to obtain access to the culture of the community in terms of a particular ethos. It is up to the representatives of normative disciplines and, ultimately, up to the politicians, to take advantage of our findings. Our data should enable them to pass fair judgments and give needed directives. However, we must not be diverted from our position of total objectivity by noting the consequences of different possible political moves. In our reasoning here, we might follow the lead of Le Page in *The national language question* (1966:82).

Because of the fact that Burundi has a long tradition of linguistic unity on the national level (which is rare in Africa as well as in the world at large), it might be thought that Kirundi could be selected for all types of usage for reasons of unification and authenticity. If this were the case, the foreign language, French, would still be taught but its domain of usage would become more and more restricted. Such a solution would preserve cultural traditions, and primary education would be facilitated. Children would not be cut off from their parents any more than would one social stratum be cut off from another. However, higher education would meet with greater difficulties. Enormous sums of money would have to be set aside for the training of teachers and for translation work. The standardization of the orthography and grammar of the Rundi language would have to be pushed forward at a quite rapid rate, of course. And at the very least, the country would be isolated from the rest of the world in many areas because of this kind of program. This is no doubt the reason why the Burundi government has rejected this solution.

As an alternative program, an international language could be instituted for all uses. The language selected, probably French, would most likely be taught almost exclusively, starting at the primary level. This requires adequate resources as far as teachers are concerned as well as textbooks adapted specifically for this kind of program. If these requirements are not met, it is most probable that the international language will change to a great extent (and this of course would increase its inefficiency) at lower levels of the social ladder and at greater distances from centers of instruction. This second way of proceeding would inevitably result in a divorce between the new generation's culture and that of its parents. It could be the cause of popular resistance for nationalistic or ideological reasons. Doubtlessly, the Burundi government would want to avoid this, in spite of suggestions from foreign experts — somewhat dated suggestions, to be sure — who have recommended such a course of action.

A third plan favored by Burundi leaders would entail instituting both a national and an international language. The goal of this would be the rapid expansion of elementary education. The national language would thus be the starting point since it would be used in the primary schools, but the high schools would employ the international language. Thus, contact would still be maintained with the outside world. However, it must be pointed out that this plan might create an elite composed of those people who managed to learn French well, especially if a situation of diglossia were to accompany that of bilingualism. What we refer to here is the situation existing in several European countries before World War I. French was then the language of an elite, the common folk using another language. All in all, bilingualism at the individual level was not common, especially among people living in the country, poor city-dwellers, and the elderly, i.e. the majority of the population. The more ambitious people — and who is not ambitious, at least for his own children? — have always preferred education in an international language. Thus the effort to modernize and reinforce the local language was almost completely abandoned. It should be stressed that this is the situation today in the ex-French colonies of Africa; however, there is a new trend to give more importance to the national language.

If the Burundi government really wants to be logical and stress both French and Kirundi, they should be made aware of the difficulties attached to such a program. It is a question of balance, always unstable and in need of being reviewed regularly. This is why we shall conclude once again by adopting suggestions of A. Mioni (the UNESCO expert in Burundi):

1. At the primary level of education, to go from the known to the unknown entails first stressing Kirundi before beginning French.

2. In official documents, use French and Kirundi side by side.

3. In public affairs, Rundi names should be given to everything having to do with daily life (i.e. names of streets, offices, ministries, military rankings, etc.).

4. In naming things, the original Rundi form should be restored for names of people and places that were incorrectly transcribed in colonial days; in like manner, the Rundi form should replace the French for Christian names (*Yohaani* and *Ludooviko* instead of *Jean* and *Louis*).

5. In publication procedures, the printing of books in Kirundi should be promoted.

Of course all of this will entail a resurrection of the *Académie rundi*. It is quite true that we lack any comparative studies on the working methods of this kind of institution. However, at Dar-es-Salaam there is a National Swahili Council which works quite well already.

Finally, we can hope that the *École normale supérieure* — and especially the University — will soon take an important role in promoting research and education in the fields we have just explored.[11]

In conclusion, we hope that the *Survey of language use and language teaching in eastern Africa*, which has previously been concerned only with the specific problems of Ethiopia, Kenya, Tanzania, Uganda, and Zambia, will identify as soon as possible those elements which might solve the problems of a national language. And we should add that Burundi should also be included in such a research project in the future.

---

[11]   Concerning this subject, see the contribution of A. Laffut, Professor of Psychopedagogy at the École normale supérieure of Burundi, reproduced in *Revue nationale d'éducation du Burundi* 25 (1968–1969), 17–24. Laffut applies to the field of individual psychology the ideas of H. Stern in *Les langues étrangères dans l'enseignement primaire* (Hamburg: UNESCO, 1965).

REFERENCES

A Study of polylingual school children
   Survey of Language use and language teaching in Eastern Africa 1(10):10.
BAECK, L.
   1957   "Etude socio-économique du centre extracoutumier d'Usambura," in *Collection of the Académie Coloniale*.
BASTIN, R.
   1966   *Pour un nouvel apprentissage du francais au Burundi*. Mimeographed. Bujumbura: Ecole normale supérieure.
BOYAYO, ABRAHAM
   1966   Comment sauvegarder notre culture rundi. *Revue nationale d'éducation du Burundi* 6(6).
D'HERTEFELT, M., A. TROUWBORST *et al.*
   1962   *Les anciens royaumes de la zone interlacustre méridionale*. Tervuren: Musée royal de l'Afrique centrale.
FISHMAN, J.
   1968   "National languages and languages of wider communication in the developing nations." Paper prepared for the Seminar on the Social Implications of Multilingualism, Dar-es-Salaam, Tanzania, December.
NUWINKWARE, PIERRE-CLAVER
   1962   *Prince Louis Rwagasore*. Bujumbura: Ministère de la Justice.
LE PAGE, ROBERT B.
   1966   *The national language question*. London: Oxford University Press.
VERDOODT, A.
   1966   Influence des structures ethniques et linguistique des pays membres des Nations-Unies sur la rédaction da la Déclaration universelle des droits de l'homme. Evian: Sixth World Meeting of Sociology (Second section, Group C: the Sociology of International Relations).
   1968   Zweisprachige nachbarn? Die deutschen Hochsprach- und Mundartgruppen in Ost-Belgien, dem Elsass, Ost-Lothringen und Luxemburg. Vienna, Stuttgart: W. Braumüller, Universitäts-Verlagsbuchhandlung.

The Sociolinguistic Structure of the Danube Basin

GYULA DÉCSY

"Danube basin" is used here to refer to the territory of the so-called "old" Hungary in its boundaries up until 1918. This territory may be considered as one of the linguistically most complex areas of Europe. During the preceding thousand years the following languages have played a role there in varying degrees: Hungarian, Slovak, Rumanian, Ukrainian, Serbo-Croatian, German, Latin, Greek, Church Slavonic, Turkish, Czech, Russian, Bulgarian, French, English, Yiddish, Ladino, Alan (Iaşian), Pechenegan, Cuman, and Armenian. This article will characterize the ethnic and social function of the individual languages.

1. ETHNOLINGUISTIC UNITS

This term is used to mean the spoken language of the permanently settled rural and urban populations.

1.1. *Hungarian*

Approximately twelve million speakers in a territory of roughly 120,000 square kilometers (46,332 square miles); for the most part in the central region of the Danube basin. Brought to the area by Hungarians settling the area at the end of the ninth century, the language spread quickly; by the end of the eleventh century it was probably the only language of civil organization. It was subsequently superseded by Latin, although it was employed as the colloquial language of the bureaucracy throughout the Middle Ages. It is dialectically differentiated only little and possesses a great inner coherence.

1.2. *Slovak*

Four million speakers in the north, for the most part in the mountainous areas (ca. 40,000 square kilometers; 15,440 square miles). Introduced in the sixth and seventh centuries from the original Slavic homeland (north of the Carpathians) by migrating Slavs. A tripartite dialect division with strong divergences: the west dialect close to Czech, the east dialect close to Polish, the middle dialect archaic with many special developments which set it apart from the other West Slavic languages and relate it in part with South Slavic. The language unit today has come about by and large through integration, whereby the three originally varying dialects have grown together as a result of homogeneous cultural influences.

1.3. *Ukrainian*

Ca. 800,000 people in the northeast in the Carpathian Ukraine (Trans-carpathia), a subdialect of Ukrainian, verifiable since the thirteenth century. The small area in the vicinity of the Polish, (East) Slovak, Hungarian, and Rumanian languages was exposed to a multitude of ethnolinguistic as well as cultural linguistic influences.

1.4. *Rumanian*

Four million speakers, ca. 40,000 square kilometers (15,440 square miles) in Transylvania (presently western Rumania). According to the continuity theory autochthonous, according to the migration theory a residual language of the east Roman Latinity imported from the south (Central Balkans). The nomadic mountain shepherds, organized in shepherd communities, were in the Middle Ages the main class which preserved its use. Minimal dialectical differentiation; by means of direct ties to the West and in particular to Rome important to the "occidentaliz-ing" of the whole of Rumania (today ca. twenty million speakers).

1.5. *Serbo-Croatian*

Ca. one million speakers, area ca. 15,000 square kilometers (5,792 square miles) in the south (the autonomous region of Vojvodina in Yugoslavia). Colonized since the seventeenth century by migration from areas situated to the south (flight from the Turks). Dialectically mini-mally differentiated, a culturally important factor for the whole of the Serbo-Croatian-speaking area (15.5 million speakers). The language of the numerous Serbian trade settlements along the Danube (Ofen, Szentendre, Vienna), which controlled the shipping trade on the Danube in the seventeenth through the nineteenth centuries.

1.6. *German*

Colonial dialects in numerous groups which hardly cohere temporally or spatially with one another. The cities and rural communities of the Transylvanian Saxons were founded in the twelfth century; also old are the Zips communities in east Slovakia. The medieval German populations of the west Hungarian and west Slovakian cities were early assimilated or annihilated as a result of the Turkish Wars in the sixteenth century (in the south). The new rural settlements in Hungary and Yugoslavia (Vojvodina) came into being in the framework of institutional colonization in the eighteenth century. The settlers continued to speak their native dialects, which in many places produced a special city or rural dialect, for which various High German elements (mainly Bavarian, Austrian and Alemannic) and, to a lesser degree, Middle German and Rhine-Franconian elements were basic. The ethnolinguistically heterogeneous German nationalities only became a homogeneous language group through the expansion of the standard literary language, which became established at various times after the sixteenth century. The home dialects nevertheless remain in use as the language of the home in the rural communities to this day. There are presently some 600,000 German descendants in the area.

1.7. *Yiddish*

In 1910 still spoken by approximately 600,000 people. It was imported following the middle of the nineteenth century for the most part in an intensive immigration from Galicia. As a result of assimilation (taking over of High German, Hungarian, Slovak, Rumanian, Serbo-Croatian, etc.) the language has practically disappeared, there being today only about 30,000 speakers.

1.8. *Speech Islands*

Today there remain only Slovenian (in west Hungary, ca. 10,000 speakers) and Gypsy (since the fifteenth century, today ca. 50,000 speakers). The following languages have disappeared: Alan (Iaşian, still spoken in the fifteenth century between the Tisza and the Danube); Pechenegan and Cuman (in the thirteenth century between the Tisza and the Danube); Ladino (during the time of the Turks spoken in Ofen and perhaps other cities); Croatian (settlements in the time of the Turks in Slovakia and other realms of the Hapsburg Monarchy); Greek (language of businessmen and refugees of various periods); Armenian (large communities in Transylvania, Szamosújvár, etc.). The old Slavic nation (indigenous since the sixth and seventh centuries), which in the ninth and tenth centuries had a West Slavic character (probably Slovakian to the north of Lake Balaton and a Slovenian character to the south thereof), was absorbed in the twelfth century by the Hungarian nation. In the region between the Tisza and the Danube and in eastern Transylvania a large Slavic population must be assumed for the Middle Ages, which however was likewise assimilated (i.e. Romanized or absorbed by the Hungarians) by the thirteenth century. The Slavs of east Transylvania probably spoke dialects of a Bulgarian type, although this cannot be proven on the basis of the preserved linguistic material (for the most part place names) in Rumanian and Hungarian. Special groups were the Csergeder-Bulgarians (settlements in the thirteenth century, became Lutheran in the sixteenth century, died out in the nineteenth century) as well as new Bulgarian colonists in the eighteenth century in Banat, who are today by and large assimilated.

2. CULTURAL LINGUISTIC UNITS

Here are indicated dialects which can be viewed primarily as literary standards, cultural languages, teaching and school languages, the language of educated speakers, documentary languages, church languages (sacral languages), written languages, etc., and which customarily had international or interregional distribution. In relation to the area under investigation it is a matter of autochthonous languages (e.g. Hungarian) or imported languages (Latin, Greek, Czech, etc.).

2.1. *Hungarian*

As a standard language Hungarian arose on the basis of the ethnolinguistic unit discussed under Section 1.1. In the tenth and eleventh centuries it was, in its spoken form (colloquial Hungarian of the Middle Ages) the language of civil organization, and in this use it was employed in the non-Magyar parts of the area as well, at least until the sixteenth century. Proof of this is provided by the approximately 1,000 loanwords and place names which were borrowed into Slovak, Carpathian Ukrainian, Rumanian, etc. Numerous lexical Balkanisms and a series of expressions in the language of the nomadic mountain shepherds (Walachians) have their origin in this colloquial Hungarian of the Middle Ages. Possessing but a sparse written record in the Middle Ages, followed by a literary flowering in the sixteenth and seventeenth centuries, then superseded again in the eighteenth century by German and Latin as the standard and official languages as well as by the new national languages, Hungarian then achieved an interregional expansion in the period 1867 to 1918, only subsequently to contract back upon its ethnolinguistic foundation after World War I.

2.2. Latin in Hungary

Latin was introduced in the eleventh century with Christianization as written and church language, probably in the north Italian pronunciation of that time. Transmittal was by the Germans, the Croatians, and the Slovenians. The most typical characteristic was $š$ for Latin s. Its use was for the most part written; in the documents and the chronicles of the Middle Ages it is interwoven with the peculiarities of the local colloquial languages of the inhabitants (Hungarian, Slovak, German, etc.). In the sixteenth and seventeenth centuries with the Reformation and the Counter-Reformation its use was restricted particularly in the Protestant areas, but it remained nevertheless the main language of officialdom and of the intelligensia though it was written and spoken only by the educated class (jurists, churchmen, teachers, writers, officials). It was certainly also a supranational tool for understanding in a state having many dialects. In Hungary Latin never became a true language in the home or for everyday usage. It experienced a rebirth in the eighteenth century as a language of the educated; it was officially replaced by Hungarian as the language of officialdom only in 1868, after which it retained importance only as the liturgical language of the Roman Catholic Church. Latin instruction was very intensive in advanced schooling in the area until the end of World War II.

2.3. Greek

Greek arrived in Hungary as a language of culture from Constantinople in the tenth and eleventh centuries. For a while it served as a written language, to a certain extent perhaps also as a spoken language among that portion of the leading class which had received its education in Constantinople (e.g. King Béla III, 1173–1179). New impulses for its use came from the Greek Orthodox Church (particularly in Transylvania through Rumania) as well as from Humanism in the sixteenth century, when in Kronstadt (Brassó) numerous Greek grammars and other works were published. Later Greek was only fostered by theologians and philologists within the confines of an intensive classical education.

2.4. High German

Brought to the country in the sixteenth century with the Reformation, the Lutheran Church of the German-speaking areas provided High German at first with its most important social basis. It soon became the unified language of the heterogeneous German dialects. With the stabilization of the Hapsburg hegemony in the seventeenth century it acquired an especial importance as a cultural language. Officially German never became a bureaucratic language in Hungary, though it practically achieved an international importance as a means of communication among the highest governing offices (situated in Vienna) and as the common language of the educated world in Central Europe. In the age of the Dual Monarchy (1867–1918) German was the language of the so-called communal institutions of the Austro-Hungarian Monarchy (military, foreign service) and served as the most important foreign language for the press, the sciences, international trade, etc.

2.5. Church Slavonic

Church Slavonic was used only in the areas of the Orthodox Church (Carpathian Ukraine, Transylvania, Vojvodina) in local variants as a sacral and documentary language. The first use of Church Slavonic in West Slovakia was between 863 and 880 (the activity of Cyril and Methodius in the Greater Moravian Empire). It cannot be determined whether the old Slavic population of east Transylvania (see Section 1.8.) was christianized and Church Slavonic was used as a liturgical language. It may be presumed so for the Greek Orthodox areas of the Carpathian Ukraine and east Transylvania at least since the thirteenth century.

2.6. Czech

Czech was probably introduced by scribes in the fourteenth and fifteenth centuries into the cities of Slovakia, which at this time must have had an important Slovak-speaking population. The oldest records are law books, documents, linguistically completely identical with the written Czech standard, which was generally in use at that time in the vicinity of Prague. There existed under Matthias Corvinus (1457–1490) a royal Bohemian

(Czech) chancellery in Ofen (Buda, Czech Budín), which issued a series of documents (letters) in the Czech language, by and large addressed to recipients in Moravia and Bohemia. At the end of the sixteenth century Czech in the norm of the Kralitz Bible (1579–1593) became the liturgical language of the Slovak Lutherans. For the Slovaks, Czech was always considered an imported standard used only by the educated, and it was never assimilated by the mass of the people.

2.7. *Turkish*

Turkish was the language of the Turkish military government from 1541 to about 1680. The written form was strictly normalized following the practice at Istanbul; the spoken form was used by and large in the Bosnian pronunciation (West Balkan Turkish) by hardly more than 50,000 speakers (Military personnel, officials, businessmen), who were compelled to leave the area at the end of the seventeenth century.

2.8. *Russian*

As a result of confessional and cultural ties, Russian entered (in the eighteenth and nineteenth centuries,) the Carpathian Ukraine and Vojvidina, where some Russian educational institutions were established. They had however only limited influence. Since 1945 Russian serves as the common second language of high-level political and economic organizations.

3. THE DANUBE BASIN SITUATION TODAY

The contemporary situation in the Danube Basin is characterized by the following features: decisive importance is maintained only by the Hungarian, Slovak, Ukrainian, Rumanian, and Serbo-Croatian, (ethnolinguistic units) which are all today highly developed cultural languages and are used in the corresponding states either exclusively or preeminently. German as a common second language of the educated class lost greatly in prestige following 1918 and lost still more after 1945; it could however in no way be completely eliminated, although the social class which preserved it was weakened also by the transfer of populations. In spite of intensive governmental support Russian was not able to establish itself as a common second language, not least of all because it had no noteworthy tradition in the area. French has been very popular among the Rumanians but is hardly employed by the other people of the area as a foreign language. In itself, English — like Russian — has scarcely any tradition in the area, but encountered a ready acceptance after 1945 nevertheless. Its spread is limited however. Since classical education was practically eliminated after 1945, knowledge of Greek and Latin is no longer the general rule among the educated.

The Danube basin is today perhaps the only extensive area in Europe (ca. 250,000 square kilometers; 96,525 square miles, 25 million people) which does not presently possess a common supranational language. For international linguistic communication there is a particular importance therefore in bilingualism and in interpreters and translating.

The five dominating ethnolinguistic units (Hungarian, Slovak, Ukrainian, Rumanian, Serbo-Croatian) form today — each for itself — socially coherent language communities in which there exists no friction between literary standard and popular speech. The dialects are dying out and the standard is establishing itself in the lower social levels everywhere. The social stratifications, recognizable in language use in the oppositions bourgeois/worker, city dweller/country inhabitant, landowner/peasant, have been eradicated following 1945. Language no longer serves in the area as a differentiating feature. Modern mass media (television, radio) greatly intensify verbal communication, which has led to internal equalization in the spoken language. The written language remains everywhere behind the rapid tempo of development in the spoken language; the gulf between verbal and written communication is deepening — an occurrence which is generally characteristic for language development in the industrial nations.

Language Unification in Taiwan: Present and Future

ROBERT L. CHENG

INTRODUCTION

For the past twenty-eight years the Nationalist government has promoted Mandarin in Taiwan under two assumptions: (1) Taiwan is a province of China, and (2) Mandarin is the national language of China. Without challenging either of these assumptions, this paper examines the Nationalist language policy in Taiwan and shows that the policy neglects proper planning for other vernaculars[1] and, in practice, seeks language unification through monolingualism rather than through bilingualism. This paper presents the view that unification through bilingualism will achieve the government's proclaimed goals of national harmony, political unity, democracy, and social progress much better than through monolingualism, both in Taiwan and in the whole of China.[2]

The policy of language unification in China through bilingualism takes the following positions. In the non-Mandarin areas both Mandarin and the mother tongue will be recognized as official languages of the respective areas. This means that Mandarin is to be learned as a second language by people of non-Mandarin areas and is to be used for communication among people who do not speak the same tongue. The non-Mandarin mother tongues remain the major communication tools in the schools, homes, communities, courts, and local governments. These languages (or

---

[1] Whether or not Taiwanese, Hakka, Cantonese, and Mandarin, etc., are different languages or different dialects of the same language is a problem. Western linguists have regarded them as different languages on the ground that they are not mutually intelligible. Some Chinese patriots view this to be an attempt by imperialists to divide China. I use the two terms, "language" and "dialect" interchangeably. For language-planning in general, see Fishman (1968), Rubin (1971).

[2] For the general background of language policy in China, see DeFrancis (1950).

dialects) may eventually die a natural death, but this will not be the result of any man-made policy. In the Mandarin areas, Mandarin will be the only official language. Mandarin speakers need not learn a second language unless they want to reside in a non-Mandarin area.

Quite in contrast with the above policy is one which attempts to unify the language of China through suppression of all non-Mandarin tongues. This has as its eventual goal the learning and use of Mandarin as the FIRST language by all people in even the non-Mandarin areas. Non-Mandarin tongues would be officially illegal anywhere in public: in schools, in the courts, and at all levels of government. Non-Mandarin tongues would be allowed in communities with the understanding that they will be used temporarily only so long as non-Mandarin monolinguals are living. To see to it that non-Mandarin tongues are extinguished as soon as possible, Mandarin will be used between all bilinguals who can speak Mandarin. The well-being of any older members of the community who can speak only a non-Mandarin tongue is to be sacrificed for the sake of national linguistic unity.

Language planning for a population that speaks different languages but has to live under one government is a worldwide problem. Even though my discussion focuses mainly on Taiwan, this paper is intended as a contribution to the joint efforts of scholars in various disciplines to deal with this problem.

My arguments for the promotion of bilingualism are based on the following assumptions about language and its role in society and I claim them to be universally applicable.

1. An individual's native language is his best communication tool. It becomes an inseparable part of his ego, once his nerve system has internalized it.

2. Old people rarely can sufficiently acquire a second language and only a small portion of younger adults are especially talented in learning a second language.

3. A normal individual has a sense of linguistic loyalty to his speech community; if this loyalty is destroyed, there is a danger of losing his love for and confidence in both his local culture and the culture he acquires later.

4. Linguistic differences have come into existence as a natural result of man's efforts to adjust to different environments. Linguistic as well as other human differences are not in themselves evil or causes of problems.

5. Many nonlinguistic features (geographical, cultural, institutional, etc.), which are also important to group identification can be responsible for linguistic changes. It is useless to destroy linguistic differences in order to obtain a monolithic group identity unless differences in these other features are also eliminated.

6. That linguistic unity through monolingualism is a prerequisite of

political unity is a political conviction, not a proven fact. Far more essential for political unity are attitudes of tolerance, understanding, harmony, and lawfulness, together with common interests. To attempt to eliminate language differences because of such a mistaken conviction is no more proper than to attempt to eliminate other facets of social life for the sake of purely religious beliefs of what is "best." Not only is the attempt expensive, but there is also the risk of losing essential features of political unity in order to attain less essential features of political unity.

7. When any two speech groups are in contact, there is a tendency for the dominant group to feel superior and the dominated group to feel inferior because of their language differences. Education should not further intensify these superior–inferior feelings which result in social disharmony. People should be educated to tolerate and respect linguistic differences and at the same time to increase their ability to communicate with other people.

8. Man instinctively fears people of another linguistic community. He fears contamination of his own linguistic system by alien linguistic elements, and views such innovations as evil. But man is capable of being bilingual, and bilingual individuals are more ready to tolerate differences and to benefit from cultural interchange than are monolinguals.

While the population of Taiwan shares many features with others in similar conditions and hence is subject to the application of the above assumptions, it has certain peculiar features that will be of special interest to language-planning specialists: it has a recent history of the consecutive imposition of two languages upon the local populace — the implication of the Japanese language policy to "assimilate the Taiwan population in order to expand the Japanese population" and of the Nationalist policy to assimilate the population of Taiwan into the Chinese population lest Taiwan should be "alienated from her mother country again." Both of these language policies aimed at assimilative monolingualism and are in sharp contrast with the British colonial policy which aimed at segregated monolingualism. The latter was euphemistically "separate but equal," but may only have been a strategy to divide and rule.[3] Both also differ from the integrated bilingual policy in Singapore today.

Taiwan's literate population now uses Chinese characters which, though they take much longer to master than a second spoken language, have the magical power of making their users believe that they belong to the people of the characters — the Chinese. As soon as such literate speakers of different "dialects" attempt oral communication, however,

---

[3] I am referring to the British policy of allowing different schools for different vernaculars. Under the Japanese and Nationalists only the national language was used at all school levels. The main difference between the two is that the Japanese set up separate schools for Japanese children and Taiwanese children, whereas the Nationalists mix children of different language backgrounds in the same classes.

they may discover their speech to be so different that they feel they belong to different peoples.

To my knowledge, no case study of language planning in Taiwan has been done from the viewpoint of modern sociolinguistics.

The Nationalist government has urged solidarity and harmony among the different speech groups in Taiwan in order to cope with its present internal and external political crises. It particularly advocates national unity, love for and confidence in Chinese culture, democracy, social progress, and science as the major goals of government and education. It is timely that specialists in the behavioral sciences discuss the relevance of language planning with regard to these proclaimed goals. No attempt will be made here to go beyond these proclaimed goals and the Nationalists' claim that the language policy being practiced in Taiwan is identical with its policy for the whole of China.[4]

Brief descriptions of the sociolinguistic situations of Taiwan twenty-eight years ago when the Nationalists first took over Taiwan and of the present time are given in Section 1. In Section 2, I evaluate various aspects of the Nationalists' language planning with particular attention given to whether or not their proclaimed goals can be achieved by either of the two alternative means of language unification: bilingualism and monolingualism. My arguments in favor of bilingualism are presented during this evaluation.

1. SOCIOLINGUISTIC SITUATIONS IN TAIWAN

The Situation in 1945

After the end of World War II, the population of Taiwan was about 6,000,000. Except for the 5 percent Japanese who did not return to Japan immediately and the 2.5 percent Austronesians who were the earliest settlers, the majority of the population spoke either Taiwanese (a Chin-

---

[4]   There are views that the Nationalists intend to divide various groups to prevent united opposition, that the Nationalists at this time want to alienate the population of Taiwan from China so as to cope with Peking's efforts to take over Taiwan and that Taiwan has been a separate political entity and its dwellers desire independence. Discussion of such political goals will go beyond the scope of this paper. I do believe, however, that bilingualism should be the choice for any population that is similar to that of Taiwan under any responsible government that knows the nature of language and human groups. When Taiwan is treated as a political entity separated from China, the sociolinguistic goals of language planning may change slightly. The basic principle of unification through bilingualism should not change.

Whether the Taipei or Peking government or people active in the Taiwanese Independence Movement like it or not, bilingualism of the Taiwan variety of Mandarin, Hakka, and Min is a reality which serves as a feature of group identity in addition to other features of group identity, geographical, institutional, educational, etc.

ese dialect developed through the mixture of South Min or South Hok-kien dialects such as Amoy, Ch'üan chou and Chang chou)[5] or Hakka as their first language. The ratio between Taiwanese and Hakka is estimated to be seven to one. A great portion of the population were bilinguals, with their first tongue either Taiwanese or Hakka and their second Japanese because under the Japanese theirs was the only language allowed at all school levels.

The proportion of such bilinguals compared with monolinguals, and also the degree of Japanese proficiency of these bilinguals varies greatly according to age groups. Resistance to formal education was stronger in the earlier part of the fifty years of Japanese rule; Japanese was rarely used in the local community until much later in the 1930s when compulsory six-year Japanese education was put in effect.

Under the policy of Japanization of the Taiwanese (the so-called policy of assimilating the Taiwanese population into the population of the Japanese Emperor's subjects) toward the end of World War II, there were a few families in which Japanese was used. Such families were called "National-Language" families and enjoyed some privileges that other Taiwanese families did not have. The children in these families tended to speak Japanese better than they did either Hakka or Taiwanese. Rarely were they unable to speak Taiwanese or Hakka if they lived in ordinary communities. In the northern urban areas, where Taiwanese- and Hakka-speakers were mixed or in government housing areas where the Japanese population was proportionally higher, Japanese was used more frequently and monolingual Japanese children existed even in Taiwanese families.

When the Japanese later evacuated, immigrants from China came to Taiwan. It was mainly into these two types of areas that they moved. Therefore the newcomers unfortunately miscalculated the success of the language policy of the Japanese rulers. Japanese was frequently heard in the urban areas because many people in either the Taiwanese or Hakka group were able to communicate with people in the other group only in Japanese. In the government housing areas, Japanese was often heard more frequently because Japanese monolinguals lived there. For bilingual adults, the habit of using Japanese was impossible to erase overnight. For their monolingual Japanese-speaking children the learning of Taiwanese or Hakka takes a longer time.

Another reason for the newcomers' underestimation of the Taiwanese

---

[5] The terms Taiwanese and South Min (or South Hokkien) are both problematic. In the south of the Min (or Hokkien) provinces, Hakka is also spoken, and the south Min dialects are also spoken in the province of Canton. I follow the general use of the term, namely, the Taiwanese people include Taiwanese and Hakka speakers who immigrated to Taiwan before World War II. When referring to language, the term includes only the Min variety of Chinese spoken in Taiwan.

people's desire to maintain their own mother tongue despite the Japanese language policy came from the fact that Japanese loan words were used frequently in both Taiwanese and Hakka speech by a majority of the people. Such speech was often thought to be Japanese by the newcomers who did not understand Hakka or Taiwanese.

In spite of official Japanese discouragement of learning and use of Taiwanese by Hakka-speakers and vice versa, Hakka–Taiwanese bilinguals and trilinguals (those who could also speak Japanese) did exist as a natural result of social contacts.

Among the Austronesian people in the mountains, Japanese was used very much as a lingua franca because there were several small speech communities which could not otherwise communicate with each other.

As for writing, Japanese was used by almost all literates in all speech communities toward the end of World War II. Romanization of Taiwanese was used by churchgoers. Taiwanese texts in Chinese characters were available only in the Bible and hymn books. If one could read romanization, one generally could also write romanized Taiwanese, which contrasted sharply with writing in Chinese characters. Romanized Taiwanese was most frequently used for communication among those church members who did not know Japanese.

Outside of the churches there were only two uses of Chinese characters for Taiwanese or Hakka: in the writing of folk songs and the reading of Chinese classics. In neither case was the writing of the vernacular language in Chinese characters a means of mass communication. It takes several years to learn enough Chinese characters to read and write in the vernacular language, and no school was allowed to give any classes for such training. Only in high schools did students receive instruction in Chinese classics; even then they had the option of reading it in Japanese or Taiwanese. Though Chinese classics reflect the earlier stages of both Taiwanese and Hakka, their language differs from these just as Latin does from French. Limited study in high school might be sufficient for reading certain selected texts but not enough to learn to write in classical Chinese.

Romanization would have been easier for people to learn and use but it was never allowed in any publication outside of churches. The ability to use romanization was almost taken as synonymous with being a Christian.

There were quite a few studies done on the vernacular languages with a view to popularizing them so as to achieve a higher rate of literacy. No such effort succeeded, because the Japanese authorities discouraged their use.[6]

---

[6]   For accomplishments in the study of the languages of Taiwan, see Wu (1963).

Major Factors of Sociolinguistic Change

Since the end of World War II, when the Nationalist Chinese government took over Taiwan, it has enforced its policy of spreading the use of Mandarin. Since the government's move to Taiwan in 1950, the policy has been carried out without much open opposition, and may be summarized as follows:

1. To survive as the legitimate government of the whole of China, the Nationalists have to maintain Mandarin as the national language in Taiwan.

2. Because Mandarin-speakers are in the minority, the government has to take extraordinary steps to maintain the status of Mandarin against the natural tendency of Mandarin-speakers to be assimilated into the Taiwanese majority.

In addition to this language policy and the evacuation of the central government of the Nationalists to Taiwan, new emigration from various parts of the Chinese mainland has been an important factor in the sociolinguistic changes in Taiwan during the past twenty-eight years. The new emigration started even before the departure of the Japanese. It reached its peak around the time of the Communist take-over of the Chinese mainland in 1949. The new emigrants are estimated to be 15 percent of the total population, including 600,000 Nationalist troops.

The increase of the population of Taiwan from 6 million to 15 million, however, has been chiefly due to natural increase rather than to new immigration (Hsieh 1964:205–228). Furthermore, natural increase is greater among the old settlers than among the new immigrants. One of the reasons for the lower rate of population increase in the latter group is that quite a few were male adults, unmarried or separated from their wives. It was not until recent years that marriage began to take place with any frequency between the old and new settlers.

The sociolinguistic implication of the general natural increase of population is that there are more younger people than older people in Taiwan. Since younger people learn a second language more easily than older people, it is easier for each language group to have more bilinguals than monolinguals. A sociolinguistic implication of a lower rate of natural increase among the new settlers is that the proportion of Taiwanese- or Hakka-speakers among the younger generation is even higher than that among the older generation. This means the social pressure on the new settlers' children to learn and use Taiwanese or Hakka in addition to Mandarin is pretty high because they are so greatly outnumbered by their Taiwanese- and Hakka-speaking peers.

The Situation in 1973

Due to the language policy of the Nationalist government and new emigration of Chinese Mainlanders, the sociolinguistic situation of Taiwan has undergone a drastic change. A brief description of the present-day situation follows.

About 75 percent of the population still speak Taiwanese as the mother tongue and 10 percent speak Hakka. The number of native speakers of Mandarin is hard to estimate. Chinese Mainlanders who went to Taiwan after the Communist take-over were not necessarily Mandarin-speakers at the time of their immigration. Even among Mandarin-speakers, dialect differences are often so great that communication is very difficult, if not entirely impossible.

Since each group among the Mainlanders is relatively very small and since this category of people has generally engaged in occupations that require much contact with other groups (government employees, teachers, and soldiers) there is a tendency for this group to use Mandarin (very frequently with a heavy accent) more frequently than do other groups in their daily life. Marriage has tended to take place within this group even though husband and wife may speak entirely different mother tongues. More than half of non-Mandarin-speaking Mainlanders' children give up their mother tongues for Mandarin.

Even if the parents are both from a Mandarin area, there is a strong tendency for the Mainlanders' children to speak a Mandarin that is different from that of their parents. Unlike the Mandarin of their parents which differs from person to person (i.e. a speaker from Shantung may have some difficulty in understanding one from Szechwan), the Mandarin in their children's speech is more uniform. This is a Mandarin that maintains most of the phonemic distinctions of the Peking dialect but is different from it in many phonetic and grammatical features. Even children of Pekingese parents speak Taiwan Mandarin except when they are asked to speak "authentic Pekingese."

The border lines separating the three speech groups are somewhat blurred because marriages take place between speech groups and because individuals do not live in separate speech communities. In rural areas the people of a village are generally either Taiwanese- or Hakka-speakers, while residential areas for military and government employees are occupied mainly by Mainlanders. Except for these two cases it is very rare for a child to speak a first language that is different from that of his parents. In the cases of mixed marriage or residence, the child tends to pick up the mother's language as the first language and the father's language or the language of the neighborhood as the second language. No statistics are available for making generalizations about the pressure of the family, relatives, neighborhood, speech community or government on the choice of first language for children in the abovementioned situations. The bilingual situations of each speech group will be described from four different aspects — the ability to understand, to speak, read and write, the frequency of use, and literacy.

Figure 1 shows my estimate of the distribution of trilinguals and bilinguals (passive knowledge only is considered here) among Taiwanese-speakers according to year of birth. It is equated with ages at 1945, when the war ended, and the year 1973. Among those who were born in 1965, more than 90 percent are capable of understanding Mandarin and hence are included in the bilingual group of TM (Taiwanese–Mandarin). Less than 10 percent of those born in that year are monolinguals in Taiwanese (T).

Age in 1973	Age in 1945	Year of Birth
88	60	1885
78	50	1895
68	40	1905
58	30	1915
48	20	1925
38	10	1935
28	0	1945
18		1955
8		1965
0		1973

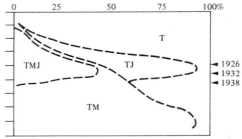

Figure 1. Percentage of Taiwanese speakers with listening ability in Mandarin and Japanese

Key: T   = Taiwanese monolinguals
      TJ   = Taiwanese–Japanese bilinguals
      TM   = Taiwanese–Mandarin bilinguals
      TMJ = Taiwanese–Mandarin–Japanese trilinguals

Those who were born between 1933 and 1938 experienced a sudden language shift while they were in primary school (seven to twelve), where they were exposed to both Japanese and Mandarin at different times. Some retained Japanese and failed to pick up Mandarin because they graduated too soon to learn Mandarin in school or failed to pick it up elsewhere afterward. These are usually the people whose occupations do not require much contact with a wide variety of people. Some forgot Japanese because they had not used it in school long enough before the time of the shift, or else they have had little opportunity to use it since then. There is a high proportion of monolinguals in this age group because compulsory education was not enforced after the war, and also because, especially in the countryside, their teachers' Mandarin was in general not sufficient.

Those who were born between 1926 and 1932 were thirteen to nineteen years old at the time of shift. If these attended high school, they usually picked up both Japanese and Mandarin, though a few older ones may have failed to learn Mandarin (only if they never served in government) and a few younger ones may have forgotten their Japanese. If they attended a middle school, they tend to be trilingual in Japanese, Mandarin and Taiwanese. If they did not, they tend to be bilingual in Taiwanese and Japanese. Monolinguals in Taiwanese are few among this group because compulsory education was imposed on them.

Quite a large proportion of the older people have picked up Mandarin mainly through social contacts. These are usually trilinguals. Those who did not learn Japanese at school but succeeded in picking up Mandarin are more numerous than those who did the reverse, because Mandarin is easier to pick up than Japanese for Taiwanese-speakers. Among the young people those who understand Japanese without even a listening ability in Mandarin are relatively few among this age group because they are exposed to both Japanese and Mandarin through similar channels: mass communication, business contacts, and in government institutions in the urban areas. Some Taiwanese speakers also speak Hakka.

In the above description, my criterion for a bilingual is listening ability in two languages. If we use the criterion of fluent speaking ability, the percentage of bilinguals in Mandarin or Japanese would be reduced by half. Many people's speaking ability is limited to simple conversation. The proportion of those who can speak up in Mandarin even in small meetings is quite low. Four reasons can be given for this: (1) There is a great educational emphasis on writing and an undue neglect of speaking ability. (2) The whole educational system trains students to listen and repeat rather than speak and discuss (because of large classes, lecture-type teaching methods, and an inadequate way of evaluating student achievement). (3) Most children's ability to express themselves is under-developed because the use of their native language is prohibited at school at the time when they are developing their ability to express themselves. (4) Except in some special areas and on some particular occasions, their mother tongue is used in their daily life.

The use of Mandarin between Taiwanese-speakers generally occurs in two situations: in schools or the armed forces, where the ban on any non-Mandarin tongue is strictly enforced, and among children when they play games which they have learned at school.

The use of Mandarin among children varies according to where they live. It is used more frequently in urban than rural areas and in mixed areas than in the monolingual areas where Taiwanese is exclusively used.

There are parents who encourage their children to use Mandarin so that they can achieve a higher academic standing at school. Competition to get into good schools at the higher levels is extremely fierce. Children are compelled to prepare for entrance examinations at the expense even of physical growth. It is common for students to study for twelve hours a day, seven days a week for more than a year preceding an entrance examination. If parents have to bear the idea of having their children sacrifice their health for better schooling, some parents do not mind taking the risk of sacrificing even their children's relationships with their families and relatives. Though small in number, some Taiwanese-speaking parents are beginning to speak to their children in Mandarin in the hope of helping their children to get better grades in school.

In regard to reading ability the population is divided much less clearly horizontally. If one can speak Taiwanese and read Japanese, one has a very good chance of developing a sufficient reading knowledge of Mandarin Chinese. This is because the syntax of Mandarin is quite similar to that of Taiwanese. The lexicons of the two dialects may be very different but they do overlap sufficiently so that at least 70 percent of their monosyllabic etymons are the same. Terms for modern concepts are generally shared by Japanese, Mandarin, and Taiwanese. Many of the same combinations of etymons represented by the same Chinese characters are used in the three languages. So far as such combinations are concerned differences are mainly matters of pronunciation. There is even a high degree of regularity in the similarities and differences among the pronunciations of the same etymons in the three languages.

Compared to people in Japan or English-speaking countries, people of Taiwan are not so dependent on writing for their daily life.

A relatively small portion of the literate depend on reading to acquire knowledge in the arts and crafts, sports, farming, and the like. Books written for the general public are generally in Chinese. Quite a few Taiwanese read Japanese and English for practical knowledge.

Writing ability is much less common than reading ability. Unlike reading Chinese, writing Chinese is not a skill one can pick up through self-study. My estimate is that less than 5 percent of those who have developed a reading knowledge BY THEMSELVES ever write in Chinese for purposes other than personal communication. Many primary school graduates cannot write even family letters. I have often heard of younger men attending cram courses in letter-writing before they are drafted so that they can write letters home when they are away. Even among college graduates, those who can write articles suitable for newspaper publication are the exception rather than the rule.

There are several reasons for this unbalanced ability in Chinese writing and reading. First, it is difficult for the average person to write correctly because of the huge number and complexity of the Chinese characters. Secondly, there is a custom of evaluating one's scholarship by one's own calligraphy; one feels discouraged to write if one feels his calligraphy is not presentable. Next, the norm of modern Chinese is still in flux. Idiom, grammar, and vocabulary from different stages of the development of

Mandarin and different dialects are all combined in varying proportions and differing styles in modern Mandarin. Grammar is rarely taught as a guide for writing clear, precise, and simple Chinese. Only the talented who have long years of practice have some confidence in their own writing ability. Lastly, the idea that writing is an ornament and a display of learning still haunts people in general. When people read official documents which are full of classical diction strange to modern grammar, it is hard to convince them that simpler and easier writing is good writing because it communicates better. Government business letters have usually been in classical Chinese; not until recently has there been a movement to use modern Chinese for these.

The proportion of those who use romanization of the Taiwanese vernacular has not increased, because the government has banned the teaching of Taiwanese romanization and the printing of new romanized texts. No systematic investigation has been done on the actual use of romanized Taiwanese, so as to compare the efficiency of a phonetic writing such as romanization and logographic writing such as Chinese characters. Such an investigation is very desirable in view of the fact that romanization is rarely used in any other Chinese community![7]

The bilingual situations of the Hakka in Taiwan are quite similar to those of Taiwanese-speakers, especially in the distribution of those who can speak and write Japanese or Mandarin according to age group. There is a higher proportion of Hakka people capable of using Taiwanese than vice versa since the Hakka population is smaller than the Taiwanese-speakers' and since they therefore need to contact outsiders more frequently than the Taiwanese. Since neither Taiwanese nor Hakka is taught at any school in Taiwan, many Hakka people have to use Japanese or Mandarin to communicate with Taiwanese speakers. Some Hakka tend to use Japanese or Mandarin among themselves when non-Hakka speakers are present. This has led to the mistaken belief that the Hakka want to identify themselves with the Japanese or Mainlanders.

The number of those who speak the various Austronesian languages as native tongues is very hard to estimate. The Austronesian peoples have suffered more than the Han (i.e. Chinese) people from the drastic shift of the national language from Japanese to Mandarin. First, Mandarin is a Chinese dialect and is easier for Taiwanese- or Hakka-speakers to learn and use than for the Austronesian population. Secondly, the Austronesian population has relied upon Japanese much more than the Han people; each of their speech communities is very small and Japanese is the only language they can use to communicate with outsiders, i.e. either other Austronesian tribes or their Han neighbors.

---

[7]   Romanized Chinese was once learned and used by Chinese communities in the Soviet Union. It was short-lived, mainly because the Chinese population was soon absorbed into the host communities (DeFrancis 1950:87–108).

2. EVALUATION OF NATIONALIST LANGUAGE PLANNING

My examination of the Nationalist language policy and its practice will center on the question of whether it plans language unification through bilingualism or through suppression of linguistic differences.

According to both the description of language policy given by the Ministry of Education at the central level and also its practice in Mainland China before the Communists took over, one would say that it was a policy for bilingualism. But judging from what is being practiced in Taiwan, especially in the entire education system, one must conclude that the official language policy is of the second type. However, the official standing of the provincial government on this is not clear.

My claim that the practice of the Nationalists in Taiwan is that of language unification through suppression of linguistic differences is based on the following observations:

1. Neither Taiwanese nor Hakka are allowed as mediums of instruction at any level of school except in the beginning months of instruction of first-graders.

2. No instruction in Taiwanese or Hakka is given at school to help Mainlanders' children communicate with Taiwanese or Hakka monolinguals. Even though, from political, economical, and social points of view, bilinguals and trilinguals are more effective and desired in Taiwan than monolinguals, the present educational system discourages Mandarin monolinguals from becoming bilinguals by offering them no facilities to learn Taiwanese or Hakka and by prohibiting the use of Taiwanese and Hakka in school. Therefore, Mandarin-speaking children do not feel the necessity of learning Taiwanese or Hakka.

Surrounded by Taiwanese-speakers, a Mandarin-speaker should be able to use Taiwanese or Hakka if either is taught at school for three months, five hours a week. Not a single class is available at school, however, for those who want to learn Taiwanese for immediate daily use. Quite in contrast with this neglect of teaching a language of daily use is the teaching of English, which is rarely used in ordinary life. English is required for every student in middle school (i.e. intermediate and high school) five hours a week every year. More than 80 percent of those who spend three years or more on English never use English in their entire lives, however.

3. No instruction in Hakka or Taiwanese is given to help community members communicate, trust, cooperate, and appreciate each other better in and through their mother languages.

4. No effort is made to teach the linguistic structure of Taiwanese and Hakka so that one can teach or learn Mandarin, Taiwanese, Hakka more efficiently. There is no effort, moreover, to correct the erroneous notion that Taiwanese or Hakka has no grammar and therefore cannot be taught

at school. Such an erroneous notion will be an important psychological factor for an earlier extinction of Taiwanese and Hakka.

5. No attempt to popularize the vernacular writing in Taiwanese or Hakka is allowed. The government has banned the printing of romanized texts. Romanization or Chinese phonetic script is easier for Taiwanese and Hakka illiterates to learn than are Chinese characters. For cultural and political reasons the phonetic script has been opposed as orthography for any Chinese dialect. But its value as a pronunciation aid has been recognized even by conservatives. In Taiwan's public schools, the Chinese phonetic script has in fact been taught with great success as an aid in learning Mandarin pronunciation. There is a greater cultural and pedagogical need for the teaching of a similar system not only as a device to indicate Taiwanese or Hakka pronunciation of Chinese characters but also as a supplement to the present orthography using Chinese characters for folk literature. Many Taiwanese and Hakka words either have no characters to represent them or are represented by characters which the average people do not know. Attempts to write down Taiwanese or Hakka are allowed only in folk poetry and proverbs but not in prose. On scholarly subjects written Chinese in characters may not vary much for Taiwanese or Hakka or Mandarin. But writing in Taiwanese or Hakka, when it is intended to faithfully reflect speech, differs as drastically from Mandarin as English from German or French. A language without an efficient and widely-used system to indicate its pronunciation would be of little value and would tend to extinction more easily than a language with such a system. Prohibition or discouragement of efforts to design or promote such a device in the vernacular should be interpreted as an attempt to eliminate it.

6. The public use of Taiwanese or Hakka, with few exceptions, is disallowed officially in the military, and in schools, and government. Use on private occasions is prohibited in many schools in order to promote Mandarin.

Taiwanese and Hakka are prohibited at some schools mainly on the ground that, in doing so, students will be forced to practice in Mandarin. The unfortunate result is that students speak inaccurate Mandarin. Because prohibition of expression in a mother tongue is too much for the average child to adjust to, except for a few talented ones, students cannot speak any language, even their native language, fluently. When students are forced to use Mandarin without sufficiently correct awareness of structural differences, they form the habit of speaking Mandarin with many Taiwanese or Hakka syntactic and phonological features. Undesirable habits of speaking inaccurate Mandarin are reinforced by conversations between students with similar habits.

Since there are regular relationships among Taiwanese, Hakka, and Mandarin the major learning problem is in accuracy rather than fluency.

After fluency in the mother tongue is firmly acquired, fluent and accurate Mandarin can be acquired with the help of modern techniques in teaching a second language, especially in making students aware of structural differences in Hakka, Taiwanese, and Mandarin.

Among teachers of Mandarin and written Chinese, there is a general lack of knowledge about the structural relations between Mandarin and Taiwanese or Hakka and their pedagogical implications. There is even fear that study of the Taiwanese dialect will result in its promotion, thereby affecting adversely the promotion of Mandarin.

In elementary classes where all students understand Taiwanese, Taiwanese teachers may read textbooks of all subjects in Mandarin but explain and discuss them in Taiwanese. Though the teaching is very effective because Taiwanese is the best tool for the students and the teachers and though parents welcome it, such a practice is forbidden from the second grade on and is seldom known to the authorities.

7. No efforts are made so that basic scientific knowledge about the structure and history of Taiwanese and Hakka can be available to students and the general public. Many people still believe that Taiwanese and Hakka have no grammar, can never be put into writing, or are inadequate and unsuitable for cultivated discussion. They are miserably ignorant of the truth that Mandarin, Taiwanese, and Hakka were once one and the same language, and that languages change as environments change — not because of community members' evil ways, disloyalty, incompetence, or inferiority, but because of their ability to innovate as language is passed down from one generation to another. Without such ability to innovate, human beings would make no progress and have no culture. Few efforts have been made to reinforce the idea that Mandarin is no more authentic, correct, or efficient than Taiwanese or Hakka, that Mandarin has been chosen as the national language of China merely because there are more people who speak Mandarin (or its varieties) than those who speak other tongues, and that Taiwanese and Hakka are not deviant forms of Mandarin.

The concept of the standard authentic language and culture results in the following unfortunate value judgment: differences from the "authentic" culture and language of the Mainlanders are undesirable. If there are differences due to innovation in the "authentic" culture of the Mainlanders, then the conservative feature in the Taiwanese language or culture is viewed as "backward." If it has been due to innovations in the Taiwanese culture or language, then the innovative features are to be viewed as the results of the "Foreign Devil's" evil influence, or as the deviated development peculiar to vulgar people.

Many school hours have been used to emphasize the common history of the Chinese population in Taiwan, and much has been said about the importance of solidarity between different speech groups. Nothing serves to prove the common history of the Chinese more effectively than the systematic relations that exist between Mandarin, Hakka, and Taiwanese and the common body of vocabulary represented by the same Chinese characters. If history is to be studied to help people understand the present and solve immediate problems, rather than to make them forget the present, the history of the three languages should be included in the curriculum. A language tends to extinguish more easily if its speakers are ignorant about its history and structure than if they are well informed about it and thereby cultivate a sense of respect and love for it.

8. No legal status is given for either Taiwanese, spoken as a native language by more than 75 percent of the population of Taiwan, of Hakka, spoken by 10 percent. Government subsidies are given for the production of Mandarin TV and radio programs and films. Taiwanese TV programs, which are the major source of information and entertainment for the great majority, have been limited to one hour a day. Mandarin is an important qualification for getting any governmental position, or for getting into any high level of school. Taiwanese or Hakka is not required of even those government employees who have to serve Taiwanese or Hakka monolinguals in person (clerks, policemen, receptionists in information booths, etc.).

The above measures, positive or negative, on Taiwanese and Hakka, have been taken in order to promote Mandarin. Whether the Nationalists intend to eliminate Hakka or Taiwanese is a debatable question, and I do not mean to claim that they have such an intention. I only claim that the combination of the above actions or neglects of action will lead to the eventual extinction of Hakka and Taiwanese. I do also claim that the population of Taiwan is big enough, civilized enough, and wealthy enough to use its taxes to provide lessons in and on Taiwanese or Hakka in addition to Mandarin and on how to write down their speech and study about the structure and history of the languages they are using every day. Taiwan has a population bigger than two-thirds of the U.N. member nations. It has nine years of compulsory education and sends a higher proportion of its children to college than most civilized nations.

Through the rest of this paper I shall discuss the various types of work needed in language planning, alternatives in major issues with the source of the discrepancies, and various aspects of Nationalist language planning in Taiwan.[8]

Selection of Planning and Implementation Agencies

The main government agency that has a role similar to that of language planning in Taiwan is the Commission on the Promotion of Mandarin

[8]   The headings to be used are adopted from Rubin (1971) who has attempted to identify a language-planner's work and an evaluator's work.

(CPM). It is affiliated with the Education Department of the Taiwan Provincial Government (ROC 1948:1162–1177). The CPM was formed in 1946 by the decree of the CPM in the Ministry of Education of the central government of the Nationalists. The CPM on either level of government was an executive body in charge of designing, investigating, and coordinating the teaching of the national language, Mandarin, in the areas within the jurisdiction of each.

The policy to adopt Mandarin as the national language and to seek linguistic unification by spreading the use of Mandarin over all of China was decided on long ago by the Planning Committee for Linguistic Unification through a National Language, first organized in 1929. Even so, the Taiwan Provincial CPM has had much independent power because it was not bound to observe any particular method or schedule of implementing the prescribed policy. In fact, the policy was carried out in varying degrees of intensity and using various methods in different provinces. In Canton and many other provinces the languages of school instruction were the native languages, up to the twelfth grade. This continued under the Nationalist government until it evacuated to Taiwan in 1950. Taiwan is the only place among the non-Mandarin areas where all subjects in Mandarin were ever taught at all school levels including even the first grade. What has been practiced in Taiwan regarding the status of non-Mandarin dialects in fact contradicts previous policies and practices of the Nationalist central government.

In 1951, soon after the evacuation from the Chinese mainland to Taiwan, the CPM was dissolved at the national level. There were some reasons for the Nationalists to dissolve the CPM at this level instead of the provincial level or instead of maintaining it on both levels. First, Mandarin was far better promoted in Taiwan than in any other place. Second, the attitude of the central CPM toward non-Mandarin dialects had been too lenient, in the mind of those in power, for the nation to achieve the goal of language unity. It had recognized that each Chinese dialect is one of the national languages in the broad sense. It had decided on Pekingese as the present-day standard, or national, language in the narrower sense. It viewed Pekingese merely as one of the Chinese dialects. It even encouraged the study of various dialects so as to enrich and improve the national language and to evolve a more lively national literature. It also stressed that the study of dialects could help improve the teaching of Mandarin (ROC 1948:1162).

All these views except the last one might have sounded too conservative or out-of-date to those authorities who were anxious to see that no language but Mandarin be recognized as the official language of Taiwan. They might have feared that Taiwanese and Hakka could stand in the way of promoting the teaching and use of Mandarin further in Taiwan.

Two questions can be asked concerning the selection of those CPM committee members who were to be in charge of language-planning and its implementation.

1. In selecting the committee members was consideration given so that the interests of each speech group could be best protected? The conflicts of interest between speech communities were NOT taken into consideration. Qualifications and interest in administering the teaching of Mandarin were and are the major consideration. Efforts have been made to appoint Taiwanese- and Hakka-speakers, but only because of their qualifications to spread Mandarin and not so they might study the interests of their respective speech communities regarding language policy and its implementation.

2. Do various speech communities have control over the appointment of the committee members? The committee members of the provincial CPM were appointed by the Governor of Taiwan. The provincial government ruled that there be an Institute for the Promotion of Mandarin in each district and city. Even the promoters of each such institute are appointed by the head of the Educational Department of the provincial government. Since both the Governor of Taiwan and the head of the Educational Department under him were not elected by the people but appointed by the central government, the people of Taiwan have NO control over these organizations.[9]

Theoretically, the people may have their voices heard through representatives in the city, district, or provincial councils.[10] Any bill which such councils might pass, however, would be nullified if it should conflict with the decrees of the central or provincial government. Even if the legislators pass bills that do not conflict with decrees on a higher level, they may not be seriously implemented because neither promoters nor their superiors are responsible to the council representatives in the administrative hierarchy.

There is no special organization at any legislative level that systematically studies the problems of language planning or examines the social, political, cultural, and educational implications of the government's policy of spreading Mandarin. The legislators as well as the public are poorly informed of views on language planning that differ from those of the government.

[9]   It also ruled that each mayor automatically be the director of the city's Institute for the Spread of Mandarin. Though the mayors are elected by the people, the mayors have no control over personnel action, policy making, or administration of the Institute; they must follow the plan for promoting Mandarin prescribed by the provincial government. Each mayor's record in carrying out the orders of the provincial government is part of the provincial government's evaluation of his service.

   Very frequently the mayor himself does not speak Mandarin at all or can speak it only very poorly.

   Incidentally, election campaign speeches are almost invariably in the vernacular, as candidates try to woo votes from the 85 percent Taiwanese population.

[10]   Meetings of such councils are usually conducted in Taiwanese rather than Mandarin.

The fact that neither the population nor its representatives had direct control over planning explains why the original policy of unification through bilingualism in school and community was changed without any serious public deliberation.

Fact-Finding

Any planning requires a thorough knowledge of facts. With the present knowledge of various fields of linguistics and applied linguistics, one must seek findings about the following types of facts in order to propose or carry out any language planning.

1. The sociolinguistic situation of each speech community to be affected by language planning.
   a. Analysis of various types of bilingualism of Taiwanese-, Hakka-, and Mandarin-speakers.
   b. Analysis of the general ability to speak, understand, write, read and translate in each language, and the actual amount of use of the various languages in each of the language skills.
   c. Analysis of the use of writing by various groups of speakers for different types of subject matter.
2. Linguistic study of languages involved.
   a. Description of Mandarin, Taiwanese, and Hakka.
   b. Historical study of the language changes that have occurred in the past due to mutual influences.
   c. Analysis of words borrowed from Mandarin and Japanese into Hakka and Taiwanese, including the two major types of borrowings: (1) compounds pronounced according to Hakka or Taiwanese pronunciation of etymons used in the compounds, and (2) compounds of etymons pronounced according to Japanese or Mandarin.
   d. Identification of most frequently used lexical items and sentence patterns in each language.
3. Contrastive analysis between languages.
   a. Collection and analysis of errors frequently made by students.
   b. Differences and similarities of each pair of languages.
   c. Degree of difficulty of various learning items.
4. Psychological analysis of various types of language users.
   a. Attitude toward own language and other languages, toward monolinguals and bilinguals in and outside one's own speech group. Use of native, national language, other languages and various types of address on different types of occasions.
   b. The intelligence and personal traits of bilinguals and monolinguals, especially those who have not had formal education in their native language.

5. The experiences of other countries in language planning.
   a. The social, cultural, political, economical, and psychological implications of various approaches to language planning.
   b. The achievements, problems, methodology, and theories of language planning in other countries.
   c. Limitations of language planning.
      i. Limitations of man's knowledge about the economical, cultural, political, and social goals in the future.
      ii. Limitation of man's prediction about sociolinguistic changes aimed at in each alternative plan.
      iii. Limitations in man's ability and facilities to carry out a proposed plan.

With such a highly developed system of government and education in Taiwan, one would expect that a lot must have been done to implement the above points. From what I have seen so far, I may say that work on points (4) and (5) is rather scarce, work on points (2) and (3) is inadequate from modern linguistic or pedagogical points of view, and much has been done on point (1) but a good deal of such work was done rather unscientifically. There is a lack both of overall coordination of efforts and of objective study through fieldwork and using methods and theories of modern behavioral science. I have not found good documentation of the work on facts relevant to language planning.

There are two statements in an official report on the language situation of Taiwan (ROC 1948:1178), which I would like to comment on because they have some bearing on the main issue of this paper — language unification through bilingualism rather than through suppression of linguistic differences.

This report describes the vernaculars of Taiwan as inadequate for academic and cultural communication because these vernaculars stopped developing and absorbing new elements during the fifty years of Japanese rule. The writer(s) did not seem to be aware that no language can ever stop growing, especially when there is intensive contact with other cultures. There has been intensive mutual borrowing of vocabulary between Japanese and Mandarin. Most Chinese compounds which are used for modern concepts were first coined in Japan by putting together Chinese etymons which were then borrowed by the Chinese (e.g. *ching chi* 'economics', *lo chi* 'logic'). What was borrowed by the Taiwanese might not be entirely identical with what was borrowed by the Mainlanders, however, since each group might have coined its own compounds for new concepts instead of borrowing entirely from Japanese or other sources. When new words were created for new concepts existing only in China (e.g. *Chung hua Min Kuo* 'Republic of China', and *Kuo Fu* 'National Father') borrowing was a matter of a very short time since all Mandarin words are represented in Chinese characters and all Chinese characters have at least their dictionary pronunciations in Taiwanese or Hakka. As for the grammar of Taiwanese or Hakka, both are even more precise than Mandarin because Mandarin has many patterns taken in from other dialects which have not been normalized into the structures of Mandarin.

The same report also says that people in Taiwan were generally more competent in Japanese than in Taiwanese or Hakka. If this had been a scientific investigation, the report would have said that people of a certain age group in certain types of areas tend to speak more fluent Japanese than Taiwanese or Hakka. Usage of words, even function words, borrowed from Japanese into Taiwanese or Hakka speech by certain age groups is very common all over Taiwan. As I have described in the first part of this paper, incorrect interpretation of data by the Nationalists has resulted in an overestimation of the power of language planning to work and an underestimation of the universal love and respect for one's own native language. The Taiwanese did not abandon their languages easily; it can be proven that Taiwanese and Hakka are still the main means of communication in their communities, in spite of the fact that their use is banned from grade school onward. The government has tried with all its power to spread Mandarin at the expense of Taiwanese and Hakka.

Identification of Purposes

Granted that changes in people's ability in and use of languages can be planned in spite of many unknowns, one must still ask what is the purpose of such language planning.

Much has been said to justify the policy of language unification through Mandarin in order to convince people in general to support government policy. This has been necessary since language unification itself should not be the eventual goal of language planning. If language unity is a sociolinguistic goal, there should be some nonsocial linguistic goals as well. To my knowledge there has been no systematized proposal for the purposes of language unification with clear concepts about their cause–effect relations, and with the priority of each purpose well-defined. These clearly stated purposes should be the guiding principles in selecting among alternative plans and evaluating the implementation of the plan adopted.

There has been a lack of a balanced analysis of the costs of unifying the language of China compared with the benefits of having a Chinese linguistic unity. While many people see the benefits of language unification, only a few have seen that changing people's language costs a lot in many respects because it brings with it many undesired side-effects, and that linguistic unity should not be an end in itself.

Among the purposes given for the language unification of China are typically the following. In accordance with the three Nationalist People's Principles of nationalism, democracy, and livelihood, these purposes are: (1) national harmony and integration of various speech communities and patriotism so as to have a stronger nation; (2) political unity and equal opportunity in order to make democracy work better; and (3) social progress for attainment of a better livelihood for all members of the nation.

The relationships between language unity and some of these goals are seldom mentioned. For example, the existence of minority speech groups alongside a dominant group often results in discrimination in job opportunities. Differences in language require a high cost in communication efforts and stands in the way of communication and cooperation between speech groups, and, hence, slow down the rate of social progress. These goals are, in my opinion, legitimate ones since they are all desired goals of government and education in general and linguistic unity does result in these goals, other things being equal.

In addition to the above goals it should be clearly understood, however, that language planning and its results should not contradict any of the general goals of education and government. For the goals of education are, among other things, that government and education should aim at the cultivation of self-respect and self-confidence for the nation as well as for the individual, and that education should aim at healthy development of the individual's body and mind. The constitutions of the Republic of China recognize equality among various ethnic or linguistic groups within China. Since language planning and its implementation are merely one task of government and education, they should not contradict any of these goals. Even with such an understanding, the interests and well-being of such a huge number of people are so much at stake when language changes are planned that I think it proper to identify such goals as negatively-stated goals of language planning lest any language policy should result in abuses.

Identification of Long-Range Goals

The main body of language planning should include sociolinguistic goals, the strategy to achieve such goals, and non-sociolinguistic goals. While the identification of non-sociolinguistic goals (such as national harmony, political unity, etc.) is not the sole responsibility of a language planner, the identification of sociolinguistic goals should be. Since the goals of government and education, especially the priority of each of these goals, are not clearly given, a language planner usually needs to present alternative plans, with his prediction of how each educational and government goal can be achieved by each alternative. As a strategy one may set up several phases of planned sociolinguistic change, and specify the sociolinguistic goals of each phase as will be discussed under the heading of short-range goals.

What is the eventual goal of the Nationalists with regard to the question of who learns and uses what language(s) in Taiwan? The clearly agreed-upon goal is that eventually everybody should be able to use Mandarin. With regard to the eventual goal of Taiwanese and Hakka, there is no agreement. Three alternatives can be considered: (1) each of the major languages is to be used by its respective community without interference; (2) each of the major languages shall eventually become extinct; (3) no decision need be made.

On paper, the central government adopted the first position for the whole country (ROC 1948:1162–1163). In Taiwan, there is no legal status of Taiwanese and Hakka, however, and there is no clear written indication as to whether Taiwanese and Hakka are to be eventually wiped out or not.

I shall now evaluate the merits of each of the above alternatives in terms of how each helps to achieve the claimed purposes of language planning.

Two reasons have been given for the second alternative: that the final goal be the extinction of non-Mandarin tongues. These reasons, and counterarguments for each, are as follows:

1. In order to assimilate the people of Taiwan into the Mandarin people without any discriminatory features, it is said, the mere ability to use Mandarin by everyone is not enough, since language functions not only as a means of communication but also as a symbol of group identification. So long as there is language difference there is variance in group identity.

This argument can be countered as follows: though a single language group identity is very desirable, the cost of achieving it is far greater than its benefits.

Taiwanese, Hakka, and Mandarin were once one and the same language. They are different today because each speech group has developed geographical, cultural, and institutional differences over the past several thousand years. One might attain the goal of a single speech group without internal linguistic differences over all of China by extraordinary means, such as killing off all the adults, or by mixing up the members of each group. An extraordinary means is needed to attain such a goal because normal people usually learn a second language with features carried over from their native tongue. It is conceivable even then that each speech group might speak Mandarin with features peculiar to that group. New dialect differences would be bound to develop even if the goal should be reached temporarily, unless all extralinguistic differences were also wiped away.

Language, moreover, is not the only means of group identification. Even if human technology should so develop that linguistic differences would not develop, yet geographical, cultural, and institutional differences are themselves also features of group identity.

Monolingualism in the same language, to be sure, is not a necessary condition for political unity or national identity. The peoples of Switzerland and Singapore[11] have national harmony and political unity without language unity. Nor is language unity through monolingualism itself a sufficient condition for true unity: Nationalist and Communist Chinese both speak the same language, but they are deadly enemies. The Irish speak English, but they adamantly refuse to be part of Great Britain. Suppression of their own language is one of the unpleasant experiences with the British that the Irish will not forget.

It is not so much for a monolithic group identity as for communication that Mandarin is to be learned by the people of Taiwan or elsewhere. To advocate elimination of linguistic differences for the purpose of eliminating all non-Mandarin group identity in a country bigger than the whole of Europe shows great naïvité about the nature of language learning, of language change, and of group identity. Among the older generations in Taiwan different group identifications are made whenever these people speak Mandarin. Young people in Taiwan, moreover, are already using a Mandarin which is different from that used in Peking. By their language alone they have an identity which is different from that of young people in China.

Given that linguistic differences cannot be eliminated entirely and that there are linguistic as well as extralinguistic features that are pertinent in group identity, it is more realistic for education to play the role of enhancing people's ability to tolerate and respect human differences than to make people look down upon differences as some evil to be eliminated. Unless people are educated to accept that Taiwanese, Hakka, Cantonese, etc. are all languages of China, and monolingualism in Mandarin is not a requirement of political unity of China, the Chinese will live in a constant fear that China will soon be divided.

2. If Mandarin is to be learned by future generations of those who are now non-Mandarin speakers, it is more economical in the long run to have Mandarin learned as a native language by everyone as soon as possible. The costs for learning Mandarin as a second language can be saved once and for all.

Treated as an economic issue the above argument is valid. But elimination of the use of a language is not purely an economic issue, either for an individual or for a government. In an extraordinary situation an indi-

[11]   Race riots that took place in Singapore were symptoms of racial conflicts. It was due to the multilingual and multiracial policy, not a policy to suppress human differences, that racial conflicts have been eased off.

vidual may decide to teach Mandarin to his children as a first language purely on the basis of long-run economy. A normal adult will, however, also consider the change of language within his family as a moral and social issue as well. He will ask: do I have an obligation to maintain my father's language? If I should give up my father's language for the language of others, what else can I give up also? What principles are involved in giving up what my family has cherished for something strange to our family tradition? Will differences in language, or differences in degree of competence in Mandarin cause wider generation gaps and isolation of the old from the young and, consequently, from the new developments of our community and the world? By alienating my children from my parents do I violate my filial piety, the highest virtue of the Chinese people? Will my children be socially acceptable to their community which still speaks Taiwanese or Hakka? Even if I do shift my identification from the Taiwanese or Hakka community to the Mandarin one, can I be accepted by the latter without discrimination? Which is more desirable, to belong to both or to either of the communities? A responsible government should, by its knowledge and ability, provide unbiased guidance so that each individual can make a balanced deliberation and make the best decision from economic, moral, and social points of view.

If it is not a purely economic issue for an individual to give up his own language, it is even less a government right to make its goal the elimination of the major native language of 13,000,000 people.

Several noneconomic problems must be considered by a government thinking of eliminating Taiwanese and Hakka.

1. The cultivation of confidence in and respect for one's own community, culture, and people is an important task of a changing community which aims at modernization. This confidence and respect include a desire that one's community undergo only healthy cultural changes, that it not give up its own system blindly, nor slavishly accept any system imposed from the outside. To achieve such a confidence, a community should develop the ability to compare the new thing with the old intelligently before it abandons the latter. An old system should be abandoned when and only when it is certain that the new system is better. Unless a community is able to exercise such a judgment, its members may tend to value any cultural feature of a dominating group from inside or outside the country as superior to that of their own group. Many Nationalist leaders themselves have been able to see the importance of self-respect and self-confidence during their process of modernization. While they see standardization or unification of language as a feature for modernization, they have generally failed to see that in their efforts to persuade people to learn and use the national language, they often commit errors.

For example, individuals of local communities are not given enough chance to compare carefully whatever they are considering adopting with what they traditionally have. Localisms are generally suppressed as being backward and reactionary. The Nationalists have not emphasized the point that a local language can be abandoned only when it is no longer used by the majority — not because it is inferior to Mandarin as a symbolic system. As a result, individuals may lose confidence in and respect for the culture, tradition and people of their own community. Some national leaders may not be worried about such cultural suicide on the local level; but lack of confidence in one's own community may extend to one's own nation, too. People who are once indoctrinated to abandon their own system for that of others because of the other's prestige rather than its superiority may tend to admire all things that are used by any other nation that has higher prestige. Nationalists of course do not want cultural suicide on the national level.[12] But they should know that language loyalty is the most important basis of cultural confidence for individuals. Once it is destroyed, cultural confidence is apt to be destroyed on the national level as well as the local level. If Taiwanese can be given up for Mandarin, why not Mandarin for English? Is not English used more widely internationally? It is noteworthy that those Mainlanders who gave up their mother tongues for Mandarin tend to either overestimate or underestimate Chinese culture, often to the extent of either fanatic glorification or desperate condemnation. The rate of brain drainage is especially high among this category of people. They tend to glorify the recent achievement of either China, but few care to return.

It is also noteworthy that those who spoke Japanese most of the time under Japanese rule now tend to speak Mandarin in Taiwan and English when they come to the United States more than they speak Taiwanese or Hakka. This shows that people do tend to seek after the language and culture of a group with more prestige once their primary language loyalty is destroyed.

Japanese tend to borrow words from cultures of greater prestige very rapidly. This seems to be a symptom of a similar trait — eagerness to adopt features having such prestige. Japan has been able to borrow rapidly from other cultures without causing too much internal disruption because her people have a strong sense of social responsibility. Those who adopt a new feature from a foreign culture make efforts to speak it to their fellow countrymen. Their fellow countrymen also make an effort to follow the change lest they should be thought lagging behind.

In a country like China, which is so big in territory and population and so burdened with the cultures of the past, to attempt a cultural change is always hard. But when it is attempted without cultivating cultural confi-

---

[12]   Symptoms of cultural suicide, which can be caused by many other factors, include opportunism among talented individuals, neurotic condemnation or glorification of one's own culture and extreme attitudes toward other cultures.

dence, group loyalty and a strong sense of social responsibility, a danger of national disruption and social confusion is added to the difficulty.

If people are taught to subordinate their own sentiments and interests to those of the nation, as they are taught in Nationalist China they do not learn to understand and work for the interests of their local community, nor do they get much experience in negotiation with other groups for the best interests of various groups. If one is not trained to understand and work for the interests of one's own community in the midst of other communities, one tends to be incapable of doing so for one's own country. The whole nation can then break down into separate groups that can be easily controlled by any powerful group that monopolizes the interpretation of national interests.

Loyalty and confidence in local community are important safeguards against the tendency for the strong to suppress the weak domestically and internationally. In order to spread Mandarin, however, the Nationalists seem to have overemphasized the following theme adapted from a Chinese proverb: since the rule is that the bigger fish swallows up the smaller fish, people should join into bigger groups and thus become the big fish which swallows rather than remain as the many small fish which are swallowed.

Japan's own success in the standardization of its language may be the envy of developing countries. However, her harsh measures in suppressing dialectal differences in Japan or in her colonies are not worth copying. Some people in Japan even committed suicide because they were put to shame when they violated the rule against using their local speech.[13] Such measures have resulted from, and have reinforced the jungle law of suppression of the weak by the strong rather than the civilized tradition of tolerance of differences and respect for the interests of one's own group and other groups. Japan's past aggression in Asia might not be purely accidental.

2. Men are blessed with the capacity to change their language according to their environment. Such an ability to change makes human progress possible. Each language is undergoing constant changes and linguistic differences are a fact of men's evolution. It is therefore totally wrong to regard Taiwanese or Hakka as a deviation from an authentic language and therefore an evil to be eliminated.

3. If the citizens of a country are equal before their law, it is hard to justify the view that the languages of that country are not equal before the same law. It is also hard to justify the fact that some parents are forbidden to teach their own language to their own children while others may, and that some cannot receive education in their own language while others can.

---

[13] Nobayashi (personal communication).

4. Since the Taiwanese people are regarded as Chinese, their language should be regarded as a Chinese language. The Nationalists took over Taiwan on the very grounds that the languages spoken by the people of Taiwan are Chinese. It would be an irony to eliminate Taiwanese languages in order to give the Taiwanese "complete" identification with China. If bilingualism in Mandarin and Taiwanese or Hakka is not enough to identify the Taiwanese as Chinese citizens, that is, if Mandarin monolingualism is the essential requirement for being a Chinese citizen, then the Taiwanese people should not be considered Chinese citizens at all.

5. There is a natural tendency for the members of a minority group to develop an inferiority complex about their own language in the midst of the majority group. If mass education is used to promote Mandarin with the final goal of eliminating Taiwanese and Hakka, it is playing the role of reinforcing such an inferiority complex among the underprivileged people. When there are human differences and group conflicts, education in a democratic society should rather play the role of emancipating people from fear, ignorance, suspicion and misunderstanding.

Identification of Short-Range Goals

The eventual status of Taiwanese and Hakka is not clearly defined by provincial government but there are three alternatives that might be considered as goals: (1) official recognition of their legal status for a clearly stated period of time, (2) immediate official denial of their legal status, or (3) no official position.

The second alternative would be justifiable if Taiwanese and Hakka speakers were too few in numbers to be granted any lawful status or if these languages were spoken primarily by newly arrived immigrants who expected to adopt the customs of the host community. Since Taiwanese and Hakka are in neither of these categories, this alternative should not be adopted.

The first alternative might be argued against on two grounds: first, if the Taiwanese and Hakka are given legal status Mandarin will never be learned, and second, the length of the transitional period during which Taiwanese and Hakka should have a legal status would be hard to determine.

The first ground might stand if Taiwan were a closed community which has resisted learning any language having a wider communication value. On the contrary, Taiwan has modern facilities for the spread of Mandarin. Its population, though not willing to give up its own language, has been quite ready psychologically to learn Mandarin for its wider communication possibilities. This readiness was a result of its experience with

Japanese, which they at first refused to learn but later found to be of benefit after they did learn it. Taiwan is a modernized society which should not risk the danger of changing too fast. Some measures are needed to slow down its cultural changes if the evils of too rapid sociolinguistic changes are to be avoided.

If a period of transition from Taiwanese and Hakka cannot be defined absolutely, it might be stated on the basis of various conditions. For example, the legal status of Taiwanese and Hakka could be recognized for seventy-five years (this is not arbitrary; it takes seventy-five years for a generation to die out) with possible consecutive seventy-five year extensions until certain sociolinguistic conditions are met and the peoples approve the denial of legal status to Taiwanese and Hakka.

There are several reasons for setting up a plan which would state unequivocable sociolinguistic goals for Mandarin, Taiwanese and Hakka at each stage. In the first place, confusion and disputes could thereby be avoided. There has been a general lack of agreement on what to do with Taiwanese, Hakka and Mandarin; such uncertainty results in suspicion and fear. The majority of Taiwanese suspect that the Mainlanders are attempting to maintain their superior position by banning Taiwanese and Hakka. The Mainlanders fear that the continued prevalence of Taiwanese is a symptom of Taiwanese nationalism which could result in persecution of the Mainlander minority.

Secondly, a concrete plan would enable efficient implementation and fair evaluation of its results. Finally, it would safeguard against undesirable side-effects of too-rapid sociolinguistic changes and abuses of language-planning through self interest.

The following are some of the possible undesirable side-effects of language planning in the event that bilingualism is not legally recognized, as it has not been in Taiwan, at least for a considerable period of time.

1. The policy of encouraging Mandarin at the expense of Taiwanese and Hakka brought incalculable advantages to both Mandarin speakers and those who learned it before others did; it also brought disadvantages to the Taiwanese and Hakka speakers which were felt in almost all aspects of their lives — economic, political, social, and educational. Many teachers and government officials lost their jobs or could not get promoted merely because of their language backgrounds. Taiwanese and Hakka children have less chance of succeeding in college and high school entrance examinations than do Mandarin children — mainly because Mandarin is the language of instruction and in such examinations. One such examination had a Mandarin composition topic written with three Chinese characters: *huo ch'e tou*. These characters mean 'locomotive' in Mandarin but 'railway station' in Taiwanese. Taiwanese parents naturally felt very bitter since this examination discriminated against their children's educational opportunities. Similar inequalities in opportunities for

jobs, in government and in schooling have naturally resulted in group conflicts.

2. Wide generation gaps are a problem common to changing societies. The problem is much worse in Taiwanese and Hakka families and communities because the parents were given their schooling in Japanese but their children are given theirs in Mandarin. Thus, sometimes, the children use a language which the older generation cannot understand. Such generation gaps would be much smaller if Taiwanese and Hakka were used in schools at least for the beginning four years, as these are languages which would be common to both parents and children. Parents could thus be of some help in both their children's homework and their application of school learning to life at home. As communication on school-related topics between generations is poor both at home and in the community, many parents' care for their own children tends to be limited to the provision of food, clothing and shelter. This is a great loss to a community, because it is the parents and not the teachers who should best be able to guide their children in their personal lives and problems. What has made things worse is the tendency for schools in Taiwan to teach too many things about the "then and there" rather that the "here and now" and its application to their daily life. Taiwan is producing new generations who are isolated from their own community, who know very little about the history, the function, the problems and the hopes, the sorrows and joys of their own people and who, instead, must learn by heart the names of territories of different dynasties and get excited over Western, Russian, and Japanese aggressions against China.

The new generation has been indoctrinated to the effect that localism and provincialism are bad, narrowminded, and backward, and constitute barriers to national unity and national modernization and progress. Even the recognition of differences is regarded as evil and intolerable. In creating high student motivation to learn Mandarin (which has no use in the community or at home), some teachers tend to discourage a real understanding and tolerance of cultural and linguistic differences among different localities; they think tolerance may encourage indifference toward or even opposition to the promotion of Mandarin and thus decrease students' drives to learn Mandarin.

3. The following psychological problems may occur among Taiwanese and Hakka children who begin to attend a school where they have to use a strange, new tongue.

Their ability to express themselves orally in public may never be developed. As has been pointed out in a UNESCO report (1953:47):

Ideas which have been formulated in one language are so difficult to express through the modes of another, that a person habitually faced with this task can readily lose his facility to express himself. A child faced with this task at an age when his powers of self-expression even in his native tongue are but incompletely developed, may possibly never achieve adequate self-expression.

A guilt complex may be developed and their self-confidence and self-respect affected when the use of their own mother tongue (a very important part of one's ego) is either forbidden or discouraged at school.

Frustration may result due to the generation gap. This gap is especially felt when parents want to check their children's progress at school and when children want help from their parents.

Mainlanders' children are psychologically no better off, even though they are privileged in many other senses. Their language privilege becomes the target of envy and resentment by the Taiwanese majority, for example. Not until recently, when Mainlanders and Taiwanese speakers began to speak the same type of Mandarin (i.e. a Taiwanese variety of Mandarin), were they accepted by their Taiwanese peers at school. An ability to use Taiwanese or Hakka is still needed for social acceptance in many Taiwanese and Hakka areas.

The older generations in Taiwanese and Hakka communities are the unhappiest of all, psychologically speaking, because of the generation gap and the lack of status of their own language. They feel left behind by the changing society and alienated from their own children. No one is unhappier than the elderly person in a Chinese community whose prestige is not respected by the younger ones.

The older Mainlanders have had similar negative psychological experiences with their children. They are actually in a worse position because, without proper facilities, they cannot pick up Taiwanese or Hakka as easily as their children do. They are very slow in regarding Taiwan as their home. It is rather embarrassing for them to claim that they want to serve the community without knowing its language.

4. Taiwan has witnessed rapid economic growth in the past two decades. This does not mean, however, that what has been done is the best among all alternatives with regard to language planning and other aspects of government. I believe that if the alternative of language unification through bilingualism is adopted, there will be more rapid economic growth and a healthier outlook in other aspects of social progress. A population that left the isolated village life on the Chinese mainland and sought adventure in the new land — a population that has been stimulated by the intermingling of new and old settlers and has had the impact of modern ideas through intensive contacts with American and Japanese peoples — such a population should have made more social progress than it has. Social progress may be deterred by language planning that neglects a proper coordination of the language of the school with the language of the community and between the languages of various speech

groups. Too great a portion of school time is spent on learning Mandarin. For children, especially, language is best learned through life rather than only in class. Less time could be spent on Mandarin if the language of school were coordinated with the language of the community. Instruction in a student's second language is not so effective as in his first language.[14] Lack of direct application of school learning to the students' community and home environment usually leads to lack of interest, of motivation, and of effectiveness in learning.

Students in Taiwan, indeed, spend too much time on books, partly because of the ineffective learning mentioned above. The exclusive use of Mandarin at school separates the school from the local community. By not teaching students to express themselves in Taiwanese or Hakka, teachers are discouraging them from contacting their own community leaders and receiving benefits from their community experiences. Any education that aims at suppression of linguistic differences tends to teach more about national events than about local matters. Students are thus ill-trained to locate and solve the problems of their own communities or to understand and serve their own people. Love, respect, and concern for their immediate environment are not cultivated along with nationally oriented interests.

A serious lack of coordination and cooperation between generations is a result of the wide generation gap described above. The young think that the old are unqualified and uninformed because they cannot even understand the official language. The old think the young know too little because they seldom take advice from their elders.

Because the medium of mass communication is mostly Mandarin, Taiwanese and Hakka monolinguals are poorly informed about happenings of the changing society. Their business tends to be limited in scale, and their ways of production slow in improvement. Farmers in isolated villages who have depended heavily upon TV for entertainment and information found themselves suddenly left behind when Taiwanese programs were drastically cut. Their inability to understand Mandarin weather forecasts has resulted in failure to take precautionary measures for their crops against bad weather.

5. The newer generations are less outspoken in public in either their native tongue or Mandarin. Through too much emphasis on learning Mandarin in addition to the memory work on Chinese characters, students have lost much of the time which could have been used to learn other subjects that would improve their creativity and critical thinking

---

[14] The principle of using vernacular language in education was stressed in UNESCO (1953:11). The difficulties in carrying out the principle of teaching in the students' vernacular language are discussed by the same writer and by Le Page (1964) also. Few of the difficulties are applicable to Taiwan, which has highly developed educational facilities and large, uniform speech communities that can financially afford bilingual education.

abilities. Thus the people tend to become a mass that blindly follows and worships its leaders, both on the local and national level.

People know too little about their own community to serve as public servants or to exercise their right to control their local government. But democracy only works when people know their own interests and their own desires as well as those of other groups, when they are prepared to compromise and tolerate differences, and when they are bound by laws in their struggle for their own interests.

On the national level, democracy is also likely to fail. If people of various local communities have insufficient training and experience in the practice of democracy on the local level, they are even less prepared for it on the national level. There, people cannot see what is going on easily, because national matters are more complex. Even if they do know the interests of their own communities and those of others, they may not be able to act for the best of all communities because they lack experience in acting similarly on a smaller scale. If people are taught to suppress their most natural group instinct — their language loyalty — they are at the same time being trained to suppress their own interests and dignity as individuals, as members of their local community, and as citizens of their country. Such suppression is euphemized by the motto which says, "Sacrifice the small ego to accomplish the big ego." The people are being prepared to follow anyone who can dictate the big ego.

Feedback

All good planning should leave some room for constant revision by checking output against both the input and the expected output. If there is good work on feedback, the practice of aiming toward monolingualism might be rectified.

Because the policy on spreading Mandarin brings so many advantages to Mainlanders and so many disadvantages to the Taiwanese people, it is to be expected that arguments such as I have presented would be raised and demands based on these arguments for a more enlightened policy would be voiced. But voices for a more rational and humane policy are heard only in private conversations.

In newspapers and radio broadcasts, however, themes such as the following are reiterated: (a) the "language unification" of Taiwan has been too slow, it is said. Taiwan should learn from Italy, where language unification was accomplished in ten years; (b) it is progressive and patriotic to use Mandarin, one is told. Many Taiwanese feel ashamed and inferior for being unable to do so. They are very enthusiastic in participating in speech contests in Mandarin as a gesture of support for the policy of promoting Mandarin; (c) the government has been considerate toward

Taiwanese, one hears, often to the extent that it is too lenient toward the use of dialects. Taiwanese people have been very thankful for the government's moderate approach on the matter of language unification.

One of few voices I have heard urging the protection of the interests of Taiwanese speakers was that of J. Bruce Jacobs, an American graduate student doing research work in rural Taiwan. In a letter (January 19, 1973) to the editor of the *Central Daily News*, a Nationalist newspaper, Jacobs pointed out that half of the population of Taiwan were farmers, most of whom do not understand Mandarin. Although one out of every three families has a TV set, farmers could not get enough information and entertainment through TV after Taiwanese programs were drastically limited, Jacobs said, and many farmers once suffered a great loss of crops which could have been saved if news and weather forecasts were also reported in Taiwanese.[15]

The lack of open opposition to the government's policy for promoting Mandarin at the expense of Taiwanese or Hakka is due, for one thing, to a general lack of scientific knowledge about language and language change. There is also a general incompetence in identifying and working for local and national interests with respect to language planning. The political, economic, social, and cultural implications of language planning are only vaguely understood. Practical aspects of language education are not fully understood. Further, there is no opposition because the traditional emphasis on the written language and classical Chinese tends to make people think that so long as their children have competence in writing, they have an equal opportunity in education, and because of an internal and external political situation, which has given rise to a phobia against any open disruption or disharmony between the Taiwanese and the Mainlanders. Language policy is one of the most touchy issues. People are afraid of raising this issue lest they be accused of causing group conflicts, a serious crime under the martial law which is still in effect in Taiwan. Promotion of Mandarin is equated to patriotism, and use of Taiwanese or Hakka is being taken as standing in the way of language unification. Advocation of study of dialects could be taken as advocation of a divided China. Finally, the government's Mandarin policy is unopposed because mass communication media are almost exclusively in the hands of Mainlanders, and because censorship has been very strict.

A lack of reliable estimate of sociolinguistic changes in the past is another cause of the failure in feedback in Taiwan. Reliance on impressions rather than on an objective investigation has characterized sources of information on sociolinguistic situations of the past and present.

Those in charge of language planning tend to exaggerate the success of the promotion of Mandarin in order to claim more credit for their own

---

[15]   Another such voice was that of Peihuo Ts'ai (1969, Introduction).

service, and to encourage people to use more Mandarin. Those in power are happy with these exaggerated reports because they serve to confirm their own impressions. They tend to have contact only with Mandarin speakers because monolinguals in Taiwanese or Hakka either live in different areas or keep quiet in the presence of Mandarin speakers. They tend to be misled in their judgments by their own wishful thinking that soon Taiwan will be peopled by only Mandarin monolinguals. Businessmen are more realistic; they support Taiwanese rather than Mandarin programs on TV or radio for their commercial advertisements.

There are also certain facts that the Nationalist government prefers not to reveal in public even though they know that these have close relationships with language planning. Unequal job and education opportunities and conflicts between groups, for example, have never been admitted to be the results of language policy.

Evaluation

I shall discuss the Nationalist government's evaluation of its own language planning mainly on the basis of its own criteria for evaluation and the relative weight put on each criterion.

To my knowledge, there is no set of criteria to evaluate how such non-sociolinguistic goals of language planning as were mentioned in the section on fact-finding are being realized. This is unfortunate because language unity itself is merely a means to some goals. Regular evaluation of the achievement of such goals as national harmony, political unity through democracy, and social progress is needed for improving language planning and planning implementation. Criteria such as the following might be considered for measuring the achievement of these goals.

1. The attitude toward the individuals, speech, and ways of life of different speech groups.

2. The frequency of contacts between individuals of different speech groups.

3. The range of subject matter in the verbal communication between generations of the same speech groups and different speech groups.

4. Equity in job and educational opportunities.

5. The proportion of individuals of different speech groups who have access to encoding and decoding various modes of exchange of ideas, including mass communication.

6. The proportion of individuals of different speech groups who participate in various types of political and social activities.

The whole official concern with evaluation of language planning and its practice in Taiwan has been skewed toward the spread of Mandarin. The number of people who can speak Mandarin, their proficiency and frequency in the use of Mandarin, the maximum use of Mandarin and the minimum use of Taiwanese or Hakka are almost the sole criteria for evaluating the achievement of language planning. A situation with 100 percent Mandarin monolinguals and zero percent Taiwanese or Hakka monolinguals would be most highly valued. One gets the impression that the spread of Mandarin has been taken as the eventual goal of language planning in itself. There is no concern with whether knowledge in Taiwanese or Hakka is a desirable thing to have or not.

If it is recognized that old Taiwanese or Hakka speakers cannot learn Mandarin easily while young Mainlanders can easily learn Taiwanese or Hakka, a bilingual ability among the latter should be highly valued to promote interspeech group harmony, integration, and cooperation.

The Nationalists' failure to evaluate the overall effect of language planning results from the fact that there is no government organization that has anything to do with such planning except the CPM. Assigned the task of spreading the use of Mandarin, the CPM has no concern or jurisdiction beyond this task.

CONCLUSION

I have defended the earlier official Nationalist position of language unification through bilingualism rather than the present practice of working toward linguistic unity through monolingualism. I discussed possible language planning alternatives. The main source of problems in Taiwan's language planning has been the misconception that the promotion of Mandarin is its sole task. My suggestions for improvement for the future of language planning in Taiwan have been implicit in my discussion. The following points summarize my main suggestions.

1. In place of, or in addition to the present CPM, a commission on language planning should be established at both the central and the provincial level and should be charged with the task of comprehensive language planning in Taiwan.

2. The legal status of the Austronesian, Taiwanese, and Hakka languages should be clarified; the interests of their speakers should be protected by law for at least a clearly defined period.

3. Taiwan should officially carry out the 1953 UNESCO recommendations for the use of vernacular languages in education. To this end, instruction in Mandarin should be delayed until students in primary school have firmly acquired the skills to express themselves in their mother tongue. Instruction in Mandarin can be introduced fairly early, however. Instruction in Taiwanese and Hakka should be continued in some way so that students can use both their native tongues and Mandarin for the discussion of all subject matters. Study should be made on such

prohibited but prevailing practices as reading textbooks in Mandarin but explaining and discussing in the students' and teachers' own mother tongue so as to improve the teaching material and methodology on all subjects including the speaking skill in the mother tongue and Mandarin.

4. The reality that a bilingual or trilingual is a more effective and desirable member of the community than a monolingual in Taiwanese, Hakka, or Mandarin should be officially recognized and education should take up responsibility for producing competent bilinguals and translators from one language to another.

5. Basic scientific knowledge of the history and structure of Mandarin, Taiwanese, and Hakka should be made available to students so that all language teachers and high school and college students may have an unbiased view toward the various vernaculars, use their own mother tongue more effectively, and learn a second language more efficiently.[16]

6. The plan of the central CPM to promote vernacular literature should be carried out. This includes: (a) instruction in folk literature at school and through mass media to help the population appreciate and create folk literature authentically; (b) instruction in a phonetic writing system of Taiwanese or Hakka (in romanization or in Chinese phonetic symbols) as is being done for Mandarin; and (c) study of Chinese characters that have been newly created or that have special usage in Taiwanese or Hakka folk literature.

The principle of a uniform writing script need not be done away with except in literature intended for faithful representation of the spoken language,[17] which in fact is merely a new style of written Chinese already emerging in Taiwan. The present colloquial style of writing is closer to various Chinese dialects than to any classical style, especially in vocabulary. A decrease of instruction in classical Chinese in favor of more instruction in Taiwanese and Hakka is justifiable because the language of the living is more important than the language of the dead, and it helps for better understanding of the latter. This innovation should make language education much more interesting and meaningful.

To sum up, I propose a comprehensive language planning that aims at integration and bilingualism in society and at school. It will bring some changes in the school system for which the population of Taiwan has sufficient financial, technological, and manpower resources. More than 85 percent of the present elementary school teachers are competent bilinguals, for example. Outside of schools it will greatly increase understanding and cooperation between different speech groups without much

---

[16] I have discussed elsewhere the relevance of degree of remoteness between the lexicons of related languages and the degree of difficulty for speakers of one language to learn the lexicon of another (1972, 1973).

[17] A writing that represents Taiwanese or Hakka faithfully needs to be discussed separately. I am for a writing combining the use of Chinese characters and a phonetic script.

cost to the government. The present colloquial style of written language will not be affected except for an increase in literary works which appeal more to the general population and use of phonetic writing to represent Taiwanese and Hakka in the elementary schools in addition to the present phonetic writing for Mandarin.

REFERENCES

CHENG, ROBERT L.
 1972   "Memorizing the pronunciation of cognates in a target language," in *Papers in linguistics in honor of A. A. Hill*. Edited by C. T. C. Tang, Jeffrey C. H. Tung and A. Y. T. Wu, 33–62.
 1973   "Second-language learner's classification of Chinese dialects and related languages," in *Gengo Kenkyu*. Tokyo: Linguistic Society of Japan.
DE FRANCIS, JOHN
 1950   *Nationalism and language reform in China*. Princeton, N.J.: Octagon.
FISHMAN, JOSHUA A., CHARLES A. FERGUSON, JYOTIRNDRA DAS GUPTA, *editors*
 1968   *Language problems of developing nations*, pp. 521ff. New York: John Wiley and Sons.
HSIEH, CHIAO-MIN
 1964   *Taiwan — Ilha Formosa, a geographic in perspective*. Taipei.
LE PAGE, R. B.
 1964   *The national language question: linguistic problems of newly independent states*. London: Oxford University Press.
ROC [Republic of China]
 1948   *Second yearbook of Chinese education*. Shanghai: Ministry of Education.
RUBIN, JOAN
 1971   "Evaluation and language planning," in *Can language be planned?* Edited by J. Rubin and B. H. Jernudd, 217–252. Honolulu: University Press of Hawaii.
TS'AI, PEIHUO
 1969   *Taiwanese-Mandarin dictionary of commonly used words*. Taipei: Chengchung Book Company.
UNESCO
 1953   The use of vernacular languages in education. Monographs on Fundamental Education 8. Paris: UNESCO.
WU, SHOU-LI
 1963   "Bibliography of studies on the vernaculars of Taiwan," in *Taipei Wenhsien*, 67–88. Taipei.

The Persistence of the Ideographic Script in the Far East: Its Competitive Values Versus the Alphabet

FOSCO MARAINI

Most of East Asia used to be an ideographic empire. Signs invented by the Chinese since the third millennium B.C., which subsequently developed into highly stylized or totally abstract and conventional graphs, reached nearly complete standardization during the Han dynasty and were used over an area which, in time, became immense. During the Ming and Ch'ing dynasties books written and printed in Peking were read not only all over China but in Korea, Japan, Vietnam, and in parts of or among some classes in Manchuria, Mongolia, Tibet, and other countries bordering upon the Chinese realm.

These signs, formally the same in the East, West, North, and South, were read in a myriad of different ways. The reader perceived the meaning through the eye, but his pronunciation was a matter of country, province, class, period, and style. A simple parallel comes at once to mind in the West in the notation of arithmetic and mathematics. A random date, say 1973, can be read as *nineteen hundred seventy-three, mille neuf-cent-soixante-treize, milleno-vecentosettantatre, neunzehnhundert-drei-und-seibzig, sen-kyuhyaku-nanajusan,* and so on, eventually running through the whole list of human languages, living and dead.

At present the ancient and impressive unity of the ideographic empire is collapsing. The Japanese have simplified some 320 characters and the Chinese have done the same but, alas, independently, acting upon a larger number of signs (some 2,300) with a much more drastic hand.[1] On the island of Formosa and in Hong Kong the old unabbreviated system still holds sway; the Koreans have substituted their native *hangul* alphabet for the ideograms and the Vietnamese started romanizing their script (the *quŏc-ngù* system) in the last century along principles which

[1]   See the booklet *Jianhuazi Zongbiao Jianzi*

ultimately go back to the works of Father Alessandro da Rodi (1615). The very name of Mao Tse-tung is now written in three different ways.[2] The ideographic area is therefore not only reduced, but fragmented. The system itself, however, is very much alive and serves the needs of nearly a billion human beings.

Many travelers now visit Japan. Upon landing at Haneda airport one notices a conspicuous array of signs in *roma-ji* (roman characters) advertising Sony tape recorders, National radios, Nikon cameras, and so on. The visitor sighs with relief; the inscrutable East is not so inscrutable after all! But let him leave the airport and proceed to the center of Tokyo or any other Japanese city and the polite romanized welcome is there no more; ideograms and *kana* signs assault him from every side. The poor foreigner not only feels linguistically isolated, but is suddenly pushed back to the humiliating status of a complete analphabet (in Japanese *monmō* 'blind to letters, to culture'). The vitality of the ideogram is unmistakable and formidable. It is also infuriating. Is it not obvious, one would like to shout, that twenty-five or thirty signs are more practical than 2,000?

In this paper I will try to examine some of the reasons why the ideogram shows such buoyant vitality in its confrontation with the alphabet or with other syllabic substitutes. I will look at the problem with the eye of the Japanologist, but this limitation, I confide, is not a serious drawback. We shall presently consider the very principles by means of which an ideogram functions, and in this case examples taken from Japanese are quite as valid as those taken from Chinese. In some ways they may be even better. Considering the ideogram from the Japanese angle, one is implicitly looking at the system in its universal aspects. After all, the single graphs were adapted from the original Chinese to a completely different language, Japanese, just as they could be adapted to write, say, Norwegian or Italian. Leibniz, it is well known, saw in these graphs the ideal elementary units of a universal language.

Many reasons are given to explain the persistence of the ideogram in the Far East. It is quite obvious that the number of homophones in Chinese and Japanese creates serious problems of transcription. In Japanese, for example, according to a medium-sized dictionary, the word *kōsei* has twenty-five different meanings.[3] The ideogram is also a unifying

[2]   毛泽东 in China, 毛沢東 in Japan, 毛澤東 in Taiwan.

[3]   In Kenkyusha's *new Japanese–English dictionary*, 1970 edition, *kosei* may mean:

extract of rice bran	(糠 精)	epigenesis	(後 成)
a fixed star	(恒 星)	unparalleled	(曠 世)
a planet	(行 星)	composition	(構 成)
a loud voice	(高 声)	aggression	(攻 勢)
justice	(公 正)	proofreading	(校 正)
revision	(更 正)	fine weather	(好 晴)

cultural factor. This may have little importance in Japan, which is racially, culturally, and linguistically homogeneous, but it is significant in China, a large country populated by people who speak a variety of dialects and languages, in some cases quite unrelated.

These are all valid arguments. But the real reason is — it would seem — quite another, and much more simple. To put it briefly: the ideogram is vastly superior to the alphabet as a visual device for conveying information.

To understand this point I propose that we observe Figure 1. Let us postulate at level (A) the undifferentiated flow of life. Conceivably one could just live in it, and find one's way about at a very elementary level, but normally symbols of some sort are necessary to isolate and analyze the complex web of things, events, and situations, and, what is more important, to communicate with other people.

The symbols we use belong to many classes. The arch-symbol, of course, is the spoken word. The vocabulary of an advanced culture contains many tens of thousands of such symbols. The spoken word, however, has one serious drawback: its utility is confined to limited human groups. Some languages (English, Russian, Chinese, French, Arabic, Spanish . . .) are spoken or understood by large sections of the human race, others (for instance, Ainu in Asia, Tlapanec in America, Zande' in Africa) by a few hundred or a few thousand people. No language is truly universal.

Gestures constitute a class of symbols less clearly defined, although quite as valid as the spoken word. Normally gestures accompany words, but in some cases (e.g. among the deaf and dumb) they may act as total substitutes. It has been observed that Trappist monks, who are supposed to pass most of their time in strict silence, have developed a sign language including over 1,300 gestures (Guiraud 1971:58).

Speech consists of symbols transmitted by means of sound; gestures are visual. A large number of visual symbols depend upon written or painted signs. Numbers and musical notations are two classes with which we are all familiar. The Western notations are not universal, but they are definitely supranational. Both are highly synthetic notations which directly suggest arithmetical, mathematical, geometric, or musical ideas and can be said, pronounced, in a variety of ways. A German mathematician may

rebirth	(更	生)	firmness	(好	勢)
public welfare	(厚	生)	aptitude	(向	情)
antibiosis	(抗	生)	porosity	(孔	性)
incarnation	(降	生)	a winze	(坑	井)
young fellows	(後	生)	hardness	(硬	性)
posterity	(後	世)	checking	(控	制)
			constancy	(恒	性)

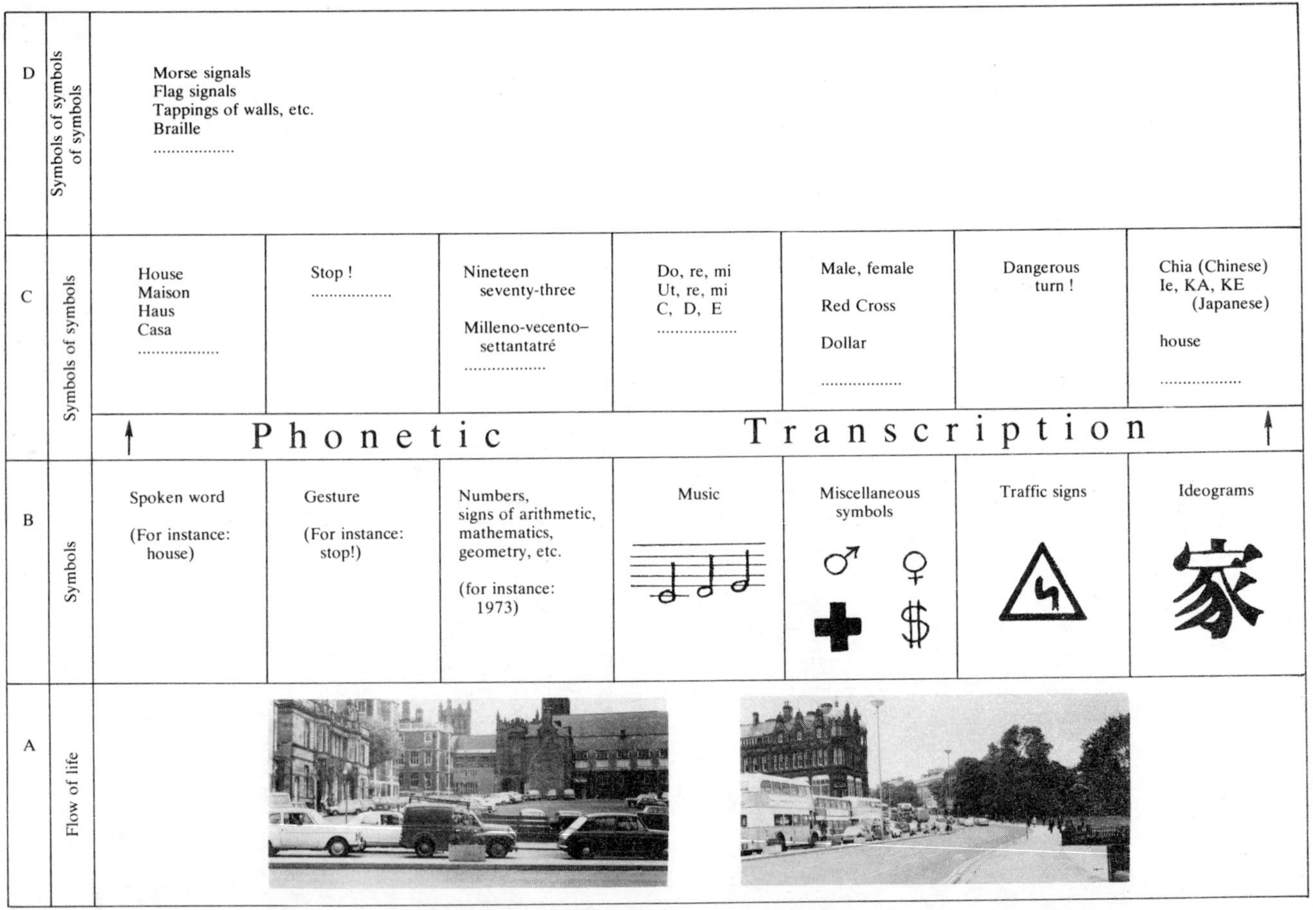

	Phonetic			Transcription			
D Symbols of symbols of symbols	Morse signals / Flag signals / Tappings of walls, etc. / Braille						
C Symbols of symbols	Spoken word (For instance: house)	Stop!	House / Maison / Haus / Casa	Nineteen seventy-three / Milleno-vecento-settantatré	Do, re, mi / Ut, re, mi / C, D, E	Male, female / Red Cross / Dollar	Dangerous turn!	Chia (Chinese) / Ie, KA, KE (Japanese) / house ....
B Symbols	Gesture (For instance: stop!)			Numbers, signs of arithmetic, mathematics, geometry, etc. (for instance: 1973)	Music	Miscellaneous symbols	Traffic signs	Ideograms
A Flow of life								

Figure 1. Visual devices for conveying information

not know how to pronounce the formula $x^2y = 4a^2(2a-y)$ if met in a French or a Russian text, but he knows exactly what it means. A Japanese musician observing the notation:

will immediately be able to hum the celebrated theme of Brahm's *First Symphony*, even if he knows no European language.

Other classes of symbols, less clearly defined, surround us on all sides. We rarely think about them or realize how important they are. These include scientific symbols (chemistry offers an impressive repository); signs such as the Red Cross, or a skull and bones to signify "poison"; national, political, and religious flags and emblems; astrological signs; military ranks and so on.

A special class, which is becoming more and more systematized and international, includes traffic signs. This is a particularly interesting group because it offers an excellent opportunity to understand the inner workings of the ideogram as a semantic unit. Traffic signs are essentially nascent Western ideograms. They are simple, direct, translinguistic. Some are authentic pictograms (children crossing a road for "school") and others are entirely abstract ("one-way traffic"); All have official "readings" which must be known when one takes an examination to obtain a driving license.

Let us imagine we are traveling at eighty or ninety miles an hour along an unknown road. Suddenly the corner of an eye catches a sign (Figure 2) announcing a dangerous turn somewhere ahead. A foot puts pressure on the brakes and the dangerous bend is negotiated in complete safety. If the same information *"Dangerous Turn,"* had been conveyed by means of a

Figure 2.   "Dangerous turn"

phonetic script, either there would have been too little time to comprehend it completely, or the attention required would have created a distraction from the act of driving. In both cases the danger of ending up in a ditch would have been multiplied by a considerable factor. Moreover, a French, Venezuelan, or Greek driver might have been handicapped by his ignorance of the English language — a problem which may seem marginal in the United States, but becomes crucial in that strange conglomeration of twenty or more major languages called Europe.

Ideograms function exactly like traffic signs. The essence of the message is transmitted with immediacy and clarity, often with a stunning punch. Reading a page of ideographic script (once the code is known) is like traveling at great speed through a maze of traffic signs of the mind. The Japanese say of their language, when transcribed into roman letters, that *pinto ga awanai* 'it is out of focus': a most appropriate comment.

Traffic signs still form a comparatively limited code, although G. Mounin (1959) says that a driver on a French national highway "reads" some 200 or 250 different signs on a journey of about 100 kilometers (60 miles). Mounin also adds that the purposes of regulating urban traffic require the use of somewhere between 800 and 1,000 different signs. Ideograms constitute a much more formidable code. A large classical Chinese dictionary produced in 1716 under the emperor K'ang Hsi contains some 40,000 characters. Wieger (1965:7) says that only about 6,000 were ever practically employed and that the remaining 34,000 are "monstrosities of no practical use." In recent times there have been many attempts to limit the number of ideograms to a definite set. The Japanese government published in 1946 a list of "ideograms for normal use" (*tōyō-kanji*) numbering 1,850. Even learning this reduced number of characters requires much effort. For a foreigner it may be a very great effort.

All symbols of register (B) in Figure 1 have this in common: they are only one step removed from the flow of life. In this sense the ideogram is not so much a parallel of the written word as of the spoken word. Spoken words are audible symbols of reality and experience; ideograms are visual symbols.

All symbols of register (B) are convertible into sound, into some form of verbal expression. At this point a further analysis may take place and the results can then be written down as phonetic script (syllabic or alphabetic). This brings us to a third (C) register. Here the spoken word *house* will appear written as "house," the gesture *stop* as "stop!", *1973* as "nineteen seventy-three," the signs used in biology ♂ ♀ will become "male" and "female," a traffic sign will be spelled as "dangerous turn," and the ideogram for *house* may be read *chia* in Chinese, *ie*, *KA* or *KE* in Japanese, but also (quite correctly) "house" in English.

Eventually a fourth (D) register can be imagined in which shorthand, Morse signals, marine flag signals, the tapping sounds made by prisoners on their walls or radiators, the Braille alphabet, and other codes find their place.

If we now look at Figure 1 again, the advantages of the ideogram as an instrument in the transmission of information become apparent. Ideograms are direct symbols of reality, of experience; they hug the world. Phonetic transcriptions are two steps removed from the flow of life; they are symbols of symbols. Morse signals, or taps on the wall, are even worse, they are symbols of symbols of symbols, three steps removed from the base.

When all this is taken into consideration, a comparison between the ideographic and the phonetic scripts show them to be roughly equal as instruments for the transmission of information; certain advantages and defects on both sides cancel each other out. The alphabet is simpler to learn but, as a symbol of symbols, it is far removed from experience and hence "opaque." It is also cumbersome because it requires a continuous coding and decoding from sound to sign and vice versa. Moreover, it is rigidly tied to the limitations of the spoken language, which may be extraordinarily narrow (Basque, Albanian, etc.). Ideograms are difficult to learn, but they transmit information directly, transparently, like instant flashes, and, with some limitations resulting from differences of grammar and syntax, may transcend the barriers of the spoken language.

The superiority of the ideogram as a means of transmitting information is confirmed by a curious development: with every year, every month, that goes by, the West is adopting more and more ideograms. The signs are not generally called ideograms (does it sound too exotic?) but they are undeniably such. The growing pace of life, the increase of international contacts, require that information be conveyed through new channels — rapid, clear, possibly beyond the narrow barriers of language. The newest types of signs turn out to be in actuality, the oldest: good, simple, archaic ideograms. An airport, a timetable, a busy city intersection, and a railway station are intensive loci of ideographic evolution. The two little figures (Figure 3a) painted on the toilet door may have seemed a bright invention to someone, although they are merely exact duplicates of ideograms (Figure 3b) with twenty or more centuries of life behind them. It may confidently be said that the distant future of mankind looks much more ideographic than alphabetic.

Figure 3.   Ideograms

Returning to the Far East, can some limited forecast be attempted? Here most readers, with sure ethnocentric instinct, will ask about the state of romanization. The phonetic transcription of Chinese and Japanese has a long history, which goes back to attempts at it made by the Jesuits since the sixteenth and seventeenth centuries. Japanese is very satisfactorily transcribed following the rules set down by Hepburn in 1885, and much less clearly by means of the *Nippon* and *Kunrei* systems: Mount Fuji becomes Mount Hudi in one and Huzi in the other, which sounds "dyust hulish" (Miller 1967:229). Unfortunately, the Japanese government has adopted the *Kunrei* system, which sometimes produces ludicrous effects, as when the Chichibu Maru (a ship named after Prince Chichibu) appeared in the ports of the world as Titibu Maru.

In China the history is much more complex, partly because the language is phonetically less amenable to an alphabetic transcription, partly because the government has actively sponsored romanization more than once. The Wade-Giles system is the oldest and the one most widely used, but it has been supplanted by *Pīnyīn*, the official system since 1958. A very accurate, but difficult, system is called *Gwoyen Romatzyh* (GR); it was invented by a group of Chinese scholars in 1926 and had official backing for some time after 1928 (see Newnham 1971:169–175).

The effects of romanization are practically nil in Japan; in China there appears to be some enthusiasm, but progress is slow. "Plus de dix ans après l'institution du *pīnyīn*, un voyageur en Chine ne s'apercevra presque pas de l'existence de ce système alphabetique" (Alleton 1970:124). Such a situation seems to be more easily explained by the inherent virtues of the ideogram than by any serious flaws in the systems of romanization. If one pauses for a moment of reflection it will appear clearly that the act of romanizing a well-developed system of ideograms is really a step backward, not a form of progress. What would we say if one fine morning we had to write "nineteen hundred and seventy-three" instead of 1973? Business, banks, and scientific laboratories would collapse immediately. We are going toward the ideogram, toward synthetic, first-degree operational symbols. Those who have them at home, who have formidable codes with centuries of tradition, naturally tend to keep them, even if the logic of a refusal to change may still appear obscure.

We have mentioned all this without considering some marginal advantages, some fringe benefits of the system. For instance, the special training it gives the eye, the way it develops accuracy of perception, the capacity of instant visual analysis. A child must learn early to distinguish signs of great complexity in which some minor graphic detail entirely alters the meaning. The subtle relationship between the ideogram as a cultural instrument and the fall of some famous ancient German optical firms under the pressure of competition from the Far East might offer subject matter for more than one fascinating doctoral thesis.

The royal road leading to a solution of a more or less permanent nature seems necessarily to pass through various steps of simplification. Much has been done in this direction. More could be achieved. The ideal solution would be for the Chinese and Japanese governments to put their brains together and manage to devise a scientific, unified system of simplifications, based on a new and rational series of radicals. All the advantages of the ideogram would be retained, avoiding most of its defects. Alphabets, especially if complicated and burdened by too many diacritical signs, isolate people and encourage narrow nationalism. Any serious effort to restore the ancient area of ideographic script in the Far East to its pristine unity should be hailed as a most felicitous event, a step broadening the cultural brotherhood of man.

REFERENCES

ALLETON, V.
   1970   *L'ecriture chinoise.* Paris: Presses Universitaires de France.
GUIRAUD, P.
   1971   *La semiologie.* Paris: Presses Universitaires de France.
KENKYUSHA
   1970   *New Japanese–English dictionary.* Tokyo: Kenkyusha.
MILLER, R. A.
   1967   *The Japanese language.* Chicago: University of Chicago Press.
MOUNIN, G.
   1959   *Les systemes de communication non-linguistiques.* BSLP.LIV
NEWNHAM, R.
   1971   *About Chinese.* Harmondsworth: Penguin.
WIEGER, L.
   1965   *Chinese characters, their origin, etymology, history, classification and signification.* New York: Dover.
Jianhuazi Zongbiao Jianzi
   1971   *Jianhuazi Zongbiao Jianzi.* Tokyo: Sankeisha.

Prestige Speech Styles: The Imposed Norm and Inherent Value Hypotheses

HOWARD GILES, RICHARD BOURHIS and ANN DAVIES

A number of studies in the United States have found that listeners can identify a speaker's social class from his speech patterns (Putnam and O'Hern 1955; Harms 1961, 1963; Shuy, Baratz and Wolfram 1969). For instance, Ellis (1967) found that a correlation of $+0.80$ existed between listeners' judgments of perceived status and speakers' objective status. Labov (1966) has presented evidence which suggests that the ability to identify prestigious speech forms correctly is dependent on the listeners' social status and linguistic usage also. Moreover, speaking the "standard" or prestigious form allows the individual to be stereotyped favorably along many personality dimensions, particularly those of perceived competence relative to nonstandard speakers of the language (Buck 1968; Tucker and Lambert 1969; Williams 1970).

In French Canada, speakers of French are also stereotyped differently depending on the particular accent they adopt (Lambert, Hodgson, Gardner and Fillenbaum, 1960). More recently, d'Anglejan and Tucker (1973) found that European French-speakers were perceived by French Canadians as more intelligent, likeable and ambitious (but less tough) than speakers of middle- and working-class Canadian French. Also, Bourhis, Giles and Lambert (1975) have found that a French-Canadian-speaker is perceived as more intelligent and educated when he shifts from a Canadian to a more European style of French in the presence of a Continental-French-speaker.

In Britain, it has been found that listeners were able to assign various accents along continua of pleasantness and prestige and that the "standard" accent, Received Pronunciation (RP), occupied the superior position on both these dimensions (Giles 1970). Indeed, in another study (Giles 1972), it was shown that the broader (or less standard) a regional accent became the less status and pleasantness it was afforded even by listeners from the region concerned. Furthermore, speakers of RP have been found to be stereotyped as more competent (although less socially attractive) than speakers of nonstandard, regional accents (Strongman and Woosley 1967; Cheyne 1970; Giles 1971a).

It is, to a certain extent, current fashion in these three cultures to propose that nonstandard speakers should be taught to speak the prestige dialect[1] in order that they may reap the benefits of speaking the culturally-valued code. However, there are two schools of thought concerning nonstandard usage (see Williams 1971), namely the DEFICIT and DIFFERENCE arguments. DEFICIT theorists would claim in very broad terms that nonstandard speech is inferior and underdeveloped along a number of linguistic dimensions while the DIFFERENCE theorists would hold no such value judgment but simply suggest that nonstandard dialects are normal, well-developed codes having their own distinct structural rules. It is well-known that lower-class children do not perform so well in school as do middle-class children. Advocates of the deficiency position (e.g. Deutsch 1967; Hunt 1964) suggest that this is because the lower-class child's nonstandard language is not linguistically sophisticated enough to cope with traditional educational training. The difference theorists (e.g. Baratz 1970; Steward 1970) argue on the other hand that

the lowerclass child speaks a complex and subtle form of English that may not be used or understood by his middleclass teacher who speaks a standard form of English. These discrepancies often result in a lack of mutual understanding between the lowerclass child and his teacher. Because of this communication gap, the child does poorly in school (Bruck and Tucker 1972).

Both schools do nevertheless propose that nonstandard speakers should extend their speech repertoire to include the prestigious speech style although their rationale and emphases are of course somewhat different. Yet little explicit attention has been drawn to esthetic considerations of nonstandard speech by these schools, especially at the phonological levels. It could be argued that one might view the origins of nonstandard speech from two quite different perspectives which may be related to the DEFICIT and DIFFERENCE arguments; these will be termed the IMPOSED NORM and INHERENT VALUE hypotheses. Let us deal with them in turn.

In most cultural contexts the users of the prestigious code of a language are to a large extent the most powerful social group. The essence of our problem may be stated in terms of whether this powerful group adopted their particular speech patterns in a more or less arbitrary manner or whether they consciously (or unconsciously) selected the universally more esthetic code. The IMPOSED NORM hypothesis would claim that the

[1] For discussions of such language extension programs in the United States, see Bereiter and Englemann (1966), in Quebec see Chantefort (1970) and in Britain see Giles (1971b). For disadvantages of such programs, see Sledd (1969).

former would be the case and that the code they speak attained its status through the prestige of its users. Indeed, Spencer (1958) has also said that the prestige of a standard pronunciation "is due directly and solely to the prestige of the class or group which possesses it." In this sense then a culture has a speech norm imposed within it which often forces nonstandard speakers to accept an inferior status and often to believe that their style of speaking is relatively less pleasing to the ear. The IMPOSED NORM hypothesis would say that the elevation of a code to the prestige position is likely to have been a cultural and historical accident. For instance, Malmstrom has claimed (1967) that the RP accent in Britain won its prestige over the other regional varieties because it was the speech style characteristic of the commercial and political center (London) in medieval times. And so, had the Court in the Middle Ages arisen in Yorkshire, BBC newcasters would now be relating the day's events in a Northern brogue. It could be argued that the DIFFERENCE theorists' position would implicitly reflect the notion that accents and dialects are in fact equally pleasing to the ear, and that subjective judgments differentially distinguishing accents on esthetic and prestige grounds are based purely on normative factors in the particular culture concerned.

The INHERENT VALUE hypothesis on the other hand would claim that the adoption of the standard accent is based on esthetic considerations. For instance, Wyld (1934), discussing British accent usage, said:

. . . if it were possible to compare systematically every vowel sound in Received Standard with the corresponding sound in a number of provincial and other dialects, assuming that the comparison could be made, as is only fair, between speakers who possessed equal qualities of voice, and the knowledge how to use it, I believe no unbiased listener would hesitate in preferring RS as the most pleasing and sonorous form, and the best suited to be the medium of poetry and oratory.

Indeed, if it was somehow objectively found to be the case that the socially-accepted mode of speaking in a given context was in fact the most pleasing way of pronouncing that language to most people, then it may be that standard accents across cultures could have phonological features in common. Similarly, it could be argued that nonstandard accents of North America and Europe may have certain phonological features in common also, such as perhaps nasality or perceived harshness. Certainly, it could be proposed that the adherence to an INHERENT VALUE hypothesis would be in line with the DEFICIT theorists' position concerning standard–nonstandard usage when they suppose there is only one "correct" manner of speaking a given language.

One way of empirically testing which is the more tenable hypothesis may be to have listeners evaluate standard and nonstandard accents of a language they do not understand. Indeed, such accents would not provide listeners directly with cues to speakers' social group membership as they would to native users of the language. If listeners could differentiate speech styles in terms of perceived pleasantness and status in the same direction as speakers of this language, then this would, to a certain extent, substantiate the INHERENT VALUE hypothesis. However, if non-native listeners could not differentiate the speech styles along these dimensions then the data would be in line with the IMPOSED NORM hypothesis. The present study adopted this technique with Welsh subjects (Ss) who were asked to make such judgments of various styles of speech heard in Quebec — European French (EF), educated Canadian French (FC) and working-class French Canadian (FCJ). Earlier, it was stated that French Canadians categorize speakers of French in terms of personality quite differently depending on the dialect they use (d'Anglejan and Tucker 1973). The present study was also designed to determine whether Welsh Ss, who had no knowledge of French, would attribute personality in the same way to speakers of those French styles as do French Canadians themselves.

METHOD

Subjects

The listener-subjects for this study were thirty-five Welshmen (eleven male and twenty-four female) who were learning Welsh as a second language at evening classes in South Wales. They could be regarded as a predominantly middle-class sample between the ages of 22 and 56 years (mean age — 36 years). Their self-reported French skills on 9-point rating scales were 1.6 and 1.2 for comprehension and speaking respectively (a score of 1 indicated absolutely no knowledge of French whatsoever).

Materials

The materials consisted of a stimulus tape and a subject questionnaire. The tape comprised six target French voices and six "filler" voices. The French voices were those edited from a previous study by Bourhis, Giles and Lambert (1972). These voices were produced by the same tridialectal speaker using the "matched-guise" technique.[2] She produced two passages of thirty seconds each in the three guises of EF, FC and FCJ so that the accent stimuli were controlled for content and paralinguistic features.

---

[2]   For a review of some work using this technique, see Lambert (1967) and Giles and Powesland (1975).

The taped filler voices consisted of six different females speaking in a native language other than French for thirty seconds on a standard topic. These filler voices were introduced into the stimulus tape so as to deter Ss from recognizing the fact that the same female speaker was producing all the French versions. The order of presentation of these voices was as follows:
(1) Spanish, (2) FC(a), (3) Gijrati, (4) EF(a), (5) Urdu, (6) FCJ(a), (7) Italian, (8) FC(b), (9) Persian, (10) FCJ(b), (11) German, (12) EF(b).

The subject-questionnaire consisted of a booklet requiring listeners to name the language and rate the pleasantness and prestige of each of the twelve stimulus voices on 9-point rating scales. In addition, Ss were also required to evaluate speakers on the traits of intelligence, likeability, ambition and toughness. These were the four traits that d'Anglejan and Tucker (1973) found salient for French Canadian Ss in evaluating speakers in Quebec. At the end of this questionnaire, demographic details including Ss' self-rated French skills were asked for.

Procedure

The stimulus tape was group-administered to Ss by means of a female experimenter. Ss were told that they would hear a series of different languages on tape and they were informed that the study was concerned with determining whether people could identify these languages, attribute labels of pleasantness and prestige to the voices and personality characteristics to the speaker. After Ss had heard a voice, they were instructed to name the language spoken and rate the voice and speaker on the six scales provided in the questionnaire. The listeners appeared to treat the procedure as a kind of novel game and reported enjoying it as such. Having rated the last speaker, Ss were asked to fill in their demographic details including a rating of their ability to speak and understand French on 9-point rating scales.

RESULTS AND DISCUSSION

Each subject was allocated a single score on each of the six evaluative dimensions for the EF, FC and FCJ voices by taking mean ratings for each accent variant. One-way analyses of variance were computed on these scales, and no significant trend emerged on any ($F_s < 1.00$). Only two and three Ss respectively did not identify at least one of the FCJ and EF accents as representing the French language, whereas somewhat surprisingly eleven Ss did not recognize FC as French. The reason why this accent rather than FCJ should not be so readily identified is totally unclear.[3]

The results would appear to support the IMPOSED NORM hypothesis in the sense that French accents having highly distinctive and salient social meaning to French Canadians in Quebec have no such meaning to non-users outside that culture. Naturally, before any general statement regarding the origins of nonstandard usage universally can be made, this type of study needs to be replicated with many different languages in many different cultural contexts and preferably using languages that listeners cannot identify at all. Nevertheless, this preliminary data does at least suggest that an INHERENT VALUE hypothesis about French language usage in Quebec may be untenable. However, future research may point to the fact that for certain languages the INHERENT VALUE hypothesis may hold whilst for others the IMPOSED NORM hypothesis may be best suited.

It could also be suggested that the second-language-learner undergoes a kind of "developmental" process of attributing pleasantness and status to accents within the new language he is learning. More often than not, we learn a foreign language via the medium of the prestige form and as we become more familiar with this speech style it could be suggested that other varieties of this language may be perceived as "substandard." A preliminary amount of support for this process comes from a pilot study conducted at Cardiff with us and Neil Hagues using the above stimulus material.[4] It was found that student Ss who had some knowledge of French (self-rated knowledge of French on the 9-point scale of 3.96; $n = 13$) did, unlike our naive Ss, significantly attribute status and pleasantness in the same direction as would French Canadians. And so, studies may also be designed to investigate the second-language-learning process developmentally and determine if attributions of status and pleasantness do evolve along the lines indicated, and if they do, determine at what point in the learning of this new language they begin to emerge.

If, eventually, enough data accrues which supports the IMPOSED VALUE hypothesis across various languages then such evidence should support the more general ideas of the difference theorists in suggesting that nonstandard dialects are different but in no sense inferior forms of a language. Such a finding could provide nonstandard dialect users with a more positive self-image and identity and a feeling that their mode of communication is undeniably as pleasant and as rich as the more prestigious variety.

---

[3]   In subsequent statistical treatment of the data, it was found that language recognition did not affect evaluative trends.
[4]   This pilot data has been reported elsewhere (Giles and Bourhis 1973).

REFERENCES

BARATZ, J.
1970   "Teaching reading in an urban Negro school system," in *Language and poverty*. Edited by F. Williams, 11–24. Chicago: Markham.
BEREITER, C., S. ENGLEMANN
1966   *Teaching disadvantaged children in the preschool*. Englewood Cliffs, N.J.: Prentice Hall.
BOURHIS, R., H. GILES, W. E. LAMBERT
1975   Social consequences of accommodating one's style of speech: a cross-national investigation. *International Journal of the Sociology of Language* 6:55–71.
BRUCK, M., R. TUCKER
1972   Lower class language: deficient or different? Mimeographed Report. Montreal: McGill University.
BUCK, J. E.
1968   The effects of Negro and White dialectal variations upon attitudes of college students. *Speech Monographs* 35, 181–186.
CHANTEFORT, R.
1970   *Diglossie au Quebec: Limites et tendances actuelles*. Québec: Les Presses de l'Université Laval.
CHEYNE, W.
1970   Stereotyped reactions to speakers with Scottish and English regional accents. *British Journal of Social and Clinical Psychology* 9:77–79.
D'ANGLEJAN, A., R. TUCKER
1973   "Sociolinguistic correlates of speech style in Quebec," in *Language attitudes: current trends and prospects*. Edited by R. Shuy and R. Fafold, 1–27. Washington, D.C.: Georgetown University Press.
DEUTSCH, M. *et al.*
1967   *The disadvantaged child*. New York: Basic Books.
ELLIS, D. S.
1967   Speech and social status in America. *Social Forces* 45:431–437.
GILES, H.
1970   Evaluative reactions to accents. *Educational Review* 22:211–227.
1971a   Patterns of evaluation in reactions to RP, South Welsh and Somerset accented speech. *British Journal of Social and Clinical Psychology* 10:280–281.
1971b   Teachers' attitudes towards accent usage and change. *Educational Review* 24:11–25.
1972   The effect of stimulus mildness–broadness in the evaluation of accents. *Language and Speech* 15:262–269.
GILES, H., R. BOURHIS
1973   Dialect perception revisited. *Quarterly Journal of Speech* 59:337–342.
GILES, H., P. F. POWESLAND
1975   *Speech style and social evaluation characteristics*. London: Academic Press.
HARMS, L. S.
1961   Listener judgments of status cues in speech. *Quarterly Journal of Speech* 47:164–168.
1963   Status cues in speech: extra-race and extra-region identification. *Lingua* 12:300–306.

HUNT, J. McV.
1964   The psychological basis for using pre-school enrichment as an antidote for cultural deprivation. *Merrill-Palmer Quarterly* 10:209–243.

LABOV, W.
1966   *The social stratification of English in New York City.* Washington, D.C.: Center for Applied Linguistics.

LAMBERT, W. E.
1967   The social psychology of bilingualism. *Journal of Social Issues* 23:91–109.

LAMBERT, W. E., R. C. HODGSON, R. C. GARDNER, S. FILLENBAUM
1960   Evaluational reactions to spoken languages. *Journal of Abnormal and Social Psychology* 60:44–51.

MALMSTROM, J.
1967   Dialects. *Florida FL Reporter* 5.

PUTNAM, G. W., E. M. O'HERN
1955   The status significance of an isolated Urban dialect. *Language* 31: diss. suppl. no. 53.

SHUY, R. W., J. C. BARATZ, W. A. WOLFRAM
1969   *Sociolinguistic factors in speech identification.* National Institute of Mental Health Research Project MH-15048-01. Washington, D.C.: Center for Applied Linguistics.

SLEDD, J.
1969   Bidialectalism: the linguistics of white supremacy. *College English* 58: 1307–1316.

SPENCER, J.
1958   RP — some problems of interpretation. *Lingua* 7:7–29.

STEWART, W. A.
1970   "Toward a history of American Negro dialect," in *Language and poverty.* Edited by F. Williams. 351–379. Chicago: Markham.

STRONGMAN, K., J. WOOSLEY
1967   Stereotyped reactions to regional accents. *British Journal of Social and Clinical Psychology* 6:164–167.

TUCKER, R., W. E. LAMBERT
1969   White and Negro listeners' reactions to various American-English dialects. *Social Forces* 47:463–468.

WILLIAMS, F.
1970   The psychological correlates of speech characteristics: on sounding disadvantaged. *Journal of speech and hearing research* 13:472–488.

WILLIAMS, F.
1971   "Some preliminaries and prospects," in *Language and poverty.* Edited by F. Williams, 1–10. Chicago: Markham.

WYLD, H. C.
1934   The best English — A claim for the superiority of Received Standard English. *S.P.E. Tract* 39.

Attitudes Toward the Adoption of an International Language

ELLEN-MARIE SILVERMAN and FRANKLIN H. SILVERMAN

> And the whole earth was of one language, and of one speech. And it came to pass, as they journeyed from the east, that they found a plain in the land of Shinar; and they dwelt there. And they said one to another, "Go to, let us make brick, and burn them thoroughly." And they had brick for stone, and slime had they for mortar. And they said, "Go to, let us build us a city and a tower, whose top may reach unto heaven; and let us make us a name, lest we be scattered abroad upon the face of the whole earth." And the Lord came down to see the city and the tower, which the children of men builded. And the Lord said, "Behold, the people is one, and they have all one language; and this they begin to do: and now nothing will be restrained from them, which they have imagined to do. Go to, let us go down, and there confound their language, that they may not understand one another's speech." So the Lord scattered them abroad from thence upon the face of all the earth: and they left off to build the city. Therefore is the name of it called Babel; because the Lord did there confound the language of all the earth: and from thence did the Lord scatter them abroad upon the face of all the earth.
>
> GENESIS 11:1–9.

> What would happen if all the children in the world learned another language along with their own? Not just ANOTHER language, but the SAME language?
>
> MARIO PEI

There are over 2,700 languages in current use, no one of which can be understood by more than 25 percent of the earth's population (Pei 1958). Since biblical times, it appears to have been fairly well accepted that man has been handicapped by his lack of a common, universal language. The lack of such a language obviously both impedes communication and influences the extent to which one can utilize cogitatively the observations and ideas of others.

Many proposals have been offered during the past 2,000 years for solving the international language problem (Pei 1958:63–175). It has been suggested that various national languages, including English, be adopted for international communication. In addition, a number of "artificial" languages have been formulated specifically for this purpose including Volapük, Esperanto, Ido, and Interlingua. A sufficiently large scholarly literature has been concerned with this problem for it to be designated a subdiscipline of linguistics, i.e. interlinguistics.

What are the current prospects for the international language movement? How aware are people of the movement? How strongly do they feel the need for an international language? How possible do they feel it would be for an international language to be adopted? While there has been considerable speculation concerning the answers to these questions, almost no relevant empirical data have been reported. The only relevant studies that are cited in the contemporary international language literature (judging by an examination of the articles that have been published in the *International Language Reporter*) are two Gallup Institute of Public Opinion Polls (1950 and 1961) and a poll conducted in Japan in 1959 by the International Language Institute of Tokyo. According to Pei (1969:5):

In 1950 the Gallup Institute of Public Opinion conducted a poll in the United States, Canada, Norway, the Netherlands, and Finland. Two questions were asked. The first was: "It has been suggested that every school child in every country should be required to learn one other language besides his own, which would be understood in all countries. Do you think this is a good idea or a poor idea?" The response was about 76 percent "good idea" in all five countries, with 15 percent opposed and 9 percent undecided.

The poll, repeated in 1961 in the United States alone, indicated that the majority in favor of the proposition had grown by eight percentage points to 84 percent, while the opposition and the undecided group had correspondingly dwindled.

A poll conducted in Japan in 1959 by the International Language Institute of Tokyo, a Japanese society interested in promoting a world language for international use, was conducted among some 400 foreign tourists in Japan and Japanese students at the University of Tokyo. Three out of four replied that they favored a world tongue.

Our primary objective in this paper is to stimulate research on these questions. We describe several tasks for obtaining the data needed to answer them. In addition, tentative answers to the questions are presented that were based upon responses of university students in the United States to the tasks.

AWARENESS OF THE INTERNATIONAL LANGUAGE MOVEMENT

The current prospects for the international language movement obviously are influenced by the number of persons who are aware that such a movement exists. In particular, the prospects for the movement would be expected to be influenced by how aware college and university students are of it, since it is from this group that leaders who will have the power to advance the objectives of the movement are most likely to come.

To begin to assess the level of awareness of university students in the United States of the international language movement, we attempted to determine how many would recognize that Esperanto is an international language (Silverman 1969, 1972). In this research we assumed that an individual who did not recognize "Esperanto" would be unlikely to be even minimally aware of the movement. Esperanto is generally acknowledged to be the best known of the constructed languages on the basis of the number of persons who can speak it, the frequency with which it is mentioned in "popular" magazine articles on international language, and the number of books and periodicals published in it.

Each of thirty-four students who were enrolled in an introductory speech course at the University of Illinois at Urbana-Champaign was asked by their instructor to perform the following task: "Please define the word 'Esperanto' [the instructor wrote Esperanto on the blackboard] on the card that was handed to you. If you are uncertain about the meaning of the word make a guess." Of the thirty-four students in the course, only four (12 percent) indicated that Esperanto was a language. The following are the four "correct" definitions:

"Esperanto is the name of a universal language that was hoped to ease communications between different nationalities."

"Esperanto: An artificial language which combines roots common to the Indo-European languages."

"Esperanto — universal language that was synthesized out of others; not too successful or too well-known or adapted."

"Esperanto: An international language — thought to combine all the major languages of the world into one — interlingua."

The most frequent associations noted in the "incorrect" definitions were (1) a Spanish word and (2) a technical speech term.

While we did not expect these students to know very much about Esperanto, we did expect the majority to at least know that it is a language. We, therefore, decided to duplicate the study using a larger sample of students and a more direct wording of the task statement. Professor Lynn Minor of Eastern Illinois University collaborated with us in the collection of the data.

A total of 427 students enrolled in speech courses at Eastern Illinois University and the University of Illinois at Urbana-Champaign were asked to complete the following sentence: "The word Esperanto refers to . . ." The sentence was printed on I.B.M. cards. Only nineteen of the 427 students (4.4 percent) indicated in their response that Esperanto is a language. As in the earlier survey, the most frequent associations noted in the "incorrect" responses were (1) a Spanish word and (2) a technical speech term. The finding of this survey, therefore, duplicates that of the earlier one.

While the findings of these surveys obviously must be interpreted with considerable caution since students at only two universities were sampled, they do suggest that only a small proportion of the current university student population in the United States is aware of the existence of the international language movement. Since this is the population from which the future leaders of the United States are most likely to come, it seems crucial that they be made aware of the movement if it is to achieve at least some of its objectives during the coming generation.

If it is generally true that only a small proportion of most populations knows of the existence of such international languages as Esperanto, this could partially explain why these languages have had as little impact as they apparently have. Obviously, the more people who know of the existence of such a language, the more people there will be who are likely to become interested in it.

ANTICIPATED REWARDS FROM KNOWING AN INTERNATIONAL LANGUAGE

The adoption of an international language would probably require a tremendous investment of time, energy, and money. Human beings usually are not willing to invest unless they feel their investment will result in a "positive" regard. That is, they are usually not willing to invest unless they EXPECT, or anticipate, that their investment will have a positive effect upon their lives. Whether or not their expectation is realistic, it will influence their behavior (Johnson 1946).

What effect(s) do people expect the knowledge of an international language to have upon their lives? One approach to answering this question would be through the analysis of responses to the following: "If you woke up tomorrow morning and found that you knew a language in addition to the ones you previously knew that would permit you to communicate both orally and in writing with ALL people in ALL countries of the world (i.e. an international language), what immediate and long-term effects do you feel knowing this language would have upon your life?" The types of effects mentioned in the responses would provide some insight into how supportive of an international language respondents could be expected to be. The more positive effect they would expect knowing such a language to have upon their lives, the more supportive they probably would tend to be of it.

In order to begin to determine the degree of effect university students in the United States would expect knowledge of an international language to have upon their lives, we obtained responses to the hypothetical question from forty Marquette University students (twenty-three males and seventeen females) who, with a few exceptions, were majoring in applied behavioral sciences which place considerable emphasis upon communication including journalism, radio and television broadcasting, business administration, political science, interpersonal communication, theater and speech pathology. We assumed if knowing an international language would have positive effects on the lives of any group of students, it would be on the members of such a group.

The vast majority of the students (90 percent) indicated in their responses they would expect knowing an international language to have immediate and/or long-term positive effects upon their lives. None indicated that knowing such a language would have a negative effect upon his life. The students varied considerably with respect to the amount of effect they indicated knowing an international language would have upon their lives. The following responses are representative:

a. "It's hard to tell at this time. If I traveled to other countries at any time in my life it would definitely be an advantage, but for right now I don't see my life as being drastically affected."

b. ". . . would be excited because I could communicate with everyone to get my thoughts across."

c. "I think that I would travel to get to know different people if I could afford to. I would like to know about different people and how they think and why. I think that being able to speak an international language would make life more interesting."

d. "A greater understanding of people all over the world. If you cannot communicate with someone, you cannot learn to understand him."

e. "I would transfer to Georgetown University and become a diplomat."

f. "Nothing, unless you were in a position to use it. If you were a diplomat, it would be a great asset but as for me, I don't think it would have much effect on me at all."

g. "Make it easier to get a job."

h. "It would provide me with common symbols with which I could attempt to communicate to learn other cultures and life styles which would enable me to be more understanding of people in these cultures."

i. "Probably, I would expand my career to include other countries in my dealings."

j. "I would feel that I had reached an optimum in my capabilities to speak. However, until I learned about the culture and the people, I would feel I knew very little . . . I would feel that my life was just beginning and I was beginning to learn about life all over again. New experiences would abound."

The findings of this study, as the previous one, must be interpreted with considerable caution because of the limited, non-random nature of the sample. However, from the responses it appears likely that a substantial number of university students in the United States would expect knowing an international language to have some positive effect upon their lives and, therefore, probably would react favorably to legislation for the adoption of such a language. The finding of this study, therefore, is consistent with those of the Gallup Institute of Public Opinion polls and the International Language Institute of Tokyo poll cited previously.

REACTIONS TO PEI'S PROPOSAL

Professor Mario Pei of Columbia University probably has written more about the international language movement than any of his contemporaries in the United States. (A bibliography of his writings since 1943 concerned with the movement was published in the *International Language Reporter* for the Third Quarter of 1969.) Pei has proposed in a number of his writings (including his book, *One language for the world*, and popular articles in such magazines as the *New York Times Magazine, Holiday*, and the *Saturday Review*) that all children in all countries be raised bilingually with their own national language and a single international language besides. Since his proposal for the adoption of an international language is probably the one best known in the United States, we felt it would be of some interest to determine how people in the U.S. react to it. We therefore constructed an attitude measurement device — a semantic differential (Osgood et al. 1957) — that could be used for this purpose (see Figure 1).

The semantic differential technique for the measurement of "meaning" was developed by Professor Charles Osgood and his associates at the University of Illinois in the 1940s. With this approach subjects are provided with a set of seven-step bipolar scales and are instructed to indicate for each scale the direction and intensity of its association with the stimulus being rated. Analyses of the subjects' ratings can provide information concerning the overall "tone" (e.g. acceptance or rejection) of their reactions to the stimulus as well as help to identify factors which may have influenced their reactions.

The semantic differential constructed to assess reactions to Pei's proposal consists of thirty-eight scales. Most of these scales were selected from a list that had been compiled from the adjectives included in Roget's *Thesaurus*, 1941 edition (Osgood et al. 1957:53–61). Space was provided on the form for subjects to write in additional scales they felt might be descriptive of their reactions to the proposal. The scales were reproduced on University of Illinois *Semantic Differential Digitek Answer Sheets* to facilitate computer processing of the ratings.

AGE: SEX: OCCUPATION:
WHAT LANGUAGES CAN YOU SPEAK?
HAVE YOU EVER VISITED A COUNTRY IN WHICH YOU COULDN'T SPEAK AND/OR UNDERSTAND THE LANGUAGE?
HAVING ALL CHILDREN IN ALL COUNTRIES RAISED BILINGUALLY WITH THEIR OWN NATIONAL LANGUAGE AND A SINGLE INTERNATIONAL LANGUAGE BESIDES

meaningful	|| || || || ||	meaningless
timely	|| || || || ||	untimely
foolish	|| || || || ||	wise
impossible	|| || || || ||	possible
competitive	|| || || || ||	cooperative
disreputable	|| || || || ||	reputable
not subversive	|| || || || ||	subversive
warranted	|| || || || ||	unwarranted
capitalistic	|| || || || ||	communistic
religious idea	|| || || || ||	secular idea
idealistic	|| || || || ||	realistic
pleasurable	|| || || || ||	painful
complex	|| || || || ||	simple
kind	|| || || || ||	cruel
eastern idea	|| || || || ||	western idea
important	|| || || || ||	unimportant
dangerous	|| || || || ||	safe
probable	|| || || || ||	improbable
not naive	|| || || || ||	naive
difficult	|| || || || ||	easy
skeptical	|| || || || ||	not skeptical
disadvantageous	|| || || || ||	advantageous
accept idea	|| || || || ||	reject idea
irrational	|| || || || ||	rational
	|| || || || ||	
pessimistic	|| || || || ||	optimistic
unselfish	|| || || || ||	selfish
regressive	|| || || || ||	progressive
relevant	|| || || || ||	irrelevant
far	|| || || || ||	near
insane	|| || || || ||	sane
practical	|| || || || ||	impractical
warlike	|| || || || ||	peaceable
interesting	|| || || || ||	boring
good idea	|| || || || ||	bad idea
ambiguous	|| || || || ||	unambiguous
useful	|| || || || ||	useless
necessary	|| || || || ||	unnecessary
undesirable	|| || || || ||	desirable

Write any other scales below that would be descriptive of your attitude and mark them.

```
|| || || || ||
|| || || || ||
|| || || || ||
|| || || || ||
|| || || || ||
|| || || || ||
|| || || || ||
|| || || || ||
|| || || || ||
```

USE PENCIL ONLY — MARK ONLY ONE RESPONSE PER ITEM — ERASE CLEANLY

Figure 1. Semantic differential used to assess reactions to Pei's proposal

The semantic differential was administered to sixty students (thirty-one males and twenty-nine females) who were enrolled in an introductory speech course at Marquette University. Most reacted favorably to Pei's proposal. Specifically 75 percent or more indicated by their ratings they considered his proposal meaningful, wise, reputable, important, advantageous, optimistic, progressive, relevant, sane, practical, peaceable, interesting, a good idea, useful, and desirable. In addition, the majority of the subjects indicated that the proposal was timely, possible, cooperative, warranted, idealistic, pleasurable, kind, safe, not naive, rational, unselfish and necessary. Almost all the remaining scales were rated by the majority of subjects as neutral with regard to Pei's proposal. Based upon these responses, it seems likely that many university students in the United States would be supportive of an attempt to implement Pei's proposal.

CONCLUSION

From the findings of the three studies reported in this paper it appears reasonable to conclude that many university students in the United States would be supportive of the goals of the international language movement if they were made aware of its existence. Perhaps, this conclusion also would be valid for the remainder of the population of the United States and those of other countries as well. If this were the case, just publicizing the movement more would improve its prospects.

REFERENCES

JOHNSON, W.
  1946   *People in quandaries.* New York: Harper and Row.
OSGOOD, C. E., G. J. SUCI, P. H. TANNENBAUM
  1957   *The measurement of meaning.* Urbana: University of Illinois Press.
PEI, MARIO
  1958   *One language for the world.* New York: Devin-Adair.
  1969   Wanted: a world language. *International Language Reporter* 15:3–8.
SILVERMAN, FRANKLIN
  1969   Letter to the editor. *International Language Reporter* 15:17–18.
  1972   Letter to the editor. *Eco-logos* 18:15.

East Europeans and the Politics of Multiculturalism in Alberta

BAHA ABU-LABAN

The recent revival of ethnicity in Canadian society is in large measure a manifestation of the tension between achievement and ascription as two distinct principles of resource allocation. Although individual achievement represents a strong value commitment in Canadian society, there are strong indications that this principle has in practice been undermined. Canadian census data, along with contemporary research evidence, show that ethnicity has not been an irrelevant criterion of selection, with English-Canadians being the most favored group (see, for example, Porter 1965; Royal Commission on Bilingualism and Biculturalism 1969a; and Milner and Milner 1972). Faced with a systematic disadvantage in the resource allocative process, many Canadian minorities have organized and called attention to ethnic inequalities in access to desired goods and services. The most vigorous challenge to the status quo came from French-Canadians, but it soon spread to include other minority groups. Porter (1972:193) has properly characterized the 1970s as the decade of organized minorities.

The strength of French nationalism in Quebec, coupled with the threat of separatism, prompted the government in 1963 to establish the Royal Commission on Bilingualism and Biculturalism "to inquire into and report upon the existing state of bilingualism and biculturalism in Canada and to recommend what steps should be taken to develop the Canadian Confederation on the basis of an equal partnership between the two founding races" (Royal Commission on Bilingualism and Biculturalism 1965:151). But in this inquiry the government could ill afford to ignore about one-fourth of the Canadian population, specifically those who were

Presented at the 1973 annual meeting of the Western Association of Sociology and Anthropology, Banff, Alberta.

neither English nor French in origin, especially in the face of strong protests and political pressure from representatives of vocal ethnic groups such as the Ukrainian and Polish, among others. Thus the Commission was also instructed to take "into account the contribution made by the other ethnic groups to the cultural enrichment of Canada and the measures that should be taken to safeguard that contribution" (Royal Commission on Bilingualism and Biculturalism 1965:151).

Since the establishment of the Royal Commission on Bilingualism and Biculturalism, advocates of minority group rights have had a field day. The Commission's efforts have resulted in the publication of several books, including *The cultural contribution of the other ethnic groups* (1969b). Further, the federal government was soon to adopt a multicultural policy which received widespread support, sponsor several cultural heritage conferences and institute a large program of financial assistance to facilitate the development of ethnic cultures and the sharing of these cultures with other Canadians. Some provinces, notably Alberta and Ontario, have adopted a similar policy aimed at the facilitation or preservation of an "ethnic mosaic." With reference to Alberta, the government sponsored two cultural heritage conferences in 1971 and 1972, respectively. Also, acting on resolutions adopted at the latter conference, the government of Alberta underwrote the publication of *Heritage* — a new ethnically relevant journal — and established an advisory Cultural Heritage Council. Clearly, some form of Canadian multiculturalism is in the making.

The concept of multiculturalism appears to mean different things to different people. At one extreme, multiculturalism may mean relative autonomy and separate existence of ethnic groups, thereby encompassing what Breton (1968) has called institutional completeness. At the other extreme, multiculturalism may mean a joint sharing by ethnic groups of a national Canadian culture which represents a synthesis of the "essence" of diverse ethnic cultures, but allowing for some ethnic group variations across the country. Between these two polar extremes, multiculturalism may assume varying degrees of cultural and structural separation from the mainstream of Canadian culture and society. The specific implications of Canada's developing multiculturalism are not altogether clear, mainly because the issues involved have not been settled yet. However, it has been suggested by some social scientists, notably Porter (1972), that multiculturalism will restrict the upward social mobility of minority group members.

The purpose of this paper is twofold. First, it will attempt to determine the nature of multiculturalism which is being advocated by a vocal segment of the so-called "Third Force," namely, representatives of East European communities in Alberta. Second, on the basis of this analysis, an attempt will be made to evaluate the validity of the proposition that multiculturalism is detrimental to the upward social mobility of minority group members.

SOURCES OF DATA

The present paper is based on content analysis of sixteen briefs submitted by representatives of Alberta's East European communities to the 1972 Alberta Cultural Heritage Conference. One-half of these briefs were signed by ethnic organizations, and the remainder were signed by individuals of East European origin. Organizational submissions came from the Ukrainian Professional and Businessmen's Club of Edmonton; the Ukrainian Self-Reliance League (which is a federation of several Ukrainian organizations); the Canadian Polish Congress, Alberta Branch; the Czechoslovak National Association of Canada; the Czechoslovak National Association of Canada, Calgary Branch; the Hungarian Cultural Society; the United Doukhobors of Mossleigh and District; and Club Austria.

The briefs under examination constitute over one-fourth of the total of fifty-nine briefs prepared for the Conference. All briefs were submitted freely in response to a public invitation in the form of an advertisement published in daily newspapers throughout the province in early 1972 and signed by the Director of Cultural Development, Alberta Department of Culture, Youth and Recreation. The briefs were distributed at the Conference where the present author was assigned the role of Discussion Group Leader. The sources of the briefs were variable, including individuals, groups, ethnic and other voluntary associations (with few, in some instances, making joint submissions), and private and governmental agencies.

With reference to the briefs under study, there is no claim that they reliably reflect public opinion of Alberta's East European residents. However, the significance of these briefs derives not so much from any claims to representativeness as from identification of deeply felt individual and group needs and strongly held beliefs regarding Alberta's cultural heritage. The contents of the briefs represent an important part of the contemporary intellectual and sociopolitical climate regarding multiculturalism in Canadian society. Since in this investigation we are interested in range of expressions which define multiculturalism rather than the quantitative structure of these expressions, no attempt was made to record the frequency with which these expressions were made in the briefs. The obvious outcome of this analysis is a qualitative description of multiculturalism from the point of view of representatives of East European communities in Alberta.

Multiculturalism and the East European Community

Without exception, representatives of Alberta's East European communities reject a bicultural Canadian society and advocate the development of a multicultural society in which members of all culture groups are accorded equal treatment. Far from being divisive, the brand of multiculturalism which they advocate assumes integration and unity within the context of diversity. None of the briefs advocates structural separation or autonomous existence of ethnic groups, although there is some lack of clarity and apparent differences in the degree of institutional completeness which different groups may wish to achieve. Nevertheless, the briefs contain many suggestions and program proposals designed to facilitate interethnic contacts and mutual appreciation of Canada's constituent ethnic cultures. Either implicitly or explicitly, the briefs underline the expectation of social, economic and political integration of ethnic groups into Canadian society, but there is no indication of preference of assimilation. The submission by the Canadian Polish Congress sums it up as follows:

Alberta, as well as other provinces of Canada, possesses a rich diversity of people. We are not a melting pot of nations, but a unique union of minorities. Each of us is proud of his or her origins, but also equally proud, or maybe prouder to be a Canadian.
    As Polish representation we wish to stress strongly that the Polish minority rejects separatistic tendencies or inclinations, be it eastern or western. We treasure the unity and integrity of the Canadian Federation. Seeking cultural equality with other minorities of Alberta, or Canada, we are deeply convinced that Canadian cultural diversity and plurality represents an immense asset, which has to be preserved and developed.

In the absence of an appropriate measure of integration, it would be difficult to determine the precise degree of integration into or separateness from Canadian society which different East European communities would like to achieve. However, it is evident from the briefs under examination that none of these ethnic communities wants to be isolated or institutionally complete. Differences in perspective, as may exist among them, seem to be slight.

It has often been remarked that the Canadian identity tends to take a negative form, indicating what Canadians are not rather than what they are (e.g. we are NOT American). To inject a positive element into the definition of Canadian identity, some briefs have strongly argued that the development of multiculturalism would provide a positive response to Canada's identity crisis. Further, it is believed, with justification, that retention of and pride in ethnic identity will help alleviate many problems of personal identity. Thus multiculturalism is viewed as a double-edged sword, with positive identificational functions both for society and the individual.

Another important defining characteristic of the multiculturalism advocated by representatives of East European communities in Alberta is its commitment to universalistic principles in matters of work and employment. In one brief, submitted by the Ukrainian Professional and Businessmen's Club of Edmonton, it is noted that the principle of individual achievement or merit has not been applied impartially. Rather than demand preferential treatment or positive discrimination to correct for past "injustices," the brief, significantly, underlines the need for recommitment to the merit principle. To quote from this brief:

No Canadian and no Albertan would favor appointments to boards and tribunals on anything but a person's merits. However, it is truly staggering to note how few individuals of Ukrainian ancestry are appointed to provincial boards and tribunals. Only very recently has the first Ukrainian been appointed to the Board of Governors of the University of Alberta — and this, even though Albertans of Ukrainian origin constitute twelve percent of Edmonton's population and about eight percent of that in the province. No Albertans of Ukrainian origin have served on the provincial planning boards, the Utilities Commission, the Universities Commission or the Liquor Control Board. WHY? Surely the reason cannot be that we lack the necessary education, talents, or merits.

The policy of the government in the above matter is crucial, for we believe that once the government creates a favorable atmosphere or climate in its appointments, the same atmosphere or climate will permeate the private sector and affect appointments to senior management and boards of directors. Accordingly, we RECOMMEND that the provincial government go on record publicly (and through the Alberta Civil Service) as a proponent of the principle of employment on the merit principle, regardless of place of origin or ancestry.

The Human Rights Act of Alberta states: "It is recognized in Alberta as a fundamental principle that all persons are equal in dignity and human rights without regard to race, religious beliefs, color, ancestry or place of origin." Important and necessary as they may be, constitutional guarantees of individual rights do not by themselves adequately meet the minimum constitutional requirements of a multicultural society. While acknowledging the need for constitutional guarantees of individual rights, at least two briefs emphasize the need for similar guarantees of ethnic group rights. One brief explicitly notes the kind of stipulation which must be contained in the Bill of Rights: "Every ethnic group in Canada has a natural right to the pursuit of its own language, religion and cultural identity." Thus, multiculturalism will receive not only social and political but also necessary legal sanctioning.

In order for multiculturalism as an articulated goal-system in society to succeed, it must receive numerous structural supports. Altogether, the briefs under study contain a very large number of suggestions, some very specific and others not so specific, concerning needed institutional supports. In some sense, these suggestions elaborate the definition of multiculturalism which we are attempting to circumscribe. Following is a general summary, in outline form, of various institutional areas and related changes which, according to the briefs, must receive special attention in order to facilitate the development of multiculturalism:

1. EDUCATION. Relevant changes in the educational system should include appropriate modification of curricula; development of an atmosphere of mutual trust and understanding of ethnic groups; development of student exchange programs; founding of ethnic studies centers; development of ethnic studies programs at the university level; and, above all, teaching of ethnic languages at all levels where there is sufficient demand. (The expectation is that incentive grants will be given to School Boards for the purpose of facilitating language instruction.)

2. MASS MEDIA. Educational television, radio and television programming and the press should all recognize and nourish the multicultural goal-system. Further, the government should assist in the development of audiovisual aids and special cultural programs, including language instruction.

3. GOVERNMENT. In addition to its important legislative role, the governmental institution should also assist materially in the preservation of ethnic cultures, particularly in their expressive forms (e.g. arts and letters, music, drama, etc.), and work towards relevant enrichment of museums, archives and art galleries. The government should, in addition, make a special effort to support smaller ethnic groups (e.g. by establishing cultural centers) and participate actively in the enhancement of multiculturalism through various kinds of programs and activities. Above all, the government should finance research programs dealing with various aspects of Alberta's cultural heritage.

Multiculturalism and Social Mobility of Minority Group Members

One of the most pressing problems to which organized minorities have drawn attention concerns discriminatory treatment which they have been accorded in virtually all major areas of social life. Available evidence shows that minority status has often been associated with abridged social, political and legal rights, as well as various forms of economic deprivation. Ethnic stratification has found minority group members to be underrepresented in elite positions and higher nonmanual occupations and overrepresented in manual occupations. Also, compared to majority group members, minority group members have tended to face more barriers to upward social mobility.

Notwithstanding such constitutional guarantees as human rights and fair employment practices legislation, inequalities and economic deprivation based on ethnicity have persisted in North American society. As a result, minority group members have had to organize in order to redress grievances. Additionally, militant minorities have raised serious questions about the value of the merit principle in light of their disadvantaged position in the process of selection. Such minorities have emphasized the need for a new principle which would further protect them from discriminatory practices; hence, the frequent reference in recent years to the principle of minority group rights. Whether or not an individual agrees with the principle of minority group rights (either as a substitute for or as a principle which augments that of individual achievement), the important point is that ethnic minorities have organized and used the rhetoric of group rights precisely for the purpose of eradicating some of the barriers to their economic well-being and upward social mobility.

Paradoxically, some social scientists have recently argued that the perpetuation of ethnic identity will restrict minority group members' chances for upward social mobility (see, for example, Porter 1972; Vallee and Shulman 1969; and Zubrzycki 1973). According to Porter (1972:196):

It would seem then that the promotion of flourishing ethnic communities is directly opposed to absorption, assimilation, integration, and acculturation and could lead to a permanent ethnic stratification and thus is likely to interfere with the political goal of individual equality.

Since ethnic groups are viewed as descent groups, multiculturalism will inevitably promote a return to endogamy and exclusiveness (Porter 1972:200). "It seems to me," says Porter (1972:199), "that making descent groups of such importance because they are carriers of culture borders on racism with all the confused and emotional reactions that that term brings. If races have been evaluated as inferior and superior, so can cultures be." Thus, while ethnic groups may provide their members with psychic supports, this advantage is achieved at the expense of perpetuating ethnic stratification; also, while pride in one's culture or national origin may compensate for low status in society, it diminishes the need for programs of ameliorative change aimed at reducing inequalities associated with ethnic stratification (Porter 1972:201).

Ethnic and linguistic distinctions are believed to have a detrimental effect on minority group members for another important reason. Vallee and Shulman (1969) observe that ethnicity will reduce minority group members' motivation to aspire to higher social and occupational positions in the larger society, unless the group in question distinctly emphasizes achievement. The contention is that many minority groups do not provide their members with a range of experiences and role models appropriate for higher achievement orientation.

The validity of the proposition that the preservation of cultural and linguistic distinctions among ethnic minority groups will interfere with the political goal of individual equality appears to rest on three main but questionable assumptions:

1. The view that ethnic minority status is an all-or-none phenomenon, rather than a variable capable of assuming different degrees of cultural and structural separation from the mainstream of Canadian culture and society.

2. The view that the effects of multiculturalism on different ethnic minority groups will be essentially the same.

3. The view that the political goal of individual equality can be attained only through assimilation (with the result of a racially and culturally homogeneous society). Given its context, this assumption involves a belief that the route to assimilation is not only open but equally so to all minority groups.

Each of these assumptions will be discussed briefly in turn.

Porter's discussion (1972) of the dilemmas of a multiethnic society appears to ignore possible variability in the extent to which ethnic minority groups may maintain social distance from each other and from the majority group. While the perpetuation and rigidification of ethnic stratification could be a possible outcome of extreme pluralism, there is little evidence to suggest that Canadian minorities are striving to achieve that extreme. The evidence derived from this study indicates a strong opposition on the part of representatives of Alberta's East European communities to absorption and assimilation, but not to integration and acculturation (although the precise degree of integration and acculturation which they want is indeterminate at this time). Significantly, the briefs which we have examined do not demand positive discrimination or preferential treatment. On the contrary, there is explicit commitment to the principle of merit. Nor do Alberta's East European communities appear to be striving for exclusiveness, endogamy or institutional completeness. Evidently, their strategy and demands have been designed to enhance their political power in society, and they seem to have achieved some measure of success in this area. Given this evidence, as well as the present trends in Canadian society, it is highly questionable that multiculturalism will inevitably undermine the political goal of individual equality.

With reference to the second assumption, it is possible that an ethnic minority group intent on maintaining a high degree of social distance in relation to other groups in society may achieve its goal at a relatively high sacrifice. However, ethnic groups are characteristically different from each other in immigration history and settlement patterns, socioeconomic backgrounds, cultural and linguistic affinity with one of Canada's Charter groups, and relationship to country of origin. These differences are likely to bring about different results for different ethnic groups. But this question cannot be resolved without empirical research. The third assumption inherent in Porter's proposition is most controversial. Because it presumably enhances individual and group opportunities for better jobs and upward social mobility, assimilation has been "viewed as the embodiment of democratic ethos" (Metzger 1971). In a similarly critical vein, Horton (1966:707–708) notes that "equality is won by conformity to a dominant set of values and behavior. Equality means equal opportunity to achieve the same American values; in other words, equality is gained by losing one identity and conforming at some level to another demand by a dominant group." Also, within the context of the functional view in sociology, the transition from particularistic to universalistic norms has led to viewing "ethnicity as a survival of primary, quasi-tribal loyalties, which can have only a dysfunctional place in the achievement-oriented, rationalized, and impersonal social relationships of the modern, industrial-bureaucratic order" (Metzger 1971:635). Judging from these critical observations, it seems clear that the assimilationist position is ideologically rather than empirically based, reflecting optimism and legitimizing the elitist ideology concerning the future of ethnic groups. On these grounds, the empirical validity of the third assumption is highly questionable (cf. Abu-Laban and Abu-Laban 1973).

The string which Porter attaches to the extension of equality to ethnic minority groups is assimilation. This means that the desirable model of Canadian society is one of cultural homogeneity, a melting pot, in which ethnics aspire to internalize the Canadian norm, however that norm is defined, in order to be accepted and liked. Contemporary sociological knowledge, however, indicates that there is a differential in the dominant group's willingness to allow the structural, if not cultural, assimilation of different minority groups (see, for example, Woodsworth 1972; Palmer 1972; and Gordon 1964). Thus, even if a certain minority group is agreeable to assimilation and absorption, the dominant group may not allow its structural assimilation. Accordingly, the implicit assumption that the doors of assimilation are equally open to all ethnic minorities cannot be sustained.

It seems clear that the social and political implications of multiculturalism, as suggested in the recent literature, are based on assumptions of questionable validity. It would be necessary to investigate empirically the nature and conditions of the developing Canadian multiculturalism in order to reliably determine its social and political consequences. While commitment to the ideology of assimilation is a matter of personal preference, the advancement of this ideology with sociological garb is misleading.

SUMMARY AND CONCLUSIONS

There is a strong belief among representatives of Alberta's East European communities in the viability of a multicultural Canadian society. Content analysis of briefs presented at the 1972 Alberta Cultural Heritage Conference reveals that the multiculturalism sought by East European communities does not encompass the notion of institutional completeness. Rather, it allows for acculturation and integration into the mainstream of Canadian culture and society. The rhetoric of the developing ideology of multiculturalism involves rejection of biculturalism as the defining characteristic of Canadian society and elevation of all Canadian ethnic groups to a position of equality. While institutional bilingualism is not seriously challenged, there is a clear demand for individual bilingualism, whereby a person's second language should preferably be the language of his ethnic group. To achieve a genuinely multicultural society, the briefs advocate the attuning of the educational, mass media and governmental institutions to the minimum requirements of multiculturalism. Many relevant suggestions for institutional support of multiculturalism are contained in the briefs.

Some social scientists have recently argued that multiculturalism will inevitably perpetuate ethnic stratification and interfere with the upward social mobility of minority group members. Further, it has been argued that the political goal of individual equality can be achieved only by assimilation of minority groups. The evidence derived from this study points to serious flaws in these arguments and questions the assumptions, explicit or implicit, which underlie them. Accordingly, the proposition that multiculturalism is inevitably dysfunctional for upward social mobility of minority group members requires qualification and modification.

REFERENCES

ABU-LABAN, BAHA, SHARON Mc IRVIN ABU-LABAN
1973   The social context of American sociology and the violence of the sixties. *International Review of Sociology*, Second Series, 9(1–2): 38–62.
BRETON, RAYMOND
1968   "Institutional completeness of ethnic communities and the personal relations of immigrants," in *Canadian Society: Sociological perspectives*. Edited by Bernard Blishen, *et al.*, 77–94. Toronto: Macmillan of Canada. (Also published in American Journal of Sociology 70 (2) 193–205).
GORDON, MILTON
1964   *Assimilation in American life*. New York: Oxford University Press.
HORTON, JOHN
1966   Order and conflict theories of social problems as competing ideologies. *American Journal of Sociology* 71:701–713.

METZGER, L. PAUL
1971   American sociology and Black assimilation: conflicting perspectives. *American Journal of Sociology* 76:627–647.
MILNER, SHEILAGH HODGINS, HENRY MILNER
1972   *The decolonization of Quebec.* Toronto: McClelland and Stewart.
PALMER, HOWARD
1972   "Mosaic versus melting pot: reality or illusion?" Unpublished manuscript.
PORTER, JOHN
1965   *The vertical mosaic.* Toronto: University of Toronto Press.
1972   "Dilemmas and contradictions of a multi-ethnic society." Transactions of the Royal Society of Canada (Series 4) 10:193–205.
ROYAL COMMISSION ON BILINGUALISM AND BICULTURALISM
1965   *A preliminary report.* Ottawa: Queen's Printer.
1969a *The work world.* Book III. Ottawa: Queen's Printer.
1969b *The cultural contribution of the other ethnic groups.* Book IV. Ottawa: Queen's Printer.
VALLEE, FRANK G., NORMAN SHULMAN
1969   "The viability of French groupings outside Quebec," in *Regionalism in the Canadian community, 1867–1967.* Edited by Mason Wade, 95. Toronto: University of Toronto Press.
WOODSWORTH, J. S.
1972   *Strangers within our gates.* Toronto: University of Toronto Press.
ZUBRZYCKI, J.
1973   Seminar presentation at the Department of Sociology, University of Alberta, Edmonton.

Universal Literacy of the Formerly Backward Peoples of the Soviet Union: A Factor of Their Social Self-Awareness

V. A. KUMANËV

Man has instinctively longed for knowledge throughout his history. The course of history, however, has invariably barred the overwhelming majority of people from acquiring education.

Even today over 740 million adults cannot read and write, and according to certain estimates, the total number of illiterates far exceeds even this impressive figure. As R. Maheu, UNESCO Director General, put it, these figures are shameful both for moral reasons, as evidence of injustice, and for economic reasons, as testifying to tremendous wastage of intellectual resources (*UNESCO Courier* 1963:31). The number of adult illiterates rises by thirty to thirty-three million persons annually.

Mass illiteracy thus remains one of the most pressing problems of the world today. With a considerable proportion of mankind illiterate and deprived of access to written knowledge, social justice is out of the question. It becomes increasingly obvious that the steps taken today in different parts of the world to eradicate ignorance and backwardness will fall flat unless they are accompanied by drastic sociopolitical and economic changes providing a basis for the unhindered development of the masses.

In prerevolutionary Russia, a country of unparalleled ethnic diversity,[1] with the population scattered over a vast territory, the socioeconomic and cultural conditions of the toiling masses were extremely varied. Nomadic peoples, for example, had barely entered the initial phase of feudalism in their social development. In the course of the nineteenth century some tribes ceased to exist; a number of others were doomed to extinction. The

---

[1] Up to 57 percent of tsarist Russia's population was made up of the so-called *inorodtsy*, 'aliens' — minor peoples.

country's non-Russian outlying areas lagged behind the central regions of the Russian Empire by centuries.

The oppressed condition of Russia's peoples was borne out by the almost total illiteracy among non-Russians; shortly before the 1917 October Revolution the proportion of those able to read and write among adult Tajiks was only 0.5 percent; among the adult Kirghiz, 0.6 percent; among the Yakuts, 0.7 percent; among the Turkmen, 0.7 percent, and so forth. In the far north there were no people among the aboriginal population who could read and write.[2] As a direct consequence of the tsarist colonialist policy, almost fifty distinct peoples and ethnic groups of the Russian Empire had no writing systems of their own. Illiteracy was an additional factor which compounded the burden of social oppression and poverty. The tsarist administration banned national tongues as the medium of instruction, vetoed newspaper- and book-printing in ethnic areas and prevented even elementary knowledge from spreading among the masses.

The essence of the administration's education policies in regard to the non-Russian peoples of the Empire found its expression in a cynical statement made at the end of the nineteenth century by the then Minister of Education D. A. Tolstoy: "The ultimate goal of education of all inorodtsy living within the boundaries of our country should unquestionably be their Russification" (Natŝional'nye Shkoly ... 1958:14). The Seventh Congress of the Gentry (Moscow, 1911) was equally outspoken on this point:

The official school should exhibit no alien features; it must be dominated by the official language of the state and no concessions can be made in this respect, Russian must be the medium of instruction. ... We, the gentry hereby declare that the school must be Russian — and Russia must be for the Russians.

According to the data supplied by officials of the Ministry of Education, in 1911, out of 900,000 school-age children of non-Russian peoples living in the Volga and the cis-Urals areas that had no writing systems of their own, 870,000 could not attend school; in Siberia only 3 percent of the children of ethnic minorities had access to education. No schools or other cultural facilities were provided for the aboriginal population of the north. There was a single school in the vast Turukhan Territory — Siberia (Vestnik vospitaniĩa 1906:91). In Turkestan per capita outlays on education averaged 1.1 kopeck; early in the present century all elementary

---

[2]   Russian statisticians and historians of public education were hard put to even to define "literacy." The mere fact that Russian civil legislation regarded as illiterates only people who could not sign their names clearly shows the degree to which even the above literacy figures were exaggerated.

schools in Borisov District, Byelorussia, were closed down because of "lack of local funds."[3]

The above statistics need no comment. The ignorance of the working people, zealously maintained by the tsarist regime, had an adverse effect on the pace of the country's development and kept it technologically and economically backward.

The first serious attempts to attract public opinion to the problem of teaching the non-Russian peoples with no writing systems of their own to read and write were made in the second half of the nineteenth century. In 1896 a collection of articles was published entitled *An economic appraisal of public education*. It was built around academician I. Ianzhul's article "The role of education in industrial and commercial progress" as well as on papers discussed by the second Conference on Technical and Vocational Training (1895). The authors wrote:

> Under present-day conditions public education of Russians and of minor peoples is the only correct path toward introducing the masses in a short time to improved production techniques; and in this sense it is a mighty factor of augmenting public wealth. . . . There are many causes retarding progress in the Russian national economy; of these pride of place belongs to the almost total illiteracy which so strikingly distinguishes our motherland from all, if only a little cultured, nations of Europe and America (Ianzhul, Chuprov, Ianzhul 1896:35, 50).

The tsarist regime turned a deaf ear to the appeals of progressive-minded thinkers who could not reconcile themselves to the plight of public education in Russia, particularly as far as the non-Russian peoples without writing systems of their own were concerned. Pursuing their selfish goals, the colonialists only took care to train (in Russian) a strictly limited number of literates from among well-to-do "natives" who became the loyal officers of the tsarist administration. There did emerge the so-called Sunday and evening schools, but they were strictly stunted in their development by the monarchy which followed the guideline of Prince Dolgoruky, Chief of the Third Bureau (gendarmerie): "It is paramount that the government should without delay take effective steps to control this movement and prevent its succumbing to subversive elements . . ." (*Narodnoe obrazovanie . . .* 1912:22). Even the circular letter addressed to the parish schools said that the very teaching of literacy harbored a threat to the regime and that instruction in elementary schools "should not pursue secondary ends, such as, for instance, information about the outside world" (*Pravila i programmy . . .* 1894). It was therefore not fortuitous that in 1891 control of all schools was given to the clergy.

However, at the turn of the century Russia produced a social force

---

[3]   Judging by the Zemstvo reports and ethnographic studies, elementary schools in the countryside generally counted their graduates among the well-to-do section of the village population (see *Selo Viriatino . . .* 1958; Borisov 1899).

destined to overthrow the old order and close the gap which separated the people and education. The Russian Marxists led by V. I. Lenin put forward from the very start a number of goals in the field of education in addition to sociopolitical and economic goals. In 1895 Lenin, in his article entitled "What are our ministers thinking about?", stressed that at the core of the "educational" policy of the Romanov House lay a mortal fear of "the working people acquiring knowledge" (Lenin n.d.a.:92). Nicholas II, upon being informed that almost none of the army conscripts, particularly from non-Russian areas, could read and write, actually exclaimed, "Thank God!" (*Narodnoe obrazovanie* 1967:83).

As they entered the twentieth century the peoples of Russia were increasingly aware of the vital need of literacy. Access to elementary knowledge was regarded by Lenin as a sure means of involving the masses in the struggle for emancipation and enlisting their active participation in the construction of a new society. The Program of the Russian Social-Democratic Labor Party (1903) contained clauses demanding free and compulsory general and vocational education for young people. The party set itself the task of ensuring the people the right of receiving instruction in their mother tongue.

The two decades following the first All-Russia Population Census of 1897 evinced no change: on the eve of the 1917 October Revolution Russia was below all the countries of Europe in the literacy level. The real tragedy of Russia was not dearth of talent or lack of cultural and scientific achievements but the fact that cultural treasures were out of the people's reach, that the working masses had no access to them and were doomed by the existing political system to intellectual poverty.

The triumph of the October Revolution marked the beginning of a cultural rejuvenation of society unprecedented in depth and scale. Soviet power set itself the task of dispensing with the cultural debt of centuries in a matter of decades. All the peoples were to become truly equal; they were to be given equal access to cultural treasures and culture was to be genuinely democratized.

The mass illiteracy which faced the new system was a danger threatening the destinies of the Revolution: it clashed with the political awakening of the citizens of the Soviet Republic. People who could not read and write could not take part in organizing and managing the national economy and the state. As V. I. Lenin wrote, "Our idea is that a state is strong when . . . the people know everything, can form an opinion of everything and do everything consciously" (Lenin n.d.b:256). We resolutely reject the superstition, declared Lenin, that representatives of backward peoples liberated by the Revolution are incapable of managing the state and the economy; provided they acquire knowledge and education, they will learn the necessary know-how, learn to run things and take a conscious part in social life.

The budding new society aimed not only at teaching the masses to read and write, but at introducing to them mankind's entire spiritual wealth. Lenin laid down the underlying principles for a system of education of the country's peoples: education was to be universal, ideologically oriented, and connected with productive labor, with the efforts of the masses striving to reconstruct their existence.

Shortly after the Provisional government had been overthrown, the Council of People's Commissars adopted the "Declaration of Rights of the Peoples of Russia." This proclaimed equality and sovereignity of peoples, abolition of all national and national–religious privileges and restrictions, free development of national minorities and ethnographic groups living in the territory of Russia, and the right of peoples to self-determination.

On December 26, 1919, Lenin signed a government decree "On the Eradication of Illiteracy among the Population of the Russian Federation." With a view to enabling the entire population of the Republic, said the decree,

... TO TAKE A CONSCIOUS PART IN THE COUNTRY'S POLITICAL LIFE the Council of People's Commissars hereby decrees; the entire population aged from 8 to 50 who cannot read and write is obligated to learn to read and write either in their mother tongue or in the Russian language, as they choose (*Direktivy VKP (b)* . . . 1947:118, emphasis added).

According to an eyewitness account by the American journalist A. R. Williams, the whole country set itself to learn to read and write. ABC books for adults were infused with sharp political contents; they were integrally related to the people's labor efforts, and their first line read, "Slaves are we not, we are not slaves."

The working people gave wholehearted support to the revolutionary legislative acts of the new government aimed at combating cultural retardation. Speaking about the masses' insatiable thirst for knowledge Lenin pointed out that millions of men and women belonging to different nationalities and races and standing at different stages of cultural development were now aspiring to a new life (Tsetkin, 1925:26). The non-Russian peoples were bound "to overtake the more advanced Central Russia at the cultural level in order to continue common progress abreast of each other" (*Deputaty Sovetskoĭ vlasti* 1957:39). Under the decisions of the Tenth Congress of the Russian Communist Party (1921) the Party worked out a program of cultural assistance to the peoples of what had been known as the non-Russian outlying areas.

The mass movement which unfolded under the motto, "If you can read and write, teach someone who cannot," successfully overcame the formidable difficulties, e.g. an acute shortage of writing material, ABC books, classrooms, and teachers. The campaign was obstructed by superstition, prejudice, and the actions of class enemies. It took a tremendous effort to draw the vast majority of the non-Russian adult population in the countryside, and above all women, into the campaign. Particular difficulties were encountered among those peoples who had no writing systems of their own. For out of the 130 languages used by the country's peoples only twenty had more or less developed writing systems; only Russians, Georgians, and Armenians used their own original alphabets.

The feat accomplished by the Soviet teachers, who were not only the first educators in the true sense of the word, but who also had to create ABC books and alphabets in the tongues of the peoples who previously had had no writing systems of their own, was a civic achievement — but it was also a scientific one, because for the first time in human history and within an unprecedentedly short period, alphabets were designed for scores of peoples separated from one another by thousands of miles and by ethnolinguistic barriers. The teachers, moreover, had to break through the prejudices of the most backward sections of the population who doubted the usefulness of learning. Thus, the far north Nentsy would reason in those days something like this: "A deer or a dog must be taught, of course; but why teach a man? He knows for himself how to hunt and live, and what else could school teach him?" (*Sovetskiĭ Sever* 1932:94).

In the 1920s many Soviet peoples switched over to latinized alphabets (the first to do so, were the Azerbaijan), which were regarded as the most internationalistic. The Institute of Languages and Writing Systems of the USSR Academy of Sciences (at present the USSR Academy of Sciences Institute of Linguistics) was to play a leading role in the development of writing systems and the compilation of ABC books. Speaking about the tasks of the read-and-write schools and circles set up throughout the country, the leaders of the People's Commissariat of Education of the Russian Federation urged the teachers not only to provide their pupils with keys to knowledge, but also to point out to them the doors those keys would open. Along with teaching the pupils to read and write, the teachers were required to expand the former's outlook (Krupskaĭà 1922:175).

When the Union of Soviet Socialist Republics was formed in 1922, the campaign to eradicate illiteracy became even more systematic. The government attached tremendous importance to the spontaneous activity of the masses in this field; accordingly, in 1923, a voluntary society "Down with Illiteracy" was set up under the presidency of M. I. Kalinin, Chairman of the Central Executive Council of the USSR.

The fact that learning and culture largely determined the people's political awareness was graphically demonstrated. It was estimated, for example, that during the election of the Soviets directly preceding the First Five-Year Plan (1928–1932) sixty-six out of every one hundred peasants (men) came to the polls — largely those who could read and write; at that time the rate of adult literacy in the countryside was about seventy per hundred. This was no mere coincidence, for among women the correlation between literacy and voting activity was about the same (*Za gramotu,* 1928:2).

The years of the First Five-Year Plan were the crucial period in the campaign to overcome cultural backwardness. The battle for eradication of illiteracy was won primarily thanks to the introduction of universal primary education for children and adolescents. The masses themselves took a valuable initiative by launching a nationwide cultural movement for literacy and a new way of life. Not only did this movement rally all public organizations, but it also mobilized millions of people who could read and write to teach the illiterates on a voluntary basis. Those years were also marked by a considerable increase in the amount of cultural assistance given by the towns to the countryside and the non-Russian regions.

The history of those days abounds in examples of heroism and high civic consciousness. There was hardly a single settlement in the country that did not have illiterates who followed up their working with ABC lessons. In the mountain *auls* of the Caucasus and the *kishlaks* of Tajikistan, in the nomadic tents of the Kazakhs and Kalmyks, in the *chooms* of Chukotsky Peninsula, toilers of all nationalities were learning to read and write.[4] The growing social awareness of the people manifested itself not only in the voluntary teaching of illiterates; people also placed their dwellings at the disposal, free of charge, of ABC schools, helped to lay in fuel for these schools, raise funds (money, part of the crop, writing material, etc.). In this connection M. I. Kalinin noted:

We are witnessing a tremendous rise in social consciousness, a tremendous rise in literacy. Who has worked this miracle? It has been worked by our public movement. ... An illiterate person cannot take up intensive social work in any organization (Kalinin 1938:59).

Under the Second and Third Five-Year Plans illiteracy was largely eradicated in the Soviet Union.[5] Thus, close to sixty million people who had not been able to read and write at all and an additional thirty million semi-illiterates learned to read and write within about two decades.

ABC schools opened the door into the realm of knowledge for the peoples of the Soviet Union; they not only helped them to learn to read

---

[4]   At the request of the peoples of the North and East of the Soviet Union, their writing systems had been converted to the Russian alphabet by the early 1940s. This helped eliminate alphabetical heterogeneity in many non-Russian schools and provided for faster rates of learning both in the native tongues and in Russian — which was increasingly becoming a medium of interethnic communication.
[5]   In 1906 the magazine *Vestnik vospitaniia* (No. 1:42) had predicted in an article on the prospects of development of Russian culture that it would take some 300 years to wipe out illiteracy in Russia.

and write and shake off their ignorance but became genuine centers of political and cultural development, helping to do away with inequality in the field of education. Eradication of illiteracy aided in ending the shortage of skilled personnel; it served to draw the larger and lesser Soviet peoples into the country's political and production life, and it opened broad vistas to the working people of all nationalities who were now able to raise their social awareness and cultural level and apply their efforts more productively. Many graduates of ABC schools have worked successfully in factories and at farms; others became engineers, scientists, and statesmen. Their ABC books, whose contents were closely related to the building of a new life, had been the first step on the path to education.

The 1970 Census has once again shown that as a result of the measures taken by the government to achieve a cultural advance in the Soviet Union, a land of many nations and languages, there is 100 percent literacy in all the constituent republics. Henri Jeannes, a French engineer who visited Bashkiria in the late 1960s, noted:

Here is a people who at the time when Citroën was building its first automobiles had no alphabet of their own; now they have a university where their children receive instruction equal to that provided by the best-known higher schools of the West (Beloded 1972:46).

Today Bashkiria has thousands of grade schools, sixty-four technical schools and nine institutes of higher learning; one out of every four Bashkirs is a student.

A statement made by Adlai Stevenson is also noteworthy. During his visit to the Soviet Union, he said, he had seen proof of its remarkable achievement in the field of education; within the lifetime of one generation this vast and formerly backward country, where the Russian language is native to only one half of the population, achieved almost total literacy; it has, moreover, caught up with or outstripped the rest of the world in the field of natural science (Stevenson 1959:74).

Half a century is a period sufficiently long to appraise the cultural achievements of the Soviet Union since the start of its campaign to eradicate illiteracy and thus lay the foundation of the edifice of culture.

Today over eighty million people in the country (i.e. one out of every three citizens) study under various education systems. The number of scientists has topped the one million mark; more than half of the working population have a higher or secondary education. For example, in number of students per 1,000 population the Kirghiz Republic has surpassed the most highly developed countries of the world, e.g. the United States, Britain, and France.

In a socialist country, universal literacy is obligatory. It taps enormous resources for the progress of culture, science, and the economy, and is an important factor in the expansion of the people's horizons, in the development of the ability to think and act independently in keeping with the interests of society; it is an essential condition for inculcating a scientific world outlook and Communist moral principles.

REFERENCES

BELODED, I. K.
1972 *Leninskaĭa teoriĭa natsional'no-ĭazykovogo stroitel'stva v sotsialisticheskom obshchestve* [Lenin's theory of national-linguistic construction in socialist society]. Moscow.

BORISOV, N.
1899 *K voprosu o vliĭanii zanĭatiĭa, ekonomicheskogo polozheniĭa i gramotnosti sel'skogo naseleniia na nekotorye storony nachal'nogo narodnogo obrazovaniia* [On the question of the influence of occupation, economic position and literacy of the rural population on some aspects of elementary popular education].

Deputaty Sovetskoĭ vlasti
1957 *Deputaty Sovetskoĭ vlasti* [Deputies of the Soviet government]. volume one. Moscow.

Direktivy VKP (b)
1947 *Direktivy VKP (b) i postanovleniĭa Sovetskogo pravitel'stva o narodnom obrazovanii* [Directives of the V.K.P. (b) and the resolutions of the Soviet government on popular education], volume 2 . Moscow, Leningrad.

IANZHUL, I. I., A. I. CHUPROV, E. N. IANZHUL
1896 *Ekonomicheskaĭa otsenka narodnogo obrazovanie. Ocherki.* [An economic appraisal of public education. Essays]. St Petersburg.

KALININ, M. I.
1938 *O voprosakh sotsialisticheskoĭ kul'tury* [On question of socialist culture]. Moscow.

KRUPSKAĬA, N. K.
1922 *Voprosy narodnogo obrazovaniĭa* [Questions of popular education]. Berlin.

LENIN, V. I.
n.d.a *Collected works* 2. Moscow
n.d.b *Collected works* 26. Moscow.

Narodnoe obrazovanie
1967 *Narodnoe obrazovanie* [Popular education] 11.

Narodnoe obrazovanie v Rossii
1912 *Narodnoe obrazovanie v Rossii s 60-kh godov XIX veka* [Popular education in Russia since the 1860s]. Moscow.

Natsional'nye shkoly
1958 *Natsional'nye shkoly RSFSR za 40 let* [National schools of the R.S.F.S.R. over forty years]. Moscow.

Pravila i programmy
1894 *Pravila i programmy dlĭa tserkovno-prikhodskikh shkol i shkol gramoty* [Rules and programs for parish schools and literary schools]. St Petersburg.

Selo Virĭatino
1958 *Selo Viriatino v proshlom i nastoĭashchem. Opyt ètnograficheskogo*

izucheniiᾶ russkoĭ kolkhoznoĭ derevni [The village Veriatino in the past and present. An attempted ethnographic study of a Russian *kolkhoz* village]. Moscow.

Sovetskiĭ Sever
   1932   *Sovetskiĭ Sever* [The Soviet North] 4.

STEVENSON, ADLAI E.
   1959   *Friends and enemies. What I learned in Russia*. New York.

T͡SETKIN, K.
   1925   *O Lenine* [On Lenin]. Moscow.

UNESCO COURIER
   1963   UNESCO *Courier* 3.

Vestnik vospitaniiᾶ
   1906   *Vestnik vospitaniiᾶ* [Education herald] 7:91.

Za gramotu
   1928   *Za gramotu* [For literacy] 12.

Communication in an Indian Village

J. S. YADAVA

Communication among human beings is the process of transmitting information, ideas, and attitudes from one person to another or to a group of persons. It is an essential ingredient of organized human life. To a large extent social life in a community is dependent upon the communication systems available to its members. The communication system with its more or less well defined channels is, in a sense, the skeleton of social life and the content of communications is, of course, the very substance of social intercourse. The flow of communications determines the dynamics of human existence and social development. Hence, it will be worthwhile to investigate and discuss some aspects of communications, the focus in this case an Indian village. The discussion will cover (1) the village social structure and communication, (2) the media of mass communication in the village context and (3) the role and place of "group meetings" in communications in the village.[1]

THE SETTING

Mandothi, the village which forms the focus of this study, is located 42 kilometers west of the city of Delhi. Administratively, it comes under the Bahadurgarh Block of Rohtak district in Haryana State. It is easily accessible by road; one drives on the Delhi–Rohtak road up to the town of Bahadurgarh, roughly 30 kilometers from Delhi, where a link road in the southwest direction leads to the village of Mandothi. Link roads also connect the village to the neighboring towns of Jhajjar and Sampla. Thus,

---

[1]   The present paper is based largely upon the data collected during a field study (Yadava 1971).

Mandothi is well-connected by means of good road links with the three neighboring towns — Bahadurgarh, Jhajjar, and Sampla.

The population of the village is 8,347 according to the 1971 provisional census report. It is a multicaste, nucleated village. In all, there are twenty-two castes; the higher castes — Jat, Brahmin and Bania — constitute a majority (about 66 percent) of the village population. Jats, the landowning cultivators, alone are 57 percent. Kumhar, Khati, Nai, and a number of other lower castes form a sizeable number (about 15 percent) in the village. The Harijans too are well represented as they form approximately 18 percent of the total village population.

There are three residential areas or wards, locally known as *pannas* — Pachosia, Kabosia, and Matendia — in the village. Generally a *panna* comprises a number of *mohallas,* each of which in turn is composed of a number of *kunbas.* The *kunba* is a kin unit consisting of closely related households whose members are descended from a common male ancestor only a few generations back. But when the number of generations becomes large, the area in which the kinsmen live is called a *mohalla* or *tholla* by the villagers. Thus, the members of a caste in a *panna* are patrilineally-related kinsmen. There is more social interaction within a *panna* than between the *pannas.* This is also true in regard to the *mohallas* and *kunbas.* Broadly speaking, social interaction becomes more intensive in the kin units as one moves down from the *panna* to the households. These units, based upon kinship ties, function as important cohesive and corporate units in socioeconomic, political, and religious activities.

Nowadays, however, social alliances are increasingly formed across the traditional lines of caste and kinship. In sociological literature, such loosely formed new alliances are referred to as factions (Nicholas 1965; Yadava 1968). In Mandothi the factions play an important role in social and political life. One can identify two major factions in this village; one led by the Sarpanch (*Uday Singh*) of the village Panchayat and the other by another important Jat leader (*Kaval Singh*). In addition, there are a number of smaller factions or subfactions that sometimes merge their identity in the large factions and sometimes maintain their identity, independent operations, and functions.

VILLAGE SOCIAL STRUCTURE AND COMMUNICATION

The social structure of the village community affects the pattern of communication in the village to a large extent. There is a traditional network of personal word-of-mouth communication and there are built-in channels and blockades for communication in the village social system itself. Communication tends to be channelled along the traditional grooves of caste and kinship groups. Within the village there is far more social communication among the members of a caste than between castes, because of the traditional norms of intercaste commensality.[2] There is usually a much faster flow of information horizontally, that is, among the members of a caste, than vertically, that is, across caste lines in the village.

In kinship-based groups such as *kunba, thola* and *panna* there are spokesmen who are listened to by their kinsmen, who disseminate new ideas and information among them. As the social interaction among kinsmen is intensive as well as extensive there is a much greater flow of communication among the kinsmen. However, sometimes communication is equally hampered due to quarrels and confrontation.

At the household level the pattern of communication is directed by the traditional social norms of respect, distance, and indulgence among members of a familial group. For instance, according to village norms, the daughter-in-law is expected to maintain a respectable distance from her father-in-law and, as a result, communication between them is very restricted. Further, wife and husband are not expected to be very free with each other in the presence of others. This is carried to the extent that the wife covers her face and does not talk to her husband in the presence of the elders.

Communication within any segment or group in a village is facilitated by the opinion leaders (Katz and Lazarsfeld 1955; Sen 1969). They are usually more knowledgeable than other members of the community, who often come to seek their advice. Mass media may provide the villagers with basic information, but before they act on such information they need to be encouraged by someone in their immediate environment whom they know and respect. A farmer may come to know about new agricultural practices through a radio broadcast or the village-level worker. But the chances of his adopting the innovation will be greater if he is encouraged by some known person whose reputation is high in his social circle. Of course, the influence of an opinion leader varies, depending upon his knowledgeability, his position in the caste hierarchy, and his place in the kinship network.

Here it may not be out of place to mention the role of factions in communication in the village community. In certain situations the factional ties facilitate communication, while in others they act as inhibitors of communication. Information flows fast and effectively among the members of a faction. While faction leaders may distort the news and add local colors to suit their interest, they do make social communication more interesting and effective among the members of a faction. This facilitates communication both horizontally and vertically in the context of the village social system.

[2] The point has been well made in most of the village studies dealing with the caste system in India. See particularly Majumdar (1958).

MASS COMMUNICATION IN THE VILLAGE

Radio

In view of the low literacy, the radio occupies a unique place as a medium of mass communication in India. It is now technologically feasible to reach every nook and corner of the country through radio. As of December, 1970, there were 11,836,653 licensed listening sets[3] in addition to a large number of sets which were not registered. It is difficult to make any estimate of the number of radio sets available in rural areas. However, the government of India, under its scheme of subsidized radio sets for rural areas, has supplied 142,451 community sets in rural areas. Different stations of the All India Radio regularly broadcast special programs for the rural audience. These programs cover all aspects of rural life and provide useful information to the villagers through dialogues, discussions, plays, news, weather reports, etc. Special talks by experts are arranged to discuss specific problems relating to agriculture, health, family planning, and education. To increase the effectiveness of radio broadcasts a nationwide scheme of Radio Rural Forums, providing listening-*cum*-discussion-*cum*-action programs, was launched in November, 1959. About 25,800 such forums are functioning at present; the participants discuss the broadcasts regularly and send their suggestions and criticism to the broadcasting station.

But notwithstanding the availability of radio sets in villages, does the radio serve the desired purpose of disseminating information to the rural masses? Or does it end up being merely a source of entertainment? A series of in-depth case studies should be undertaken to investigate this question. On the basis of limited field experience in the village of Mandothi, it may be reported that radio, by and large, does not serve the purpose of disseminating information except in situations of crisis, like war,[4] and it is used largely for entertainment purposes.

In Mandothi, with its population of 8,347 people, there are 138 radio sets.[5] A large number of these (75 percent) are owned by the higher castes in the village. The lower castes and the Harijans own 11 and 14 percent of the radios respectively. One can classify the radios in Mandothi into two categories: (1) family radios and (2) group radios. Family radios are primarily used for entertainment while group radios are for listening to news and agricultural information programs. Further, family radios are

[3]   These figures are taken from (India 1972).
[4]   In *Perception of Indo-Pakistan war at the village level* (1972) it was revealed that 76 percent of the informants in Mandothi village came to know about the war first through the medium of radio.
[5]   Of 138 radio sets only seventy-eight were registered and the remaining sixty (43.5 percent) were without a license.

generally listened to in homes by the young boys while group radios are listened to by the male elders in *baithaks* [men's quarters]. There are ninety-three (67 percent) family radios and forty-five (33 percent) group radios in Mandothi.

It was observed that the *dehati* program [special program for the rural audience, 6:45–7:30 P.M.] and the evening news broadcasts were very popular with the village male elders. These programs were listened to almost regularly by groups of villagers in the *baithaks*. The *dehati* program is popular mainly because it relates to agriculture and allied fields. As this program is in the local dialect and idiom it is easily understood by the villagers. However, in the case of the news broadcasts only spectacular news was grasped. Of course, factors like education, information level, and interest of the listeners have significant bearing upon comprehension and retention of a particular news item. The village listener generally picks up the main point of the sensational item in the news broadcasts and skips most of its details, and lesser news is lost on him. There could be many reasons for this. First, the villagers do not seem to comprehend fully the language or the text of the news broadcasts. Secondly, they do not have the necessary background information. However, the villager, whatever spectacular bits he manages to pick up from the radio broadcasts, seems to have a very strong tendency to share them with other villagers. He thereby sets in motion a chain-reaction of communication flow through word-of-mouth in the village community.

Of course, these are only tentative observations which certainly call for further intensive and systematic research over a period of time before one can postulate specific formulations about the process of communication through radio in rural areas.

Film and Television

The reach of film as a medium is very limited in rural India. The cinemas are located in towns and cities only. In the vicinity of Mandothi village there is only one cinema at Bahadurgarh, which is about 12 kilometers from the village. The villagers can hardly afford to visit the cinemas in cities. Further, the villagers in general do not seem to be very enthusiastic about seeing films. The older people disapprove of films and think that they have a "corrupting" influence. The younger persons may manage to see films in towns once in a while without the knowledge of the elders.

It is difficult to assess precisely the extent of exposure of films. However, as a part of another study, *Perception of Indo-Pakistan War at the village level* (1972), 596 persons selected at random were asked whether they had seen films. About 40 percent of them had, mostly once or twice only, and a few regularly. Further, it was found that none of the persons interviewed could recollect the titles, not to mention contents, of the two films exhibited in the village by the Field Publicity Division of the state government. This suggests that documentary films, under present circumstances, do not make much impact on rural audiences. Similar conclusions were reached by Rehman (1970) in a systematic study of reactions of rural audiences to three documentary films; it emerged that the messages of the films were generally not understood by the rural audiences.

Television is a revolutionary communication device and has great potentialities for rural India. However, at the moment broadcasting is confined to the Delhi region. There are only eighty rural "teleclubs" in Delhi villages, and twenty in villages in the neighboring states of Uttar Pradesh and Haryana. In Mandothi village there is no television set and hence exposure to this new medium is largely out of the question.

Newspapers

The Press has a very limited role in rural India because of the low literacy in the villages. The Press Commission headed by Shri Justice G. S. Rajadhyaksha has pointed out in its report (*Report of the Press Commission* 1954) that the daily newspapers in India are published mainly for metropolitan areas. Out of the total circulation of newspapers in English and major Indian languages about 55 percent are sold in the large cities and towns only. These cities and towns account for only 7 percent of the total population of the country. The circulation of newspapers in rural areas, where the bulk of India's population lives, is negligible. In Mandothi, only six newspapers were subscribed to and their readership confined only to a few educated persons. Of these six newspapers, three were subscribed to by institutions: two by the village high school and one by the primary health center. Only one Urdu newspaper was regularly shared by a few other villagers. The assumption often made that one newspaper in rural areas is shared by a large number of persons did not hold true in Mandothi village.

Printed and Visual Publicity

Printed and visual publicity material brought out by the various concerned organizations of the state, as well as the central government, hardly ever reaches the villages. Even during the course of the Parliamentary election campaign in 1971, the most publicized election campaign in

India up until that time, the reach of printed and visual publicity material was very limited in Mandothi. In all, sixty-three copies of eleven different posters reached the village. Two different wall stencils were used to print the name of the candidates and their election symbols at twenty-five places. In addition, three different folders, two leaflets and four handbills reached the village. It was not possible to assess the number of copies of the folders and leaflets; however, since not many copies were to be seen in the village one could safely say that not many reached there.

But on the basis of close observation, one could argue that while the reach of printed and visual publicity material during the election was very limited, it had potentialities of playing an important role in communication in rural areas. Low literacy in the village was a limiting factor in communication through the printed word, but it did not seem to be a paramount hindrance. If an illiterate could not read the message in posters, pamphlets, etc., the newspaper excepted, he sought the assistance of someone who could read it for him. Further, he could "sense" the message of a poster largely through its visual element. The villagers wanted to have and even preserve printed and visual publicity material. They often used publicity material with visuals for decoration in their houses. This tendency to possess a poster and the ability to sense the meaning largely through its visuals suggests that publicity material with good visuals can be used effectively to communicate with the semiliterate and even illiterate masses in rural India.

Fairs and Festivals

Fairs and festivals provide good opportunities for communication with the villagers. With the improvement of transportation, fairs and festivals attract villagers from great distances. In *melas* [fairs] there are usually, among other things, exhibitions about various new agricultural practices. The *melas* serve religious, economic, entertainment, and learning functions and help in widening the world views of the villagers. The *melas* have been used by the Fertilizer Corporation of India and the Family Planning Department to communicate new ideas and information in different parts of the country, including the Bahadurgarh Development Block where Mandothi is located.

GROUP MEETINGS AND COMMUNICATION IN THE VILLAGE

Having discussed briefly the village social structure and communication, as well as mass communication in the context of Mandothi village, we now turn to a discussion of the place and role of "group meetings"[6] in the communication pattern of the village. By group meeting we mean any group of persons sitting and informally discussing something. One generally finds such groups at various convenient and strategic places such as teashops, street corners and *baithaks* [men's quarters]. They may be playing cards, puffing a *hooka*, taking tea or just basking in the sun, but even so they are usually engaged in some sort of informal discussion. Someone makes a point, others strongly contradict it, others support either of the views expressed during the course of discussion. Occasionally all burst into laughter and then again proceed with their chit-chat. Such group meetings are a common feature of the social life in the village and serve important functions of dissemination and, to an extent, assimilation of information in the village community.

The composition of a group meeting need not be a fixed one, as persons join or withdraw from it quite casually. But the process of group formation is not entirely as casual as it may seem. Principles of social organization operate even in such informal gatherings, and caste, kinship, and factions become important considerations. Usually, a group comprises mainly persons of one particular caste or of the castes having near-equal status in the traditional caste hierarchy. However, sometimes persons from widely different caste status may also be present in such group discussions. The members of other castes are generally faction associates.

Any new information, particularly a startling news item, is likely to be shared with others and can become a topic for discussion in such group meetings. Radio news broadcasts, newspapers, pamphlets, and posters, etc., may also figure in the group discussion. The themes may vary in nature, and may be social, economic, political, religious, or pertaining to sex and morality. Local, regional, national, or international affairs may be discussed. But more often current issues (whatever these may be) form the substance of such discussions. For instance, during the election campaign the villagers in Mandothi tended to discuss election politics more often in such group meetings.

Opinion leaders often give interpretations of news which serve their interest. For instance, the decision of the Election Commission to count the votes polled by the entire constituency rather than counting them by polling booth was distorted by the village *Pradhan* to mean that the new rules would be applicable only in future elections, and in the present elections counting would be done by polling booth, as in the past. In doing so he intended to put pressure on some voters as counting by polling booth has possibilities of providing some clues to the voter's identity.

The villagers often cite some folk or other cultural story to make their

---

[6]   For lack of a better term we are using the term "group meeting" though it has neither the structural and organizational characteristics associated with the concept of GROUP nor does it function as a MEETING having purpose, decorum, agenda, etc.

points. This facilitates greatly the process of communication. Things told in local idioms and in terms of cultural experiences are easy to comprehend and remember.

Thus, these group meetings serve an important function of disseminating information through cultural idioms that facilitate comprehension and assimilation of the information. Hence, group meetings occupy a vital place among the communication channels available in the village and play a significant role through word-of-mouth in the communication process.

CONCLUSIONS

It emerges from the study that personal word-of-mouth communication occupies a prime place in the communication system existing in villages. There are channels and blockades for communication in a village social system itself. Caste, kinship and factional ties tend to influence the speed and direction of communication flow in the village. Opinion leaders play a significant role in the communication process. Informal group discussion, which is a usual phenomenon of village community life, helps in dissemination and assimilation of new information and ideas in the village community. But the reach of the mass media, by and large, is very limited.

REFERENCES

India
1972   India — 1971–1972. New Delhi: The Publication Division, Government of India.
KATZ, ELIHU, PAUL F. LAZARSFELD
1955   *Personal influence: the part played by the people in the flow of mass communication.* Glencoe, Illinois: The Free Press.
MAJUMDAR
1958   *Caste and communication in an Indian village.* New Delhi: Asian Publishing House.
NICHOLAS, RALPH W.
1965   "Factions: a comparative analysis," in *Political systems and distribution of power.* A.S.A. Monograph 2, 21–61. London: Tavistock.
Perception of Indo-Pakistan war at the village level
1972   New Delhi: Indian Institute of Mass Communication.
REHMAN, S.
1970   *Evaluation of audience reaction to documentary films — a report.* New Delhi: Indian Institute of Mass Communication.
Report of the Press Commission
1954   Report of the Press Commission. Government of India.
SEN, LALIT K.
1969   *Opinion leadership in India: a study of interpersonal communication in*

eight villages. Hyderabad: National Institute of Community Development.

YADAVA, J. S.
  1968 Factionalism in a Haryana village. *American Anthropologist* 70 (5):898–910.
  1971 *Communication and parliamentary elections.* New Delhi: Indian Institute of Mass Communication.

Emerging Patterns of Communication Networks in a Developing Society

C. LAKSHMANNA

INTRODUCTION

The importance of effective communications for rapid economic development and social transformation has been adequately recognized by both developed and developing societies. The need for streamlining the communicative processes in order to involve the various societal strata has been one of the major focusses in the policy formulation of the developing societies. It goes without saying that the participative style of governance will be a reality only when the least privileged units of social organization are drawn into the idiom of the management of the affairs of the society; this is possible only when these sections are within the circuit of the information-flow. Even knowledge and awareness of national goals alone can evoke a spontaneous response and readiness to join the pilgrimage of national reconstruction. While such knowledge and aware-ness are no sufficient guarantee for total involvement in such develop-mental activities, there is no doubt that they are an essential prerequisite for the successful implementation of any developmental program.

The drama of development in all the less fortunate societies has involved massive programs of urbanization, industrialization and moder-nization which, to a large extent, have underlined in turn the necessity for the promotion of mass communication networks. Janowitz rightly points out (1968:88–89) that

The present study forms part of a major project on "Sociocultural Change in Village India," a restudy of an Indian (Shamirpet) village which is sponsored by the Indian Council of Social Science Research, New Delhi. I have drawn generous help from my wife Mamata Laksh-manna, a Senior Research Fellow in the Department of Sociology, Osmania University, and my friend N. S. Narasimha Rao, a Research Lecturer in the Department of Sociology, Osmania University (under the ABOCS program) for which I thank them both. I am also thankful to N. Suryanarayana Rao for his painstaking efforts to do a neat typing job.

... mass communication comprises the institutions and techniques by which specialized social groups employ technological devices (press, radio, films, etc.) to disseminate symbolic content to large heterogeneous and widely dispersed audience.

To achieve the triple goal of urbanization, industrialization and modernization, the less developed societies have had to resort to heavy doses of complex technology as inputs. This has underscored the necessity of competent and effective organization of mass communication programs which, as is evident, serve vital functions in the society.

Societies in transition from tradition to modernity have been experiencing several types of problems. In traditional societies, communication media were interwoven into the religious and socioeconomic life of the people. This was possible in simple societies with very little specialization and professionalization. In complex societies, communication media become delinked from such integrated life styles; they can even serve as disparate multidirectional vehicles of ideas, sometimes transmitting conflicting ideas in sequence. The pace of this process of delinking, however, depends on several factors such as the capacity of a given society to usher in a faster economic growth rate, response to meaningful social change, and stabilization of sound political institutions. Further, in a traditional and caste-bound society, the capacity and willingness to be aware of and utilize communication networks is bound to vary considerably from one social level to another. Under such circumstances, the process of modernization, which cultivates the rationalistic and scientific temper, suffers, as a result of which the developing societies must struggle hard to keep up with the pace of technological revolution taking place elsewhere. It is rightly said that

... it is one of the tragedies of underdeveloped countries that their underdevelopment results in an inadequate growth of the media of mass communication and this in turn retards their economic and social progress. It is a vicious circle from which there is no easy escape (Editorial Board 1967:10–14).

COMMUNICATIONS DEVELOPMENT AND THE INDIAN SITUATION

The development of communication networks should normally help mobility and movement among all classes of people (Chapin 1928:279). It should facilitate the people's opting for any occupation which offers scope to their growth and development. But the improvement of communications in India with the introduction of postal service, printing, newspapers, rail and road transport and telegraph, strange as it may seem, created mostly horizontal mobility with very little vertical mobility.

Castes living in different areas which were hitherto experiencing minimum communication could now come together to discuss the common interests and common problems confronting them (Srinivas 1962:74–75); this led to caste solidarity, giving a fresh lease of life to caste organization. Caste associations sprang up in several parts of the country which in subsequent years became active political instruments.

Be that as it may, the attainment of independence brought home the fact that the problem of reconstruction of Indian society was considerably dependent upon the improvement of the communication process in the country. Thus the policy formulations in the post-independence period have laid stress on these aspects. The community development programs which were initiated in October, 1952, among other things clearly envisaged a greater role for transportation networks and communication facilities. They emphasized the importance of the improvement in physical communication networks and the flow of ideas and innovations. The necessity was felt to link far-flung, isolated and moribund villages which were then steeped in traditions and superstitions and lacked a free flow of goods or communications. The appalling level of illiteracy created communication gaps between societal layers. This was accentuated further by the practice of social distance through ritual purity and caste hierarchy — dividing Indian society into innumerable and uncommunicable divisions and very often fostering antagonism and antipathy between these strata.

Such schisms could become inevitable bottlenecks in the process of development and change. It was realized that they would prove stumbling blocks in the realization of egalitarianism and socialism, the cherished goals of the Indian people.

Apart from creating and developing the channels and agencies of communication, it was also felt necessary to develop two categories of communication agents to gear the programs of social regeneration into satisfactory position. First, it was felt that there was an urgent need to develop a cadre of workers, proficient in the technical know-how of different dimensions of development, who could effectively disseminate information and innovations in the rural areas. They were also expected to serve as local community leaders in view of their accessibility to all sections of the society. But gradually it was realized that in order to win acceptance of new ideas and innovations, these change agents should be part of the local ethos and idiom. The professional competence of the cadre had to be supplemented by the spontaneity of response evoked by leadership springing from the local soil. In short, the effective spread of communication, it was realized, greatly depended on the creation and location of opinion leaders and change agents (Page 1963:25). Successive evaluation committees, including the Balwantarai Mehta Committee, stressed the need for the people's participation in the planning and development process. The Community Development Programs had created a big role for leadership and the training and development of grass root leaders from the soil in their formulations; this was further emphasized with the introduction of the Panchayati Raj pattern of local administration. Thus it can be seen that there was adequate stress on the improvement of communication processes in the blueprints of India's planned development, both in terms of the improvement of physical communications and the efficient deployment of communication agents.

THE INDIAN EXPERIMENT: SOME BOTTLENECKS

The Indian experiment in the development of communications as an effective means of national reconstruction experienced difficulties at three levels: First, the vastness of the area to be covered on the one hand and the competing priorities for limited resources on the other accounted for the major difficulty. Many areas of India are still not serviced even by fair weather roads. Highways and other means of rapid transport are out of reach for a major part of the population. Where they have been developed, such communication media have failed to become an integral part of the development process. They are unable to serve as catalytic agents of change; they were unsuccessful in fostering a faster growth rate (Taylor et al. 1965:537).

For instance, the development of roads and centralized markets in semi-urban growth centers did not encourage the farmer to transport his commodities to such places. The role of the middle man continued to plague the economy. Trade and commerce continued to operate almost at the primitive level. This is equally true of other means of communications. The bonds of tradition and religion strengthened with the development in communication facilities like roadways and railways. The increase in travel for pilgrimage has been considerable with the growth of communication networks. The horizontal consolidation of religious and caste groups, earlier mentioned, was made possible through the growth of the communication process — as is often evident in the way local disturbances spread with lightning speed to various parts of the country. Unfortunate as it may be, the development of communications helped broaden the pathway of obscurantism in India. Very often, it failed, thus, to become the intended vehicle of social transformation.

In spite of such failures, however, this development in communication networks should be viewed as a definite step forward in progress. With all its drawbacks, it has helped Indian society to "open up." Maybe, in the long run, only massive communication development programs alone can break the hold of tradition and obscurantism, though in the initial stages they may take undue advantage of the situation through inadequate stress of enlightened educational effort. When once this hold is broken, the wheels of progress and development may run faster. Thus the need for increased effort in developing communication media in India is urgent and pressing. The side-effects have to be processed and analysed so as to devise ways and means to eliminate them.

Secondly, another bottleneck in development came about through large-scale efforts to develop communication processes for the diffusion of innovations in the fields of socioeconomic development, this through the promotion of an articulate and efficient administrative elite. Various schemes such as "Grow More Food" campaigns, "Community Development" programs, the "Organization of Agricultural Universities," the "National Demonstration Schemes," and so forth, attempted to evolve this administrative elite and use it to disseminate new ideas and a "package of practices" in the vital segments of socioeconomic growth, covering a wide range of human activities from agriculture to cooperation. The whole idea was to motivate the illiterate, ignorant but willing villagers to better ways of living and to lift the entire nation from pathetic levels of penury in the direction of plenty. This important project failed because the newly developed administrative elite lacked the mission and zeal so necessary for the success of such an enterprise. It could not generate the active participation of the people and make them adopt the program because it could not talk to the common man "in his own idiom." "Wave lengths" in communication did not synchronize, resulting in a wide communication gap. Subsequently efforts were made to fill this vacuum with ill-conceived schemes of incentives through subsidies which only succeeded in making the people highly dependent upon government sources for the successful completion of projects undertaken. Once these subsidies ceased, efforts to develop the countryside also came to a standstill. Thus the administrative elite failed to integrate themselves into the main stream of Indian life, and only stood aloof gaping at the colossal failure of the organized effort to establish a self-generation process in socioeconomic growth.

The third major bottleneck to development was witnessed in efforts to promote a grassroots political elite which would step into the gap created by the inability of the administrative elite to enthuse the people into effective participation in nation-building tasks. This was based upon the sound principle that people's representatives alone can feel the pulse of the people and represent their aspirations and needs, and on the supposition that the problem of alienation, so obvious in the case of the administrative elite, would not arise because the political elite would be drawn from the rank-and-file of the people themselves. It was expected that they would be effectively in tune with priorities in the developmental needs of the common man. It was expected that they would be backed by all sections of the society, for they shared with the people the same strong desire to improve the deplorable conditions of their lifestyles.

While it is true that the political elite, so entrusted with developmental tasks, had the power and authority to command the support of the people, the project floundered, to a large extent, because this leadership had a vested interest in the continuance of the backward economy. By and large, the leadership was comprised of the traditional caste leaders and they could not completely identify with the goals and objectives of development for this also meant the undermining of their own authority and power, once the pace of development was accelerated. It is, therefore, observed that though this traditional leadership showed considerable eagerness to jump into the void to breach it, yet it did not become an effective agent of planned change. The political elite utilized the new opportunities to foster their own interests, serving the interests of their people with only lip service and empty slogans.

If Indian developmental efforts are to ultimately succeed, it largely depends upon the nation's capacity to disengage from the grip of such vested interests and develop a purposeful and socially forward-looking leadership. In the area of the development of efficient communication channels, this is a major challenge.

COMMUNICATION NETWORKS AND SHAMIRPET VILLAGE

Shamirpet Village, like any other Indian Village, has been in the throes of development. Within easy reach of the twin cities of Hyderabad and Secunderabad in Andhra Pradesh, it is situated 32 kilometers northeast of Hyderabad on Karimnagar Road. Shamirpet has been covered by the National Extension Services, Community Development Program and Panchayatiraj administration, successively. Further, it forms part of the jurisdiction of the Block Level Extension Officer of Andhra Pradesh Agricultural University under the District Extension Program. It is clear, therefore, that Shamirpet has had several varied inputs of socioeconomic development, and since it is located on an urban fringe, all the opportunities to develop into a bustling metropolitan suburb.

Communication and Developmental Facilities

As just said, Shamirpet is only 32 kilometers away from the twin cities. It is situated at a distance of 1 kilometer from the main road which connects Hyderabad with the district town of Karimnagar. A regular bus service runs between these two places as it also runs between Hyderabad and Siddipet. More than twenty buses make the run every day in both directions. The nearest railway station is Bolaram, about 10 kilometers from Shamirpet. It is a fairly large village with a population of 3,670 by the

1971 census, (including the two hamlets Babuguda and Upparapalli). Shamirpet is served by a branch post office maintained by a priest family. A runner brings mail from Hakimpet for distribution in the village by a postman. It takes only a few hours for the villager to receive his mail from Hakimpet. There is an upper primary school in Shamirpet (about 150 students and seven teachers). The police station is in the charge of a sub-inspector of police, has a strength of one head constable, one S.W.P.C., and fifteen constables. Shamirpet police station also serves thirty-five villages in the vicinity. Under Community Development Programs, a primary health center was established here in 1959 under the control of a medical officer assisted by one compounder, one health supervisor, and one health visitor. The hospital operates four important programs including the National Malaria Eradicating Program, the National Leprosy Control program and the family planning program. Since November 1958, Shamirpet has functioned as one of the centers under a Key Village scheme intended for intensive cattle development in the area. The *gram-panchayat* of the village maintains a community radio set, but there is no library with newspapers available for the use of the villagers. The nearest cinema is located 10 kilometers away in Bolarum.

Knowledge and Communication Networks

The present study is an attempt to analyze the impact of communications networks in Shamirpet. It mainly focusses on three aspects of the problem: (1) local knowledge about the existence of communication facilities and the utilization of them and the other mass media by the people; (2) the peoples' awareness about their key change agents, such as the political leaders of different levels (results obtained through field investigations); (3) the spread of information concerning certain developmental activities through the traditional and modern communication media. Thus the scope of the present study is delimited to these three major concerns, through which it is hoped to outline the emerging patterns at the end of the discussion. Data pertaining to 270 households[1] fairly representative of the total study have been undertaken for the purposes of the present discussion. Table 1 shows the distribution of the sample by variables such as caste, education and age of the respondents.

---

[1]   However, the total households in the village were 470. For full discussion, see my project report on the study (forthcoming). A similar study, sponsored by Aachen Bochum Osmania Cooperation Scheme Research Project Board with the sole emphasis on communication networks, spreads and linkages in Telangana villages is under progress in the Department of Sociology, Osmania University, Hyderabad.

Table 1. Distribution of the Shamirpet sample by caste, education and age

Caste groups	No.	%	Educational levels	No.	%	Age groups	No.	%
1. Upper castes	72	26.7	Illiterate	222	82.2	25 and below	25	9.3
2. Middle castes	93	34.4	Literate	48	17.8	26 to 40	94	34.8
3. Lower castes	82	30.4				41 and above	151	55.9
4. Muslims	23	8.5						
Total	270	100.0	Total	270	100.0	Total	270	100.0

CASTE COMPOSITION.[2]   The distribution of the sample by caste shows that the Middle Castes group is the major group with 34.4 percent while the Muslims constitute the minor group with 8.5 percent respondents. However the Upper Castes and the Lower Castes lie in between with 26.7 percent and 30.4 percent, respectively.

LITERACY COMPOSITION.   It is seen that 82.2 percent of the sample are illiterates and 17.8 percent are literates.

AGE COMPOSITION.   More than half of the sample (55.9 percent) falls in the age group of 41 years and above, while about a third (34.8 percent) belong to the age group of 26 to 40 years. Only 9.3 percent are in the age group of 25 years and below. Since the study enlisted the cooperation of heads of households and the decision-makers in the family, the distribution of the population under these categories should reflect that in the country as a whole.

Knowledge and Utilization of Some Communication Networks

One of the objectives of the study is to assess the knowledge among the people in Shamirpet village about the existence (and utilization) of certain communication facilities such as the post office, railway station and the roadway bus stop as well as their use of mass media like the newspapers, the radio and the cinema.

Table 2 shows that as far as the location of the post office, railway station and bus stop are concerned, the Upper Castes, the Middle Castes and the Muslims have 100 percent knowledge, except in the case of the Middle Castes with regard to the post office; 1.9 percent of Middle Caste respondents did not know where it was. In the case of the Lower Castes, 2.4 percent, and 6.1 percent of the respondents did not know about the existence, respectively, of the post office and the railway station and bus stop. On the whole 98 percent (even a little more) of the respondents were aware of the existence of these communication networks.

While knowledge about the existence and location of these facilities is very high, Table 3 shows that they were not put to good use. Only 27.7 percent of the respondents used the post office, while 76.2 percent used the railways and 92.8 percent the buses for travel. It is significant that a

---

[2]   For the purposes of this discussion, Upper Castes include the Brahmins, the Rajus, the Vaisyas, the Kapus, the Reddis, the Padmasalis, the Munnuru Kapus, the Katikas and the Chippas. The Middle Castes comprise the smiths (called the Pancha Brahma group consisting of the Avusula, Kammari, Vadia, Kanchari and Silpi), the Goundlas, the Mutrasis, the Kummaris, the Chakalis and the Mangalis. The Lower Castes consist of the Vadderas, the Erukulas, the Pichiguntlas, the Malas and the Madigas. The last two castes also count themselves among Harijans.

Table 2.   Knowledge about the communication networks among different caste groups in Shamirpet

Caste groups		Post office			Railway station			Roadway bus stop		
		Yes	No	Total	Yes	No	Total	Yes	No	Total
1. Upper castes		72	0	72	72	0	72	72	0	72
	%	100	0	100	100	0	100	100	0	100
2. Middle castes		92	1	93	93	0	93	93	0	93
	%	98.1	1.9	100	100	0	100	100	0	100
3. Lower castes		80	2	82	77	5	82	77	5	82
	%	97.6	2.4	100	93.9	6.1	100	93.9	6.1	100
4. Muslims		23	0	23	23	0	23	23	0	23
	%	100	0	100	100	0	100	100	0	100
Total		267	3	270	265	5	270	265	5	270
	%	98.9	1.1	100	98.2	1.8	100	98.2	1.8	100

Table 3. Utilization of the communication networks among different caste groups in Shamirpet

Caste groups		Post office			Railway station			Roadway bus stop		
		Yes	No	Total	Yes	No	Total	Yes	No	Total
1. Upper castes		23	49	72	55	17	72	64	8	72
	%	31.9	68.1	100	76.4	23.6	100	88.9	11.1	100
2. Middle castes		26	66	92	76	17	93	91	2	93
	%	28.3	71.7	100	81.7	18.3	100	97.8	2.2	100
3. Lower castes		7	73	80	52	25	77	69	8	77
	%	8.8	91.2	100	67.5	32.5	100	89.6	10.4	100
4. Muslims		18	5	23	19	4	23	22	1	23
	%	78.3	21.7	100	82.6	17.4	100	95.6	4.4	100
Total		74	193	267	202	63	265	246	19	265
	%	27.7	72.3	100	76.2	23.8	100	92.8	7.2	100

very high percentage of Muslims utilized all these services, including the post office; the Upper and Middle Castes used the railways and roadways considerably. In the case of the post office, only 31.9 percent of the Upper Castes and 29.3 percent of the Middle Castes used this communication facility. Lower Caste utilization of the post office is very insignificant but they put the railways and road to comparatively good use. If we add up the figures of those who did not even know about the existence and location of these networks, the non-utilization among this group becomes really significant.

The post office can have, obviously, great reach and coverage as a communication network. It can connect any point of the world with the place where it is located. Hence we attempted to find out the extent of the distance of the destination of letters posted and received through this medium in Shamirpet, as shown in Table 4.

Significantly, we find that among the respondents using the post office the Muslims did so to communicate with people at all distances and levels — from the *taluk* to foreign lands. The Lower Castes correspond only at two levels — within the district and the state. The Upper and Middle Castes corresponded all over the whole country. In the case of correspondence with people within the country, the Upper Castes account for a good percentage among users of this facility.

The larger spread in correspondence among the Muslims can perhaps be attributed to two reasons. First, the Muslims' being a minority community on the one hand and on the other a ruling community in the area under the erstwhile Nizam's dominion about two and a half decades back might make them outward-looking in attitudes and consequently account for their correspondence with people all over India — incidentally proving our earlier thesis about horizontal mobility resulting from the strengthening of communication networks — and also outside India. Secondly, a large number of the Muslims in this area have relatives in Pakistan and the Middle East, which means correspondence with such relatives. While Upper Castes utilize this medium even for correspondence within the *taluk*, the Middle and Lower Castes do not use it to such an extent at this level. This could be because the people belonging to these castes use personal visits to communicate with people at the *taluk* level. But what is significant is the effective utilization of the post office for correspondence within the district, which only shows that the villagers are gradually "opening up" to the outside world.

In terms of age groups, the large number of people belonging to older age groups have wider correspondence spreads. This prompted us to look into the age groups among the Muslims and the destination of their correspondence. While older groups among them carried on long distance correspondence, younger groups (not only Muslims) had a correspondence spread only to the district level. The post office is one facility

Table 4. Destination of letters (by caste, age and education of sender) from Shamirpet

	0		1		2		3		4		5		Total	
	No.	%	No.	%	No.	%	No.	%	No.	%	No.	%	No.	%
Caste group:														
Upper castes	2	8.7	5	21.7	3	13.1	10	43.4	3	13.1	0	0.0	23	100.0
Middle castes	0	0.0	2	7.7	5	19.2	17	65.4	2	7.7	0	0.0	26	100.0
Lower castes	0	0.0	0	0.0	2	28.6	5	71.4	0	0.0	0	0.0	7	100.0
Muslims	1	5.5	1	5.5	2	11.2	12	66.7	1	5.5	1	5.5	18	100.0
Total	3	4.0	8	10.8	12	16.2	44	59.5	6	8.1	1	1.4	74	100.0
Age groups:														
25 and below	0	0.0	0	0.0	1	11.1	7	77.8	1	11.1	0	0.0	9	100.0
26–40	0	0.0	3	15.8	2	10.5	11	57.9	2	10.5	1	5.3	19	100.0
41 and above	3	6.5	5	10.9	9	19.6	26	56.5	3	6.5	0	0.0	46	100.0
Total	3	4.0	8	10.8	12	16.2	44	59.5	6	8.1	1	1.4	74	100.0
Educational levels:														
Literates	0	0.0	3	10.0	7	23.3	17	56.7	2	6.7	1	3.3	30	100.0
Illiterates	3	6.8	5	11.4	5	11.4	27	61.3	4	9.1	0	0.0	44	100.0
Total	3	4.0	8	10.8	12	16.2	44	59.5	6	8.1	1	1.4	74	100.0

Key:
0 = no response;   1 = within the *taluk*;   2 = within the district;
3 = within the state;   4 = within the country;   5 = outside the country.

which can be utilized even by illiterates for they can get letters written or read by others; thus we found a good number of illiterates were also availing themselves of this facility.

Use of Mass Media by the Villagers

Among the communications channels, mass media also play a significant part in building up the climate for socioeconomic change. We have attempted in this study to determine the utilization of some of these media by Shamirpet villagers. We have confined ourselves, for the purpose of analysis, to the media of newspapers, radio broadcasts, and cinema. It is seen from Table 5 that only 17 percent of the respondents read newspapers (this figure may include those who listen to news read by others for their benefit). Only 29.3 percent of the respondents went to cinemas, though the twin cities have a large number of cinema houses. But 44.1 percent of the respondents listened to the radio. Lower Castes have utilized very little of these media while the Muslims put them to greater use. The Upper Castes show an indifferent attitude, mainly from fear that development may ultimately pose a challenge to their power and authority. This has led to a sort of "inward looking" attitude in them, and an attempt to consolidate their position within the village and the region so as to safeguard their interests in the future.

The other castes are gradually gaining ascendancy in the power structure in India, which may be reflected in their greater use of cinema and radio. The Middle Castes, as in the case with the Muslims, are slowly developing "outward looking" attitudes so as to take advantage of the benefits available to them in the new political processes. It may perhaps take some more time for the Lower Castes, especially Harijans, to reach this level, though there are already some indications in this direction. The twin cities have two or three well-established Urdu newspapers, whereas there is only one fairly good Telegu newspaper. This may be one of the reasons for the greater utilization of newspapers by the Muslims.

Political Elites and the Villagers

As discussed earlier, official political leaders have a significant part to play as effective communication and change agents in India. The communication between these leaders and the people should be a "two-way flow." The leaders should maintain contacts with the people so as to provide an effective feedback mechanism about the impact of the developmental programs on the people. In turn, the people should be able to confide in the leaders so that they can express their needs properly

Table 5. Use of mass media in Shamirpet

Caste groups		Newspapers			Radio			Cinema		
		Yes	No	Total	Yes	No	Total	Yes	No	Total
1. Upper castes		13	59	72	32	40	72	32	40	72
	%	18.0	82.0	100	44.4	55.6	100	44.4	55.6	100
2. Middle castes		15	78	93	51	42	93	36	57	93
	%	16.1	83.9	100	54.8	45.2	100	63.2	36.8	100
3. Lower castes		4	78	82	23	59	82	1	81	82
	%	4.9	95.1	100	28.0	72.0	100	1.2	98.8	100
4. Muslims		14	9	23	13	10	23	10	13	23
	%	60.9	39.1	100	56.5	43.5	100	43.5	56.5	100
Total		46	224	270	119	151	270	79	191	270
	%	17.0	83.0	100	44.1	55.9	100	29.3	70.7	100

through these leaders. Thus it was felt desirable to find out about how this two-way flow with these leaders actually worked among different groups in Shamirpet.

These leaders are classified as local and regional leader groups and state and national leader groups. As is seen from Table 6, the Lower Castes have minimum contacts with leaders at different levels except the *gram panchayat* members. Muslims' contacts taper down from *gram panchayat* members to Zilla Parishad Chairman. However 30.4 percent of them maintain contacts with the M.L.A. and the M.P. The contacts of Upper Castes with these leaders vary from 16.7 percent to 4.2 percent, excepting *gram panchayat* members (84.7 percent). The Lower and Middle Castes have better contacts with the M.L.A. of the region. On the whole Middle Castes show greater desire for such contacts than the Upper Castes. Incidentally, it must be stated here that the M.L.A. of the region hails from the Harijans (of the Lower Castes), and the M.P. is a Muslim. Perhaps this accounts for the indifference of the Upper Castes, or perhaps they are making contacts through the administrative personnel with whom they deal. Since Muslims belong to the minority group they might be taking advantage of local political elites in seeing to their needs. Or, the Muslims of older age groups being better educated, they may be in a better position to make use of political contacts. From the table and the foregoing discussion, it could be inferred that political leaders do not really evince sufficient interest in getting in touch with the people and maintaining contacts. Where the contacts exist they exist on the basis of caste and communal considerations. Since the communication programs can succeed only if they identify with the people, there is a need for political leaders to make greater efforts at this in order to become effective vehicles of planned social change.

Development Programs and the Administrative Elite as the Communication and Adoption Agents

The various Indian developmental activities needed technical experts to convey the importance of these programs and to win acceptance of them by the people. However, more often than not, these experts have not succeeded in carrying the people. This is shown in Table 7. As far as the awareness about the Indian family planning program is concerned, all the caste groups are well informed about it, but few make use of it. In this connection, it is worth recalling that there are massive Indian efforts to propagate the family planning program, both by government agencies and government-aided voluntary organizations. But it is seen from the table that only a very low percentage of the people have adopted the family planning methods. This means that the administrative and techni-

Table 6. Contacts with the political leaders in Shamirpet

Caste groups		Local and regional leaders									State and national leaders					
		Gram panchayat member			Panchayat samithi president			Zilla parishad chairman			M.L.A.			M.P.		
		Yes	No	Total	Yes	No	Total	Yes	No	Total	Yes	No	Total	Yes	No	Total
1. Upper castes		61	11	72	12	60	72	9	63	72	7	65	72	3	69	72
	%	84.7	15.3	100	16.7	83.3	100	12.5	87.5	100	9.7	90.3	100	4.2	95.8	100
2. Middle castes		79	14	93	16	77	93	7	86	93	15	78	93	3	90	93
	%	85.0	15.0	100	17.2	82.8	100	7.5	92.5	100	16.1	83.9	100	3.2	96.8	100
3. Lower castes		65	17	82	4	78	82	2	80	82	11	71	82	0	82	82
	%	79.3	20.7	100	4.9	95.1	100	2.4	97.6	100	13.4	86.6	100	0	100	100
4. Muslims		20	3	23	11	12	23	9	14	23	7	16	23	7	16	23
	%	87	13	100	47.8	52.2	100	39.1	60.9	100	30.4	69.6	100	30.4	69.6	100
Total		225	45	270	43	227	270	27	243	270	40	230	270	13	257	270
	%	82.33	17.67	100	15.3	84.7	100	10	90	100	14.8	85.2	100	4.8	95.2	100

Table 7. Family planning and applied nutrition programs in Shamirpet

Caste groups		Knowledge about family planning			Use of family planning methods			Knowledge about applied nutrition programs		
		Yes	No	Total	Yes	No	Total	Yes	No	Total
1. Upper castes		60	10	72	4	56	60	1	71	72
	%	83.3	16.7	100	6.7	93.3	100	1.4	98.6	100
2. Middle castes		84	9	93	9	75	84	3	93	93
	%	90.3	9.7	100	10.7	89.3	100	3.2	96.8	100
3. Lower castes		72	10	82	6	66	72	0	82	82
	%	87.8	12.2	100	8.3	91.7	100	0	100	100
4. Muslims		23	0	23	1	22	23	0	23	23
	%	100	0	100	7.4	92.6	100	0	100	100
Total		239	31	270	20	219	239	4	266	270
	%	88.5	11.5	100	8.4	91.6	100	1.5	98.5	100

cal officers in the family planning program have failed to impress upon the people the urgency and the magnitude of the population problem. About the applied nutrition program, the picture is also very dismal. The organizers of this program have failed to create in Shamirpet even an awareness about its existence. This is evident from the table because it shows that only four (1.5 percent) people among the respondents had any idea about this all-important program. The future of India is not only dependent upon the control of its population but also on promoting the health of its citizens. In this connection, the importance of nutrition is obvious.

Further, from the field investigations in Shamirpet, it was clear that the developmental agencies utilized the traditional modes of communication like the *Burrakathas*, dances and puppet shows for popularizing these programs. Most of the respondents from all caste groups acknowledged this fact. But what is significant is that while these traditional modes helped to bring about an awareness of the developmental processes, they did not offer enough incentives to make people adopt the suggested innovations. This means that more strenuous efforts have to be made to locate, in addition, other traditional modes and modernize them in order to bring about the desired change in the basic attitudes of the people. This perhaps could act as a lever for change in future.

REFERENCES

CHAPIN, F. S.
1928   *Cultural change.* New York: Century.
EDITORIAL BOARD
1967   The problem — A statement posing the many facets involved in media. *Seminar* (issue on Mass Communication), New Delhi.
JANOWITZ, MORRIS
1968   "The study of mass communication," in *International Encyclopaedia of Social Sciences.*
PAGE, L. W.
1963   "Models of traditional, transitional and modern communication systems," in *Communication and Political Development.* Princeton, New Jersey: Princeton University Press.
SRINIVAS, M. N.
1962   *Caste in modern India.* Bombay: Asia Publishing House.
TAYLOR, CARL C., *et al.*
1965   *India's roots of democracy.* Bombay: Orient Longman's.

Network Concepts in the Sociology of Language

EVANGELOS A. AFENDRAS

In a comparative study of two very different communities in northwestern Europe and India respectively, Gumperz (1964) came upon the concept of social network developed by Barnes ten years before that in a study of class structure and political processes in a Norwegian community. Barnes' work (1954) inspired a continuous tradition of anthropological and sociological effort with what some practitioners saw as a dynamic research tool, a tool which could parallel that of kinship analysis in the study of tribal societies, and be used in the study of "fluid" social systems undergoing rapid change. But, in spite of Gumperz' discovery, what happened in the study of language and society was different: the attention of ethno- and sociolinguists to network concepts has been quite sparse and while mention of networks has been there, work actually utilizing them has also been more or less sporadic.

In the belief that rather than reflecting the usefulness of network analysis to sociolinguistic research this absence is accidental, I would like to present here in summary form the cases where networks WERE used, the explanatory uses to which they were put, the conceptual systems based on networks in some cognate fields, and suggestions for further cross-disciplinary links.

The discussion will be limited to those instances in which network concepts are explicit and not to instances which, although of a related

The idea of boundary has been touched on in this paper — where the network may stop, where the speech community or area fades out. A volume edited by Barth (1969) contains a number of papers on boundaries which are directly pertinent to many of the concepts which I have presented here, e.g. recruitment, interaction, etc. Sociometric methodology will be found in Borgatta (1968), formal aspects of networks in Barnes (1969), the role of spatial constraints to communication and interaction and additional formal models in Olsson (1965).

nature, do not draw on any formalized and explicit network notions as such.

CLOSED–OPEN NETWORKS, SWITCHING AND CHANGE: GUMPERZ

The pioneer work of Gumperz on the community of Hemnesberget (based on previous sociological analysis) focused on an attempt to relate different kinds of interaction networks to different kinds of "codeswitching" and the entry points of linguistic innovation in the local verbal repertoire.

The cluster of binary concepts with which Gumperz operated is as follows:

SUPERPOSED (intrapersonal) variation — ". . . shifts in the language of single individuals" and its opposite, DIALECTAL variation; PERSONAL interaction in which individuals act as such rather than for limited apparent goals, and TRANSACTIONAL in which the goals are limited, individuality is suspended, and status is enacted. Specific interactions, however, are not exclusively personal or transactional but MAINLY one or the other, and shift to secondary interaction can take place. Next, depending on the MAIN type of interaction in which superposed variation occurs, we distinguish personal or transactional SWITCHING. Finally, in order to study the locus of superposed variation, Gumperz follows Barnes in rejecting the segmentation of the community into classes defined by sociodemographic criteria and proposes the study of superposed variation "by means of the interaction patterns through which social relationships are maintained" (1964:34). SOCIAL NETWORKS, which are introduced at this point, are also split into two types:

Given three individuals A , B, and C, if A and B are acquainted, and B and C are also acquainted, the network is CLOSED if there is a HIGH PROBABILITY that A also knows C. If on the other hand, there is a HIGH PROBABILITY that A will not know C, the network is said to be OPEN (1966:34–35; emphasis added).

Ultimately, Gumperz observes that PERSONAL SWITCHING is more responsible for language shift, borrowing (at a word level or higher), i.e. change of a nongradual, noninternal type, and that "personal switching is confined to open networks." He further remarks that the study of the incidence of types of networks, and of types of switching within them, in a bilingual speech community could provide us with further clues for its stability over time.

Gumperz comments that ". . . Hemnesberget residents of socio-economic group one were found to be LARGELY part of closed networks; . . . MANY members of group(s) two, . . . showed open network characteristics . . ." (1966:35; emphasis added). In contrasting Khalapur to Hemnesberget, he remarks the relative absence of open networks in the former — CLOSURE is more typical. There are, however, mentions of the rich in Khalapur having friendlier relations with wealthy merchants from neighboring villages than with poorer caste brothers (1964:142), a comment which can be interpreted as implying the existence of some open networks for the merchants of Khalapur.

There is also something in the difference between the two communities beyond the difference in closure, which is not captured in the above model of networks; this may be because of its initial use and development to account for the Norwegian case. What I mean is the fact that there is a very strong element of hierarchization in the Indian case (largely absent in Norway) a dimension apart from closure. This is certainly reflected in the kinds of networks one encounters, as in the description of the hierarchical sitting and smoking arrangement in Khalapur. I will discuss subsequently other kinds of network models which may prove more adequate in this respect. (As Neustupný points out in his papers, we obviously have here pyramidal or pivotal kinds of networks.) Part of the social change affecting Khalapur is also what we could refer to as the recruitment of members of the population into open networks and this among groups in which traditionally such members were not recruited. This recruitment is done through increased educational opportunities, and is affected by external changes: for instance, the overall improvement of the transport and communication systems. The nature and distribution of open networks may well depend on the educational, administrative, economic and other systems and services available and this is supported by Gumperz' comments on the interurban network of transport and communication.

From the preceding comments it is clear that networks lie on a continuum of closeness–openness and we may say that the distinction of two types according to the poles of this continuum may be arbitrary and perhaps even unnecessary. Certainly many networks will display the extremely high or extremely low transitivity of friendship which defines closure. But we can expect as many to have nonextremal transitivity values. For this, it seems advantageous to study DEGREE of closure of networks rather than a binary classification.

An application of Gumperz' conceptual framework for the study of change has appeared in an article by Basso (1973) on change in the terminological system of relation-kinship. Basso probes the position of the concept of network in the field of concepts surrounding that of speech community, and draws in part on Hymes' definition article (1968). Having pointed out the features of the Kalapalo (Upper Xingu) setting, linguistic diversity, systems of intervillage trade, kinship ties, intermarriage, common mythology, "the shared set of normative expectations on the conduct of social relationships," the lack of widespread bilingualism or of a lingua franca and the fact that verbal interaction within the community is appropriate only among kinsmen, Basso concludes that such cannot be called a speech community in Bloomfield's sense of a community characterized by intensive, frequent verbal interaction among all its members (Gumperz 1966:28). Her discussion leads eventually to the substitution for speech community of the term COMMUNICATIONS NETWORK, defined as:

... a system consisting of several kinds of linkages between individuals and groups, in which verbal and nonverbal codes are present but not necessarily shared by the total set of participants. The use of these various codes results in intersecting lines of communication by which any message can be ultimately transmitted to, and understood by, any local group or individual. (1973:5).

Basso relates next the enactment of communication networks to different types of situations, namely, personal and nonpersonal (Gumperz' transactional), according to the participants, codes, and the content. She analyzes, furthermore, the kinds of SETTINGS, events and relationships that characterize the two types of situations. The introduction of Portuguese terms is examined in the context of changes in the network characteristics because of external pressures (such as resettlement). These changes consisted in activation of existing links of kinship, friendship and affinity; such activation effected other linkages, for instance, recruitment into new networks through intermarriage and/or "concrete assistance in major work projects." These links being characterized by egalitarian relationships, linguistic experimentation and innovation became possible, and the "impartial" Portuguese terms were used to label the new links — and eliminate "designative inadequacy."

Thus Basso introduces the notion of somehow extended networks which cut across intelligibility boundaries and do not rely on a lingua franca except in the sense that they establish a LINGUA FRANCA OF KINSHIP TERMS (of Portuguese derivation); she connects the formation of either fresh networks or links with the rise of lexical needs to label these as part of the communicative behavior that allows their enactment (in addition to kinesic or other activities such as embracing and flirting). Ritualized enactment in nonpersonal situations is irrelevant to the study of change.

NETWORK DIFFERENCES AND LANGUAGE DIFFERENCES: LABOV

Basing his analysis on data collected in his survey, Labov has given us (1968) an interesting example of the application of sociometric techniques to the study of social (and speech) networks. His criticism of data from so-called "judgment samples," "random samples," and "stratified

random samples" in face-to-face interviews which skew the context of
language use recall Gumperz' similar comments (e.g. 1966:30). Labov's
study focusses on two types of populations: individuals who are members
of clearcut CLOSED NETWORKS (gangs) and a group who are by contrast
isolated, the so-called "lames":

> ... even in the most solid workingclass areas, there are many isolated children
> who grow up without being members of any vernacular peer-group and a steadily
> increasing number of individuals split away from the vernacular culture in their
> adolescent years (1968:84).

As with Basso, Labov touches on the notion of speech community (e.g.
p. 113) but how it differs from a speech network is not clear: other than
that the former is defined by frequency of interaction and CLOSURE of the
networks involved. If we consider criteria of interaction frequency we end
up with one kind of speech community; if we weigh criteria of some sort of
symbolic identification (Fishman's definition), we end up with another
kind of speech community. One possibility is to distinguish between
MICRO- and MACRO-SPEECH COMMUNITIES, or CONTACT and REFERENCE
(Fishman 1971a:233).

Another problem we encounter in Labov's use of the network concept
is of a similar nature as we have encountered in the previous paragraphs.
Although he contrasts "lames" and gang members as basically isolated
individuals versus members of a network, he does occasionally mention
that a "lame" too may partake of various interaction networks:

> ... A lame may not achieve full competence in any one vernacular dialect, since
> HE INTERACTS AS AN INDIVIDUAL WITH MANY OTHER INDIVIDUALS AND SMALL GROUPS
> rather than participate fully in any primary group ... (1968:113; emphasis
> added).

In examining the differences between these two populations (members
and lames), Labov attempts to characterize members by some network
features (p. 99; diagram, p. 100; sociometric data, p. 102; socioeconomic
data, p. 105). But while he distinguishes between types of members,
lames are treated as an amorphous residual group: its individuals enjoy
identical contexts of social isolation! However, it is obvious from the
sociometric diagrams provided (e.g. p. 100) that there are some lames
who have "weak" connections to the hang-out groups, among other
possible network links (see Labov 1968:113, and his Note 11, p. 92). The
very methodology used for the collection of data, the naming technique,
may be of limited use with other populations (other than urban, adolescent New Yorkers); for instance, groups of immigrants. Here, we may
also have totally different TYPES of networks and totally different participation patterns for the individual than the all-encompassing gang and
hang-out groups of the adolescents, involving work, intermarriage,

encounter networks, etc. (see also Ervin-Tripp in Fishman 1971a:70). A method for collecting data must be found that will tap information which may slip through naming questionnaires, such as a daily-activities or communication questionnaire, or the "language diary" used by Ure (1971:136–156).

As for a statement of the linguistic differences among lames and members, in Labov's words:

CATEGORICAL OR SEMICATEGORICAL RULES OF BE [Black English] ARE WEAKENED TO VARIABLE RULES BY THE LAMES; VARIABLE RULES THAT ARE IN STRONG USE IN BE ARE REDUCED TO A LOW LEVEL BY THE LAMES. Whenever there is a contrast between SE and BE, the language of the Lames is shifted dramatically towards SE [Standard English] (1968:98; original emphasis).

And concerning discourse and verbal interaction skills,

If we are interested in toasts, jokes, sounds, the dozens, riffing or capping, we cannot turn to the lames . . . proficiency at these verbal skills is achieved only by daily practice and constant immersion in the flow of speech (p. 111).

ON OTHER DIMENSIONS OF SPEECH NETWORKS: HYMES AND NEUSTUPNÝ

Hymes and Neustupný have contributed to the definition of the conceptual field within which speech network could be viewed in a more proper perspective. Their suggestions on the many faces of communicative similarity/distance could in fact be followed through with a more rigorous study of the TYPES OF SOCIAL NETWORKS that may yield (or favor) the different types of such distance. Some pertinent data and discussion will be found in Clyne (1972:107–110), Sorensen (1967), and Fishman (1971a:283–284), and of course even in older linguistic or ethnographic work on traditional *Sprachbünde*. I consider Hymes' series of definitions (below) as the starting point for the systematization of this conceptual field. He has related the notion of SPEECH NETWORK to a number of other notions partly along the lines which we have been following here.

. . . I would tentatively define the basic notion of SPEECH COMMUNITY in terms of shared knowledge of rules for the interpretation of at least one common code. Common rules of use but none of code would imply a SPEECH AREA . . . Common rules of code but not of use, might be taken to imply one aspect of SPEECH FIELD, that range of settings in which one's knowledge or rules makes communication potentially possible. For a given person, or group, one would have to investigate empirically the variety of settings in which the PERSONAL (or group) REPERTOIRE of codes and rules of use would permit communication. A distinctive hierarchy, or array, or profile of speech fields might result. In this respect one might want also to distinguish SPEECH NETWORK, as the particular linkages of communication actively participated in by a person or group (1968:37; original emphasis).

Neustupný's work on social networks, to my knowledge, represents the most elaborate and extensive application of this concept. Not only does he touch on a number of different aspects of networks, but he also uses them in the context of both micro- and macrosociolinguistic investigations. He is among the first to breach the subject of network membership, and formation maintenance, or, in terms of the network jargon, RECRUIT-MENT. He touches, for instance, on Japanese intergroup contact (and potential recruitment) when he points out that a Japanese may bridge social distance by ". . . declaring one's social group and position within the group . . . looking for mutual friends . . . speaking about them and supplying new information about their contemporary alliances" (1972, 1973a:19). Elsewhere (1972:84, etc.) he implies the importance of friendship since socialization time for in-groupness; equality of status, sharing of working situation and sharing of entertainment situations. The above attributes, if not directly involved in recruitment, appear important in qualifying potential "recruits" in a (Japanese) friendship network.

Neustupný also discusses network characteristics other than openness and their relation to particular social systems (1971:119) and furthermore, the relation to speech rules, for instance:

. . . the rule that there is only one pivot within a network seems to be related with the impossibility to pay respect to two superiors within a situation in which one is subject and one is the object of the same predicate (1972, 1973a:21).

He relies on network attributes and terminology elaborated by Bavelas and his followers on which we will present more subsequently. Neustupný hints also at the appropriateness of particular communicative routines for given networks (1973a:23). In related work, Ervin-Tripp (1971:21) has pointed out differences in rules for address depending on network, as for instance, in the output of the TLN rule, where T = (Mr., Dr., Prof.) and is known, but LN is not:

T + LN → T = Ø → Ø   (academic speakers)
        → T   (nonacademic speakers)

Another interesting suggestion that Neustupný makes relates to the idea of combination of various network attributes, something that seems worth exploring further and to which we will return. He observes, specifically, that open networks have a tendency to be also nonhierarchical and homogeneous and, if I understand him correctly, are not found embedded in network hierarchies (1973a:25). He introduces the distinction between ENCOUNTER and GROUP networks, meaning "the particular arrangement of personnel in a communicative situation" and the group of "individuals who usually communicate" (1973b:13). With regard to language treatment networks, he calls for the study of formation rules, recruitment, internal structure, flow of information etc. He examines DIFFERENTIATION, i.e. types occurring with regard to institutional, social level, from folk to private association to professional to governmental. He makes some diachronic observations, such as, folk networks (characterized as SCATTERED) become WHEEL during encounter and in case of divergent opinion, resolve the conflict through split, and are, furthermore, characterized by PARTICULARISTIC RECRUITMENT. In contrast, some modern professional or government networks are characterized as ALL-CHANNEL and less hierarchical (1973b:18).

INTEGRATIVE STUDIES: FISHMAN, ERVIN-TRIPP

We also find the occasional discussion of the network concept in the integrative works of Fishman and Ervin-Tripp (from two different perspectives). Fishman (1971a:233ff.) introduces the term NETWORK RANGE in a sense that seems to be equivalent to that of network REPERTOIRE or Hymes' use of the term speech network itself (Hymes 1968:37). He classifies types according to domain of interaction: family, occupation, interest, friendship, etc. and according to another important attribute, REDUNDANCY, which refers to interaction over different roles between the same people. In this context he states that small total communities differ from small networks within larger communities in displaying a higher degree of redundancy, and both may be accompanied by functional linguistic differentiation and occasional bilingualism. Network SIZE is introduced as another attribute at this point. Finally, Fishman discusses the important EXPERIENTIAL versus REFERENTIAL dimensions:

. . . One of the characteristics of large and diversified speech communities is that some of the varieties within their verbal repertoires are primarily experientially acquired and reinforced by dint of actual verbal interaction within particular networks, while others are primarily referentially acquired and reinforced by dint of symbolic integration within reference-networks which may rarely or never exist in any physical sense (1971a:233).

I will return subsequently to a fuller discussion of network attributes in the context of explanation.

Ervin-Tripp broadens the frame of Gumperz' pioneer work and probes issues of network formation, make-up and communicative content as well as the role networks could play in sociolinguistic explanation. Network formation is approached from a variety of perspectives. For instance, in her own work with Japanese wives of Americans ("war-brides"), whose linguistic and social integration (i.e. recruitment into American networks) seems to have depended on their conservatism while still in Japan, and attitudes to intermarriage within their Japanese networks: ". . . Women who shifted to American responses . . . identified with American women, had close American friends, read American magazines . . ." etc. (Fishman 1971a:72). The comment, however, that "people select 'similar' addressees for social interaction" (p. 67) is too general and would have to be modified for different types of social networks or different cultural contexts. At least, this similarity of the interlocutors would have to be specified (e.g. it may be ideological rather than sociodemographic) and the basis for judging similarity may well shift across networks within the same community. NETWORK STABILITY is brought up in the discussion of evidence that durability of redundant networks, i.e. networks with overlapping membership, is lessened where conflict in interaction practices is involved (1971a:70). Implications for language use in redundant networks must be investigated and one should keep in mind at this point Fishman's discussion of SITUATIONAL CONGRUENCY and switching (1971a:244–248).

Concerning the internal characteristics of networks, Ervin-Tripp discusses a paper by Hammer et al. (1965, reprinted in Fishman 1972) in which central individuals among the regular clientele of a New York coffee shop ". . . were the most predictable and each person most successfully predicted the omitted items from the speech of persons with whom he interacted most . . . the hidden variable seems to have been COHESIVENESS" (p. 69; emphasis added). The work of Bernstein and his associates is also discussed, regarding the controversial question of the impact of family interaction patterns and networks on verbal socialization and the emerging verbal repertoire of the child: ". . . communicative patterns . . . are related to the character of a family's social network . . . emphasis on different function of language . . . use of pronouns with external referents, and an ability to switch style with task . . ." (p. 70).

Ervin-Tripp's comments on particular communicative functions within various types of networks, such as, "a high frequency of requests for social reinforcement, and of expressive speech" in cohesive networks point the way to important research questions. We may, for instance, investigate network membership (network features of the individual and the group) and verbal behavior (switching, acculturation, etc.). This leads us to Ervin-Tripp's next pivotal theme, namely, INTERACTIONAL INTENSITY (or frequency), NETWORK COHESIVENESS and implications for the DIFFUSION OF CODES in part or in whole as well as of ATTITUDES TO CODE FEATURES. We see here the role networks play in language shift, internal or contactual language change, change in the rules for language use, and finally, the formation or change of language attitudes and behavior to language (see also the work of Neustupný discussed above). Cases of dissimilarity, even though in the context of intensive communication, are adduced in order to illustrate the fact that the desire to maintain a distinct identity may result in a desire for linguistic (or, as Fishman has amply shown, writing system) difference. Here again, the work of Gumperz concerning situational constraints to change — personal versus transactional interaction — must be remembered (see discussion above and also in Gumperz 1972:220–221). In many such cases, we encounter interaction within HIERARCHICAL NETWORKS and the individual's shifting from a nonhierarchical to a hierarchical network is accompanied by a switch in varieties.

The impact of family networks and socialization on language behavior has been the main focus in the work of the Bernstein school-data analyzed by Fishman from the immigrant case (e.g. 1971a:311) and can perhaps be related to this research as well. We also have a recent article of the "Monash school" (see Neustupný) by Phillips (1973) which focusses on interaction within an Australian (extended) family; the types of networks observed, the flow of conversation and the locus and flow of power; address and reference usage, and a detailed analysis of conversational topics: initiation, intra/extra-familial content, taboos, duration and sequence.

This work is important because it contributes to our understanding of network formation and situational enactment (encounter), the topical and (possibly) functional content of interactions within. One would have wished some additional information on verbal socialization during family encounters of the last generation. A promising area of research would be the study of links between functions (and topics) among immigrants and the verbal enculturation of both family and the children. For instance, the reflection of family network formality and interaction on lexical acculturation and on the particular shape of linguistic routines functionally differentiated. Horner and Gussow (1972) present findings on in-family communication frequency (intensity) and direction of flow, as well as functional content (in Skinner's rather than Hymes' sense), from their observations of two Black-American households.

Further integrative work in which networks appear in the context of a broader sociolinguistic model can be found in the contribution of Cooper to the Moncton Seminar (in Kelly 1969) in which we see the analysis of speech events/acts according to domain, situation, role relationships and interaction type. Gumperz' conceptualization underlies Cooper's model. An integrated (formal) model for the study of language related diffusion, i.e. both language change and language shift, has been presented by the author elsewhere (Afendras 1970, 1971, 1978). In that work I have relied heavily on the accomplishments of social geographers and rural sociologists who have addressed themselves to questions of human interaction and the diffusion of innovations. We turn now to the development of network theory and methodology outside of sociolinguistics and their possible interpretation for use in sociolinguistic research.

NETWORK CONCEPTUALIZING OUTSIDE THE LANGUAGE SCIENCES

A number of very pertinent papers are reprinted in Smith (1966) and especially in Ch. 6, "Networks, directions and distances." Among them we single out Bavelas' theoretical contribution, "A mathematical model of group structures" (pp. 212–222), on the organization of psychological situations and small group communication networks. Bavelas points out the two aspects one must keep in mind: the network of communicating individuals and the network in the CONTENT transmitted during the interaction, i.e. the weaving of ideas, attitudes, and in our case, (socio) linguistic features and rules. He outlines in his model a geometry of networks — a geometry of life space — and their points (cells) and defines cell-boundaries, cell-regions, cell-closure and structure, chains of cells, distances between cells and between cells and regions, outer- and inner-most regions of a structure, structure diameter, and structure and peripheral regions. These notions should be applicable to sociolinguistic research in redefining speech networks. We may, for instance, consider distances of an individual from given groups (ethnic, social, etc.) or from given networks (consider "lames" from the various hang-out groups in Labov's work); or distance between groups or speech communities and the manifestations of these distances on the verbal repertoires involved, on linguistic similarity etc.

Of interest also is Leavitt's article "Some effects of certain communication patterns on group performance" (in Smith 1966:222–243). Following Bavelas' model, Leavitt explores the effect of an individual's position in a (laboratory) network on his task performance and the way the "geometry" of the network itself affected group performance as well as "enjoyment of the job."

The network patterns with which he experimented were as given below (they all involved five individuals):

circle   chain   Y   wheel

The differences among the above patterns are as follows: chain, Y and wheel have a most central position C (the one closest to all other positions) while all positions of the circle are equal as to centrality. The SUM OF NEIGHBORS for one entire pattern, defined by Bavelas as the summation one position away from each position is: circle, 10, and all others 8 each. Similarly, the SUM OF DISTANCES is the summation for all positions of the shortest distances in links from every position to every other one: circle, 30, chain, 30, Y, 36 and wheel, 32. To quote from Leavitt's findings (in Smith 1966:242–243):

The communication patterns within which our groups worked affected their behavior. The major behavioral differences attributable to communication patterns were differences in accuracy, total activity, satisfaction of group members, emergence of a leader, and organization of the group. There may also be differences . . . in . . . self-correcting tendencies, and durability of the group as a group.

Similar conclusions were drawn with regard to the individual positions within a pattern. The strongest determiner of differences in behavior was CENTRALITY for both the overall patterns and individual positions.

While the types of networks studied above are characteristic of, for instance, occupational organizations (perhaps even gangs), they still include elements that are undeniably present even in larger, less organized interaction networks.

Guetzkow and Simon (in Smith 1966:244–253) criticized some aspects of Leavitt's work and suggested an alternative explanation; that the performance of the group is limited by the pattern of the network indirectly, by affecting the group's organizational ability. An additional pattern is introduced (which we have seen in the work of Neustupný above) the all-channel network in which there are no restrictions as to WHO talks with whom.

Coming from a different perspective, questions of social network theory and methodology are the theme of a collection edited by Aronson (1970), and much will be found of usefulness to sociolinguistics in the articles included. Extensive anthropological and sociological literature on the subject is reviewed by the various contributors and a wealth of relevant concepts is exposed. Wolfe's "On structural comparisons of networks" (1970:226–244) provides guidelines for the collection of data, coding and comparison, with a view to testing "processual hypotheses" which concern networks. In his taxonomy of network concepts (p. 229), he gives a number of definitions: SOCIAL NETWORK; LIMITED or UNLIMITED NETWORK (particular extracts of the total network); and a variety of SETS: PERSONAL — limited to the links of one person; CATEGORICAL — "links involving a type of person"; ACTION — "links purposefully created for a specific end"; ROLE SYSTEM — "links involved in an organized role system or group"; FIELD — "links with a certain content (e.g. economic, political, etc.)." Subsequently, Wolfe introduces twelve variables which may characterize the links. We also find a discussion of problems arising in the coding of links from any given data source on these variables.

In brief, these variables are as follows (Aronson 1970:239ff.):
1. Dependence on other links (from none to at least one)

2. Dependence of other links (from none to at least one)
3. Communication pathways (from direct plus additional number of paths)
4. Uniqueness (from unique-to-none to unique-to-both)
5. Functional diffuseness (from specific to diffuse)
6. Hierarchical status imbalance (alike to different in general status)
7. Inequality of rights and duties (identical–different–unequal)
8. External sanctions (negative to positive EXTERNAL sanctioning of rights and duties relevant to link)
9. Situational contingency (rights and duties contingent or not on situation)
10. Structuring (degree of formal patterning of rights and duties)
11. Scale (within one community or between communities)
12. Urbanity (from rural only to urban only).

We note Chrisman's paper "Situation and social network in cities" (Aronson 1970:245–257) on questions of LINK CONTENT, RECRUITMENT into PERSONAL INTERACTION networks from potential or institutional networks and the SITUATIONS in which such relations are activated. Illustrations are from fieldwork among Danish Americans in California.

Aronson's article "Social networks: towards structure or process?" (1970:258–268) and "Editor's preface" to the volume (pp. 221–225) provide additional theoretical perspective, as does Whitten's article (pp. 269–280) which, in addition, because of its focus on the role of the investigator, should provide an interesting complement to the work of Labov on linguists' "lameness."

Jakobson's paper, "Network analysis in East Africa: The social organization of urbal transients" (in Aronson 1970:281–286), may prove helpful to those sociolinguists who are working with geographic mobility and urbanization, and especially to the many who are involved in the massive language-use surveys of East Africa (see Whiteley 1971). I also would like to point out a complementary paper by Criper, "Sprachliche Komplexität und Mobilität in Uganda" (1971:157–172).

CONCLUSIONS

In conclusion, I would like to present a number of observations and suggestions on the concept of network. As the present divergence of usage may be a source of confusion, at least of communicative "noise," we must attempt to reach some explicitness and common ground without necessarily falling into the restrictiveness of standardized use. Networks must be viewed from the perspective of the cluster of related notions that Hymes (1968) and Neustupný (1971) have discussed. Moreover, the available conceptual resources of other fields can be turned to innovative use in sociolinguistics with regard to theory and explanation as well as methodology (see also Fishman 1971a, Preface).

Among the issues that deserve attention the most are characterization of networks and their distribution in larger groups. We must isolate the important network attributes and resolve the question of measurement, i.e. choose an appropriate model, whether discrete (e.g. the binary closure model) or continuous. And we must certainly investigate the co-occurrence of network attributes.

Processes of network formation present another important topic — consider, for instance, the case of migrant integration or the assimilation of ethnic minorities. We can systematically investigate NETWORKS AND THE INDIVIDUAL (recruitment, range, redundancy, AND verbal repertoire) and also the DISTRIBUTION, COUPLING AND HIERARCHIES of networks in the tribe or the polity. A number of questions can be asked here on the relation of network types to communicative similarity (in any of Hymes' manifestations, 1968:37), to attitudes and behavior towards the system of communication, and, consequently, to language planning. Finally, we can design the appropriate research with which to test the explanatory power of our interaction network models and the present alternative sociolinguistic models.

REFERENCES

AFENDRAS, E. A.
    1970   "Diffusion processes in language: prediction and planning." Paper presented to the Section on Sociolinguistics, 7th World Congress on Sociology, Varna (Bulgaria). Available as research document, International Center for Research on Bilingualism, Université Laval, Quebec, Canada.
    1971   "Diffusionsprozesse der Sprache: Vorhersage und Planung," in Zur Soziologie der sprache. Koelner Zeitschrift fuer Soziologie und sozialpsychologie (Special Issue 15). Edited by R. Kjolseth and F. Sack, 104–119. Opladen: Westdeutscher.
    1978   "Some formal models for the sociology of language: diffusion, prediction and planning of change." Publication B-43. Quebec: International Center for Research on Bilingualism.
ARONSON, D. R., editor
    1970   Social Networks. Special Issue of the Canadian Journal of Sociology and Anthropology 7(4).
BARNES, J. A.
    1954   Class and committees in a Norwegian island parish. Human Relations 7:39–58.
    1969   Graph theory and social networks. Sociology 3:215–232.
BARTH, F., editor
    1969   Ethnic groups and boundaries: the social organization of culture difference. Boston: Little, Brown.

BASSO, E. B.
1973 The use of Portuguese relationship terms in Kalapalo (Xingu Carib) encounters: changes in a central Brazilian communications network. *Language in Society* 2:1–21.

BORGATTA, E. F.
1968 "Sociometry," in *The Encyclopedia of the Social Sciences* 15:53–57.

BOTT, E.
1957 *Family and social network.* London: Tavistock.

CLYNE, M.
1972 *Perspectives on language contact: based on a study of German in Australia.* Melbourne: Hawthorne Press.

CRIPER, C.
1971 "Sprachliche Komplexitaet und Mobilitaet in Uganda," in *Zur Soziologie der Sprache. Koelner Zeitschrift fuer Soziologie und sozialpsychologie* (Special Issue 15). Edited by R. Kjolseth and F. Sack, 157–172. Opladen: Westdeutscher.

ERVIN-TRIPP, SUSAN M.
1969 "Sociolinguistics," in *Advances in experimental social psychology,* volume four. Edited by L. Berkowitz, 91–165. New York: Academic Press.

FISHMAN, J. A., *editor*
1971a *Advances in the sociology of language,* volume one. The Hague: Mouton.
1971b "The sociology of language: an interdisciplinary social science approach to language in society," in Fishman (1971a:217–404).
1972 *Advances in the sociology of language,* volume two. The Hague: Mouton.
1978 *Advances in the study of societal multilingualism.* The Hague: Mouton.

GUMPERZ, J. J.
1964 Linguistic and social interaction in two communities. *American Anthropologist* 66(2):137–153.
1966 "On the ethnology of linguistic change," in *Sociolinguistics.* Edited by W. Bright, 28–49. The Hague: Mouton.
1972 "Sociolinguistics and communication in small groups," in *Sociolinguistics: selected readings.* Edited by J. B. Pride and J. Holmes (Originally published in 1970 in *Penguin modern linguistics readings,* 203–224.)

HAMMER, M., S. POLGAR, K. SALZINGER
1965 "Comparison of data sources in a sociolinguistic study," in *Advances in the sociology of language,* volume two. Edited by J. A. Fishman. The Hague: Mouton.

HORNER, V. M., J. D. GUSSOW
1972 "John and Mary: a pilot study in linguistic ecology," in *Functions of language in the classroom.* Edited by C. B. Cazden, V. P. John and D. Hymes, 155–194. New York: Teachers College Press.

HYMES, D.
1968 "Linguistic problems in defining the concept of the 'tribe'," in *Essays on the problem of the tribe.* Edited by J. Helm, 83–101. Proceedings of the 1967 annual spring meeting of the American Ethnological Society, University of Washington, Seattle.

KELLY, L. G., *editor*
1969 *Description and measurement of bilingualism: an international seminar.* Toronto: UNESCO and University of Toronto Press.

KJOLSETH, R., F. SACK, *editors*
1971   *Zur Soziologie der Sprache. Koelner Zeitschrift fuer Soziologie und Sozialpsychologie* (Special Issue 15). Opladen: Westdeutscher Verlag.

LABOV, W.
1973   The linguistic consequences of being a lame. *Language in Society* 2(1):81–115.

LABOV, W., P. COHEN, C. ROBINS, J. LEWIS
1968   "A study of the non-standard English of Negro and Puerto-rican speakers in New York City," in *The uses of language in the speech community*. Cooperative research project No. 3268 (Office of Education), volume two. New York: Columbia University Press.

NEUSTUPNÝ, J. V.
1968   "Politeness patterns in the system of communication." Paper presented at the Symposium *Usages of honorific language*, VIIIth International Congress of Anthropological and Ethnological Sciences, Tokyo and Kyoto, September 3–10, 1968.
1971   Toward a model of linguistic distance. *Linguistic Communications* 5:115–132.
1972   Remarks on Japanese honorifics. *Linguistic Communications* 7:78–117.
1973a "Personnel in Japanese language treatment." Unpublished manuscript.
1973b The modernization of the Japanese system of communication. *Linguistic Communications* 9.

OLSSON, G.
1965   *Distance and human interaction*. (Bibliography series 2). Philadelphia: Regional Science Research Institute.

PHILLIPS, D. J.
1973   How an Australian family communicates: networks and topics. *Linguistic Communications* 10:1–35.

SMITH, A. G., *editor*
1966   *Communication and culture: readings in the codes of human interaction*. New York: Holt, Rinehart and Winston.

SORENSEN, A. P., JR.
1967   Multilingualism in the N.W. Amazon. *American Anthropologist* 69:670–684.

URE, J.
1971   "Eine Untersuchung des Sprachgebrauchs in Ghana," in *Zur Soziologie der Sprache*. Edited by R. Kjolseth and F. Sack, 136–156. Opladen: Westdeutscher Verlag.

WHITELEY, W. H., *editor*
1971   *Language use and social change: problems of multilingualism with special reference to Eastern Africa*. International African Institute and Oxford University Press.

Problems of Language Standardization in India

BH. KRISHNAMURTI

1. INTRODUCTION

Anthropologists and sociologists trace the entire growth of human civilization based on science and technology and the complex sociopolitical systems to the invention of the writing system (Goody and Watt 1972). While language is as old as man, human civilization, as we now understand it, is hardly 4,000 years old. The progressive evolution of the alphabet from pictographic writing with distinctive symbols for vowels and consonants has made both the representation and the transmission of oral messages more efficient. The printing press and the mass media have made universal education not only a possible concept but also a goal of democratic citizenship.

The notions of "standard" and "nonstandard" usage are a direct consequence of the introduction of the writing system and the creation of written literature. These terms are used sometimes synonymously with "correct," "incorrect," "grammatical," and "ungrammatical" by laymen as well as language pedagogues.

What the layman and the school teacher characterize as "grammatical" is in fact the socially acceptable or respectable choice of usage. Here a complex pattern of social values is projected onto linguistic usage to provide a judgment as to its validation or invalidation and this is represented as though the judgment is basically linguistic. These terms and concepts should therefore be understood as primarily nonlinguistic factors which are transferred from the value system of a literate society. These nonlinguistic factors include values and aspects such as educated–uneducated, cultured–uncultured, urban–rural, and "forward" and "backward" in the socioeconomic hierarchy. According to Bloomfield (1964):

The nearest approach to an explanation of "good" and "bad" language seems to be this, then, that, by a cumulation of obvious superiorities, both of character and standing, as well as of language, some persons are felt to be better models of conduct and speech than others (p. 396).

In the emergence of standard languages, two attitudes of speakers play an important role — what is "high" and "imitation-worthy" and what is "low" and therefore not a "model" for imitation, and what is worthy of the written form and what is not. The speech behavior of a small segment of the population who are highly literate and who wield social, economic and political power thus becomes fashionable and respectable and sets the model for others to imitate. Since such groups are usually concentrated in or around a metropolis, standard speech spreads from the urban centers with a centrifugal force absorbing the surrounding provincial varieties of rural populations. It is therefore no accident of history that standard English, French and Latin evolved from the speech of the elite of London, Paris, and Rome respectively. Mass media and the modern means of communication accelerate the pace of dissemination of the "standard language." There is always a constant interaction between standard language and nonstandard usage. What is deemed nonstandard and provincial at one time may later become part of the standard language through the medium of powerful creative writing. Standardization is not a process to be determined by a group of scholars or by committees of governments.

2. THE PROPERTIES OF A STANDARD LANGUAGE

The properties of a standard language are said to be "flexible stability" and "intellectualization." Clarifying these concepts, Paul Garvin (1964) says:

Flexible stability here refers to the requirement that a standard language be stabilized by appropriate codification, and that the codification be flexible enough "to allow for modification in line with culture change." Intellectualization here refers to the requirement of increasing accuracy along an ascending scale of functional dialects from conversational to scientific (p. 521).

Furthermore, according to Garvin, a standard language has to fulfill three functions: the unifying function, the prestige function, and the frame-of-reference function (Garvin 1964:522). By its unifying function a standard language links up several dialect regions into a single standard language community which can be identified as a separate entity from other neighboring languages. The prestige function gives a standard language a superiority over nonstandard local varieties, and its possession lends a degree of social prestige to its speakers when compared to those that do not possess it. As a frame-of-reference the standard language is the tool to judge degrees of appropriateness (correctness) in social context.

Ferguson (1962:23–27) proposes two dimensions for the classification of world languages, viz. the degrees of utilization in writing (W 0, 1, 2, 3) and the degrees of standardization (St. 0, 1, 2). They are defined as follows:

W 0. Not used for normal written purposes.

W 1. Used for normal written purposes.

W 2. Original research in physical sciences regularly published.

W 3. Translations and resumés of scientific work in other languages are regularly published.

St 0. There is no important amount of standardization. No particular norm has wide acceptance.

St 1. This is not defined but explained as obtaining in languages with one or more implicit standard forms with a wide range of variation.

St 2. A single, widely accepted norm which is felt to be appropriate with only minor modifications or variations for all purposes for which the language is used.

This is an oversimplified matrix requiring sub-classifying scales under each category.

Haugen (1972) refers to these two as aspects governing the form and the function of a language, one representing codification (standardization) and the other elaboration (utilization in writing). "As the ideal goals of a standard language, codification may be defined as MINIMAL VARIATION IN FORM elaboration as MAXIMAL VARIATION IN FUNCTION" (Haugen 1972:107).

An absolute standard with uniform spelling, grammar, and lexicon has never been attained by any known language (Bloomfield 1964:393). A high degree of uniformity backed by social prestige is what is to be aimed at.

3. DIGLOSSIA AND STANDARD-WITH-DIALECT

In languages having a rich literary heritage a situation characterized by Ferguson (1964) as "diglossia" will arise: He maintains that:

DIGLOSSIA is a relatively stable language situation in which, in addition to the primary dialects of the language (which may include a standard or regional standards), there is a very divergent, highly codified (often grammatically more complex) superposed variety, the vehicle of a large and respected body of written literature, either of an earlier period or in another speech community, which is learned largely by formal education and is used for most written and formal spoken purposes but is not used by any sector of the community for ordinary conversation (p. 435).

In this situation two varieties of a language exist side by side throughout the community, each having a definite role to play. One of these exists as a superposed variety for certain higher roles — formal speeches, rituals, poetry, newspaper writing, and broadcasting, etc. The low variety is used in conversation and folk literature, in informal talks, and as captions in political cartoons, etc. In the case of Arabic, Greek and Tamil such a situation exists. The high variety has its origin in history, is several centuries old and has only marginally changed. This variety is acquired through formal education in what nearly amounts to a second language (Ferguson 1964:433). The superposed variety here is the standard language though it is not the elite counterpart of contemporary speech as in the case of English, French, etc. With the spread of literacy there is bound to be a prolonged conflict, and as in the case of the emergence of Romance languages breaking away with the superposed Latin the diglossia situation may eventually give way to the standard-with-dialect situation.

4.   STANDARD VERSUS NONSTANDARD IN INDIAN LANGUAGES

Against the above conceptual background we may examine the standard and the nonstandard varieties of some typical Indian languages.

The Constitution of India recognizes fifteen languages, including Sanskrit, which account for 88 percent of the total population of the country. Of the fourteen modern languages, eleven belong to the Indo-Aryan family and four to the Dravidian. With the exception of Sindhi and Urdu, the rest of the modern Indian languages are the dominant regional languages in one or more States.

All these languages have rich poetic literature and fiction and almost all of these had been in use as media of instruction up to the secondary level long before 1947. Since independence (1947) and, later, since the formation of the linguistic States (1956) the regional languages have gained increasing importance in local administration and higher education. During the 1960s most of the States recognized the regional languages as official languages for local administration. University education, being a State concern, has fallen in line with the changing trend; the universities introduced regional languages as media of higher education up to the first degree level during the late 1960s. Although English still remains as an inter-State link-language at the higher levels of intellectual communication (all-India conferences, etc.), its role has significantly changed at the State level. Hindi is intended to replace English eventually as the link-language for inter-State communication in administration and higher education. But it will take a long time to accomplish this. Meanwhile the functions of the regional State-level languages have considerably increased and this has led to problems of ACCEPTANCE and SELECTION of one variety as a standard form over others. In the natural process of culture change, implicit standard forms have emerged for nearly all the regional languages, though the nature and degree of standardization is not as institutionalized for Indian languages as it is for Western languages like English, Swedish, and German. In terms of Ferguson's typology, modern Indian languages can be classified as W1 St1 moving fast in the direction of W2 St2 (see Section 2 above).

It would appear that a supradialectal norm of St2 type is necessary for each of the modern Indian languages for the following purposes:

1. To spread literacy among illiterates who constitute, on the average, 80 percent of the total population,
2. To serve as an effective vehicle of intra-State administration,
3. To spread modern knowledge at all levels of formal education,
4. To facilitate intertranslatability with the other Indian languages for exchange of information and knowledge, and
5. To make bilingualism and multilingualism feasible as a means of preserving national integrity and nationhood.

It is necessary to examine if these objectives are fulfilled by the existing standard forms of Indian languages and, if not, what steps are needed for planned standardization. Five languages are taken for case study, Telugu, Tamil, Marathi, Bengali and Hindi.

4.1. *Telugu*

According to the 1961 Census Telugu is spoken by 38 million people, second only to Hindi in numbers. The ratio of rural to urban population is 80 percent:20 percent. Only 25 percent of the population is literate.

Sharp differences appear from the beginning of literature (in the eleventh century) between the literary language and the contemporary spoken language as revealed from inscriptions (ca. 6th century onwards). All classical literature was poetry but there is no evidence for the literary dialect ever being used for formal speech roles, even by the upper class. Grammars were written for the high variety and the spoken language was banned from usage in poetry where the two differed. The spread of prose literature in the nineteenth and twentieth centuries necessitated the growth of a current standard variety. Attempts to create a diglossia situation where there had been no such tradition failed with the emergence of the mass media and modern forms of literature like the novel, the essay, and the social play. The variety widely used in the newspapers, the radio, and fiction is based on the speech of the educated middle and upper classes of Central Andhra (Guntur, Krishna, East and

West Godavari districts). For more information on this, see Figure 1.[1] This area has produced the largest number of writers who have influenced the direction of standard usage and their pattern is widely imitated.

Differences between standard and the nonstandard can be linguistically formulated mainly in phonology, verb and noun inflexion, and the choice of certain lexical items.

The following features are significant in distinguishing modern standard from nonstandard (Krishnamurti 1962, 1971).

		STANDARD	NONSTANDARD
1.	Deaspiration	p:ph; b:bh, d:dh, etc.	p, b, d, etc.
		h-	ø-
2.	Semi-vowel loss	w [front vowel	ø-
3.	Cluster-simplification	consonant clusters, e.g.	simplified through (a) assimilation or (b) anaptyxis; e.g.
		st-	tt-
		pr-	par-
4.	Sibilant reduction	s: ś: ṣ	s
5.	Deretroflexion	n: ṇ	n
		l: ḷ	l
6.	Affricate fricative alternation	č	s
7.	Fricative-stop alternation	f	p

The above phonological variations show that "the ability to use borrowed words from Sanskrit and English without assimilating them to the native system distinguishes standard from nonstandard" (Krishnamurti 1972:3).

---

[1] Figure 1 gives a glimpse into the social stratification and speech variation in Telugu. The primary classification is into SPOKEN and WRITTEN. Under the SPOKEN there are four regional dialects in Telugu (numbered 1 to 4) ascertained on the basis of an extensive survey of the terms used in native occupations like agriculture, weaving, carpentry, etc. (Krishnamurti 1962). This is also partly supported by variation in the speech of the urban educated classes. The educated speech of the central area (No. 4 in the diagram) is the basis of modern standard written language. The educated speech of the other three areas is extensively influenced by the standard colloquial and written forms. Phonological differences between the educated and the uneducated follow the general pattern shown in Krishnamurti's standard — nonstandard phonological features of Telugu, irrespective of region, economic class, or caste. Besides these, there may be other phonological variations restricted to regional dialects; e.g. in Dialect 3 (Visakhapatnam and Srikakulam districts) the uneducated replace initial *l* of the educated variety by *n*, e.g. *lēdu* (educated) : *nēdu* (uneducated)

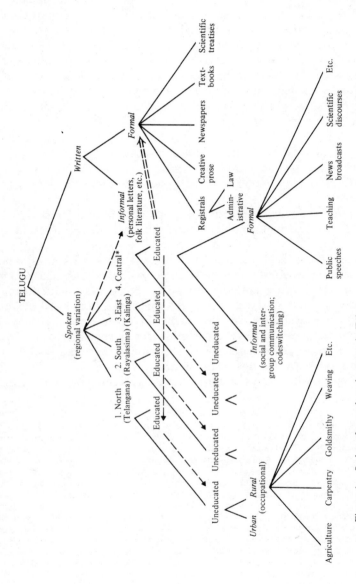

Figure 1. Styles of speech and writing in Telugu
* The educated speech of this area (central coastal districts) is the basis of modern written standards.

The hierarchy of politeness reflected in the choice of appropriate pronouns and honorific clitics like *-gāru* and *-aṇḍi* distinguish the standard formal usage from the nonstandard informal. In word-coining the educated speakers draw on English and Sanskrit whereas the uneducated coin compounds with native components. This area is still unexplored as to the community's sensitivity to notions of standardness. The controversy over the style to be used in school and college textbooks is not yet totally resolved, although for course books the State Government Institute of Telugu (Telugu Akademi) uses only the standard colloquial language.

SOME ISSUES IN THE STANDARDIZATION OF TELUGU

1. The writing system is fairly phonemic. Symbols have to be provided for *ǣ* and *f*. Certain symbols of archaic phonemes occasionally used can be discarded.

2. Popularized Sanskrit words have regional variation in the pronunciation of educated speakers. Such variation need not be represented in spelling.

3. Deaspiration is the major phonological marker of nonstandard pronunciation though its function is limited to a small vocabulary. When the majority of nonstandard speakers are exposed to formal education, the flooding of textbooks with technical terms drawn from Sanskrit would demand greater attention from the teacher in correcting the spelling and pronunciation mistakes. It is even possible that a new batch of *tadbhavas* will come into vogue if the teacher's scholastic background is such as to make him insensitive to this phenomenon.

4. Variation within the standard language is much more in the case of

---

'it is not'; similarly, in Dialect 1 (Telangana), initial *w* is lost before low vowels (*a, ā*). The loss of *w* before high and mid vowels (*i, ī, e, ē*) is a common feature of the uneducated speech throughout the state as opposed to its retention in educated speech. Among the educated, the INFORMAL SPOKEN style has a greater degree of codemixing and codeswitching than the FORMAL. The uneducated speakers are subclassified as URBAN and RURAL. The URBAN uneducated are exposed to the educated speech and other spoken media which make them much more sensitive than the RURAL uneducated to upward mobility in their speech patterns. Occupational division comes below RURAL; even here speech variation is mainly in the lexicon and not in phonology and morphology. Carpenters use terms germane to their occupation which are not understood by speakers of other professions. Caste, if it has any significance, comes at the bottom of the chart underneath occupational groups. There are two sects engaged in the handloom industry, *sātāni* and *padmasāli*, who maintain and use distinct terms for some of the common tools used in weaving. Beyond such lexical differences, caste-wise variation in phonology and grammar is totally baseless.

Under INFORMAL WRITTEN come personal letters and folksongs, and also recently, writers of social plays have introduced uneducated regional dialects appropriate to their characters. Under FORMAL WRITTEN, administrative and judiciary registers are yet to develop. Regional variation obtaining in the speech of the educated is accepted in writing and it is mostly in the area of morphology and lexicon, and marginally in phonology, e.g. past tense *inā* (Dialect 2)/*iā* (Dialect 4); durative *tū* (Dialect 4)/*tā* (Dialect 2), etc.

Telugu than, say, English. Efforts to choose one standard form over the other may not be advisable since it has no function to serve in so far as intelligibility or social prestige are concerned, e.g. *tināle, tināli* 'one should eat'; *ceppǣḍu/ceppināḍu* 'he said', etc.

5. Dictionaries and grammars for modern standard Telugu are yet to come out.

4.2. Tamil

Tamil is spoken by 31 million people and is the dominant regional language of Tamilnaḍu. It has one of the oldest literatures, dating back to the early Christian era. There is a definite tradition of diglossia in Tamil (Ferguson 1964:435–436). The language used on formal occasions (teaching, platform lectures, radio broadcasts, etc.) and in writing (newspapers, poetry, fiction, etc.) is *cen-tamiẓ* [literary Tamil] which is not based on the contemporary spoken variety of any section of the population. It is acquired only through education. There are several regional and social varieties used for informal purposes — at home, in the bazaar — and rarely in movie dialogues, and fiction. Formal Tamil is closer to the written classical variety which does not take into account sound changes that have taken place in speech since the time of Cangam literature (Shanmugam Pillai 1960:28–35). Even in morphology, literary Tamil and common Tamil differ widely (35–40). It must, however, be noted that the modern formal Tamil forms, particularly in the case of compound verbs, reflect deliberate substitution of Classical Tamil inflections for their modern counterparts, working backward, although such compound verb forms are not attested in the literary texts; e.g. colloquial *senjigiṭrikē* 'I had done it for myself' is rendered into *ceytu-koṇṭ-irukkirēn* in formal Tamil. The reconstructed literary form does not derive from the literary dialect. Taking such as these into account Ramanujan (1968:463) assumes that the written form "furnishes us with the underlying, even historically prior, base-forms." What is important to note is the impact of the spoken form on the written. In other words, formal Tamil follows the syntactic rules of colloquial Tamil but the phonological (morphophonemic and phonemic) rules of literary Tamil. In this respect, the case of Tamil may be different from that of Arabic and Greek cited by Ferguson (1964:435–436). The DMK political party has, in power, given a new boost and stability to the "superposed variety." Even literal translation of originally Sanskrit proper names into Tamil is attempted as a mark of political and cultural emancipation of Tamil and its distinctness from Aryan Sanskrit. Tamilization of technical terms — of even English loan words which are otherwise popular — is comparable to the current Hindi situation where extensive borrowing of *tatsamas* is undertaken deliberately by writers motivated more by sociopolitical considerations than educational. Whether the new stability given to Tamil by the DMK party is apparent or real, only time can judge.

Tamil "diglossia" has tremendous implications for the spread of literacy. Illiterates have to acquire reading and writing skills with literary Tamil as the target language, which naturally involves greater exposure time and effort. It is practically like learning a second language (Shanmugam Pillai 1960:40). The diglossic situation has inhibited the growth of an educated spoken variety as a vehicle of formal communication. The polarization is between a superposed literary Tamil and many regional and social varieties, none of which has any particular superiority and prestige over the others (Ramanujan 1968). A change for the choice of a spoken variety for purposes of writing can only come from the educated who are keenly aware of the problems of mass literacy. Even linguists of Tamilnadu are afraid of advocating a modern dialect form for formal written communication — for fear of reprisals from the party in power.

4.3. *Marathi*

Marathi is the mother tongue of 33.3 million speakers and the dominant regional language of Maharashtra. The standard language is based on the educated middleclass speech of Poona. Standard and nonstandard have the following phonological differences (Apte 1962:8–13).

	STANDARD	NONSTANDARD
1. Deaspiration	b:bh, d:dh, k:kh, etc.	b, d, k, etc.
	h-	ø-
2. Deretroflexion	s:ṣ	s
	n:ṇ	n
3. Semi-vowel loss	w [front vowel	ø
	y [ə	ø
4. Cluster simplification	pr-	pər-
	mru-	mur-

Occasionally nonstandard speakers (perhaps, in the process of acquiring standard speech) acquire hyperstandard forms:

puḍhə   *phuḍ* 'in front of'.

Apte mainly contrasts Brahmin standard with non-Brahmin dialects equating the Brahmin speech with standard. He indicates education and urban dwelling as factors influencing the nonstandard speech toward standard. Recent in-depth studies show that speakers are more sensitive to "education" than to "caste" as a determiner of standard or nonstandard speech (Berntsen 1973:1–24).

4.4. *Bengali*

Bengali is spoken by 34 million people according to the 1961 Census and is the dominant regional language of West Bengal. There existed two recognized styles, *Sādhu-bhāṣā* [SB: literary language] and *Calit-bhāṣā* [CB: colloquial language]. The SB is never spoken as the *grānthika* [bookish] style of Telugu, whether on formal or informal occasions. The CB whose base is the educated speech of the middle and upper classes of Calcutta has gradually spread as the modern written vehicle, restricting the use of the SB. The SB had earlier Bengali morphology but predominantly Sanskrit vocabulary, including inflected nouns (*śāstrataḥ, lokataḥ*: 'from science', 'from world'). As in the case of Telugu, the earlier form of literature was poetry confined to a small section of pundits well-versed in Sanskrit. When prose developed as a literary form and the mass media spread under social change the CB could hardly be prevented from entering the written language in the twentieth century. The modern SB is also influenced by CB and is "far less definable grammatically than it was a century ago" (Dimock 1960:43–63).

4.5. *Hindi*

According to the 1961 Census Hindi is the mother tongue of 133 million speakers, excluding Bihari and Rajasthani which account for 32 million speakers. It is the dominant language of seven States: Uttar Pradesh, Madhya Pradesh, Rajasthan, Bihar, Haryana, Delhi, and Himachal Pradesh. Hindi (also called Hindwi and Hindusthani) originated as a trade language during the Moghul rule in Western Uttar Pradesh and Punjab and spread as the urban vernacular of Northern India (Chatterji 1960:192ff.) known as *Kharī bolī*, which constitutes the basis of modern standard Hindi. By the beginning of the nineteenth century Hindusthani had already become the vehicle of prose in two styles — Nagari Hindi and Urdu (Chatterji 1960:212). Because of different scripts and other socioreligious differences reflected in the choice of sources of borrowing (Sanskrit versus Perso-Arabic), Hindi and Urdu came to be treated as two different languages, although in syntax they are practically identical. This difference in styles between High Hindi and Urdu became further accentuated after Hindi became the official language of independent India and Urdu the official language of Pakistan after 1947.

Although the regional and subregional varieties used within the Hindi area are mutually unintelligible at distant points, *khaṛi bolī* serves as an urban vernacular and lingua franca throughout the Hindi area. It is also widely understood as a bazaar language in important cities like Bombay, Calcutta, Hyderabad and Madras outside the Hindi area (Gumperz and Naim 1960:100). Standard Hindi based on this vernacular has recently become highly Sanskritized in its derivational morphology and lexicon. Even popular Hindusthani expressions are being systematically replaced by Sanskrit forms, thereby needlessly interfering with the essential communication of a day-to-day nature.[2] The Sanskritized style thus gives an air of superiority and exclusiveness to writers, enabling them to maintain their control of the standard language and their social distance from the uneducated or the moderately educated.

4.6. *Summary*

To summarize, two historical processes are evident in the evolution of standard norms for writing among the dominant Indian languages:

1. A spoken form of the educated classes with clearly identifiable geographical boundaries constitutes the base of the modern written form, e.g. Hindi, Bengali, Marathi, and Telugu.

2. A literary dialect which is not the spoken form of any section of speakers superposed on several regional and social dialects is accepted as standard for formal communication, e.g. Tamil.

5.   CASTE DIALECTS VERSUS STANDARD LANGUAGE

Sociolinguistic work on Indian languages by American linguists has emphasized "caste" as a factor in the shaping of standard languages, particularly in southern India. These studies are sketchy and have not taken other variables into account (Bright 1960; Sjoberg 1962; McCormack 1960; Southworth 1972). More recent studies in some of these languages have shown that nonstandard speakers correlate standard speech with higher educational level than with caste (e.g. Pandit 1972; Krishnamurti 1962, 1971; Berntsen 1973). The model presented for Telugu would broadly suit the other Dravidian and Indo-Aryan lan-

---

[2]   The following are some examples of replacements of popular words of Indo-Aryan and Persian origin by Sanskrit *tatsamas* in standard Hind (popular:standard) *kapḍā* : *vastr*/'cloth', *ākh* : *netr* 'eye', *ke bād* : *paścāt* 'after', *aur* : *evam* 'and', *havā* : *vāyu* 'air', *davākhānā* : *cikitsālay* 'hospital', *tārīkh* : *dinānk* 'date', *bijlī* : *vidyut* 'electricity', *kheti* : *kṛṣi* 'agriculture', *bukhār* : *jvar* 'fever', *gussā* : *krodh* 'anger', *khūn* : *rakt* 'blood', *khālī* : *rikt* 'empty', 'vacant'. Elaborate discussions of this trend are found in Gumperz and Naim (1960) and Gumperz and Das Gupta (1971).

guages. Caste has never been a static model in India and to establish speech variation along caste lines presupposes the absence of communication between one caste and another. Pandit maintains that caste is not a "relevant speech group" and variation in speech is functional, simultaneously facilitating communication and maintaining social distance between the educated and the uneducated (1972:55–56). Krishnamurti (1971) noticed no distinction in phonology between the uneducated Brahmin and non-Brahmin varieties in Telangana Telugu. If we were characterizing the speech varieties of Indian languages at a point in history when Brahmins were the only educated class, perhaps caste would be a relevant variable in speech variation. But this is no longer true of modern Indian languages.

At least one linguistic aspect seems to be dominant in distinguishing standard from nonstandard. In Marathi (Apte 1962; Berntsen 1973), Telugu (Krishnamurti 1962), and Kannada (Bright 1960; McCormack 1960) the standard language has a much larger inventory of phonemes incorporating the phonologies of borrowed words from Sanskrit and English. This phenomenon indicates that bilingualism and multilingualism are a function of education in India and the bilingual's phonology naturally sets the model for the monolingual illiterates.

6. PROBLEMS IN THE STANDARDIZATION OF INDIAN LANGUAGES

Parallel phonological differences between standard and nonstandard among three mutually unintelligible languages like Kannada, Telugu and Marathi is a striking phenomenon which needs investigation. In the case of Marathi, Southworth traces this and similar parallels to a Dravidian substratum and the consequent hybridization (1968:45–55). In the process of modernization of Indian languages, Sanskrit is the main source language for lexical expansion. The distance between educated standard, on the one hand, and the illiterate varieties, on the other, will be further increased and accentuated with the influx of a large body of Sanskrit-based technical terms in textbooks and treatises on science and technology. Either terms with native constituents or borrowed international terms would do less to widen the existing social gap between standard and nonstandard, since a feature like aspiration, reminiscent of social distance, would be absent here. In this respect, fewer phonetic adaptations are required in a language like Tamil between standard and nonstandard speakers, since all lexical expansion is devoid of Indo-Aryan influence.

Whether the standardization of a language can be planned by committees or governmental agencies is a question relevant for the Indian situation. Where no standard norms exist this is perhaps possible as in the case of Israeli Hebrew and Finnish.

Finland's was an unwritten vernacular, Israel's an unspoken standard. Today both are standards capable of conveying every concept of modern learning and every subtlety of modern literature. Whatever they may lack is being supplied by deliberate planning, which in modern states is an important part of the development process (Haugen 1972:105).

This process will not be very successful in the case of Indian languages where widely accepted regional norms have developed long before their functional range has expanded. The only type of planning that seems to be within the range of planners is modernization, which, according to Ferguson, is "lexical expansion and developing new styles and forms of discourse" (1968:32–33). The question boils down to one of finding technical terms and promoting rigorous styles of writing for scientific and technological subjects. Language planning in these areas has been defective for the Indian languages. The Scientific and Technical Terms Commission has manufactured nearly 300,000 terms with a Sanskrit base for different branches of knowledge and these are avidly used by Government agencies and law-makers. The users of modern knowledge should have participated in the creation of such terminologies. This has not happened except in the form of associating a few experts with each branch of knowledge.

A better beginning could have been made by encouraging the bilingual style of instruction in schools and colleges without a bar on codeswitching and without insisting on the production of textbooks. Technical terms could have come into vogue by exploiting the natural processes of language growth, viz. borrowing through phonetic adaptation, coining with native components and expanding the meanings of the existing terms wherever possible. In subjects like agriculture, fisheries, etc., a survey of occupational vocabularies, like that for Telugu, could provide the basis for coining new terms. The UNESCO paper on the use of vernacular languages in education proposes six principles for the creation of terminologies (Tanner 1968:707–708):

1. Begin by making a study of vocabulary already in use, including recent borrowed words and native expressions recently formed to describe new concepts. The principal methods used include giving new meanings to old terms, using native descriptive expressions or derivatives, adopting foreign terms, modelling native descriptive expressions after convenient foreign models. The problem, then, is to determine which of these procedures are most generally used and in what way they tend to be applied to different sets of concepts.
2. Avoid coining new words where native words are already in general use or where there are words which could easily be stretched to include the new concept without special confusion. If the native word is mainly used by people in a given section of the country or by specialists in some particular craft, then the problem

would be simply that of generalizing its use. Along with the employment of words of strictly native tradition, one must give full consideration to relatively new words adopted from other languages, particularly if they already have general currency.

3. Before adding a word to the vocabulary, be sure that it is really needed either at once or in the relatively near future. It is not wise to prescribe words which will not be used with some frequency, since such needs can be met by using brief descriptions. People generally will not bother to learn special words in such cases, and those few persons who go out of their way to use the prescribed terms may not be understood. A difference should be made in the case of new terms whose meaning is reasonably self-evident.

4. Where a whole set of terms applying to a given field of science has to be adopted, try to maintain general consistency among them — consistency as to type of formation and language of origin. The international terms from Latin and Greek, and other terms in widespread usage through the world, should be given special consideration.

5. Make necessary adaptations to the phonemic structure and grammar of the language.

6. Once the new terms have been chosen, try them out on a number of people to see how readily they take to them. If possible, experiment with the use of the new terms in lectures, class instruction and general conversation for a while before publishing.

These principles are hardly followed in modernizing Indian languages. Most of the new coinings are loan translations of international terms, word-to-word or even morpheme-to-morpheme with Sanskrit components.[3] Even popular terms of established usage have been replaced by Sanskrit-based loan translations. The so-called pan-Indian terminologies prepared by the Scientific and Technical Terms Commission have not found favor with the educational agencies of State governments even in the Indo-Aryan area.

7. RESEARCH STRATEGIES IN LANGUAGE STANDARDIZATIONS

At present in-depth studies are lacking on the exact form and function of standard languages in India. I would like to identify some of the areas in which research is needed.

1. Cross-linguistic comparisons of the sociological and historical processes underlying the emergence of one or more norms for written communication should be made. Written norms in Hindi, Bengali, and

---

[3] Here are a few specimens of technical terms used in Telugu collegiate level textbooks: equator belt (*bhūmadhyarēkhāmēkhala*); reciprocal value (*wyutkramamūlyamu*), dipolemoment (*dwidhruva bhrāmakamu*), diaphragm (*wibhājaka paṭalamu*), spectrometer (*warṇapaṭala māpakam*), spark (*sphulṅgamu*), magnetic meridian (*ayaskāntakṣitijasamāntara rēkha*), inorganic (*ajaiwika*), horizontal (*samastalīya*). These specimens are from the *Provisional list of technical terms* (Telugu Akademi, Hyderabad 1973).

Marathi originated from the spoken languages around metropolitan centers (Dehli, Calcutta, Poona). The standard norm in Telugu is more diffuse, its place of origin being the rich Krishna–Godavari delta from which most modern writers have come and evolved a written standard based on their colloquial speech. Telugu and Bengali are again comparable in that a classical language is progressively being replaced by a modern standard of the educated middle class. The standard language of Tamil stands on a different footing altogether, being a superposed classical variety which some consider as an underlying and even historically older form, from which modern dialects can be derived by a set of regular phonological rules (Ramanujan 1968).

2. A study should be made of the extent of use of the standard language in terms of the number of readers and listeners exposed to mass media, the number of prose publications, creative and scientific, and whether unimodal or multimodal standards are used in different spheres of written communication.

3. A critical and comparative study should be made of the procedures of modernizing the languages and their impact on the acquisition of knowledge and the saving effected in terms of learning time, comprehension, and concept formation. The consequences of language planning by the national and state institutes of languages in the production of college level textbooks should be examined. The extent to which this reform has accelerated the learning process as compared to the use of English as the medium should be assessed.

4. Social acceptability does not necessarily guarantee wider intelligibility of a norm. Intelligibility surveys of the language and styles used in mass media (newspapers, radio broadcasts, etc.) should be undertaken for different languages to see what factors matter most in comprehension. Phonological, grammatical and lexical features interfering with intelligibility should be listed to quantify the degrees of comprehension of the standard language in different social, regional, and educational groups.

5. An assessment should be made of the role played by the language of the newspapers and the new literati, who, prompted by political power and nationalist sentiment, systematically ban the process of borrowing as a means of enriching the language for modern concepts and its impact on the shaping of the standard language. Gumperz and Das Gupta (1970:142–146) fear that the increasing classicization of Hindi by Eastern U.P. scholars under the aegis of the Hindi Sahitya Sammelan has widened the gap "between the media of elite communication and mass comprehension." New rules of derivational morphology have been introduced by such coinings as *varjit, prakaaśit, sthaapit*, etc., causing uneasiness even among the educated speakers of Hindi regarding their control of the new standard.

8. ATTITUDES CONDUCIVE TO THE GROWTH OF STANDARD LANGUAGE

The following attitudes seem to help in the development of modern standard languages:

1. As long as the spelling is uniform, regional variation in pronunciation should be tolerated where it does not signal information of strata along the social scale, e.g. in Telugu *ty* and *dy* are pronounced by educated speakers as *ccε, jjε* and *ttε, ddε*, respectively, in different regions.

Spelling   Pronunciation
padyam   *pajjεm paddεm*   'poem'
satyam   *saccεm sattεm*   'truth'

The differences in regional variation are therefore derivable by a set of regular phonetic rules applied to spelling. Variation in morphology and lexicon should be tolerated where it does not correlate with social variation; different modes of addressing kinsmen and words in common parlance for daily essentials show a great deal of regional variation even within the standard language.

2. In the coining of technical terms natural processes of language growth should be exploited including promotion of extensive borrowing. "A technical vocabulary can be equally effective whether it comes from the language's own processes of word formation or from extensive borrowing from another language" (Ferguson 1968:33).

3. Efforts should be made to promote multimodal standards for different roles. A local educated standard would be more suitable as a medium of instruction at the primary school level and in adult literacy programs, to enable the learners to have smooth transition from their workingclass home dialect to an "elaborated code" of the standard language. Bernstein maintains (1968:224) that "the lower the social strata, the greater the resistance to formal education and learning" and that this is a function of the social structure of the strata. Although there are practical difficulties in publishing textbooks in local standard dialects, the cost is worth it when compared to the devastating effects of exposing socially backward children to a totally unfamiliar variety, called the standard language.

4. A standard language, once established, should absorb a larger number of regionalisms by planned efforts of creative writers to expand its comprehensibility. In Norway the elitist *riksmål* and the popular *landsmål* are thus being brought together by the planned efforts of government agencies and academic institutions. There are cases where standard languages died out by their exclusiveness, e.g. Sanskrit and Latin, but no instance of a standard language losing its acceptability by being brought closer to the regional dialects. The mass media and powerful writers have a crucial role to play in this process. It is said that Bahasa

Indonesia has enhanced its acceptability by its relative flexibility (Tanner 1972:133–135).

1. Standard Indonesian shows signs of becoming more acceptable for polite speech — as indicating respect and social distance.
2. Slangs based on regional codes are being incorporated into daily Indonesian in order to make it "swing," to mute its public, utilitarian, colourless and stiff connotations, and transform it into a flexible, informal style capable of promoting subgroup solidarities.
3. Through vocabulary expression it has begun the process of becoming an adequate vehicle for technical discussions and for advanced as well as elementary education.

When this happens, several standard varieties develop within a standard language for different functional roles overlaid by a major standard for highly formal communication and rigorous writing.
5. In scientific and technical discourses, informal codeswitching should be encouraged between an Indian language and English so that concept formation takes precedence over word formation. This process will lead to free borrowing of terminology from the source language with necessary adaptation and assimilation into the phonological and syntactic patterns of the borrowing language.

REFERENCES

APTE, MAHADEV L.
  1962   Linguistic acculturation and its relation to urbanization and socioeconomic factors. *Indian Linguistics* 23:5–25.
BERNSTEIN, B.
  1968   "Some sociological determinants of perception: an inquiry into subcultural differences," in *Readings in the sociology of language*. Edited by Joshua A. Fishman, 223–239. The Hague: Mouton.
BERNTSEN, MAXINE
  1973   "Social stratification in the Marathi speech of Phaltan. Mimeographed report, 1–24.
BLOOMFIELD, LEONARD
  1964   "Literate and illiterate speech," in *Language in culture and society*. Edited by Dell Hymes, 391–396. New York: Harper and Row.
BRIGHT, WILLIAM
  1960   "Linguistic change in some Indian caste dialects," in *Linguistic diversity in South Asia: studies in regional, social and functional variation*. Edited by Charles A. Ferguson and John J. Gumperz, 19–26. Research Center in Anthropology, Folklore and Linguistics Publication 13. Bloomington: Indiana University.
BRIGHT, WILLIAM, A. K. RAMANUJAN
  1964   "Sociolinguistic variation and language change," in *Proceedings of the ninth international congress of linguists* 1962, 1107–1114. The Hague: Mouton.

CHATTERJI, SUNITI KUMAR
1960   *Indo-Aryan and Hindi* (second edition). Calcutta.
DIMOCK, EDWARD C.
1960   "Literary and colloquial Bengali in modern Bengali prose," in *Linguistic diversity in South Asia: studies in regional, social and functional variation*. Edited by Charles A. Ferguson and John J. Gumperz, 43–63. Research Center in Anthropology, Folklore and Linguistics Publication 13. Bloomington: Indiana University.
FERGUSON, CHARLES A.
1962   The language factor in national development. *Anthropological linguistics* 4(1):23–27. (Reprinted 1966. New York: Kraus Reprint Corporation.)
1964   "Diglossia," in *Language in culture and society*. Edited by Dell Hymes, 429–439. New York: Harper and Row.
1968   "Language development," in *Language problems of developing nations*. Edited by Joshua A. Fishman, Charles A. Ferguson and Jyotirindra Das Gupta, 27–35. New York: John Wiley.
FERGUSON, CHARLES A., JOHN J. GUMPERZ, *editors*
1960   *Linguistic diversity in South Asia: studies in regional, social and functional variation*. Research Center in Anthropology, Folklore and Linguistics Publication 13. Bloomington: Indiana University.
FISHMAN, JOSHUA A.
1968   *Readings in the sociology of language*. The Hague: Mouton.
FISHMAN, JOSHUA A., CHARLES A. FERGUSON, JYOTIRINDRA DAS GUPTA, *editors*
1968   *Language problems of developing nations*. New York: John Wiley.
GARVIN, PAUL L.
1964   "The standard language problem: concepts and methods," in *Language in culture and society*. Edited by Dell Hymes, 521–523. New York: Harper and Row.
GIGLIOLI, PIER PAOLO, *editor*
1972   *Language and social context*. Harmondsworth: Penguin.
GOODY, J., I. WATT
1972   "The consequences of literacy," in *Language and social context*. Edited by Pier Paolo Giglioli, 311–357. Harmondsworth: Penguin.
GUMPERZ, JOHN J., J. DAS GUPTA
1971   "Language, communication and control," in *Language in social groups: essays by J. Gumperz*. Introduced and selected by Anwar S. Dil, 129–150. Stanford, Calif.: Stanford University Press.
GUMPERZ, JOHN J., C. M. NAIM
1960   "Formal and informal standards in the Hindi regional language area," in *Linguistic diversity in South Asia: studies in regional, social and functional variation*. Edited by Charles A. Ferguson and John J. Gumperz, 92–118. Research Center in Anthropology, Folklore and Linguistics Publication 13. Bloomington: Indiana University.
HAUGEN, EINAR
1968   "Language planning in modern Norway," in *Readings in the sociology of language*. Edited by Joshua A. Fishman, 673–687. The Hague: Mouton.
1972   "Dialect, language, nation," in *Sociolinguistics*. Edited by J. B. Pride and Janet Holmes, 97–111. Harmondsworth: Penguin.
HYMES, DELL, *editor*
1964   *Language in culture and society (a reader in linguistics and anthropology)*. New York: Harper and Row.

KRISHNAMURTI, BH.
1962   "A survey of Telugu dialect vocabulary," in *A Telugu dialect dictionary of occupational vocabularies,* 99–130. Hyderabad: Andhra Pradesh Sahitya Akademi.
1971   Telugu māṇḍalikālu: Karīmnagaru wāḍuka. *Telugu Dialect Bulletin* 1, 7–25. Hyderabad: Telugu Akademi.
1972   "Bilingualism and social dialects in Tle Telugu." Mimeographed report, 1–14.

McCORMACK, WILLIAM
1960   "Social dialects in Dharwar Kannada," in *Linguistic diversity in South Asia: studies in regional, social and functional variation.* Edited by Charles A. Ferguson and John J. Gumperz, 79–81. Research Center in Anthropology, Folklore and Linguistics Publication 13, Bloomington: Indiana University.

PANDIT, P. B.
1972   *India as a sociolinguistic area.* Poona: University of Poona.

PRIDE, J. B., JANET HOLMES, *editors*
1972   *Sociolinguistics.* Harmondsworth: Penguin.

RAMANUJAN, A. K.
1968   "The structure of variation: a study in caste dialects," in *Structure and change in Indian society.* Edited by Milton Singer and Bernard S. Cohn. Chicago: Aldine.

SHANMUGAM PILLAI, M.
1960   "Tamil literary and colloquial," in *Linguistic diversity in South Asia: studies in regional, social and functional variation.* Edited by Charles A. Ferguson and John J. Gumperz, 27–42. Research Center in Anthropology, Folklore and Linguistics Publication 13. Bloomington: Indiana University.

SJOBERG, ANDRÉE F.
1962   Coexistent phonemic systems in Telugu: a sociocultural perspective. *Word* 18:269–279.

SOUTHWORTH, FRANKLIN C.
1968   "Detecting prior pidginization: an analysis of the historical origins of Marathi." Mimeographed report, 1–67.
1972   Problems in defining the standard languages in India, England and the United States. *International Journal of Dravidian Linguistics* 1:29–37.

TANNER, N.
1968   "The use of vernacular languages in education: report of the UNESCO meeting of specialists, 1951," in *Readings in the sociology of language.* Edited by Joshua A. Fishman, 688–716. The Hague: Mouton.
1972   "Speech and society among the Indonesian elite: a case study of a multilingual community," in *Sociolinguistics.* Edited by J. B. Pride and Janet Holmes, 125–141. Harmondsworth: Penguin.

Universals of Language Planning in National Development

CHARLES A. FERGUSON and ANWAR S. DIL

Language is a universal element in human societies, and we must carefully examine the role of language in society if we are ever to reach any understanding of the processes of social change which we see in operation around us. The study of language in society on a broad macrolevel is a vast field of inquiry, and the role of language in social change has been examined at different times and places with such highly varied philosophical and political assumptions as those of Aśoka's edicts of third century B.C., Ibn Khaldun's fourteenth century *Muqaddimah*, and Lenin's classic *O Prave Nacij na Samoopredelenie*. In this paper we will attempt only one of many possible approaches — the combination of the conceptual framework of national development with the viewpoint of language universals. In spite of the limitations of the present state of sociolinguistic knowledge, it is possible to attempt a listing of some language universals of national development, in the hope that they will promptly be challenged and will become the starting point for extensive investigations. We may also hope that even at this very tentative stage of formulation they may be of some value for policy-making and action programs in a wide range of national settings.

The whole question of language is beginning to occupy a more central position in national development planning, even in highly developed countries language problems are becoming increasingly urgent. Tensions between different social groups are an inevitable concomitant of social and technological change in the developing countries of Asia and Africa, and often language, as the most salient marker of such groups, is important in a direct way as the channel of communication and indirectly as a symbol of group identity or aspirations. In some nations of Europe and the Americas new forces of ethnicity and new demands of linguistically-identified groups are posing severe problems, not only in countries such as Belgium, Canada, and Yugoslavia where the tensions have long been recognized, but also in nations such as Great Britain, Spain, and the United States, where language questions were generally assumed to be very minor. Soviet scholarship has recently emphasized the importance of sociolinguistic research and a number of Latin American countries are experimenting with new patterns of education to cope with widespread illiteracy and substantial Indian-language populations.

The notion of "national development" is open to many interpretations and is subject to many criticisms, but nations certainly vary widely in such indicators as the rate of growth of per capita income, the degree of mass mobilization and participation in political processes, or the amount of differentiation and specialization in occupational categories, and it is generally possible to agree that a particular nation is "more highly developed" or is "developing more rapidly" than some other nation in some identifiable respects. Accordingly, our "universals" here will be stated as though the notion of development were quite clear, and we will use the phrasing "as development accelerates" and "trends are strengthened" to refer to a systematic relation of some kind between development processes and the language phenomena under discussion, without defining acceleration or making explicit qualification of either side of the equation. We shall use the expression "center of development" to refer to a city or region which serves as a focal point for the spreading and acceleration of developmental processes. Also, from the point of view of the economist or the anthropologist the nation may not always be the best unit of development to be analyzed since a larger or smaller economy or society may be more appropriate. Here, however, we shall state our universals in terms of the nation as the most obvious unit of planned social change, although occasionally a smaller or larger unit will be cited as an example.

The viewpoint of "language universals," in the attempt to find generalizations about human language, examines particular phenomena in large numbers of languages. As such, it is in part a reaction against linguists' earlier concern with the enormous diversity of structure among languages and a corresponding attempt to find fundamental common features shared by all languages. In part, too, it is a way to make use of the accumulated data of grammatical descriptions of hundreds of languages by testing significant hypotheses of linguistic theory. In this paper we are looking for generalizations about changes in the attitudes about and the use of language which are related to the processes of national development. We do this with the expectation that in spite of the sociocultural differences among different nations and among the same nations at different times as well as the great differences in language situations, we can find common features which are not only of interest in themselves but can prove of value to policy makers and language planners. Our combined approach of language universals and national development inevitably reveals tensions between the two viewpoints. Also, the phenomenon of inadequate communication between Western and non-Western participants in international development exchange and intellectual undertakings is well known. The authors hope, however, that the merits of the combined approach, even with all the risks of compromise, will outweigh the doubts and contradictions inherent in it. We find support in the history of man's cooperation across linguistic and cultural barriers for the improvement of the human condition.

The generalizations of this study are stated in the form of hypotheses, some of which may be merely surface outcomes of principles operating at a deeper level, while others may be nearer to the underlying principles.

Hypothesis 1

THE DEVELOPMENT PROCESS REQUIRES THE USE OF ONE OR MORE "LANGUAGES OF DEVELOPMENT." Like any other identifiable set of institutions or processes in a society, development involves the use of language. Uses which are clearly related to development include among others management, technical access, governmental services, education. Thus, management policy decisions are discussed and made and transmitted to lower echelons in some language; and one language or another may be the source language for needed scientific and technological information. The government uses language in the administration of financial and technical operations associated with development, and one language or another is the medium of instruction in schools. While the definition may be fuzzy, it is generally possible to identify the languages or language varieties which serve as the languages of development in a particular nation as opposed to languages used in ordinary conversation, religious activities, and so on.

Hypothesis 2

THE DEVELOPMENT PROCESS TENDS TOWARD THE DOMINANCE OF A SINGLE LANGUAGE OF DEVELOPMENT IN A NATION. This means that, as development accelerates, trends toward language unification in these developmental uses are strengthened. Conversely, the entry of additional languages of development onto the scene, other things being equal, tends to retard development. Nowhere in the world does a nation use only a single language of development, and in some of the highly developed smaller countries of Western Europe (e.g. Luxembourg) there may be very complex patterns of use of different languages of development. Nevertheless it seems clear that the very processes of development do tend toward communicative standardization at certain levels, and in some general theory of development a hypothesis of this sort should be a provable theorem.

Hypothesis 3

THE DEVELOPMENT PROCESS TENDS TOWARD MAKING AVAILABLE A SINGLE LANGUAGE OF NATIONAL COMMUNICATION. There is no full correlation between unilingualism and national development, and there are instances of multilingual, highly developed nations (e.g. Switzerland) and unilingual, poorly developed nations (e.g. Costa Rica). Nevertheless the correlation is high, and it seems clear that, as development accelerates in a multilingual nation, trends toward a single dominant national communication network increase or else social tensions and communication problems increase between language groups, retarding development. The development of networks of communication utilizing bilingual linkages which is an instance of this tendency, may, however, stabilize for long periods of time at a point far short of a single language. Also, languages may function as nationwide means of intercommunication at various levels, ranging from an official national language publicly recognized by law or custom (e.g. Amharic in Ethiopia) to a low-prestige informal lingua franca (e.g. pidgin English in some West African nations).

Hypothesis 4

THE DEVELOPMENT PROCESS TENDS TOWARD STANDARDIZATION OF LANGUAGES OF DEVELOPMENT AND OFFICIAL LANGUAGES OF NATIONAL COMMUNICATION. Speech communities differ greatly in the amount of their internal diversity, i.e. dialect variations and the use of different languages in the community. Development processes tend to unify and disseminate a single norm of pronunciation, orthography, basic grammatical categories, basic vocabulary, and semantic areas related to development activities. This standardization process represents the same integrating, standardizing force of development processes reflected in Hypotheses 2 and 3. There is no single path to language standardization, but the direction of the changes is clear. Most of the attitudinal and behavioral changes subsumed under the term language standardization are unconscious, but much of this kind of social change may be subjected to conscious planning (cf. Hypothesis 13 below).

The principal kinds of variation which are reduced or eliminated by this process are regional variation and variation between educated conversational language and special literary varieties (e.g. Bengali, where the

Standard Colloquial is displacing both the traditional literary variety and the regional dialects). Regional and social differentiation may remain or even arise in relation to the development process but it will be at a quite different level, such as variation in the pronunciation of certain sounds within an established norm of pronunciation and grammar rather than extreme variation in morphology and lexicon. Also, the tendency will be to reduce or eliminate the gap between a highly divergent, archaic, literary language accessible only to an elite and the everyday conversational language of educated people, whether by the emergence of intermediate varieties or the reduction of functions of the high literary form. Development may lead to new literary styles, but these also will tend to be at a different level, such as choice of particular words or constructions within a basically unified norm (cf. Hypothesis 5 below).

Hypothesis 5

THE LANGUAGE WHICH IS THE PRINCIPAL VEHICLE OF TECHNICAL INNOVATION AND MANAGERIAL DECISION-MAKING TENDS TO BECOME THE DOMINANT LANGUAGE OF DEVELOPMENT. Many factors are involved in the spread of a language or the diffusion of elements from one language to another, but this hypothesis suggests that when there is a discrepancy between a managerial/technical language and a language of common use the former will continue to spread to more and more uses related to development and will only be successfully resisted and replaced when the managerial/technical innovation and decision-making is carried out by people for whom the replacement language is a more natural means of communication. Thus, German was replaced by Hungarian as the language of Hungarian national development in the nineteenth and twentieth centuries not only because of Hungarian ethnic and linguistic consciousness but also because the crucial managerial/technical activities came to be carried out by native speakers of Hungarian. This same process of linguistic diffusion can be seen at the intralanguage level (cf. Hypothesis 6 below). The movement of a language into this kind of dominance may constitute a disruption of the existing language equilibrium and thus be accompanied by severe tensions of adjustment among the competing languages or language varieties of the nation and different responses tending to the resolution of the conflict.

Hypothesis 6

THE LANGUAGE OR VARIETY WHICH IS THE PRINCIPAL VEHICLE OF TECHNICAL INNOVATION AND MANAGERIAL DECISION-MAKING WILL TEND TO BE THE

MAJOR SOURCE OF LEXICAL EXPANSION. Every language has its own patterns of lexical innovation. As new words are needed they are created, often unconsciously but sometimes with detailed conscious consideration. The patterns may involve word compounding, various forms of derivation by affixes, vowel alternations, and so on, or a "borrowing" from a classical language or modern foreign language. The point of this hypothesis is that the managerial/technical language will be a major determinant of lexical innovation. Thus, if a new technology for road-building is developing in an Asian country and the technical innovators are all English-speaking, and technically trained in English, and they include some essentially monolingual English-speakers, the likelihood is great that new terms related to road-building will be English loanwords or modeled on English words and expressions, while in a country where the road-building innovators are basically trained in their own language the lexical expansion is very likely to be based on local patterns of lexical innovation.

This hypothesis also relates to the issue of different centers of development in the same language, either in the same or different nations. For example, railroad technology developed to a large extent independently in Great Britain and the United States and the lexical innovations, while all based on patterns of the English language, ended up in two very different technical vocabularies (switch:point, freight car:goods wagon, caboose:brake van). Thus intralanguage differences and lexical innovation may result from different source languages or different centers of development with the same source language. The source language in the first case may be different colonial languages in the same language community (e.g. French versus English source in Lebanon and Jordan). The source language in the second case may even be the same, as in the railroad example, and may even be a foreign or colonial language (e.g. different English-origin innovations in Egypt and Iraq).

Hypothesis 7

THE DOMINANT LANGUAGE AT THE CENTER OF DEVELOPMENT TENDS TO BECOME THE DOMINANT OFFICIAL LANGUAGE OF NATIONAL COMMUNICATION. There are a number of well-known sources for incipient national languages, such as language of the traditional elite (e.g. Amharic in Ethiopia), overwhelming numerical predominance (e.g. Malagasy in the Malagasy Republic), trade language (e.g. Malay in Indonesia). This hypothesis merely calls attention to the importance of the center of development as a factor in the emergence of the national language. The hypothesis is suggested by the history of national languages in Europe (e.g. French and Russian). Hypothesis 8 is another aspect of the linguistic importance of a center of development.

Hypothesis 8

THE VARIETY OF LANGUAGE DOMINANT AT THE CENTER OF DEVELOPMENT
TENDS TO BECOME THE NORM FOR THAT LANGUAGE THROUGHOUT THE NATION.
It may safely be assumed that all speech communities have variations
associated with prestige, i.e. some varieties of the language are widely
held to be in some sense "better" than other varieties and are used by
people or in settings which may be regarded as prestigious. As the
development process accelerates, a traditional locus of prestigious language will tend to be eclipsed by a center of development (e.g. the variety of
Amharic which is rapidly spreading in Ethiopia as the prestige norm is not
the traditional model of Gojjan but the Amharic spoken in Addis Ababa).

Hypothesis 9

THE DEVELOPMENT PROCESS TENDS TOWARD DIFFERENTIATION OF LANGUAGE
ALONG FUNCTIONAL LINES, resulting in the expansion of technical vocabularies and the appearance of new forms of discourse; the differentiation may be within single languages or may be by the use of one or more
additional languages with different functional allocations. This functional
differentiation contrasts sharply with the unifying and standardizing process of Hypotheses 2, 3, and 4. Here reference is made, for example, to
the expansion of the total lexicon of the language. In a small nonliterate
society of high social homogeneity it may be assumed that the total
lexicon of the language tends to be available to everyone, and the distinctive vocabularies of specialists in the society is minimal. It seems likely
that the working vocabulary of the ordinary person is roughly of the same
order no matter what the level of development of a society, but the
development process may add enormously to the specialized ways of
speaking, vocabularies, and forms of written discourse known only to
specialist groups in the society.

Hypothesis 10

THE DEVELOPMENT PROCESS WILL TEND TO STRENGTHEN THE USE OF A CLASSI-
CAL LANGUAGE FELT TO BE A POWERFUL MARKER OF ETHNIC OR NATIONAL
IDENTITY. If a nation is conscious of a special religious or cultural tradition
of which it believes it is an inheritor and that tradition is linked with a
classical language, then in a period of accelerated development the nation
will attempt to revive and extend the use of the classical language as a
priority field of planning and development (e.g. since independence the
process of Sanskritization in India and Arabicization in Algeria).

Hypothesis 11

THE PROCESS OF DEVELOPMENT TENDS TO CREATE OR INTENSIFY SOCIAL TENSION RELATED TO THE USE OF TRADITIONAL AND MODERNIZING LANGUAGES. If sociocultural revivalism centering on the use of a language in a nation becomes linked with traditionalism and orthodoxy, while the use of another language (local or foreign) is linked with the process of modernization, loyalties to the respective languages can become a salient focus of social conflict (e.g. Sinhalese versus English in postindependence Ceylon).

Hypothesis 12

DEVELOPMENT TIED TO ETHNIC IDENTITY WILL TEND TO UPGRADE THE STATUS OF THE LANGUAGE OR LANGUAGE VARIETY OF THE ETHNIC GROUP. As a new center of development in a nation is linked to feelings of ethnic identity and oppression by the people of another center, language use will reflect this by such phenomena as the emergence of a new standard language, even if it is extremely close to an existing standard language (e.g. Slovak separating from modern Czech) and the overt political recognition of new uses of the subordinate ethnic language (e.g. new uses of French in Canadian national life).

Hypothesis 13

THE DEVELOPMENT PROCESS TENDS TO INCREASE LANGUAGE PLANNING ACTIVITIES. In periods of rapid national development, new language planning functions are undertaken, either by extending the functions of existing institutions or by the emergence of new language planning activities such as increased language learning (national and international), script reform, translation, creation of language societies or academies (e.g. fifteenth–sixteenth century England, the Islamic world under the Abbasids, Turkey of Ataturk). In some larger theory of national development this kind of hypothesis should be a provable theorem inasmuch as planning activities in general tend to increase as development accelerates although in quite different ways in different nations.

Hypothesis 14

THE DEVELOPMENT PROCESS TENDS TO PRODUCE INDIVIDUALS OF BILINGUAL OR BIREGISTRAL COMPETENCE. In periods of rapid national development in a nation where the languages of development differ from local languages, the number of bilingual speakers will increase to meet the new communication needs. These bilinguals often play key roles of innovation within the nation and communication between interacting social groups and development agencies. This is only the larger version of the familiar phenomenon that rapid development in a unilingual setting requires more "interpreters" who are able to communicate between management and labor or between other segments of the population where new patterns of communication are being established.

The Dimensionality and Predictability of Responses to Language Planning Activities

JOSHUA A. FISHMAN

The International Research Project on Language Planning Processes (IRPLPP) represents an attempt to provide comparative data on the effectiveness of certain major aspects of language planning: lexical elaboration for modernization and influencing knowledge and attitudes toward the central agencies charged with the responsibility for such elaboration. All in all, therefore, the IRPLPP is concerned with the code-planning rather than with the status-function planning aspects of language planning (Kloss 1969), although these two aspects are always to some extent interrelated. Furthermore, the IRPLPP represents an attempt to compare the ACCEPTANCE (attitudinal and overt) of language-planning products within national group boundaries rather than an attempt to study the international spread of such products (Spathaky 1970; Felber 1970) or their local comprehensibility in comparison to their preplanning predecessors (Jamias 1970). The project as a whole is primarily explanatory in purpose rather than theoretically integrative in view of its preliminary nature.[1]

The project has involved five senior researchers acting as coordinators in five locales (Charles A. Ferguson, administrative coordination, United States; Joshua A. Fishman, research coordination and Israeli data; Joan Rubin, Indonesian data; Jyotirindra Das Gupta, Indian data; Bjorn Jernudd, originally East Pakistani and ultimately Swedish data), as well as a rather large number of local study directors, associates, consultants, and assistants. The material presented in this report deals only with one aspect of the total theoretical, methodological, and substantive coverage of the project.

[1] This presentation attempts to summarize and integrate a far more detailed but less conceptually integrated report (Fishman 1972).

DESIGN

The IRPLPP has focussed upon several different but related populations in each of the countries in which it has been active. Thus, in each country, the members and senior staff of the national Language Planning Agencies (LPAs) have been intensively studied with respect to their language planning views and work routines. Textbook writers and educational officers have been similarly subjected to lengthy questionnaires and interviews, as have representatives of certain other populations in a particular country (e.g. driving instructors [Fainberg 1972] and industrial chemists [Hofman 1972] in Israel), that are possibly indicators of language planning problems or successes.

That part of the IRPLPP to be reported upon here may be outlined as follows:

1. THREE COUNTRIES: India, Indonesia, Israel.
2. THREE SCHOOL-RELATED POPULATIONS: TEACHERS (at high school and college levels), STUDENTS (at high school and college levels), and ADULTS (represented, in part, by parents of the above students and, in part, by a sample of whitecollar workers).
3. THREE ATTITUDINAL-INFORMATIONAL CRITERIA OF "SUCCESSFUL" LANGUAGE PLANNING:

   a. accurate knowledge and favorable attitudes with respect to the officially recognized and centrally supported national Language Planning Agency or Agencies (based on replies to sixty questions),
   b. accurate knowledge and favorable attitudes re ADVOCATORY AGENCIES generally supporting the work or the goals of the Language Planning Agencies (based on totaling replies to thirty-five questions), and
   c. accurate knowledge and unfavorable attitudes re OPPOSING AGENCIES generally counteracting the work or the goals of the Language Planning Agency or Agencies (based on replies to twelve questions).

4. THREE WORD-USAGE CRITERIA OF "SUCCESSFUL" LANGUAGE PLANNING: giving (in a word-naming task) "LPA approved" words[2] in

   a. a humanities field (GRAMMAR),
   b. a natural sciences field (CHEMISTRY), and
   c. a social sciences field (CIVICS).

Thus, the findings to be reviewed here are based upon a three-country by three-population by six-criteria design which AIMS AT DISCOVERING WHETHER THERE ARE SIGNIFICANT SIMILARITIES AND/OR DIFFERENCES BE-

---

[2]   In some instances it was possible to determine whether words named by our respondents were "LPA-approved" by consulting officially published lists of such terms; in others (where no lists were available) judges well acquainted with LPA views or principles pertaining to neologisms in particular substantive fields determined whether the words named by our respondents were such as would be approved by the LPA.

TWEEN CERTAIN SCHOOL RELATED POPULATIONS WITH RESPECT TO LEXICAL (AND RELATED INFORMATIONAL/ATTITUDINAL) LANGUAGE PLANNING SUCCESS, AS REFLECTED BY THE SIX CRITERIA UTILIZED. It was hoped that an initial explanatory investigation such as this would prepare the ground conceptually and methodologically for more detailed as well as more integrated hypothesis-testing research in the future.

DATA COLLECTION

In connection with the above design, two-to-six hour questionnaires were administered to teachers, students, and parents associated with the UNIVERSITIES AND THE "BETTER HIGH SCHOOLS" IN THE CAPITAL CITY in particular and, where possible, in similar institutions in one or more other major cities. In both Indonesia and Israel, roughly 250 teachers, 2,000 students, and 400 adults were questioned, as were smaller samples of each population in India (where our research was focussed more on the capital alone). The following independent variables were assessed by the instruments employed, as potential predictors of the criteria mentioned above.

1. PERSONAL BACKGROUND, particularly in connection with the language repertoires of respondents and their immediate family members, but also including considerable other personal and demographic information dealing with ethnicity, religion, education, travel, reading, and radio/television preferences, etc.

2. ATTITUDES, particularly in connection with modernization, national consciousness, language consciousness, and the designation of particularly good and bad speakers, writers, or references *re* Indonesian, Hindi, or Hebrew.[3]

3. LEXICAL PREFERENCES ("word evaluation"), particularly in connection with usage claims and attitudinal reactions to a twenty-five-word sample of academy-approved terms[4] in at least one of the three substantive fields for which work-naming criterion scores were obtained, as well

---

[3] Respondents were asked whether there were regional varieties, social class or group varieties, groups or well-known individuals who spoke the indicated language particularly well or poorly, whether there were any who wrote it particularly well or poorly, whether there were any really good dictionaries or grammars for the language, etc. In each case those responding affirmatively were also asked to name the groups, regions, individuals, or references involved. This entire set of questions sought to determine if a dimension of sociolinguistic sensitivity and discrimination existed among our respondents. A similar dimension had been factorially derived in prior work among New York Puerto Ricans by Fishman, Cooper and Ma et al. (1971).

[4] "Academy-approved" terms in connection with the study of lexical preference were located by methods similar to those utilized in scoring WORD-NAMING for "LPA-approved" terms, i.e. either by referring to approved lists or to expert judges. No attempt was made to locate identical terms or terms of identical difficulty in each language. On the other hand, a conscious (and largely successful) effort was made to locate "academy-approved" terms that still had active "unapproved" rivals in popular and/or scientific usage.

as in connection with INDIGENOUSNESS OF SCHEDULED LANGUAGE (SL) VOCABULARY in general.[5]

DATA ANALYSIS

In view of the huge amount of data collected by the IRPLPP, the data analysis and interpretation methods selected rely upon quantitative data-reduction and compositing. Thus, for example, the roughly 1,200 coded responses per respondent in our TEACHER study were intercorrelated and then factor analyzed (via the varimax orthogonal structure method). As a result, twelve major factors (representing the twelve largest and maximally different dimensions in our data) as well as from twenty to thirty "minor factors" (i.e. individual items that seemed both unrelated to each other or to any of the foregoing twelve factors) were identified in each country. The items selected as being most representative of the twelve major factors (from twelve to sixteen in each country) plus the items most clearly unrelated to any of these factors (from twenty to thirty) were then utilized via cumulative multiple correlation methods to predict each of the six criteria mentioned earlier. Similar procedures were followed in connection with the student and adult data. All in all, nine different factor analyses were performed (for three populations in each of three countries) and the factor-representing items identified thereby were then utilized in predicting the aforementioned criteria in each population-by-country combination.

In addition to the predictors derived by factor analysis just mentioned, several *a priori* predictors (i.e. predictors chosen on the basis prior assumptions as to their usefulness) were also regularly employed in view of their intrinsic interest as well as apparent "face validity" with respect to our criteria:number of languages respondents claim to speak, number of languages respondents claim to read, number of languages respondents claim father knows, number of languages respondents claim mother knows, and respondents' overall or general attitudinal preference for indigenousness of SL vocabulary. In addition, TOTAL WORD-NAMING SCORES (as measures of total lexical availability) in each substantive field were also employed as *a priori* predictors, as were all five remaining criterion scores, in the cumulative multiple prediction of any particular criterion. A stepwise forced procedure was employed in determining

---

[5]   A scheduled language is any one of the particular languages with whose lexical elaboration we were concerned. For the three countries from which our final data were obtained it might have been equally accurate to refer to NL (=national language). However, because we initially sought to obtain East Pakistani data as well, and both Urdu and Bengali were then the national languages of Pakistan, and because the positions of Hindi, Indonesian, and Hebrew as national languages differs in significant ways, we choose instead the more neutral designation "scheduled language" (SL) for the particular languages of interest to us.

cumulative multiple prediction of any given criterion so that all predictors (factorial and *a priori*) were entered FIRST, the five additional criteria were entered NEXT, and total word-naming scores were entered LAST (because of their conceivable necessary correlation with "approved" word-naming).[6]

Given the kinds of predictor measures and criterion measures employed by the IRPLPP, it is the goal of this study to provide empirical data concerning the DIFFERENTIAL SUCCESS OF LANGUAGE PLANNING ACTIVITY (pertaining to lexical usage and attendant information and attitudes) *vis-à-vis* the populations here studied. If this can be done, the IRPLPP may be considered a step ahead in attacking the following general question: Do the explanatory factors related to differential success in language planning tend to be the same or different, and do they tend to be equally powerful or not, across countries, across populations, across usage criteria, and across attitudinal–informational criteria?

FINDINGS *RE* DIMENSIONALITY OF PREDICTOR DATA

Via a compositing method (factor analysis[7]) the many hundreds or thousands of bits of predictor information obtained from our subjects were reduced to a MUCH smaller set of maximally different dimensions needed to reproduce the data for each population-by-country combination. All in all, across all countries and populations, eighteen recurring major dimensions or factors were discovered in this fashion (see Table 1) as well as a somewhat larger number of recurring and nonrecurring minor dimensions. That such a high degree of compositing proved to be POSSIBLE (and, as we will soon see, also PROFITABLE for the purposes of prediction and explanation) is an important finding in and of itself, as an indication that a reasonably small number of behavioral regularities underlie the seemingly endless array of socially patterned cognitive, affective, and overt responses to language planning efforts.

Approximately half of the composited major dimensions that were located dealt with language repertoire matters (e.g., 1, 3, 4, 5, 6, 9, 10, 11 — numbers refer to labels in Table 1) the remainder being rather equally divided between attitudinal/informational dimensions (7, 8, 12,

---

[6]   "Total word-naming" and "approved word-naming" do NOT stand in any predictable part–whole relationship with each other. Individuals naming MORE words in any lexical field do not thereby necessarily need to name more APPROVED words and, indeed, may very well name FEWER approved words. The latter would obtain where more informed individuals with respect to a particular field of endeavor were particularly opposed to or uninformed about LPA-approved nomenclatures for that field.

[7]   The particular variety of factor analysis employed was that known as "varimax orthogonal rotation" (see Nie, Bent, Hull 1970:208–244 for a discussion of programs for factor analysis in general and varimax orthogonal rotation in particular). For a nontechnical introduction of factor analysis, see Rozeboom (1966) or Rummel (1967).

Table 1. Major factors across countries and populations*

Labels given to conceptually composited higher order factors	Populations	Indonesia	India	Israel
1. Breadth of language repertoire	T	X (III) (VII)		VIII
	S	V	V	IX
	P	XI		I,X
2. Educational status (of ego/resp.) (also see Number 4, below)	T		VII	I,X
	P	VII	XI	
3. Education via European languages of wider communication (also see Number 4, below)	T	III		
	P			VI
4. English:interest/professional	T		XII	
	S		X	
	P		VI	
5. Language of instruction	S	Chemistry/English: IX, non-Chemistry/ SL:VIII	Chemistry/SL:XI	
6. Language and ethnicity	T	IV (VII)	I, VI	VI, VII, X, XI
	S	I, III, IV, VI	II, III	II, III, VII
	P	II, V, VIII		II
7. Modernization orientation	S		II	I(XII)
	P	IV		

Table 1 (*continued*)

Labels given to conceptually composited higher order factors	Populations	Indonesia	India	Israel
8. National ideology (nationalism) and language ideology	T	XI	XI	V, IX
	S	(VII)	X, XII	VII
	P			
9. Out-of-school formal study of SL	S	X		X
10. Regional language literacy	T	V		IX
	S	VI		
	P			
11. SL first language of ego/parents	T	II	I	I
	S	I	(IX)	(XI)
	P	III	(VII)	(XI)
12. Social change problems	P		VIII, IX	XII
13. Social class/mobility	T	VI	VII	VIII
	P	I (XII)		
14. SL training and normativism (also see Number 15 below)	T		V	XII
	S		IX	
15. SL orientation and implementation (also see Number 16 below)	T		VI	XII
	S		(VII)	

Table 1 (*continued*)

Labels given to conceptually composited higher order factors	Populations	Indonesia	India	Israel
16. Sophistication/differentiation	T	VIII, IX	III	III
re good/bad	S		III, IV, VIII	IV, V, VIII
SL location/users	P	IX, X	I,IV	IV, V
17. Subject matter	T	I/Chemistry	II/Chemistry X/Physical sciences	II/Chemistry
	S	VIII/non-Chemistry	V/Civics	VI/non-Chemistry (XII/Civics)
18. Writing/reading	T	XIII	IV, (VIII),IX	IV

* Roman numerals pertain to major factors located in particular country-by-population factor analyses. Parentheses are used to indicate more tentative assignments of individual country-by-population factors to "higher order" factors.

The first cell in this table should be read as follows: The factor analyses of data EACH Indonesian population yielded a major factor which appears to be relatable to breadth of language repertoire. Among teachers (T) this was major factor X; among students (S): V; among pupils (P): XI. Factors III and VII among teachers are less clearly classifiable as pertaining to this particular "higher order" factor and are, therefore also classified elsewhere in the table.

14, 15, 16) and dimensions concerned with other "demographic" characteristics of the respondents (2, 13, 17, 18). Although no dimension occured in every single population-by-country combination, there were three that were encountered in eight out of the nine such combinations: (Number 6) Language and ethnicity of respondents; (Number 11) SL as first or early language of respondents and/or their parents; (Number 16) Respondent's sophistication differentiation *re* location (social/geographic) and users of particularly good or bad SL. Other factors that occur in at least two-thirds of all possible population/country combinations are: (Number 1) breadth of respondent's language repertoire, (Number 17) subject-matter field with which respondent/offspring is associated; and (Number 8) national and language ideology.

All in all (and in marked contrast to the findings of Jacob et al. [1972] in cross-national studies of leadership values), there was greater DIMENSIONAL SIMILARITY BETWEEN COUNTRIES when all populations were combined (median r=.68) THAN BETWEEN POPULATIONS when all countries were combined (median r=.42) (see Table 2). Thus, for our data it is more fruitful to make between-population comparisons (because there are more differences there) than to make between-country comparisons, all the more so because our samples were not selected so as to be nationally

Table 2. Dimensional similarity: correlations between factor distributions shown in Table 1*

(a) Between countries across populations		*Indonesia*	*Israel*
	India	0.36	0.85
	Indonesia	–	0.68
(b) Between populations across countries		*Students*	*Pupils*
	Teachers	0.53	0.37
	Students	–	0.42

* The r for the teacher factor structures in Indonesia and India, for example, is based on cell entries in Table 1 that begin as follows: 3.0; 0.1; 1.0; 0.0; 2.0; 0.0; etc. The intercorrelations arrived to give an objective estimate of the similarities between the various between-country and between-population factor distributions shown in Table 1.

representative (but rather, so as to tap the populations related to the better schools and universities). It would seem to be more instructive (as well as more valid) in our case to indicate that the dimensions most frequently encountered in our adult samples were of the language repertoire type, while those most frequently encountered for our student samples were of the attitudinal/informational type, than to point out that an overall Indonesian–Indian contrast also exists exactly along these lines.[8] All in all, the low between-population dimensional similarity suggests that both degree of education and generation are important deter-

---

[8]   Israeli data more frequently reveal dimensions of the "Other (demographic) characteristics of respondents" type.

minants of differential response to language planning. The recurringly greater similarity between teachers and students than between either teachers and parents or between students and parents suggests that of these two, for our populations, degree of education is the more powerful dimension.

PREDICTABILITY OF CRITERIA OF "SUCCESS"

The derivation of parsimonious dimensionality for a body of data does not at all guarantee the utility of the dimensions encountered with respect to explaining or accounting for (=predicting) variability on criterion measures ("dependent variables") that are of prime interest. In the present case it is quite clear, however, that the dimensions located were also extremely valuable ones *vis-à-vis* the criteria specified.

Using predictions based upon these dimensions as well as upon those selected on an *a priori* basis, quite high cumulative multiple correlations with the criteria were obtained (yielding a median CR of .52). When other criterion scores were also added into the cumulative prediction the median CR rose to .62. Finally, when total word-naming scores were also involved as predictors the median CR became .88 (see Tables 3, 4, and 5). All in all, the cumulative predictability OF CRITERIA for adults (whether teachers or parents) was about .20 higher than it was for students, as long as total word-naming scores were not employed. When such scores were employed too no noteworthy generational differences remained.

Almost without exception the three word-naming criteria were more fully predicted (median cumulative multiple correlation based upon predictors plus other criteria of .71) than were the three attitudinal informational criteria (median cumulative multiple correlation based upon predictors plus other criteria of .61). The difference is partially the result of the greater reliability and validity of overt verbal measurement in comparison to that of attitudinal measurement, and partially the result of the existence of untapped attitudinal dimensions in response to language, some of which Hofman has subsequently explored (1972). Among the word-naming criteria per se, the one that was regularly most predictable was approved word-naming in chemistry (median cumulative multiple correlation of .79). This resulted largely from the greater variance on this criterion, given the fact that chemistry majors and nonmajors and students differed so greatly and so reliably in connection with their performance on this criterion.[9]

[9]   The most predictable attitudinal/informational criterion was regularly the one dealing with the LPA (medium cumulative multiple correlation based upon predictors plus other criteria of .70). This is largely a result of the fact that no opposing agencies function today in either Indonesia or Israel, while no advocatory agencies function in Indonesia or are active in Israel. As a result, the range of response on the latter two criteria in Indonesia and Israel was extremely limited.

Table 3.   The cumulative multiple prediction of criteria for teachers

		LPA	AA	OA	Ap WN:Gr	Ap WN:Ch	Ap WN:Ci
Predictors alone	Indonesia	0.67	0.49	0.34	0.63	0.82	0.47
	India	0.75	0.61	0.53	0.73	0.89	0.73
	Israel	0.72	0.47	0.49	0.66	0.60	0.54
P + Criteria	Indonesia	0.75	0.61	0.37	0.68	0.82	0.49
	India	0.80	0.70	0.58	0.81	0.91	0.85
	Israel	0.77	0.62	0.54	0.72	0.76	0.69
P + C + TWN	Indonesia	0.76	0.62	0.37	0.93	0.92	0.81
	India*	–	–	–	–	–	–
	Israel	0.77	0.64	0.54	0.95	0.94	0.89

* India word-naming (WN) data were scored as the PERCENTAGE of all words that were LPA-approved (rather than as separate scores for total and approved words), thus making it impossible to derive SEPARATE scores for NUMBER of APPROVED words and NUMBER of TOTAL words.

Key: AA = Advocatory agencies
   OA = Opposing agencies
   Ap WN:G = Approved word-naming:grammar
   Ap WN:Ch = Approved word-naming:chemistry
   Ap WN:Ci = Approved word-naming:civics
   P = Predictors
   C = Criteria
   TWN = Total word-naming

Table 4.   The cumulative multiple prediction of criteria for students

		LPA	AA	OA	Ap WN:Gr	Ap WN:Ch	Ap WN:Ci
Predictors alone	Indonesia	0.36	0.27	0.14	0.46	0.41	0.33
	India	0.39	0.52	0.43	0.79	0.86	0.81
	Israel	0.54	0.30	0.22	0.31	0.31	0.27
P + Criteria	Indonesia	0.66	0.63	0.19	0.55	0.53	0.51
	India	0.44	0.53	0.49	0.95	0.95	0.94
	Israel	0.60	0.44	0.28	0.49	0.62	0.58
P + C + TWN	Indonesia	0.67	0.63	0.19	0.93	0.90	0.89
	India*	–	–	–	–	–	–
	Israel	0.61	0.44	0.28	0.87	0.85	0.71

* India word-naming (WN) data were scored as the PERCENTAGE of all words that were LPA-approved (rather than as separate scores for total and approved words), thus making it impossible to derive SEPARATE scores for NUMBER of APPROVED words and NUMBER of TOTAL words.

Key: AA = Advocatory agencies
   OA = Opposing agencies
   Ap WN:Gr = Approved word-naming:grammar
   Ap WN:Ch = Approved word-naming:chemistry
   Ap WN:Ci = Approved word-naming:civics
   P = Predictors
   C = Criteria
   TWN = Total word-naming

Table 5. The cumulative multiple prediction of criteria for adults*

		LPA	AA	OA
Predictors alone	Indonesia	0.52	0.49	0.48
	India	0.84	0.78	0.75
	Israel	0.58	0.50	0.36
P + Criteria	Indonesia	0.70	0.66	0.50
	India	0.86	0.78	0.75
	Israel	0.67	0.60	0.39

* No word-naming data were obtained for adults.
Key: AA = Advocatory agencies.
    OA = Opposing agencies.
    P = Predictors.

It is important to stress that the various criterion measures were them-selves highly useful in helping to predict one another. Thus, there is an appreciable complementary or circular relationship between them; i.e. attitudinal/informational factors DO significantly help predict variance in approved word-naming usage (just as approved word-naming usage scores help significantly to predict attitudinal/informational variance). Nevertheless, each subset of criteria is more highly predictive of other members of that subset. Thus, it is both correct to consider LPA-relevant attitudes/information on the one hand and usage of approved nomencla-tures on the other hand as clearly SEPARATE criteria of success, while at the same time they are also reliably and importantly RELATED to each other.

INTERCORRELATIONS INVOLVING CRITERION MEASURES

While knowledge and attitudes *re* LPAs were everywhere markedly low, interesting between-country differences appeared in connection with the intercorrelations among the three approved word-naming scores obtained for all teachers and students (see Tables 6 and 7). In Israel, all three scores were consistently positively related to each other. In India, on the contrary, they were consistently negatively related to each other. Finally, in Indonesia, a different pattern emerged for teachers and stu-dents. Among teachers the approved word-naming scores in SL grammar and in civics were positively related to each other but negatively related to approved word-naming in chemistry. Among students consistently posi-tive interrelationships were obtained. The first-mentioned pattern (that in Israel) indicates the most GENERALIZED response to academy-approved nomenclatures whereby individuals either utilize or fail to master them regardless of whether they be in one's own specialized field or not. The second pattern mentioned (that in India), on the other hand, reveals the

Table 6.   Intercorrelations between criterion measures for teachers (means and s.d.s ON diagonal; intercorrelations BELOW diagonal)

		LPA	Ap WN:Gr	Ap WN:Ch	Ap WN:Ci
LPA	Indonesia	7.74/10.82			
	India	6.88/ 6.84			
	Israel	14.38/11.01			
Ap WN:Gr	Indonesia	0.50*	14.10/ 8.13		
	India	0.36*	8.11/13.90***		
	Israel	-0.03	12.14/11.20		
Ap WN:Ch	Indonesia	-0.26*	-0.23*	15.10/10.07	
	India	-0.35*	-0.39*	1.74/ 2.61***	
	Israel	-0.02	0.47	11.50/ 8.42	
Ap WN:Ci	Indonesia	0.11**	0.18	-0.03	16.65/6.20
	India	-0.18	-0.38*	-0.43*	1.72/2.69***
	Israel	-0.05	0.42*	0.60*	12.84/8.11

* Significant at 0.01 level: Indonesia, $r = 0.15$ ($n = 288$); India, $r = 0.26$ ($n = 113$); Israel, $r = 0.18$ ($n = 232$)
** Significant at 0.05 level: Indonesia, $r = 0.11$; India, $r = 0.20$; Israel, $r = 0.14$
*** India word-naming (WN) means and s.d.s are based upon a different scale than that employed in Indonesia and Israel. This difference does NOT effect intercorrelations but DOES make comparisons between means/s.d.s impossible.

Key: Ap WN:Gr = Approved word-naming:grammar
      Ap WN:Ch = Approved word-naming:chemistry
      Ap WN:Ci = Approved word-naming:civics

Table 7. Intercorrelations between criterion measures for students (means and s.d.s ON diagonal; intercorrelations BELOW diagonal)

		LPA	Ap WN:Gr	Ap WN:Ch	Ap WN:Ci
LPA****	Indonesia	0.92/3.69			
	India	1.18/3.22			
	Israel	4.18/6.85			
Ap Wn:Gr	Indonesia	0.19*	13.75/ 5.51		
	India	0.08	10.10/15.26***		
	Israel	0.06**	15.14/ 9.12		
Ap WN:Ch	Indonesia	−0.10*	0.24*	14.74/ 7.68	
	India	−0.09	−0.44*	10.69/16.06***	
	Israel	0.07**	0.38*	14.55/ 6.52	
Ap WN:Ci	Indonesia	0.06**	0.36*	0.37*	14.50/ 5.42
	India	0.04	−0.46*	−0.46*	11.47/16.53***
	Israel	0.13*	0.33*	0.54*	13.52/ 6.07

* Significant at 0.01 level: Indonesia, $r = 0.08$ ($n = 2212$); India, $r = 0.15$ ($n = 245$); Israel, $r = 0.08$ ($n = 1982$)
** Significant at 0.05 level: Indonesia, $r = 0.08$; India, $r = 0.11$; Israel, $r = 0.06$
*** India word-naming (WN) means and s.d.s are based upon a different scale than that employed in Indonesia and Israel. This difference does not affect intercorrelations but DOES make comparisons between means and s.d.s impossible.
**** Adult means and s.d.s with respect to knowledge and attitudes toward LPA were Indonesia = 1.04/4.41; India 3.30/5.55; Israel = 5.19/7.36. No word-naming data were collected on adults.
Key: Ap WN:Gr = Approved word-naming:grammar
Ap WN:Ch = Approved word-naming:chemistry
Ap WN:Ci = Approved word-naming:civics

most SPECIALIZED response to academy-approved nomenclatures. In this pattern the more one utilizes such approved nomenclatures in one's own field, the less one masters them in any other. The third pattern mentioned (that among Indonesian teachers) is INTERMEDIATE between the foregoing two. In this pattern the humanities/social sciences are on one side and the natural sciences on the other. The more humanities and social science specialists utilize their own and each other's approved specialized nomenclatures, the less they master those in the natural sciences and, similarly, the more natural science specialists utilize approved terminology in their own field, the less they master in either of the others.

In Indonesia and India there occur significant NEGATIVE correlations between knowledge/attitudes toward the LPAs and approved word-naming in chemistry, whereas in the other two lexical fields approved word-naming and knowledge/attitudes re LPA are POSITIVELY intercorrelated. This is another reflection of a possible natural science opposition or resistance directed to LPA/lexical elaboration as already implied by the Indonesian teacher data mentioned above.

A recurring positive relationship is encountered between claimed language repertoire size of respondents (and, to a lesser extent between that claimed by respondents on behalf of their parents, particularly their

Table 8. Intercorrelations between claimed language repertoire size and criterion variables

Among teachers		LPA	Ap WN:Gr	Ap WN:Ch	Ap WN:Ci
Total languages ego sps.	Indonesia	0.16*	0.09	−0.16*	0.10
	India	0.01	−0.04	−0.09	0.09
	Israel	0.24*	−0.06	−0.11	−0.09
Total languages ego rts.	Indonesia	0.20*	0.15*	−0.05	0.15*
	India	0.28*	0.19**	−0.28*	0.19**
	Israel	0.32*	0.05	−0.02	0.01
Among students					
Total languages ego sps.	Indonesia	0.07**	0.08*	0.02	0.07**
	India	−0.10	−0.07	0.14**	0.03
	Israel	0.22*	0.15*	0.15*	0.10*
Total languages ego rts.	Indonesia	0.09*	0.08*	0.04	0.12*
	India	−0.01	−0.03	0.14**	−0.01
	Israel	0.21*	0.10*	0.06*	0.03
Among adults					
Total languages ego sps.	Indonesia	0.06			
	India	0.32*			
	Israel	0.15*			
Total languages ego rts.	Indonesia	0.14*			
	India	0.01			
	Israel	0.22*			

* Significant at 0.01 level (see Table 6 for *n*'s and minimal required *r*'s).
** Significant at 0.05 level (see Table 7 for *n*'s and minimal required *r*'s).
Key: Ap WN:Gr = Approved word-naming:grammar
    Ap WN:Ch = Approved word-naming:chemistry
    Ap WN:Ci = Approved word-naming: civics

fathers), and knowledge/attitudes towards the LPAs (see Table 8). To a lesser extent such a relationship also exists between repertoire size and approved word-naming scores. This positive relationship is suggestive of the importance of experiential non-parochiality in influencing behavior toward central language planning and its terminological products. In our populations the larger the language repertoires claimed, the more likely the individual was to know about and to be positive toward his country's central LPAs and to utilize the lexicons these agencies have fashioned or approved (even though membership in certain ethnic–religious–language communities was also commonly of great importance in these very same connections).[10]

RANK ORDER OF IMPORTANCE OF PREDICTORS

For both of the adult populations sampled (adults and teachers), the demographic and language repertoire predictors are usually much more important (i.e., both stronger and more frequently appearing) than the attitudinal/informational ones, particularly in conjunction with the word-naming criteria (for teachers). For the student populations, quite the contrary seems to be the case; the attitudinal/informational predictors most often seem to be of primary importance (i.e. they are recurringly the most powerful predictors).

Table 9. Claimed repertoire sizes for respondents and their parents (means/s.d.s)

		Indonesia	India	Israel
TLES	Teachers	2.22/0.97	1.44/0.64	2.66/1.39
	Students	1.60/0.86	1.20/0.96	1.21/0.85
	Adults	2.07/0.96	1.31/0.92	1.88/1.12
TLER	Teachers	2.26/1.03	1.53/0.87	1.71/0.89
	Students	1.34/0.85	1.05/0.54	1.05/1.01
	Adults	1.87/1.11	1.21/0.52	1.45/1.26
TLFK	Teachers	2.23/0.76	1.56/1.32	2.42/1.22
	Students	2.37/0.77	1.83/1.09	1.78/1.32
	Adults	–	–	–
TLMK	Teachers	1.93/0.80	–	1.50/1.06
	Students	2.22/0.80	–	1.67/1.32
	Adults	–	–	–

[10] Two additional minor observations are prompted by Tables 8 and 9: (a) Among teachers larger repertoire size is negatively related to ApWN:Ch and in Indonesia and India these negative correlations attain significance; (b) In all three countries the between-population progressions are (from most to least) teachers, respondents' parents, adults, and students. The first observation fits in with the subject matter field differences mentioned above; the second, with the generational differences to be mentioned below.

Apparently, for adults their primary group memberships (ethnic, religious, linguistic) and basic social experiences (education, occupation) most strongly determine their attitudinal/cognitive and overt usage responses to language planning. On the other hand, students are (still) responding largely on attitudinal/informational bases, and, therefore, are perhaps more open to attitudinal/informational influences. Practically speaking, therefore, it would seem to be most advisable for language planning implementation-campaigns to focus on younger rather than on older populations (see, for example, Etzioni and Remp 1972) as well as to focus upon generationally different motivations/sanctions (because informational/attitudinal manipulation is generally easier than fostering demographic change in occupation, social class, education, etc). Adults may require basic changes in their opportunity system and role-repertoire, whereas younger subjects may respond more readily to organized attitude-shaping communications per se.

SIGNIFICANT DIFFERENCES ON CRITERION AND RELATED MEASURES

With respect to the attitudinal/informational criteria of language planning "success," the between-population differences noted are usually greater than the between-country differences. The standard between-population progression in this connection is teachers, adults, and students. Thus, the teachers are normally most informed and most positive toward LPAs, adults next most so, and students least so (note, for example, the means in Tables 6 and 7). Thus, there is an inverse relationship between the importance of attitudinal/informational factors in predicting criterion behaviors in our populations and the level or standing of these populations with respect to criterial attitudes and information.

With respect to the approved word-naming criteria, between-country differences are recurringly greater than between-population differences (except for approved word-naming in civics, where the reverse is true). The most usual between-country progression is Indonesia–Israel. The most usual between-population progression on approved word-naming is teachers, students (with adults presumably in third place) in Indonesia, and students, teachers (with adults presumably in third place in Israel).[11] Although these progressions may be the result primarily of sampling factors (i.e. of differences in the extent to which students have recently

[11]   With respect to total (rather than approved) word-naming, the between-country progression is invariably Israel–Indonesia, and the between-population progression in both countries is students–teachers (–adults) for grammar and chemistry and teachers–students (–adults) for civics. Unfortunately, Indian word-naming data were so scored as not to be readily comparable with the Indonesian and Israeli data.

studied the lexical fields tested and differences in the extent to which teachers are foreign-educated) the impression of crucial generational (or generational/educational) differences is furthered. It would seem, particularly in Israel, that the populations most positive attitudinally toward LPA activity (teachers, parents) are not at all necessarily the ones that are most "approved"-usage oriented, while the populations most in control of approved word-naming (students) are not necessarily attitudinally/informationally the most positive. A similar impression derives from the related Israeli work of Fainberg (1972), with respect to older and younger auto drivers; Hungier and Katz (1971–1972), with respect to older and younger teachers; and Hofman (1972), with respect to older and younger chemists.

That the educational dimension is sometimes rather similar to and at other times rather distinct from the generational one is evident from a consideration of attitudes toward indigenousness of vocabulary in general (rather than specifically in relation to the LPAs' work). Here we find an interesting reversal of the former progression that obtained in conjunction with the LPAs (teachers, adults, students) and find, instead, an overall tendency toward the progression adults, students, teachers (Table 10). Thus teachers would appear to be a population somewhat in conflict.

Table 10.   Attitudes toward indigenousness of vocabulary (weighted and adjusted scores*; means/standard deviations)

	Teachers	Students	Adults
Indonesia	43.56/12.09	48.40/11.11	44.95/10.83
India	30.16/ 5.29	29.87/17.05	33.16/18.96
Israel	24.80/16.20	25.57/24.57	38.51/14.56

Source	SS	df	Mss	F
A: Countries	470.77	2	235.38	200.75**
B: Populations	57.69	2	28.85	24.60**
AB: Country and population	80.03	4	20.01	17.06**
Within SS (Adj)	7002.17	5972	1.17	

* Attitudes toward indigenousness of vocabulary scores are based upon twelve items for students and adults and upon eighteen items for teachers. Responses were weighted along a scale from 5 to 1 in such fashion that 5 was assigned to SL preferences and 1 to English preferences.
** Significant at 0.1 level.

Although most knowledgeable and positive with respect to the LPAs and their work, they nevertheless are most likely to make functional/situational distinctions with respect to the necessity for indigenous vocabulary. Their own professional reading, writing, and meetings with foreign colleagues inclines them toward such differentiations and, indeed, their students are already closer to them in this respect than they are to whitecollar adults in general. Actually, therefore, there are three progressions to keep in mind: that which pertains to the attitudinal/informational criteria relating to the LPA and its work (teachers, adults, students), that which pertains to the approved word-naming criteria (teachers, students, adults in Indonesia and students, teachers, adults in Israel), and that which pertains to general attitudes toward indigenousness of vocabulary (adults, students, teachers) and which may, in a sense, be intermediate between the other two.[12]

CONCLUSIONS

Response to central agency language-planning activity in connection with lexical elaboration — whether attitudinal/informational or approved word-naming usage — appear to be VERY APPRECIABLY PREDICTABLE across countries and across populations on the basis of a rather SMALL SET OF PREDICTOR DIMENSIONS. Such prediction is somewhat better for teachers and adults than it is for students, being based primarily on demographic and language repertoire characteristics in the first two populations and on attitudinal/informational characteristics in the third.

Nevertheless, there is reason to conclude that in the three countries reported on, the attitudinal/informational goals of language planning tend to be best approximated by an older generation of users (who were themselves young adults when language planning activity may have been less routinized and more ideologically embedded), whereas its approved usage goals often tend to be best approximated by a younger generation of users (who acquire the new terminologies as part of normal and institutionalized educational experiences with much more minor attitudinal/informational overtones). Although significant between-country differences and country-by-population interactions exist in all of these connections, the regularity and size of the between-group differences encountered is suggestive of recurring routinization trends as language situations that initially elicited ideologized central planning slowly normalize and stabilize and as languages of wider communication formerly viewed locally as competitors for various official or unofficial functions are no longer as widely regarded as such.

---

[12]   The significant interaction effect shown in Table 10 is largely the result of the higher than expected score of students in Indonesia.

REFERENCES

ETZIONI, AMITAI, RICHARD REMP
  1972 Technological "shortcuts" to social change. *Science* 175:31–38.
FAINBERG, YAFA ALLONI
  1972 "Official Hebrew terms for parts of the car: a study of knowledge, usage and attitudes," in *Language planning processes, September 1972, draft report.*
FELBER, HELMUT
  1970 Standardization of terminology in USSR. A cursory review. *Babel* 16(4):197–203
FISHMAN, JOSHUA A.
  1972 "Comparative dimensionality and predictability of attitudinal/informational and usage behaviors related to certain language planning activities," in *Language planning processes, September 1972, draft report.* (Revised: International Journal of the Sociology of Language, 1974, 1:67–94.)
FISHMAN, JOSHUA A., ROBERT L. COOPER, ROXANA MA, *et al.*
  1971 *Bilingualism in the barrio.* Language Sciences Monograph 7. Bloomington: Research Center for the Language Sciences, Indiana University.
HOFMAN, JOHN
  1972 "The prediction of success in language planning: the case of chemists in Israel," in *Language planning processes, September 1972, draft report.* (Revised: International Journal of the Sociology of Language, 1974, 1:39–66.)
HUNGIER, MEDINA, DEBORA KATZ
  1971–1972 "Where do new Hebrew terms come from?" Seminar paper for a language planning course, Hebrew University, 1971–1972.
JACOB, PHILIP E. *et al.*
  1972 *Values and the active community.* New York: Free Press.
JAMIAS, JEAN F. *et al.*
  1970 The comprehensibility of modernized versus traditional Tagalog. *Asian Studies* 8:187–195.
KLOSS, HEINZ
  1969 *Research possibilities on group bilingualism: a report.* Publication b–18, Quebec: International Center for Research on Bilingualism (Laval University).
NIE, NORMAN H., DALE H. BENT, C. HADLAI HULL
  1970 *Statistical package for the social sciences.* New York: McGraw-Hill.
ROZEBOOM, W. W.
  1966 *Foundations of the theory of prediction.* Homewood, Ill.: Dorsey Press.
RUMMEL, R. J.
  1967 Understanding factor analysis. *Conflict Resolution* 11:444–480.
SPATHAKY, RONALD
  1970 The international scientific vocabulary and the new national languages. *Linguistics* 61:92–94.

SECTION SIX

Discussion

Summary of Discussion

The central issue emerging from the totality of discussion of language in anthropology, and in fact one of the major subjects to which much of the discussions was devoted, was the importance attributed to the study of language in its social and cultural setting and the recognition of the paramount role of sociolinguistic approaches in studies involving language in its function as a means of intercommunication, and also in studies dealing with the nature of language itself. Approaches widely regarded as valid, especially transformational–generative approaches, came under severe criticism, and their artifically restrictive nature in their dissociating the subject matters studied by them from the social and cultural background in which these subject matters were functioning was regarded as a severe drawback, putting the value of their findings into question. It was argued that these subject matters of study had a real existence only in the social and cultural settings in which they appeared, and against the background of these settings, and it was pointed out that approaches to the study of language which ignored these settings and backgrounds in the light of their orientation could only produce results of doubtful validity, or results which lacked in relevance. In other words, they indicated WHAT was going on in language, but not HOW it related to the world.

Other views put forward admitted that a distance was present between the transformational–generative approach and sociolinguistics which was increasingly being hailed as THE linguistics, but it was suggested that the transformational–generative approach could be extended to include sociolinguistic factors in its system of description. This was countered by holders of the opposite view: that the sociolinguistic approach involved the utilization of methods which belonged basically to realms lying outside the field of linguistics.

In general, there was wide agreement that it was necessary to include a fundamental tenet of sociolinguistics, that of the study of variation and sociocultural setting, into the study of language, but there was disagreement as to the nature of the approach, and the essence of the opposition was the view that (a) such an extension required the utilization of methods which came into linguistics from outside, from other disciplines, whereas (b) the adherents of the transformational–generativist schools argued that it could be achieved from within linguistics through an application of linguistic methods to the study of social factors impinging on language.

While this facet of the totality of discussion on language in anthropology was of great importance for the contents of the other three *World Anthropology* volumes resulting from this General Session (i.e. *Language and Man, Language and Thought,* and *Approaches to Language*), it was even more central to the contents of the present volume on *Language and Society,* which, then, can perhaps be regarded as the most important and topical of the four volumes in dealing most thoroughly with what appears to have become the central issue of the study of language today.

In this volume, the papers included in Section 1 exemplify how the field of sociolinguistics has made increasing use of social science concepts, for explanatory purposes, in the last decade, whereas those combined into Section 2 serve to demonstrate the more and more quantitative nature of our sociological and linguistic knowledge of speech variation, and at the same time offer arguments for the avoidance of psychologisms in developing methodology. The papers appearing in Section 3 provide new, comparative, cultural and historical perspectives on languages functioning to denote the cultural identity of human groups, and point out the difficulties of predicting trends of language use in complex multicultural societies if the local situation is unknown or not adequately known. Some of the papers in Section 3 demonstrate the relevance of social historical investigations for interpreting the role of language in society. The papers in Section 4 demonstrate the increasing capability of sociolinguistics to predict and improve the performance and results of language planners in their efforts to advance the goals of modernization.

While all of the papers included in this volume are valuable in adding new perspectives to, and increasing our knowledge in, fields of sociolinguistics which constitute known areas of research endeavor, several of them offer topics of study and discussion which are largely novel in their orientation.

Much of the discussion on the papers of the present volume was provided by the two formal discussants, Professor Michael A. K. Halliday, of the University of Illinois at Chicago Circle, and Dr. John B. Pride, of the Victoria University of Wellington in New Zealand.

Halliday started by saying that the papers forming part of the session to which he was addressing himself represented a large number of different themes; he thought it best to extract a few dominant ones among these and comment on them, seeing that they were relevant and central to our interests today. He suggested six headings under which his remarks would fall: (1) Language as Social Semiotic; (2) Semiotic Styles and Habits of Meaning, leading to language and subculture as a subheading; (3) Social Context or Situation Type; (4) Variation as Choice; (5) Multilingualism and Language Planning; and (6) Restricted Communication?

Turning toward Language as Social Semiotic, he pointed out that in many of the papers he found a tendency towards an interpretation of language in the context of the social system, with the latter interpreted as a system of meanings. This, he felt, was an indication that what he called the myth of an autonomous linguistics was on the way out. He noted on this that, in his paper, Khubchandani argued that far from peoples' sense of identity being determined by their language, their sense of language was determined by their identity. Halliday also mentioned Guboglo as pointing out that ethnic consciousness was a multistage identification of the individual with the ethos, with language being a major factor only when the ethnicity was threatened (as was the case for instance in some urban communities) and as saying that the attitudes towards a traditional culture depended on whether it was carried by a particular language or not. Turning to Vanek's paper, Halliday stressed the importance of Vanek's statement that linguistic rules had to take recourse to nonlinguistic interpretations.

Summarizing from these remarks, Halliday points out that the papers under discussion had in common the interpretation of language as a projection or realization of the social system—something familiar in semiotics, and in fact being the semiotic perspective in language.

Halliday points out that this perspective of the culture or the social system as a system of meaning is nothing new, but what is important is that this perspective includes language, and that in the language–culture perspective, we interpret language as a form of the realization of the social semiotic. He mentions that, in this, the question as to whether it is primary or not need not be argued.

This leads Halliday to the second heading of Semiotic Styles and Habits of Meaning. He feels that the papers falling under this heading range from high semiotic to low semiotic, with Armstrong's paper stressing the importance of peak phenomena of thought and speech, and of obtaining adequate documentation. Halliday points out that he feels that high semantics is not so much a category as an assemblage of cultural attributes. He feels that Smith's paper is similar in its orientation. In proceeding to low semiotics, Halliday makes the general point that linguists have been rather frightened off the Whorfian notion of fashions of speaking or

730 S. A. WURM

semantic styles because they had been taught that anything that could not be expressed in formal rules was not respectable. However, he maintains that linguists know that a deep underlying reality is behind these notions. Pointing to Warshay's remarks about the different semiotic habits of males and females, including those before and after marriage, and to Pandit's references to speech variation being functional in maintaining identity, Halliday says that it is clear that a great deal of the linguistic variation that linguists are attempting to interpret in a cultural context is not variation on a phonological, grammatical, or lexical level as such, but variation in semantic styles.

Proceeding to the next heading of Social Context or Situation Type, Halliday raises the question as to how we characterize the social background or context of the variations just mentioned. Referring to the paper by Pascasio and Hidalgo in which social contexts are characterized by domain, role relationship and language situation, Halliday points out that there are different ways of taxonomizing, of classifying situation types, but in the past it was very difficult to know what theoretical status to assign to them. However, it is possible to make predictions about the linguistic situations assigned to them, e.g. predictions about the choice of one language as opposed to another, or predictions about the subject matter and semantic configurations that are typically associated with these variables. These are interpretations of the social context as a semiotic structure — this results in the interpretation of language use by characterizing situations as being themselves semiotic structures, i.e. structures of meaning relations. Yamamoto's paper, he says, discusses a typology of culture space which is a closely related context.

This leads Halliday to his fourth heading, that of Variation as Choice. He mentions the frequent reference in the papers to the meaning inherent in variation which includes code, dialect and language switching. At one end of the scale lies the situation of lack of choice which is discussed in Albó's paper with relation to oppressed languages of diminished vitality spoken in a subculture of poverty. Ornstein's paper discusses a situation of complexity of choice, whereas Giles, Bourhis and Davies talk about imposed norms which will affect choice. Scotton interprets language switching as an expression of the value that is inherent in the choice of language, with language mixing constituting a course leading to a safe return. Muthiani feels that the choice of a language by an individual depends on his, the individual's, social–functional interpretation of the situation, and he interprets it as a semiotic structure.

Turning to the fifth heading, Multilingualism and Language Planning, Halliday mentions Lewis' paper and the primary, determining factors listed by the latter such as geography, economics, professional migration, urbanization, etc. Fishman's paper on consumer reaction to language planning, Halliday feels, is an important contribution to a little studied field. Halliday points out that much of language planning concerned with "extension of vocabulary" is in fact much more than that and is a very fundamental semantic development which has effects on the semantic and semiotic patterns of these languages which have only begun to be studied in an insightful way.

The last heading, Restricted Communication?, brings Halliday to speak about Pandit's paper which refers to, and criticizes, the myth that speech differences such as dialect divergence are caused by restricted communication. Halliday feels that there is nothing special about social hierarchies leading to different semantic styles, and points out that everybody is a multilingual, i.e. may have typical semantic configurations which he associates with certain social contexts. The norm is variation. Halliday then mentions Dakubu's paper which discusses the extensive use of foreign languages, especially Akan, in Gã singing. Akan tends to be associated in this with things which are tabu in some form, and its use has a distancing effect, a semiotic opposition, between Gã and non-Gã in Gã songs.

Halliday concludes his discussion remarks by saying that it is particularly in anthropological and sociological contexts that the perspective of language as a realization of culture is stressed, but adds that to him as a linguist this is also the only valid perspective: this is the necessary first step not only to the understanding of culture but also to the understanding of the nature of the linguistic system. In order to begin to understand why human language has its specific properties, it is necessary to see it as a realization of the social system, in other words, to see it as one form of the social semiotic.

Pride started his comments as a formal discussant by saying that he intended to cast his views on what he had read of the papers in a particularly social anthropological light, with considerable linguistic potentialities, without mentioning individual papers much. He mentioned that language can serve as a means of conveying a picture of oneself which is as favorable as possible. Language, in this, can be one means of transacting "bargains" in which considerable value can be gained.

This overall value is made up of different kinds of value — different ways of discriminating between, or juxtaposing, or emphasizing, or de-emphasizing, or ignoring otherwise institutionalized statuses, along with their associated rights and duties. In this, Pride refers to statuses as points on status dimensions at which particular combinations of rights and duties apply. Role-relationships may be characterized therefore not only in terms of the various statuses which the society in question assigns to them, but also by the ways in which values of one sort or another are applied, on particular occasions, to modify, or to highlight, particular aspects of the essentially normative status structure. The particular rights and duties which are selected in this interplay between values and statuses are likely to be linguistic in nature. Pride refers to them therefore as "transactional language behaviors" and raises the question of what form these might take. He feels that codeswitching is one obvious kind of potentially transactional behavior, with the word "code" implying system; therefore codes can be systematically distinct languages or dialects or stylistic levels; they may even be nonlinguistic — as in the case of kinesic systems. It is possible, for instance, for somebody to speak the English language while simultaneously communicating some elements of the kinesics of native speakers of French. Pride points out that stylistic codeswitching is well illustrated in Yamamoto's analysis of semantic features appropriate to particular status relationships in one kind of situation in Japanese and also in Vanek's description of thou-ing and he-ing and so forth in Czech. The transactional component of everyday speech functions should not be ignored either. Labels such as "command," "request," "advice," "disagreement," and the like, point toward particular clustering of statuses which speakers may wish to express or not express on some particular occasion. Assertions ABOUT language behavior may also have transactional intent, and this indeed may frequently amount to the real truth behind the data that emerge from questionnaires, self-reports, censuses, and the like; Pride points out that this is well shown, for example, for the 1951 and 1961 Indian censuses in Khubchandani's paper.

Pride mentions that transactional bargaining in the currencies of language is, almost by definition, not easy. "Dilemmas of choice," he feels, may very likely be disturbing both for the larger group and for the individual. For this very reason, they may also be quite strategically important for the way things are going. At the large-scale level, he thinks that the problem is essentially that of identifying and translating between values which may often appear to be irreconcilable, or simply untranslatable. Whether or not with a view to change, he says that a first step is that of presenting a balanced and comprehensive account of apparently opposing views, or unsuspected sides, to the problem. He mentions papers from South America and Taiwan of this broadly appraising sort, written by Albó and Cheng, respectively. Ultimately, Pride points out, one always hopes to see the emergence of "overarching values" — as, most obviously, in the case of emergent and successful national languages. He adds that at the individual level, it pays no less to be able to appreciate different value systems and to make good use of this knowledge in one's own choice of language.

Pride thinks that there are two crucial aspects to what he has been saying up to this point. First, if language and culture are processes as well as (or indeed rather than) stable configurations or traditions, then to that extent one should be watching out for "dilemmas of choice" at all levels of language use. And secondly, there is the closely related methodological principle that this kind of data can best be obtained with the aid of participant analysis of natural language. There are signs, however, that the study of language and culture will increasingly rely on written questionnaires, on rigorously uniform interviewing techniques, even on observation which makes no reference to the opinions or reactions of participants. In all such techniques the participant himself responds within the investigator's already formulated terms of reference. It is no accident, Pride thinks, that transactional language behavior does not figure very large — if at all — in work of this sort. The main reason is that informants are not often asked this sort of question. It is also a difficult sort of question to answer: firstly, the informant has to appreciate the fact that the behavior in question could apply to him; secondly, he has to recollect particular occasions on which it did apply; and thirdly, he has the difficult job of interpreting this behavior. Nor does information on transactional behavior, when it is obtained, easily lend itself to correlational analysis. And why indeed should it?, Pride asks. Language is often the only expression or overt sign of transactional bargaining. It is certainly valuable to have data on normative patterns of one sort or another, but Pride asserts that it is equally valuable to know what people do with these norms, i.e. how they use them, and for what ends. Pride also questions whether some of our current methodologies do not tend to elicit mere statistical averages of what people think are the norms that as it were "govern" their use of language. Another kind of methodological question thrown up by Pride is therefore this: how do we find out about the many ways in which, knowingly and unknowingly, people manipulate language to their own (and indeed to others') advantage, how do they control situations, and change the status quo?

Apart from these prepared remarks by Halliday and Pride, comments had been made on Lindenfeld's paper by two of the formal discussants to the preceding IXth ICAES subsession, published as *Approaches to Language*, since at the time of the Congress Lindenfeld's paper had been included in the latter subsession as well. Valerie Makkai had mentioned Lindenfeld's paper as one of those which emphasized the need to look at extralinguistic contexts of language to reach a fuller treatment of language itself. Hamp too had referred specifically to it, saying that it treated more the boundaries of the field of linguistics.

Following the remarks by Halliday and Pride, points made in discussions from the floor were generally in support of, or elaborations to, the comments in these formal discussions, e.g. those of M. Guboglo. Lindenfeld, responding now to Hamp's earlier remarks as they impinged on her concern with the question of the opposition in linguistics today between the ethnography of communication and correlational linguistics, elaborated on her paper by saying that she had tried to actually apply what she was advocating, i.e. the use of Hymes' broad flexible framework and, within it, the use of methods derived from correlational linguistics: she was applying them to the analysis of conversation over lunch in a provincial French middleclass home, a communicative situation which she could view from the inside as a native participant as well as from the outside as an investigator. In the work, directed towards the description of the speech components, she felt that recourse could be had to the notions of covariation and correlation used by Labov and other sociolinguists, without losing sight of the fact that the situation was not one of simple one-to-one correspondences. Regarding Hamp's remarks that there might not be any major differences between correlational sociolinguistics, the ethnography of communication and generative semantics, Lindenfeld felt that the three approaches had the same ultimate goal, i.e. a better understanding of the way in which people communicated, but she thought that this did not mean that correlational sociolinguistics, the ethnography of communication and generative semantics were either equivalent or interchangeable approaches.

Other special points were concerned with the question of bilingualism, and disappointment was expressed, e.g. by Jacob Ornstein, at the fact that no more papers were concerned with it. The opinion was voiced that this might still be the result of a trauma, of a situation in which the study of problems of bilingualism was not regarded as respectable. It was suggested that linguists might have to look to bilinguals for the answers to some questions concerning universals, and that attempts would have to be made to find bilingual universals.

Another topic touched upon in the discussions was that of international language models, with a view to the development of a trade and documentation interlanguage. It was argued, e.g. by Wendy Allen, that ideally, such an interlanguage should be capable of expressing the finest nuances of each and every national language. Various existing interlanguages including computer languages were touched upon and found lacking, and it was suggested that the phoneme system of an ideal interlanguage would be a set of existing natural language phonemes, with its core vocabulary built on those most prevalent or common to the greatest number of speakers. Its syntax or grammar would be both elaborate with every device of natural languages available, and at the same time with no mandatory feature which would not be common to all natural languages.

Special consideration was given, in this question of an international language, to ideographic script. It was argued, e.g. by Robert Cheng, that it was time for scholars in the field of semiotics to think more seriously about man's capability to develop a graphic symbolic system which had a semantic structure much closer to the universal thinking structure than that of a natural language and was much less bound to the linearity of natural language than any conventional writing system or a symbolic logic was. Some such international visual symbols which represent directly semantic units which are rather universal in nature do already exist, but are only sporadically used. Expression was given to the feeling that man has the potentiality to develop a graphic system which is even more comprehensive, accurate and powerful than any natural language in communicating man's thought, and less language-specific and therefore less subject to semiotic and graphic changes. It was suggested that research in this area could result in our understanding of a semantic structure which was developed through and manifested by a linearity-bound natural language, and of one which was associated with a two-dimensional representation of a graphic system. It was pointed out that the Chinese script was far from being such a universal graphic system — it was language-specific and very culture-specific.

The question of the success of language planning with a view to Fishman's paper was also raised at the discussions, for instance by István Fodor, and the suggestion was made by him that the word-stock of a language was elastic enough to follow a not too rapid rate of development — however, with a quite rapid social development, it was felt that the growth of the vocabulary could not keep pace with it because of the rather conservative character of linguistic development, with the resulting and considerable deficiency which only an intensive and planned linguistic reform movement could help. It was pointed out that the dominant type of word formation for the creation of new vocabulary items depended on historical, cultural and other criteria, not only linguistic, with most of these factors attributable to foreign cultural linguistic impact. It was said that composition, derivation, semantic change, dialectal borrowing, and sometimes arbitrary modification of the word shape belonged to the proper means of word formation, whereas formation utilizing foreign sources included simple word-borrowing, calque, semantic borrowing and sometimes borrowing of affixes or other structural elements.

In addition to such discussion during subsessions, written comments were forthcoming from J. B. Pride on Pandit's and Smith's papers. He praised the first as a wide-ranging synthesis of recent work, including that of the author himself, and pointed out that the discussion of the role of the conscious versus unconscious factor, and that of literacy, in linguistic innovation was of great interest in sociolinguistics generally. Pride mentioned that Pandit seems to accept without further question Bright's formula of phonological and morphological change being less conscious, and borrowing and semantic extensions more conscious, but he feels that there are a number of problems in this. He thinks that it may be very different to separate these particular levels of analysis in practical description and observation, that phonology, morphology, borrowing, and semantic extension do not account for all of the linguist's levels of analysis, and that the interdependence of various levels makes it difficult to label change at one or the other level as more, or less, conscious. On

Smith's paper, Pride feels that further substantiation and clarification of some of its main points are called for. For instance, he thinks that on the matter of bidialectalism, it is necessary to go into the whole question of different functions, and therefore possibly limited structural ranges, of the dialects concerned. He agrees that readers of Smith's paper who are not already familiar with current work on the general topic of Black English may not catch more than a very slight glimpse of the real scope of this work from it.

Interestingly enough, all four of the ad hoc informal sessions which self-constituted themselves in Chicago for purposes of further discussing topics of current importance relevant to language in anthropology focussed on subject matter most appropriate to this volume on *Language and Society* — or, as this subject matter was termed in Chicago, "language in many ways." Thus, though summaries of the discussions in the ad hoc sessions were presented verbally at various times to the formal subsessions, all the summaries are recorded in this volume, below.

One of these ad hoc sessions had for its main theme "What Is Sociolinguistics — With Special Reference to Correlational and Interactional Approaches?" and this session was characterized by discussion so lively and extended that the central issues emerging from it have been stated by this present writer at the outset of his Summary of Discussion to all four of the *World Anthropology* volumes resulting from the General Session on "Language in Anthropology."

At the formal subsession Language in Many Ways, it was Dr. J. B. Pride, and Professor Albert Verdoodt of Louvain who reported on the conclusions of this ad hoc session. In his report, Pride said that in one sense, sociolinguistics was just one of a number of disciplinary or interdisciplinary labels applied to the study of language in its widest cultural and social contexts. Thus there were sociolinguistics, linguistics, the sociology of language, anthropological linguistics, and others. It was generally felt, he said, that these terminological distinctions could blind us to the fact that language was a societal phenomenon demanding for its study a "Hegelian synthesis" of insights from many disciplines — irrespective of how they were labelled. One immediate question was: do we need an alternative cover term for "sociolinguistics" in view of the fact that more than linguistics plus sociology is involved? Having regard to the existence of nonverbal and animal communication, "communication" itself was suggested; but was regretfully dismissed as already connoting a more narrow range of academic interests. "The ethnography of communication" and "human linguistics" were noted as other possibilities. Several among those present felt that the transformational model of linguistics, particularly in its generative semantic form, would eventually be able to accommodate all kinds of relevant information. The question was raised, however, as to whether and to what extent the notational system or systems of transformational linguistics would forbid its incorporation of many such factors as role relationships, values, and purposes for the use of language generally. So that if one has to recognize a distinction in the foreseeable future between a theory of grammar and a theory of language use, then the task of sociolinguistics is quite clearly to show how each throws light on the other. And in the immediate future there are pragmatic problems to be solved, so that it might perhaps be better to get on with these rather than wait for some super-model to emerge.

Pride then proceeded to say that he himself held strong views concerning the rather basic distinction in sociolinguistic methodology between correlational and interactional approaches. In this, correlational sociolinguistics assumes that language and society constitute different kinds of reality, whereas interactional sociolinguistics states that while this may in some respects be the case, it is not always so. Interactional sociolinguistics is interested in cases in which linguistic variation can be observed without there being any observable change of a nonlinguistic sort on the occasion in question. In other words, language itself may on such occasions constitute the only real evidence for whatever nonlinguistic variation there might be. The simplest kind of example is that in which codeswitching between different languages takes place without other observable changes in the situation. Pride pointed out that the late W. H. Whiteley had shown this well in his book *Language in Kenya*. Thus a man seeking an interview may select or alternate between English and Swahili according to such factors as his degree of acquaintanceship with the typist at the reception desk, her apparent cooperativeness, how busy they both are, their proficiencies in the languages, his sense of self-importance, and so on. Other good examples are Geertz's account of style-switching in Javanese, Salisbury's account of choice of host and of guest language in parts of New Guinea — apparently according to how both parties want to see their relationship and/or to display their bilingual competence, Basso's interpretation of silence among American Indians as ultimately explainable in terms of ambiguities in the situation, and Mitchell-Kernan's studies of Black English–White English switching in Oakland, California.

Pride feels that the behavior involved in these and in many other such cases could be called transactional: namely the use of language as a sort of bargaining in which speakers strive to establish the kind of role-relationships which they want. Language is manipulated rather than, or in addition to, being used in predictable ways according to dominant norms. Pride said that he would go further and suggest that such interpersonal linguistic fluctuation was by no means necessarily a random matter of momentary inclination, and by no means of only microsociolinguistic interest, but quite the opposite: these behaviors might be precisely those that are most significant for the larger speech community. "Significant," he explained to mean indicative of change in the use of language and correspondingly in the society itself. But, he said, there was no need for interactional sociolinguistics to be OPPOSED to correlational sociolinguistics, and concluded by uttering the warning that we must beware of adding yet another false dichotomy to the army of dichotomies that were misleading us.

After Pride, Verdoodt gave a report of his impression of the informal session, with his own comments added. He mentioned that in order to solve the numerous problems of linguistic variations, several members of the discussion group recognized the need to use sociological methods and even sociological theories of explanation. Nevertheless, the question remained open as to whether this type of research could be successfully conducted without leaving the field of linguistics as such (grammar, phonetics, speech behavior, and so forth).

On the one side it was said that Chomsky had endeavored to use logical models in his transformational grammar without leaving linguistics — thus, analogously, sociolinguistics could make use of sociology without leaving linguistics. On the other side it was argued that sociology was not an overall abstract and general discipline such as logic was. However, sociology is a well-established and positive science with its own methods and theories: in consequence, sociolinguistics is an interdisciplinary approach and not only sociology or linguistics. Just as sociologists do not claim that grammar, phonetics, etc. are sociology, simply because language is social, so the linguist who wishes to throw light on the social aspect of language should not claim that the study of ideologies, values, power and so forth are per se linguistics simply because speech is an aspect of social behavior.

Moreover, it was stressed that sociology would suffer if the specificity of its methods (let alone its concepts and theories) were not fully recognized by the linguists using them.

This point was challenged, but in the last part of the discussion, concerning the relation between biology and language, it was generally recognized that biologists would have to be involved and consulted by linguists as fully respected specialists in a different and rigorous scientific discipline — and not simply imitated independently. By analogy, Verdoodt pointed out, it was felt that sociology should not be treated by the linguists as an easy-going sort of discipline.

Verdoodt added as a personal comment that he thought that with regard to the dependence of the linguist in relation to sampling methods, many studies could have gained in breadth and depth if serious account could have been taken of the social stratification of the area under study. He said that it was a rather good sign that scholars like Haugen, Fishman and Labov had taken this point into consideration.

Another ad hoc informal session was devoted to the problem of language acquisition, and was reported on to formal subsessions by S. A. Wurm. Technically, its subject matter belonged to the orbit of the *World Anthropology* volume *Language and Man*, but the nature of the discussion so impinged on matters discussed under the present aegis of *Language and Society* that an account of this informal session occurs in the "Summary of Discussion" in both these volumes.

The discussion very quickly concentrated on the question of what was referred to as nature versus nurture, i.e. the question of innate versus learning, nativism versus environmentalism. This led to some confrontation between adherents and opponents of the transformational–generativist school; it was pointed out the environment had a very strong influence and was responsible for much that could not be explained through the innate approach. It was largely agreed that both factors were vital though there was disagreement as to which of the two was more vital. It was mentioned that for instance in grammatical descriptions, the issue was not only whether sentences were linguistically acceptable, but also which of these were culturally acceptable.

It was argued that the issue revolved on the opposition of universals on one side and the question of cultural acquisition on the other, but it was quickly stressed that there were universals which were not based on genetic factors, and the existence of linguistic means of addressing a group was mentioned as an example. This led to the question as to how nature affected nurture and vice versa, and it was accepted that our knowledge as to what belonged to which of these two was inadequate. It was agreed that, while language certainly depended on both nature and nurture, it was possible that some feature which had been thought to depend on nature, i.e. to be innate, might depend on nurture instead. It was also stressed that it was important to keep apart the phylogeny of language, its ontogeny as based on nature and nurture (or environment), and the history of language as a cultural product.

Another informal session was devoted to the discussion of dichotomies. Pride reported on this session to the formal subsessions. He said that, at it, several prevailing dichotomies of a closely related sort were looked at. These were such as: "theory" and "relevance," "theoretical" and "empirical," "objectivity" and "commitment," "deductive" and "inductive," "outsider" and "insider," and so forth.

The discussion had opened with what was to prove its dominant theme, namely the motivation felt by, as it were, the "insider," to CHANGE the situation. Sociolinguistics, it was said, was the area where change was possible. Aalsen's comparisons of Norwegian dialects, for example, sprang from a desire to create a new Norwegian language; and generally, it could be said that pioneering work was often done by those who wanted to change things. "Commitment" then should entail, at the very least, recognition of this fact. At the same time, it had to be conceded that "language planning" itself was usually carried on from positions of strength, notably financial strength — "picking on the little guys," as someone put it. It was therefore all the more important that members of the speech community concerned should be brought into the picture.

Various points were made on this score. The creation of new orthographies, for example, independently of the feelings of those for whom they were designed, might thereby prove faulty even on linguistic grounds. Pride said that he was reminded in this of what Albó had said in his outstanding paper for the IXth ICAES Congress: "The invading oppression of Spanish has obliged the more accepted alphabets up to now, almost irrevocably, to ignore the very contrastive systems of the Quechua and Aymara phonology and to distort them in order to adapt incongruously the contrasts — and the inconsistencies — of the Spanish alphabet because it is the dominating one." Ultimately, Pride continued, the best way to bring the insider into the picture was to make the picture more clear to HIM —while, at the same time, learning all one could FROM him. Both parties, in other words, should be engaged in a two-way process. Pride said that perhaps he might be forgiven for mentioning that one-third of his own paper discussed the value and the drawbacks of informant and opinion, or, as he had put it, "talk about talk." And what the insider said certainly might have its drawbacks — unless, that was, one could find out how best to interpret it. The problem of interpreting what the informant said became particularly acute when native informants disagreed among themselves on the direction and goals of change.

Interpretation, in this sense, Pride continued, came down then to a question of COMMUNICATION with the members of the speech community. If only one native language was involved there might be relatively little difficulty. If however there were fifty or sixty, as in Mexico, or hundreds, as in New Guinea, the factor of bias from the translator would intrude, a bias which had its social–psychological as well as its more purely linguistic sides. This was one of the contexts which demanded also the use of methods which might rather broadly be termed "objective." In effect, the various "objective" methods that had been used could be regarded as experiments in a kind of laboratory situation, and, it was felt, might yield false information for this very reason. Returns from questionnaires for example might prove to be false in many respects, the use of methods from experimental psychology might lead to spurious behavior, and observation would necessarily be limited — possibly more than would the introspection of informants — to the small population sampled. Accordingly, the statistical presentation of results might well be superficial. In order therefore to overcome this general problem, it was necessary to double-check by using a variety of such techniques. A point was made, however, specifically about the use of questionnaires. This was that not all questionnaires operated only in yes–no, or true–false terms, or even in terms of graded points on a scale. Questionnaires could take the form of prepared stimuli designed to elicit genuine opinions.

With all these potential drawbacks, methodological approaches from as it were the inside, and from the outside, aimed to achieve depth and breadth, respectively; or, as it was also put, insight and perspective. But, Pride warned, we should beware once again of falling foul of a host of further dichotomies. If for example you took the whole of India, what did "inside" mean? In some settings, and in some respects, the English language might be more welcome "inside" than Hindi was. So we returned to the need for a Hegelian synthesis — or, to bring the whole matter down to earth, the need (as it was expressed by an Indian member of the group) for the would-be researcher to work in his own backyard for a while before venturing outside.

Another of the four informal sessions was concerned with the theme of binary and/or bilogical or multilogical analysis of linguistics, and was reported to the formal subsessions by S. A. Wurm. The discussion during this informal session turned on very much the same points set forth at the opening of the present Summary of Discussion as being the central subjects of much of the discussions at the IXth ICAES Congress.

In addition to those issues, it was argued that the question of a binary opposition was a characteristic trait of the Western culture, and that it constituted an abstraction from an infinite string of possibilities, along which two sufficiently disparate points of contrast were arbitrarily chosen. These points constituted foci for global extensions of modified possibilities which in one direction extended towards each other resulting ultimately in the creation of a fuzzy area between the two points. It was pointed out that Oriental culture did not embrace the concept of binary opposition to the extent to which it dominated Western culture.

The notion of a binary opposition was seen by several as a manifestation of "common sense" which was guiding our thinking, without a definition of this "common sense" emerging from the discussion.

Finally, a short period between two formal subsessions was devoted to an ad hoc informal discussion on language planning, which was regarded as one of the burning questions of the practical application of subject matters coming under the heading of "Language in Many Ways" in many parts of the world at present such as Africa, Indonesia and New Guinea. There was some discussion as to what constituted language planning, and various past examples such as that affecting Hungarian in the nineteenth century were briefly touched upon. The question of attempts in China to consider the eventual introduction of Roman script, with the simultaneous standardization in two-syllable rather than one-syllable words was mentioned as a little-publicized and little-known approach, in contrast to the well-known procedure of the simplification of Chinese characters. It was agreed that for procedures to qualify to be called "language plan-

ning" they had to be either centrally organized, directed and/or super-
vised, or at least carried out by some bodies with example status.

The question was raised whether language planning might go beyond
the obvious levels of vocabulary and grammar which impinged on semantics, and following the wider present notion of what language was about,
would go into fields of sociolinguistics, and other fields. This led to an
animated discussion on whether basic logic was different among different
cultures. It was argued, especially by Oswald Werner, that there was very
poor evidence for the existence of basic differences in cross-cultural and
cross-linguistic logic, but this was strongly opposed by others, especially
Magoroh Maruyama.

Biographical Notes

BAHA ABU-LABAN (1931–   ) was born in Jaffa, Palestine. He received his B.A. (1953) and M.A. (1956) in sociology from the American University of Beirut and his Ph.D. (1960) from the University of Washington (Seattle). He has taught at the University of Washington, Stanford University, the American University of Beirut, and the University of Alberta. He is now Professor of Sociology and Associate Dean (Social Sciences) in the Faculty of Arts, University of Alberta. His publications include works on community power, settler regimes in Africa and the Middle East, the Arab minority in North America, Canadian multiculturalism, Canadian education, Canadian drinking behavior, the Lebanese press, Lebanese and Arab youth, the Egyptian revolution, and cultural and educational development in the Arab world.

EVANGELOS ANGELOU AFENDRAS (1943–   ) was born in Levadeia, Greece. He studied electrical engineering, classics and linguistics at the Johns Hopkins University where he received his B.A. (1965) and Ph.D. (1968) in interdepartmental studies with concentration in linguistics. He has held teaching and research posts at the Johns Hopkins University, University of Oklahoma (Munich), Université Laval and International Center for Research on Bilingualism (Quebec), the East West Center (Senior Fellow Affiliate), the University of Hawaii, Universiti Sains Malaysia and the Regional Language Centre (Singapore). His major research interests are: multilingualism, formal models for language change and shift, language planning with special reference to Southeast Asia. He has published extensively in these areas.

XAVIER ALBÓ (1934–   ) is Director of the Centro de Investigación y Promoción del Campesinado (CIPCA) in La Paz, Bolivia. His interests include Andean sociolinguistics and ethnolinguistics, Quechua language and culture, Andean social change and modernization, and contemporary Andean ethnography. His publications include *Social constraints on Cochabamba Quecha, El Quechua a su Alcance*, and "Dinámica en la Estructura Intercomunitaria de Jesus de Machaca."

MAHADEV L. APTE (1931–   ) received his M.A. degrees from Bombay and London Universities and his Ph.D. from the University of Wisconsin at Madison, Wisconsin. He has taught at the University of Wisconsin, the University of Poona, India, and is currently on the faculty of the Department of Anthropology at Duke University in Durham, North Carolina. His major research interests include sociolinguistics, South Asian languages, societies and cultures, ethnography of humor, acculturation and ethnicity, and Marathi language and literature. His publications include two books and several articles on sociolinguistics of South Asia and on the society and culture in Maharashtra.

ROBERT GELSTON ARMSTRONG (1917–   ) was born in Danville, Indiana, and grew up in Cincinnati, Ohio, U.S.A. He received his B.A. in sociology at Miami University, Oxford, Ohio, his M.A. in social anthropology at the University of Oklahoma, and his Ph.D in social anthropology at the University of Chicago in 1952. He taught anthropology at Atlanta University and the University of Puerto Rico. From 1950 to 1953, he was a Fellow of the Colonial Science Research Council, London, and studied the Idoma people of (present) Benue State, Nigeria. He also spent a year in research and writing at the University of Oxford, England. He was appointed Professor of Anthropology at Atlanta University in 1958. He was Field Director of the West African Languages Survey (Ford Foundation) from 1960 to 1963, when he joined the Institute of African Studies, University of Ibadan, Nigeria, as Research Professor of Linguistics, a post he still holds. He directed the Institute for eleven years, between 1966 and 1977. His major research interests are the Eastern Kwa languages, especially Idoma and Yoruba, African oral literature, and the social anthropology of the Idoma. He tries to maintain the fructifying co-existence of linguistics, ethnography, and social anthropology in his work and has published widely in these fields.

RICHARD Y. BOURHIS (1950–   ) born in Montreal Quebec. He received a B.Sc in psychology from McGill University (1972) and his Ph.D in social psychology from the University of Bristol, England in 1977. He has taught at McGill University and is now Assistant Professor in Psychology at McMaster University, Ontario, Canada. Current research is mainly concerned with the social psychology of intergroup relations, with special interest in ethnic identity and the role of language in ethnic interaction. A recent series of studies explored the dynamics of language usage as "speech strategies" in multilingual and multidialectal settings including Quebec, Wales, Belgium, and Switzerland. Other areas of research include social categorization, stereotypes, ethnic humor and sociolinguistics.

CONRAD MAS BENEDICT BRANN (1925–   ) was born in Germany and educated in Hamburg, Rome, Oxford, Paris, and Bruges in modern languages and international studies. He lectured in English at Hamburg University prior to joining the educational and cultural administration of Unesco, Paris from 1958 to 1965. He was Senior Lecturer and Head of the language education unit, University of Ibadan from 1966 to 1977 and has been Professor and Head, Department of Languages and Linguistics, Dean of Arts, University of Maiduguri since 1978. His research interests and publications concern multilingualism in education and society, especially in sub-Saharan Africa. He is founder-editor of the *West African Journal of Modern Languages* (no. 3[1978] Language in Society in West Africa) and associate editor (sub-Saharan Africa) of the *Sociolinguistics Newsletter* (ISA Research Committee on Sociolinguistics).

ROBERT L. CHENG (1931–   ) was born in Taiwan. He studied linguistics at Indiana University and received his Ph.D (1966) with the dissertation "Some Aspects of Mandarin Syntax." He has taught at the University of York and is now Professor of Chinese and Japanese at the University of Hawaii. His major research interests are Chinese linguistics, especially Mandarin and Taiwanese grammar and lexicon, and comparison of Chinese and Japanese in such areas as language change, writing, sociolinguistics, and language planning.

HARRY J. CROCKETT, JR. (1927–   ) is Professor of Sociology at the University of Nebraska.

REGNA DARNELL (1943–   ) received her Ph.D. from the University of Pennsylvania in 1969. She is currently Associate Professor at the University of Alberta, Canada. Her primary interests are history of American anthropology, Cree language and culture, language, culture, and sociolinguistics in North America, and Doukhobor Russian language and culture. Her publications include Readings in the history of anthropology, "The social context of Cree narration," and "The bilingual speech community: a Cree example."

ANN DAVIES. No biographical data available.

GYULA DÉCSY (1925–   ) was born in the Hungarian minority territory of Czechoslovakia, studied at the universities of Budapest, Bratislava Prague and Sofia, and took his Ph.D. (1948) at the University of Budapest and his *cand. sc. lingu.* at the Hungarian Academy of Sciences (1955). He taught at the University of Göttingen from 1957 to 1959, and at the University of Hamburg from 1959 to 1977. He is presently Professor of Uralic and Altaic Studies at Indiana University, Bloomington. He is Founder and Secretary General of the Commission for Language Problems of the European Unification (Hamburg, currently in Bloomington, Indiana). He was Secretary General of the Societas Uralo-Altaica (1958–1977) and has been Editor-in-Chief of the Ural-Altaische Jahrbücher since 1967. Among his publications are the manuals *Einführung in die finnisch-ugrische Sprachwissenschaft* (1965) and *Die linguistische Struktur Europas* (1973). Other publications concern genetic and areal linguistics, Ural-Altaic studies, Slavic languages language universals, and nostratic linguistics.

ANWAR S. DIL (1928–   ) studied English language and literature, applied linguistics, history of language and science, and sociolinguistics at the University of the Panjab, University of Peshawar, and University of Michigan, before receiving his Ph.D. degree from Indiana University. He served as Professor and Language Specialist at the Education Extension Centre for West Pakistan, Lahore (1959–1965), and the Institute of Education and Research, University of the Panjab, Lahore (1965–1969). He was Visiting Scholar in Linguistics at Stanford University (1969–1972). During 1971–1972 he served as Consultant in Language Science and Educational Development to Unesco and helped in the establishment of the ALSED (Anthropology and Language Science in Educational Development) Program. He is the Founder-Director of the Linguistic Research Group of Pakistan (1961–   ). LRGP has sponsored, among other publications, the Pakistani Linguistics Series, and the distinguished Language Science and National Development Series. Since 1973 he has been Professor of Language Science and Communication at the United States International University, San Diego, California. His special interests and publications are in the history and development of Pakistani languages, the application of language science to problems of national development, and strategies of developing communicative resources for greater individual and societal development.

CHARLES A. FERGUSON. No biographical data available.

JOSHUA A. FISHMAN (1926–   ) is a Professor at Yeshiva University, New York. His main interests include language maintenance and shift in the United States and Israel, language planning, language and nationalism, bilingual education, societal bilingualism, and language attitudes. He is the Editor of the *International Journal of the Sociology of Language* and has published extensively in the field of sociolinguistics.

HOWARD GILES. No biographical data available.

M. GUBOGLO. No biographical data available.

JÜRGEN HEYE (1939–   ) was born in Germany and studied translation and Romance languages in Zurich and Italy. He received his Ph.D. in linguistics from Georgetown University in 1970 and held teaching posts at Georgetown and the State University of New York at Buffalo. Since 1972 he has held a joint appointment as Associate Professor of Linguistics at the Pontifícia Universidade Católica and the Universidade Federal do Rio de Janeiro, where he also coordinates the Graduate Program in Linguistics. He has been co-editor of the Revista Brasileira de Linguística since its founding in 1974. His major research interests include the study of bilingualism and language maintenance among immigrants, and the influence of African languages in Brazilian Portuguese.

GRACE JOLLY. No biographical data available.

LACHMAN M. KHUBCHANDANI (1932–   ) was born in Karachi; studied Hindi literature and journalism at the Panjab University, and linguistics and anthropology at the University of Pennsylvania where he received his doctorate (1963) with a dissertation on bilingualism among Sindhi immigrants in India. He is now Director of the Centre for Language and Communication Studies in Poona. Currently, he is also Second Vice-President of the Research Committee on Sociolinguistics, and Chairman of the Quetelet Workgroup on Language Statistics, RCS. He is also Founder-Chairman of the Afro-Asia Education Trust, engaged in rural literacy programmes in the Third World. Formerly a journalist with the Indian Press Information Bureau in Delhi, Professor of Indian Linguistics at Zagreb University, and Senior Fellow at the East-West Center Honolulu, he has held teaching and research posts at Deccan College Poona, Indian Institute of Advanced Study Simla, University College London, SEAMEO Regional English Language Centre Singapore, and University of Khartoum. He also held visiting assignments at several universities in India (Karnataka, Osmania, Kerala, Baroda, Bombay), the Südasien Institüt Heidelberg, and the University of Hawaii. His major research interests are: sociolinguistic theory in relation to multilingual societies, pragmatics, language communication, language modernization and planning, language demography, literacy and language education, policy, teaching of English, Hindi–Urdu as second language, and Indo–Aryan linguistics (particularly Sindhi and Hindi-Urdu phonology and semantics). He has published extensively in these fields.

BHADRIRAJU KRISHNAMURTI (1928–   ) has been Professor and Head of the Department of Linguistics, Osmania University, Hyderabad, India since 1962. He studied Telugu language and literature at Andhra University (1945–1948) and linguistics at the University of Pennsylvania and the University of California, Berkeley (1954–1956). Previously he taught at Andhra University and Sri Venkateswara University and held visiting positions in teaching and research at the University of California, Berkeley (1960–1961), Cornell University (1967 spring, 1970 fall), the University of Michigan, Ann Arbor (1967 summer), the Australian National University, Canberra (1974 winter), and the University of Illinois, Urbana (1978 summer). He has been a Fulbright scholar (1954–1957), Fellow of the Rockefeller Foundation (1955–1956), Asian Fellow at Australia National University (1974), Fellow at the Center for Advanced Study in the Behavioral Sciences, Stanford (1975–1976), and President of the Linguistic Society of India in 1970. His major interests are comparative linguistics with special reference to Dravidian, Telugu linguistics, lexicography, sociolinguistics, and language typology. He has published nine books and thirty research papers in Indian and foreign journals, which include: *Telugu verbal bases: a comparative and descriptive study* (University of California Press, 1961); *A Telugu dialect dictionary of occupational vocabularies* (A. P. Sahitya Akademi, Hyderabad, 1962, 1972); *Koṇḍa or Kūbi: a Dravidian language* (Tribal Cultural Research and Training Institute, Hyderabad, 1969); *A history of the Telugu language* (ed.) (A. P. Sahitya Akademi, Hyderabad, 1974); "Areal and lexical diffusion of sound change: evidence from Dravidian," *Language* 54, 1–20 (1978).

MARY ESTHER KROPP DAKUBU (1938–   ) studied English and philosophy at Queen's University (Kingston, Canada), linguistics at the University of Pennsylvania, and received her doctorate in West African languages from the University of London (S.O.A.S.). Since 1964 she has taught and done research at the University of Ghana, where she is now Senior Research Fellow in the Institute of African Studies. Her major fields of research and publication have been historical linguistics, sociolinguistics, phonology, and grammar and verbal art of languages spoken in and around Ghana, especially the Ga and Dangme languages.

VICTOR ALEXANDROVICH KUMANEV (1931–   ) was born in Gorky and graduated from Gorky University in 1954. He received a Ph.D. (1971) in history from the Institute of Ethnography, Academy of Sciences of the USSR. He has lectured at Moscow State University and other higher educational institutions in the USSR. He is an N.K. Krupskaya Prize winner. His publications include works on the history of soviet society and science and culture. He is a member of the editorial board of *Social Sciences Today.*

CHINTAMANI LAKSHMANNA (1935–) studied at Loyola College, Madras, and sociology at Lucknow University. His Ph.D. dissertation was on "Intercaste relations in rural Andhra." He has taught at Lucknow University, Lucknow, Andhra Pradesh Agricultural University, Hyderabad and Osmania University, Hyderabad. He has been visiting Professor at Pittsburgh University, Pittsburgh (U.S.A.), Professor and Head, Department of Sociology Osmania University, Hyderabad, and Principal, University College of Arts and Social Sciences, Osmania University. His main areas of research interest are stratification, social change, deprived groups, and women studies, and he has published widely in the national and international journals and books. Major publications (books): *Caste dynamics in village India, Democratic planning: problems and processes, Depressed group students, Harijans and social discrimination,* and *Sociology in India.*

LEWIS LEVINE (1927–) is Professor of Linguistics and Chairman of the Department of Linguistics at New York University.

EVAN GLYN LEWIS (1910–) studied English and Celtic at the Universities of Wales and Oxford. He has taught at the University College of Wales at Swansea before becoming Her Majesty's Inspector of Schools (H.M.I.) with responsibility for research in languages in education. He has lectured on bilingual education and the sociology of language at various North American universities and in European universities, and has studied bilingualism in the Soviet Union, Africa and the United States. His principal publications are *The place of Welsh and English in the schools of Wales* (1953), *Bilingualism in education* (Unesco U.K. Commission 1963), *English as a foreign language in ten countries* (1970), *Multilingualism in the Soviet Union* (1972) and has at present a volume in press (University of New Mexico), *Bilingualism and bilingual education — a comparative study.*

JACQUELINE LINDENFELD (1934–) was born in France. After receiving a French degree in English studies and going to the United States to train and work as an interpreter-translator, she studied linguistics at the University of California at Los Angeles and obtained a Ph.D. in 1969. She has been teaching in the department of Anthropology at California State University, Northridge since 1971. Her main research interests are anthropological linguistics, American Indian languages, psycholinguistics and especially sociolinguistics. She has many publications in English and French.

FOSCO MARAINI (1912–   ) was born in Florence. He took a degree in natural sciences from the University of Florence in 1938. He was an exchange Assistant Professor at Hokkaido University, Japan from 1938 to 1941, where he studied the Ainu. From 1941 to 1943 he was a Reader in Italian at the University of Kyoto. In 1946, after spending two years in a Japanese internment camp and a year as an interpreter for the United States Army in Tokyo, he returned to Italy. Between 1946 and 1959 he spent most of his time writing and travelling in Japan and Tibet. From 1959 to 1952 he was a Fellow at St. Antony's College, Oxford. Writing and travel again occupied his time from 1963 to 1972. In 1972 he became a Lecturer in Japanese and Japanese history at the University of Florence. His publications include *Secret Tibet, Meeting with Japan, Karakoram,* and *Japan, patterns of continuity.*

WILLIAM C. MCCORMACK (1929–   ), a Canadian, is Professor of Anthropology and Linguistics at the University of Calgary. Born in the U.S.A., he received a B.A. in liberal arts from the University of Chicago in 1948, a B.A. with distinction in psychology from Stanford University in 1949, an M.A. in anthropology from Stanford in 1950, and, after also studying at the University of California (Berkeley, 1950–1951), a Ph.D. in anthropology from the University of Chicago in 1956. Having studied linguistics, he took part in a Summer Institute at the University of Michigan (Ann Arbor, 1956), then taught and researched in linguistics during 1956–1958 at Deccan College, Poona, India, with special reference to Kannada ethnolinguistics and sociolinguistics. He is author of *Kannada: a cultural introduction to the spoken styles of the language* (1966) and of many articles on language in relation to society, religion, and identity in India. Since his fieldwork in Friesland and Scotland in 1967–1968, his research orientations have been comparative over forms of religious communication among Lingayats of South India and selected Calvinists of the West.

RAVEN I. MCDAVID, JR. (1911–   ), a tenth-generation South Carolinian born in Greenville, received his B.A. in English at Furman (1931) and his Ph.D. as a Miltonist at Duke University (1935). He studied linguistics at the University of Michigan and University of North Carolina and Yale University (chiefly in linguistic institutes), informally as a participant in the Intensive Language Program of World War II and in the regional linguistic atlases as informant, fieldworker, editor and adviser. He has taught linguistics at the University of Michigan, Western Reserve University, University of Chicago, Rutgers University, Michigan

State University, Illinois Institute of Technology, University of South Carolina, and Louisiana State University. His major interests are in American English and its cultural affiliations, particularly regional and social dialectology and lexicography.

JOSEPH MUTHIANI (1936–   ) was born in Machakos, Kenya, where he was a school teacher for eight years. In 1959 he went to the U.S.A. for further studies. He received a B.A. in political science, an M.A. in sociology and applied anthropology, an M.A. in linguistics and a D.D. in comparative religion. He also did course-work for doctorates in sociology, linguistics, and in educational leadership. He participated in Peace Corps training programmes more than a dozen times, as Language Instructor, Instructor and Coordinator for Language and Cross-Cultural Training and as a consultant. For six years, he was an instructor at Western Michigan University where he used to teach in five departments, Linguistics, Religion, Social Sciences, History and Humanities and served as Chairman of African Studies, before returning to Kenya in 1975. Currently, he is a lecturer in languages and linguistics at Kenyatta University College. He has published a book and over twenty articles in religion, history, social anthropology and linguistics. He has two books forthcoming in anthropology and linguistics. His research interests are concerned with theoretical/descriptive linguistics and areas of sociolinguistics, and anything to do with sociocultural milieu, especially having to do with social change. Basically, Africa is his area of interest.

JACOB ORNSTEIN received a B.S. and M.A. at Ohio State University and a Ph.D. at the University of Wisconsin. He is a Professor of Modern Languages and Linguistics, University of Texas at El Paso. His writings include numerous articles and longer studies on Hispanic and Slavic languages and literatures, teaching methodology, theoretical and applied linguistics. His books and monographs include *The ABC's of languages and linguistics* (with W. W. Gage), *Elements of Russian* (with R. C. Howes), *Luis de Lucena and his repetición de amores, Slavic and East European studies: their development and status in the western hemisphere, Studies in language and linguistics 1970–1971* (co-edited with R. W. Ewton), and *Programmed instruction and educational technology in the language teaching field* (with R. W. Ewton and Theodore H. Mueller).

PRABODH B. PANDIT (1923–1978) was born in Gujarat State, India, and educated at Ahmedabad, Bombay, Paris and London. He received his Ph.D. in IndoAryan from the University of London in 1949. From 1955 to 1956 he held a Rockefeller Post-Doctoral Fellowship at Yale University. He taught linguistics at Gujarat University and was Visiting Professor of Linguistics at the Deccan College, Poona, from 1956 to 1957 and later became Professor at the Centre of Advanced Studies in Linguistics at Deccan College, Poona. Since 1966 he was Professor and Chairman of the Department of Linguistics at the University of Delhi. He had also been Visiting Professor of Linguistics at the University of Michigan, Ann Arbor, and Cornell University. His publications include papers on various aspects of IndoAryan linguistics, phonemics, historical linguistics, and sociolinguistics, which appeared mainly in *Indian Linguistics* (Linguistic Society of India) and *Language* (Linguistic Society of America), and the books *Structure and change in Gujarati* (in Gujarati), *Phonemic and morphemic frequencies in Gujarati,* and *India as a Sociolinguistic Area.*

EMY. M. PASCASIO. No biographical data available.

J. B. PRIDE. No biographical data available.

WILLIAM PULTE. No biographical data available.

JOHN ROSS (1938–   ) studied French language and literature, phonetics and romance linguistics in Toulouse, Paris and his native Edinburgh, where he received his Ph.D. with the dissertation *La réduction du R géminé dans le domaine galloroman, et problèmes annexes.* The said *problèmes* led him away from historical phonology, unwittingly in the direction of sociolinguistics. He has taught at the University of Essex since its foundation in 1964: French language (theoretical and practical) at all levels from beginners' to post-graduate, sociolinguistics of French, and general sociolinguistics (post-graduate). Apart from papers on language teaching and sociolinguistic methodology, his publications are dominated by translations from French, Italian and Spanish, and by a series of BBC radio/TV French courses. Research interests focus mainly on the syntax of spoken French, bilingualism, creolization, and lect/register variation in English, French, and Italian.

GLORIA PAULIK SAMPSON (1939–   ) received her A.B. in English from the University of Chicago in 1961. She subsequently taught for two years in the Philippines. She received her Ph.D. in linguistics from the University of Michigan in 1969. From 1970 to 1977 she taught at the University of Alberta in Canada, specializing in English as a second language. She is currently an Associate Professor in the Faculty of Education at Simon Fraser University in British Columbia, Canada. She has published articles on English as a second language and has written and edited the six-level ESL series *New Routes to English.*

CAROL MYERS SCOTTON (1934–   ) was born in Harvey, North Dakota, U.S.A. She received her Ph.D. in linguistics from the University of Wisconsin (1967). She has spent over five years teaching at universities and doing field studies in Africa, including Tanzania, Uganda, Kenya, and Nigeria. She has taught at Howard University, Makerere University (Uganda), the University of Nairobi, and Yale University. She is now Associate Professor in the Department of Linguistics and Oriental and African Languages at Michigan State University. Her major teaching and research interests are in sociolinguistics and in Bantu linguistics, with a specialty in Swahili.

ELLEN-MARIE SILVERMAN (1942–   ) studied communicative disorders at the University of Iowa where she received her doctorate in psycholinguistics at the University of Illinois at Urbana–Champaign where she was a Post-Doctoral Fellow and Research Associate. Since 1973 she has been an Assistant Professor of Speech at Marquette University. She is also an Assistant Professor of Otolaryngology at the Medical College of Wisconsin. Her major research interests are: stuttering, articulation disorders, voice disorders, and gender differences in communication. She has published more than twenty-five papers in these areas.

FRANKLIN H. SILVERMAN (1933–   ) studied communicative disorders and research methodology at the University of Iowa where he received his doctorate. He has held teaching and research posts at the University of Iowa and the University of Illinois at Urbana–Champaign. Since 1971 he has been on the Faculty of Marquette University and is now Professor of Speech at that institution. He is Associate Editor of the *Journal of Speech and Hearing Research*. His major research interests are: stuttering, nonvocal communication, research methodology, general semantics, and interlinguistics. He has published two books and more than eighty papers in these areas.

RILEY B. SMITH. No biographical data available.

FRANKLIN C. SOUTHWORTH (1929–   ) received his doctorate in linguistics from Yale University. Since 1959 he has taught linguistics and South Asian languages at the University of Pennsylvania, where he is now Professor of South Asian Linguistics. He has also taught at Columbia University and Swarthmore College. He has spent about six years in the field in South Asia, doing linguistic and sociolinguistic fieldwork in Marathi, Hindi-Urdu, Nepali, Tamil, and Malayalam. He has published in the areas of general linguistics, descriptive linguistics, historical linguistics, semantics, and sociolinguistics.

HENRY TORRES TRUEBA (1931–   ) was born in Mexico City, Mexico. He obtained his M.A. from Stanford University, and his Ph.D. in social anthropology from the University of Pittsburgh. He taught at Western Illinois University (1969–1971), California State University at Sacramento (1971–1973), the University of Illinois (1973–1978), and is currently Head of the Multicultural Education Department at San Diego State University since January of 1979. He has directed and executed research projects on bilingual education, especially with regard to the sociocultural environment of linguistic minority children in the U.S.A., and the relation of this environment to their learning achievement. His preferred research methodology is microethnographic through the use of audio-visual equipment. He has edited a five-book series on bilingual education which attempts to present to the public a compendium of the status quo of our knowledge in bilingual education from a sociolinguistic perspective, published by Newberry House.

JEAN URE teaches in the Department of English Studies, University of Edinburgh.

ANTHONY L. VANEK (1931–   ) is Associate Professor of Slavic Linguistics at the University of Alberta, Editor of *Papers in Linguistics*, and Director of Linguistic Research, Inc. He received his Ph.D. in linguistics from the University of Illinois, and has also taught at the University of Florida in Tallahassee. He is currently doing fieldwork with Doukhobor Russian speakers in western Canada and with Cree Indians.

ALBERT F. VERDOODT (1925–   ) was born in Brussels, Belgium. He studied sociology, political science, and linguistics at the Catholic University of Louvain, where he received his Ph.D. (1964). He held teaching and research posts at the Laval University (Quebec), the Official University of Burundi (Bujumbura), the International Institute for Human Rights (Strasbourg), and the Netherlands Institute for Advanced Study in the Humanities and Social Sciences. He is presently teaching sociolinguistics at the Catholic University of Louvain.

DIANA WORTMAN WARSHAY. No biographical data available.

STEPHEN A. WURM (1922–   ) studied linguistics, anthropology and Oriental languages at the University of Vienna where he received his doctorate. He held teaching and research posts at the University of Vienna, the Central Asian Research Centre (associated with St. Antony's College, Oxford University), Sydney University, and the Australian National University, and visiting appointments at Northwestern University, Indiana University, and the University of Hawaii. Since 1958, he has been in charge of the extensive research program in Pacific Linguistics at the Australian National University and was appointed to the Chair of Linguistics in the School of Pacific Studies of that University in 1968. He has been Editor of the serial publication *Pacific Linguistics* since its inception in 1963. His major research interests are concerned with the Papuan, Australian, South Western Pacific Austronesian, and pidgin languages of the Pacific, as well as with sociolinguistics (formerly he studied Turkic languages as well). He has published widely in these fields.

JASWANT SINGH YADAVA (1942–   ) studied social anthropology at the University of Delhi (India) and received his Ph.D. in 1968. He held research posts with the Anthropological Survey of India (1967–1968), and the Calcutta and the Ford Foundation, New Delhi (1968–1969). He was Associate Professor and Chairman Department of Social Anthropology, Punjabi University, Patiala (1969–1971). Since 1971 he has been Professor of Research at the Indian Institute of Mass Communication, New Delhi. His publications include works on social anthropology and cultural change. His main interest is mass communication and development in village India.

AKIRA YAMAMOTO (1940–   ) was born in Shimane, Japan. He received his B.A. in education from Shimane University in 1962. He studied linguistics and anthropology at Indiana University where he received his M.A. in linguistics in 1970 and his Ph.D. in anthropology in 1974. He is now Associate Professor of linguistics and anthropology at the University of Kansas. His major research interests are: American Indian linguistics, Japanese linguistics, sociolinguistics, culture theory, anthropology of education and bilingual/bicultural education. He has continuously done his fieldwork with the Hualapai Indian people in Arizona, the Kickapoo in Kansas, and the Japanese in Arizona and in Japan.

Index of Names

Index of Subjects